About Pearson

Pearson is the world's learning company, with presence across 70 countries worldwide. Our unique insights and world-class expertise comes from a long history of working closely with renowned teachers, authors and thought leaders, as a result of which, we have emerged as the preferred choice for millions of teachers and learners across the world.

We believe learning opens up opportunities, creates fulfilling careers and hence better lives. We hence collaborate with the best of minds to deliver you class-leading products, spread across the Higher Education and K12 spectrum.

Superior learning experience and improved outcomes are at the heart of everything we do. This product is the result of one such effort.

Your feedback plays a critical role in the evolution of our products and you can reachus@pearson.com. We look forward to it.

Global Marketing Management

Warren Keegan is to global marketing what Philip Kotler is to marketing. As a student, then as a teacher, Keegan was my hero, and there is still no one who comes anywhere near him for depth, excitement, clarity, and vision. This eighth edition is a book that stands head and shoulders above all others. It pushes the state of the art to even new frontiers. For anyone interested in global marketing, whether student, teacher, or practitioner, this book is a must.

—PROFESSOR MALCOLM H. B. MCDONALD

Emeritus Professor at Cranfield School of Management and Visiting Professor at Henley, Warwick, Aston, and Bradford Business Schools

Companies doing business in the Asia Pacific region, both local and global, need marketing today more than ever. In this new business environment, marketing will be the key to success and prosperity, and Keegan's eighth edition is the key to global marketing. His book stands out as a clear leader. If you want to be a world-class global marketer, this book shows the way.

—HERMAWAN KARTAJAYA

Hermawan Kartajaya, founder of MarkPlus, Inc. Jakarta, Indonesia is the President of World Marketing Association. In 2003, he was named by the United Kingdom Chartered Institute of Marketing as one of the "50 Gurus Who Have Shaped the Future of Marketing".

Eighth Edition

GLOBAL MARKETING MANAGEMENT

Eighth Edition

GLOBAL MARKETING MANAGEMENT

Warren J. Keegan
Professor Emeritus, Lubin School of Business,
Pace University, New York City and Westchester
Fellow, Academy of International Business

With Elyse Arnow Brill

Gautam Dutta
Assistant Professor, Marketing
Indian Institute of Foreign Trade
Delhi, Kolkata

Pearson

Credits and acknowledgments borrowed from other sources and reproduced, with permission, in this textbook appear on the appropriate page within text.

Authorized adaptation from the United States edition, entitled *Global Marketing Management, 8th Edition*, ISBN 9780136157397, by Warren J. Keegan, with Elyse Arnow Brill, published by Pearson Education, Inc, Copyright © 2014.

Indian Subcontinent Adaptation

ISBN 978-93-325-8432-7

First Impression, 2017
Seventh Impression, 2024
Eighth Impression, 2026

Published by Pearson India Education Services Pvt. Ltd, CIN: U72200TN2005PTC057128.

Head Office: 1st Floor, Berger Tower, Plot No. C-001A/2, Sector 16B, Noida - 201 301, Uttar Pradesh, India.

Registered Office: 6th Floor, Tower A, Unit A and B, International Tech Park, CapitaLand Chennai, 200 Feet Radial Road,Zamin Pallavaram, Old Pallavaram Chennai – 600117, Tamil Nadu, India

Website: in.pearson.com; Email: companysecretary.india@pearson.com

Digitally printed in India by Trinity Academy for Corporate Training Ltd, New Delhi in the year of 2026

In memory of my parents, Donald Rayfield Keegan
and Edla Sigrid Polson

BRIEF CONTENTS

CONTENTS

PREFACE

Global Marketing Management, Eighth Edition, traces its ancestry to *Multinational Marketing Management,* a book that broke new ground in the field of international marketing when it was published in 1974. The first edition departed from the traditional export trade focus in the field of international marketing and adopted a strategic approach that reflected the growing importance of multinational corporations, the latest findings of research, and the most advanced experience of practitioners. The book combined text with classroom tested graduate-level cases and was an immediate worldwide success. The objective of each revision has been to not only reflect current practice but to anticipate the direction of development of the field and maintain the book's authoritative position as the leading MBA graduate-level and reference text for practitioners of international marketing. Considered one of the most comprehensive and visionary books on the subject for three and a half decades, the eighth edition continues this legacy by introducing a fresh perspective grounded in real world experience and a truly global vision of marketing and its evolving role in business.

Powerful trends are sweeping the marketing field today. Developing a global point of view and keeping pace with the changing environment is challenging every industry and every organization from new start-ups to established global giants. *Global Marketing Management,* Eighth Edition, presents the latest developments in global marketing within the context of the whole organization, making internal and external connections where appropriate for a deeper understanding of global business from a managerial point of view.

A special focus is placed on the big emerging markets—China and India, in particular, but also Brazil, Russia, South Africa, Indonesia, and Turkey (the BRIC-ITs) and countries in all of the emerging world regions from the Americas, Asia, Europe, the Middle East, and Africa. From the latest market statistics to the global trends in consumer tastes, attention is given to the dominant cultural, social, economic, and competitive forces that are shaping marketing worldwide.

Combining solid academic research with a strategic business perspective is another distinguishing feature of this edition. Updated with the most recent and relevant research and concepts from top scholarly journals and respected business publications, *Global Marketing Management,* Eighth Edition, provides theories, concepts, tools, and insights into global marketing that enable the student, teacher, and practitioner to identify global market opportunities, threats, and issues.

Through an updated page design, significantly more visual presentations, and many new features such as chapter outlines, marginal annotations, and bulleted summaries, this edition is more readable and engaging. The completely redone presentations and the addition of other supporting materials such as short closing cases, anecdotal stories, and experiential and application exercises for each chapter successfully illustrates the application of theoretical concepts to real-world situations and extend the student's understanding.

New to the eighth edition:

- Integrated discussion of Internet marketing throughout the book.
- Intensified focus on culture's influence on marketing communications both from the customer's and manager's perspective.
- New chapter—Global Social and Environmental Responsibility.
- Latest research and theory from the leading academic and business publications.
- Illustrative stories adapted from current business management press.

- Experiential exercises that require students to apply concepts presented in the chapter to realistic business situations.
- Chapter-at-a-glance outline for easy identification of the chapter structure and main topics.
- Completely revised and updated lecture slides that include access to websites and other relevant multimedia sources and teaching aids.
- Updated chapter organization to reflect current global marketing priorities and themes.
- Extensive coverage of topics matching with Indian syllabus requirements by adding new cases and up-to-date text.

The book is organized into six parts: Part I is an introduction to global marketing. Part II covers the major dimensions of the environment of global marketing—economic; social and cultural; and political, legal, and regulatory. Part III is devoted to analyzing and targeting global market opportunities. Part IV focuses on global marketing strategy, and Part V covers the global marketing mix of product, pricing, place, and promotion decisions. Part VI concludes the book with a focus on implementation. It addresses the tasks of leading, organizing, and monitoring the global strategy; the future of global marketing; and careers in global marketing. The topic of e-marketing, which was addressed in a separate chapter in the seventh edition, is now integrated into every chapter in the book.

A TOTAL TEACHING AND LEARNING PACKAGE

A successful global marketing management course requires more than a well-written book. Today's classroom requires well-prepared instructors and a fully integrated learning system. A total package of instructor supplements extends this edition's emphasis on creating value for your classroom. The following aids support *Global Marketing Management,* Eighth Edition:

Instructor PowerPoint Slides (Download Only)

A comprehensive set of PowerPoint slides that can be used by instructors for class presentations or by students for lecture preview or review is available for download.

Instructor's Manual (Download Only)

A complete instructor's manual which can be used to prepare a lecture or class presentations, find answers to the end of chapter exercises, and even design the course syllabus.

Test Item File (Download Only)

The test bank for the eighth edition contains over 50 questions per chapter. Questions are provided in a multiple-choice and true/false format. This Test Item File supports Association to Advance Collegiate Schools of Business (AACSB) learning standards. Where appropriate, the answer line of each question indicates a category within which the question fails. This AACSB reference helps instructors identify those test questions that support learning goals.

ACKNOWLEDGMENTS

This edition, like the previous seven, reflects the contributions, insights, and labor of many persons. My colleagues, associates, and students at the Lubin School of Business, Pace University, New York University, The George Washington University, Baruch College, Columbia Business School, and at many other universities around the world; the fellows and members of the Academy of International Business; clients, past and present, have all contributed.

Although many colleagues, students, clients, and others have contributed to this and to previous editions, I especially want to thank Elyse Arnow Brill, my former student and now good friend and partner on earlier book projects. She has been an invaluable partner in the writing of this edition. Elyse combines a great grasp of the marketing discipline, enthusiasm for tracking down new insights and experience, extraordinary energy and focus and organizational skills, and an ability to meet deadlines. She has worked with me on every chapter in the book and has made an invaluable contribution to this exciting new edition.

Special thanks are also due to my good friend Steven Burgess, Director and Professor of Marketing at Nelson Mandela Metropolitan University, South Africa. Steven is one of the world's leading global marketing scholars and has managed to find the time in his very busy schedule of teaching, research, consulting, and writing to make a major contribution to this edition by agreeing to coauthor a complete revision and update of Chapter 4, The Global Cultural Environment.

The reference librarian at Pace, Michelle Lang, is an author's dream come true: no matter how difficult the request, she always finds the information. If the information is out there, Michelle will find it.

Hermawan Kartajaya, President of the Asia Pacific Marketing Federation and Chief Service Officer of MarkPlus, Jakarta, has been a friend for almost two decades and is a knowledgeable and perceptive guide to marketing in Asia and the world and a source of insight and creative thinking about the marketing concept and discipline. Hermawan's remarkable rise as a leader in marketing is an impressive accomplishment and an inspiration to marketers all over the world. He has contributed the opening appendix to Chapter 1, The 18 Guiding Principles of Legacy Marketing, and the 12 Cs of New Wave Marketing.

Professor Bodo B. Schlegelmilch, Vice-Dean International and Chair of International Marketing and Management, Vienna University of Economics and Business Administration (WU-Wien), former Editor-in-Chief of the *Journal of International Marketing,* and my coauthor of *Global Marketing Management: A European Perspective,* has generously shared his thoughts, experience, and insights.

Special thanks go to all those of you who reviewed the early drafts of this edition and provided your insights.

Joyce Claterbos	Kansas University
Debbie Gaspard	Southeast Community College
Michael Goldberg	Berkeley College
Daekwan Kim	Florida State University
Ruby Pui Wan Lee	Florida State University
Michael Mayo	Kent State University

Others who have made special contributions to this revision include Mark Keegan, my partner, and Anthony Donato, my associate at Keegan & Company; Mark Green, Professor, Simpson College and my coauthor of *Global Marketing.* Svend Hollensen,

Professor, University of Southern Denmark, has been a good friend since we met during his residence at Pace as a visiting scholar and has been a very helpful supporter of this edition. Thomas D'Angelo, a former Pace DPS doctoral student, made an important contribution to Chapter 3, The Political. Legal, and Regulatory Environments of Global Marketing, based on his research on global bribery and corruption. Christopher "Kit" Nagel is a Professor at Concordia University in California. He was Marketing Manager-Asia for International Paper Company before joining the Concordia faculty and has drawn on this experience in his contribution to Chapter 8, Global Entry and Expansion Strategies. Niklas Myhr, Assistant Professor of Marketing, Argyros School of Business and Economics, Chapman University, provided encouragement and contributed to the chapter on Global Distribution. Noel Capon, Professor of Marketing, Columbia Business School, former colleague and friend who has shared his research and insights on managing global accounts; Dave Heenan, Trustee of the Estate of James Campbell, Visiting Professor, Georgetown University Business School is a longtime friend who has shared his experience and insights for this and every preceding edition of this book; Jean Boddewyn, Professor Emeritus, Baruch College and former Dean of the Fellows of the Academy of Business; Malcolm McDonald, Cranfield University, my coauthor for *Marketing Plans that Work,* and colleague at Cranfield; Joseph Ganitsky, Professor of International Business, Loyola University–New Orleans; Donald Gibson, Professor, Macquarie University; H. Donald Hopkins, Associate Professor, Temple University–Philadelphia; Raj Komaran, National University of Singapore; Hermann Kopp, Professor, Norwegian School of Management; James A. F. Stoner, Fordham University; and Dinker Raval and Bala Subramanian of Morgan State University.

Finally, my greatest debt is to my readers: the faculty who adopt this book and the students and executives who purchase the book to study and learn about how to be a successful player in the exciting world of global marketing. To all of you I say, thank you for your support and inspiration and best wishes for every success in your global marketing programs.

Warren J. Keegan

Contributor's Acknowledgment

I would like to record my thanks to Indian Institute of Foreign Trade, several export promotion organizations like Federation of Indian Export Organization (FIEO), Export Promotion Council for Handicrafts (EPCH), Engineering Export Promotion Council (EEPC) etc, and many internationalized Indian companies who allowed me to learn the finer points of international marketing. I am also thankful to my colleagues at Indian Institute of Foreign Trade who helped me with continuous supports and academic inputs.

I am highly obliged to the editorial team at Pearson India for their hard work and encouragement. Mr Varun Goenka, Editor, constantly encouraged me to come out with this edition. Ms Sailza Kumari, Assistant Editor, deserves credit for sustained cooperation and hard work.

Finally, my special thanks to my wife Elora, son Abhishek and brother Uttam for their emotional support and making it all worthwhile.

Gautam Dutta

We would like to thank Dr Gautam Dutta, Assistant Professor, Faculty of Indian Institute of Foreign Trade, for making the book more relevant and contextual for Indian students.

ABOUT THE AUTHOR

DR. WARREN J. KEEGAN

Fellow, Academy of International Business

Dr. Keegan is Professor Emeritus of International Business and Marketing at the Lubin School of Business of Pace University, New York, and is a current or former Visiting Professor at Cranfield University School of Management (UK), CEIBS (China European International Business School)–Shanghai, Wharton Executive Programs, University of Pennsylvania, ESSEC, Cergy-Pontoise, INSEAD, Fontainbleau, Stockholm School of Economics, University of Hawaii Executive Programs, and GE's John F. Welch Leadership Center. He is the founder of Warren Keegan Associates, Inc., a consulting consortium of experts in global strategy formulation and implementation. The firm is affiliated with Marketing Strategy & Planning, Inc. in New York and MarkPlus, Indonesia's leading marketing consulting firm. Dr. Keegan is Chairman of the Markplus Global Institute–Singapore. He is the cofounder of Keegan & Company LLC.

He wrote the first multinational marketing textbook and is one of the world's leading experts on marketing and global business. He holds BS and MS degrees in economics from Kansas State University and an MBA and doctorate in marketing and international business from the Harvard Business School. He has held faculty positions at a number of business schools including Columbia, George Washington University, New York University, INSEAD, IMD, and the Stockholm School of Economics.

His experience includes consulting with Boston Consulting Group and Arthur D. Little, marketing planning with the Pontiac Division of General Motors, and Chairman of Douglas A. Edwards, Inc., a New York commercial real estate firm. He is a consultant to a number of global firms. Current or former clients include AT&T, GE, Microsoft, Bertelsmann, IBM, Citicorp, Bad Boy Entertainment, General Electric, J. Walter Thompson, PurduePharma, Philips, Reckitt & Colman, Singapore International Airlines, and the Singapore Trade Development Board.

Dr. Keegan is the author or coauthor of many books, including *Global Marketing Management: A European Perspective* (Financial Times/Prentice Hall, 2001), *Marketing Plans That Work: Targeting Growth and Profitability* (Butterworth Heinemann, 1997), *Global Marketing* (7th ed., Prentice Hall, 2012), *Marketing* (2nd ed., Prentice Hall, 1996), *Marketing Sans Frontiers* (InterEditions, 1994), *Advertising Worldwide* (Prentice Hall, 1991), and *Judgments, Choices, and Decisions: Effective Management Through Self-Knowledge* (John Wiley & Sons, 1984). He has published numerous articles in leading journals including *Harvard Business Review, Administrative Science Quarterly, Journal of Marketing, Journal of International Business Studies,* and *The Columbia Journal of World Business.*

Dr. Keegan is a former MIT Fellow in Africa; Assistant Secretary, Ministry of Development Planning; Secretary of the Economic Development Commission, Government of Tanzania; consultant with Boston Consulting Group and Arthur D. Little; and Chairman of Douglas A. Edwards, a New York corporate real estate firm.

He is a Lifetime Fellow of the Academy of International Business; Individual Eminent Person (IEP) appointed by Asian Global Business Leaders Society (other awardees include Noel Tichy, Rosabeth Moss Kanter, and Gary Wendt); a current or former member of the International Advisory Board of École des Hautes Études Commerciales (HEC)–Montreal; Editorial Advisory Board, Cranfield School of Management and Financial Times/Prentice Hall Management Monograph Series, *The International Journal of Medical Marketing;* commissioner of PT Indofood Sukses Makmur (Jakarta); The S.M. Stoller Company, Inc.; The Cooper Companies, Inc. (NYSE); Inter-Ad, Inc.; American Thermal Corporation, Inc.; Halfway Houses of Westchester, Inc.; Wainwright House; and The Rye Arts Center.

DR. GAUTAM DUTTA

Professor, Indian Institute of Foreign Trade

Professor Gautam Dutta has been teaching international marketing at Indian Institute of Foreign Trade for more than a decade. Prior to that, he served as Director of Indian Institute of Entrepreneurship (an organization under the Ministry of MSME, Government of India), and Professor and Head, Department of Management Studies, Sikkim Manipal University. He is a mechanical engineer with Masters in Business Management. He received his doctoral degree from Indian Institute of Technology (IIT). He has about 30 years of experience in post graduate teaching in management, training, research and project consultancy on SME enterprise development and trade promotion.

Professor Dutta's research interest is in international business, borderland studies and international entrepreneurship with special focus on internationalization of Indian businesses. His research work has been published as journal articles in peer reviewed reputed journals, teaching cases, and book chapters.

Part I Introduction and Overview

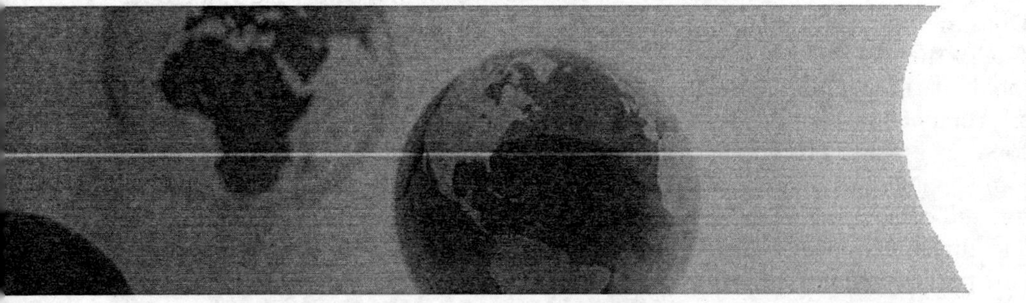

CHAPTER 1

Introduction to Global Marketing

The new electronic interdependence re-creates the world in the image of a global village.

—MARSHALL HERBERT MCLUHAN *The Medium is the Message* (1967)

Marketing is too important to be left to the marketing department.

—DAVID PACKARD *Cofounder of HP*

Learning Objectives

1. Summarize the evolution of marketing (3–6).
2. Identify the three basic principles of marketing (6–7).
3. Discuss global marketing practices and strategies (7–11).
4. Discuss the growth of global market opportunities (14–21).
5. Compare and contrast management orientations (24–26).
6. Describe the driving forces behind the increased pace of global integration (26–32).
7. Identify three restraining forces that hinder global marketing efforts (35–36).

INTRODUCTION

We live in a fast-paced, global marketplace. Wherever we live, whether it is in Europe, the Americas, Asia, Africa, or the Middle East, we take for granted products and services that come from around the world. From our laptops, cell phones, tablets, cars, furniture, artwork, and food, to our shoes, jeans, tee shirts, and watches, the world and its products are ours. A myriad of cultural influences and shared interests have become a backdrop to our daily lives as technology and travel push the envelope to provide us with faster and deeper connections with just about everyone and everything on the planet.

In this context, where does marketing fit—what role does it play and what value does it add? Does the field and practice of marketing globally contribute to or detract from the welfare of the global population?

Global marketing management requires a strategically integrated focus on customers, competition, technology, regulation, and economic, political, and social trends and factors…in a word, everything. An aligned marketing effort in a global enterprise requires an alignment of organizational design, corporate culture, leadership, employee motivation and compensation, creativity and innovation, and the rethinking of traditionally distinct functional policies and programs.

In the past two centuries, a sweeping transformation has profoundly affected the world economy. Prior to 1840, students sitting at their desks would not have had any item in their possession that was manufactured more than a day's horseback ride from where they lived—with the possible exception of the books they were reading. Many countries—most notably Great Britain—were actively involved in international trade in the mid-nineteenth century. This involvement increased until the world withdrew into autarky as a response to the collapse of aggregate demand that resulted in the global depression of 1929–1939.

The world economy began its recovery in the 1930s with military spending in Germany and Japan followed by military spending in the US, the UK, and USSR. At the end of World War II, Germany, Japan, Eastern Europe, and Western USSR were in ruins; Britain was broke and exhausted. The US mainland had been untouched by any enemy invasion or bombardment and had recovered from the Great Depression to become the most productive, innovative and richest country in the world. In the war-torn countries, the challenge was reconstruction. For the United States, the challenge was converting a wartime economy that had supplied not only its own military forces, but also those of its British and Soviet allies, to peacetime needs and wants. Remarkably, both the victors and the defeated made a remarkably speedy recovery in rebuilding their peacetime economies. The United States became a colossus with more than half of global GDP, and Japan and Germany rapidly became the second and third largest countries in the world in GDP after the United States. The USSR and the dream of a communist utopia eventually collapsed, and the threat of international communism fell into the dustbin of history.

Since World War II, there has been an unparalleled expansion into global markets by companies that previously focused principally on customers located in their home country. Three decades ago, the phrase *global marketing* did not even exist. Today, businesses look to global marketing for the realization of their full commercial and societal potential. However, there is another even more critical reason why companies need to take global marketing seriously: survival. A company that fails to become global in outlook and practice risks losing its domestic business to competitors who have lower costs, more relevant experience, and better products.

What is global marketing? How does it differ from domestic marketing? Marketing can be defined as a series of activities leading to an exchange between a seller and a buyer at a profit. Marketing activities center on an organization's efforts to satisfy customer wants and needs with products and services that offer competitive value. The marketing mix—product, price, place, and promotion—is a marketer's primary tool. Marketing is a discipline, as applicable in Australia as it is in Zanzibar, in all industries and sectors from high to low tech and from for-profit to not-for-profit firms and for all products from consumer to industrial.

This book is about global marketing, its context, concepts, tools, and practice. An organization that engages in global marketing focuses its resources on global market opportunities and threats. One difference between domestic marketing and global marketing is in the scope of activities. A company that engages in global marketing conducts key marketing activities outside the home-country market. These activities include marketing intelligence gathering, which provides the information foundation for a market-driven, integrated marketing mix that address the opportunity and competition in every addressed global market. Another difference is that global marketing involves an understanding of specific concepts, considerations, and strategies that must be skillfully applied, in conjunction with universal marketing fundamentals, to ensure success in global markets. This book concentrates on the major dimensions of global marketing. A brief overview of marketing is presented next, although the author assumes the reader has completed introductory marketing and international business courses or has equivalent experience.

MARKETING: A UNIVERSAL DISCIPLINE

The foundation for a successful global marketing program is a sound understanding of the marketing discipline. Marketing is the process of focusing the resources and objectives of an organization on environmental opportunities and needs. The first and most fundamental fact about marketing is that it is a universal discipline. Marketing is a set of concepts, tools, theories, practices and procedures, and experience. Together, these elements constitute a teachable and learnable body of knowledge. Although marketing is universal, marketing practice, of course, varies from country to country, region to region, and across markets within a single country. Just as each person is unique, each country or market is unique. This reality of differences means that, as marketers, we cannot always directly apply experience from one country to another or from one market to another. It is certain that if customers, competitors, channels of distribution, and available media are different, to name only a few of the varying contingencies that exist in diverse markets, it will be necessary to change our marketing plan. On the other hand, even though markets are unique, each shares many similarities with other markets. The astute global marketer recognizes these similarities and creates greater value by extending elements of the marketing program wherever possible. Successful global companies recognize that one product can serve needs worldwide and that the global product is more competitive because it provides greater value to customers at a lower cost. Of course, global products are adapted to local languages, laws, regulations, and the physical and cultural environments of markets, when adaptation is required and when the cost of adaptation does not exceed the gain in competitiveness achieved by adaptation.

The Marketing Concept

During the past century, the concept of marketing has changed dramatically. As shown in Figure 1-1, it has evolved from a focus on the product and on producing a better product based on internal standards and values defined by the company in isolation from the customer. An example of this stage of the marketing concept was Henry Ford's famous reply to executives who wanted Ford to offer the Model T in colors other than the standard black in order to better compete with General Motors. Ford's reply: "Any customer can have a car painted any color that he wants so long as it is black." In Ford's mind, the Model T was a perfect car, and there was no point in wasting money on offering different colors. Profitability was the sole objective of product-focused marketing. The means was a sale based on persuading the customer to exchange his or her money for the company offering. Messaging involved 'pushing' the product into the market space and to the end user by mass advertising in print, on TV, or through in-store promotion.

Marketing Is Everything

	Marketing Concept		
	Old	"New" (1960's)	Strategic (Emerging)
Focus →	Product	Customer	Way of Doing Business
Means →	Telling and Selling	Integrated Marketing Mix	Knowledge and Experience
End →	Profit	Profit	Mutually Beneficial Relationship
Marketing Is... →	Selling	A Function	Everything

© Dr. Warren J.keegan

FIGURE 1-1 Marketing is Everything

THE NEW CONCEPT OF MARKETING AND THE FOUR PS The new concept of marketing, which appeared about 1960, shifted the focus of marketing from the product to the customer. The objective was still profit, but the means of achieving the objective expanded to include the entire marketing mix, or the Four Ps as they became known: product, price, place (channels of distribution), and promotion. For a discussion of the new concept of marketing see "The 18 Guiding Principles of Legacy Marketing" in the appendix at the end of this chapter.

THE STRATEGIC CONCEPT OF MARKETING By the 1990s, it was clear that the new concept of marketing was outdated and that the times demanded a strategic concept. The strategic concept of marketing, a major evolution in the history of marketing thought, shifted the focus of marketing from the customer or the product to the customer in the context of the broader external environment. Knowing everything there is to know about the customer is not enough. To succeed, marketers must know the customer in a context including the competition, regulation and government policy, and the broader economic, social, political, scientific, and technological macro forces that shape particular markets and their evolution. The strategic concept of marketing recognizes that sustainable profitability is the reward for performance, which must be achieved by satisfying customers in a socially and environmentally responsible and sustainable way.[1] In the final chapter of this book, I discuss the Big New Idea in marketing: creating shared value. Today, is it urgent for marketers to understand that real success can only be realized by creating an economic value for both customers and society. Social and community needs and challenges must be an integral part of the economic value-creation process. In the strategic concept of marketing, addressing social needs is not an exercise in corporate philanthropy but rather an exercise in creating shared value. What society needs is a healthy enterprise system that creates

[1] Regis McKenna, "Marketing is Everything," *Harvard Business Review* (January–February 1991).

competitive products and jobs that sustain employees. When a company is creating shared value, employees and suppliers will be directly supporting community needs with strong, secure families, tax-supported government community projects, and their own private contributions.

A revolutionary development in the shift to the strategic concept of marketing is in the marketing objective—which shifts from profit to stakeholder benefits. Stakeholders are individuals or groups who have an interest in the activity of a company. They include the employees and management, customers, society, government, and shareholders, to mention only the most prominent. For example, to compete in today's market, it is necessary to have an employee team committed to continuing innovation and to producing quality products in an environmentally sustainable manner. In other words, marketing must focus on the customer in context and deliver value by creating stakeholder benefits for customers, employees, and the communities they serve and, in turn, affect.

Profitability is not forgotten in the strategic concept. Indeed, it is a critical means to the end of creating stakeholder benefits. The means of the strategic marketing concept is strategic management, which integrates marketing with the other management functions. One of the tasks of strategic management is to make a profit, which can be a source of funds for investing in the business and for rewarding shareholders and management. Thus, profit is still a critical objective and measure of marketing success, but it is not an end in itself. The aim of marketing is to create value for stakeholders, and the key stakeholder is the customer. If your customer can get greater value from your competitor because your competitor is willing to accept a lower level of profit reward for investors and management, the customer will choose your competitor, and you will be out of business. The spectacular entry of Apple, the new North American player, into the global cell phone market has been responsible for the precipitous decline in market share and revenue of the former leaders from Europe, the "cradle of innovation and scale in mobile," in the words of one leading consultant. Nokia, the former leader, is now a distant third in sales trailing Apple and Samsung. This massive market shift occurred because Apple and RIM pioneered the design and deployment of smartphones, which have completely displaced traditional phones in the top end of the market. Apple pulls in more than half of the profits in the world's mobile industry despite having only a 4 percent share of the world market in units. Apple's success is based on its ability to create value for customers. Stephen Elop, Nokia's new boss, underlined what a threat this is to the former world leader. "We are standing on a burning platform," he wrote in a memo to all 132,000 Nokia employees.[2]

Finally, the strategic concept of marketing has shifted the focus of marketing from a company-centric maximization paradigm to managing strategic partnerships and positioning the firm in the value chain to create value for customers. This expanded concept of marketing was termed *boundaryless marketing* by Jack Welch, former chairperson and chief executive officer (CEO) of General Electric. The notion of *boundaryless* marketing is shown in Figure 1-2.

Figure 1-2 depicts marketing's set of activities as encompassing the business processes, from the initial identification of customer needs and wants to the end product or service offering that creates the best relative customer value vis-à-vis the competition. Marketing can be conceptualized as the process of focusing the resources and objectives of an enterprise on customer and consumer needs. Market-driven firms are focused, agile, and tactically responsive both through differentiated marketing planning strategies and marketing mix elements. It is ultimately the marketing mix

[2] "Blazing Platforms," *The Economist,* February 12, 2011, 69.

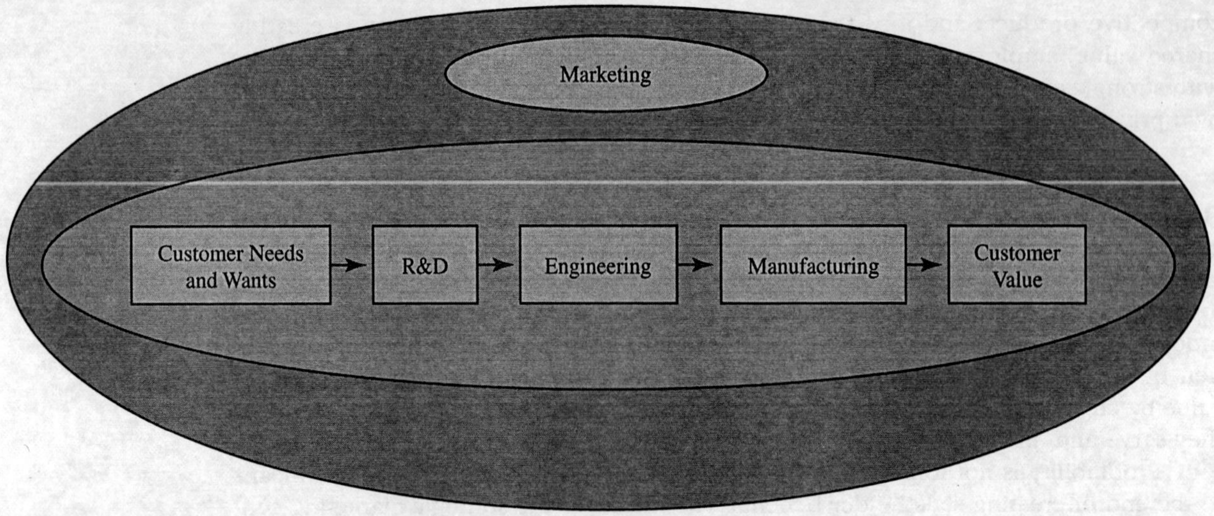

FIGURE 1-2 Value Chain Boundaryless Marketing

that integrates the organization's offers, logistics, and communications into a viable offering, which is, in turn, experienced by the customer as the overall marketing strategy. The three basic principles that underlie marketing are discussed next.

THE THREE PRINCIPLES OF MARKETING

The essence of marketing can be summarized in three great principles. The first principle identifies the purpose and task of marketing, the second identifies the competitive reality of marketing, and the third identifies the essential requirement for achieving the first two principles.

Customer Value and the Value Equation

The task of marketing is to create customer value that is greater than the value created by competitors. The value equation, shown in Figure 1-3, is a guide to this task. As suggested in the equation, value for the customer can be increased by expanding or improving product and/or service benefits, by reducing the price, or by a combination of these elements. Companies with a cost advantage can use this advantage to gain a sustainable competitive edge in any of the marketing mix elements: product, price, promotion, or place. Knowledge of the customer combined with innovation and creativity can lead to a total offering that offers superior customer value. If the benefits

Key Marketing Principles

Action	***Knowledge***
• Customer Value = Benefits/Price (B/P)	• **Company**
• Focus	• **Customer**
• Comptitive Advantage	• **Competition**

FIGURE 1-3 Key Marketing Principles

are strong enough and valued enough by customers, a company does not need to be the low-price competitor to win customers. On the other hand, the value equation may lead to a focus on price as the key element of competitive advantage.

Competitive or Differential Advantage

The second great principle of marketing is competitive advantage. A competitive advantage is a total offer, vis-à-vis relevant competition that is more attractive to customers. The advantage can exist in any element of the company's offer: the product, the price, advertising and point-of-sale promotion, or the distribution of the product. One of the most powerful strategies for penetrating a new national market is to offer a superior product at a lower price. The price advantage will get immediate customer attention and, for those customers who purchase the product, the superior quality will make an impression.

Focus

The third great principle of marketing is focus, or the concentration of attention. Focus is required to succeed in the task of creating customer value at a competitive advantage through the mobilization of organizational effort and resources. All great enterprises, large and small, are successful because they understand and apply this principle.

Apple retains its edge as a leader in product design and benefits, often disrupting older technologies, because it is more clearly focused on how to take advantage of technology to design and make products that offer unique consumer benefits, and because it knows how to position and communicate unique benefits to target markets. Apple's selection and integration of marketing activities, including brand-building retail stores that offer not only value-creating products but unique services for existing and prospective customers, contribute to its continuing distinctive advantage. Starbucks is another example of driven focus and often obsessive attention to every element of branding behavior and consistent customer experience. This attention to detail can be seen in Starbucks' ads, in-store promotions, décor and ambiance, products, product sizes, brand messaging, and training of the baristas behind the counter. Such laser focus and brand experience sometimes comes from an entrepreneurial leader who himself embodies the values of the brand, such as Starbucks' Howard D. Schultz.[3]

GLOBAL MARKETING: WHAT IT IS AND WHAT IT IS NOT

Although the marketing discipline is universal, markets and customers are quite differentiated. This means that marketing practice must vary not only from region to region but also from country to country, and even between the different market segments within a country. Companies that attempt to transfer irrelevant or inappropriate experience from one market to another will suffer a loss both in investment, credibility, and market share. One famous example involves Nestlé's attempt to create a market for iced tea in India. Nestlé received a cold response, as Indian consumers traditionally like to have their tea beverages hot. Procter and Gamble provides another well-known example with its attempted introduction of Cheer laundry detergent in Japan. P&G overlooked the fact that the Japanese wash their clothes in cold water. Accordingly, the advertising campaign highlighting washing clothes at "all temperatures" was meaningless to this target audience.

---

[3] Scott Bedbury and Stephen Fenischell, *A New Brand World: 8 Principles for Achieving Brand Leadership in the 21st Century* (New York: Penguin Book Group, 2002).

A major issue in global marketing practice and theory involves the extent of adaptation or standardization of products for diverse markets. With the growth of the global, competitive marketplace, international marketing has transformed into integrated global marketing. The global marketing manager's focus has shifted from a focus on the functional differences between national or regional markets to a focus on understanding the transnational differences and similarities of target markets.[4] The prime driver of marketing globally is the synergistic benefits and productivity improvements obtained through global marketing initiatives. These value-creating initiatives include each of the elements of the marketing mix as well as other supporting business functions, such as accounting, procurement and channel management, production, and research and development (R&D).

The Standardization Debate

Robert Buzzell offered the first theoretical discussion of standardization as an international marketing strategy in 1968.[5] He argued that dissimilarities among countries led multinational firms to perceive marketing planning in each country as a local problem with localized solutions. Buzzell provided several rationales for an international standardization strategy, most importantly, cost savings arising from standardization of the marketing mix elements and the creation of a single marketing strategy spanning the globe. Following Buzzell's work, Professor Theodore Levitt's 1983 seminal article in the *Harvard Business Review*, "The Globalization of Markets," argued that marketers were confronted with a "homogenous global village."[6] Levitt advised organizations to develop standardized, high-quality world products and market them around the globe using standardized advertising, pricing, and distribution. He recognized that "success in a world with homogenized demand requires a search for sales opportunities in similar segments across the globe." In fact, he contended that "the most effective world competitors incorporate superior quality and reliability into their cost structures.... They compete on the basis of appropriate value—the best combinations of price, quality, reliability, and delivery for products that are globally identical with respect to design, function, and even fashion." Levitt introduced the importance of creating value by offering functional, quality, low-priced products. One way of doing this is through the use of standardization of the marketing mix and marketing process.

Some well-publicized failures by companies seeking to follow Levitt's advice brought his proposals into question. The business press frequently quoted industry observers who disputed Levitt's views. For example, Carl Spielvogel, chairman and CEO of the Backer Spielvogel Bates Worldwide advertising agency, told *The Wall Street Journal,* "Theodore Levitt's comment about the world becoming homogenized is bunk. There are about two products that lend themselves to global marketing—and one of them is Coca-Cola."[7] Indeed, it was global marketing that made Coke a worldwide success. However, that success was not based on a total standardization of marketing mix elements. In his book

---

[4] Jagdish N. Sheth and Atul Parvatiyar, "The Antecedents and Consequences of Integrated Global Marketing," *International Marketing Review*, 18, iss. 1 (2001): 16–29. See also, Hongsik John Cheon, Chang-Hoan Cho, and John Sutherland, "A Meta-Analysis of Studies on the Determinants of Standardization and Localization of International Marketing and Advertising Strategies," *Journal of International Consumer Marketing*, 19, no. 4 (2007): 109.

[5] R. D. Buzzell, "Can You Standardize Multinational Marketing?," *Harvard Business Review*, 46, no. 6 (1968): 102–133.

[6] Theodore Levitt, "The Globalization of Markets," *Harvard Business Review*, 61, no. 3 (1983): 92–102.

[7] Joanne Lipman, "Ad Fad: Marketers Turn Sour on Global Sales Pitch Harvard Guru Makes," *The Wall Street Journal,* May 12, 1988, 1.

The Borderless World,[8] Kenichi Ohmae explains that Coke's success in Japan could be achieved only by spending a great deal of time and money becoming an "insider" to that market. That is, the company built a complete local infrastructure with its sales force and vending machine operations. Coke's success in Japan, according to Ohmae, was a function of its ability to achieve "global localization," the ability to be as much of an insider as a local company, but still reap the benefits that result from world-scale operations.

What does the phrase *global localization* really mean? In a nutshell, it means a successful global marketer must have the ability to "think globally and act locally." As we will see many times in this book, global marketing may include a combination of standard (e.g., the actual product) and nonstandard (e.g., distribution, messaging, or packaging) approaches. A global product may be the same product everywhere and yet different. Global marketing requires marketers to behave in a way that is global and local at the same time by responding to similarities and differences in world markets. This being the case, a review of the literature reflects an evolving state of knowledge and practice with respect to a multidimensional view of global marketing strategy when it comes to standardization/adaptation decisions. In 1969, Keegan, using the global marketing mix, identified four strategic alternatives based on product standardization versus adaptation and promotion standardization versus adaptation dimensions.[9] Much literature in the field of international marketing builds on this initial multidimensional perspective[10] and looks beyond single-strategy dimensions. Heterogeneity among various cross-border markets does not allow standardization in any absolute sense. Important variables of differentiated markets include cultural, legal, and social dictates, as well as differences in local media and distribution vehicles and capabilities, trade restrictions, and government regulation. Yet, the expense involved in adaptation of many of the elements of the marketing program can be prohibitively expensive. Finding the balance and merging the benefits of standardization and adaptation may be a key determinant of successful integrated global marketing campaigns.[11]

Indeed, the Coca-Cola Company has demonstrated that its ability to think globally and act locally can be a source of competitive advantage. By adapting taste and product elements, sales promotion, distribution, and customer service initiatives to local needs, Coke established a strong brand preference.

Not only is tailoring the global marketing concept to fit a particular product, business, or market of crucial importance, it is necessary to understand that global marketing does not mean entering every country or region in the world. Global marketing requires widening business horizons to encompass the world while scanning for opportunity and threat. The decision to enter markets outside the home country depends on a company's resources and its stage of development, its managerial mind-set, and the nature of opportunities along with existing competitive threats. Globalization challenges companies to recognize what they do well within the global marketplace and be where they have competitive strength. For example, the most globally successful auto companies have been gaining market share. Toyota, Mercedes, and BMW rely on a strong single- or dual-brand strategy across all their markets. They bring their branding strengths to new markets as compared with GM, which lost market share over the

---

[8] Kenichi Ohmae, *Borderless World: Power and Strategy in the Interlinked Economy* (New York: HarperCollins, 1999).

[9] W. J. Keegan, "Multinational Product Planning: Strategic Alternatives," *Journal of Marketing*, 33, no. 1 (1969): 58–62.

[10] See, for example, J. A. Quelch and E. J. Hoff, "Customizing Global Marketing," *Harvard Business Review*, 64, no. 3 (1986): 59–68.

[11] See, for example, Cheon, Cho, Sutherland, "A Meta-Analysis of Studies"; and Andreas Birnik and Cliff Bowman, "Marketing Mix Standardization in Multinational Corporations: A Review of the Evidence," *International Journal of Management Reviews*, 9, no. 4 (2007): 303–324 (22).

past five decades with its failure to apply the three principles of marketing. Any understanding of these principles would have led GM to the conclusion that in order to be competitive, it needed to reduce the number of brands in its global product portfolio. It is only after being forced into bankruptcy and a government bailout that GM finally sold or closed the brand franchises that stood between them and a chance at competitive global parity. As this example shows, globalization is not a one-size-fits-all solution for companies. Remaining domestic or regional rather than becoming weakened by expanding focus and expending resources globally may be the best strategy for some companies. Indeed, by remaining a predominantly regional company until recently, Fiat, based in Turin, Italy, was able to enter the US market with a controlling investment in Chrysler, America's third largest car company.

Many other companies have successfully pursued global marketing by creating strong global brands. In the automotive industry, Daimler has gained global recognition for its Mercedes nameplate, as has its competitor, Bayerische Motoren Werke Aktiengesellschaft, Munich, for its nameplate BMW automobiles and motorcycles. However, as shown in Table 1-1, global marketing strategies can also be based on product or system design and innovation, product positioning, packaging, distribution and logistics, customer service, and sourcing considerations. For example, McDonald's has designed a restaurant system that can be set up virtually anywhere in the world, but, like Coca-Cola, McDonald's customizes its menu offerings in accordance with local eating and entertainment customs. In Jakarta, Indonesia, for example, McDonald's is positioned as upscale dining. In Israel, Big Macs are served without cheese in many outlets to permit the separation of meat and dairy products required by kosher dietary laws. Unilever formerly used a teddy bear in various world markets to communicate the benefits of the company's fabric softener and now relies on the tag line "Brands for Life" and a strong Internet and Facebook presence to support its sales in over 170 countries worldwide. Harley-Davidson's motorcycles are positioned around the world as the all-American bike. Italy's Benetton and Spain's Zara utilize a sophisticated distribution system to quickly deliver the latest fashions to its worldwide network of stores. The backbone of Caterpillar's global success is a network of dealers that supports a promise of "24 hour parts and service" anywhere in the world. China's Foxconn's sourcing strategies have made it an indispensable partner to the likes of IBM, Microsoft, Nokia, Sony, Hewlett-Packard, and Apple. Information technology has given CEMEX of Mexico its competitive advantage in delivery of cement and building products in the 50 countries

TABLE 1-1 Examples of Global Marketing Strategies

Global Marketing Strategy	Company/Home Country
Brand Name	Coca-Cola (US), Apple (US), BMW (Germany)
Product Design	McDonald's (US), Toyota (Japan), Apple (US), Google (US)
Product positioning	Unilever (Great Britain/Netherlands), Harley-Davidson (US), Apple (US), Samsung (S. Korea)
Packaging	Gillette (US), Apple (US)
Distribution	IKEA (Sweden), Apple (US), H&M (Sweden)
Customer service	Caterpillar (US), Dell (US), Brother (Japan), Apple (US), Lexus (Japan)
Sourcing	Toyota (Japan), Honda (Japan), Nike (US), Wal-Mart (US), Apple (US), Foxconn (China)
Innovation	Apple (US), Google (US), Samsung (S. Korea), Tata (India), Ford (US)

in which it operates. Southwest Airlines, the largest US-based airline, is known throughout the aviation industry as a "low-cost carrier" because of its unique business model. Over the past several years, Ford successfully repaired its struggling business through the innovation of styling, fit and finish, safety, and fuel economy technology. The success of Honda and Toyota in world markets was initially based on exporting cars from factories in Japan. Now, both companies have invested in extensive assembly and manufacturing facilities abroad, including the United States and major markets.

The particular approach to global marketing that a company adopts will depend on industry conditions and its source or sources of competitive advantage. Should Harley-Davidson start manufacturing motorcycles in a low-wage country such as Mexico or China (Box 1-1)? Because Harley's competitive advantage is based in part on its "Made in the USA" positioning, shifting production outside the United States may not be advisable. Toyota and Honda's historic success abroad is partly attributable to their ability to transfer world-class manufacturing skills to global markets while using advertising to stress that its products are built in market countries with components manufactured and purchased in the market countries. Toyota and Honda have positioned themselves as global brands independent of the location of manufacture and assembly. A Toyota is a Toyota wherever it is made. Similarly, Hyundai is a recent example of an Asian automaker that entered the North American market three decades ago with quality problems and with unit volumes similar to Chinese competition of today. It took the company almost two decades to establish a presence in the mature North American market through competing on price and building its sales network and brand image. Today, Hyundai is moving toward successfully positioning its brand independent of country of origin. Yet, there remain brands, such as Harley-Davidson motorcycles that, if made abroad, would clash with the brand image linking Harley to its country of origin, the USA.

BOX 1-1

Side Bar: Harley Davidson Looking for Level Playing Field in India and China

How can a global company be present in different countries of the world and create customer value in the same way? It is not so easy because different marketing–related, country–specific, environmental variables force a global company to struggle for recreating identical marketing programmes. Let us put it simply with example for better understanding. Harley-Davidson Motor Company, an American manufacturer of motorcycles based in Milwaukee, Wisconsin has been successful in creating customer value in an identical way in 90 countries of the world where it is present. Harley-Davidson was founded way back in 1903 and initially took time to finally come out with the world winning heavyweight motorcycle and there was no looking back. With considerable ease, it kept its target consumers enthused in different countries of the world. Initially it started with countries of Europe since the company felt that it would be easy to market American macho image of the motorcycle in these countries, particularly to its core target group – the baby boomers. The company was not mistaken. Though the company earned its major share of revenue from its home country, it did manage to bring in a considerable amount of revenue from other parts of the world. For example, during the financial year ending December 2010, countries other than USA, contributed to 28.58 percent of the total revenue of $4858 million of the company. During the financial year ending December 2011 this contribution marginally went up to 28.59 percent, out of the total increased revenue of $5,311.7 million indicating growth of revenue from countries other than USA as shown in the Table 1-2. More recently during financial year ending December 2014, the company was able to increase other than home country contribution to its revenue stream to about 29.36 percent. Interestingly, during 2014 the total revenue of the company also shot up to $6229 million which was about 17.27 percent

TABLE 1-2 Contribution of Revenue Other than Home Country

Region	Revenue in USD ml (FY 2010)	Share of region % (FY 2010)	Revenue in USD ml (FY 2011)	Share of region % (FY 2011)	Revenue in USD ml (FY 2014)	Share of region in % (FY 2014)
USA	3469.485	71.42	3,774.80	71.10	4400.4	70.64
Japan	234.3207	4.82	229.4	4.30	197.8	3.18
Canada	183.9632	3.79	180.1	3.40	218.1	3.50
Australia	136.2235	2.80	141.4	2.70	190	3.05
EMEA	702.9517	14.47	785.9	14.80	875.8	14.06
Other Foreign Countries	131.0413	2.70	200.1	3.70	346.8	5.57
Total	**4857.99**	**100**	**5,311.70**	**100**	**6228.9**	**100**

Source: Data from Harley Davidson annual report available at http://media.corporate-ir.net/media_files/IROL/87/87981/HD.pdf.

rise over its total revenue of 2011. The greatest contribution came from other foreign countries with growth of revenue to the tune of 73.31 percent (Figure 1-4).

The company's journey to the other countries of the world has not been without fighting out the competitors. Harley Davidson had to fight with other big names of the world equally competent to produce heavyweight motorcycles, like Bayerische Motoren Werke (BMW) AG; Honda Motor Co Ltd; Suzuki Motor Corporation; Polaris Industries Inc.; Yamaha Motor Co Ltd; Ducati Motor Holding; and Honda Motor Co Ltd of Japan is the largest motorcycle manufacturer of the world. BMW and Kawasaki directly competes with Harley Davidson in global market as both of them manufactures heavyweight touring motorcycles. A case to this point is the acute competition that the company faces in two most populous countries of the world, India and China. The economic progress of

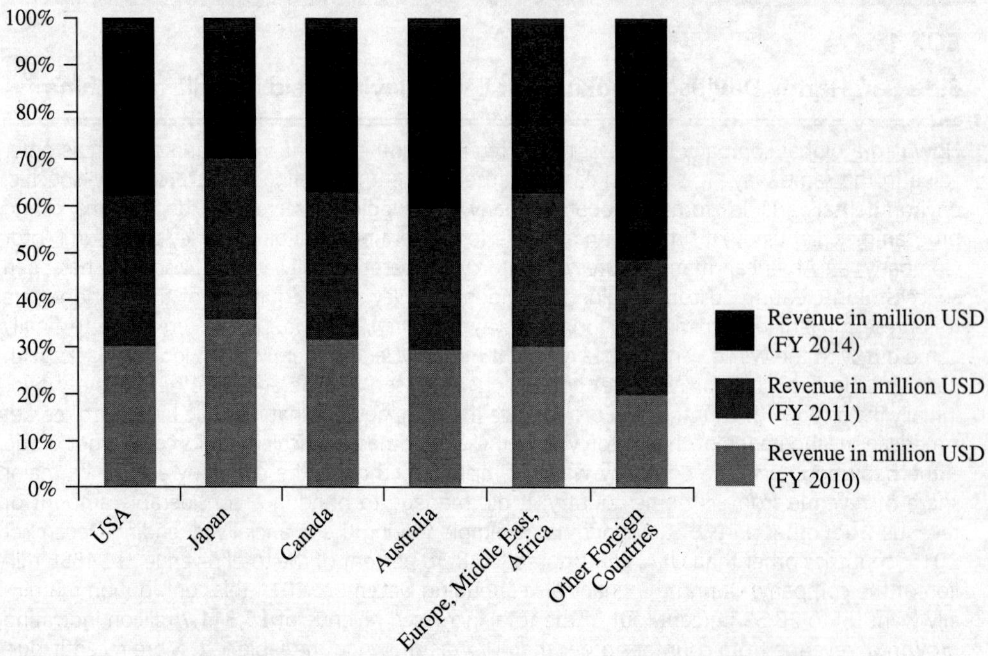

FIGURE 1-4 Other Foreign Countries Revenue Increased Substantially During 2014

Adapted from Harley Davidson annual report available at http://media.corporate-ir.net/media_files/IROL/87/87981/HD.pdf, as accessed on 10 January 2017 at 6pm.

China always attracted Harley Davidson but it took a long time to prepare itself for a culturally dissimilar country like China. During 2005, the company made a cautious start in China by opening a marketing office in Shanghai. But very soon the company understood that in order to take advantage of the economic boom and fight out competition from the local as well as global players it required intense involvement in the country. A wholly owned foreign enterprise (WOFE) of Harley Davidson came up just after five years of its entry in to the country. It also equipped itself with a well-knit network of dealership to cover almost whole of the country. It also readied its product line, the most important component of marketing mix, with 14 models from five distinct families of motorcycles. The company made a very cautious entry in India during 2009. It readied itself with its best global selling 11 models to enthuse Indian affluent baby boomers. But customer value creation process of global companies requires that they must have level playing field in every country market to replicate marketing success and beat the competition from local as well as global players. For global automobile giant Harley Davidson level playing field in both China and India, possibly the best two markets for the future years, was denied initially. In China it was a combination of two factors; first, road registration permit restrictions for the running Harley Davidson heavyweight motorcycles across different cities of China and second, comparatively high import duty. In India, Harley Davidson was struck with the exceptionally high import duty of heavyduty motorcycles.

Considering the fact that on an average only about 30 percent of the sales matured from markets outside USA during 2010–14, Harley Davidson was eager to get level playing field at the earliest in these two important countries. The company found that the import tariff structure in India was too skewed which ultimately effected the pricing of the product. 100 percent ad-velorem Indian customs duty for heavyduty motorcycle under the designated harmonised system code (HS code 871150) was high enough to keep market price for Haley Davidson motorcycle out of reach for the Indian customers (Table 1-3). The import duty structure in case of China was also considerably high with 30 percent ad-velorem but the main problem came from a major non-tariff barrier prevailing in China. In China, an age-old regulations in motorcycle registration process prevailed which did not permit motorcycles to be driven in many cities and on elevated motorways. Getting the motorcycle registration was a big hurdle for the prospective buyers causing a dampening effect on the spree of owning the iconic American Harley Davidson brand motorcycles of the Chinese customers.

TABLE 1-3 Harley Davidson Faced High Import Duty in Many Countries

Importing country	Total ad valorem equivalents tariff, 2013	Export from USA to partner country (value in US$ `000) during 2013
China	30.00%	13,445
Cook Islands	200.00%	14
Ethiopia	30.00%	0
Gabon	30.00%	250
Lao Republic	40.00%	0
Maldives	100.00%	0
Nepal	30.00%	0
Pakistan	65.00%	249
Philippines	30.00%	553
Sudan	40.00%	8
Syrian Arab Republic	50.00%	0
Thailand	60.00%	9,971
Uzbekistan	30.00%	0
Viet Nam	57.50%	254
India	100.00%	503

Adapted from http://tao.wto.org/report/TariffLines.aspx and put them in tabular format, as accessed on 10 January 2017 at 6pm.

Apple is a world leader in every category of marketing strategy highlighted in Table 1-1 and had an equity market value of more than $500 billion in 2012.[12] With its iconic music player the iPod, Apple confirmed its reputation for innovation and fueled its financial success. The iPhone sold 3.8 million units in three months in 2009 during the height of the Great Recession, attesting to its strong marketing program and product value. And with the 2010 launch of Apple's iPad positioned in a new category, the tablet, Apple added to its family of tech gadgets creating mobile platforms for digital communication, information, and entertainment. The explosive growth of mobile apps since Apple's App Store launch in 2008 has increased innovation in the product categories as well as competition. From computers to smartphones, Apple products are known for their style, uncluttered ease of use, technical sophistication, and power. Apple innovation involves leaping ahead of existing technology, anticipating needs, and "delivering capabilities that redefine product categories."[13] Driving these offerings was the marketing genius of Steve Jobs, "a gifted marketer and showman, but also a skilled listener to the technology....to judge when an intriguing innovation is ready for the marketplace. Technical progress, affordable pricing and consumer demand must jell to produce a blockbuster product."[14] Jobs knew that controlling the product is less important than controlling our desire.[15]

GLOBALIZATION AND GLOBAL MARKETING

The largest national market in the world, the United States, today represents roughly 25 percent of the total world market for all products and services. Despite significant economic growth over the last 40 years in Asia and India, with advances in innovation, technology, and productivity, the United States' share of total world output has remained constant. US companies wishing to achieve maximum growth potential must go global, as three quarters of world market potential is in the rest of the world (ROW).

Non-US companies have an even greater motivation to seek market opportunities beyond their own borders—their opportunities include the 308 million people in the United States. Non-Chinese firms have the greatest market opportunity by globally targeting China's 1.34 billion consumers. China surpassed Japan's market value in August 2010 to become the second largest economy after the United States, leading both India and Germany in fourth and fifth position, respectively. Goldman Sachs estimates that China will overtake the United States in total GDP in 2019, although estimates vary.[16] Japanese firms now have 85 percent of world market potential outside their home market, while German firms have 94 percent of world market potential outside of their borders. Non-EU companies have just over 500 million people in the member states of the EU to target with their products and services.

Thousands of companies have recognized the importance of conducting business activities outside their home country. Industries that were strictly national in scope only a few years ago are dominated today by global companies with home bases on all continents and in all world regions. The rise of the global corporation closely parallels the rise of the national corporation, which emerged from the local and regional corporation in the 1880s and the 1890s in the United States. The auto industry provides a dramatic example. In the first quarter of the twentieth century, there were thousands of auto

---

[12] As of December 12, 2012.

[13] David B. Yoffie, cited in "The Apple in His Eye," *The New York Times*, January 31, 2010.

[14] Ibid.

[15] Devin Leonard, "The Last Pitchman," *Businessweek*, June 14–20, 2010.

[16] http://www.istockanalyst.com/article/viewarticle/articleid/4894427

companies in the world and more than 500 in the United States alone. In most industries, the companies that will survive and prosper in this century will be global enterprises. Companies that do not respond to the challenges and opportunities of globalization will be absorbed by more dynamic enterprises. As Thomas Middelhoff, chairman of Bertelsmann AG, said recently, "There are no German and American companies. There are only successful and unsuccessful companies."[17]

Table 1-4 shows the top 10 of the Forbes Global 2000, a list of global companies for 2016 ranked in terms of market capitalization, that is the market value of all shares of stock outstanding. Table 1-5 provides a different perspective: the top 10 of Forbes 2016 ranking of the largest global firms by revenues. Comparing the top 10 companies in each table, it is striking to note that while all 10 of the largest global firms measured by market value are North American, on the most profitable list of the Forbes 2000, 2016 ranked companies, the top 10 global firms are from more diverse countries, including Netherlands, UK, Japan, China and Germany. In light of china's growth as an industrial exporter of the past decade, it is not surprising that 2 of the top 10 biggest global competitors are from China: Petro China, and Sinopec China are engaged in oil and gas extraction. Out of the top 10 global firms in terms of revenue, four are from oil and gas sector clearly showing dominance by beating out other industries such as banking, automobile, retail and hi-tech services and equipment. Toyota of Japan and Volkswagen Group of Germany are the two automobile companies proudly figuring in the top 10 list in terms of revenue generation and signalling their superior global business strategy performance over the traditional past performers in automobile industry like General Motors, Daimler Chrysler and Ford Motor Company. Wal-Mart store being the largest global company based on the sales revenue is successfully demonstrating its ability to thwart the competition from mushrooming online retail firms. It has organically grown to the top sales position over the past decade through the growth strategy of retail expansion and not through mergers and acquisitions.

TABLE 1-4 The World's Largest Corporation by Market Value, 2016

Rank	Company	Country	Sales	Profits	Assets	Market Value	Industry
1	Apple	United States	$233.3 B	$53.7 B	$293.3 B	$586 B	Tech, hardware, Equip
2	Alphabet	United States	$77.2 B	$17 B	$149.7 B	$500.1 B	Conglomerate
3	Microsoft	United States	$86.6 B	$10.2 B	$181.9 B	$407 B	Software service
4	ExxonMobil	United States	$236.8 B	$16.2 B	$336.8 B	$363.3 B	Oil and Gas
5	Berkshire Hathaway	United States	$210.8 B	$24.1 B	$561.1 B	$360.1 B	Financials
6	Face book	United States	$17.9 B	$3.7 B	$49.4 B	$314.8 B	Communication
7	Johnson & Johnson	United States	$70.2 B	$15.4 B	$133.4 B	$312.6 B	Medical Equipments and Supplies
8	Amazon.com	United States	$107 B	$596 M	$67.7 B	$292.6 B	Internet & Catalogue Retail
9	General Electric	United States	$122.4 B	$1.7 B	$492.7 B	$285.6 B	Conglomerates
10	Wells Fargo	United States	$91.4 B	$22.7 B	$1,849.2 B	$256 B	Major Banks

Source: Forbes, The World's Biggest Public Companies, 2016, accessed 29 August, 2016 http://www.forbes.com/global2000/list/#tab:overall

[17] As quoted in "Global Mall," *The Wall Street Journal*, May 7, 1998, 1.

TABLE 1-5 The World's Largest Corporation by Revenue, 2016

Rank	Company	Country	Sales Revenue	Profits	Assets	Market Value	Industry
1	Wal-Mart Stores	United States	$482.1 B	$14.7 B	$199.6 B	$215.7 B	Discount Stores
2	Sinopec	China	$283.6 B	$5.1 B	$223.7 B	$89.9 B	Oil & Gas Operations
3	Petro China	China	$274.6 B	$5.7 B	$368.7 B	$203.8 B	Oil & Gas Operations
4	Royal Dutch Shell	Netherlands	$264.9 B	$2.1 B	$340.2 B	$210 B	Oil & Gas Operations
5	Volkswagen Group	Germany	$246.2 B	$7.1 B	$414.6 B	$73.1 B	Auto & Truck Manufacturers
6	ExxonMobil	United States	$236.8 B	$16.2 B	$336.8 B	$363.3 B	Oil & Gas Operations
7	Toyota Motor	Japan	$235.8 B	$19.3 B	$406.7 B	$177 B	Auto & Truck Manufacturers
8	Apple	United States	$233.3 B	$53.7 B	$293.3 B	$586 B	Computer Hardware
9	BP	United Kingdom	$218.7 B	$–6.5 B	$261.8 B	$99 B	Oil & Gas Operations
10	Berkshire Hathaway	United States	$210.8 B	$24.1 B	$561.1 B	$360.1 B	Investment Services

INDIAN-CHINA GROWTH STORY FOR AUTOMOBILE SECTOR

Indian automobile sector in the 1980s depicted a story of piggybacking on the foreign automobile companies with the executions of a number of joint venture agreements. The global automobile majors were also to a great extent, sceptical about the country's true potential and hence desired to reduce their involvement as minority partners or as technology tie- ups. The radical policy changes during the post 1991 period brought a face change to the automobile sector in India. A number of foreign automobile companies like Hyundai, Toyota etc took active interest in entering the country with manufacturing set up. During 2015 the country ranked 6th top automobile manufacturer in the world with about 4.13 millions unit production. China ranked number one with mammoth production size of 24.5 million followed by USA (12.1 million), Japan (9.28 million), Germany (6.03 million), South Korea (4.56 million) and India (4.13 million) (see Table 1-6 and Figure 1-5). However, in terms of yearly growth rate India ranked only second after Spain with 7.3 percent, amongst the top ten countries who recorded positive growth followed by Mexico (5.90%), USA (3.8 %), China (3.3 %), Germany (2.1%), and South Korea (0.7%) (Table 1-7).

However, in the Asia Oceania region, India is (2015) the 4th largest manufacturers of motor vehicle after countries like China, Japan and South Korea as shown in the Table 1-7. China topped the list with 24.5 million vehicle productions followed by Japan of 9.28 million productions during the year 2015. South Korea is marginally higher than India with production of 4.56 million vehicles during 2015. India clocked 4.13 million vehicle productions during 2015 which was about 7.13 percent more than its production during 2014. The Table 1-7 also indicates that India registered a handsome production growth rate (year on year from 2014 to 2015) of 7.31 percent which is even more than that of China at 3.25 percent.

Motorisation rate is a good indicator of vehicle penetration in a country, which is expressed as the number of passenger cars per 1000 inhabitants. Here, passenger car indicates a road motor vehicle used for the carriage of passengers and designed to seat no more than nine persons (including the driver). The term "passenger car" therefore includes very small cars to taxis to pick-ups and hired passenger cars with

TABLE 1-6 Top 10 Automobile Producers of the World, 2015

Country	Production of cars in nos)	Production of Commercial Vehicle in nos	Total (Nos)	Percentage change in production (y-o-y)
China	210,79,427	34,23,899	245,03,326	3.30%
USA	41,63,679	79,36,416	121,00,095	3.80%
Japan	78,30,722	14,47,516	92,78,238	-5.10%
Germany	57,07,938	3,25,226	60,33,164	2.10%
South Korea	41,35,108	4,20,849	45,55,957	0.70%
India	33,78,063	7,47,681	41,25,744	7.30%
Mexico	19,68,054	15,97,415	35,65,469	5.90%
Spain	22,18,980	5,14,221	27,33,201	13.70%
Brazil	20,18,954	4,10,509	24,29,463	–22.80%
Canada	8,88,565	13,94,909	22,83,474	–4.60%

Adapted from Organisation Internationale des Constructeursd'Automobiles (OICA): http://www.oica.net/category/production-statistics/, as accessed on 10 January 2017 at 6pm.

seating capacity less than 10 persons but exclude motorcycles. The Table 1-8 indicates the motorisation rate of few prominent passenger car producing countries located in the Asia Oceania region. The Table 1-8 indicates that Australia topped the list with as much as 714 passenger cars per 1000 inhabitants living in that country whereas, Bangladesh has very low motorisation rate of 5 passenger cars per 1000 inhabitants during 2014. Malaysia and South Korea are going neck to neck with 405 and 406 as motorisation rate. China with a motorisation rate of 102 is waiting like a

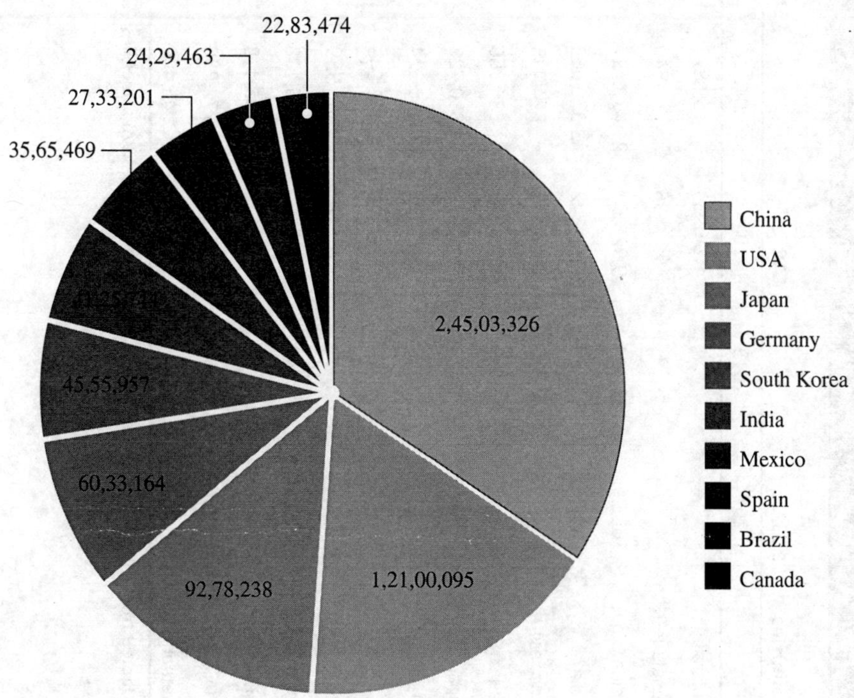

FIGURE 1-5 Top 10 Automobile Producers of the World, 2015

TABLE 1-7 World Motor Vehicle Production in Asia-Oceania Region in Units

Countries	BUS		CAR		Heavy Trucks		LCV		Total		% Change (y-o-y)
	2014	2015	2014	2015	2014	2015	2014	2015	2014	2015	
Australia			166,933	159,872	5,325	5,471	8,053	7,666	180,311	173,009	−4.05
Bangladesh			536	540					536	540	0.75
China	162,292	163,894	19,928,505	21,079,427	1,770,109	1467217	1,870,694	1,792,788	23,731,600	24,503,326	3.25
India	44,062	53,223	3,162,372	3,378,063	204,578	267,224	433,845	427,234	3,844,857	4,125,744	7.31
Indonesia	4,105	3,873	1,013,172	824,445	120,014	70,747	161,232	199,715	1,298,523	1,098,780	−15.38
Iran	417	685	925,975	884,866	15,757	14,159	148,697	82,627	1,090,846	982,337	−9.95
Japan	9,402	11,425	8,277,070	7,830,722	604,768	586,562	883,425	849,529	9,774,665	9,278,238	−5.08
Malaysia	683	517	545,122	558,324	5,123	3,460	44,206	52,370	595,134	614,671	3.28
Pakistan	563	773	126,020	182,548	3,375	4,635	18,788	41,730	148,746	229,686	54.41
Philippines			74,322	77,539	10,227	10,960	22,389	23,994	106,938	112,493	5.19
South Korea	17,304	17,948	4,124,116	4,135,108	95,560	94,029	287,952	308,872	4,524,932	4,555,957	0.69
Taiwan			332,629	298,418	3,713	4,418	42,881	48,249	379,223	351,085	−7.42
Thailand	563	4,590	743,258	772,250	17,527	22,700	1,119,239	1,115,880	1,880,587	1,915,420	1.85
Vietnam			44,328	45,400	4,543	4,600			48,871	50,000	2.31

Adapted from Organisation Internationale des Constructeursd'Automobiles (OICA): http://www.oica.net/category/production-statistics/, as accessed on 10 January 2017 at 6pm.

TABLE 1-8 Motorisation Rate of Few Prominent Countries Located in the Asia Oceania Region.

Country	Motorization rate 2013 (/1000 population.)	Motorization rate 2014 (/1000 population.)
Afghanistan	50	49
Australia	705	714
Bangladesh	4	5
Brunei	416	482
China	91	102
Hong-Kong	88	90
India	20	22
Indonesia	77	83
Iran	164	170
Japan	602	607
Malaysia	398	405
Pakistan	15	16
Philippines	35	35
Singapore	154	150
South Korea	394	406
Sri Lanka	49	50
Taiwan	314	320
Thailand	208	232
Vietnam	21	22

Source: Organisation Internationale des Constructeursd'Automobiles" (OICA).http://www.oica.net/category/production-statistics/

TABLE 1-9 Projected Motorisation Rate of Selected Countries of the World

Selected Countries	Motorization Rate 2013 (/1000inh.)	Motorization Rate 2014 (/1000inh.)	Motorization Rate 2025 (/1000inh.)	Change	Growth Rate %
United Kingdom	569	575	602	27	4.62
Russia	337	354	388	34	9.48
USA	797	808	930	122	15.14
Brazil	198	207	221	14	7.00
China	91	102	187	85	83.04
India	20	22	72	50	225.94
Japan	602	607	553	–54	–8.94
South Korea	394	406	553	147	36.07

Source: Author's calculation, data from OICA and projected 2025 motorisation data from Roland Berger strategy report.

TABLE 1-10 Future Markets of Automobile in the World

Selected Countries	Motorization rate 2025 (/1000 inh.)	Population 2025 (000)	Size of automobile market 2025 in number of units
United Kingdom	602	61,243	36,868,286
Russia	388	1,25,687	48,766,556
USA	930	3,97,063	369,268,590
Brazil	221	2,18,980	48,394,580
China	187	14,70,787	275,037,169
India	72	13,51,801	97,329,672
Japan	553	1,23,798	68,460,294
South Korea	553	52,065	28,791,945

Source: Author's calculation

sleeping tiger for the future surge.[18] In terms of motorisation rate, India clocked only 22 during the year 2014 which may be considered as low and does not commensurate with its recent economic progress. Experts are of the opinion that the country's poor motorisation rate is not the true reflection of its potential. India's motorisation rate can be perceived to be very low when one considers the highest motorisation rate in the world, which during 2014 was recorded as 808 in the USA. The average motorisation rate in Europe was 464 during 2014. In Asia the highest motorisation rate of 607 was achieved by Japan during 2014. However, when one looks at vehicle concentration in the cities of India, the low motorisation picture of the country gets changed. In India the big cities are clocking motorisation rate more than 100 and interestingly are fast increasing. Delhi, Chennai, and Coimbatore have more than 100 cars per 1,000 population. The city of Delhi itself has 157 cars per 1000 population while other cities like Bangalore, Pune, Thane etc. are also not lagging far behind. The recent study report on future motorisation rate of the emerging countries of the world released by strategy consultant Roland Berger suggest, that backed by the city led increasing motor vehicle ownership India is going to clock 72 as motorisation rate by 2025.

The Table 1-9 has been constructed with the help of OICA data on motorisation rates of few emerging economies of the world during 2014 and motorisation rate of these countries by 2025 as projected by strategy consultant Roland Berger. The Table 1-9 and 1-10 indicate towards a few important understandings so far as the potential demand of the automobiles in the world and where the automobile marketers should concentrate their marketing attention. It shows that during the period 2014 to 2025 India would be catching up the motorisation rate with huge growth rate of 226 percent and during the same period China would clock in second with 83 percent growth rate. Japan would have a sluggish negative growth rate of 8.94 percent. Interestingly, USA would still be growing at the rate of 15.14 percent during the same period and almost achieve 100 percent motorisation with 930 automobile per 1000 population. South Korea would be another country with prospects as it would also grow fairly well with a growth rate of about 36 percent.

---

[18] The Economic Times, October, 2014 available at http://economictimes.indiatimes.com/industry/indias-passenger-vehicle-and-two-wheeler-market-steer-towards-a-double-digit-growth-report/articleshow/44989399.cms

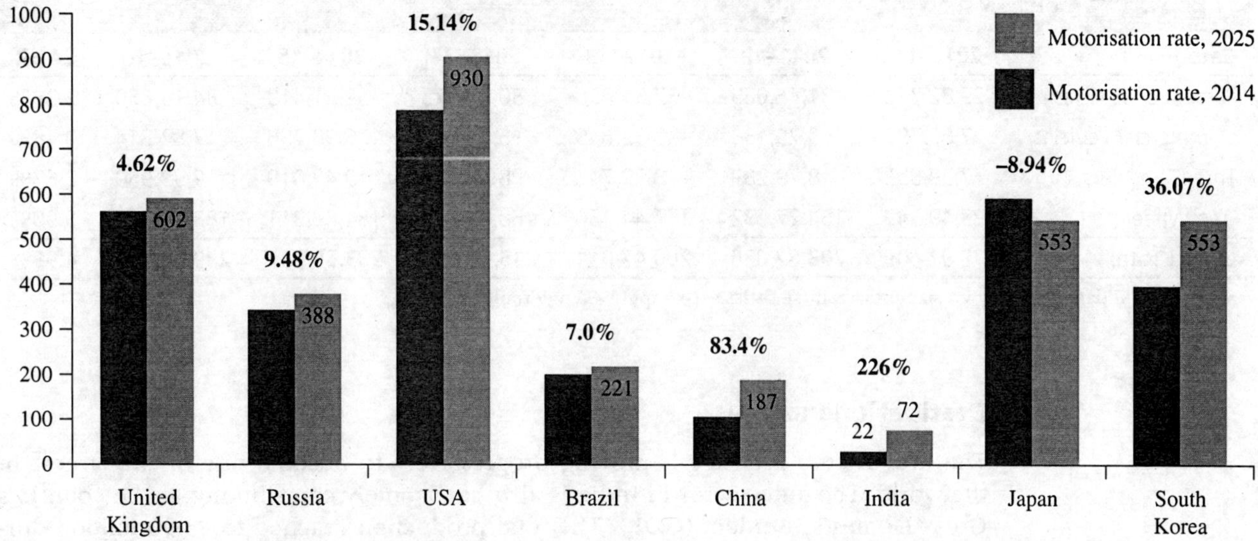

FIGURE 1-6 Future Motorisation Rate and India Catching Up.
Source: Author's calculation

The Figure 1-6 shows that India and China with a growth rate of 226 percent and 83 percent respectively are going to draw all the attention of the automobile marketers of the world. Therefore, Asia will be leading from the front in generating the automobile demand for the global level auto companies of the world. Surely, the auto marketers are not missing these facts and hence equipping themselves adequately throughout the last decade to reap benefits of the future by believing in the good old global marketing saying, "we are there where market is".

FUTURE MARKETS OF AUTOMOBILE IN THE WORLD

What could be the future market size in some of the leading auto demand countries of the world? The global auto marketers need to know about it in order to reposition their marketing strategy. A notional estimate can be made out of the 2025 projected market size of some of the prospective countries of the world from motorisation rate (projected) and population size (projected) for the year 2025 for the countries. The Table 1-10 shows the projected size of the automobile market in number of units during the year 2025 in some selected countries of the world.

The Table 1-10 shows that USA continues to lead the pack by being the country to have about 369 million passenger cars. China would be the second largest country, to be the abode of about 275 million passenger cars during 2025. India would also not be lagging far behind with about 97 million passenger cars of the world by 2025 and even surpassing about 68 million passenger cars which Japan would be housing by then. Brazil and Russia, with about 48 million passenger cars in their respective countries continues to attract the global auto marketers during these periods up to 2025. Moreover, China and India together would be the star attraction of the major global level marketers as these two countries together will surpass even USA with about 372 million passengers in their countries.

TABLE 1-11 Production in Number of Units

Category	2010–11	2011–12	2012–13	2013–14	2014–15	2015–16	CAGR
Passenger Vehicles	29,82,772	31,46,069	32,31,058	30,87,973	32,21,419	34,13,859	2.28%
Commercial Vehicles	7,60,735	9,29,136	8,32,649	6,99,035	6,98,298	7,82,814	0.48%
Three Wheelers	7,99,553	8,79,289	8,39,748	8,30,108	9,49,019	9,33,950	2.62%
Two Wheelers	133,49,349	154,27,532	157,44,156	168,83,049	184,89,311	188,29,786	5.90%
Grand Total	**178,92,409**	**203,82,026**	**206,47,611**	**215,00,165**	**233,58,047**	**239,60,409**	**4.99%**

Source: SIAM data (http://www.siamindia.com/statistics.aspx?mpgid=8&pgidtrail=14)

Destination India

The Indian auto industry is moving progressively to become one of the largest in the world. The auto sector in India is also handsomely contributing to the country's Gross Domestic Product (GDP). The total production reached to 23.96 million during 2015–16 from 17.89 million during 2010–11 and thereby registering CAGR of about 5 percent as shown in the Table 1–11. Two Wheelers grew faster from 13.35 million during 2010–11 to 18.83 million during 2015–16 at CAGR 5.9 percent. Out of the total production of automobile during 2015–16 about 81 per cent are two wheeler productions which indicated a demand of the middleclass population as well as a rural demand.

Two wheelers recorded a strong domestic sales growth with 16.46 million during 2015–16 from 15.98 million last year. Overall sectoral sales grew at the rate 4.76 percent CAGR as shown in the Table 1-12 below. The sales of passenger vehicles also grew moderately and registered a CAGR of 2.28 percent. Though the passenger car sector got hit by the ban of Diesel cars in some cities of the country but it shows that the Industry could still maintain a moderate growth rate.

India is looked upon by the major global level auto players as a convenient location to produce and export the same to the different markets of the world. During the period 2014–15 to 2015–16 the export of commercial vehicle grew sharply from 0.09 million to 1.02 million thereby registering a growth of about 17 percent as shown in the Table 1-13. During the year 2016–16 the country exported about 2.5 million two wheelers to the different countries of the world, out of 3.64 million sectoral exports constituting to about 67.54 percent of the total automobile export of the country. Countries like Colombia, Sri Lanka, Nigeria, Bangladesh, Philippines, Nepal, Mexico, Iran, Guatemala, and Argentina remained the top ten export destination of two wheelers from the country during 2015–16.

TABLE 1-12 Trend of Domestic Sales of Automobile in India

Category	2010–11	2011–12	2012–13	2013–14	2014–15	2015–16	CAGR
Passenger Vehicles	25,01,542	26,29,839	26,65,015	25,03,509	26,01,236	27,89,678	1.83%
Commercial Vehicles	6,84,905	8,09,499	7,93,211	6,32,851	6,14,948	6,85,704	0.02%
Three Wheelers	5,26,024	5,13,281	5,38,290	4,80,085	5,32,626	5,38,092	0.38%
Two Wheelers	1,17,68,910	1,34,09,150	137,97,185	148,06,778	159,75,561	164,55,911	5.75%
Grand Total	**154,81,381**	**173,61,769**	**177,93,701**	**184,23,223**	**197,24,371**	**204,69,385**	**4.76%**

TABLE 1-13 Export of Automobile from India

Category	2010–11	2011–12	2012–13	2013–14	2014–15	2015–16	CAGR
Passenger Vehicles	4,44,326	5,08,783	5,59,414	5,96,142	6,21,341	6,53,889	6.65%
Commercial Vehicles	74,043	92,258	80,027	77,050	86,939	1,01,689	5.43%
Three Wheelers	2,69,968	3,61,753	3,03,088	3,53,392	4,07,600	4,04,441	6.97%
Two Wheelers	15,31,619	19,75,111	19,56,378	20,84,000	24,57,466	24,81,193	8.37%
Grand Total	**23,19,956**	**29,37,905**	**28,98,907**	**31,10,584**	**35,73,346**	**36,41,212**	**7.80%**

NEW INVESTMENT IN INDIA

Buoyed with the potential of Indian automobile sector many global companies are investing in India to reap future benefits. It is estimated that about ₹278.3 billion of investments are planned by the major passenger car manufacturers of the world. The Suzuki motor corporation of Japan topped the list with about ₹85 billion, followed by Renault –Nissan (₹50 billion), Ford Motor (₹40 billion), Isuzu (₹30 billion), Foton (₹30 billion), Fiat –Chrysler (₹20 billion), Honda (₹13.8 billion), Volvo (₹7 billion), Mercedes Benz (₹1.5 billion), and BMW (₹1 billion). Suzuki motors of Japan would enhance its production capacity with 7.5 lakh units more to cater to the future demand. Ford Motor of USA, is planning to set up its Research and Development centre in India. Renault –Nissan, is going to invest in its Chennai plant for supplying of more small cars for Indian market. Isuzu of Japan, is already producing passenger vehicles with a contract manufacture agreement with Hindustan Motors and plans to invest more to set up its first car plant in Sri City (SEZ near Chennai) to produce 120,000 units of light commercial vehicles

TABLE 1-14 New Investment in Passenger Vehicle Manufacturing in India

Auto companies	Country of origin	Proposed investment In Rs million	Expansion proposed
Suzuki Motors	Japan	85000	To set up facility with 7.5 lakh unit capacity in phases
Ford Motor	USA	40000	To set up R&D centre
Renault -Nissan	Franco-Japanese	50000	To expand capacity of Chennai plant
Isuzu	Japan	30000	To set up its first car plant in Sri City (SEZ near Chennai) to produce 120,000 units of light commercial vehicles and sports utility vehicles by 2020.
Foton	China	30000	To set up manufacturing plant at Chakan and then expansion.
Fiat –Chrysler	Italy	20000	To manufacture luxury SUV.
Volkswagen	Germany		To increase production capacity of Chakan plant to 20000 units.
Volvo	Sweden	7000	To expand present capacity.
BMW	Germany	1000	For localisation of cars
Honda	Japan	13800	To set up new plan and expand capacity of Tapukura plant (Rajasthan).
Mercedes Benz	Germany	1500	To add a new manufacturing line at its Chakan plant for production capacity enhancement.

Source: http://economictimes.indiatimes.com/industry/auto/news/industry/automobile-companies-are-betting-big-on-india-investing-in-building-new-capacity/articleshow/47621633.cms

and sports utility vehicles by 2020. The big Chinese auto brand Foton, the world's second largest commercial vehicle manufacturer, is all set to start up a manufacturing plant at Chakan near Pune city and then plans to expand. Fiat Chrysler Automobiles (FCA), the seventh-largest automaker in the world, is investing in India to manufacture its famous Jeep Vehicles in the country. The Japanese car maker Honda, is all set for a new plant and intents to expand the capacity of its existing manufacturing plant at Tapukura (Rajasthan).

MANAGEMENT ORIENTATIONS

The form and substance of a company's response to global market opportunities depend greatly on management's assumptions or beliefs—both conscious and unconscious—about the nature of the world. The worldview of a company's personnel can be described as ethnocentric, polycentric, regiocentric, or geocentric.[19] Management at a company with a prevailing ethnocentric orientation may consciously make a decision to move in the direction of geocentricism. The orientations—collectively known as the EPRG framework—are summarized in Figure 1-7.

Recent studies have demonstrated that the cognitive orientation of top-level management can either help propel organizations toward fast track internationalization—born globals—or toward lower-risk, international commitments such as exporting in the early phases of internationalization. These domestic mind-sets refer to management's knowledge and knowledge structures prior to going international and are based on cultural values and managerial experience and learning. They are the lens through which management perceives the environment and makes decisions. Activities that cultivate greater learning and knowledge creation can lead to a management mind-set which fosters, for example, new ways to compete and differentiate offerings from competitors. In other words, a more complex knowledge base can lead to stronger and often faster or earlier international commitment and risk taking. In contrast, consistent

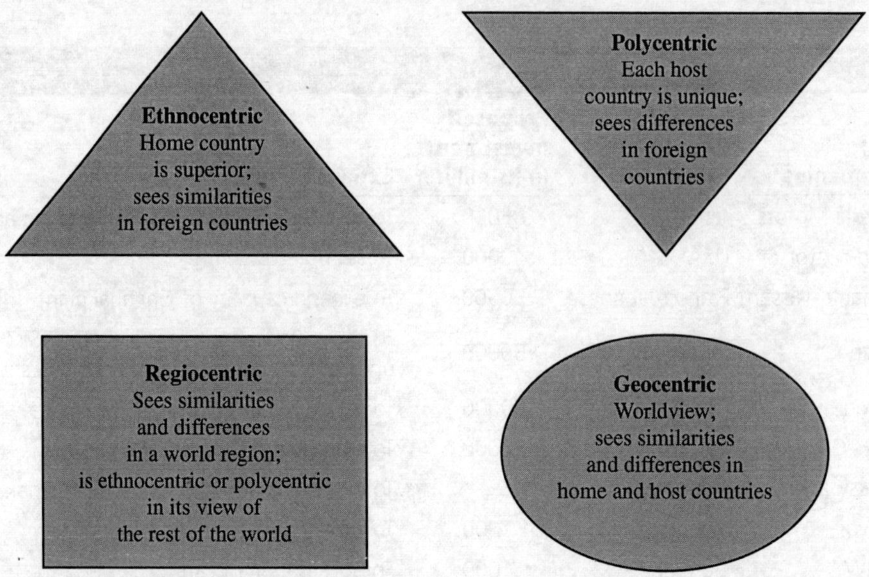

FIGURE 1-7 Orientation of Management and Companies

19 Adapted from Howard Perlmutter, "The Tortuous Evolution of the Multinational Corporation," *Columbia Journal of Business* (January–February 1969).

use of the same home market patterns of competition and business activity can lead to inertia, which may prevent firms from expanding both their mind-sets and markets.[20]

In later chapters, we will discuss global organizational design and the importance of management of human resources and talent capital worldwide. For now, it is important to note that cognitive orientations of management are vital to enterprise-wide growth and expansion strategies.[21]

Ethnocentric Orientation

A person who assumes his or her home country is superior compared with the rest of the world is said to have an ethnocentric orientation. The ethnocentric orientation means company personnel see only similarities in markets and assume the products and practices that succeed in the home country will, due to their demonstrated superiority, be successful anywhere. At some companies, the ethnocentric orientation means that opportunities outside the home country are ignored. Such companies are sometimes called domestic companies. Ethnocentric companies that do conduct business outside the home country can be described as international companies; they adhere to the notion that the products that succeed in the home country are superior and, therefore, can be sold everywhere without adaptation.

In the ethnocentric international company, foreign operations are viewed as being secondary or subordinate to domestic operations. An ethnocentric company operates under the assumption that tried and true headquarters' knowledge and organizational capabilities can be applied in other parts of the world. Although this can sometimes work to a company's advantage, valuable managerial knowledge and experience in local markets may go unnoticed. For a manufacturing firm, ethnocentrism means foreign markets are viewed as a means of disposing of surplus domestic production. Plans for overseas markets are developed utilizing policies and procedures identical to those employed at home. No systematic marketing research is conducted outside the home country, and no major modifications are made to products. Even if consumer needs or wants in international markets differ from those in the home country, those differences are ignored at headquarters.

Fifty years ago, most business enterprises—and especially those located in a large country such as the United States—could operate successfully with an ethnocentric orientation. Today, ethnocentrism is a fatal orientation for companies who are competing in a global or globalizing industry.

Polycentric Orientation

The polycentric orientation is the opposite of ethnocentrism. The term *polycentric* describes management's often unconscious belief or assumption that each country in which a company does business is unique. This assumption lays the groundwork for each subsidiary to develop its own unique business and marketing strategies in order to succeed; the term *multinational company* is often used to describe such a structure. An executive offered the following description of his polycentric company: "We were like a medieval state. There was the king and his court, but it was the in-country barons who were in charge. The king and his court might declare this or that, but the land barons went and did their thing."

---

[20] Sucheta Nadkarni and Pedro David Perez, "Prior Conditions and Early International Commitment: The Mediating Role of Domestic Mindset," *Journal of International Business Studies*, 38 (2007): 160–170.

[21] See, for example, Orly Levy, Schon Beechler, et al., "What We Talk About When We Talk About 'Global Mindset': Managerial Cognition in Multinational Corporations," *Journal of International Business Studies*, 38 (2007): 231–258.

Regiocentric and Geocentric Orientations

In a company with a regiocentric orientation, management views regions as unique and seeks to develop an integrated regional strategy. For example, a European company that focuses its attention on the EU or Europe is regiocentric. A company with a geocentric orientation views the entire world as a potential market and strives to develop integrated world market strategies. A company whose management has a regiocentric or geocentric orientation is a global or transnational company.[22]

The geocentric orientation represents a synthesis of ethnocentrism and polycentrism; it is a worldview that sees similarities and differences in markets and countries and seeks to create a global strategy that is fully responsive to local needs and wants. A regiocentric manager might be said to have a worldview on a regional scale; the world outside the region of interest will be viewed with an ethnocentric or a polycentric orientation, or a combination of the two. Many companies seek to strengthen their regional competitiveness as a first stage in globalization rather than moving directly to worldwide operations. These companies have a global strategy and are focusing on establishing a regional competitive advantage as the first stage of globalization.

The ethnocentric company is centralized in its marketing management, the polycentric company is decentralized, and the regiocentric and geocentric companies are integrated on a regional and global scale, respectively. A crucial difference between the orientations is the underlying assumption for each. The ethnocentric orientation is based on a belief in home-country superiority. The underlying assumption of the polycentric approach is that there are so many differences in cultural, economic, and marketing conditions in the world that it is impossible and futile to attempt to transfer experience across national boundaries, except in exceptional cases where the product or service is driven to global standards and has become a truly global product. The geocentric company believes that there are similarities and differences in markets and that they can create the greatest value by recognizing when to extend a global element of their offer and when to adapt to regional, national, and subnational differences.

DRIVING AND RESTRAINING FORCES

The remarkable growth of the global economy over the past 60 years has been shaped by the dynamic interplay of various driving and restraining forces. During most of those decades, companies from different parts of the world in different industries achieved great success by pursuing international, multinational, or global strategies. Over the past two decades, changes in the global business environment have presented significant challenges to the more industrial-age, purely domestic ways of doing business. The growing importance of global marketing stems from the fact that driving forces have significantly more momentum than restraining forces in defining the competitive global environment. The forces affecting global integration are shown in Figure 1-8.

---

[22] Although the definitions provided here are important, to avoid confusion we will use the term *global marketing* when describing the general activities of global companies. Another note of caution is in order: usage of the terms *international, multinational,* and *global* varies widely. Alert readers of the business press are likely to recognize inconsistencies; usage does not always reflect the definitions provided here. In particular, companies that are global as defined in this book are often described as multinational enterprises (abbreviated MNE) or multinational corporations (abbreviated MNC). The United Nations prefers the term *transnational company* rather than *global company.* When we refer to an international company or a multinational, we will do so in a way that maintains the distinctions described in the text.

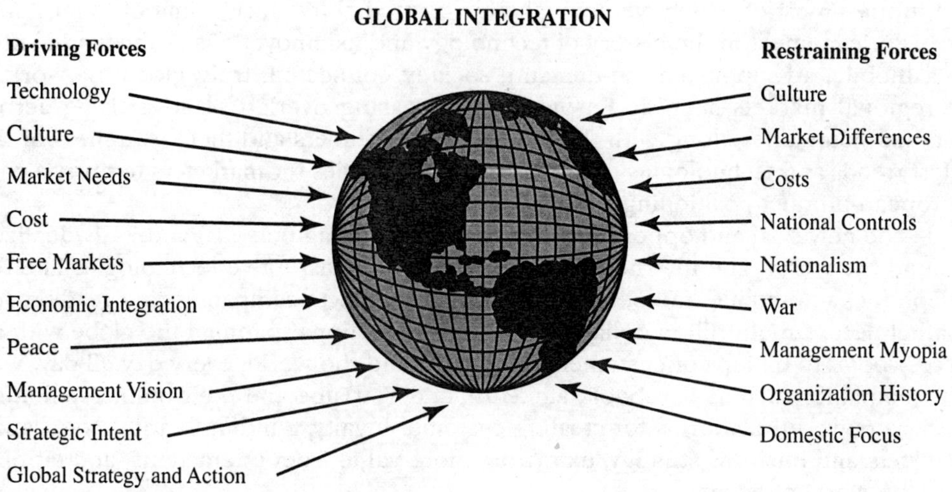

FIGURE 1-8 Global Integration

Driving Forces

Converging market needs and wants; technology advances; pressure to cut costs; pressure to improve quality; access to labor, talent, raw materials and energy needs; dramatic improvements in communication and transportation technologies; global economic growth; and opportunities for leverage, all represent important driving forces. Almost all industries are subject to these forces and, therefore, are candidates for globalization.

TECHNOLOGY Technology is a significant, universal factor that crosses national, regional, and cultural boundaries. Technology is truly stateless; there are no cultural boundaries limiting its application. Once a technology is developed, it soon becomes available everywhere in the world. With 43 percent of the world's online population residing in Asia, China accounts for 17 percent of the global online population. China will have 1.3 billion subscribers and 957 million mobile web users by 2014 and has already surpassed the United States in the use of mobile Internet apps.[23] India's Internet population has grown to 71 million. Japan has about 21.8 million social network users, with about one-half actively managing their profiles. The Philippines has more than 106 million Facebook users and is ranked eighth in the world for countries with the highest number of residents using the social networking site. This growing phenomenon of online and mobile use supports Levitt's prediction concerning the emergence of global markets for standardized products. In his landmark Harvard Business Review article, Levitt anticipated the communication revolution that has, in fact, become a driving force behind global marketing[24] and the emergence of a true global village. The Internet's first ad appeared in October 1994 on Wired magazine's news site. It was part of the AT&T's "You Will" campaign showcasing technologies of

[23] The Nielsen Company, as reported by Jack Marshall, ClickZ online newsletter (August 6, 2010), accessed August 8, 2010.
[24] Levitt, "The Globalization of Markets."

the future—most of which we now take for granted.[25] It's "tech's time of tumult" and an historic moment in the history of technology and its innovations as the world shifts to a mobile, ad-supported, on-demand, socially connected, truly global network.[26] In regional markets such as Europe, the increasing overlap of advertising across national boundaries along with the mobility of consumers and their awareness of the latest trends and technologies have created opportunities for marketers to pursue pan-European product positioning.

The new goal and opportunity is to make marketing personal and individualized around the world. The Internet differs from previous disruptive technologies like the telephone, automobile, radio, and television. It connects companies to a ready-made marketplace: a multitrillion dollar network of connections spanning the globe with an access point to billions of customers located around the world, every day all day. Web 2.0 companies such as Facebook, LinkedIn, and YouTube and their online communities are powerful platforms for creating customer loyalty, building brands, co-creating products and business strategy, extracting more value from interactions, and tapping into the world of talent.

REGIONAL ECONOMIC AND POLITICAL AGREEMENTS A number of multilateral trade agreements have accelerated the pace of global integration. Examples include the mother of all regional unions, the European Union, which began after World War II as a free trade union and is today an economic and political union with a common currency, the euro. The EU includes 27 countries, 17 of which are in the euro zone. In addition, there are four candidate member states: Turkey, Croatia, Iceland, and the Former Yugoslav Republic of Macedonia.

The North American Free Trade Agreement (NAFTA) was signed by the governments of Canada, Mexico, and the United States, creating a free trade area in North America. The agreement came into force on January 1, 1994. It superseded the Canada–United States Free Trade Agreement signed in 1989.

The General Agreement on Tariffs and Trade (GATT), which was ratified by more than 120 nations in 1994, was replaced by the World Trade Organization to promote and protect free trade, but has come under attack by developing countries. The goal of several of the multilateral agreements is to facilitate South–South trade such as between Latin American (Mercosur also known as the Southern Common Markets) or African countries. The Commonwealth of Independent States (CIS) exists between 11 of the former 15 Soviet Republics. APEC (Asia-Pacific Economic Cooperation) is made up of 21 members, most with a coastline on the Pacific Ocean. The ASEAN Free Trade Area was created to promote regional stability and foster economic growth among its 10 Southeast Asian country members.

MARKET NEEDS AND WANTS A study of markets around the world reveals cultural universals as well as cultural differences. The common elements of human nature provide an underlying basis for the opportunity to create and serve global markets.

[25] Just over ten years ago, Sir Tim Berners-Lee, the inventor of the web, said, "I have a dream for the web [in which computers] become capable of analyzing all the data on the web—the content, links, and transactions between people and computers. A 'Semantic Web' which should make this possible, has yet to emerge, but when it does, the day-to-day mechanisms of trade, bureaucracy, and our daily lives will be handled by machines talking to machines. The 'intelligent agents' people have touted for ages will finally materialize." As reported by Vin Crosbie, "The New Media Stone Age," ClickZ online newsletter (February 6, 2009), accessed February 6, 2009, http://www.clickz.com/clickz/column/1709191/the-new-media-stone-age.

[26] David Kirkpatrick, "Tech's Time of Tumult," CNNMoney Fast Forward Newsletter (October 19, 2007), accessed October 19, 2007, CNNMoney.com.

The word *create* is deliberate. Most global markets do not exist in nature; they must be created by marketing effort. For example, no one needs soft drinks, and yet today, in some countries, per capita soft-drink consumption exceeds the consumption of water. Marketing has driven this change in behavior, and today the soft-drink industry is global. Consumer needs and wants around the world are converging today as never before. This creates an opportunity for global marketing. Multinational, multicountry strategy companies pursuing strategies of product adaptation run the risk of being overtaken by global competitors that have recognized opportunities to serve global customers with global products. Philips Lighting, the world's largest producer of industrial and consumer lighting products, is playing a large role in the ongoing global transformation from incandescent to solid-state lighting using LED technology. Focusing on worldwide innovation, Philips understands that new technology is "just a vehicle to respond to needs.…It's really about [looking] outside and understanding what the market needs are, what the future applications are, what the requirements are for lighting solutions and experiences in various places and spaces."[27]

Market needs and consumer desires will, in great part, be defined by the growing middle class of emerging economies. Until recently, the world's middle class has been located in the triad of Europe, North America, and Japan. In 2000, developing countries accounted for 56 percent of the global middle class. By 2030, this figure is expected to reach 93 percent, with China and India accounting for two-thirds of the growth. As a result, multinationals, which have viewed developing economies largely as a source of cheap labor, are now in the position to benefit from workers now able to afford more than life's necessities. In almost every country, the growing middle class spurs market trends and the creation of new products.[28] The global push to address this growing worldwide, middle-class, consumer audience is comprised of multifaceted integrating forces, such as digital information networks and globally integrated R&D, marketing programs, and distribution channels.[29]

Global customers, and not only those in the middle class, are suddenly beginning to look similar across international markets, and this similarity itself is an integrating force. For example, Japanese consumers are similar to consumers in Europe and the United States in their interest in seeking quality, value, and convenience and a less expensive product. Japanese consumers, like their European and North American counterparts, are flocking to discount and online retailers. Affordable private-label foods have increased significantly, and many consumers across the globe, despite smaller living spaces, are purchasing in bulk, eating at home instead of at restaurants, and packing their own lunches. This shift in attitude toward more cost consciousness and economy is projected to continue despite any longer term, global economic recovery.[30]

TRANSPORTATION AND COMMUNICATION IMPROVEMENTS The time and cost barriers associated with distance have fallen tremendously over the past 100 years. The jet airplane revolutionized communication by making it possible for people to travel around the world in just over one day's time. Tourism enables people from many countries to see and experience the newest products being sold abroad. One essential characteristic

---

[27] "Philips Lighting CEO Rudy Provost: Innovation Means Putting Consumers' Needs First," Knowledge@Wharton (February 20, 2008), accessed February 25, 2008, http://knowledge.wharton.upenn.edu/article.

[28] "The New Global Middle Class: Potentially Profitable—But Also Unpredictable," Knowledge@Wharton (July 9, 2008), accessed August 25, 2008, http://knowledge.wharton.upenn.edu/article.

[29] See, for example, Christopher P. Beshouri, "A Grassroots Approach to Emerging-Market Consumers," *The McKinsey Quarterly*, no. 4 (2006), accessed January 15, 2007, http://www.mckinseyquarterly.com/article.

[30] Brian Salsberg, "The New Japanese Consumer," *The McKinsey Quarterly* (March 2010), accessed March 12, 2010, http://www.mckinseyquarterly.com/article.

of the effective global business is face-to-face, real-time communication among business leadership and employees and between the company and its customers. Along with modern jet travel, communication technologies, which range from simple point-to-point voice communication to multiparty, multichannel, and multimedia applications, are reducing the barriers of distance and time. Examples of communications technology platforms include cellular systems, wireless LANs, and wireless personal area networks. Basic communications technology such as e-mail, fax, and pagers are found worldwide. Skype is a popular example of a VoIP (Voice over Internet Protocol) product,[31] with an estimated 600 million accounts worldwide. VoIP allows customers, executives, and managers to conduct business face-to-face in real time from virtually any part of the globe at almost no cost.

A similar revolution has occurred in transportation technology. Physical distribution has declined in terms of cost; the time required for shipment has been greatly reduced. For example, a distributor of a tablet PC located in Austin, Texas, can have the product shipped from a manufacturer outside Shanghai by FedEx Corp. in a total of five days. With finished product delivered to a truck, loaded on a plane in Shanghai to Anchorage, and then delivered by a series of flights and trucks to Austin, FedEx has become a de facto partner in thousands of retail operations around the globe, eliminating warehousing and inventory costs and offering competitive air express rates. This just-in-time value proposition offered by FedEx has made it number one in the China–US air express market.[32] With transport capabilities increasing and cost decreasing, distance factors matter less. For example, the per-unit cost of shipping automobiles from Japan and Korea to the United States by specially designed auto-transport ships is less than the cost of overland shipping from Detroit to either US coast.

PRODUCT DEVELOPMENT COSTS The pressure for globalization is intense when new products require major investments and long periods of development time. The pharmaceuticals industry provides a striking illustration of this driving force. According to the Pharmaceutical Manufacturers Association (PMA), the cost of developing a new drug in 1976 was $54 million; by 1982, the cost had increased to $87 million. By 1993, the cost of discovering, developing, and launching a new drug had reached $359 million,[33] and by 2003, studies indicate the cost had more than doubled to $802 million.[34] Other estimates indicate that costs may have more than quadrupled during the same time period to 1.7 billion.[35] The same kind of expenditures and development times are common in other industries. These outlays provide an incentive to expand globally to recover costs of discovery and development and realize the potential returns of additional market revenue.

QUALITY Global marketing strategies can generate greater revenue and greater operating margins, which, in turn, support the cost of world-class design and manufacturing quality. A global and a domestic company may each spend 5 percent of sales on R&D, but the global company will have many times the total revenue of the domestic because it serves the world market. Global companies raise the bar for all competitors in an industry.

---

[31] Skype was first released in 2003, written by Estonian developers Ahti Heinla, Priit Kasesalu, and Jaan Tallinn. It has developed into a platform with over 600 million users and was acquired by Microsoft in 2011 for $8.5 billion; Wikipedia, Skype, accessed December 12, 2012.

[32] Dean Foust, "Taking Off Like 'A Rocket Ship,'" *Businessweek*, April 3, 2006, 76.

[33] PMA figures cited in T. W. Malnight, "Globalization of an Ethnocentric Firm: An Evolutionary Perspective," *Strategic Management Journal*, 16, no. 2 (2006): 123.

[34] Joseph A. DiMasi, Ronald W. Hansen, and Henry G. Grabowski, "The Price of Innovation: New Estimates of Drug Development Costs," *Journal of Health Economics* (February 2003).

[35] "Has the Pharmaceutical Blockbuster Model Gone Bust?," Bain & Company press release (December 8, 2008).

Global competition has forced all companies to improve quality. For truly global products, uniformity can drive down research, engineering, design, and production costs across business functions. Quality, uniformity, and cost reduction were all driving forces behind Ford's development of its "World Car." Manufacturing of the 2012 Focus, an all-new sedan and five-door hatchback, ramped up at Wayne Assembly in Michigan. Across the Atlantic, Ford's Saarlouis factory in Germany built virtually the same cars for Europeans. Manufacturing plants in Louisville, Kentucky (US), Vsevolozhsk, St Petersburg (Russia), and the Valencia plant in Spain were also scheduled to build the new-shape models. The global Focus is built and sold in the United States; the availability of diesel engines and a wagon body style in Europe will be the only significant regional differentiators for the model series in global markets.[36]

The global success or failure of this new Focus, the idea of engineering one car, one platform, one set of powertrains for one model that will be sold in the same segment the world over, is the true test of Ford's goal to become a global vehicle manufacturer.

WORLD ECONOMIC TRENDS There are three reasons why economic growth has been a driving force in the expansion of the international economy and the growth of global marketing. First, world growth has created market opportunities that provide a major incentive for companies to expand globally. At the same time, slower growth in a company's domestic market can signal the need to look abroad for opportunities in nations or regions with high rates of growth.

Second, economic growth has reduced resistance that might otherwise have developed in response to the entry of foreign firms into domestic economies. When a country is growing rapidly, policy makers are likely to look favorably on outsiders. A growing country means growing markets; there is often plenty of opportunity for everyone. In a growing market, it is possible for a foreign company to enter a domestic economy and establish itself without taking business away from local firms. Without economic growth, global enterprises may indeed take business away from domestic ones. Domestic businesses are more likely to seek governmental intervention to protect their local position if markets are not growing.

Worldwide movement toward deregulation and privatization is another driving force. The trend toward privatization is opening up formerly closed markets significantly, and tremendous opportunities are being created as a result. For example, when a nation's telephone company is a state monopoly, it is much easier to require it to buy only from national companies. An independent, private company will be more inclined to look for the best offer, regardless of the nationality of the supplier. Privatization of telephone systems around the world is creating opportunities and threats for every company in the industry.

LEVERAGE A global company possesses the unique opportunity to develop leverage. Leverage is simply some type of advantage that a company enjoys by virtue of the fact that it conducts business in more than one country. Four important types of leverage are experience transfers, scale economies, resource utilization, and global strategy (see Box 1-2).

1. *Experience transfers.* A global company can leverage its experience in any market in the world. It can draw on management practices, strategies, products, advertising appeals, or sales or promotional ideas that have been tested in actual markets and apply them in other comparable markets.

[36] Glenn Brooks, "All Eyes Focus on Alan Mulally's One Ford Strategy," AutomotiveWorld.com (March 17, 2011), http://www.automotiveworld.com/news//86323-all-eyes-focus-on-alan-mulally-s-one-ford-strategy

2. *Scale economies.* The global company can take advantage of its greater manufacturing volume to obtain traditional scale advantages within a single factory. Also, finished products can be produced by combining components manufactured in scale-efficient plants in different countries. Globalizing firms continue to look to economies of scale in their merger and acquisition activities as well as their overall global manufacturing strategy.

   Leverage from scale economies is not limited to manufacturing. Economies of scope, advantages gained by providing services across several product categories or geographical markets, drive industries toward globalization. For example, global firms such as Procter and Gamble, Colgate-Palmolive, and Unilever, in the household and personal care product categories, derive significant benefits from sharing the same distribution, marketing, design, and research capabilities across product categories and customer needs. By centralizing functional activities, global firms also create opportunities to improve corporate staff competence and quality, and affect worldwide corporate culture.
3. *Resource utilization.* A major strength of the global company is its ability to scan the entire world to identify people, money, and raw materials and use them effectively to compete in world markets. For many, if not all companies, talented people are a prime source of competitive advantage. The digital global economy is fueled by intellectual capital and the sharing of knowledge across worldwide enterprises. Global managers recognize that flat and networked organizations populated by empowered employees and managers are indispensable to quick decision making and response to rapidly changing marketplace demands. This is equally true for established companies and start-ups. Executives worldwide rank human performance and attracting and retaining people as their number one strategic priority. Global investment in human performance areas will be critical to building cross-cultural human talent. These include creating a high–performance workforce by matching talent with the right global opportunities, measuring and developing talent in real time and across borders, and linking workforce goals to business strategy and results. Building human assets involves understanding how a new generation of employees and corporate leadership from all points of the globe will function.
4. *Global strategy.* The global company's greatest single advantage can be its global strategy. A global strategy is built on an information system that scans the world business environment to identify opportunities, trends, threats, and resources. When opportunities are identified, the global company adheres to the three principles identified earlier in the chapter. It leverages its skills and focuses its resources to create superior perceived value for customers and achieve competitive advantage. The global strategy is a design to create a winning offering on a global scale. This takes great discipline, much creativity, and constant effort. The reward is not just success—it is survival.

BOX 1-2

Tata Auto Looking for More Intense Internationalization

It is important that a company has the twin characteristics of low-cost as well as quality manufacturing capability in order win over markets, country after country. TATA Motors Limited, (formerly known as Tata Engineering and Locomotive Company) is mastering this twin arts to become a true Indian multinational automotive manufacturing company. Though TATA Group is a household name in India with credible existence in the domestic market, it never lost sight of foreign markets. Since its inception in 1945 it grew in strength, establishing supremacy in the domestic market and finally went international in 1961. As of 2015, it marketed different types of automobile in more than 50 countries of Africa, Latin America, Europe, Russia, Asia Pacific, Middle East. In terms of number of countries, it has most presence in African countries where so far 19 countries have been invaded followed by Asia Pacific (12 countries), Middle East (9 countries), Latin America (4 countries), and 3 countries each in Europe and Russia as shown in the Table 1-15.

TABLE 1-15 Tata's Internationalisation in 50 Countries

Africa	South Africa, Angola, Algeria, Democratic Republic of Congo, Ghana, Kenya, Morocco, Mozambique, Nigeria, Seychelles, Tanzania, Tunisia, Uganda, Zambia, and Zimbabwe, Djibouti, Ethiopia, Senegal, Sudan, (19 countries)	Africa attracted more TATA automobiles like cars, buses, SUVs and trucks than any other continents of the world. TATA also customised its products to abide by country-specific legal requirement of these countries. To compete more effectively the company set up assembly plant at Rosslyn, South Africa, for assembling trucks ranging from 7 to 75 tonnes from semi knocked down parts exported from India.
Latin America	Bolivia, Chilli, Uruguay, Ecuador (4 countries)	Tata Motors entered the Bolivian market with its passenger cars during Feb 2016 partnering with local auto major Bolivian Auto Motors. During 2009 Tata made alliance with Chilean auto company SKBergé to market its products in the country. Tata Motors entered Uruguay with its import partner local auto giant Fiancar Group. Tata entered Ecuador with an importing and distributing partnership with local automobile company Central Motors.
Europe	Italy, Poland, Spain (3 countries)	TATA relies on private importers to import and sell its automobile to Italy, Poland, Spain.
Russia	Russia, Turkmenistan, Ukraine (3 countries)	Russia, Turkmenistan and Ukraine are increasingly becoming fond of wide range of TATA trucks. The company maintains a strong dealer's and distributor's network to provide customer services.
Asia Pacific	Afghanistan,Australia, Bangladesh,Bhutan, Indonesia, Malaysia,Myanmar,Nepal, Philippines, Sri Lanka, Thailand, Vietnam (12 countries)	Tata Motors first entered Sri Lanka in 1961 and has never looked backed. Countries like Bangladesh, Nepal, Myanmar, Bhutan, Afghanistan, Indonesia, Malaysia, Philippines, Thailand and Vietnam started welcoming the vehicles from the TATA stable as its excellent domestic image crossed over to the other countries.
Middle East	UAE, Oman, Kuwait, Qatar, Saudi Arabia, Iraq Turkey. Abu Dhabi, and Bahrain (9 countries)	Tata Motors has been present in the Middle East geography since 1971. It made sales and distribution partnership with Dubai-based auto major United Diesel of Al Rostamani Group.

Adapted from Different TATA Motor's websites, annual reports, and SIAM website available at TATA Motors.

TABLE 1-16 Domestic Sales of Automobile in Units

Category	2011–12	2012–13	2013–14	2014–15	2015–16	CAGR in %
Passenger Vehicles	26,29,839	26,65,015	25,03,509	26,01,236	2,7,89,678	2
Commercial Vehicles	8,09,499	7,93,211	6,32,851	6,14,948	6,85,704	0
Three Wheelers	5,13,281	5,38,290	4,80,085	5,32,626	5,38,092	0
Two Wheelers	1,34,09,150	1,37,97,185	1,48,06,778	1,59,75,561	1,64,55,911	6
Grand Total	1,73,61,769	1,77,93,701	1,84,23,223	1,97,24,371	20.469,385	5

Source: SIAM data and author's calculation

India is converting into an automobile export hub

Tata Motors limited continued its prosperous journey towards internationalisation since 1961 and by now has demonstrated its marketing success in foreign markets. As this individual company progressed, India as a whole also progressed fast to become an automobile export hub for the world. Not only the large domestic market size but also low-cost production facilities are attracting many other automobile majors to set up manufacturing facilities in India and export from there to the world. Companies like Hyundai, Ford, Volkswagen, Toyota, Suzuki etc., are increasingly putting their firm feet in the country and using India as their global sourcing point. Table 1-16 indicates that the domestic sales of different types of automobiles in Indian market in terms of compound annual growth rate. Except for the two wheelers segment, others have been subdued to some extent. The compounded annual growth rate (CAGR) in total sales of automobile in India increased at the rate of 5 percent during 2011–12 to 2015–16 basically due to increase in the sales of two wheelers in the country during the same period.

However, the Table 1-17 shows that export of automobiles from India grew quite handsomely by registering a CAGR of 8 percent during 2011–12 to 2015–16. Passenger cars sector and three wheelers sector both grew at a CAGR of 7 percent each during the same years.

During the fiscal year 2011–12 Indian automobile companies sold 17.36 million vehicles in the domestic market which was 12 percent more than what they did a year before. This when compared with export from automobile companies during the same year, a huge rise of 27 percent year -on-year export growth was registered. Next fiscal year, i.e., during 2012–13 both export and domestic market were subdued. In fact, export during 2012–13 declined by 1 percent from the last year. During the same period domestic sales also declined and somehow managed to register a meagre 2 percent year-on-year growth. During 2013 –14 the industry could manage to increase domestic sales to about 18.23 million units which was a 4 percent year on year growth. However, there was cheers on the export front with sale of 3.11 million units which was a 7 percent increase from the previous year. The year 2014 –15 was a great year for the automobile producers as they could export about 3.57 million units which was about 15 percent increase on year-on-year basis. This rise of export eased out the pressure of the domestic market slump to a great extent. However, 2015–16

TABLE 1-17 Export Sales in Automobiles in Units

Category	2010–11	2011–12	2012–13	2013–14	2014–15	2015–16	CAGR in %
Passenger Vehicles	4,44,326	5,08,783	5,59,414	5,96,142	6,21,341	6,53,889	7
Commercial Vehicles	74,043	92,258	80,027	77,050	86,939	1,01,689	5
Three Wheelers	2,69,968	3,61,753	3,03,088	3,53,392	4,07,600	4,04,441	7
Two Wheelers	15,31,619	19,75,111	19,56,378	20,84,000	24,57,466	24,81,193	8
Grand Total	23,19,956	29,37,905	28,98,907	31,10,584	35,73,346	3,6,41,212	8

Source : SIAM data and author's calculation

TABLE 1-18 Ups and Downs in the Export Market for Indian Exporters

Fiscal Year	Export Sales In nos	Y-O-Y Growth (%)	Domestic Sales In nos	Y-O-Y Growth (%)
2010–11	2319956	–	15481381	–
2011–12	2937905	27	17361769	12
2012–13	2898907	−1	17793701	2
2013–14	3110584	7	18423223	4
2014–15	3573346	15	19724371	7
2015–16	3641212	2	20469385	4

Adapted from Society of Indian Automobile Manufacturers (SIAM) available at http://www.siamindia.com/statistics.aspx?mpgid=8&pgidtrail=15, as accessed on 20 January 2017 at 2pm.

was a bad year for the automobile producers in India like Tata motors, Daewoo, Suzuki, Ford etc., who have been investing in the country to still upgrade their production capacities either with the hope to take advantage of the domestic market demand or using the country as an export-destined manufacturing base. During 2015–16 the year-on-year growth registered a tepid rate of 4 percent. But more dampening news came from the export frontier, where year-on-year growth rate touched only 2 percent with an export of 3.64 million vehicles in the fiscal year as shown in the Table 1-18.

Internationalisation push for Tata Motors

The experts feel that motorisation rate as expressed by number of vehicle owned by per thousand of population will increase in the coming years and hence the domestic demand of automobiles would increase. Tata motors, being the Indian multinational, would like to take advantage of the demand rise. Tata with such a huge network of distributors, spread across more than 50 countries of the world, has opportunities to beat the present slump of demand in the domestic market. Companies from US and other European countries have successfully demonstrated in the past how the overdrive to reach foreign markets because of a slump in the domestic market actually rewarded them in the long run. Southeast Asia, the Middle East and Africa focussed approach with a more aggressive internationalisation drive would make these Indian multinational truly international in the years to come.

Source: All the information collected from different TATA Motor"s websites, annual reports, and SIAM website available at Tata Motors.

THE GLOBAL/TRANSNATIONAL CORPORATION The global/transnational corporation, or any business enterprise that pursues global business objectives by linking world resources to world market opportunity, is the organization that has responded to the driving, restraining, and underlying forces in the world. Within the international financial framework and under the umbrella of global peace, the global corporation has taken advantage of the expanding communications and information technologies to pursue market opportunities and serve needs and wants on a global scale. The global enterprise has both responded to market opportunity and competitive threat by going global and, simultaneously, has been one of the forces driving the world toward greater globalization.

Restraining Forces

Despite the impact of the driving forces identified earlier in the chapter, several restraining forces may slow a company's efforts to engage in global marketing. Three important restraining forces are management myopia, organizational culture, and national controls. As we have noted, however, in today's world the driving forces predominate over the restraining forces. That is why the importance of global marketing continues to grow.

MANAGEMENT MYOPIA AND ORGANIZATIONAL CULTURE In many cases, management simply ignores opportunities to pursue global marketing. A company that is nearsighted and ethnocentric will not expand geographically. Myopia is also a recipe for market disaster if headquarters attempts to dictate when it should listen and to whom it should listen. Global marketing is not effective without strong country market teams that can creatively respond to local market opportunities and threats. A global company needs to be able to respond creatively in all markets: home and the rest of the world. New ideas and initiatives in a global company should come from the entire world, not just from the home market. It is the failure to develop this capability that has been the downfall of many once-leading companies such as Sears and JC Penney in retail, Wang and DEC in computing, and Sony in portable personal sound. Now, as opposed to thirty years ago, competitors in all regions of the world come from everywhere.

In companies in which subsidiary management knows it all, there is no room for vision from the top. As we will see in Chapter 16, executives and managers at successful global companies have learned how to integrate global vision and perspective with local market initiative and input. A striking theme emerged during interviews conducted by the author with executives of successful global companies: respect for local initiative and input by headquarters executives, and corresponding respect for headquarters' vision by local executives.

NATIONAL CONTROLS AND BARRIERS Every country protects local enterprise and interests by maintaining control over market access and entry in both low- and high-tech industries and advertising. Such control ranges from a monopoly controlling access to certain markets to national government control of broadcast, equipment, and data transmission markets. Today, tariff barriers have been largely removed in the high-income countries, thanks to the World Trade Organization (WTO), NAFTA, and other regional and bilateral economic agreements. However, nontariff barriers (NTBs) still make it more difficult for outside companies to succeed in foreign markets. The only way global companies can overcome these barriers is to become insiders in every country in which they do business.

Global advertising and promotion are also hampered by government regulations. It is illegal in some countries to use comparative advertising. In other countries, such as Germany, premiums and sweepstakes are illegal. Also working against global advertising is the use of different technical standards around the world. However, over the past 20 years, digital compatibility has helped facilitate global marketing programs and market insight. And continuing improvement of the mobile web, the growth of smartphones, and the success of tablets, as well as improved user experience across devices with the roll out of 4G and carrier improvements, will only serve to strengthen mobile's growth as one of the most powerful platforms available to global marketers.

OUTLINE OF THIS BOOK

The book is divided into six parts. Part I is an introduction and overview of Global Marketing Management.

Part II addresses the Global Marketing Environment: socioeconomic conditions including the location of income and population; patterns of trade and investment; stages of market development; and social, political, legal and regulatory, and cultural elements.

Part III, Analyzing and Targeting Market Opportunities, begins with Chapter 5 which focuses on global customers and marketing across global diversity, Chapter 6, outlines global marketing information systems and research and chapter 7 addresses Global segmentation, targeting, and positioning.

Part IV, Global Marketing Strategy, is the bridge between the first seven chapters which address the external environment of global marketing, and the next nine chapters which address the formulation of a competitive global marketing strategy. Chapter 8 outlines alternative entry and expansion strategies and the key concepts and frameworks needed to formulate global competitive analysis and strategy.

Part V focuses on the global marketing mix: the formulation and integration of product, price, channel, and marketing communications decisions to create value for customers and a sustainable global competitive advantage for the firm.

Part VI, Managing the Global Marketing Program, focuses on the implementation of a global strategy and the future of global marketing. It begins with a chapter on global structure, organization and leadership and continues with a chapter that is new to this edition: corporate social and environmental responsibility. Chapter 16 concludes the book with a discussion of the the major forces and concepts that will shape the future of global marketing.

CASE 1-1

Internationalisation of KFC in Emerging Markets like India

Colonel Harland Sanders found himself frustrated after trying his luck in different jobs ranging from helper in a blacksmith's workshop to cleaner in a railroad company in USA after completing his scheduled stint with US army. When nothing clicked to his satisfaction he decided to try his luck in entrepreneurship. Colonel made a humble beginning by opening a roadside restaurant in Kentucky, USA in the year 1950 and soon found that the fried Chicken items are in much demand in the country. In the year 1952, Colonel opened a more professional outlet in Salt Lake City, Utah. This was the first outlet of "Kentucky Fried Chicken (KFC)" which eventually internationalised at such a pace that the entire international business community appreciated. As of 2015 KFC expanded its outlets in 118 countries of the world. Colonel always considered Asia to have great business potential and accordingly it entered Philippines way back in 1967. Three years later it established its first outlet in Japan followed by Malaysia (1973), Singapore (1977), Indonesia (1979), Thailand (1984), Hong Kong (1985), China (1987) and in 1995 it entered India and Sri Lanka simultaneously. The growth of the outlets in these Asian countries was also very satisfying for the Colonel.

However, the growth of KFC outlets in terms of outlets per million populations across Asian countries has been uneven. As it can be seen from Table 1-19 that the highest concentration of KFC has been in Malaysia followed by followed by Singapore, Hong Kong, Japan, Thailand, China, Philippines, Indonesia, Sri Lanka and India. The company noticed with grave concern that the second most populous country of the world has an abysmally low KFC outlet concentration and stands at 0.22 outlets per million population. The company painfully observed that neighbouring countries of India, like China and Sri Lanka have considerably good outlet concentration which stood at 3.58 and 1.31 respectively. The company management was wondering about the cause of low penetration of the company in India and a possible strategy to reverse the situation. China growth story for KFC was very much encouraging for the company where already 4889 outlets were functioning to meet the demand but in comparison KFC could open up only 342 outlets in India. The American company look perplexed and nervous and wanted the situation to be reversed.

KFC ENTRY IN INDIA

The entry of KFC in India during the 1995 was filled with uncertainties. It opened its first outlet in Bangalore after the country took policy level decision regarding entry ease of foreign companies in India. The decision to open its first outlet in Bangalore was also very strategic as the city was fast progressing to host a sizable rich and modern middle class. KFC was aware of the fact that though the newly introduced policy of economic

TABLE 1-19 Growth of the KFC Outlets in Some Asian Countries

Country	Year of entering	Number of outlet (2015)	Outlet concentration during 2015 (Outlets per million population)
Philippines	1967	241	2.43, (99.1)*
Japan	1977	1152	8.85, (127.1)
Malaysia	1973	607	20.3, (29.9)
Singapore	1977	88	16, (5.5)
Indonesia	1979	501	1.97, (254.5)
Thailand	1984	493	7.28, (67.7)
Hong Kong	1985	67	9.31, (7.2)
China	1987	4889	3.58, (1,364.3)
India	1995	342	0.26, (1,295.3)
Sri Lanka	1995	27	1.31, (20.6)

*Figures in the bracket are the country population during 2015

Source: Country populations obtained from The World Bank as of 2014 and number of KFC outlets from http://www.yum.com/company/ accessed on 2.08.2016.

liberalisation welcomed the multinational companies (MNCs) but there are some nongovernmental organisations (NGOs) that were determined to challenge the government policy. But despite that how could a multinational like KFC avoid being present in the second most populous country of the world. So the management of KFC was determined to challenge the challenges. The first KFC outlet was opened in the Garden city of Bangalore on 18th June, 1995 under the full protection from security forces. But neither KFC management nor security forces could rightly assess the pattern of confrontation. As a result the activists of the so called anti-MNC nationalists attacked and ransacked the outlet freely causing a setback for the brand to take off. The seasoned international business managers of KFC initially refused to budge under pressure. In fact, by 1995, KFC consolidated its presence in more than 69 countries of the world and the managers at KFC believed that even if the marketing environment was hostile in some countries, a global company needed to face them with requisite business strategy in place. So, the reaction from its management team was not a knee jerk but on the contrary they decided to continue operating with police picket posted permanently outside the retail outlet at Bangalore. The management wanted to counter the onslaught of anti-MNC nationalists by opening a new outlet in the capital of India. The KFC outlet opened in Delhi with high hope to garner quick popularity which could be used strategically to counter the ill effects of the anti – KFC propaganda unleashed by the ultra-nationalist groups present in India. However, before, the KFC management could really present its products to the prospective population of the capital city a two pronged attack was unleashed. First, there was a strong rumour which spread quickly that KFC used porkfat in cooking and frying its products. Second, the products of KFC contained more than permissible level of monosodium glutamate which if consumed by human beings could even cause diseases like cancer. The double blows too damaging and dampening to attract Indian customers to the KFC outlets, both at Bangalore and Delhi. The result was obvious, the global management decided to shut its Indian operation at least for a few years to cool down the situation.

To prevent further onslaughts on the KFC outlet, the management of the KFC outlet demanded a police van to be permanently parked outside for almost a year. Another KFC outlet was soon opened in Delhi in the same year. However, the combined revenue of both the Bangalore and Delhi outlets was not sufficient to continue the KFC business in India.

Anti-KFC movements accusing KFC of using illegally high amounts of monosodium glutamate, which are injurious to health, was the reason why KFC didn't gain popularity. Also, the anti-KFC movements claimed that KFC sold food that was cooked and fried in pork fat. Under these circumstances, the fast food restaurant did not reap satisfactory revenue to continue its operations in India. Consequently, KFC had to abandon the Indian market.

MARKETING ENVIRONMENT IN CHINA AND INDIA: A COMPARISON

On the contrary to the Indian entry debacle, China entry of KFC was smoother. KFC entered China almost a decade earlier than India and thereafter the company was on the songs. As of 2015, the outlet concentration of KFC as measured by number of outlets per million population stood at a 3.58 as against a dismal 0.26 in India. It dominated the Chinese fast food market with 40 percent market share. During 2015 it proudly opened its 4889th outlet in China as against 342 outlets in India. Why could the global fast food giant not maintain its not maintain its juggernaut advance in India the same way it had done in China? What are the requirements to replicate success for a global company in different country markets? How can a company understand and assess the factors that bring different marketing results in different countries. The answer to all these questions lie in the differential marketing environment prevailing in different country markets. Let's understand the differences in India and China and how that environmental factors created result differences in these two most populous countries of the world for the global fast food retailers.

Economic Environment

During 1995 when KFC entered India, the country just came out of long conservative economic system, trying to position itself as an open-market. But traces of its past autarkic policies remained. The country heavily depended on agriculture and services as sources of economic growth. During KFC entry the economic environment of the country was shrouded with challenges from increasing poverty, unemployment and fiscal insolvency. On the other hand China moved steadily from 1970 to form a market-oriented economy accompanied with aggressively pursued industrial development to cater to the demand of global market through exportation. The matching changes effected on the economic policy front started pouring results in terms with increase in GDP. The country was adequately addressing challenges arising out of increasing population and unemployment problems, rapid rural–urban migration. As a result, the living standards of the aspiring population improved dramatically. The trend was continuing and reportedly the per-household disposable income went up from approximately 1510 Yuan during 1990 to 6800 Yuan during 2015.

Technology Environment

The Indian telecom sector was entirely under government ownership until 1984, when the private sector was allowed in telecommunication equipment manufacturing only. As per World Bank data, Internet penetration as measured by Internet users (per 100 people) was zero during 1995 in India which was increased to 2.4 during 2005 and further to 7.5 during 2010. As per World Bank data internet penetration in China was zero during 1995 which was increased to 8.5 during 2005 and further to 34.3 during 2010. With more and more Internet penetration, the younger population fall prey easily to the strategic and witty marketing communication of western fast food retailers.

Political Environment

Political system in India requires all major reforms related to facilitating setting up of foreign companies in India in different sector, concurrence from all the political parties. China being single party could take faster decision in the interest of the country. Several political decisions were implemented fast to attract foreign companies to set up their respective business houses under the wholly owned foreign subsidiary mode. India was showing a sluggish nature in this respect. Thus there was differences in these two countries in terms of receiving foreign capital investment. By 1998, Maddison's calculations showed that China had $183 FDI per capita and India had $14. Also, India could not attract FDI from its own diaspora in comparison to China.

Competition

It is said that competition brings out the best in a company. The fast food sector where KFC operated was always a battleground where the home-grown players and foreign players continuously fought to get their piece of the pie from the growing market. As more and more foreign companies started coming to the country, the traditional culinary habit of people was put under attack. The home-grown players specialising with Chinese food were always found playing the second fiddle. The big western players tried to take advantage of the situation through firm anchoring in the country. They were expecting that with the all-round increasing economic prosperity of the country, they were expecting the rural-urban divide to fade quickly, resulting in the inroad of western-type fast food even in the rural areas of the country. This was the reason the fast food industry in China grew faster at the rate of 13% compared to just 2.9 percent in the USA. In order to survive competition from local as well as other American companies like McDonald, KFC aggressively expanded without forgetting to continuously nourish its brand image in the country. On the contrary, the Indian fast food market was growing at a slower pace than China and the most importantly during the latter half of 1990s the preference for fast food just surfaced amongst the urban population of the country.

Social/Cultural

As China made more and more economic progress, a major chunk of the population inclined to embrace western culture paving way for western fast food chains like KFC. Interestingly, in history of KFC in China, the first KFC outlet opened in Beijing during 1982 had a 50 meter long queue which even surprised the KFC strategists in USA. KFC did not miss the opportunity, and to be more close to the local food habit the company kept on localising their products rather than offering the same as available in the USA. The urban population started feeling that consumption of western fast food was a way of demonstrating their economic upsurge in the society making them feel more like global citizens. When KFC entered India the rich upper class possibly harboured the same feeling but their size was too less to create any impact on the society at large. The rich middle class which one can see in the present were almost non-existent. The large section in the society continued to look upon the entry of western fast food as a sign of western imperialism in India. In addition, the strong cultural affinity of the Indians towards home-cooked food was found difficult to dissociate from them even with aggressive marketing communication.

Pressure Group

The pressure group environment has been always very strong in India as the country's age-old democratic environment always provided a platform for free thinking and free speech, no matter if they are diagonally opposite to the government version. The presence of substantial number of political opposition groups has been the characteristic of the Indian political system. These groups were found to be actively patronising the nongovernmental organisations (NGOs) that were active in voicing protest against government moves. So, there were always NGOs in the country who never supported westernisation of Indian culture, protested against it in the form of 'Swadesi' movement or otherwise. On the contrary, NGO led protests against government move have been quite low in China. Although, the government has identified the Falungong spiritual movement and the China Democracy Party as subversive groups but their activities were not towards western multinationals.

Way Forward for KFC in India:

With 0.26 outlet concentration during 2015, the KFC headquarters at Louisville, Kentucky is very unhappy for obvious reason. The second most populous country of the world could not be penetrated in spite of huge marketing strength of the company which over the years have been adequately nourished with learning ploughed back from its different country experiences. The company, therefore, was up with all its marketing weapons to overcome the initial hiccups and chart a new journey in the country and maximise opportunities evolving out of economic progress of the country. This requires the company to rejig its marketing recipe exclusively for India to come more close to the prospective customers. The company knows that for a vast country like India there is sure to exist different sub-cultures, some of them could be too strong to break and would show no signs of getting moulded when confronted with KFC's global marketing campaign. An old saying, which is very popular for the strategy makers, goes, "When you are obstructed by the invincible, retreat, then find a new way and proceed to reach destination" In India, KFC seems to have adopted the same retreat and proceed strategy. A company globally known for its non-vegetarian food suddenly became extra careful about some Indian subculture. For example, since about 70 percent people of Gujarat are staunch vegetarian, KFC must show extra care to their religious and cultural sentiments to attract them to its fold. The result was opening "KFC veg" restaurant in the state of Gujarat. It was just like repetition of the strategy when McDonald's opened Kosher restaurants in Israel. Kosher restaurants were opened by Mc-Donald to respect the traditional Jewish dietary law. These restaurants strictly followed the religious and cultural food habit of the Jewish people and prepared food under Kosher supervision. There outlets used no dairy product and meats, etc., were served on the 'Passover buns' only, i.e., unleavened bread. KFC has literally gone for 'Kosher' for Gujarati vegetarian people. This includes introduction of separate coloured uniforms staff members, separate ordering and payment counters for vegetarian people, separate cooking areas indicated by markings on the wall, separately coloured utensils, etc., to clearly signal the vegetarian public in the state that even a global food outlet cares for their cultural and religious preferences.

Case Questions

1. What were the challenges in front of KFC while entering India?
2. Why could KFC spread fast in China but not in India?
3. How can a company like KFC, on internationalisation drive assess its success in different country markets?
4. What could be the strategies for KFC to spread fast in India? How can you be sure that such strategy would pay the company rich dividends in the long run?

Chapter Summary

Global marketing is the process of focusing the resources and objectives of a company on global marketing opportunities. Companies engage in global marketing for two reasons: to take advantage of opportunities for growth and expansion, and to survive. Companies in globalizing industries that fail to pursue global opportunities will eventually lose their domestic markets because they will be pushed aside by stronger and more competitive global competitors. This book presents the theory and practice of applying the universal discipline of marketing to the global opportunities found in world markets.

The basic goals of marketing are to create customer value and competitive advantage by maintaining focus. Company management can be classified in terms of its orientation toward the world: ethnocentric, polycentric, regiocentric, and geocentric. An ethnocentric orientation characterizes domestic and international companies; international companies pursue marketing opportunities outside the home market by extending various elements of the marketing mix. A polycentric worldview predominates at a multinational company, where the marketing mix is adapted by country managers operating autonomously. Managers at global and transnational companies are regiocentric or geocentric in their orientation and pursue both extension and adaptation strategies in global markets.

Global marketing's importance today is shaped by the dynamic interplay of several driving and restraining forces. The former include market needs and wants, technology, transportation improvements, costs, quality, global peace, world economic growth, and a recognition of opportunities to develop leverage by operating globally. Restraining forces include market differences, management myopia, organizational culture, and national controls.

Discussion Questions

1. What are the basic goals of marketing? Are these goals relevant to global marketing?
2. What is meant by global localization? Is Coca-Cola a global product? Explain.
3. Describe the differences among ethnocentric, polycentric, regiocentric, and geocentric management orientations.
4. Identify and briefly describe some of the forces that have resulted in increased global integration and the growing importance of global marketing.
5. Define leverage, and explain the different types of leverage utilized by companies with global operations.
6. What, in your view, is the future of a company such as Nokia? Will it be able to continue as an independent company? Why? Why not?
7. What are some major trends in the world that will affect marketing?

Suggested Readings

Brettel, Malte, Andreas Engelen, Florian Heinemann, and Pakpachong Vadhanasindhu. "Antecedents of Market Orientation: A Cross-Cultural Comparison." *Journal of International Marketing*, 16, no. 2 (June 2008): 120–151.

Burgess, Steven M. *The New Marketing*. Cape Town: Zebra Press, a Division of the New Holland Struik Publishing Group, (pty) Ltd, 1998.

Cavusgil, S. Tamer, Seyda Deligonul, and Attila Yaprak. "International Marketing as a Field of Study: A Critical Assessment of Earlier Development and a Look Forward. " *Journal of International Marketing*, 13, no. 4 (December 2005): 1–27.

Collins, Jim. *Good To Great: Why Some Companies Make the Leap…and Others Don't*. New York: HarperBusiness, HarperCollins Publishers, Inc., 2001. (Also *Built To Last: Successful Habits of Visionary Companies* with Jerry I. Porras, 1994).

Collins, Jim, and Morten T. Hansen. *Great By Choice: Uncertainty, Chaos, and Luck—Why Some Thrive Despite Them All*. New York: HarperCollins Publishers, 2011.

Comstock, Beth, Ranjay Gulati, and Stephen Liguori. "Unleashing the Power of Marketing." *Harvard Business Review* (October 2010): 90–98.

Day, S. George. *Market Driven Strategy: Processes for Creating Value*. New York: The Free Press, A Division of Simon & Schuster, Inc., 1999.

Douglas, Susan P., and C. Samuel Craig. "Convergence and Divergence: Developing a Semiglobal Marketing Strategy." *Journal of International Marketing*, 19, no. 1 (March 2011): 82–101.

Goldfayn, Alex L. *Evangelist Marketing: What Apple, Amazon, and Netflix Understand About Their Customers (That Your Company Probably Doesn't)*. Dallas: Ben Bella Books, Inc., 2011.

Hamel, Gary. *Leading the Revolution*. Boston: Harvard Business School Press, 2000.

Hamel, Gary, and C. K. Prahalad. *Competing for the Future*. Boston: Harvard Business School Press, 1994.

Hulbert, James, Noel Capon, and Nigel F. Piercy. *Total Integrated Marketing*. New York: Free Press, 2003.

Hult, G. Tomas M., S. Tamer Cavusgil, Tunga Kiyak, Seyda Deligonul, and Katarina Lagerström. "What Drives Performance in Globally Focused Marketing Organizations? A Three-Country Study." *Journal of International Marketing*, 15, no. 2 (June 2007): 58–85.

Kothandaraman, Prabakar, and David T. Wilson. "The Future of Competition: Value-Creating Networks." *Industrial Marketing Management*, 30, no. 4 (May 2011): 379–389.

Kotler, Philip. *Kotler On Marketing: How To Create, Win, and Dominate Markets*. New York: The Free Press, A Division of Simon & Schuster, 1999.

Kumar, Nirmalya. *Marketing As Strategy: Understanding the CEO's Agenda For Driving Growth And Innovation* Boston: Harvard Business School Press, 2004.

Leinwand, Paul, and Cesare Mainardi. *The Essential Advantage: How to Win with a Capabilities-Driven Strategy*. Boston: Booz & Company, Inc., Harvard Business School Publishing, 2011.

Levitt, Theodore. "Marketing Myopia." *Harvard Business Review* (July–August 2004): 138–149.

McKenna, Regis. *Real Time: Preparing for the Age of the Never Satisfied Customer*. Boston, Harvard Business School Press, 1997.

McKenna, Regis. *Total Access, Giving Customers What They Want in an Anytime, Anywhere World*, Boston, Harvard Business School Press, 2002.

Mintzberg, Henry, Bruce Ahlstrand, and Joseph Lampel. *Strategy Safari: A Guided Tour Through the Wilds of Strategic Management*. New York: The Free Press, A Division of Simon & Schuster, Inc., 1998.

Peters, Thomas J., and Robert H. Waterman, Jr. *In Search of Excellence: Lessons from America's Best-Run Companies*. New York: Harper & Row, Publishers, 1982.

Prahalad, C. K., and Gary Hamel. "The Core Competence of the Corporation." *Harvard Business Review* (May 1990).

Prahalad C. K., and Venkatram Ramaswamy. *The Future of Competition: Co-Creating Unique Value with Customers*. Boston: Harvard Business School Press, 2004.

Ricci, Ron, and John Volkmann. *Momentum: How Companies Become Unstoppable Market Forces*. Boston: Harvard Business School Press, 2003.

Rust, Roland T., Christine Moorman, and Guarav Bhalla. "Rethinking Marketing." *Harvard Business Review* (January–February 2010): 94–101.

Schilke, Oliver, Martin Reimann, and Jacquelyn S. Thomas. "When Does International Marketing Standardization Matter to Firm Performance?" *Journal of International Marketing*, 17, no. 4 (December 2009): 24–46.

Simon, Hermann. *Hidden Champions: Lessons from 500 of the World's Best Unknown Companies*. New York: Springer Science + Media, LLC., 2009.

Townsend, Janell D., Sengun Yeniyurt, Z. Seyda Deligonul, and S. Tamer Cavusgil. "Exploring the Marketing Program Antecedents of Performance in a Global Company." *Journal of International Marketing*, 12 no. 4 (December 2004): 1–24.

Part II The Global Marketing Environment

CHAPTER 2

The Global Economic Environment

Free trade, one of the greatest blessings which a government can confer to a people, is in almost every country unpopular.

—LORD MACAULAY, 1800–1859

Learning Objectives

1. Summarize significant historical changes in the global economic environment (45–46).
2. Identify trends in the world economy that affect global marketing decisions (46–49).
3. Describe how economic measures of freedom help drive or hinder global business expansion and growth (49–52).
4. Describe the stages of market development (55–63).
5. Explain how global income distribution and population patterns affect marketing decisions (63–68).
6. Discuss the balance of payments and global trade patterns (69–72).

INTRODUCTION

The macro dimensions of the environment are economic, social and cultural, political, regulatory and legal, scientific and technological. Each is important, but perhaps the single most important characteristic of the global market environment is the economic dimension. With money, all things (well, almost all!) are possible. Without money, many things are impossible for the marketer. Luxury products, for example, cannot be sold to low-income consumers. Hypermarkets for food, furniture, or durables require a large base of consumers with the ability to make large purchases of goods and the ability to drive away with those purchases. Sophisticated industrial products require sophisticated industries as buyers.

Today, in contrast to any previous time in the history of the world, there is global economic growth. For the first time in the history of global marketing, markets in every region of the world are potential targets for almost every company from high to low tech, across the spectrum of products from basic to luxury. Indeed, the fastest-growing markets, as we shall see later in the chapter, are in countries at earlier stages of development. The economic dimensions of this world market environment are of vital importance. This chapter examines the key characteristics of the world economic environment from a marketing perspective.

Income levels, cultural dictates, infrastructure capacities, and legal constraints or protections all are examples of macroeconomic dimensions that have major impact on strategic marketing decisions. Although significant competitive factors differ by industry, understanding and anticipating macroeconomic trends and aligning business decisions to those most critical can be the foundation for growth and sustained profitability.[1]

Economic growth was once concentrated in the high-income countries of the North Atlantic, Western Europe, and North America and then achieved in Japan and Singapore and other South East Asian countries. It has now extended to markets in every region of the world and to countries of all sizes, including the largest countries in the world, China and India.

The global marketer is fortunate in having a substantial body of data available that charts the nature of the environment on a country-by-country basis to aid in understanding economic dimensions of targeted markets. Each country has national accounts data, indicating estimates of gross national product, gross domestic product, consumption, investment, government expenditures, and price levels. Also available on a global basis are demographic data indicating the number of people, their distribution by age category, and rates of population growth.

National accounts and demographic data do not exhaust the types of economic data available. A single source, The Statistical Yearbook of the United Nations, contains global data on agriculture, mining, manufacturing, construction, energy production and consumption, internal and external trade, railroad and air transport, wages and prices, health, housing, education, and communications. This data is available for all high-income countries. The less developed a country is, the scarcer the availability of economic data. In the low-income countries of the world, one cannot be certain of obtaining anything more than basic national accounts and demographic and external trade data.

Especially in emerging markets, there are many challenges to obtaining accurate and timely micro and macro market data. Despite these issues, the marketer's problem is not one of an absence of data but rather one of abundance. Official statistical data compiled by the International Monetary Fund, the United Nations Environmental Programme, or GEO Data Portal are examples of authoritative sources for composite and comparable data that can be found online. Many business and nonprofit organizations provide online access to database sets, including Nielsen Online or GlobalEdge's database of international business statistics. These, as well as many other organizations, repackage official data from different sources including the CIA and World Factbook. Similar to many other interactive sites, comparative data is made available in a variety of user-generated formats.

This chapter will identify the most salient characteristics of the economic environment to provide the framework for further consideration of the elements of a global marketing program.[2]

---

[1] See, for example, "Going from Global Trends to Corporate Strategy," *The McKinsey Quarterly* (June 19, 2007).

[2] Chapter data is based on research completed in 2010 and 2011 from data from the latest available sources that offer data on a comparable basis.

THE WORLD ECONOMY—AN OVERVIEW

The world economy has changed profoundly since World War II. Perhaps the most fundamental change is the emergence of global markets; responding to new opportunities, global competitors have steadily displaced local ones. Concurrently, the integration of the world economy continues to increase. Economic integration stood at 10 percent at the beginning of the twentieth century; today, it exceeds 50 percent. Integration is increasing in all world regions.

Thomas Friedman discusses ten forces that have contributed to the flattening of the world.[3] This leveling of the global competitive playing field has been accomplished by a series of interlocking political, economic, and technological factors. For example, the fall of the Berlin Wall "tipped the balance of power" to countries "advocating democratic, consensual, free market-oriented governance." Open sourcing and the power of "self-organizing collaborative communities" made possible by growing computing and software power has had significant impacts on human communications, interactions, and behavior. Offshore research and development and manufacturing have been facilitated by advances in communications technology which have driven down costs and vastly increased the speed and capacity of global communications. Technology has similarly increased the speed and reduced the cost of global transportation of goods and people and has been responsible for a major shrinking of the world. As firms move to collaborative, networked relationships with the goal of realizing supply and scale efficiencies around the world, flattening continues. Important to the strategic marketer, as networked supply chains grow, common standards are fostered between companies. These common standards eliminate inefficiencies in communications and supporting technologies. The points of friction created by national boundaries become smaller as global integration expands.

Countries in emerging markets have achieved sustained high rates of growth by taking advantage of lower labor costs to produce for the global marketplace. At the same time, companies in high-income, high-labor-cost countries have been able to create sustained competitive advantages by combining their understanding of customer needs and wants with innovation in design and manufacturing to offer competitive products and services.

Supported by the flow of capital around the globe, some corporations no longer call any country home-base. With worldwide corporate functions and globally-informed consumers, these firms are linked by cyber technology.[4] Along with seeking customers in all corners of the globe, almost every global firm's strategy includes reducing costs and getting closer to fast-growing markets by locating manufacturing and production operations as well as research facilities around the world. Firms no longer make their largest capital expenditures domestically, instead they respond to customers worldwide and seek out talent to support global information technology (IT), R&D, and channel partners around the world.[5]

The automobile industry is a good example. In the past, European nameplates such as Renault, Citroën, Peugeot, Volvo, BMW, Daimler (Mercedes), VW, and others were radically different from North American and Japanese models. These companies

---

[3] Thomas Friedman, *The World Is Flat: A Brief History of the Twenty-First Century* (New York: Farrer, Straus and Giroux, 2005).

[4] See Chapter 1, Kenichi Ohmae, *Borderless World: Power and Strategy in the Interlinked Economy* (New York: HarperCollins, 1999). See also Donald A. DePalma, *Business Without Borders: A Strategic Guide to Global Marketing* (New York: John Wiley & Sons, Inc., 2002) and Lowell Bryan et al., *Race For the World: Strategies to Build a Great Global Firm* (Boston: Harvard Business School Press by McKinsey & Company, 1999).

[5] See Michael Mandel, "What Spending Slowdown?," *Businessweek*, April 23, 2007.

produced local cars built by local talent destined predominantly for local or regional markets. Today, the world car, based on global designs and components sourced from locations around the world, is a reality for every global company in the industry, including those in Korea. Ford, for example, has made the world car a centerpiece of its strategic efforts worldwide and based design and marketing efforts on data from its European customers as well as customers who purchased Hondas in the US market and Toyotas in China.[6]

Production, R&D, and product modifications reflect larger organizational changes as well: the world's largest automakers have evolved into companies which compete in a global industry with global strategies. Ford has been an international company since the early twentieth century, but its overseas divisions long operated as semi-autonomous units focused on individual markets. With a single engineering platform for its world car, operations include a development team that draws from European designers and members from Asia and the Americas. It is envisioned that by 2013, 80 percent of Ford's products will be built on global platforms which leverage its global resources and talent. Ford's marketing campaigns tied to these global platforms are limited to four or five strategies around the world. As James Farley, Ford's global marketing chief, puts it, "diversity of the marketing [program] is created by the customer we want to reach, and not by the differences in the vehicles."[7]

As a result, with the exponential growth of both global trade and investment, nations and markets have become increasingly economically interdependent. Implications of this integration are profound. The unfolding of the 2007 global credit crisis unraveled the global financial markets to an extent that was exceeded in the past century only by the Great Depression of the 1930s. As a result, the global marketplace faced the possibility of economic collapse as far-flung economies from Iceland to China to Turkey felt the impacts of systemic contraction.

THE WORLD ECONOMY: IMPORTANT TRENDS

Within the past decade, along with the growth of global markets and worldwide economic integration, there have been several remarkable changes in the world economy and related business and industry trends that hold important implications for global marketing decision making.

A business leader's ability to assess trends in a rapidly changing competitive marketplace, and use these to appropriately gauge their impact on profitability of the firm, is a critical competence. Some of the questions to consider as you read these and other important industry-specific trends are: How should strategic marketing planners go about the task of analyzing the impact of a complex global trend? What role does the marketing planning process play in identifying growth opportunities and the product portfolio mix? How can a globally integrated firm use its skills to drive the product-to-market innovations that can put it out front of important trends?

Analyzing what may appear to be an isolated trend could be a mistake. Trends are often made up of a variety of subtrends that may impact various industries in different ways or to varying degrees. For example, we will see that the growing worldwide middle class's demand for goods and services is an important factor in decisions from product design to sourcing. However, a corollary subtrend is that increased demand from this expanding consumer base will place increasing stress on already

---

[6] David Kiley, "Can Ford's 'World Car' Bet Pay Off?," *Businessweek*, Innovation and Technology, June 4, 2009, accessed April 7, 2010, http://www.businessweek.com/magazine/content/09.

[7] James Farley, Ford's Chief of Global Marketing. Bill Vlasic, "Ford's Bet: It's a Small World After All," *The New York Times*, January 10, 2010, B1.

constrained resources and create unsustainable environmental degradation.[8] How companies respond to this sustainability challenge will be critical to competitive success.

Economic Activity Will Shift from West to East

The ongoing shift in in the balance of global economic activity toward developing countries in the East and away from the developed countries in the West and the growth in the number of consumers in emerging markets represent two of the major global trends that must be recognized as critical changes that will impact business strategy and profitability.[9] Global business leaders expect the eastward shift in global business to accelerate, but many indicate their companies are not well prepared for competition from their Asian counterparts.[10] Indicative of this shift, over the next decade, it is anticipated that India and China will average GDP growth of 6.8 and 6.5 percent annually, respectively, and will far outpace the United States' projected growth of 2.5 percent.[11] It is anticipated that China's GDP, in PPP terms,[12] will rise by US$14.5 trillion[13] over the next decade, or the equivalent of the United States' entire 2010 economy. Over the same period, India is expected to add US$5.6 trillion to its GDP in PPP terms, which exceeds the current GDP of Japan.

This growth will be spurred in great part by shifting both production and marketing towards domestic consumption and away from the region's decades of successful export-driven growth. Private consumption as a proportion of GDP in China, for example, is projected to grow dramatically to 52 percent of GDP by 2020.[14] As more consumers reach US$5,000 annual income per household member, the sale of consumer goods accelerates.[15]

Global companies entering new markets will need to adapt their offerings, distribution systems, and operations to local demand and custom. As noted by Victor Fung Kwok-King, group chairman of the global trading group Li & Fung, "Preferred brands, shopping styles, distribution networks, and, therefore, opportunities change as one moves around the country."[16] China, with its highly fragmented consumer markets and varied provincial as well as regional customs and business practices, requires local knowledge and experience. Dr. Fung reiterates the important need for both Western and Asian firms to embrace new customers in these fast-growing markets while not alienating their existing market base in developed regions of the world.[17]

In fact, certain industries and corporate functions, such as manufacturing and IT, will shift even more dramatically, resulting, in great part, from economic liberalization,

---

[8] Wendy M. Becker and Vanesa M. Freeman, "Going from Global Trends to Corporate Strategy," *The McKinsey Quarterly* (August 2008), accessed July 1, 2010, http://www.mckinseyquarterly.com.

[9] "Five Forces Reshaping the Global Economy: The McKinsey Global Survey Results," *The McKinsey Quarterly* (May 2010), accessed May 9, 2010, http://www.mckinseyquarterly.com/article_print.aspx?L2=21&L3=33&ar=2581.

[10] "The Big Tilt: The Rise of the East and What it Means for Business," a special report of the Economist Intelligence Unit, *The Economist* (2010), 8.

[11] Ibid., 9.

[12] Purchasing power parity is a currency conversion rate that equalizes the purchasing power of different currencies. For example, PPP adjusts for the lower cost of living in China.

[13] The $ symbol in this text refers to US$ unless otherwise indicated.

[14] "The Big Tilt," *The Economist*, 14.

[15] Although it is clear that total income numbers of the emerging high population countries are comparable or will exceed high income countries, per capita numbers are not comparable and will take many years of growth to become comparable.

[16] "The Big Tilt," *The Economist*, 14.

[17] Ibid., 15.

demographic changes, technological advances, and capital market developments. These shifts of income and population are discussed in greater detail later in this chapter.

An argument can be made that although regulated free-market economies and capitalism have shown sustained strength for the past century, the ascendency of China demonstrates that rapid development may accompany a system where the state is a principle actor and arbiter in the national economy, driving investment and setting the rules of competition, production, and communication. Therefore, differences in the regulatory, political, and cultural business environment are major challenges for multinationals doing business, as Google found out in 2010, leaving China's mainland search engine industry to Baidu, the State-supported search engine firm, in light of strict censorship rules.[18] BlackBerry maker Research In Motion had similar challenges as it faced regulatory pressures from Middle Eastern governments to provide access to customers' messages.[19]

Aging Worldwide Population Will Demand Increasing Levels of Productivity and Efficiency

The second change highlights the aging of populations across the globe. This trend will call for higher levels of productivity and efficiency. For example, Japan's population over the age of 75 is expected to increase 36 percent from 2005 to 2015. To meet this challenge, the increase in tax burden needed to maintain benefit levels at current levels of productivity for Japan's future generations is 175 percent. In Germany, to meet the same future benefit levels as are offered today, the increase in tax burden is 90 percent. Clearly, there is a great need for innovation to offer affordable social services to worldwide aging populations. This need is a major opportunity and challenge to companies and countries.

Shifts and Growth in Consumer Segments Will Result in Changes in the Global Consumer Marketplace

Shifts in consumer segments will result in a greatly expanded consumer marketplace populated by many new consumers around the globe. Within the next decade, an estimated one billion new consumers will demand products and services made possible by economic growth in emerging markets. This means in effect that the global middle class will double. Discretionary purchasing by these new consumers will increase as more households earn over US$5,000 annually. (A threshold income level of US$5,000 has been shown to be the level of household income needed to purchase discretionary items.) Accordingly, a large increase in consumer spending will take place with respect to products whose price points are 20 to 25 percent or less of their current functional equivalents. Through 2015, consumer spending power in emerging economies will increase from $4 trillion to more than $9 trillion, almost the current spending power of Western Europe. In addition, the estimated number of Chinese households to achieve European income levels by 2020 is 100 million people, assuming a real income growth rate of 8 percent annually. The reductions of Chinese annual growth to 6 percent annually will push this date forward into the later part of the decade.

---

[18] See Bruce Einhorn, "Google and China: A Win for Liberty and Strategy," *Businessweek*, January 25, 2010, 35; Mark Landler, "Google Searches for a Foreign Policy," *The New York Times*, March 28, 2010; Miguel Helft and Michael Wines, "Making a Stand: Google Faces the Fallout," *The New York Times*, March 24, 2010; Dexter Roberts, "Closing for Business," *Businessweek*, April 5, 2010, 32. See also Eric Pfanner, "New To Russia: Google Struggles to Find Its Footing," *The New York Times*, December 18, 2006.

[19] Jenna Wortham, "BlackBerry's Maker Resists Pressure From Mideast Governments," *The New York Times*, August 4, 2010.

Consumer demographic trends in the more developed countries and regions will shift as well. For example, the purchasing power of Hispanics will rise from $1 trillion in 2010 to $1.5 trillion in 2015, accounting for nearly 11 percent of the United States' total buying power. In fact, the Hispanic market alone in the United States, at $1 trillion, is larger than the entire economies of all but 14 countries in the world—smaller than the GDP of Canada but larger than the GDP of Indonesia.[20]

Changing Industry Structures and Emerging New Models of Corporate Organization Will be Characteristic of Growing Global Competition

Shifting industry structures and emerging forms of corporate organization are characteristics of a growing competitive global economy.[21] For example, the pharmaceutical industry has been a leader in partnering to outsource product design and R&D.[22] In 2008, Daiichi Sankyo of Japan purchased a stake in Ranbaxy Laboratories, India's largest drug maker, helping to jump start the foreign drug manufacturer's push into India. Indeed, partnering can speed the growth of an emerging-market company. One example is Ranbaxy Laboratories, which cut its teeth under a unique patent regime that encouraged Indian companies to manufacture patent-protected drugs in order to make them affordable to the country's vast population of poor. Off of a demanding local market springboard of price-sensitive customers and a challenging distribution environment, Ranbaxy has become a leading generics producer in both the United States and Europe.[23]

One result of these shifting industry structures, cross-border partnerships, and the changing shape of ownership across national borders is that the heritage of many of the best known brands is morphing. Country of origin has a sometimes profound influence in brand-building; think of Toblerone and IBM's ThinkPad—originally Swiss and American, respectively—now South African and Chinese. Rover might be considered Indian as it owned by Tata Motors, which also purchased Jaguar from Ford in 2008. And although Volvo will remain based in Sweden and keep factories in Belgium, it is now owned by Chinese carmaker Geely after being purchased from Ford; Swedish automaker Saab is now owned by the Dutch manufacturer Spyker Cars.

Managing brand heritage in this complex, global environment is a challenge. From these examples, it is clear that where a company is headquartered may not be as important as its understanding and use of global branding and strategic marketing.[24]

The Demand for Natural Resources Will Continue to Grow, Resulting in Growing Pressure on an Already Strained Global, Natural Environment

The demand for natural resources will continue to grow as developing countries require fossil fuels and other resources to power their industrial growth, as did the developed world over the last century. For example, the tripling of demand in China for cooper, steel, and aluminum has made China a strong player in India's economy. Both India and China have paid a steep environmental price for rapid industrialization and population growth. Cities such as New Delhi, Chongqing, and Bombay are among the

[20] Despite recession, Hispanic and Asian buying power is expected to surge in the United States, according to the annual UGA Selig Center Multicultural Economy study, a report by the by the Selig Center for Economic Growth at the University of Georgia Terry College of Business, accessed December 12, 2012, http://www.terry.uga.edu/news/releases/2010/minority-buying-power-report.htm.

[21] Survey results published at "Acting on Global Trends: A McKinsey Global Survey," *The McKinsey Quarterly* (April 2007), http://www.mckinseyquarterly.com/article_page.aspx?ar=1998&L2=21&L3=34&srid=17.

[22] Ibid.

[23] Jayant Sinha, "Global Champions from Emerging Markets," *The McKinsey Quarterly* (May 2005), accessed July 1, 2010, http://www.mckinseyquarterly.com.

[24] David Kirkpatrick, "Gateway Wasn't Fabled, But I'll Miss It," CNNMoney.com: Fast Forward Newsletter (August 27, 2007).

world's most polluted. Forests and other natural habitat are rapidly vanishing.[25] Negative impacts of environmental degradation, among other problems, are impacting China's ability to compete as a major player on the global stage.[26]

This continuing demand for commodities will strain an already burdened global, natural environment. Among the most constrained resources are water and the atmosphere. These limited resources will require future technological innovation, worldwide regulation, and more limited use in order to support sustainable future economic growth and environmental practices over the long term.[27] In fact, price volatility and supply concerns are forcing firms to rethink their commodity exposure and strategy. For example, Chinese car and battery maker BYD purchased 18 percent of a Chinese lithium mine, while the candy company Mars has entered into a partnership with IBM and the US Agriculture Department to sequence the cacao genome to achieve a hardier cacao tree. ArcelorMittal, the world's largest steelmaker, purchases not just iron ore but coal mines in order to procure the materials it needs for iron ore production.[28]

China mines more than 95 percent of the global supply of light rare earths and metals—essential for smartphones, electric cars, computer components, and military hardware—and 99 percent of the least common rare earths, which are used in trace amounts but are important to many clean energy applications and electronics. Some rare earths now cost up to 10 times as much outside China as inside. Not coincidentally, China increasingly dominates the production of clean energy technologies that require these metals, including wind turbines and solar panels.[29]

Like providers of rare earths, key providers of oil are highly exposed to broader geopolitical instability which makes security of supply a major risk. Four countries—Iran, Iraq, Saudi Arabia, and Venezuela—hold 50 percent of known oil and gas reserves, and nationally owned oil companies control over 85 percent of those reserves.[30]

The implications are clear: Companies can no longer assume access to critical resources and relatively stable prices. With huge uncertainties looming, companies will have to consider options and outcomes under multiple scenarios.

Scrutiny of Global Firms' Worldwide Practices Will Increase as the Reach and Scale of Global Firms Expand; Increasing Regulation Will Shape the Structure and Conduct of Whole Industries

As global firms' reach and scale intensify, scrutiny of big business practices will increase. As demands on the environment grow more acute and the debilitating effects on the quality of human life worldwide become publicized through the World Wide

---

[25] Pete Engardio, "Crouching Tigers, Hidden Dragons," *Businessweek,* August 22–29, 2005, 60.

[26] See, for example, Pete Engardio et al., "Broken China," *Businessweek*, July 23, 2007, 39 and Elizabeth Economy and Kenneth Lieberthal, "Scorched Earth: Will Environmental Risks in China Overwhelm its Opportunities?," *Harvard Business Review* (June 2007): 88.

[27] See, for example, Ian Davis and Elizabeth Stephenson, "Ten Trends to Watch in 2006: Macroeconomic Factors, Environmental and Social Issues, and Business and Industry Developments Will All Profoundly Shape the Corporate Landscape in the Coming Years," *The McKinsey Quarterly* (January 2006), accessed October 13, 2010, http://www.mckinseyquarterly.com/Strategy/Globalization/Ten_trends_to_watch_in_2006_1734.

[28] See, for example, Suzanne Wooley, "How Companies are Coping with Unstable Commodities," *Businessweek*, September 30, 2010.

[29] Keith Bradsher, "Unlocking a Grip on Rare Earths," *The New York Times*, December 15, 2010; "China to Cut Rare Earths Trade in 2011," *The New York Times*, December 29, 2010; "China Restarts Rare Earth Shipments to Japan," *The New York Times*, November 20, 2010; "The Illegal Scramble for Rare Metals," *The New York Times*, December 30, 2010; and "China Tightening Control of Rare Earth Minerals," *The New York Times*, September 1, 2009. See also Todd Woody, "In the Future, Already Behind: Silicon Valley's Solar Innovators Retool to Catch Up to China," *The New York Times*, October 13, 2010.

[30] For review of sources of conflict see Thom Shanker, "Why We Might Fight, 2011 Edition," *The New York Times* (December 2010).

Web, political and regulatory backlash is likely.[31] In addition, many current businesses are experiencing increasing scrutiny of their business practices. Regulatory changes may disrupt entire value chains and business models. When and if carbon is priced, for example, it could alter more than a few industries.

Regulatory issues abound in all industries. In the power industry, there is regulation stemming from the implementation of the Kyoto Protocol along with transmission regulation, to name two. In the telecom industry, for example, there is regulation of pricing and the bundling of Voice over Internet Protocol (VoIP) and mobile license renewals; in the food industry, there is regulation of advertising of junk food and calorie and ingredient messaging. To maximize long-term value, firms must link regulatory changes and mandates with product and market strategies.

The Economics of Information Will Be Transformed as the Ubiquitous Nature of Information Expands

The ubiquitous nature of information and its dissemination across various platforms is changing the economics of knowledge. New models of knowledge creation, including open-source methods founded in community activism as opposed to individual proprietorship, change not only ownership and the means of distribution but also potentially increase information's impact across sectors of society.

Information itself has the capacity to transform global strategy. The new economics of information is eliminating the trade-off between richness of content and the reach of distribution. The spread of digital connectivity and common standards are redefining how businesses interact with their customers, channel partners, and employees and other stakeholders.[32] Flows of information and data, capital, goods, and talent create a global grid that connects geographies, economies, and social and business groups in ways that optimize interactions leading to innovation and new business models. Large-scale interactions, which support information flows around the planet, have increased exponentially; trade flows have grown 1.5 times faster than global GDP; and cross-border capital flows have increased at three times the rate of GDP growth.[33]

Talent Pools Have Become Global in Nature; Assimilating Talent into the Leadership Structure of a Global Company Will Be a Competitive Advantage

Shifts in labor pools and talent will be more far-reaching than the migration of jobs to low-wage countries over the past decade. Increasingly, as competitive advantage is based in knowledge-based assets and processes, sources of talent are becoming increasingly global. There are 33 million university-educated young professionals available in developing nations, more than double the number available in developed countries.[34] Global firms are taking advantage of high-tech centers that span innovation hubs from Eastern Europe to the Middle East and Asia. In the twentieth century, international success meant coordinating the activities of individual

---

[31] See, for example, "Too Much Corporate Power?" *Businessweek*, September 11, 2000, 144.

[32] See Philip Evans and Thomas Wurster, *Blown to Bits: How the New Economics of Information Transforms Strategy* (Boston: Harvard Business School Press, 2000).

[33] Peter Bisson, Elizabeth Stephenson, and S. Patrick Viguerie, "The Global Grid," *The McKinsey Quarterly* (June 2010), http://www.mckinseyquarterly.com/The_global_grid_2626.

[34] Ian Davis and Elizabeth Stephenson, "Ten Trends to Watch in 2006: Macroeconomic Factors, Environmental and Social Issues, and Business and Industry Developments Will All Profoundly Shape the Corporate Landscape in the Coming Years," The McKinsey Quarterly, (January 2006), accessed October 13, 2010, http://www.mckinseyquarterly.com/Strategy/Globalization/Ten_trends_to_watch_in_2006_1734.

business units through the efforts of a centralized headquarters. Now, the overarching challenge is to manage a globally dispersed workforce and the often diverse needs of multinational staff and leadership through a networked and collaborative model of work.

THE MARKET STATE: VARYING DEGREES OF ECONOMIC FREEDOM

Moving into the second decade of the twenty-first century, national economic systems vary from free-market systems with no or little government intervention to controlled systems. In the past, countries could be classified based on the dominant method of resource allocation: market allocation, command or central plan allocation, or mixed allocation. In 1948, one hundred years after the publication of *The Communist Manifesto* by Marx and Engels, half of the world's population lived in command or central plan allocation systems. Today, with the exception of North Korea, almost all countries have mixed economic systems with a major reliance on market allocation.

A pure market allocation system is one that relies on consumers to allocate resources. Consumers write the economic plan by deciding what goods will be produced by whom. The market system is an economic democracy—citizens have the right to vote with their pocketbooks for the goods of their choice. The role of the state and regulatory agencies in a market economy is to promote competition and ensure consumer protection.

In a command allocation system, the state has broad powers to serve the public interest as it determines what that public interest is to be. These include deciding which products to make and how, when, and where to make them. Consumers are free to spend their money on what is available, but decisions about what is produced and, therefore, what is available, are made by state planners. As demand exceeds supply, marketing mix elements are not utilized. Similarly, there is little reliance on marketing tools such as product differentiation, advertising, and promotion. Distribution is handled by the government to cut out exploitation by intermediaries. North Korea and, until recently, Cuba, have clung to command allocation systems. The consequences have been low economic growth, poverty, and limited economic integration with the rest of the world.

Despite the recent history of command allocation economies, a vital new picture is emerging of the Central European countries that have moved aggressively onto the global competitive stage since the Iron Curtain fell. Today, a different reality exists as Poland, the Czech Republic, Slovakia, Slovenia, Hungary, Estonia, and Bulgaria, as well as Romania, Latvia, and Lithuania, compete in the talent-and-wage wars, seeking foreign investment and growing their national competitive advantages.

There are no pure market or command allocation systems today. All market systems have a command sector; in other words, they are mixed. In a market economy, the command allocation sector is the proportion of gross domestic product (GDP) that is taxed or spent by the government. For example, in comparison with the rest of the world, the EU27 tax ratio to GDP remains generally high and has been, in recent years, more than one-third above the levels in the United States and Japan. However, among the member states, the tax burden varies considerably, ranging in 2008 from 28 percent in Romania (28.0%), Latvia (28.9%), Slovakia (29.1%), and Ireland (29.3%), to just under 50 percent in Denmark and Sweden.[35]

---

[35] "Taxation trends in the European Union3," Eurostat, the statistical office of the European Union and the Commission's Directorate-General for Taxation and Customs Union (2010), http://europa.eu/rapid/pressReleasesAction.do?reference=STAT/10/95&format=HTML&aged=0&language=en&guiLanguage=en.

Taxes come in many forms: value-added tax, personal income tax, corporate profits tax, property tax, social security, and tax on goods and services, among others. For instance, the largest source of tax revenue in the EU27 is labour taxes,[36] representing over 40 percent of total tax receipts, followed by consumption taxes at roughly one quarter and taxes on capital at just over one fifth. Social security taxes also play a major role.

In a series of yearly reports by the Washington, DC–based Heritage Foundation/ Wall Street Journal Index of Economic Freedom, more than 180 countries are ranked by degree of economic freedom. Ten key economic variables are considered indicative of economic openness, competitiveness, and the rule of law. These are trade policy, taxation policy, government consumption of economic output, monetary policy, capital flows and foreign investment, banking policy, wage and price controls, property rights, regulations, and the black market, with a composite average overall score for each. The rankings form a category continuum from "free" (scoring 80–100) to "repressed" (scoring below 50 points), with "mostly free" and "mostly unfree" in between. In 2013, only five countries earned a rating of "free." Another 29 were rated as "mostly free." The categories "moderately free" and "mostly unfree" had 47 and 58 countries, respectively. Thirty-two countries had "repressed" economies. The top ten 2011 findings are summarized in Table 2-1. This table has been picked up from http://www.heritage.org/index/topten.

Taking 2011 for example, the global average economic freedom score inched up by .3 points over 2010. The combined scores of 117 economies were stronger; the scores of 58 were weaker. Of the 117 economies whose scores improved, 102 are developing or emerging economies, many of which are in Sub-Saharan Africa and the South and Central America/Caribbean region. Indeed, all regions except Europe and North America recorded increased levels of economic freedom, with Hong Kong, Singapore, Australia, New Zealand, Switzerland, and Canada solidifying their status as the world's most free economies. Policy responses to the global economic crisis of 2008–2010 have caused a major reshuffling of the top 20 countries; both Iceland and the United Kingdom are no longer in the top 20 countries. In 2013, the United States slipped to number ten.

As with previous editions of the Index, findings confirm that not only are higher levels of economic freedom associated with higher per capita incomes, but they also strongly correlate to overall well-being measures, which take into account factors such as health, education, security, personal freedom, economic growth, and prosperity. As reflected in The Heritage Foundation's 2008 Index, the world's most free nations had twice the average per capita income of the second quintile of countries and over five times the average income of the fifth quintile.[37] Four of the five quintiles in 2008, from most free to least free, had roughly equal populations, but the fourth quintile, which included China and India, contained half of the world's population. This fact suggests that when China and India further move toward higher economic freedom measures, there will be a major increase in global economic freedom.[38]

Consider Hong Kong. This special administrative region is part of the People's Republic of China but retains its own political governance structure and economic system. It was a British colony until the 1997 transfer of sovereignty to China;

---

[36] Taxation on labour, as measured by the tax wedge, encompasses employers' social security contributions, personal income tax, and employees' social security contributions. See http://ec.europa.eu/europe2020/pdf/themes/16_tax_burden_on_labour.pdf.

[37] http://www.heritage.org/research/features/index/chapters/pdf/index2008_execsum.pdf, p. 3.

[38] Ibid., 6. See also "Real Wages and Productivity Thrive in Developing Countries that Open Their Markets," *Stanford GSB News* online newsletter (October 2008), http://www.gsb.standford.edu/research/.

TABLE 2-1 Index of Economic Freedom World Ranking, 2016 Top Ten

Country Name	World Rank	2016 Score	Change from previous	Property Rights	Freedom from Corruption	Fiscal Freedom	Business Freedom	Labor Freedom	Monetary Freedom	Trade Freedom	Investment Freedom	Financial Freedom	GDP per Capita (PPP)
Australia	5	80.3	–1.1	90.0	80.0	63.2	89.4	77.2	85.2	86.4	80	90	$46,433
Chile	7	77.7	–0.8	85.0	73.0	74.8	72.1	64.3	82.9	86.4	85	70	$22,971
Estonia	9	77.2	0.4	90.0	69.0	81.9	79	57.2	82.2	88	90	80	$26,999
Ireland	8	77.3	0.7	90.0	74.0	73.6	79.6	72.1	85.5	88	90	70	$49,195
New Zealand	3	81.6	–0.5	95.0	91.0	71.0	91.4	85.9	88.1	87.2	80	80	$35,152
Singapore	2	87.8	–1.6	90.0	84.0	91.2	95	90.7	81.8	90	85	80	$82,762
Switzerland	4	81.0	0.5	90.0	86.0	70.9	82.2	72.1	87.8	90	85	80	$58,087
United Kingdom	10	76.4	0.6	90.0	78.0	64.9	86	71.8	76.4	88	90	80	$39,511
Canada	6	78	–1	90	81.0	80.0	81.8	72.6	76.9	87.0	80.0	80.0	$44,843
Hong Kong	1	88.6	–1.0	90.0	74.0	92.6	97.4	89.0	81.8	90	90	90	$54,722

Source: http://www.heritage.org/index/, as accessed on 23 December 2016 at 4pm.

however, it maintains the rule of law, free entry of foreign capital, the repatriation of earnings, and financial transparency, all important for foreign investment and capital movement.[39] The Index rates Hong Kong's economy as the freest in the world at 89.7 percent free. With highly competitive corporate tax rates, overall taxation is a relatively small percentage of GDP and simplified business regulations are supported by a flexible labor market. Investment is encouraged through legislated policy, with non-intrusive regulation of the banking and financial industries supported by judicial protection of property rights. The Hong Kong dollar is freely convertible and there are no controls or requirements on current monetary transfers, purchase of real estate, or access to foreign exchange.

Saudi Arabia's economy, by comparison, is rated as 66.2 percent free according to the 2011 Index. It is the largest Persian Gulf kingdom and has been ruled as an absolute monarchy by the Saud Dynasty since 1932. It is the world's largest oil producer and exporter and plays a leading role in the Organization of Petroleum Exporting Countries (OPEC). Since becoming a member of the World Trade Organization in 2005, through economic reforms, the government has looked to attract foreign investment and facilitate economic diversification. It is relatively easy to start a business and licensing takes less than the world average, indicative of the streamlining of the country's regulatory framework. However, tariff rates, import bans and restrictions, export controls, services market access barriers, non-transparent and inconsistent standards implementation, and domestic bias in government procurement all add to the cost of trade. Islamic law prohibits direct price controls, but the government influences pricing through regulation, subsidies, and state-owned businesses and utilities. Foreign investors are licensed yet must work with local partners in certain sectors. Minimum capital requirements and licensing processes are cumbersome. Saudi courts do not always enforce contractual obligations, and laws protecting intellectual property rights are in the process of being revised to comply with WTO's standards. Corruption is perceived as significant.[40]

State-dictated as well as democratically defined public policies help create and set market structures including tax, fiscal, and political agendas that are the basis for many government interventions, whether direct or indirect. Such interventions set the stage nationally as well as internationally, through trade groups and cooperative agreements, for business growth and expansion strategies and their success or failure on the world competitive stage.

STAGES OF MARKET DEVELOPMENT

Country markets are at different stages of development. Gross National Product per capita provides a very useful way of categorizing countries by their level of development. GNP per capita is also a popular indicator of the relative wealth of a country's citizenry.[41] Gross National Income (GNI) represents the total amount of money that country's consumers spend on all products and services per annum, divided by that country's population. GNP per capita includes only consumption that can be measured in money; therefore, these statistics do not capture the true

---

[39] http://www.heritage.org/Index/Country/HongKong.

[40] http://www.heritage.org/Index/Country/SaudiArabia.

[41] Academic and business leaders have been critical of traditional measures of prosperity, including the GDP. See, for example, Jon Gertner, "The Rise and Fall of the GDP," *The New York Times Magazine,* May 16, 2010, 60.

quality of life in a country and should not be taken to reflect a stereotyped lifestyle of all the citizens of that country.[42]

Using GNP as a base, The World Bank divides global markets into four categories. Each of these categories corresponds to a level of economic development with distinct economic and social characteristics, capabilities, and priorities. Thus, the stages provide a useful basis for business and marketing decisions regarding global market expansion, entry, and timing of that entry as well as market segmentation, target marketing, and product and brand positioning.

The categories are shown in Table 2-2. Low, lower-middle, and upper-middle income are often generally referred to as *developing countries*, while high-income countries are considered *developed countries*. Lower-middle income and upper-middle-income countries may also be referred to as *emerging markets*, denoting their general movement towards industrialization, among other factors.

Economies are divided according to 2015 gross national income (GNI) per capita, calculated using the World Bank Atlas method.[43] It is important to note that the relative size of economies, and changes in rankings from one year to the next, depend on the choice of specific indicators included and the method used to covert local currencies to US dollars. Year-to-year changes in the level of output or income of an economy are affected by a combination of forces: real growth, price inflation, and exchange rates. Changes in any of the three can affect an economy's relative size and, therefore, its ranking in comparison to other economies. Table 2-3 shows countries listed in each income group according to 2015 World Bank data.

Number of Countries in each group:

- Low income—31 countries
- Lower-middle income—52 countries
- Upper-middle income—52 countries
- High income: 79 countries

TABLE 2-2 World Bank List of Country Income Groups According to 2015 GNI Per Capita, Calculated Using the World Bank Atlas Method[44]

Low-Income Economies	$1,025 or less
Lower Middle-Income Economies	$1,026 and $4,035
Upper Middle-Income Economies	$4,036 and $12,475
High-Income Economies	$12,476 or more

Source: http://databank.worldbank.org/data/home.aspx, as accessed on 12 December 2016 at 5pm.

[42] Gross Domestic Product (GDP) as contrasted to Gross National Product (GNP). For a country, GDP is the market value of all goods and services produced by labor and property located in that country and equals GNP minus the net inflow of labor and property incomes from abroad. Gross National Product or GNP per capita is one measure of a country's economic development, referred to also as Gross National Income (GNI). This statistic represents the total amount of money that country's consumers spend on all products and services per annum divided by that country's population. GNP per capita includes only consumption that can be measured in money; therefore, these statistics do not capture the true quality of life in a country and should not be taken to reflect a stereotyped lifestyle of all the citizens of that country.

[43] http://data.worldbank.org/about/country-classifications/world-bank-atlas-method. The World Bank's official estimates of the size of economies are based on GNI converted to current US dollars using the Atlas method. GNI takes into account all production in the domestic economy (i.e., GDP) plus the net flows of factor income (such as rents, profits, and labor income) from abroad. The Atlas method smoothes exchange rate fluctuations by using a three-year moving average, price-adjusted conversion factor.

[44] http://data.worldbank.org/about/country-classifications.

TABLE 2-3 Countries Classified by Income—2015

Low-income economies ($1,025 or less) (31)		
Afghanistan	Guinea	Rwanda
Benin	Guinea-Bissau	Senegal
Burkina Faso	Haiti	Sierra Leone
Burundi	Korea, Dem. People's Rep.	Somalia
Central African Republic	Liberia	South Sudan
Chad	Madagascar	Tanzania
Comoros	Malawi	Togo
Congo, Dem. Rep	Mali	Uganda
Eritrea	Mozambique	Zimbabwe
Ethiopia	Nepal	
Gambia, The	Niger	
Lower-Middle-Income Economies ($1,026 To $4,035) (52)		
Armenia	Kiribati	Solomon Islands
Bangladesh	Kosovo	Sri Lanka
Bhutan	Kyrgyz Republic	Sudan
Bolivia	Lao PDR	Swaziland
Cabo Verde	Lesotho	Syrian Arab Republic
Cambodia	Mauritania	Tajikistan
Cameroon	Micronesia, Fed. Sts.	Timor-Leste
Congo, Rep.	Moldova	Tonga
Côte d'Ivoire	Mongolia	Tunisia
Djibouti	Morocco	Ukraine
Egypt, Arab Rep.	Myanmar	Uzbekistan
El Salvador	Nicaragua	Vanuatu
Upper-Middle-Income Economies ($4,036 To $12,475) (55)		
Albania	Fiji	Namibia
Algeria	Gabon	Palau
American Samoa	Georgia	Panama
Angola	Grenada	Paraguay
Azerbaijan	Guyana	Peru
Belarus	Iran, Islamic Rep.	Romania
Belize	Iraq	Russian Federation
Bosnia and Herzegovina	Jamaica	Serbia
Botswana	Jordan	South Africa
Brazil	Kazakhstan	St. Lucia
Bulgaria	Lebanon	St. Vincent and the Grenadines

(continued)

TABLE 2-3 Continued

Upper-Middle-Income Economies ($4,036 To $12,475) (55)		
China	Libya	Suriname
Colombia	Macedonia, FYR	Thailand
Costa Rica	Malaysia	Turkey
Cuba	Maldives	Turkmenistan
Dominica	Marshall Islands	Tuvalu
Dominican Republic	Mauritius	Venezuela, RB
Equatorial Guinea	Mexico	
Ecuador	Montenegro	

High-income economies ($12,476 or more) (79)		
Andorra	Gibraltar	Oman
Antigua and Barbuda	Greece	Poland
Aruba	Greenland	Portugal
Australia	Guam	Puerto Rico
Austria	Hong Kong SAR, China	Qatar
Bahamas, The	Hungary	San Marino
Bahrain	Iceland	Saudi Arabia
Barbados	Ireland	Seychelles
Belgium	Isle of Man	Singapore
Bermuda	Israel	Sint Maarten (Dutch part)
British Virgin Islands	Italy	Slovak Republic
Brunei Darussalam	Japan	Slovenia
Canada	Korea, Rep.	Spain
Cayman Islands	Kuwait	St. Kitts and Nevis
Channel Islands	Latvia	St. Martin (French part)
Chile	Liechtenstein	Sweden
Croatia	Lithuania	Switzerland
Curaçao	Luxembourg	Taiwan, China
Cyprus	Macao SAR, China	Trinidad and Tobago
Czech Republic	Malta	Turks and Caicos Islands
Denmark	Monaco	United Arab Emirates
Estonia	Nauru	United Kingdom
Faroe Islands	Netherlands	United States
Finland	New Caledonia	Uruguay
France	New Zealand	Virgin Islands (U.S.)
French Polynesia	Northern Mariana Islands	

Source: http://databank.worldbank.org/data/home.aspx, as accessed on 12 December 2016 at 5pm.

Low-Income Countries

Low-income countries are those with the lowest income category (incomes of less than $1025.00 per capita). They share the following characteristics:

1. Limited industrialization and a high percentage of the population engaged in agriculture and subsistence farming
2. High birth rates and low literacy rates, especially among women and girls.
3. Heavy reliance on foreign aid
4. High levels of poverty
5. Inequality of income distribution
6. Political instability and unrest due at least in part to disenfranchised social groups

Between 1981 and 2005, the share of the population in the developing world living below US$1.25 a day was halved from 52 to 25 percent, reducing the number of the poor by 500 million (from 1.9 billion to 1.4 billion) during that period. It is projected that global extreme poverty is likely to drop to about 920 million (15 percent) by 2015, according to a World Bank 2010 baseline forecast.[45] However, in light of the slowed global economy resulting from the financial crisis of 2008–2010, the pace of poverty reduction has been slowed, with an estimated 64 million more people expected to be living in extreme poverty than would have been without the global crisis.[46]

The decline in poverty between 1981 and 2005 varied considerably across regions. Led by China, the East Asia and the Pacific Region made dramatic progress, with poverty incidence dropping from 78 percent to 17 percent, using the US$1.25 a day poverty line at 2005 prices. At the other extreme is Sub-Saharan Africa (SSA) with a poverty rate of 51 percent in 2005—not much lower than in 1981. The poverty rate fell in South Asia, Latin America and the Caribbean, Middle East, and North Africa during the same period.[47]

The bottom of the economic pyramid is made up of the 2.5 billion people living on less than $2.50 per day.[48] Economic development experts, business leaders, and academicians have suggested business models which combine development and social transformation. They see opportunity at the bottom of the pyramid in the areas of product design and brand building, among others.[49]

As we pointed out in Chapter 1, marketing is a universal discipline. As such, the marketing process of focusing an organization's resources on targeted market opportunities can be applied to diverse markets at any stage of development or industrialization. The role of marketing—to be the link between the market and the enterprise—is the same in countries at every level of the income spectrum from low to high. To capture the complexities existing in emerging markets, companies need to recognize low-income markets as value-conscious. Based on this shift in thinking, opportunities can be identified. Merely adapting products designed for high-income markets to meet the needs of emerging markets has serious limitations.

Demographics and the particularities and constraints of bottom-of-the-pyramid markets demand innovation. Lenovo's PC for rural peasant farmers is not only a simplified

---

[45] http://web.worldbank.org/WBSITE/EXTERNAL/NEWS/0,contentMDK:20040961~menuPK:34480~pagePK:64257043~piPK:437376~theSitePK:4607,00.html (Accessed September 2010).

[46] Ibid.

[47] Ibid.

[48] T. London, "The Base-of-the-Pyramid Perspective: A New Approach to Poverty Alleviation," In G. T. Solomon (Ed.), *Academy of Management Best Paper Proceedings* (2008).

[49] S Allen Hammond, William J Kramer, Julia Tran, Rob Katz, Courtland Walker *The Next 4 Billion: Market Size and Business Strategy at the Base of the Pyramid* (World Resources Institute, 2007): 164; C. K. Prahalad and S. L. Hart, "The Fortune at the Bottom of the Pyramid," *Strategy + Business,* 26: 54–67; C. K. Prahalad, *The Fortune at the Bottom of the Pyramid: Eradicating Poverty through Profits* (Upper Saddle River, NJ: Wharton School, 2005): 407.

version but will include a keyboard and use the buyer's television set as a monitor. Websites provide much needed information suited to rural lifestyles including weather reports, product pricing, and agricultural information all aligned with the social, cultural, and environmental constraints of this market. In addition, packaging innovations such as sachetized cooking oil, sold for pennies, match economic constraints.

Global firms can meet the needs of these markets in addition to those of markets at higher income levels. For example, ICICI Bank deploys 2000 ATMs in urban neighborhoods and villages in India and, similar to microcredit organizations, organizes thousands of self-help community groups that provide loans for as little as $100 to poor entrepreneurial women starting businesses. ICICI is now India's dominant consumer bank with more than 15 million customers, moving 75 percent of its transactions online. Using its in-house financial software, ICICI plans to take its low-cost base to expand into the Canadian market and other developed countries.[50] Similarly, General Electric's health-care division is marketing a first-of-its-kind electrocardiogram machine in the United States—the smallest battery-powered electrocardiogram device on the market, weighing only six pounds. This innovative product will sell for only $2,500, which represents an 80 percent savings from similar products currently on the market. Most importantly, for our purposes, this diagnostic product was originally designed for health-care professionals in India and China in 2008.[51]

Carly Fiorina, former CEO of Hewlett-Packard, championed a program of World e-Inclusion which aimed company resources to product development for developing countries and their poor. The logic behind this and other programs is that by providing technology tools, the poor can increase their earning power and, accordingly, their power to consume more expensive technology. One of the technologies in greatest demand is the cell phone. Accordingly, Motorola, with its Motofone, a product designed for emerging markets, sells for about $30.00, with up to 400 hours of standby time on one charged battery, perfect for electricity-constrained market environments. Other examples of this cross-border learning are the $100 laptop developed by Nicholas Negroponte of MIT's Media Lab for markets in Latin America, rural Asia, and Africa and the $100 iPod shuffle.[52]

Until global firms begin to explore and build competitive advantage from these new markets, emerging markets with high levels of poverty remain invisible or will not be conceived to be attractive enough to warrant investment.

Lower-Middle-Income Countries

Lower-middle-income countries, also known as emerging markets, are those with a GNP per capita of more than $1026.00 and less than $4035.00. These countries are at the early stages of industrialization. Factories supply a growing domestic market with such items as clothing, batteries, tires, building materials, and packaged foods. These countries are also locations for the production of standardized or mature products such as clothing for export markets.

Consumer markets in these countries are expanding. These countries represent an increasing competitive threat as they mobilize their relatively cheap—and often highly motivated—labor to serve target markets in the rest of the world. Emerging markets have a major competitive advantage in mature, standardized, labor-intensive products. Indonesia, the largest noncommunist country in Southeast Asia, is a good example of an *LDC (less developed country)* on the move: per capita income has risen from $250 in 1985 to $2,050 in 2009.

---

[50] Pete Engardio, "Business Prophet," *Businessweek*, January 23, 2006, 68.

[51] Reena Jana, "Inspiration from Emerging Economies," *Businessweek*, March 23 and 30, 2009, 38.

[52] David Kirkpatrick, "Tech Targets the Third World," CNNMoney.com, Fast Forward online newsletter (December 12, 2006), accessed December 22, 2006.

Vietnam is another attractive, emerging market. With GNI per capita of $930 (Atlas method, current US$), its economy is growing as briskly as is its middle class, numbering 7 million in 2003 and expected to grow to an estimated 25 million in 2013.[53] Its literacy rate stands at 92.5 percent with the number of university students doubling from 2003 to 2008. Six of its expanding cities, although mostly small, account for 40 percent of the country's sales.[54] The government estimates that retail sales attained $39.1 billion in 2009, just about twice sales five years earlier. Indeed, what Vietnamese consumers purchase is not surprising—reliable goods that enhance their daily lives. What makes Vietnam distinctive is how fast these middle-class consumers are leapfrogging, a term highlighted by Unilever's Vietnam chairman, Marijn van Tiggelen. In 2009, it was estimated that Vietnam had 5 million Internet subscribers and 18 million Internet users, impressive for a country still at the early stage of digital development. In Hanoi and Ho Chi Minh City, half the population is online, although expenditure on digital marketing for the country as a whole is still low, just $15 million. "TV is still king in Vietnam because women are the decision makers in the family and they spend a lot of time watching TV," observed Mai Huong Hoang, chairwoman of Saatchi & Saatchi.[55] To reach Vietnam's predominantly rural villages with limited country infrastructure, consumer goods company Unilever has established a model of trained, independent distributors to sell its products to these dispersed and fragmented markets.

The biggest LDC on the move of course is China, with its population of over 1.3 billion people. In 2010 it overtook Japan to become the number two global economic power. Previously unseating Germany, France, and Great Britain, China will, if it continues in successful sustained growth, one day overtake the United States, with its gross 2009 domestic product of about $14 trillion. China has passed the United States in 2009 as the largest market for passenger vehicles (in units but not in value) and is the world's largest exporter.[56] Another rapidly growing LDC, India's urban per capita GDP is projected to grow at a rate of 6 percent a year from 2005 to 2025, surpassed only by China with a projected growth rate of 7.4 percent. In light of the rapid urbanization and projected growth, market opportunities in both countries will be transportation, communications, food, and health care, followed by housing, utilities, recreation, and education.[57]

Upper-Middle-Income Countries

Upper-middle-income countries, also known as industrializing countries, are those with GNP per capita between $4036.00 and $12,475.00. In these countries, the percentage of population engaged in agriculture drops sharply as people move to the industrial sector and the degree of urbanization increases. Many of the countries in this stage—Malaysia, Argentina, Venezuela, Brazil, Mexico, and Turkey, for example, have rising wages, high rates of literacy, and advanced education, but still have significantly lower wage costs than advanced countries. These countries, and others at this stage of development, frequently become formidable competitors and experience rapid, export-driven growth and home-grown global competition.

The expanding economies of Eastern Europe belong to this category. Turkey, for example, has gone from a volatile economy and disruptive political turmoil to relative

---

[53] Marco Breu, Brian S. Salsberg, and Ha Thanh Tu, "Growing Up Fast: Vietnam Discovers the Consumer Society," *The McKinsey Quarterly* (August 2010), accessed August 22, 2010 http://www.forbes.com/2010/08/23/vietnam-retailing-consumerism-leadership-managing-mckinsey.html.

[54] Ibid.

[55] Ibid.

[56] Ibid.

[57] Richard Dobbs and Shirish Sankhe, "Comparing Urbanization in China and India," *The McKinsey Quarterly* (July 2010), accessed July 15, 2010 http://www.mckinseyquarterly.com/Comparing_urbanization_in_China_and_India_2641.

stability. Turkey has sometimes sought admission to the EU. With active foreign investment from the likes of Ford, General Electric, and joint venture investment from Chinese companies competing for public infrastructure contracts and manufacturing for Europe's expansive single market, Turkey is the T in the BRIC-IT (Brazil, Russia, India, China, Indonesia, and Turkey) group of fast-growing emerging markets.[58]

High-Income Countries

High-income countries, also known as advanced, industrialized, or postindustrial, are those with GNP per capita above $12,475.00. With the exception of the relatively new oil-rich nations, the countries in this category reached their present income level through a process of sustained economic growth.

The phrase *postindustrial countries* was first used by Daniel Bell of Harvard to describe the United States, Sweden, Japan, and other advanced, high-income societies. Bell suggests there is a difference between the industrial and the postindustrial societies or information age that goes beyond mere measures of income. Bell's thesis is that the sources of innovation in postindustrial societies are derived increasingly from the codification of theoretical knowledge rather than from random inventions of more industrial production. Later renaming this concept the *information society*, he was one of the original theorists who postulated that postindustrial nations would move from being producers of goods founded in industrialized manufacturing to service economies where theoretical knowledge, technology, and information become the major drivers of productivity gains. This move was to be supported by, in Bell's view, information processing and exchange; the ascendancy of investments in knowledge over tangible capital as a key strategic resource; the growth of intellectual over mechanical technology; and the ascendance of science and scientific pursuit, especially the newer science-based industries. Information and those who know how to create, assemble, and disseminate it as a commodity would be more valued, in Bell's view, than the more traditional labor force. Other aspects of the postindustrial society stressed by Bell's original thinking was an orientation toward the future; he stressed that postindustrialized societies would need to learn how to predict the future rather than forecast in order to increase the number of theoretical future possibilities so that they might all be addressed or explored as society changed. Although forecasting remains an important strategic tool for global business, the rise of scenario planning in corporate strategic playbooks attests to the strength of Bell's original vision.

Emerging Countries

Antoine W. van Agtmael of International Finance Corp. (IFC), during 1981 first came out with the term, "emerging countries or markets", to designate the few countries of the world with future economic growth possibilities. These countries are taking up serious reforms in policies and measures, irrespective of the fact that they are small or big, to excel in the part of fast economic development in the near future. For example, China is an emerging country with 1.37 billion population, 7925 USD as GDP per capita, life expectancy of 75 years, unemployment rate of 4.7 percent, and adult literacy rate of 96.36 percent. Whereas Tunisia is a small country with 11.1 million populations, 3873 USD as GDP per capita, life expectancy of 74 years, unemployment rate of 13.3 percent, and adult literacy rate of 81.05 percent. But both China and Tunisia can be termed as emerging countries because they are proceeding in the path of economic development and embracing globalisation.

---

[58] Steve Bryant and Ben Holland, "Turkey's Moment," *Businessweek*, April 25, 2010, 45. See also Judy Dempsey, "Building Bridges with Eastern Europe," *The New York Times*, September 22, 2010.

BRICS Countries as Big Market

Brazil, Russia, India and China (acronym BRIC) are the best known emerging countries of the world as these countries are progressing in the path of development at a faster pace. These countries have placed reforms in policies and measures in their primary agenda. They are proving themselves to be the economic power house in the world and hence attracting global companies for business. For example, Apple Inc. entered the BRIC countries and was successful in achieving its marketing dream. iPhone sales in Brazil was remarkable for the company and in Russia sales grew at a very faster pace, Indian market accepted the product with eagerness to own them and China was a dream market for the product in terms of revenue realisation. This remarkable marketing success was possible because about 40 per cent of world population lives in BRIC countries and is responsible for 25-30 per cent of world's GDP.

INCOME AND PURCHASING POWER PARITY AROUND THE GLOBE

When a company charts a strategic plan for global market expansion, it often finds that, for most products, income is the single most valuable economic variable. After all, a market can be defined as a group of people willing and able to buy a particular product or service. For some products, particularly those that have a very low unit cost—chewing gum, for example—population is a more valuable predictor of market potential than income. Nevertheless, for the vast range of industrial and consumer products in international markets today, the single most valuable and important indicator of potential is income.

Looking at Table 2-4, GNP and other measures of national income converted to US dollars can be calculated on the basis of purchasing power parities (i.e., what the currency will buy in the country of issue) or through direct comparisons of actual prices for a comparison basket of goods and services. This provides a comparison of the standards of living in the countries of the world. The reader must remember that exchange rates equate, at best, the prices of internationally traded goods and services. They often bear little relationship to the prices of those goods and services not traded internationally which form the bulk of the national product in most countries. Agricultural output and services, in particular, are often priced lower in relation to industrial output in developing countries than in industrial countries. For example, a visit to a doctor in India for an examination or treatment that costs $200 in the United States might cost $2 in India. In this example, the Indian medical dollar has 100 times the purchasing power of the US medical dollar. Furthermore, agriculture typically accounts for the largest share of output in less developed countries. Thus, the use of exchange rates tends

Table 2.4 Stages of Economic Development/Global Income and Population 2016 Edition

Income Group	GDP Per Capita (Current US$)	GDP (Current US Million $)	GDP Growth (Annual%)	GNI Current US$ (Million)	GNI Percapita (Current US$)	Total Population (Million)	Population Growth (Annual %)
High income	39,576.9	46,985,246.88	1.9	49,109,691.34	41,366	1187.2	0.6
OECD	35,783.1	45,837,975.61	2	47,945,195.37	37,428	1281	0.6
Low income	615.6	392,904.088	4.7	395.5	620	6382.86	2.7
Lower middle income	4,244.7	25,960,080.24	3.6	27,049,331.27	4,423	2,927.41	1.45
Upper middle income	7,737.4	19,732,883.63	3	20,691,643.04	8,110	2550.33	0.8

Source: http://data.worldbank.org/indicator/NY.GNP.PCAP.CD?locations=XM-XO, as accessed on 12 December 2016 at 3.30pm.

to exaggerate differences in real income and standard of living between countries at different stages of economic development. Relative price differences require the use of purchasing power estimates in order to compare the standard of living between countries. Purchasing power differences can account for differential in demand of products and services, and also provide an indication on differences in costs.

Purchasing power parity comparisons of income provide better measures of standard of living of residents of an economy because they measure the economy's output in terms of buying power. The PPP rate is defined as the number of units of a country's currency required to buy the same amount of goods and services in the comparison country. By recognizing local prices, PPP rates deliver a measure of the standard of living in a country. Table 2-5 ranks the top 20 countries in terms of 2015 GNP per capita income and total GNP, both adjusted for purchasing power parity (PPP). Although, for example, Switzerland ranks 6th in income, its standard of living—measured by what money can buy—ranks 10th.

Table 2-5 ranks the top 20 countries in terms of 2015 per capita income at the 2015 US$ exchange rate at PPP. Beyond the exchange distortion illustrated in Table 2-5, there is the distortion of money itself as an indicator of a nation's welfare and standard of living. Although per capita GNI of Canada and Austria are similar—47,540 and 47,410

TABLE 2-5 GNP and PPP Per Capita. Top 20 Countries, 2015, Atlas method

Rank	GNP per capita	GNP per capita, (US dollars)	PPP adjusted GNP per capita	PPP adjusted GNP per capita (International dollar)
1	Monaco	*	Qatar	138,480
2	Liechtenstein	*	Macao SAR, China	102,480
3	Bermuda	106,140	Kuwait	84,360
4	Norway	93,740	Brunei Darussalam	82,140
5	Channel Islands	*	Singapore	81,360
6	Switzerland	84,630	Luxembourg	70,750
7	Qatar	83,990	United Arab Emirates	70,020
8	Isle of Man	83,290	Bermuda	66,680
9	Luxembourg	77,000	Norway	64,590
10	Macao SAR, China	67,180	Switzerland	62,590
11	Australia	60,070	Hong Kong SAR, China	57,650
12	Denmark	58,550	United States	57,540
13	Sweden	57,920	Saudi Arabia	54,730
14	United States	55,980	Netherlands	48,400
15	Singapore	52,090	Germany	48,260
16	Cayman Islands	*	Denmark	47,810
17	Iceland	50,140	Austria	47,510
18	Netherlands	48,860	Sweden	47,390
19	Canada	47,540	Ireland	46,410
20	Austria	47,410	Iceland	46,120

Source: http://data.worldbank.org/data-catalog/GNI-per-capita-Atlas-and-PPP-table, as accessed on 12 December 2016 at 12pm.

*2015 data not available, but ranking based on estimate.

in 2015—PPP per capita GNI is different—44,010 versus 47,510, respectively. The typical consumer in Austria has just about 8 percent more purchasing power of the Canadian consumer.

The implications of this are profound. A visit to a mud house in Tanzania will reveal many of the things that money can buy: radios, an iron bed frame, a corrugated metal roof, beer and soft drinks, bicycles, shoes, photographs, and razor blades. What Tanzania's per capita income of $920 in 2015 does not reflect is the fact that instead of utility bills, Tanzanians have the local well and the sun. Instead of nursing homes, tradition and custom ensure that families will take care of the elderly at home. Instead of expensive doctors and hospitals, villagers can turn to traditional doctors and healers. In industrialized countries, a significant portion of national income is generated by taking goods and services that would be free in a less developed country and putting a price on them. Thus, the standard of living in many countries is often higher than income data might suggest.

The income per capita and life expectancy in the world was relatively flat 175 years ago. Then Europe, the United States, Canada, Australia, and New Zealand broke out of the world average and began a long period of steady growth which resulted in a great gap between the income in these countries and the rest of the world. Japan was the first country outside of this set of countries to achieve high-income status. These countries accounted for 80 percent of global income and were called *the triad* (Europe, United States/Canada, and Japan). Table 2-6 shows the richest countries in the world measured by GDP (PPP).

TABLE 2-6 Richest Countries of the World GDP (PPP)

Country Ranking	Economy	GDP (PPP) in 2015 (Millions of International dollars)
1	China	19,524,348
2	United States	17,946,996
3	India	7,982,528
4	Japan	4,738,294
5	Germany	3,848,272
6	Russian Federation	3,579,826
7	Brazil	3,192,398
8	Indonesia	2,842,241
9	United Kingdom	2,691,809
10	France	2,650,823
11	Mexico	2,194,431
12	Italy	2,182,580
13	Korea, Rep.	1,748,776
14	Saudi Arabia	1,685,204
15	Spain	1,602,660
16	Canada	1,588,596
17	Turkey	1,543,284
18	Iran, Islamic Rep.	1,357,025
19	Thailand	1,108,108
20	Nigeria	1,091,698

Source: http://data.worldbank.org/data-catalog/GDP-PPP-based-table, as accessed on 23 December 2016 at 12pm.

Ranking, 2015	Economy	(Millions of international dollars)	Rank in 2020
1	China	19,524,348	China
2	United States	17,946,996	United states
3	India	7,982,528	India
4	Japan	4,738,294	Japan
5	Germany	3,848,272	Russia
6	Russian Federation	3,579,826	Germany
7	Brazil	3,192,398	Brazil
8	Indonesia	2,842,241	United Kingdom
9	United Kingdom	2,691,809	France
10	France	2,650,823	Mexico
11	Mexico	2,194,431	South Korea
12	Italy	2,182,580	Indonesia
13	Korea, Rep.	1,748,776	Italy
14	Saudi Arabia	1,685,204	Canada
15	Spain	1,602,660	Spain

FIGURE 2-1 Rank Shift in GDP 2015 vs 2020

Adapted from http://data.worldbank.org/data-catalog/GDP-PPP-based-table and http://blog.euromonitor.com/2010/07/special-report-top-10-largest-economies-in-2020.html for 2020 forecast.

Ten years ago, the concentration of the world's wealth continued in the triad regions. The rapid growth of Asian countries, in particular China and India, as well as several fast-growing Latin American, Eastern European, Middle Eastern, and African countries, has led to what has been termed the "rise of the rest." This is a world where the mountain tops and valleys of income are becoming a wide plateau of high income.

By 2020 there will be a major shift in the global balance of economic power compared with 2010. Emerging economies will rise in importance and China will have overtaken the United States to lead the list of the world's top 10 largest economies by GDP measured in PPP terms. Consumer markets in emerging economies will present enormous opportunities; however, as we have begun to see today, their rapid growth poses a challenge to the sustainability of the global environment. Figure 2-1 shows rank shift in GDP 2015 vs 2020.

BOX 2-1

Side Bar: GDP or GNP Based Understanding could be Misleading!

In many developing countries of the world, the divide between rich and poor are increasing. Rich people are getting richer every day and poor people are getting poorer in a continuous process. The marketers while marketing in different countries of the world are taking a serious note about this increasing income inequality phenomenon because not only the size of the target segments are changing but also the change of taste, choice and preference are visible. One of the most important economic parameters in understanding income inequality of countries is income inequality index, better known as Gini coefficient, which helps international marketers to better understand the income inequality status of a country. Gini index actually, is a statistical representation of the distribution of national income amongst the population of a country. A little verity of the index is the Gini coefficient on disposable income which actually is more informative as it refers the after-tax distribution of income. Gini coefficient varies between 0 to 1 where 0 indicates maximum equality and 1 indicates maximum inequality. If a country has a Gini coefficient of 0 then every person living in the country earns the same whereas, 1 represent that only select few are enjoying all the income of the country.

Recently during March 2016, International Monetary Fund (IMF) in its working paper indicated that income inequality in India was increasing. In India, the Gini coefficient also rose from 0.45 during 1990 to o.51 during 2013, testifying the fact that the country had a problem of income distribution. IMF also did not forget to indicate the fact that the situation of income inequality in India was comparatively better than its neighbouring country China. According to IMF, income inequality data indicates that during the same period between 1990 to 2013, income inequality co efficient had risen faster in China. During 1990, income was comparatively fairly distributed in China with Gini co efficient stable at 0.33 but with the splendid rise in the national income with time, the wealth started accumulating in the hand of the rich segment and hence the Gini co efficient also increased to 0.53 during 2013[59].

The accumulation of dispensable income in the hands of rich segment of the population put its due pressure on the international companies. They are required to be more quality conscious to create customer value creation. One necessary evil associated with high income in equality is low price elasticity of demand. Rich population need quality product irrespective of the price so the marketers can remain adamant in increasing the price of the products without effecting the market demand of the product offered. However, a vast chunk of population with low disposable income ironically would no longer remain in the radar of the global quality producers.

ACTUAL INDIVIDUAL CONSUMPTION

Actual individual consumption is measured by the total value of household consumption expenditure, expenditures by nonprofit institutions (such as NGOs and charities) serving households, and government expenditure on individual consumption goods and services (such as education or health).

As Table 2-7 indicates, there exists a signficant gap between the living standard of the majority of people in high-income countries and those in low-income countries. In fact, looking at the distribution of world income by population quintiles demonstrates that the concentration of world income is in the wealthiest quintile (fifth) of the world's population. Despite these statistics, champions of free trade and global capital movement stress that world income distribution is becoming more equal as globalization moves forward. If statistics showed this to be true, then the "law of even development" would appear to be true also. The "law of even development" says that all national economies gain from more integration in international markets, and lower-cost, capital-scarce economies (developing countries) are likely to gain more from fuller integration than higher-cost, capital-abundant economies (developed countries).[60]

As we have seen earlier in the chapter, the gap between the richest and poorest countries provides tremendous incentive for migration, both in the form of legal and illegal immigration, to high-income countries to seek economic and educational

---

[59] 2016 International Monetary Fund Working Paper WP/16/48, March, 2016.

[60] Robert Hunter Wade, "The Rising Inequality of World Income Distribution, Finance, and Development," a quarterly magazine of the *International Monetary Fund*, 38, no. 4 (December 2001), http://imf.org/external/pubs/ft/fandd/2001/12/wade.htm.

TABLE 2-7 Actual Individual Consumption Per Capita[61]

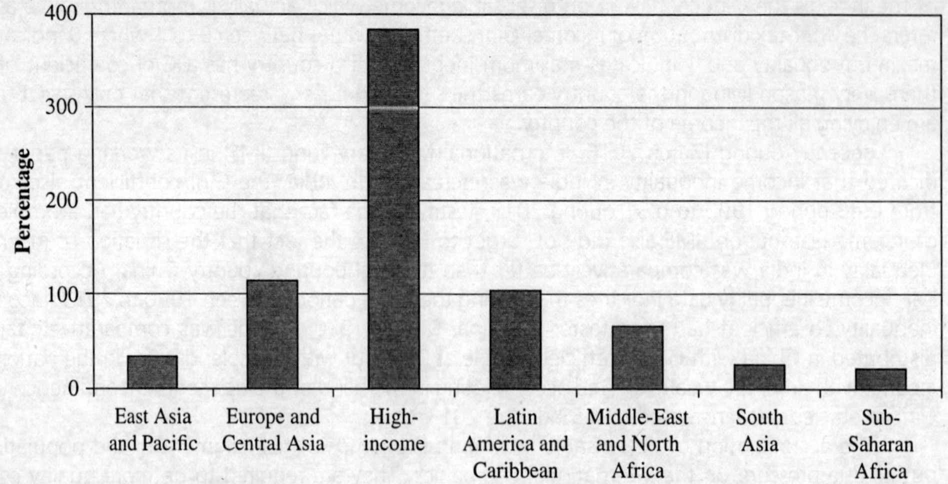

opportunities and a higher standard of living.[62] Throughout the late nineteenth and twentieth centuries, industrial countries' share of world income increased. During this period of time, annual compound rates of growth profoundly altered the world's distribution of income. The magnitude of this change as compared with the previous 6,000 years of civilized world history is enormous: over one-third of the real income and about two-thirds of the industrial output produced by people throughout recorded history were generated in the industrialized countries and regions of the world over the past century. Through what can be considered systematized growth versus more incremental, average annual growth rates, the economic geography of the world has been transformed.

The concentration of income in the high-income and large-population countries means that a company can be global, that is, derive a significant proportion of its income from countries at different stages of development, while operating in a dozen or fewer countries. Table 2-7 shows actual individual consumption per capita for major regions of the world.

THE LOCATION OF POPULATION

For products whose price is low enough, population is a more important variable than income in determining market potential and consumer demand. Although population is not as concentrated as income, there is, in terms of size of nations, a pattern of considerable concentration. As shown in Table 2-8, the 10 most promising emerging countries in the world account for roughly 47.2 percent of the world's population today. These 10 emerging countries together have GDP PPP (2015) of $32.64 trillion out of the world GDP PPP (2015) $115.14 trillion i.e., almost 30 percent of the total.

There are serious implications for the strategic marketer who has her sights only on mature, developed global markets. What worldwide opportunities are being missed? What regional strategies might be highlighted? What global partners or strategic alliances are not being assessed that might prove actionable for market entry or

[61] International Comparison Program 2005, Preliminary Results, December 17, 2007. at www.worldbank.org/data/icp.

[62] See, for example, "A World Ever More on the Move," *The New York Times*, June 27, 2010.

TABLE 2-8 Population and Per Capita Trend in Emerging Countries

Sl No.	Countries	Population (2016)	GDP (purchasing power parity): 2015 ($)	GDP per capita (PPP) ($)
1	Argentina,	43,886,748	$884.2 billion	$20,500
2	Brazil	205,823,665	$3.199 trillion	$15,600
3	China	1,373,541,278	$11.18 trillion	$14,300
4	India	1,266,883,598	$7.998 trillion	$6,200
5	Indonesia	258,316,051	$2.848 trillion	$11,100
6	Mexico	123,166,749	$2.23 trillion	$18,400
7	Poland	38,523,261	$1.007 trillion	$26,500
8	South Africa	54,300,704	$725.9 billion	$13,200
9	South Korea	50,924,172	$1.853 trillion	$36,600
10	Turkey	80,274,604	$1.596 trillion	$20,400

Source: CIA fact book.

market expansion? What product or branding opportunities are being overlooked or what product design offerings or packaging alternatives do not see the light of day because their potential users are not identified?

GLOBAL TRADE AND INVESTMENT

The Balance of Payments

The balance of payments is a record of all of the economic transactions between residents of a country and the rest of the world. It is a macro-level picture of the economic transactions of a country. The balance of payments is divided into a so-called current and capital account. The current account is a record of all of the recurring trade in merchandise and service, private gifts, and public aid transactions between countries. The capital account is a record of all long-term direct investment, portfolio investment, and other short- and long-term capital flows. The capital account exerts a lot of pressure on exchange rates, which, in turn, impacts price of goods and services. In general, a country accumulates reserves when the net of its current and capital account transactions shows a surplus; it gives up reserves when the net shows a deficit. The important fact to recognize about the overall balance of payments is that it is always in balance. Imbalances occur in subsets of the overall balance.

The Asian economies, despite a dip in 2000–2001, have seen increasingly positive current account balances, with China leading with an account balance of 293.2.5 billion, way ahead of second-ranked Germany with 285.2 billion as shown in Table 2-9. Japan follows with current account balance of 137.5 billion. The United States laces last out of 191 countries with a negative account balance of negative 484.1 billion, far outpacing the nearest negative account balance of United Kingdom with negative 123.5 billion. For the United States, the deficit on the overall balance of payments in current accounts, which includes goods, services, and foreign investment income combined, has risen since the early 1990s, worsening dramatically over the past decade.

China, Germany, and Japan offset their trade surplus with an outflow of capital. (Remember, the balance of payments always balances!) The United States

TABLE 2-9 Estimated 2015 Current Account Balance of World Top Ten Surplus Countries

Rank	Country	Current Account Balance 2015
1	China	$293,200,000,000
2	Germany	$285,200,000,000
3	Japan	$137,500,000,000
4	Korea, South	$105,900,000,000
5	Netherlands	$80,990,000,000
6	Taiwan	$76,170,000,000
7	Switzerland	$75,820,000,000
8	Russia	$65,800,000,000
9	Singapore	$57,560,000,000
10	Italy	$38,740,000,000

Source: https://www.cia.gov/library/publications/the-world-factbook/rankorder/2187rank.html, as accessed on 10 January 2017 at 9pm.

offsets its trade deficit with an inflow of capital. As trading partners, the United States owns an increasing quantity of Chinese, Japanese, and German products. These three nations own more US real estate, government securities, and publicly traded company equity. Prior to the Great Recession of 2008–2009, trade surpluses allowed many developing countries to accumulate reserve assets as a protection against global financial crisis or balance-of-payments vulnerabilities. Strong reserves help lower interest rates and reassure global lenders. China's trade and foreign exchange-rate policy has been an issue for some time for global political and business leaders seeking a transition to a more global and sustainable trade and account balance equilibrium.[63] Clearly, the present Chinese trade surpluses and offsetting trade deficits in the rest of the world (ROW) and especially in the United States are not sustainable.

GLOBAL TRADE PATTERNS

Since the end of World War II and into the first decade of the twenty-first century, world merchandise trade has grown faster than world production. In other words, over the span of years, import and export growth has outpaced the rate of increase in GNP. In fact, in most countries the share of imports and exports as a percentage of the national economy has grown. In 2007, the world's major economic regions reflected synchronized growth trends in excess of 3 percent annually, while average global trade grew in real terms at 7.7 percent.[64] A year earlier, in 2006, the volume of world merchandise trade was 8 percent, while world gross domestic product reflected a 3.5 percent increase. Both years confirm a continuing trend since 2000 in

[63] Lowell Bryan, "Globalization's Critical Imbalances," *The McKinsey Quarterly* (June 2010), accessed June 24, 2010, https://www.mckinseyquarterly.com/article. See also "Worlds Apart: What's Behind the US-China Currency Dispute?," Knowledge@Wharton (October 13, 2010), accessed October 14, 2010, http://knowledge.wharton.upenn.edu/; and David Barboza, "Chinese Leader Fields Executives' Questions," *The New York Times*, September 23, 2010, 42.

[64] Based on World Bank preliminary estimates December 2008, World Trade Indicators 2008, Benchmarking Policy and Performance, The World Bank, Washington, D.C. 2008 at http://info.worldbank.org/etools/wti2008/docs/mainpaper.pdf.

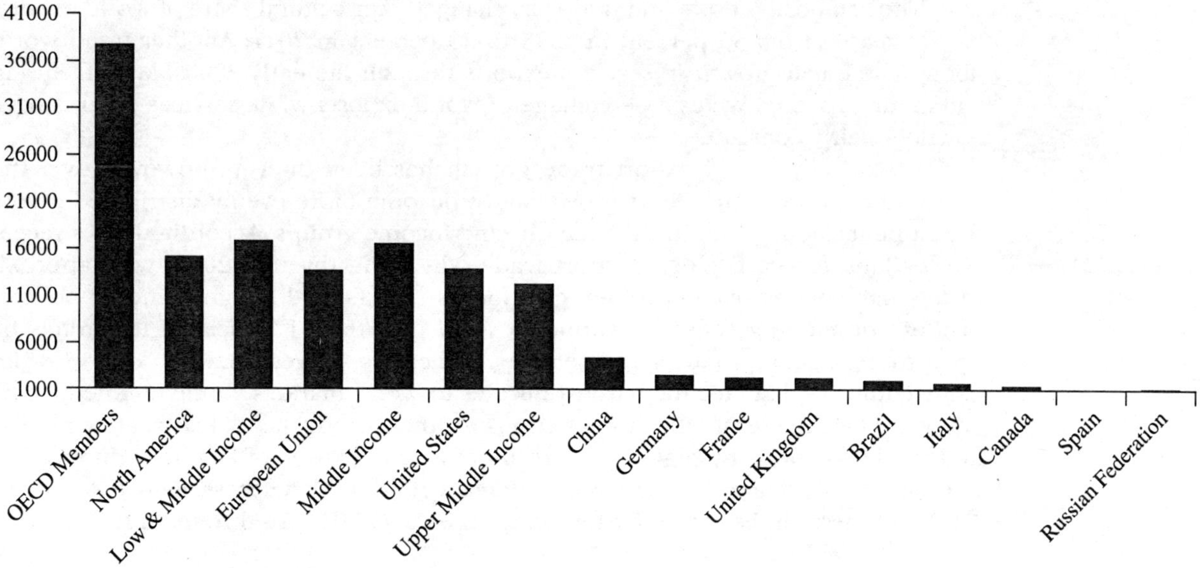

FIGURE 2-2 Average PPP Consumption Across 146 Countries
Adapted from http://databank.worldbank.org/data/home.aspx, as accessed on 23 December 2016 at 2pm.

which world merchandise trade has grown by twice the annual growth rate of output. The increase in both trade and investment flows is a major cause of economic globalization and a direct outcome of economic globalization. Figure 2-2 shows average PPP consumption in USD of some countries of the world in the range 1000 to about 38000 USD. Figure 2-3 shows growth in volume of world merchandise trade and GDP from 2007 to 2016 (provisional).

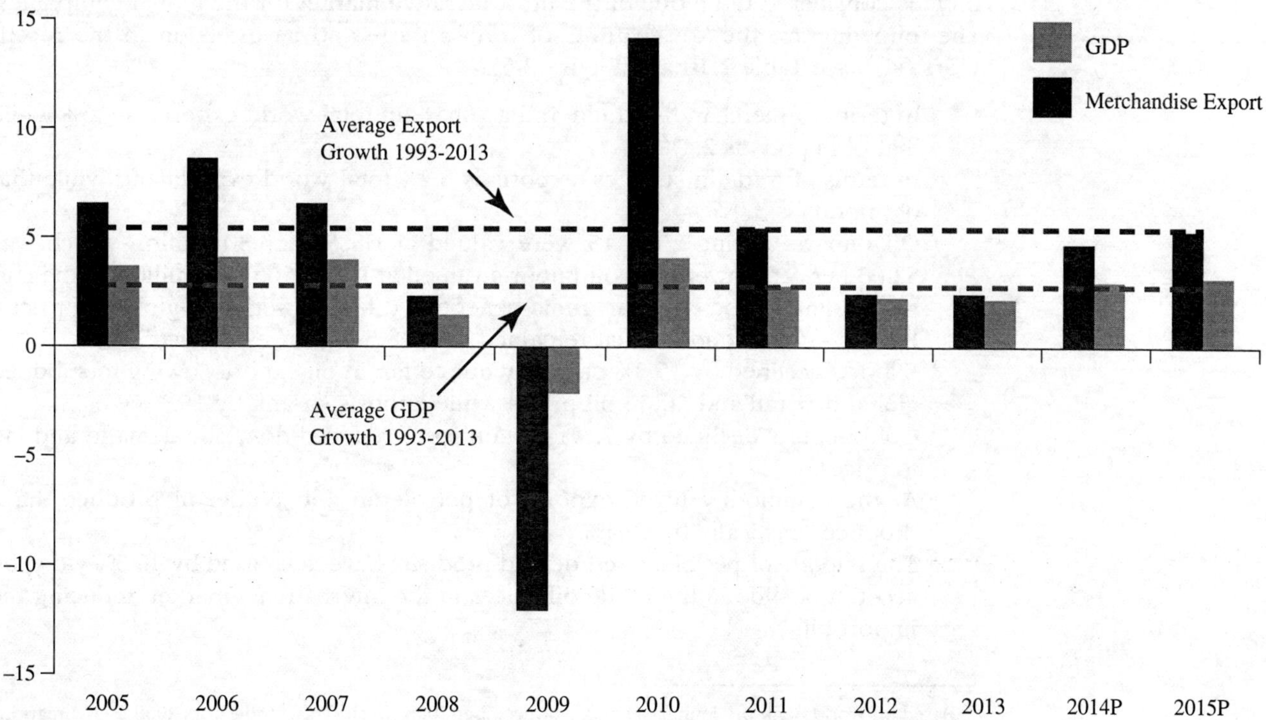

FIGURE 2-3 Growth in Volume of World Merchandise Trade and GDP 2007 to 2016 (provisional).
Courtesy: https://www.wto.org/english/res_e/statis_e/wts2016_e/wts2016_e.pdf page 18, as accessed on 23 December 2016 at 12pm.

The composition of world trade has changed. Agricultural share of world exports has decreased from 50 percent in 1995 to 28 percent in 2011. Another trend worth noting is the real growth in services exports through the early 2000s. Manufacturing and mining have grown as a percentage of world exports while services exports have remained fairly constant.

Historically, world export trade growth has been uneven; however, over the past decade, trade and export growth have become more evenly distributed across the globe including both diverse regions and income groups. Accordingly to a recent World Bank forecast, global export trade will triple through 2030, with approximately half coming from developing countries.[65] In fact, although domestic policies of these developing countries support export growth, it is crucial that markets be open to exporter's products and services. Indicators suggest that it is often low-income countries that face the hardest hurdles to world markets, while middle-income countries face the least barrier restrictions for their products.[66] Clearly, merchandise and services exports by region are a result of a combination of factors including, but not limited to, pricing, exchange rates, demand, and market access. Figure 2-4 shows GDP and merchandise trade by region for the years 2010–14 through 2015.

COMPOSITION OF INDIA'S TRADE AND DIRECTION

Since 1991, India has been adapting a path of trade liberalisation. With the opening up economy and removal of trade barriers, the country embraced foreign trade as vital tool for economic development. The country is rapidly integrating its economy with that of the world. India as a developing country depends a lot more on its exports and imports to set the pace of economic development. Though many countries of world are hit by recent slow down but still maintaining it momentum of economic development and growing at the rate of 7 to 7.5 percent rate in GDP. Naturally, then India is considered to be one of the most lucrative market for the global companies. The following are the key features of India's trade and its direction in the recent years (also see Table 2-10 and Figure 2-5).

- In terms of merchandise trade, India's share in total world exports is 1.6% while that of imports is 2.4%.
- In terms of trade in services, exports is 3.2% total world exports and while that of imports is 3.0%.
- Oil imports during 2014–15 were valued at US $ 7413.30 million which was 52.68 per cent lower than oil imports valued at US $ 15667.12 million in the corresponding period last year. India benefitted due to lowering of global oil prices. In 2015–16, the trade deficit remained at $118.5 bn, lowest in last 5 years.
- Exports declined by 15.8% primarily due to fall in oil exports, owing to subdued global demand and fall in oil prices while imports shrank by 15.3% y-o-y.
- Gold imports declined by 7.8% pertaining to reduced domestic demand and fall in prices.
- At the commodity level, exports of petroleum and crude oil products have dropped drastically by 49.4%.
- The imports of petroleum crude and products have decreased by 40.5% y-o-y, on account of slide in the crude oil prices in the international market, reducing the import bill.

---

[65] Based on World Bank preliminary estimates December 2008, World Trade Indicators 2008, Benchmarking Policy and Performance, The World Bank, Washington, D.C. 2008 at http://info.worldbank.org/etools/wti2008/docs/mainpaper.pdf.

[66] Ibid.

Exports 2010–14	Exports 2013	Exports 2014	GDP 2013	GDP 2014	GDP 2015		Imports 2010–14	Imports 2013	Imports 2014
3.5	3.0	2.5	3.3	3.3	3.8	World	3.0	2.0	2.5
4.5	2.5	4.0	2.2	2.2	3.1	North America	3.5	1.0	4.5
4.0	2.0	5.5	2.0	2.3	2.4	Canada	2.5	1.5	2.0
6.0	4.5	7.0	1.1	2.4	3.5	Mexico	6.0	3.0	7.0
4.5	2.5	3.5	2.2	2.2	3.1	United States	3.0	1.0	4.5
2.0	2.0	−1.5	2.7	1.3	2.2	South and Central America	3.5	3.5	−2.5
2.5	2.5	1.5	−0.4	0.8	1.3	Europe	1.0	0.0	2.5
2.5	2.0	2.0	0.2	1.4	1.8	European Union (28)	1.0	−0.5	3.0
−1.5	−5.0	1.5				Norway	1.5	1.5	1.0
4.5	16.0	−6.0				Switzerland	−2.5	2.0	−13.0
1.0	1.0	0.0	2.2	0.8	1.6	Commonwealth of Independent States (CIS)	2.5	−1.0	−10.0
4.5	5.0	4.5	6.6	6.5	6.6	Asia	4.5	5.0	3.5
3.5	6.0	6.0				Australia	2.5	−2.5	2.0
7.5	7.5	7.0	7.7	7.4	7.1	China	6.5	10.0	4.0
6.0	8.5	3.0	5.0	5.6	6.4	India	4.5	−0.5	3.0
−1.0	−2.0	0.5	1.5	0.9	0.8	Japan	3.0	0.5	2.5
3.5	3.0	4.0	5.2	4.7	5.4	Six East Asian traders[a]	3.0	3.5	3.0

FIGURE 2-4 GDP and Merchandise Trade by Region for the years 2010–14 through 2015

(Annual percentage change)

[a] Hong Kong, China; Malaysia; Republic of Korea; Singapore; Separate Customs Territory of Taiwan, Penghu, Kinmen and Matsu (Chinese Taipei) and Thailand.

Courtesy: https://www.wto.org/english/res_e/statis_e/its2015_e/its2015_e.pdf, page 39, as accessed on 23 December 2016 at 3pm.

TABLE 2-10 Composition of India's Trade

(US $ billion)

	2011–12	2012–13	2013–14	2014–15	2015–16	Growth (FY16/FY15)
Trade Balance	−183.4	−190.1	−134.0	−137.5	−118.5	−14.2
Exports	305.7	300.2	314.9	310.1	261.1	−15.8
POL	55.9	60.8	63.3	56.6	29.1	−48.6
Non-POL	249.9	239.4	251.5	253.5	232.0	−8.5
Imports	489.1	490.2	448.8	447.6	379.1	−15.3
POL	155.0	163.8	164.9	137.8	82.3	−40.3
Non-POL	334.2	326.4	283.9	309.8	296.8	−4.2
Gold	56.3	53.7	27.5	34.4	31.8	−7.8

Source: CMIE.

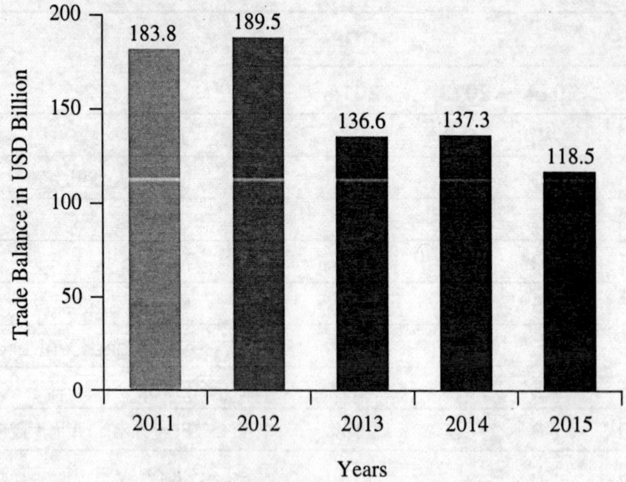

FIGURE 2-5 Indian Trade Balance from 2011–2015.

- A trade surplus is an economic measure of a positive balance of trade,where a country's exports exceed its imports. Trade deficit is an economic measure of a negative balance of trade in which a country's imports exceeds its exports. India had trade deficit of US $ 137014.46 million during 2014–15, which was higher than the deficit of US $ 135797.90 million during, 2013–14.
- The net inflows in services like travel, financial services and construction picked up while that in insurance and pension services and transport fell.
- Within services, telecommunications, computer, and information services fetched highest net inflows.

EXCHANGE RATES

Exchange rates are the price of one currency in terms of another. If exchange rates change, so do the prices of exports and imports. Countries whose exchange rates are depreciating will find their exports becoming more price competitive and their imports relatively more expensive. If a seller of products or services expects payment for exports in any denomination other than their home currency, the total home-country receipts will change depending on the exchange rate at the time payment is made.

Because exchange rates can give a price advantage to producers, governments seek to manage exchange rates. This is done by using reserves to buy or sell foreign currencies. If reserves are not used, market supply and demand will decide the value of the currency. Countries can choose to *devalue* their currency purposefully to stimulate their economy's exports and limit imports. Devaluation means that more of their currency is now needed to buy the same amount of a foreign currency. In 1997, Asian countries devalued their currencies in an attempt to save their *fixed exchange-rate system*. However, the currencies were not devalued enough and the governments of these countries were no longer able to control the exchange rates at target prices. Countries that allow their exchange rates to trade freely are said to have a *floating exchange-rate system*. The currency value will be determined by demand and supply. The United States is an example of a country with a floating exchange rate.

BOX 2-2

Side Bar: Bunfight

Over the long term, price inflation is a good indicator of changes in exchange rates. If prices are up, the country's ability to compete on price will diminish, and the currency will have to depreciate to bring prices to par. One popular measure of price differentials in different countries is the Big Mac Index (see Figure 2-6). In parts of China, for example, in 2010, a McDonald's Big Mac costs just 14.5 yuan on average, the equivalent of $2.18 at market exchange rates. In the United States, the same burger averages $3.71.

That makes China's yuan one of the most undervalued currencies in the Big Mac Index which is based on the idea of purchasing power parity; a currency's price should reflect the amount of goods and services it can buy. Since 14.5 yuan can buy as much hamburger as $3.71, a yuan should be worth $0.26 on the foreign-exchange market. However, in reality it costs $0.15, implying that it is undervalued by about 40 percent.[67]

Interest rates also exert pressure on exchange rates. Interest rates are the returns on various forms of capital. Governments often control interest rates through monetary policy to promote economic growth. Capital seeks the highest return and will gravitate towards currencies that have the highest real interest rates. This will, in turn, put pressure on the currency to appreciate. Events such as wars, changes in economic policies, and political risks can also affect the attractiveness of a currency and, therefore, its value. These types of events typically increase the volatility of the currency, making it harder to predict.

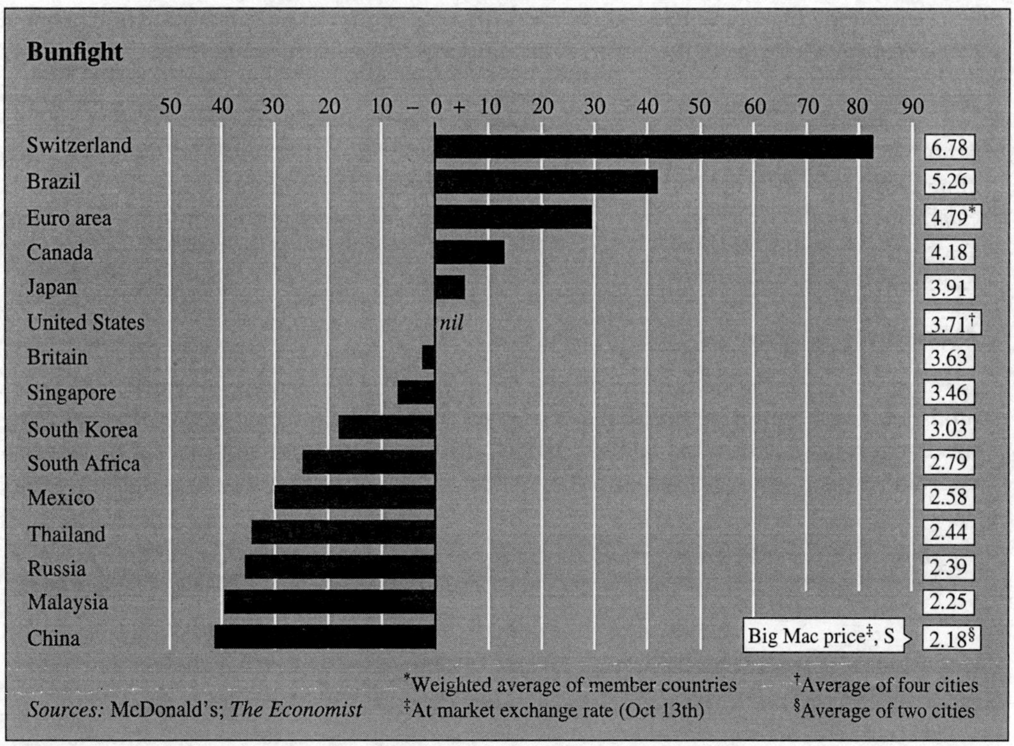

FIGURE 2-6 Big Mac Index: Local Currency Under (–)/Over (+) Valuation Against the Dollar, in Percent.
Source: http://www.economist.com/node/17275912

[67] For a list of all countries in the Index, see http://www.oanda.com/currency/big-mac-index.

If international marketers want to limit their exposure to fluctuations in exchange rates, a few options exist. (1) They can require payments to be made in dollars or, increasingly, in euros. This is typical in many contracts since dollars and euros are internationally major reserve currencies. (2) They can buy a forward contract, a contract available through a bank that guarantees the exchange rate at the time the transaction will take place. (3) They can buy an option, which is a derivative financial instrument that can give the purchaser the option to buy or sell a currency at a future point at a given price. (4) They can assume the exchange-rate risk and take the currency suggested by the international partner. Large multinational companies either hedge against exchange-rate risks or, if they are big and diversified geographically, often self insure. Smaller companies often rely on dollar-denominated or euro-denominated contracts because these currencies are perceived as stable.

DEGREES OF ECONOMIC COOPERATION

There are four degrees of economic cooperation and integration, as illustrated in Table 2-11.

A Free Trade Area

A free trade area (FTA) is a group of countries that has agreed to abolish all international barriers to trade among themselves. Countries that belong to a free trade area can and do maintain independent trade policies with countries outside of the free trade area. A system of certificates of origin is used to avoid trade diversion in favor of low-tariff members. The system discourages importing goods into the member country with the lowest tariff for shipment to countries within the area with higher external tariffs. The European Economic Area as well as the North American Free Trade Agreement (NAFTA) are FTAs.

A Customs Union

A customs union represents the logical evolution of an FTA where, in addition to eliminating the internal barriers to trade, members of a customs union agree to the establishment of common external barriers. Mercosur (Mercado Comun del Cono Sur), also known as the Southern Common Markets (SCCM), and the Andean Group are examples of customs unions.

A Common Market

A common market goes beyond the removal of internal barriers to trade and the establishment of common external barriers to the important next stage of eliminating the barriers to the flow of factors (labor and capital) within the market. It seeks to coordinate economic and social policy within the market to allow free flow of capital

TABLE 2-11 Degrees of International Economic Integration

Stage of Integration	Abolition of Tariffs and Quotas	Common Tariff and Quota System	Removal of Restrictions on Factor Movements	Harmonization of Economic, Social, and Regulatory Policies
Free trade area	Yes	No	No	No
Customs union	Yes	Yes	No	No
Common market	Yes	Yes	Yes	No
Economic union	Yes	Yes	Yes	Yes

and labor from country to country. Thus, a common market creates an open market not only for goods but also for services and capital to support investment.

The full evolution of an economic union would involve the creation of a unified central bank, the use of a single currency, and common policies on agriculture, social services and welfare, regional development, transportation, taxation, competition, legal protections, and so on. Integration requires extensive political unity.

As seen from the descriptions given above, trade blocs have a range of reasons to protect the trade interests of their grouping:

1. To establish a form of regional control that promotes the interests of nations within that region
2. To facilitate regional security and political concerns
3. To promote South-South trade such as between Latin American or African countries
4. To establish tariffs that protect intraregional trade from outside forces
5. To promote economic and technical cooperation among developing countries in the region

In addition, trade blocs utilize several measures to restrain global competition:

1. Import quotas which limit the amount of imports into the country so that domestic consumers purchase products made by the countries in their immediate region
2. Customs delays by establishing bureaucratic formalities that slow down and sometimes curtail the ability for an imported product to enter the domestic market
3. Subsidies, which are government financial assistance to sectors of the home economy to enable them to be stronger competitors
4. Boycotts and technical barriers that restrain trade
5. Bribes and voluntary restraints to external trade[68]

A selection of the better known trade blocs include the following:

THE EU OTHERWISE KNOWN AS THE EUROPEAN UNION currently includes 27 countries on the European continent from Portugal to Romania, from east to west, and five candidate member states—Turkey, Serbia, Iceland, the Former Yugoslav Republic of Macedonia, and Montenegro.[69] In theory, economic development should be the main criteria for membership, however, in reality, political issues are involved as well. The EU has grown in size through the accession of new member states, now with close to 500 million consumers. It has facilitated a single economic market through standardized laws applying to products, goods, services, capital flows, and the movement of people throughout its member states, and maintains common trade as well as regional development policies. It has also formulated a role in foreign policy and represents its members in the WTO and other organizations as well as the United Nations. The euro, its common currency, has been adopted by 15 members. The EU operates in part intergovernmentally as well as acting as a federal body in certain areas including finance and justice. Several important institutions have been created including the European Central Bank, the European Parliament, and the European Court of Justice.

THE ASIA-PACIFIC ECONOMIC COOPERATION OR APEC currently is made up of 21 member economies, which include Australia, Brunei Darussalam, Canada, Chile, China, Hong Kong (China), Indonesia, Japan, the Republic of Korea, Malaysia, Mexico, New

---

[68] Regional Trade Blocs UC Atlas of Global Inequality at http://ucatlas.usc.edu/trade/subtheme_trade_blocs.php, accessed April 7, 2008.

[69] Along with Croatia as an acceding member. For an updated list of EU members see http://europa.eu/abc/european_countries/candidate_countries/index_en.htm.

Zealand, Papua New Guinea, Peru, the Philippines, the Russian Federation, Singapore, Taiwan (China), Thailand, the United States, and Vietnam, most with a coastline on the Pacific Ocean. India has requested membership and Mongolia, Pakistan, Laos, Colombia, and Ecuador along with Guam are among those seeking membership.

THE COMMONWEALTH OF INDEPENDENT STATES OR CIS is an international organization, or alliance, consisting of 11 former Soviet Republics: Armenia, Azerbaijan, Belarus, Georgia, Kazakhstan, Kyrgyzstan, Moldova, Russia, Tajikistan, Ukraine, and Uzbekistan. The creation of the Commonwealth of Independent States in 1991 signaled the dissolution of the Soviet Union. Its purpose was to "allow a civilized divorce" between the Soviet Republics. Since its formation, the member states of CIS have signed agreements addressing issues of integration and cooperation with respect to economics, defense, and foreign policy.

THE MERCOSUR OR MERCADO COMUN DEL CONO SUR ALSO KNOWN AS SOUTHERN COMMON MARKETS (SCCM) is a regional trade agreement with four member states—Brazil, Argentina, Uruguay, and Paraguay. Bolivia, Chile, Colombia, Ecuador, and Peru currently have associate member status, and Venezuela signed a membership agreement in 2006. SCCM was established in 1991 by the Treaty of Asunción, which was later amended and updated by the 1994 Treaty of Ouro Preto. Although seeking economic integration, the progress of Mercosur was weakened by the collapse of the Argentine economy in 2001. In light of continuing internal conflicts over trade policy, the status of integration remains uncertain. However, with more than 263 million consumers and a combined gross domestic product of its full member nations in excess of $2.78 (PPP adjusted) annually, it is the fifth largest economy in the world. In December 2004, it signed a cooperation agreement with the Andean Community trade bloc (CAN) and published a joint letter of intention for a future negotiation towards integrating all of South America.

THE NORTH AMERICAN FREE TRADE AGREEMENT OR NAFTA is a trade bloc created in 1994 with three members—Canada, Mexico, and the United States. It is supplemented by two additional agreements: the North American Agreement on Environmental Cooperation and the North American Agreement on Labor Cooperation. It remains the largest trade bloc based on the total GDP of its three members. NAFTA originally eliminated tariffs on products traded between and among the three members and subsequently reduced additional tariffs. The treaty is seen as trilateral in that its terms apply equally to all members except on certain tariff reductions and the protection of selected industries, which are negotiated on a bilateral basis. Further integration has been difficult as many issues remain outstanding, including environmental protections. In light of these, nonmember states often enter into separate bilateral trade agreements with each of the three member states.

THE ASEAN OR THE ASSOCIATION OF SOUTHEAST ASIAN NATIONS was established in 1967 in Bangkok by the five original Member Countries—Indonesia, Malaysia, the Philippines, Singapore, and Thailand. Brunei Darussalam joined later in 1984, Vietnam in 1995, Lao PDR and Myanmar in 1997, and Cambodia in 1999. With a population in 2006 of about 560 million consumers, it has a combined gross domestic product of almost US$1.1 billion with total trade standing at about US$.1.4 billion. ASEAN's goals are to foster economic growth, social and cultural development among and between its member states, and to promote regional peace and stability. The ASEAN Free Trade Area of AFTA was created in 1992 with the aim of promoting the region's competitive advantage as a single production area with the elimination of tariff and nontariff barriers among the member countries. As of the beginning of 2005, most tariffs on products of six of the member countries were reduced.

As free trade agreements and foreign-trade zones develop as an important indicator of globalization and the economic interdependence between countries and across regions, global firms increasingly face decisions about where best to source and establish manufacturing. Companies need to optimize their understanding and knowledge of how best to utilize if not exploit FTAs and their regulatory, administrative, legal, and often judicial strategies for regional competitiveness in the global marketplace.[70]

Few Important Economic Partnerships Involving India

India is also following the general tendency of negotiating economic partnership agreements with the other nations of the world to primarily maximise economic benefits. India is progressing in this front strategically to reap the following benefits in particular:

1. To establish stronger trade relationships with partnered countries.
2. To go beyond elimination or reduction of tariff and to put several non tariff barriers that exists in the partnered countries under control.
3. To allow its vast SMEs to be befitted of cheaper inputs and thereafter marketing competitive products in the world market.
4. To unleash the greater agenda of complete economic liberalisation in the long run.
5. To allow industries to develop and manufacture products for India plus markets which are of regional or global standard.
6. To address the issues of intellectual property right, rules of origin, local content requirement in a bilateral set up.

With these agenda in mind, India executed a number of economic partnership agreements with different countries of the world. A few of them are as follows:

	Agreement Description	Partner Country
1	Preferential Trade Agreement (PTA)	Afghanistan
2	India entered in to trade agreements with a number of African countries, as these countries also opened up their economy considerably.	African countries like Ghana, Tanzania, South Africa, Senegal, Mauritius, Rwanda, Uganda Etc
3	Asia Pacific Trade Agreement (APTA) is the oldest PTA signed during 1975.	Bangladesh, China, Lao PDR, Mongolia, South Korea, and Sri Lanka
4	The ASEAN–India Free Trade Area (AIFTA) is a Comprehensive Economic Cooperation Agreement (CECA) which came in to effect from 2010	Ten member states of the Association of Southeast Asian Nations (ASEAN) and India.
5	It is a Preferential Trade Agreement (PTA) signed finally during 2016.	Chile
6	The Comprehensive Economic Partnership Agreement (CEPA) came in to force during 2011	Japan
7	Comprehensive Economic Partnership Agreement Between India And Republic Of Korea (CEPA) signed during 2009	Korea
8	Agreement on Trade, Commerce And Transit Between India and its neighbouring country Bhutan.	Bhutan

[70] "Global Sourcing Model Helps Companies Optimise Benefits from Free Trade Agreements," Knowledge@ SMU Operations Management (November 3, 2007), accessed December 3, 2007, http://knowledge.smu.edu.sg/index.cfm?fa=printArticle&ID=1108.

9	Comprehensive Economic Cooperation Agreement Between India And (CECA)	Malaysia
10	Preferential Trade Agreement (PTA) between India And MERCOSUR countries	MERCOSUR is trade block in Latin America comprising Brazil, Argentina, Uruguay and Paraguay.
11	FTA between India–Sri Lanka came in to force from 2000	Sri Lanka

BOX 2-3

Side Bar: India Embracing Economic Partnerships Fast!

It has become a regular feature that WTO rounds somehow would not reach towards its successful end. Expectations of the WTO member countries through multi-lateral negotiations also seem to be not getting fulfilled as expectations are varied and conflicting in the backdrop of multilateral set up. Issues like reduction of tariff, rules of intellectual property right, investment rules, government procurement rules etc. are so complicated that they always played spoil sports and hence WTO negotiations did not proceed to the conclusive end. Hence, naturally, the countries were trying to find a way out to meet their passion for free trade. This passion for free trade became so pervasive that countries are plunging in to the crisscross network of hundreds of bilateral and regional trade agreements. Like many other countries India also executed a number of economic partnership agreements. The following are the agreements and countries involved.

1. Agreement of Cooperation with Nepal to Control Unauthorised Trade
2. Agreement on Economic Cooperation between India and Finland
3. Agreement on SAARC Preferential Trading Arrangement SAPTA
4. Agreement on South Asia Free Trade Area SAFTA
5. Asia Pacific Trade Agreement APTA
6. CECA between The Republic of India and the Republic of Singapore
7. Comprehensive Economic Cooperation Agreement between India and Malaysia
8. Agreement on Economic Cooperation between India and Finland
9. Agreement on SAARC Preferential Trading Arrangement SAPTA
10. Agreement on South Asia Free Trade Area SAFTA
11. Asia Pacific Trade Agreement APTA
12. CECA between The Republic of India and the Republic of Singapore
13. India Africa Trade Agreement
14. India Chile PTA
15. India Afghanistan PTA
16. India ASEAN Agreements
17. India Bhutan Trade Agreement
18. India Japan CEPA
19. India Korea CEPA
20. India MERCOSUR PTA
21. India Nepal Trade Treaty
22. India Sri Lanka FTA
23. India Bangladesh Trade Agreement
24. India Ceylon Trade Agreement
25. India DPR Korea Trade Agreement
26. India Maldives Trade Agreement
27. India Mongolia Trade Agreement

BOX 2-4

Side Bar: India Gets Close to ASEAN Nations

The Association of Southeast Asian Nations (ASEAN) is a free trade area created by ten member states like Brunei Darussalam, Cambodia, Indonesia, Laos, Malaysia, Myanmar, Philippines, Singapore, Thailand, and Vietnam. Initially ASEAN as a regional organisation was inked by five countries like Indonesia, Malaysia, Philippines, Singapore, and Thailand. Later the organisation's membership was extended to make it ASEAN 10. The ASEAN–India Free Trade Area (AIFTA) is a free trade area among the ten member states of and India. The initiation of this agreement was made during 2003, but after several negotiations, the agreement was finally signed during August 2009 and came in to effect from January 2010. The salient features of this agreement is as follows:

- Tariff liberalisation will be effected on the traded products. First it will be affect 90 percent of products traded between ASEAN members and India and then it will also cover special products like palm oil (crude and refined), coffee, black tea and pepper. More reduction of tariff will be made by 2016.
- ASEAN and India will also work for developing private sector engagement between these two regions.
- The agreement will also make efforts to increase tourist flow between India and ASEAN member states.
- Traditionally the trade balance is in favour of ASEAN since the member states are mainly exporters. It is expected that tariff reduction further enlarges the trade balance. Since early 2000s, India has had an increasing trade deficit with ASEAN. Indian industries mainly in the plantation sector, some manufacturing industries, and the marine products industry of ASEAN would be benefitted as they could be competitive enough with reduced price and hence Indian local industries in these sectors may be disturbed.

Source: Ministry of commerce website, Govt of India.

CASE 2-1

Economic Cooperation in the Greater Mekong Subregion (GMS)[71]

THE BEGINNING

The 4,350 long Mekong River originates from Tibetan Plateau and flows through six important countries of Southeast Asia like China's Yunnan Province, Myanmar, Laos, Thailand, Cambodia, and Vietnam before it falls into South China Sea. This commonality was the inspiration behind the background effort made during 1990s to craft a prosperous and equitable economic sub regional grouping comprising of these six countries. In 1995, these six countries finally agreed to ink a pact, leading to form Greater Mekong Sub region (GMS), with the vision to develop it as a prosperous economic sub region by supporting each other with trade and investment with barrier less cross border movement of goods and people. During 1995 the head of the involved countries also developed an effective strategy to reach the goal of the GMS economic

[71]The case "Ecopnomic Cooperation in the Greater Mekong Subregion" has used different websources like (a) World Bank Governance Indicators available at http://info.worldbank.org/governance/wgi/index.aspx#home, (b) United Nations Statistics Division's MDG website.

co-operation which was popularly called 3C strategy. First 'C' talked about establishing faster Connectivity, the second 'C' wanted to develop Competitiveness by making the region barrier free in respect of cross border movement of goods and people and third 'C' envisaged to foster Community feeling amongst the 300 million people living in GMS sub region.

Benefits of Economic Cooperation

The GMS countries are expected to benefit due to economic grouping both in the long term and in the intermediate term. The intermediate term benefits can be availed by the involved countries as the partner countries would be lowering trade barriers facilitating export of goods, both raw material and value added. The value added products are likely to enjoy more benefits as the partnered countries would drift away from previous tendency to tax the finished products more. Exports from the countries are expected to increase with time as intra country trade within the GMS region increases. As such export contribution to GDP for the countries are also expected to rise. Increased trade would nourish country economy which in turn should work for poverty reduction and inclusive growth. Development would lead to inflow of more capital and better division of labour. Such benefits are not only country specific but also outflows to other countries outside the economic group. Strong economic groups also outstretch its trade power to the countries outside the economic group and thereby forging stronger cooperation especially in the field of international trade and commerce.

GMS Country Character

Few demographic indicators are always very important to understand a country's status. Major demographic indicators include fertility, mortality, and composition of population and distribution of population. Table 2-12 indicates demographic characteristics about the GMS countries which vary widely amongst them. One noticeable feature is that they all still have a major rural population except for Thailand. Thailand is a very urbanized country as well as the second highest populated amongst the five Mekong countries. Cambodia has the least urbanized population with second highest infant mortality rate. Vietnam has the highest population which has quite a respectable urbanised component. Lao PDR remains the most sparsely populated country of the region but with an alarming infant mortality rate of 50.07. Life expectancy is quite respectable in Thailand and Vietnam but LAO PDR and Myanmar still have a long way to go in this direction. While population growth rates are lowering year by year in Thailand, Myanmar and Vietnam, the same is continuing to rise in Cambodia and Lao PDR. In a Nutshell, the Table 2-12 confirms the fact that even in 2015 the Mekong countries varies a lot, as far as demographic parameters are concerned.

TABLE 2-12 Demographic Characteristics of GMS Countries

Countries	Total Population (in million) (2015) (Growth Rate)	Urban population%	Fertility Rate	Life Expectancy	Mortality Rate, Infant (per 1,000 live births) 2015	Age Structure
Thailand	67.9 (0.34%)	50.4	1.48 (2014)	74 years (2011)	9.63	0-14 years: 17.41 % 15-64 years: 72.73 % 65 years and over: 9.86 %
Lao PDR	6.9 (1.55%)	38.6	3.2 (2012)	62.39 (2011)	52.97	0–14 years :37.2%,15–64 years: 59.3%, 65 and over 3.67%
Myanmar	56 (1.01%)	34.1	2.29 (2014)	65.25	43.55	0–14 years 29.01%,15–64 years 65.12%, 65 and over 5.87% (2014)
Cambodia	15.7 (1.58%)	20.7	2.66 (2014)	69.50 (2010)	50.04	0–14 years 31.9%,15–64 years 64.3%, 65 and over 3.8%
Vietnam	94.3 (0.97%)	33.6	2.10 (2015)	73.3 (2015)	18.39	0–14 years 24.6%,15–64 years 69.8%, 65 and over 5.5%

Source: CIA Fact book and various other sources, Compiled by author.

TABLE 2-13 Economic Indicators for the GMS Countries

GMS Countries	Growth Rate of GDP Per Person Employed (% at 1990 PPP dollars) 2015	Employment-to-Population Ratio (% of population aged 15 years and above in 2013)	Proportion of Employed People Living Below $1.90 (PPP) Per Day % 2013	Internet Users Per 1000 population 2014	Per Capita Gross National Income (GNI), Atlas Method USD 2014	Trade Balance % in of GDP 2015	Total External debt Outstanding % GNI 2014
Cambodia	5.5	82.8	33.6	9.00	1,020	−19.1	33.8
Lao PDR	...	65.7	59.4	14.26	1,660	−23.3	46.9
Myanmar	6.8	...	62.3	2.10	1,270	−11.7	12.9
Thailand	2.8	69.4	0.1	34.89	5,780	8.8	35.8
Viet Nam	4.7	76.2	4.5	48.31	1,890	3.8	28.9

Courtesy: http://unstats.un.org/unsd/mdg/SeriesDetail.aspx?srid=757, as accessed on 23 December 2016 at 3.45pm.

Table 2-13 shows economic indicators for the GMS countries, including labour productivity, overall GDP, as well as the percentage of the economy in agriculture, forestry, industry, and services. The growth rate of gross domestic product (GDP) per person employed is used as a parameter to indicate the growth rate of output per unit of labour input or labour productivity. A respectable labour productivity rate indicates the ability of a country's economic environment to create and sustain decent employment opportunities with fair and equitable remuneration. A glance at the Table 2-13 indicates that excepting Thailand, in other countries the growth rate of labour productivity has been quite respectable. Employment-to-Population Ratio indicates the proportion of the country's working-age population (in between 15 to 64 years of age) that is employed and higher percentage indicates the country's ability to create employment opportunity. The Table 2-13 indicates that Thailand with 82.8 percent has been extraordinarily successful in this respect. Vietnam followed the suit with 76.2 percent. However, the other three countries Lao PDR, Myanmar, Cambodia had a dismal performance in this respect. The newly introduced international poverty line of $1.90 (2011 PPP) indicates the proportion of poor people in the country who are still below the international standard. The Table 2-13 indicates that Lao PDR, Cambodia, and Myanmar have been under reeling under extreme condition of poverty. The 62.3 percent people living below the international poverty line in Myanmar is really a matter of concern. Internet Users Per 1000 population is an indicator of development and modernisation of a country. In this front, performance of three Mekong country like Lao PDR, Cambodia, and Myanmar have been abysmal. The internet penetration in Myanmar per thousand population was only two person during 2014. Per Capita Gross National Income is a strong indicator of prosperity of a country in terms of releasing the benefit of economic growth. In this count also the Mekong countries, excepting Thailand, have not been extraordinary. Trade balance, also known as net export, as a percentage of GDP indicates its contribution to GDP of a country. A surplus figure on this account indicates GDP boost on account of net export and a deficit reduces the GDP. Trade balance as percentage of GDP in case of GMS countries indicates that these countries are widely dissimilar in the respect. While net export of Thailand and Vietnam are positively contributing to their GDP build up, the same is not happening in case of other three countries. The GDP formation are continuously being hurt by negative net export in case of Lao PDR, Cambodia, and Myanmar. External debt to Gross National Income (GNI) is a powerful economic indicator which measures the external debt of a country in relation to its capacity to generate income to relinquish the debt. For Myanmar the external debt to the GNI was 12.9 percent, as revealed in the Table 2-13, which indicates that the country only could generate income to the tune 12 percent of what the country externally borrowed during the year 2014. Surely, this is not a good economic situation in the country as piling up of external debt in the back drop of reducing national income may lead to a

TABLE 2-14 Governance Status in Mekong Countries

Countries	Control of Corruption		Rule of Law Rule of Law		Government Effectiveness	
	1998	2014	1998	2014	1998	2014
Cambodia	(–)1.08	(–)1.08	(–)1.10	(–)0.93	(–)1.1	(–)0.68
Lao PDR	(–)0.39	(–)0.76	(–)0.90	(–)0.71	(–)0.6	(–)0.39
Myanmar	(–)1.17	(–)0.92	(–)1.40	(–)1.17	(–)1.2	(–)1.08
Thailand	(+)0.00	(–)0.41	(–)0.50	(–)0.15	(–)0.1	(–)0.41
Vietnam	–0.40	(–)0.50	(–)0.40	(–)0.31	(–)0.4	(–)0.06

Source: World Bank Group. World Bank Governance Indicators.

state of bankruptcy. By far, Lao PDR and followed by Thailand had the respectable income capabilities to pay the external debt to the tune of 46.9 percent and 35.8 percent respectively during 2014.

World Bank governance indicators data shows that none of the five Mekong countries are demonstrating extraordinary performance in terms of governance since 2008 as revealed in the Table 2-14. World Bank measures and provides data on governance by using six parameters like voice & accountability, political stability and lack of violence, government effectiveness, regulatory quality, rule of law, and control of corruption prevailing in different countries of the world since 1996. The World Bank reflects the status of governance with a range from –2.5 (weak governance) to 2.5 (strong governance). The Table 2-14 captures data of governance for the five Mekong countries in respect of three key parameters like government effectiveness, rule of law, and control of corruption in this usual range of –2.5 to +2.5 in respect of year 1998 and 2014. The Table 2-14 reveals that Thailand and Vietnam, of all the five GMS countries, have only demonstrated relatively consistent middle tier governance scores since 1998. These two countries did not improve much overtime but at least did not allow governance performance to go down. Lao PDR, despite lower scores in these three parameters in the same time period performed better that Cambodia and Myanmar.

Now it is a matter of study that how much the economic grouping has contributed in overall economic development of the involved countries. Whether the high hope that the economic grouping generated in the involved countries was truly fulfilled in terms of overall economic progress achieved over the period of staying together or not. The Table 2-15 captures the economic progress of GMS countries after participating in the GMS economic grouping. The table purposefully captures data pertaining to the year 2000 when the economic grouping was in the nascent stage till the present time (2016).

TABLE 2-15 Economic Progress of GMS Countries

Countries	GDP, Current Prices, Billion $US	GDP, Current Prices, Billion $US	CAGR of GDP (2000–2016)	GDP per Capita Current US$	GDP per Capita Current US$	GDP per Capita Current US$	CAGR of GDP Per Capita (2000–2016)
	(2000)	(2016)	%	(2000)	(2010)	(2016)	%
Cambodia	3.7	19.5	10.95	293.6	821	1234.55	9
Lao PDR	1.6	13.4	14.21	326.3	1175.7	1865.07	12
Myanmar	10.3	74.0	13.12	177.6	742.4	1416.39	14
Thailand	126.4	409.7	7.63	1943.2	4610	5939.69	7
Vietnam	31.2	201.4	12.36	401.5	1191.4	2173.65	11
China	1,208.8	11,383.0	15.05	949.2	4507	8239.89	14

Source: IMF World Economic Outlook (WEO), April 2016 & Asian Development Outlook Update (2011).

It can be seen that compounded annual growth rate of GDP of the participating countries, as measured in billion $US (current prices), grew for all the participating countries more than double digit level during the period 2000 to 2016 except Thailand. However, the table also indicates that CAGR of GDP per capita during 2000 to 2016 has not been even in all the six participating countries. It has been highest in two countries like Myanmar and China. The impact of GMS grouping on China is difficult to be established because only two provinces of the country like Guangxi Zhuang, Yunnan, were involved in the GMS grouping. But for Myanmar the economic benefit could be due to economic partnership with GMS member countries. Cambodia and Thailand registered a nominal CAGR of 7 percent and 9 percent respectively in terms of GDP per capita which indicates comparative subdued performance of the respective countries during the period 2000 to 2016.

The Road Ahead

Two decades have passed since the Mekong countries inked the economic partnership agreement. These five countries have come across a long way in operationalizing the provisions of economic partnership agreement. The common macroeconomic parameters in respect of all these five countries testify that all these five countries progressed in terms of economic development since partnership agreement entered into. However, the critiques argue that the development has not been a balanced one-both in terms of geographic dispersion and sectoral perspective. Huge difference still exist in terms of economic development across the countries. Myanmar is still the laagered state economically while country like Thailand could step up its economic development with time. During 2010 Myanmar's GDP per capita was about 6 times lesser that that of Thailand which only reduced to about 4 times during 2016. Countries like Lao PDR, Myanmar, and Cambodia have still been reeling under the pressure of lower rung governance score. On the other hand, country like Thailand and Vietnam have not allowed to go their governance score below an intermediate level. So, actually it appears that intra country partnership failed in respect of equitable distribution of economic benefits across partner countries.

Case Questions

1. What were the basic objectives of GMS economic partnership? Why has it appeared beneficial for the constituent countries?
2. Review the economic and social benefits enjoyed by the partner countries during the last two decades of partnership and comment on the success or failure of GMS economic grouping.

Chapter Summary

The economic environment is a major determinant of global market potential and opportunity. Global marketers should factor into their marketing strategies the profound changes in the world economy and understand that global competition is now a feature of almost every national market. Centers of economic activity are shifting dramatically across the globe and across regions due to demographic changes, economic liberation, technological developments, and, over the next decade, an estimated one billion new consumers in emerging markets demanding products and services. Today, with the exception of North Korea, almost all countries have mixed economic systems with a major reliance on market allocation.

Countries can be categorized in terms of their stage of development: low income, lower-middle income, upper-middle income, and high income. It is possible to identify these distinct stages and formulate general estimates about the type of demand associated with a particular state of development. For many products, the single most important indicator of market potential is income; therefore, the first step in determining the potential of a country or region is to identify the total and per capita income levels. For products whose price is low enough, population may be just as important a variable as income in determining market potential and customer demand. State-dictated as well as democratically defined public policies help create and set market structures including tax, fiscal, and political agendas which are the basis for many government interventions. Such interventions set the stage for potential global business growth and expansion strategies and need to be carefully considered.

Market potential for a product can be evaluated by determining the product saturation levels in light of income levels. In general, it is appropriate to compare the saturation levels of countries or of consumer segments within countries or regions with similar income levels. Gross National Product or GNP per capita is the most widely accepted index for a country's financial success; however, purchasing power parity or PPP comparisons of income provide better measures of standard of living of residents in an economy. In addition, exchange rates tend to exaggerate differences in real income between countries at different stages of economic development, and balance-of-payments issues can also have economic impacts.

One of the ways of dealing with the complexity of a world with hundreds of national markets is to focus on economic cooperative agreements which seek to both manage and facilitate trade activities for identified regions. These agreements, of which the European Union with over 500 million consumers is the most successful example, have both economic as well as political implications. In the Asian-Pacific region, ASEAN typifies both the expansion and elimination of trade barriers in that region and throughout other regions of the world.

Discussion Questions

1. What are the stages of national market development and what percentage of world income is found in each of the stages? Why is this information important to global marketers?
2. What are the major trends in the world economy in the first two decades of the twenty-first century? How do these trends impact global marketing decisions? Cite several subtrends that relate, in your opinion, to these major trends.
3. What is the pattern of income distribution in the world today? How is it different than even 10 years ago? What are the implications of these patterns of income distribution across the globe for the strategic marketer?
4. A manufacturer of an online gaming device is assessing the world market potential for her product. She asks you if she should consider emerging countries as potential markets. What advice would you give to her?
5. Are income and standard of living the same thing? What is meant by the term standard of living; how is this best measured and why?
6. Describe the importance of international trade alliances and economic cooperation agreements. In your view, are these beneficial to the global marketer? If so, why? If not, why not?
7. Interview several local business owners to determine their attitude toward world trade. Why, in your opinion, do they hold these attitudes and on what factual information or experience are they based?

Suggested Readings

Arnold, David. *The Mirage of Global Markets: How Globalizing Companies Can Succeed as Markets Localize*. Upper Saddle River, NJ: Pearson Education, Inc. publishing as Financial Times Prentice Hall, 2004.

Bhagwati, Jagdish. *In Defense of Globalization*. New York: Oxford University Press, Inc., 2004.

Bryan, Lowell L., Jeremy Oppenheim, Wilhelm Rall, and Jane Fraser. *Race For The World: Strategies to Build a Great Global Firm*. Boston: Harvard Business School Press, 1999.

Chandler, Alfred D. Jr., and Bruce Mazlish, eds. *Leviathans: Multinational Corporations and the New Global History*. Cambridge, UK: Cambridge University Press, 2005.

Drucker, Peter. "Marketing and Economic Development." *Journal of Marketing*, 22, no. 3 (January 1958): 252–259.

Fligstein, Neil. *The Architecture of Markets: An Economic Sociology of Twenty-First Century Capitalist Societies*. Princeton, NJ: Princeton University Press, 2001.

Friedman, Thomas L. *The World Is Flat, A Brief History of the Twenty-First Century*. New York: Farrar, Straus and Giroux, 2005.

Gabel, Medard, and Henry Bruner. *Global Inc.: An Atlas of the Multinational Corporation*. New York: The New Press, 2003.

Galbraith, John Kenneth. *The Nature of Mass Poverty*. Cambridge, MA: Harvard University Press, 1979.

Garten, Jeffrey E. *The Big Ten*. New York: Basic Books, 1997.

Garten, Jeffrey E. *World View: Global Strategies for the New Economy*. Boston: Harvard Business School Press Review, 1999.

Keegan, Warren J., and Bodo B. Schlegelmilch. *Global Marketing Management: A European Perspective.* New York: Prentice Hall International, 2000.

Kennedy, Paul. *The Rise and Fall of Great Powers.* New York: Random House, 1987.

Martin, Roger L. *Fixing The Game.* (Boston: Harvard Business School Publishing, 2011.

Meyer, Christopher, and Julia Kirby. "Runaway Capitalism." *Harvard Business Review* (January–February 2012): 66.

Micklethwait, John, and Adrian Wooldridge. *A Future Perfect: The Challenge and Promise of Globalization.* New York: Random House Inc., 2003.

Nilekani, Nandan, *Imagining India: The Idea of a Renewed Nation.* London, England: Penguin Press, 2008.

Nye, Joseph S. "The Future of American Power." *Foreign Affairs,* 89, no. 6 (November–December 2010).

Ofek, Elie, and Luc Wathieu. "Are You Ignoring Trends That Could Shake Up Your Business?" *Harvard Business Review* (July–August 2010): 124.

Ohmae, Kenichi. *The End of the Nation State: The Rise of Regional Economies.* New York: The Free Press, 1995.

Ohmae Kenichi. The *Next Global Stage, Challenges and Opportunities In Our Borderless World.* Upper Saddle River, NJ: Pearson Education Inc. publishing as Wharton School Publishing, 2005.

Porter, Michael E. *The Competitive Advantage of Nations.* New York: The Free Press, 1990.

Reich, Robert B. *The Work of Nations.* New York: Vintage Books, 1992.

Reid, David McHardy. "Perspectives for International Marketers on the Japanese Market." *Journal of International Marketing,* 3, no. 1 (1995): 63–84.

Rivoli, Pietra. *The Travels of a T-Shirt in the Global Economy: An Economist Examines the Markets, Power, and Politics of World Trade.* Hoboken, NJ: John Wiley & Sons, Inc., 2009.

Rodrik, Dani. *The Globalization Paradox: Democracy and the Future of the World Economy.* New York: W.W. Norton and Company, Inc., 2011.

Sharma, Ruchir. *Breakout Nations: In Pursuit of the Next Economic Miracles.* New York: W.W. Norton & Company Inc., 2012.

Simpfendorfer, Ben. *The New Silk Road: How a Rising Arab World Is Turning Away from the West and Rediscovering China.* New York: Palgrave Macmillan, a division of St. Martin's Press, LLC., 2009.

Smick, David M. *The World Is Curved: Hidden Dangers To The Global Economy.* New York: Portfolio, a member of the Penguin Group, Inc., 2008.

Spence, Michael. *The Next Convergence: The Future of Economic Growth in a Multispeed World.* New York: Farrar, Straus and Giroux, 2011. (Winner of the Nobel Prize in economics.)

Stiglitz, Joseph E. *Globalization and Its Discontents.* New York: W.W. Norton and Company, Inc., 2003.

Taleb, Nassim Nicholas. "On Accepting Uncertainty, Embracing Volatility." *Knowledge@Wharton,* the online business journal of Wharton Business School (December 17, 2012). Accessed December 25, 2012. http://knowledge.wharton.upenn.edu.

Thurow, Lester. *Head to Head: The Coming Economic Battle Among Japan, Europe, and America.* New York: William Morrow and Company, 1992.

Waheeduzzaman, A. N. M. "Are Emerging Markets Catching Up With the Developed Markets in Terms of Consumption?" *Journal of Global Marketing,* 24, no. 2 (2011): 136–151.

Williamson, Peter J. *Winning in Asia: Strategies for Competing in the New Millennium.* Boston: Harvard Business School Press, 2004.

Yan, Rick. "To Reach China's Consumers, Adapt to Guo Qing." *Harvard Business Review* (September–October 1994): 66–74.

Zakaria, Fareed. *The Post-American World: Release 2.0.* New York: W.W. Norton and Company, Inc., 2011.

CHAPTER 3

The Political, Legal, and Regulatory Environments of Global Marketing

When you are at Rome live in the Roman style; when you are elsewhere live as they live elsewhere. Advice to St. Augustine

—St. Ambrose, AD 340–397

The global economy in which both managers and policymakers must now operate is not the neat, easily divisible sum of separate national economies. It has its own reality, its own rules, and its own logic.

—Kenichi Ohmae *The Next Global Stage* (2005)

Learning Objectives

1. Describe how the political environment affects global marketing decisions (89–98).
2. Discuss the functions of international law and the legal issues that affect global businesses (99–102).
3. Explain the significance of intellectual property rights, antitrust laws, and licensing agreements to global marketers (103–108).
4. Describe the nature of corruption in the global business environment (109–113).
5. Discuss the rising use of arbitration among international firms (115–116).
6. Explain the roles of regulatory agencies and trade agreements in international trade (116–120).

INTRODUCTION

While governments in many countries are studying environmental issues, particularly recycling, Germany already has a packaging ordinance that has shifted the cost burden for waste material disposal onto industry. The German government hopes the law, known as *Verpackungsverordnung,* will create a closed-loop economy. The goal is to force manufacturers to eliminate nonessential materials that cannot be recycled and adopt other innovative approaches to producing and packaging products. Despite the costs associated with compliance, industry appears to be making significant progress toward creating the closed-loop economy. Companies are developing new packaging that uses less material and includes more recycled content. More than 1,900 non-German companies are currently participating in the program.

The German packaging law is just one example of the impact that political, legal, and regulatory environments can have on marketing activities. Each of the world's national governments regulates trade and commerce with other countries and attempts to control the access of outside enterprises to national resources. Every country has its own unique legal and regulatory system that impacts the operations and activities of the global enterprise, including the global marketer's ability to address market opportunities. Laws and regulations constrain the cross-border movement of products, services, people, money, technology, and know-how. The global marketer must attempt to comply with each set of national—and in some instances, regional—constraints. These efforts are hampered by the fact that laws and regulations are frequently ambiguous and continually changing.

In this chapter, we consider the basic elements of the political, legal, and regulatory environments of global marketing, including current issues and some suggested approaches for dealing with those issues. Some specific topics, such as rules for exporting and importing industrial and consumer products, standards for health and safety, and regulations regarding packaging, labeling, advertising, promotion, and the Internet, are covered in later chapters devoted to individual marketing mix elements. Ethical issues are also discussed in this chapter.

THE POLITICAL ENVIRONMENT

Global marketing activities take place within the political environment of governmental institutions, political parties, and organizations through which a country's people and rulers exercise power. Any company doing business outside its home country should carefully study the government structure in the target country and analyze salient issues arising from the political environment. These include the governing party's attitude toward sovereignty, political risk, taxes, the threat of equity dilution, and expropriation.

Political Risk

Political risk—the risk of a change in government policy that would adversely impact a company's ability to operate effectively and profitably—can deter a company from investing abroad. When the perceived level of political risk is lower, a country is more likely to attract investment. The level of political risk is inversely proportional to a country's stage of economic development. All other things being equal, the less developed a country, the greater the political risk. The political risk of high-income countries, for example, is quite limited as compared with countries at earlier stages of development.

In 2011, the risk profile average for the world as measured by ECR (Euromoney Country Risk) was 44.56. The highest score in June of 2011 was Norway (92.44) and the lowest was Eritrea with 5.13 (the lower the score, the higher the risk). Russia scored 56, India and Indonesia scored 57, China 63, and Australia and New Zealand 85. Japan scored 74, South Korea 72, and Taiwan 82.

In the Americas, the United States scored 82 versus 87 for Canada and 58 for Mexico; in South America, Brazil scored 62, Argentina 43, and Chile 74. These ratings are a combination of six categories: qualitative expert opinions (30%), economic performance (30%), and four other measures. While these scores are subject to debate and discussion, most would agree that, in general, they do roughly reflect actual relative differences in levels of country risk.

Different Types of Political System in the World

Every country has a political system. The political system of a country runs its government and is responsible for policy making to ensure the state's sovereignty over a territory and people. The government is a formal structure which uses political system to run a system of governance in a particular country. The political system may be different for different country. They are broadly divided into, democracy, totalitarianism and socialism.

Democracy: This type of political system is well respected in the world. Under this system, either people govern themselves in a structure of direct democracy, or there are elected representatives of the people who form the government. People living in democracy enjoy a few benefits like frequent elections after a specified period of time through which they can change government if economic benefits are not reaching the people of the country. For example, countries like India, USA are democratic countries where periodic elections are held where people at large get the power to replace a government if they are not performing to the interest of the country.

Totalitarianism: A totalitarian government has all the power to regulate and control all aspects of private and public behaviour in the country. The country may be run by a single political party or one monarch or one dictator. North Korea is under totalitarian rule, where a single individual or entity runs the government. China, on the other hand, was considered as a totalitarian state under its leader Mao Zedong, but latter it apparently converted itself in to an authoritarian state. The difference between totalitarian and authoritarian has been in terms of tolerance level in the matter of governance. Jordan and Saudi Arabia have different system and are run by a monarchy system which is ruled by an absolute leader chosen by hereditary means. Iran is ruled by religion-based leadership.

Socialism: Under the socialism government, all the wealth and capital are owned by the state only. The industries and other productive systems that grow in a country are just intended to satisfy the economic demands and human needs. Therefore, this type of political system does not promote the idea of profit accumulation at the individual level. It believes that produced goods, profits and other resources are required to be distributed equally amongst the people so that there is no disproportionate distribution of wealth in the society. Socialist government wants to remove the rich and poor divide, and hence actively participate in removing exploitation of poor people living in the country. Pure socialism flourished in erstwhile USSR and from 1980 onwards the state economy collapsed. For example, China had a socialistic regime during and under Mao Zedong. Sweden followed a mix of socialism and democracy which can be called as a social democracy. An example of a pure socialistic nation is not there at present.

Evidences of Impact on Marketing Practice due to Political Environment

GMR Group of companies is a much respected business house in India. The entrepreneur, Mr. G.M Rao, started with a small jute mill during 1978, and by spectacular achievements he rose to the top. GMR Group now is a well known major player in the Infrastructure Sector, both in India and abroad. The GMR group is actively involved in developing projects in high growth areas such as Airports, Energy, Transportation and Urban Infrastructure. GMR operates India's busiest airport, the Indira Gandhi International Airport (IGIA) in New Delhi and has carefully build up its reputation as a performing company who can successfully handle turnkey airport construction and operation projects internationally. So, it was not surprising when the company got the contract worth 500 million USD to build and own- operate the Male airport of Maldives. In fact, the GMR group had to fight with big international infrastructure developers to win over contracts in the country. However, when the company proceeded with construction of new terminal block and operating the old one, it heard about a political conspiracy to terminate the contract mid way. The company all along grew in India where the system of political governance is democracy. The Managers at the GMR group were not prepared for such a situation, where after winning the contract and proceeding to fight a long way towards execution of the contract, there could be a termination threat. But alas! The political opponent of Maldives government, headed by Mohamed Waheed, was found to suddenly became crazy for terminating contract with the GMR Group. The company was accustomed to manage contracts by going through its legal obligations in India and in no way could even think of direct involvement of country government. GMR group was rest assured, that when the entire bidding process was conducted under the watchful eye of International Finance Corporation (IMF), so there would be no problem during the execution part in Maldives. But it was not known to them clearly that the political opponents of the present President Nasheed, were looking for an opportunity to strike discord in the country. They got an issue here and became active to flair patriotic feelings in the country by relating GMR's presence in the country as anti national. According to the contract signed by the GMR group and Maldives government, GMR group started levying a $25 per passenger charge as Airport Development Charge (ADC) for the existing terminal which would be used later for financing the new construction. Under the patronage of political opponents, the passengers using the airport first declined to pay the tax and secondly the media soon made it a national issue with patriotic flavour. Overnight, the GMR group was made as anti Maldives company. For GMR, things further worsened when President Nasheed was ousted in a midnight coup. The new government fuelled the anti GMR campaign further and successfully drabbed presence of GMR in Maldives as anti nationalistic. Finally, the Maldives government decided to scrap the agreement with GMR which the previous government signed leading to huge financial loss for the Indian company.

While doing business, the knowledge of political system is essential for international business as each political system has its own advantages and disadvantages affecting business functions. Maldives transformed itself from an authoritarian state to a democratic one during 2009. The political system was a presidential type with a directly elected president and parliament (Majlis), where multiple parties were allowed to contest elections. However, very soon the political interests started dominating over the democratic principles and democratic norms. The country became a "faulty democracy" where elections could not take place because of political interest of a group of people with vested interest.

Types of Political Risk for Global Marketers

Global businesses have always been uncomfortable to the political risk factors present in a country of investment. Political risk, by its character, falls under the category of uncontrollable factors because hardly a business can influence this type of risk for eradication or mitigation. Experts in international business have always suggested that global marketers, therefore, must develop good understanding of political risk present in a country and its possible impact on businesses to avoid mishaps arising out of investment loss. Many a time, rouge country government purposefully make political risks camouflaged in order to avoid loss of image at the international level but still continue to spite the global companies with different facets of politically motivated agenda. In order to safeguard a business from the string of politically motivated risk the global businesses must understand the different types of political risk which are as follows.

1. ***Expropriation risk:*** this type of risk happens when a country's government directly or indirectly attempts to grab the assets and prosperity of foreign companies in the name of national interest. Thereby a foreign company may lose its tangible assets overnight. In these days expropriation risk may not be acting so directly and blatantly as it may raise huge international condemnation. The countries craving for foreign investment would like to project a better face image to the foreign investors. However, there could be a case of creating very unfriendly hostile environment which compels the foreign company to sell off its property at a very low price. Generally, it all starts with politically driven campaign for uniting the ultra-nationalists under a common apolitical platform and then indirectly allowing them to create public unrest by involving the foreign companies. These create operational difficulties for the foreign companies and slowly these difficulties started taking toll on the efficient frontier. The foreign companies get threatened as the erstwhile subdued local competitors start displaying competitive might by snatching market share. The head quarter of the foreign company prescribes many remedial actions but the subsidiary fails to activate them because of purposefully crafted crippling strategy unleashed by the concerned country. The manifestation of this strategy can be felt by the foreign company in terms of measures like import and export restrictions, price controls, excessive taxation (like taxes on windfall gains, duplicate tax claims by both central and state government), stringent environmental laws or labour standards, preferential policy towards protection of domestic companies or financial institutions, etc.
2. ***Risk from change in regulatory regime:*** the best example of this type of risk can be seen in the case of GMR group of India working in Maldives. The Indian company won the contract of modernisation and operation of the international airport located in the capital city, Male, during 2010. The company was welcomed wholeheartedly by the then political regime led by President Mohamed Nasheed. However, when Mohamed Waheed Hassan took over as president, after toppling the previous regime, all the pro government political parties of the country termed the contract anti national. All sorts of politically motivated changes were made in regulatory policies or legal framework of the host government which rendered the contract as 'illegal'. Many a time such change in the guard would result in adopting policies to corner foreign companies, increase vigil on transfer pricing within companies, scrapping of privileges granted earlier, amending the some critical parts of the contract agreement signed during earlier regime, ending subsidies agreed earlier, imposing environmental fines, unleashing frequent raids by the government agencies on the ground of workers' safety etc.
3. ***Risk of hooliganism or terrorist activities:*** in recent days, no country seems to be safe from the act of terrorism and hence it is required that the political party at the helm of power must have the genuine will to fight out terrorism and provide companies fear free environment. In the same way, as income inequality in many countries is increasing at an alarming rate, many foreign companies are subjected to hooliganism often covertly supported by some political parties for narrow gains. Sometimes the hooligans are motivated to act against certain sector, foreign companies etc creating an absolute environment of lawlessness.

It is also important that the political wills are directed to check all types of acts of terrorism unleased by the dreaded terrorist organisations like ISIS or Al Qaeda and thereby creating a sense of security amongst the business community at large.

4. ***Risk of capital controls:*** Capital control is a process where the host country government imposes restrictions on free cross country movement currency, by way of either disapproving transfer of capital or by delaying the process with the pretext of administrative reasons. Free flow of capital from company headquarter to foreign subsidiaries or profit transfer from subsidiaries to headquarter is a natural process through which company survives in the international markets. But delays in approving capital transfers, imposition of limit on repatriation of profits, enforcing of different currency conversion rate for profit transfer, etc are bound in having an ill effect on the running of business in a foreign country. Venezuela provides an excellent example of political risks arising out of capital control. The Venezuelan government enforced different currency conversion rates for different purposes for foreign companies operating in the current environment. The currency conversion rate from Venezuelan currency Bolivar to Dollar, was tweaked artificially in such a way that foreign companies could transfer only a part of the profit generated in the country.
5. ***Risk of political uncertainty:*** It is difficult to run business operation in countries where political situation is very volatile due to a weak government in power and opponent political parties are up with their arms to topple the government. The foreign company may expect political revolution, protests, strikes, civil commotions, armed conflicts, military coup d'état, civil war etc at any time. These unrest give rise to an all round corruption as different unscrupulous agents take advantage of political volatility and try to fish in the troubled water. Nepotism, corruption, bribery, red-tapism, administrative laxity, etc also surfaced and creating risk for the foreign companies more than the local companies operating in the country.
6. ***Risk of judiciary bias:*** It is expected that the country's legal system should be neutral and not discriminate between local and foreign businesses. However, a judicial system of a country which can succumb to political pressure could be a potential source of danger for a foreign company while operating in such a host country's environment. Many a time for the sake of cheap publicity and rousing ultra nationalist sentiment, the political bosses may indulge in arm twisting with foreign companies by accusing them on several flimsy ground. Here, neutral behaviour of the judiciary system (including quasi-judicial bodies) are absolutely necessary which can safeguard the interest of foreign companies.

The above mentioned six types of political risks are in no way to be construed as an exhaustive list, as the manifestation of political risks is subjected to change overtime. With the progress of time, the foreign companies operating in different countries are getting exposed to different other types of political risks. For example, politically motivated cyber attacks on the companies are gaining momentum. Political bosses unleash its hackers to attack and destroy or unfold company's secret information from company server and thereby creating a situation disadvantageous for the foreign company in the host country market. Politically motivated cyber attack made in China on Australian mining companies like BHP Billiton, Fortescue Metals and Rio Tinto made head line in every newspaper during 2010. As per report, the hackers broke in to the company servers and stole vital and secret business information. The attack was so nasty that Rio Tinto had to put its Singapore office off line for consecutive three days to recover and put revitalised security system in place.

MEASURING POLITICAL RISK OF COUNTRIES

It is often said that political risks cannot be avoided by the global companies when operating in different countries of the world but if the assessesement is done in advance it can provide ways to escape. But the question arises: how to assess the political risks in advance to understand the gravity of the danger looming large on the company operation. In order to support global companies in this direction various professional companies have come up with different methodologies to measure political risks (see Box 3-1 for example).

Aon's Political Risk Assessment

Aon, a British multinational corporation with its head quarter in London, continuously make efforts to provide its proprietary live rating guide so that a company may be aware of the political risk prevailing in the country. Aon covers about 200 countries of the world where they continuously monitor actions and reactions in the political space of the concerned country and come up with structured analysis and valuable bench mark information which in turn allows a company to take informed decisions. Aon Examining, trends in more than 200 countries and territories and considering threats ranging from terrorism and sabotage, to strikes, political insurrection and civil war, the map is one of the most comprehensive tools available to those looking to better understand their exposures to these extreme risks.

The PRS Group's Risk Assessment

The PRS group, headquartered in USA, has more than a long standing history of delving in to the subject of political and country risk assessment of different countries of the world. PRS Group applies mainly International Country Risk Guide (ICRG) methodology for working out political risks prevailing in different countries and working out the political risk index.

The International Country Risk Guide (ICRG) methodology is very old and publicly available to understand how risks rating of the countries are calibrated. In this methodology the group uses 22 variables covering three sub factors of country risk i.e. political, economic and financial risks. Political risks has 13 weighted variables on which country specific data are collected, followed by 5 and 4 weighted variables under financial risk and economic risks respectively. These 22 variables are allotted monthly ratings within a specified range rates for every country. The 22 political variables are in three subcategories of risk: political, financial, and economic variables get subjecting ratings whereas economic variables gets ratings based on quantitative assessment and financial variables uses both qualitative and quantitative assessment for their ratings. Finally, these three factors are combined to give rise to the composite country risk index where the political risk rating contributes 50% and each of financial and economic risk ratings contribute 25%.

BOX 3-1

Side Bar: EIU and Political Risk: Political Instability Index

Economist Intelligence Unit (EIU), has been regularly publishing data about different countries on various aspects like country risk, economic forecast and industry reports. These reports are very useful for the global marketers to get first hand reports and future predicts of different countries of the world. The Economist Intelligence Unit (EIU) provides these services through research and analysis.

The political instability index of EIU intends to provide a comparative measure of political instability present in the countries by exploring different factors contributing to the cause like social, economic and political factors. The political instability index uses a simple model developed by the George Mason University in the US, in order to understand political instability present in a country, both qualitatively and quantitatively.

According to EIU the political instability or unrest of a country is a phenomenon that creates a serious extra-parliamentary or extra-institutional threat to governments or the existing political order. A situation of political instability occurs when there are economic distress and inequality, poor level of development, presence of neighbouring countries with track record of violent internal conflicts and inefficient regime which are neither consolidated democracies nor autocratic regimes. In addition, political instability in a country may come from factors like ethnic fragmentation, poor governance, history of labour unrest, the level of provision of public services and state strength.

The Political Instability Index of EIU comes in a 10 point scale where 0 indicates no vulnerability and 10 indicates highest vulnerability of a country. In order to arrive at this index the EIU continuously assess the following 15 indicators.

1	Economic inequality	Measured by Gini coefficient
2	State history	Measured according to date of independence
3	Corruption	Economist Intelligence Unit's own ratings
4	Ethnic fragmentation	Ethnic fractionalisation index as per methodology of "Fractionalization", NBER Working Paper 9411, 2003.
5	Trust in institutions	Percentage of population that trusts/has confidence in parliament
6	Status of minorities	As per Minorities at Risk Project (MRP) of EIU.
7	History of political instability	As per EIU task force report
8	Proclivity to labour unrest	As per EIU's own ratings
9	Level of social provision	Measured on the basis of the "expected" infant mortality rate
10	A country's neighbourhood	As per EIU's own assessment
11	Regime type	Classification of political regimes as per EIU 's Index of Democracy.
12	Regime type and factionalism	As per Polity data series widely used in political science research
13	Economic distress	As per growth rate data in real GDP per head
14	Unemployment	As per International Labour Organisation data
15	Level of income per head	GDP per head at PPP

Source: http://viewswire.eiu.com/index.asp?layout=VWArticleVW3&article_id=874361472, as accessed on 09 March 2017 at 2.10pm.

Taxes

It is not uncommon for a company to be incorporated in one place, do business in another, and maintain its corporate headquarters in a third. This type of diverse geographical activity requires special attention to tax laws. Many companies make efforts to minimize their tax liability by shifting the location of income. For example, it has been estimated that tax avoidance by foreign companies doing business in the

United States costs the US government several billion dollars each year in lost revenue. In one approach, called *earnings stripping*, foreign companies reduce earnings by making loans to US affiliates rather than using direct investment to finance US activities. The US subsidiary can deduct the interest it pays on such loans, thereby reducing its tax burden.

There are no universal, international laws governing the levy of taxes on companies that do business across national boundaries. To provide fair treatment, many governments have negotiated bilateral tax treaties to provide tax credits for taxes paid abroad. The United States has dozens of such agreements in place. In 1977, the Organization for Economic Cooperation and Development (OECD) passed the Model Double Taxation Convention on Income and Capital to help guide countries in bilateral negotiations. Generally, foreign companies are taxed by the host nation up to the level imposed in the home country, an approach that does not increase the total tax burden to the company.

Dilution of Equity Control[1]

Political pressure for national control of foreign-owned companies is a part of the environment of global business in lower-income countries. The foremost goal of national governance is to protect the right of national sovereignty, especially in all aspects of domestic business activity. Host-nation governments sometimes attempt to control ownership of foreign-owned companies operating within their borders. In underdeveloped countries, political pressures frequently cause companies to take in local partners.

Legislation that requires companies to dilute their equity is never popular in the boardroom, yet the consequences of such legislation are often surprisingly favorable. Dennis J. Encarnation and Sushil Vachani examined corporate responses to India's 1973 Foreign Exchange Regulation Act (FERA), which restricted foreign equity participation in local projects to 40 percent. The researchers identified four options available to companies faced with the threat of dilution:

- Follow the law to the letter. Colgate-Palmolive (India) took this course, became an Indian company, and maintained its dominant position in a growing market.
- Leave the country. This was IBM's response. After several years of negotiations, IBM concluded that it would lose more in shared control than it would gain from continued operations under the new rules.
- Negotiate under the law. Some companies used the equity dilution requirement to raise funds for growth and diversification. In most cases, this was done by issuing fresh equity to local investors. Ciba-Geigy increased its equity base 27 percent to $17.7 million, for example, and also negotiated an increase in production that doubled the sales of Hindustan Ciba-Geigy.
- Take preemptive action. Some foreign firms initiated defensive strategies well before FERA's passage. These included proactive diversification to take advantage of investment incentives, gradual "Indianization" of the company, and continuously updating technology and maintaining export sales.

Encarnation and Vachani's study offers some important lessons.

1. First, look at the range of possibilities. There is no single best solution, and each company should look at itself and at the country situation to decide on strategy.
2. Companies should use the law to achieve their own objectives. The experiences of many companies demonstrate that by satisfying government demands, it is possible to take advantage of government concessions, subsidies, and market protection.

[1] This section is based on Dennis J. Encarnation and Sushil Vachani, "Foreign Ownership: When Hosts Change the Rules," *Harvard Business Review* (September–October 1985): 152–160.

3. Anticipate government policy changes. Create a win–win situation. Companies that take initiative are prepared to act when the opportunity arises. It takes time to implement changes; the sooner a company identifies possible government directions and initiatives, the sooner it will be in a position to propose its own plan to help the country achieve its objectives.
4. Listen to country managers. Country managers should be encouraged to anticipate government initiatives and to propose company strategy for taking advantage of opportunities created by government policy. Local managers often have the best understanding of the political environment. They may be in the best position to know when issues are arising and how to turn potential adversity into opportunity through creative responses.

The threat of equity dilution has caused some companies to operate in host nations via joint ventures or strategic alliances. These alternatives create special legal problems. There should be clauses in the joint venture or alliance agreement regarding its subsequent dissolution, as well as for the ownership of patents, trademarks, or technology realized from the joint effort. The agreement should also include clauses related to cross-licensing of intellectual property rights developed under joint operations.

Expropriation

The ultimate threat a government can pose toward a company is expropriation. Expropriation refers to governmental action to dispossess a company or investor. Compensation is generally provided to foreign investors, although not often in the "prompt, effective, and adequate" manner provided for by international standard. Nationalization occurs if ownership of the property or assets in question is transferred to the host government. If no compensation is provided, the action is referred to as confiscation.

Short of outright expropriation or nationalization, the phrase *creeping expropriation* has been applied to severe limitations on economic activities of foreign firms in certain developing countries. These have included limitations on repatriation of profits, dividends, royalties, or technical assistance fees from local investments or technology arrangements. Other issues are increased local content requirements, quotas for hiring local nationals, price controls, and other restrictions affecting return on investment. Global companies have also suffered discriminatory tariffs and nontariff barriers that limit market entry of certain industrial and consumer goods, as well as discriminatory laws on patents and trademarks. Intellectual property restrictions have had the practical effect of eliminating or drastically reducing protection of pharmaceutical products.

When governments expropriate foreign property, there are impediments to action to reclaim that property. For example, according to the US Act of State Doctrine, if the government of a foreign state is involved in a specific act, a US court will not get involved. Representatives of expropriated companies may seek recourse through arbitration at the World Bank Investment Dispute Settlement Center (International Centre for Settlement of Investment Disputes, or ICSID). It is also possible to buy expropriation insurance, either from a private company or the US government's Overseas Private Investment Corporation (OPIC). The expropriation of copper companies operating in Chile in 1970 and 1971 shows the impact that companies can have on their own fate. Companies that strenuously resisted government efforts to introduce home-country nationals into the company management were expropriated outright; other companies that made genuine efforts to follow Chilean guidelines were allowed to remain under joint Chilean–US management.

BOX 3-2

Side Bar: Political Risk in Valenzuela Increasing!

Venezuela has been blessed with oil reserve and over the years the country has been exporting its oil to different countries of the world. But it has never been like the past few years. Rather, oil became the only commodity which the country could export as evident from the fact that oil constituted to about 95 percent of total exports in recent years. Out of total export of $63 billion during 2014, crude petroleum constituted $47.8B followed by refined petroleum $10.9B which meant that about 93.17 percent was due to these two petroleum based products only. During 2015, the country witnessed a sharp fall in export revenue when the export could reach the value of $47.54 billion only due to two prominent reasons like shrinkage of production as well as slump in oil price in the global market. Oil export earnings constituted about half of the country's GDP and hence it is predicted that Venezuelan economy would shrink by at least 10-15 percent in the coming years.

In the political front, good news came when long and torturous left brand politics, introduced by President Hugo Chavez and popularly known as "Chavismo", came to an end. Hugo Chavez's party failed to win the country wide election. But long misrule of the ''Chavismo" made various dents in the economy and it is not expected that the democratically elected new regime would be able to do some miracle for the country to realign it in the path of economic development. However, the Hugo Chavez's chosen successor, Maduro, is still very active to regain control and planning to take help of referendum to regain the power from democratic alliance.

The economy of Venezuela possibly has travelled to the lowest level; shrinkage of economy is in a fast track, drop in oil production is continuing, slump in oil price seems to be irreversible, huge debt burden looming large on the country, low foreign reserve is not even sufficient to pay for food and medicine import bill. About 7.3 percent of Venezuelan households are living under extreme poverty condition. A bulk chunk of the working population, do not even earn enough wages to be able to afford to purchase groceries for even a week per month. One immediate rescue point for the distressed economy can come from rise in oil price in the international level. But this reversal seems to be remote as petrol prices nosedived from $111 per barrel during 2014 to around $40 during 2015. The GDP per capita during 1977 shot to about USD 15581.43 which came down to a low of USD 12793 in 2015. While fighting inflation always has been a very tricky and continuous business even in well managed developed countries, but Venezuela seems to have resigned in even making effort. According to International Monetary Fund, consumer-price inflation has been forecasted to hit 480% during 2016 and thereafter might reach record high of 1,640% during 2017. To make the internal situation still worse, the law and order situation has been worsening day by day. During the present year, kidnapping, murder, theft etc have become order of the day. The country ill-famed itself when it became the second country after Honduras in the world to have maximum homicide cases.

Venezuela has been reeling under political and economic crisis for a long time but it has been intensified in the recent years. People get involved in broil to get their limited share of grocery items from stores. The country has no money even to import regular medicines and live -saving drugs for its citizen. Limited electricity supply is available because the power generation companies have no money to run their companies. These adverse situation has created a suitable opportunity where the citizens are demonstrating their anger by staging anti-government demonstration almost on a regular basis. The continuous journey of the country towards severe instability have compelled the international observers to term the country as a 'failed state'.

Courtesy: The International Monetary Fund Country Outlook. http://www.imf.org/external/pubs/ft/wp/2016/wp16159.pdf, as accessed on 10 March 2017 at 12.30pm.

INTERNATIONAL LAW

International law may be defined as the rules and principles that nation-states consider binding upon themselves. There are two categories of international law: public law, or the law of nations, and international commercial law, which is evolving. International law pertains to trade and other areas that have traditionally been under the jurisdiction of individual nations.

The roots of modern international law can be traced back to the early Middle Ages in Europe and later to the seventeenth-century Peace of Westphalia. Early international law was concerned with waging war, establishing peace, and other political issues such as diplomatic recognition of new national entities and governments. Elaborate international rules gradually emerged—covering, for example, the status of neutral nations. The creation of laws governing commerce developed on a state-by-state basis, evolving into what is termed the *law of the merchant*. International law still has the function of upholding order, although in a broader sense than dealing with problems arising from war. At first, international law was essentially an amalgam of treaties, covenants, codes, and agreements. As trade grew among nations, order in commercial affairs assumed increasing importance. Whereas the law had originally dealt only with nations as entities, a growing body of law rejected the idea that only states can be subject to international law.

Paralleling the expanding body of international case law in the twentieth century, new international judiciary organizations have contributed to the creation of an established rule of international law. These include the Permanent Court of International Justice (1920–1945); the International Court of Justice (ICJ), the judicial arm of the United Nations established by article 7 of the United Nations Charter in 1946; and the International Law Commission, established by the United States in 1947. Disputes arising between nations are issues of public international law, and they may be taken before the ICJ located in The Hague, often referred to as the World Court. Article 38 of the ICJ Statute identifies recognized sources of public international law. As described in the supplemental documents to the United Nations Charter, article 38 of the ICJ Statute defines sources of international law.

> The Court, whose function is to decide in accordance with international law such disputes as are submitted to it, shall apply:
>
> a. international conventions, whether general or particular, establishing rules expressly recognized by the contesting states;
> b. international custom, as evidence of a general practice accepted as law;
> c. the general principles of law recognized by civilized nations;
> d. subject to the provisions of Article 59, judicial decisions and the teachings of the most highly qualified publicists of the various nations, as subsidiary means for the determination of rules of law.

What happens if a nation has allowed a case against it to be brought before the ICJ and then refuses to accept a judgment against it? The plaintiff nation can seek recourse through the UN's highest political arm, the United Nations Security Council, which can use its full range of powers to enforce the judgment.

Common Versus Code Law

Private international law is the body of law that applies to interpretations of and disputes arising from commercial transactions between companies of different nations. As noted earlier in the chapter, laws governing commerce emerged gradually. Forty-nine of the 50 states of the United States, nine of Canada's 10 provinces, and other former English colonies (Australia; New Zealand; India; Hong Kong; the English-speaking former African colonies, for example, with a colonial history) founded their systems on common law. Historically, much of continental Europe was influenced by Roman law and, later, the Napoleonic Code. Asian countries are split: India, Pakistan, Malaysia, Singapore, and Hong Kong—all former British colonies—are common-law jurisdictions. Japan, Korea, Thailand, Indochina, Taiwan, Indonesia, and China are civil-law jurisdictions. Today, the majority of countries have legal systems based on civil-code traditions, although an increasing number of countries are blending concepts, and hybrid systems are emerging. Despite the differences in systems, three distinct forms of laws are common to all nations. Statutory law is codified at the national, federal, or state level; administrative law originates in regulatory bodies and local communities; and case law is the product of the court system.

Under civil or code law, the judicial system is divided into civil, commercial, and criminal law. Thus, commercial law has its own administrative structure. Property rights, for example, are established by a formal registration of the property in commercial courts. Code law uses codified, written norms, which are complemented by court decisions. Common law, on the other hand, is established by tradition and precedents, which are rulings from previous cases; until recently, commercial law was not recognized as a special entity. Differences include the definition of acts of God; under common law, this phrase can refer only to floods, storms, and other acts of nature unless expanded by contract. In code-law countries, an "unavoidable interference with performance" can be considered an act of God. In code-law countries, intellectual property rights must be registered, whereas in common-law countries, some—such as trademarks but not patents—are established by prior use.

A significant recent development is the Uniform Commercial Code (UCC), fully adopted by 49 US states, which codifies a body of specifically designed rules covering commercial conduct. (Louisiana has adopted parts of the UCC, but its laws are still heavily influenced by French civil code.) The host country's legal system—that is, common or civil law—directly affects the form a legal business entity will take. In common-law countries, companies are granted the ability to operate by public authority. In civil-law countries, companies are formed by contract between two or more parties who are fully liable for the actions of the company.

SIDESTEPPING LEGAL PROBLEMS: IMPORTANT BUSINESS ISSUES

Clearly, the global legal environment is very dynamic and complex. Therefore, the best course to follow is to get expert legal help. However, the astute, proactive global marketer can do a great deal to prevent conflicts from arising in the first place, especially concerning issues such as establishment, jurisdiction, patents and trademarks, antitrust, licensing and trade secrets, and bribery.

The services of counsel are essential for addressing these and other legal issues. The importance of international law firms is growing as national firms realize that to properly serve their clients they must have a presence in overseas jurisdictions. As in many industries, global consolidation is increasing among international law firms. One forecast is that within a decade, only 5 to 10 global law firms will exist. Table 3-1 shows the top 10 law firms in the world and the percentage of lawyers outside the home country.

Establishment

Under what conditions can trade be established (See Box 3-3 on how the Multilateral Agreement on Investment failed.)? To transact business, citizens of one country must be assured that they will be treated fairly in another country. In Western Europe, for example, the creation of the Single Market now assures that citizens from member nations get fair treatment with regard to business and economic activities carried out within the Common Market. The formulation of the governance rules for trade, business, and economic activities in the EU will provide additional substance to international law.

TABLE 3-1 The World's Largest Law Firms by 2010 Revenue[2]

Rank	Name	Revenue	Headquarters
1 ▲	Baker & McKenzie	$2,104.0m	USA (Chicago, IL)
2 ▲	Skadden, Arps, Slate, Meagher & Flom	$2,100.0m	USA (New York, NY)
3 —	Clifford Chance	$1,874.5m	UK (London)
4 ▼	Linklaters	$1,852.5m	UK (London)
5 ▲	Latham & Watkins	$1,821.0m	USA (New York)
6 ▼	Freshfields Bruckhaus Deringer	$1,787.0m	UK (London)
7 ▼	Allen & Overy	$1,644.5m	UK (London)
8 —	Jones Day	$1,520.0m	USA (Washington, DC)
9 ▲	Kirkland & Ellis	$1,428.0m	USA (Chicago)
10 ▼	Sidley Austin	$1,357.0m	USA (Chicago)

BOX 3-3

Side Bar: The Multilateral Agreement on Investment[3]

In 1995, the OECD began talks on a new initiative known as the Multilateral Agreement on Investment (MAI) that would set rules for foreign investment and provide a forum for dispute settlement. In some countries, so-called performance requirements favor local investors over foreigners. For example, foreign companies may be required to obtain some goods and services from local companies rather than the home office. Performance requirements can also take the form of stipulations that a certain number of senior managers must be local nationals or that the foreign company must export a set percentage of its production.

The existence of the MAI negotiations remained largely unknown to the general public until a Canadian consumer rights group obtained the text of MAI and posted it on the Internet. In fact, a large number of consumer and environmental action groups joined in opposition to the agreement. As Mark A. Vallianatos, an international policy analyst at Friends of the Earth, explained:

> Our fear is that MAI will give multinational corporations the opportunity to treat the whole world as their raw pool of natural resources and labor and consumer markets. It may allow them to do everything based on profit motives without environmental considerations providing sensible limits on how they operate. MAI gives new rights to corporations without addressing their responsibilities to workers and the environment. An MAI that is worth doing should deal with how investments will affect sustainable development, how they will affect workers' rights, and how they will affect excessive resource extraction—those kinds of issues.

Some industry experts downplay MAI's potential to contribute to environmental degradation. R. Garrity Baker, senior director at the Chemical Manufacturers Association, says, "When foreign companies that have better environmental performance come in and invest in a market [they] bring that know-how with them, then over time that know-how kind of trickles down to

[2] Data source: http://en.wikipedia.org/wiki/List_of_100_largest_law_firms_by_revenue. (taken from American Lawyer, a publication of ALM at http://www.americanlawyer.com/current_issue.jsp

[3] Bette Hileman, "A Globalization Conundrum," *Chemical & Engineering News,* 20 (April 1998): 45; "Bye-bye, MAI?" *Financial Times,* February 19, 1998, 13.

other companies. Foreign companies set an example that others can learn from." MAI supporters also point out that the agreement allows countries to adopt any measure deemed appropriate to ensure investment is undertaken in a manner that reflects sensitivity to environmental issues. Several years after its introduction, prospects for MAI approval in the United States were clouded by disagreements between key Washington agencies that might be affected by the agreement's provisions. The US State Department and Commerce Department are generally supportive, but the Environmental Protection Agency, the US Agency for International Development, and the Justice Department are concerned that MAI will lead to a rash of lawsuits against the United States. At the state level, a number of governors felt that MAI would impinge on state sovereignty. In February 2002, OECD released a large quantity of documents relating to the negotiations. These can be viewed at http://www1.oecd.org/daf/mai/toc.htm

The United States has signed treaties of friendship, commerce, and navigation with more than 40 countries. These agreements provide US citizens the right to nondiscriminatory treatment in trade, the reciprocal right to establish a business, and, particularly, to invest. Commercial treaties provide one with the privilege, not the right, to engage in business activities in other than one's own country. This can create problems for business managers who may still be under the jurisdiction of their own laws even when they are out of their native country. US citizens, for example, are forbidden by the Foreign Corrupt Practices Act to give bribes to an official of a foreign government or political party, even if bribes are customary for conducting business in that country.

Jurisdiction

Company personnel working abroad should understand the extent to which they are subject to the jurisdiction of host-country courts. Employees of foreign companies working in the United States must understand that courts have jurisdiction to the extent that the company can be demonstrated to be doing business in the state in which the court sits. The court may examine whether the foreign company maintains an office, solicits business, maintains bank accounts or other property, or has agents or other employees in the state in question. In a demonstrative case, Revlon Inc. sued United Overseas Ltd. (UOL), in the US District Court for the Southern District of New York. Revlon charged the British company with breach of contract, contending that UOL failed to purchase some specialty shampoos as agreed. UOL, claiming lack of jurisdiction, asked the court to dismiss the complaint. Revlon countered with the argument that UOL was, in fact, subject to the court's jurisdiction; Revlon cited the presence of a UOL sign above the entrance to the offices of a New York company in which UOL had a 50 percent ownership interest. The court denied UOL's motion to dismiss.[4]

Normally, all economic activity within a nation is governed by that nation's laws. When a transaction crosses boundaries, which nation's laws apply? If the national laws of country Q pertaining to a simple export transaction differ from those of country P, which country's laws apply to the export contract? Which apply to the letter of credit opened to finance the export transaction? The parties involved must reach agreement on such issues, and the nation whose laws apply should be specified in a jurisdictional clause. There are several alternatives from which to choose: the laws of the domicile or principal place of business of one of the parties, the place where the contract was entered, or the place of performance of the contract. If a dispute arises under such a contract, it must be heard and determined by a neutral party such as a court or

[4] Joseph Ortego and Josh Kardisch, "Foreign Companies Can Limit the Risk of Being Subject to U.S. Courts," *The National Law Journal,* 17, no. 3 (19 September 1994): C2.

an arbitration panel. If the parties fail to specify which nation's laws apply, a fairly complex set of rules governing the "conflict of laws" will be applied by the court or arbitration tribunal. Sometimes, the result will be determined with the help of "the scales of justice," with each party's criteria stacked on different sides of the scale.[5]

Intellectual Property: Patents and Trademarks

Patents and trademarks that are protected in one country are not necessarily protected in another, so global marketers must ensure that patents and trademarks are registered in each country where business is conducted (see Box 3-4). In the United States, where patents, trademarks, and copyrights are registered with the Federal Patent Office, the patent holder retains all rights for the life of the patent even if the product is not produced or sold. Patent and trademark protection in the United States is very good, and American law relies on the precedent of previously decided court cases for guidance.

Companies sometimes find ways to exploit loopholes or other unique opportunities offered by patent and trademark laws in individual nations. In France, designer Yves Saint Laurent was barred from marketing a new luxury perfume called Champagne because French laws allow the name to be applied only to sparkling wines produced in the Champagne region. Saint Laurent proceeded to launch Champagne in the United States, England, Germany, and Belgium; "Champagne" and other geographic names are not protected trademarks in the United States. In France, the perfume is sold without a name.[6]

Trademark and copyright infringement is a critical problem in global marketing and one that can take a variety of forms. *Counterfeiting* is the unauthorized copying and production of a product. An *associative counterfeit*, or imitation, uses a product name that differs slightly from a well-known brand but is close enough that consumers will associate it with the genuine product. A third type of counterfeiting is *piracy*, the unauthorized publication or reproduction of copyrighted work. Piracy is particularly damaging to the entertainment and software industries; computer programs, videotapes, cassettes, and compact discs are particularly easy to duplicate illegally. Figure 3-1 shows the percentage of pirated software in select countries. Pirating cost the software industry an estimated $51 billion in 2009.

BOX 3-4

Side Bar: Software Piracy[7]

In Lebanon, one of the largest retailers of software sells the original Microsoft Office 97 Professional for $200, but it also sells the pirated version for $7. Selling pirated versions is rationalized for the following reasons: (1) Given a per capita GNP of approximately $3,000, the $7 version is certainly more affordable. (2) Islam religion says that no one can own science. Since the software is considered science, it should belong to everyone. (3) Dealers question, given the cost of production, the large price difference. "We know how much profit Microsoft is making." (4) Is the government going to enforce trademark law and, if so, how vigorously?

[5] For a more extensive development of this point, see Robert J. Radway, "Legal Dimensions of International Business," in *International Encyclopedia of Business and Management*, Malcolm Warner, ed. (London: Thomson, 1996).

[6] Karla Vermeulen, "Champagne Perfume Launched in United States but Barred in France," *Wine Spectator* (October 31, 1994): 9.

[7] James Schofield, "Beating Software Piracy Proves to Be No Soft Touch," *Financial Times*, April 1, 1999, 7.

FIGURE 3-1 "Software Piracy Rate by Country", Fifth Annual BSA and IDC Global Software Piracy Study

Rank	Countries	Amount	Rank	Countries	Amount
1	Armenia	93%	40	Peru	71%
2	Moldova	92%	41	Uruguay	69%
2	Bangladesh	92%	41	Philippines	69%
2	Azerbaijan	92%	41	India	69%
5	Zimbabwe	91%	44	Romania	68%
6	Sri Lanka	90%	44	Macedonia, Republic of	68%
7	Yemen	89%	44	Bulgaria	68%
8	Libya	88%	44	Bosnia and Herzegovina	68%
9	Venezuela	87%	48	Morocco	67%
10	Vietnam	85%	49	Ecuador	66%
10	Iraq	85%	49	Chile	66%
12	Pakistan	84%	51	Turkey	65%
12	Indonesia	84%	52	Kuwait	62%
12	Cameroon	84%	53	Oman	61%
12	Algeria	84%	53	Mexico	61%
16	Ukraine	83%	53	Costa Rica	61%
17	Zambia	82%	56	Jordan	60%
17	Paraguay	82%	56	Egypt	60%
17	Nigeria	82%	58	Malaysia	59%
17	China	82%	58	Brazil	59%
17	Botswana	82%	60	Greece	58%
17	Bolivia	82%	60	Colombia	58%
23	Kenya	81%	62	Poland	57%
23	El Salvador	81%	62	Mauritius	57%
23	Côte d'Ivoire	81%	62	Bahrain	57%
26	Senegal	80%	65	Lithuania	56%
26	Nicaragua	80%	65	Latvia	56%
26	Guatemala	80%	67	Qatar	54%
29	Kazakhstan	79%	67	Croatia	54%
29	Dominican Republic	79%	69	Saudi Arabia	51%
31	Thailand	78%	69	Hong Kong	51%
31	Albania	78%	69	Estonia	51%
33	Tunisia	76%	72	Cyprus	50%
33	Serbia and Montenegro	76%	73	Italy	49%
35	Panama	74%	74	Slovenia	48%
35	Honduras	74%	74	Iceland	48%
35	Argentina	74%	76	Malta	46%
38	Russia	73%	77	Slovakia	45%
38	Lebanon	73%			

FIGURE 3-1 Continued

Rank	Countries	Amount	Rank	Countries	Amount
78	Puerto Rico	44%	93	Norway	29%
79	Spain	43%	94	Netherlands	28%
79	Portugal	43%	94	Australia	28%
79	Korea, South	43%	96	Germany	27%
82	Hungary	42%	97	United Kingdom	26%
82	France	42%	98	Switzerland	25%
84	Taiwan	40%	98	Sweden	25%
84	Réunion	40%	98	Finland	25%
86	Czech Republic	39%	98	Denmark	25%
87	Singapore	37%	98	Belgium	25%
88	United Arab Emirates	35%	98	Austria	25%
89	South Africa	34%	104	Japan	23%
89	Ireland	34%	105	New Zealand	22%
91	Canada	33%	106	Luxembourg	21%
92	Israel	32%	107	United States	20%

Source: Retrieved from http://www.NationMaster.com/graph/cri_sof_pir_rat-crime-software-piracy-rate.

International Trademark Filings

A record 39,945 international trademark applications were received in 2007 by the World Intellectual Property Organization (WIPO) under the Madrid system for the international registration of trademarks, representing a 9.5 percent increase on figures for 2006. The largest share of trademark applications received by WIPO in 2007 was filed by companies in Germany (6,090 applications or 15.2% of the total). These were followed by companies in France, which accounted for 3,930 applications or 9.8 percent of the total. Users in the United States ranked third with 3,741 applications, or 9.4 percent of the total, only four years after the United States joined the Madrid system. Those filing their international applications through the EC's regional Trademark Office (OHIM) were fourth, only three years after the EC acceded (with 3,371 applications or 8.4% of the total). They were followed by Italy (2,664 or 6.7%), Switzerland (2,657 or 6.7%), Benelux (2,510 or 6.3%), China (1,444 or 3.6%), the United Kingdom (1,178 or 2.9%), and Australia (1,169 or 2.9%).

China remained the most designated country in international trademark applications, reflecting increasing levels of trading activity by foreign companies in China.

WIPO Director General Dr. Kamil Idris welcomed the growing use of the "Madrid system," a user-friendly and cost-effective service that enables individuals and companies to acquire and maintain trademark protection in export markets. "The Madrid system has earned the trust and confidence of the business community as a reliable option for brands seeking export markets," he said. As Dr. Idris pointed out,

> Brand value is one of the most important assets that a business holds. From a legal perspective, brand creation and management translates into trademark protection. Trademarks are a key means by which businesses are able to add value to their day-to-day commercial operations and thereby secure their long-term financial viability.

WIPO will continue to enhance its services to the private sector to enable companies to obtain and maintain trademark protection in a timely and cost-effective way.

Since October 2004, applicants from the EC have the option to file their international applications either through their national trademark office or through the EC's regional trademark office (OHIM). In 2007, the third full year of the EU's membership in the Madrid system, the number of international applications filed by applicants from the EC through OHIM rose by 37.9 percent. The 27 countries of the European Union (EU) together accounted for 26,026 applications in 2007. These figures include both the international applications filed through the national trademark offices of the countries concerned and those filed through OHIM (3,371).

A number of countries experienced significant growth in the number of international trademark filings in 2007. The United States, for instance, enjoyed an 18.8 percent increase, enabling it to strengthen its 3rd position in the ranking of top filer countries. Other countries included the United Kingdom (+11.8%) now ranking 9th (previously 11th), Japan (+16.2%) now ranking 12th (formerly 13th), Russian Federation (+42.9%) now 13th (formerly 15th), Denmark (+19.6%) now 16th (formerly 17th), Sweden (+19.5%) now 18th (formerly 19th), and Hungary (+101.8%) now 19th (formerly 25th).

Developing countries accounted for 2,108 filings in 2007, representing 5.3 percent of total filings and a 10.5 percent growth over 2006. The developing country that witnessed the most significant growth in international trademark filings in 2007 was the Republic of Korea with 330 applications (+73.7%).[9]

In the United States, trademarks are covered by the Trademark Act of 1946, also known as the Lanham Act. President Reagan signed the Trademark Law Revision Act into law in November 1988. The law makes it easier for companies to register new trademarks; as a result, the number of filings has increased dramatically. Table 3-2 shows the increase in foreign trademark filings in the United States for the decade starting 1988. There were 385,00 total filings and 225,00 registrations in the United States in the 2011 fiscal year.

TABLE 3-2 Foreign Company Trademark Filings in The United States for Selected Countries[8]

Country	1988	1998
Belgium	111	246
Britain	1,392	2,619
Canada	2,447	4,894
Germany	1,400	2,984
Hong Kong	168	396
Israel	45	438
Japan	1,010	2,231
Mexico	126	693
South Korea	131	372
Total	6,830	14,873

[8] http://www.wipo.int/pressroom/en/articles/2008/article_0007.html
[9] US Patent and Trademark Office.

Visit the WebSites

Visit www.uspto.gov for US information.

Visit www.european-patent-office.org for information about Europe.

Antitrust

Antitrust laws are designed to combat restrictive business practices and to encourage competition. American antitrust laws are a legacy of the nineteenth-century US trust-busting era and are intended to maintain free competition by limiting the concentration of economic power. The Sherman Act of 1890 prohibits certain restrictive business practices, including fixing prices, limiting production, allocating markets, or any other scheme designed to limit or avoid competition. The law applies to foreign companies conducting business in the United States and extends to the activities of US companies outside US boundaries as well, if the company conduct is deemed to have an effect on US commerce contrary to law. Similar laws are taking on increasing importance outside of the United States.

The European Commission prohibits agreements and practices that prevent, restrict, and distort competition. The interstate trade clause of the Treaty of Rome applies to trade with third countries, so a company must be aware of the conduct of its affiliates. The commission also exempts certain cartels from articles 85 and 86 of the treaty in an effort to encourage the growth of important businesses. The intent is to allow European companies to compete on an equal footing with Japanese and US companies.

In some instances, individual country laws in Europe apply to specific marketing mix elements. For example, some countries permit selective or exclusive product distribution. However, community law can take precedence. In one case, Consten, a French company, had exclusive French rights to import and distribute consumer electronics products from the German Grundig Company. Consten sued another French firm, charging the latter with bringing parallel imports into France illegally. That is, Consten charged that the competitor bought Grundig products from various foreign suppliers without Consten's knowledge and was selling them in France. Although Consten's complaint was upheld by two French courts, the Paris court of appeals suspended the judgment, pending a ruling by the European Commission on whether the Grundig–Consten arrangement violated articles 85 and 86. The commission ruled against Consten on the grounds that "territorial protection proved to be particularly damaging to the realization of the Common Market."[10] The principle being offended was that of the free flow of goods defined in articles 24 to 30 of the Treaty of Rome.

Licensing and Trade Secrets

Licensing is a contractual agreement in which a licensor allows a licensee to use patents, trademarks, trade secrets, technology, or other intangible assets in return for royalty payments or other forms of compensation (see Chapter 8 for a discussion of licensing as a marketing strategy). In the United States, laws do not regulate the licensing process per se as do technology transfer laws in the EU, Australia, Japan, and many developing countries. The duration of the licensing agreement and the amount of royalties a company can receive are considered a matter of commercial negotiation between licensor and licensee, and there are no government restrictions on remittances of royalties abroad. In many countries, these elements of licensing are regulated by government agencies.

Important considerations in licensing include analysis of what assets a firm may offer for license, how to price the assets, and whether to grant only the right to make

[10] Detlev Vagts, *Transnational Business Problems* (Mineola, NY: The Foundation Press, 1986).

the product or to grant the rights to use and to sell the product as well. The right to sublicense is another important issue. As with distribution agreements, decisions must also be made regarding exclusive or nonexclusive arrangements and the size of the licensee's territory.

To prevent the licensee from using the licensed technology to compete directly with the licensor, the latter may try to limit the licensee to selling only in its home country. The licensor may also seek to contractually bind the licensee to discontinue use of the technology after the contract has expired. In practice, host government laws, including US and EU antitrust laws, may make such agreements impossible to obtain. Licensing is a potentially dangerous action: it may be instrumental in creating a competitor. Therefore, licensors should be careful to ensure that their own competitive position remains advantageous. This requires constant innovation. There is a simple rule: if you are licensing technology and know-how that are going to remain unchanged, it is only a matter of time before your licensee will become your competitor, not merely with your technology and know-how but with improvements on that technology and know-how. When this happens, you are history.

As noted, licensing agreements can come under antitrust scrutiny. In one recent case, Bayer AG granted an exclusive patent license for a new household insecticide to S. C. Johnson & Sons. The German firm's decision to license was based in part on the time required for Environmental Protection Agency (EPA) approval, which had stretched to three years. Bayer decided it made better business sense to let the American firm deal with regulatory authorities in return for a 5 percent royalty on sales. However, a class action suit was filed against the companies, alleging that the licensing deal would allow Johnson to monopolize the $450 million home insecticide market. Then the US Justice Department stepped in, calling the licensing agreement anticompetitive. In a statement, Anne Bingaman, head of the Justice Department's antitrust unit, said, "The cozy arrangement that Bayer and Johnson maintained is unacceptable in a highly concentrated market." Bayer agreed to offer licenses to any interested company on better terms than the original contract with Johnson. Johnson agreed to notify the US government of any future pending exclusive licensing agreements for household insecticides. If Bayer is party to any such agreements, the Justice Department has the right to veto them. Not surprisingly, the reaction from the legal community has been negative. One Washington lawyer who specializes in intellectual property law noted that the case "really attacks traditional licensing practices." As Melvin Jager, president of the Licensing Executives Society, explained, "An exclusive license is a very valuable tool to promote intellectual property and get it out into the marketplace."[11]

What happens if a licensee gains knowledge of the licensor's trade secrets? Trade secrets are confidential information or knowledge that has commercial value, is not in the public domain, and for which steps have been taken to keep secret. Trade secrets include manufacturing processes, formulas, designs, and customer lists. To prevent disclosure, the licensing of unpatented trade secrets should be linked to confidentiality contracts with each employee who has access to the protected information. In the United States, trade secrets are protected by state law rather than federal statute; most states have adopted the Uniform Trade Secrets Act (UTSA). US law provides trade secret liability against third parties that obtain confidential information through an intermediary. Remedies include damages and other forms of relief.

The 1990s saw widespread improvements in laws pertaining to trade secrets. Several countries adopted trade secret statutes for the first time. Mexico's first statute

[11] Brigid McMenamin, "Eroding Patent Rights," *Forbes,* October 24, 1994, 92.

protecting trade secrets became effective in 1991; China's first trade secret law took effect in 1993. In both countries, the new laws were part of broader revisions of intellectual property laws. Japan and South Korea also amended their intellectual property laws to include trade secrets. Many countries in Central and Eastern Europe have also enacted laws to protect trade secrets. When the North American Free Trade Agreement (NAFTA) became effective in 1994, it marked the first international trade agreement with provisions for protecting trade secrets. This milestone was quickly followed by the Agreement on Trade-Related Aspects of Intellectual Property Rights (TRIPs) that resulted from the Uruguay Round of GATT negotiations. The TRIPs agreement requires signatory countries to protect against acquisition, disclosure, or use of trade secrets "in a manner contrary to honest commercial practices."[12] Despite these formal legal developments, in practice, enforcement is the key issue. Companies transferring trade secrets across borders should apprise themselves not only of the existence of legal protection but also of the risks associated with lax enforcement.

BRIBERY AND CORRUPTION[13]

History does not record a burst of international outrage when Charles M. Schwab presented a $200,000 diamond and pearl necklace to the mistress of Czar Alexander's nephew. In return for that consideration, Bethlehem Steel won the contract to supply the rails for the trans-Siberian railroad. Today, in the post-Soviet era, Western companies are again being lured by emerging opportunities in Eastern Europe. Here, as in the Middle East and other parts of the world, they are finding that bribery is a way of life and that corruption is widespread. American companies in particular are constrained in their responses to such a situation by US government policies of the post-Watergate age.

Corruption is defined as "the misuse of entrusted power for private gain"[14] and has existed throughout recorded history and in virtually every corner of the globe. "Corruption is an outcome—a reflection of a country's political, economic, legal, and cultural institutions."[15] Corporate scandals, like those that occurred at Enron, Worldcom, and Parmalat, have demonstrated that corruption is indeed a global phenomenon which takes place in countries with developed and developing economies alike. Expansion of the global business environment and intensification of international trade have increased transnational corporations' exposure to the risk of corruption. Empirical studies have demonstrated that increased global business linkages have been accompanied by growth in the level of corruption.[16]

When companies operate abroad in the absence of home-country legal constraints, they face a continuum of choices concerning company ethics. At one extreme, they can maintain home-country ethics worldwide with absolutely no adjustment or adaptation to local practice. At the other extreme, they can abandon any attempt to maintain company ethics and adapt entirely to local conditions and circumstances as they are perceived by company managers in each local environment. Between these extremes, one approach that companies may select is to utilize varying degrees of

---

[12] Salem M. Katsh and Michael P. Dierks, "Globally, Trade Secrets Laws Are All over the Map," *The National Law Journal,* 17, no. 36 (May 8, 1995): C12.

[13] I am indebted to Tom D'Angelo, doctoral candidate at Pace University, for this section. It is adapted from his research paper on corruption which was prepared for my doctoral seminar in global strategic marketing.

[14] Transparency International, 2011, http://transparency.org, See for, example, European Neighbourhood Policy: Monitoring Azerbaijan's Anti-Corruption Commitments, March 11, 2010.

[15] J. Svensson, "Eight Questions about Corruption," *Journal of Economic Perspectives,* 19, no. 3 (2005): 19–42.

[16] R. Theobald, "Containing Corruption: Can the State Deliver?," *New Political Economy,* 7, no. 3 (2002): 435–449.

extension of home-country ethics. Alternatively, they may adapt in varying degrees to local customs and practices.

The existence of bribery as a fact of life in world markets may not change overnight because it is condemned by governments. What should a company do if competitors are offering a bribe? Three alternative courses of action are possible. One is to ignore bribery and act as if it does not exist. Another is to recognize the existence of bribery and evaluate its effect on the customer's purchase decision as if it were just another element of the marketing mix. A third is to inform the competitor that you intend to file bribery charges in his or her home country.

Complex relationships that exist among a global corporation and its suppliers, subcontractors, joint venture partners, and customers provide significant challenges to those in management responsible for corporate governance. The increasing role of the world's governments in the economies of their respective nations has resulted in higher levels of taxation, large increases in public spending, and more regulation of and controls on economic activities.[17] Given ever more competitive business conditions, transnational corporations are more likely to seek special treatment or other accommodations from bureaucrats in order to gain advantage through government-provided benefits or cost avoidance.

It is thus of critical importance that today's global business manager have an understanding of the dynamics of corruption. This includes recognizing its different forms, being familiar with the tools available for estimating its pervasiveness and magnitude, and having an awareness of characteristics that may indicate a higher probability of the existence of corruption within a country. Global managers must have knowledge of the regulations established to combat corruption, including international conventions and treaties as well as home- and host-country anticorruption laws.

Forms of Corruption

Corrupt activities take a variety of forms and can be generally categorized in a number of different ways. These range from the stereotypical bribing of a public official to highly complex, organized corruption that takes place on a large scale. Shah and Schacter segregate corruption into three broad forms: bureaucratic corruption, grand corruption, and influence peddling.[18] Bureaucratic corruption consists of isolated transactions executed by individual public officials that abuse their office. These transactions might include the demand for bribes and kickbacks, diversion or embezzlement of public funds, or the granting of favors in exchange for personal consideration. Grand corruption involves the misappropriation or misuse of large amounts of public resources by state officials who are often members of the political or administrative elite. Subsequent to the discovery of such prolonged activity, the magnitude of grand corruption often captivates the interest of the mainstream news media and these events are usually highly publicized. The grand corruption that was allegedly perpetrated during the regime of Mobutu Sese Seko, the former President of Zaire, was reported to be in excess of $5 billion. Influence peddling or state capture involves collusion between members of the private sector and public officials to gain mutual benefit. This form of corruption is also known as *state capture* because members of the private sector effectively capture the state, legislative, executive, or judicial apparatus for their own purpose.

---

[17] V. Tanzi, "Corruption around the World," *IMF Staff Papers*, 45, no. 4 (1998): 559–593.

[18] A. Shah and M. Schacter, "Combating Corruption: Look Before You Leap," *Finance and Development*, 41, no. 4 (2004): 40–43.

Further distinction among forms of corruption is made by Transparency International,[19] who suggests that the bribes that are offered to public officials constitute two types of corruption: according-to-rule corruption and against-the-rule corruption.[20] According-to-rule corruption exists when bribes are made in order to receive preferential treatment for something that a public official can legally do. This might involve paying a public official to grant a business license that has been withheld from competitors. Against-the-rule corruption occurs when a bribe is made to facilitate a service that a public official cannot legally offer. This could involve public officials illegally granting contracts to preferred firms while circumventing a fair open-bidding process.

It is important to remember that corruption is, at a minimum, a two-sided transaction, and a distinction can be made between the briber or supply side and the bribee or demand side. While much of the focus on estimating the pervasiveness of corruption in a given host country is centered on the demand for bribes, there is equal culpability on the side of the bribe payer, whether domestic or foreign-based. Analogous to efforts to curtail the international trafficking of illegal drugs, understanding the distinction between the supply and demand sides of corruption is critical in the design of programs to effectively combat it.

Both centralized corruption and decentralized corruption can affect growth.[21] Centralized corruption is well organized, and the amount of bribes demanded as well as each participant's share of ill-gotten gains are determined by a central figure. Decentralized corruption involves the uncoordinated activity of individuals in which each participant seeks to maximize the amount extorted. Decentralized corruption is seen as a greater deterrent to growth because of the higher rate of bribes demanded and the lower likelihood of prosecution due to the relative weakness of the state.[22]

Estimating the Pervasiveness and Magnitude of Corruption

Unlike legitimate business transactions, corruption involves secrecy and a high level of risk. Public officials and private actors engaging in such activities are not likely to provide a paper trail documenting corrupt transactions nor will they report the details to government statistical bureaus. Therefore, disagreements exist among researchers regarding the overall magnitude of global corruption and the most accurate way to estimate it.

The World Bank estimated that worldwide bribery totaled in excess of $1 trillion or more than 3 percent of world income during 2002.[23] While this in itself is a staggering sum, it is an estimate that includes only the volume of bribes paid, not the total economic impact of corruption on growth and income. The cost of corruption is not merely limited to bribes paid but also must include the social costs, economic opportunity costs, environmental costs, and other immeasurable factors, such as the loss of confidence in a government.[24]

[19] Transparency International's website provides the following organizational description: "Transparency International, the global civil society organization leading the fight against corruption, brings people together in a powerful worldwide coalition to end the devastating impact of corruption on men, women, and children around the world. Transparency International's mission is to create change towards a world free of corruption." http://transparency.org (2011).

[20] Transparency International, 2011.

[21] W. Easterly, *The Elusive Quest for Growth: Economist' Adventures and Misadventures in the Tropics*, (Cambridge, MA: MIT Press, 2002): 49–69.

[22] Ibid.

[23] World Bank, 2003, http://worldbank.org.

[24] Transparency International, 2011.

Although the very nature of corruption makes it difficult to quantify with any acceptable measure of precision, a number of resources exist that can be useful in estimating the pervasiveness of corruption within a particular country. One of the most prominent of these is the Corruption Perception Index published by Transparency International. The Corruption Perception Index ranks individual countries by the level of perceived corruption compiled from a variety of sources, including managers of transnational corporations, consultants, chambers of commerce, and members of the local population.[25] The organization also publishes the Global Corruption Barometer and the Bribe Payers Index, the latter publication evaluates the supply side of corruption. Other popular tools which provide estimates of the pervasiveness and magnitude of corruption are published by the World Bank, Global Integrity, and a number of private risk-assessment firms.

The sources cited in this section are helpful to the global manager in providing directional, if not quantifiable, information regarding corruption. These indices tend to be rough measures of the difficulty one might encounter while attempting to do business internationally but should not be used to make precise bilateral comparisons between closely ranked countries.[26]

Characteristics of Countries with High Perceived Levels of Corruption

A review of the scholarly literature pertaining to corruption reveals the complex nature of the subject matter and the often blurred distinctions among its various causes and consequences. This chicken or egg type of quandary can be demonstrated by considering the relative level of a country's income and wealth and the pervasiveness of corruption within that country. Higher levels of income and wealth tend to be inversely correlated to perceived levels of corruption.[27] Does the lack of income and wealth cause corruption or does corruption have an adverse effect on income and wealth? Is there some degree of simultaneity? The answers are far from clear. One approach to circumventing some of the confusion inherent in the corruption cause-and-effect conundrum is to simply identify characteristics commonly associated with countries that tend to have pervasive corruption. These include certain economic, governmental, social, historic, geographic, and cultural characteristics which, given the presence or absence of such characteristics, can be useful in predicting the potential risk of corruption.

While the spectrum of national characteristics is broad, perhaps the most likely incentives that influence individuals to engage in corrupt behavior are those rooted in economic activity. There are a number of economic attributes that are shared by countries that have a high perceived level of corruption. As discussed previously in the chapter, empirical studies associate low economic growth rates and higher levels of poverty with corruption.[28] Low national average income leads to economic uncertainty, which tends to create structural incentives for corrupt behavior.[29]

[25] W. Sandholtz and W. Koetzle, "Accounting for Corruption: Economic Structure, Democracy, and Trade," *International Studies Quarterly*, 44 (2000): 31–50.

[26] S. Rose-Ackerman, "The Challenge of Poor Governance and Corruption," *World Bank Copenhagen Consensus 2004* (2004): 1–48.

[27] S. D. Beets, "Understanding the Demand-Side Issues of International Corruption," *Journal of Business Ethics*, 57 (2005): 65–81.

[28] Ibid.

[29] Sandholtz and Koetzle, "Accounting for Corruption."

A common economic characteristic of countries with pervasive corruption is a lack of integration with the global economy.[30] This may result from restrictive trade policies or other tight government controls exerted on the economy. High import tariffs might provide incentives to bribe customs officials.[31] This may also be manifest in low levels of foreign direct investment and other capital inflows, since transnational corporations avoid investing in countries where the risks of expropriation or confiscation are high. Large budget deficits are often present as politicians choose public works based on the opportunity they present for bribes and kickbacks rather than their intrinsic economic worth.[32] Other economic attributes include lower productivity, less effective industrial policies, and larger unofficial economies than commonly found in countries with less corruption.

In addition to economic attributes, similar observations may be made regarding governmental, social, historic, geographic, cultural, and other national characteristics associated with countries with high perceived levels of corruption. Critically, an understanding of the quality of a nation's institutions will provide some indication of the potential for the existence of corruption. A lack of transparency in regulations, rules, and laws can create conditions that increase the risk of corruption.[33] Considering a broad matrix of country characteristics is likely to be a more effective approach in assessing corruption risk than attempting to evaluate individual characteristics in isolation.

Competition Commission of India as Market Regulator in India

The market place of any country should be an open market which allows free and fair competition and thereby ensures that the consumers are the recipient of the benefits in terms of quality and cost. When competition is free and fair it ensures level playing field to the participating companies which foils attempts of such companies who desire to tax consumers by undue means. The objective of CCI is to play an overarching role as a market regulator across all sectors with the focus on anti-competitive behaviour of enterprises that may distort competition. As put by Adam Smith in his book "The wealth of Nations", that in the sphere of competition the participating companies are bound to get benefits only after hard work and the fittest companies will come up with better products at lower prices which in turn allow the consumers to maximise their benefits. The Indian market, therefore, also desired to have a free market environment facilitating competition amongst the companies so that efficiency prevails and quality goods and services at reasonable prices are coming out for the consumers. The need was very acutely felt after the 1991 reforms program which saw growth momentum of the country being unleashed in an unprecedented manner.

Competition commission of India (CCI) was set up by Government of India in 2003 to act as a body of the responsible for enforcing the Competition Act, 2002 and competition (Amendment) Act, 2007 in India and to prevent activities that have an adverse effect on the Competitive landscape of the country. The Competition (Amendment) Act, 2007 has the following four major objectives:

1. To prohibit anti-competitive agreements, including cartels;
2. To prevent abuse of dominant position;
3. To regulate combinations (acquisition, acquiring of control and Merger and acquisition); and
4. To propagate competition advocacy

---

30 Rose-Ackerman, "The Challenge of Poor Governance."

31 Easterly, *The Elusive Quest for Growth*.

32 V. Tanzi and H. Davoodi, "Roads to Nowhere: How Corruption in Public Investment Hurts Growth," *IMF Working Paper* (1998).

33 V. Tanzi, "Corruption around the World," *IMF Staff Papers*, 45, vol. 4 (1998): 559–593.

The CCI in order to ensure level playing field for the companies in a vast marketplace like India and exercise of powers vested under the act in case of threat of breach of competitive equilibrium has been armed with the powers vested in a Civil Court under the Code of Civil Procedure. By dint of this power CCI can summon or enforce attendance of any person and examine him on oath, requiring discovery and production of documents and receive evidence of affidavit. Also the body is entitled to pass inter-alia any or all of the following orders under section 27 of the act. The CCI can also, if the situation warrant may temporarily enforce restriction on any party from continuing with the alleged contravention, till enquiry is conducted to arrive at a meaningful finding.

The global marketers are required to understand the competition regulations prevailing in a country while discharging marketing functions. Take the case of global South Korean automobile giant Hyundai's spare parts marketing drive exclusively through its dealers in India. According to CCI this action was market distorting as the independent automobile repairers would not be able to compete with Hyundai authorised as spare parts and diagnostic equipments were only available to the exclusive company dealers. Hence, the after sales market of the automobile sector would not have the level playing field which in a sense deprives the automobile owners to make a free choice of selecting repairing centre between company authorised automobile centres and independent automobile repairers. The CCI found that such action of the Hyundai led to a situation where the customers were made to pay higher by distorting fair competition. The CCI levied a penalty of about Rs. 420 crores, calculated on the basis of 2% of its average turnover on Hyundai through their Indian operation as price for distorting the market competition and instructed to company for immediate change of spare parts distribution system.

CONFLICT RESOLUTION, DISPUTE SETTLEMENT, AND LITIGATION

Countries vary in their approach toward conflict resolution. Table 3-3 shows the number of practicing lawyers per 100,000 population in selected countries. The United States has more lawyers than any other country in the world and is arguably the most litigious nation on earth. In part, this is a reflection of the low-context nature of American culture, a spirit of confrontational competitiveness, and the absence

TABLE 3-3 Lawyers: An International Comparison[34]

Country	People per Lawyer
United States	265
Brazil	326
New Zealand	391
Spain	395
UK	401
Italy	488
Germany	593
France	1403

[34] http://wiki.answers.com/Q/What_country_in_the_world_has_most_lawyers_per_capita, Data for 2007-2008.

of one important principle of code law: the loser pays all court costs for all parties. The degree of legal cooperation and harmony in the EU is unique and stems in part from the existence of code law as a common bond. Other regional organizations have made far less progress toward harmonization.

Conflicts will inevitably arise in business anywhere, especially when different cultures come together to buy, sell, establish joint ventures, compete, and cooperate in global markets. For American companies, the dispute with a foreign party is frequently in the home-country jurisdiction. The issue can be litigated in the United States, where a company and its attorneys might be said to enjoy home court advantage. Litigation in foreign courts, however, becomes vastly more complex. This is due in part to differences in language, legal systems, currencies, and traditional business customs and patterns. In addition, problems arise from differences in procedures relating to discovery. In essence, discovery is the process of obtaining evidence to prove claims and determining which evidence may be admissible in which countries under which conditions. A further complication is the fact that judgments handed down in courts in another country may not be enforceable in the home country. For all these reasons, many companies prefer to pursue arbitration before proceeding to litigate.

Alternatives to Litigation for Dispute Settlement[35]

Extrajudicial, alternative approaches often provide a faster, easier, and less expensive way to resolve commercial disputes than litigation. Indeed, alternative approaches have a tradition that is centuries old. Chambers of trade and commerce first began to hear and resolve disputes as trade developed between different tribes or nations. Settlement of modern trade disputes takes various forms and occurs in many locations. Formal arbitration is one means of settling international business disputes outside the courtroom. Arbitration generally involves a hearing of all parties before a three-member panel. The result is usually a decision by which the parties agree in advance to abide. Courts of arbitration have long existed in London and Zurich. For decades, business arbitration has also been promoted through the Paris-based International Chamber of Commerce (ICC). The ICC recently modernized some of its older rules. However, because it is the best-known international business organization, it has the biggest backlog of cases. Thus, the ICC has gained a reputation for being slower, more expensive, and more cumbersome than some alternatives. The United Nations Convention on the Recognition and Enforcement of Foreign Arbitral Awards (also known as the New York Convention) has more than 50 signatories. The New York Convention facilitates arbitration when disputes arise, and signatories agree to abide by decisions reached through arbitration.

Some firms and lawyers, inexperienced in the practice of international commercial arbitration, have used standard boilerplate arbitration clauses in contracts that cover merger, severability, choice of law, and other issues. US companies may stipulate that arbitration will take place in the United States; companies in other countries may choose their home country courts. Arbitration can be a minefield due to the number of issues that must be addressed. For example, if the parties to a patent licensing agreement agree in the arbitration clause that the validity of the patent cannot be contested, such a provision may not be enforceable in some countries. In a disagreement, which country's laws will be used as the standard for validity?

---

[35] This section draws heavily on the work of Radway, Robert J., "United States Regulations and Acquisitions", 14 Vanderbilt Journal of Transnational Law 1981. Publication indicates that author is a practicing New York Attorney specializing in international law; formerly International Counsel to the McKee Corp. and Legal Advisor to the Council of the Americas.

Pursuing such an issue on a country-by-country basis would be inordinately time consuming. In addition, there is the issue of acceptance: By law, US courts must accept an arbitrator's decision in patent disputes; in other countries, however, there is no general rule of acceptance. To reduce delays relating to such issues, one expert suggests drafting arbitration clauses with as much specificity as possible. To the extent possible, for example, patent policies in various countries should be addressed; persons drafting arbitration clauses may also include a provision that all foreign patent issues will be judged according to the standard of home-country law. Another provision could forbid the parties from commencing separate legal actions in other countries. The goal is to help the arbitration tribunal zero in on the express intentions of the parties.[36]

As US involvement in global commerce grew dramatically during the post-World War II period, the American Arbitration Association (AAA) became recognized as a very effective institution within which to resolve disputes. Each year, the AAA uses mediation to help resolve thousands of disputes. The AAA has entered into cooperation agreements with the ICC and other global organizations to promote the use of alternative dispute resolution methods; it serves as the agent to administer arbitration in the United States under ICC auspices. In 1992, the AAA signed a cooperation agreement with China's Beijing Conciliation Center.

Other agencies for settling disputes include the Swedish Arbitration Institute of the Stockholm Chamber of Commerce. This agency frequently administered disputes between Western and socialist countries and has gained credibility for its even-handed administration. Other alternatives have proliferated in recent years. In addition to those mentioned, active centers for arbitration exist in Vancouver, Hong Kong, Cairo, Kuala Lumpur, Singapore, Buenos Aires, Bogotá, and Mexico City. The World Arbitration Institute was established in New York; in the United Kingdom, the Advisory, Conciliation, and Arbitration Service (ACAS) has achieved great success at handling industrial disputes. The International Council for Commercial Arbitration (ICCA) was established to coordinate the far-flung activities of arbitration organizations. The ICCA meets in different locations around the world every four years.

The United Nations Conference on International Trade Law (UNCITRAL) has also been a significant force in the area of arbitration. UNCITRAL rules have become more or less standard, as many of the organizations named previously have adopted them with some modifications. Many developing countries, for example, long held prejudices against the ICC, AAA, and other organizations in developed countries. Representatives of developing nations assumed that such organizations would be biased in favor of multinational corporations. Developing nations insisted on settlement in national courts, which was unacceptable to the multinational firms. This was especially true in Latin America, where the Calvo Doctrine required disputes arising with foreign investors to be resolved in national courts under national laws. The growing influence of the ICCA and UNCITRAL rules, coupled with the proliferation of regional arbitration centers, has contributed to changing attitudes in developing countries and has resulted in the increased use of arbitration around the world.

THE REGULATORY ENVIRONMENT

The regulatory environment of global marketing consists of a variety of agencies, both governmental and nongovernmental, that enforce laws or set guidelines for conducting business. These organizations/agencies address a wide range of marketing issues,

---

[36] Bruce Londa, "An Agreement to Arbitrate Disputes Isn't the Same in Every Language," *Brandweek* September 18, 1994, 18. See also John M. Allen, Jr. and Bruce G. Merritt, "Drafters of Arbitration Clauses Face a Variety of Unforeseen Perils," *National Law Journal,* 17, no. 33 (April 17, 1995): C6–C7.

including price control, valuation of imports and exports, trade practices, labeling, food and drug regulations, employment conditions, collective bargaining, advertising content, competitive practices, and so on. The decisions are binding and are carried out by the global marketers (see Box 3-5 regarding EU regulation for chemicals).[37]

BOX 3-5

Side Bar: EU Regulations on Chemicals

Registration, Evaluation, Authorisation and Restriction of Chemicals (REACH) is an European Union regulation enacted in 2006. REACH aims to improve the protection of human health and the environment through the better and earlier identification of the intrinsic properties of chemical substances. This is done by the four processes of REACH, namely the registration, evaluation, authorisation and restriction of chemicals. REACH also aims to enhance innovation and competitiveness of the EU chemicals industry.

REACH simply believes in "No data no market". It means that unless the company provides relevant data on the different parameters regarding the risk of use of the chemical and those data are analysed and assessed properly towards the impact on human life till then the products are not allowed to do business in EU countries. REACH, therefore, transfers the responsibility on industry to manage the risks from chemicals and to provide safety information on the substances. Manufacturers and importers are required to gather information on the properties of their chemical substances, which will allow their safe handling, and to register the information in a central database in the European Chemicals Agency (ECHA) in Helsinki. The Agency is the central point in the REACH system: it manages the databases necessary to operate the system, co-ordinates the in-depth evaluation of suspicious chemicals and is building up a public database in which consumers and professionals can find hazardous information.

The Regulation also calls for the progressive substitution of the most dangerous chemicals (referred to as "substances of very high concern") when suitable alternatives have been identified.

One of the main reasons for developing and adopting the REACH Regulation was that a large number of substances have been manufactured and placed on the market in Europe for many years, sometimes in very high amounts, and yet there is insufficient information on the hazards that they pose to human health and the environment. There is a need to fill these information gaps to ensure that industry is able to assess hazards and risks of the substances, and to identify and implement the risk management measures to protect humans and the environment.

Adapted from https://echa.europa.eu/regulations/reach/understanding-reach; https://echa.europa.eu/regulations/reach/evaluation, as accessed on 10 March 2017 at 2pm.

The influence of regulatory agencies is pervasive, and an understanding of how they operate is essential to protect business interests and advance new programs. For example, in the United States, the International Trade Commission administers the Tariff Act of 1930. Section 337 prohibits "unfair methods of competition" if the effect of this competition is to destroy or substantially injure an industry. To seek relief or defend access to the US market if challenged under this act, a company should retain the services of specialized legal talent, supported by technical expertise in patents and in international marketing. It is useful to call on the assistance of home-country diplomatic staff to assist and support the effort to obtain a favorable ruling.

[37] See Sergei A. Voitovich, "Normative Acts of International Economic Organizations in International Law Making," *Journal of World Trade* (August 1990): 21–38.

The European Union

The Treaty of Rome established the European Economic Community (EEC), the precursor to the EU. The treaty contains hundreds of articles, several of which are directly applicable to global companies and global marketers. Articles 30 to 36 establish the general policy referred to as "Free Flow of Goods, People, Capital, and Technology." Articles 85 and 86 contain competition rules, as amended by various directives of the EU Commission. These articles and directives constitute community law, which is somewhat analogous to US federal law.

The European Court of Justice, based in Luxembourg, hears disputes that arise among the 15 EU member nations on trade issues such as mergers, monopolies, and trade barriers. The court is also empowered to resolve conflicts between national law and EU law. In most cases, the latter supersedes national laws of individual European countries. Marketers must be aware, however, that national laws should always be consulted. National laws may be more strict than community law, especially in such areas as competition and antitrust. Community law is intended to harmonize, to the extent possible, national laws to promote the purposes defined in articles 30 to 36. The goal is to bring the lax laws of some member states up to designated minimum standards. However, more restrictive positions may still exist in some national laws.

The 1987 Single European Act amended the Treaty of Rome and provided strong impetus for the creation of a Single Market by December 31, 1992. Although technically the target was not completely met, approximately 85 percent of the new recommendations were implemented into national law by most member states by the target date, resulting in substantial harmonization.

One function of the European Union is to harmonize business regulations so as to facilitate business (See Box 3-6). Rather than conforming to individual country laws, a company now must follow the laws established by the legal arm that apply to all member countries. One law relates to product guarantees and became effective January 1, 2002. The EU countries agreed to a two-year guarantee on goods purchased. This quadrupled the guarantee period in Austria, Germany, Greece, Portugal, and Spain. In countries with longer guarantee periods (in the United Kingdom it is six years and in France and the Netherlands there are no limits), those time periods may be maintained.[38] Although harmonization is occurring, companies must comply with the laws of the individual countries.

BOX 3-6

Side Bar: EU Regulation on Food Products

European Union ensures that no sub standard food reaches EU countries by enacting regulation No 1169/2011. This regulation contains the provisions which the food businesses, food retailers and wholesalers must abide by in all stages of the food chain so that right type of food products can be made available to the consumers. By dint of the provisions of regulation number 1169/2011 the EU ensured that consumers also remain aware of the food products they are consuming so that there could be full proof system in place. The regulations made the food and beverage manufacturers responsible for:

[38] Michael Smith, "Accord on Product Guarantees," *Financial Times*, March 23, 1999, 2.

1. Manufacturers must display EU 1169/2011 compliant information on all product packaging. The directive specifies a list of mandatory information and details on how the information should be formatted—covering ingredients, allergens and nutritional values.
2. Manufacturers must provide the following information online to the consumers before purchase:

   a. The name of the food
   b. The list of ingredients
   c. Any ingredient or processing aid or derived from a substance or product causing allergies or intolerances used in the manufacture or preparation of a food and still present in the finished product, even if it is in an altered form
   d. The quantity of certain ingredients or categories of ingredients
   e. The net quantity of the food
   f. The date of minimum durability or the 'use by' date
   g. Any special storage conditions and/or conditions of use
   h. The name or business name and address of the food business operator.
   i. The country of origin or place of provenance.
   j. Instructions for use where it would be difficult to make appropriate use of the food in the absence of such instructions
   k. With respect to beverages containing more than 1.2% by volume of alcohol, the actual alcoholic strength by volume
   l. A nutrition declaration;

3. Retailers have a joint duty with manufacturer to ensure that food and beverage products retailed comply with this new legislation. Wherever required product information must be provided to the consumers at point of sale, be it in-store or online retailing. For more details refer to International Monetary Fund country outlook. http://www.imf.org/external/pubs/ft/wp/2016/wp16159.pdf.

World Trade Organisation as Regulator

World trade organisation (WTO) also plays a critical role as regulator in international trade. All countries have different specific regulations which can govern local businesses but when the stake holders are from different countries and a single country regulation is not enough to do the justice then international organisation like WTO can play a critical role as regulator. During 2010, Government of India under its Jawaharlal Nehru National Solar Mission (NSM) set an ambitious target of generating 100,000 MW of grid connected solar power by 2022 in India. The government also wanted to develop country's manufacturing capabilities of solar cell along with it so that at the peak of demand, the generation of solar power is not handicapped due to short supply of solar cells. Though internationally, countries like USA and China have the capacity to supply the product but indigenous production is required to avoid disruption of power generation due to causes like import delay, sudden price rise etc. So, a mandatory domestic content requirement (DCR) clause was included for global tender inviting participation of the solar power developers. This DCR clause put many global solar power developers on the back foot as materials used in the NSM must be manufactured in India and more importantly, India extended the DCR clause to include solar thin film technologies, where USA already had proficiency and hence had to set up production here. So, the DCR clause put US companies in a 'catch twenty-two' situation. If they agree to the DCR clause then they would be, in a sense, involved in a process of developing competitors for US company and if they do not then they would missing a huge business opportunity. During 2013, USA approached WTO with a complain that the DCR clause directly or indirectly disturbed the level playing field where US companies were pushed to the disadvantageous position to participate in the process of developing solar power in India. The WTO referred the case to its dispute settlement body to hear argument from both the sides and come to a conclusion. The Dispute Settlement Panel heard both sides and observed that mandatory DCR clause had violated WTO's National Treatment Clause. Under National treatment (GATT Article III) clause, WTO desires that members must not resort to discriminatory tactics between imports and domestic products. WTO, therefore, contented that the DCR clause was not tenable in this instant case. The observation of WTO in this case came as a direct blow to the optimistic plan of Government of India to slowly switch over from fossil fuel based electricity generation to clean solar energy and thereby stepping a bold step towards sustainable development.

ETHICAL ISSUES

Ethics, just as the legal environment, vary around the world. What is acceptable in one country may be considered unethical in another. In addition to the obvious moral questions, companies may suffer when negative publicity is generated. A case in point is the use of child labor or allegations of its use. Nike is well aware of this problem. Nike sources its goods in countries with low wages and poor labor regulations. Although Nike does not directly employ children in its overseas manufacturing, the sourcing agent may. A program has been established by Nike to monitor its suppliers but it is difficult when some locals may argue in favor of child labor. Regarding child labor in Pakistan, "trade bans on goods produced by child labor could have the unintended effect of forcing the children into other paid work at a lower wage"[39] and/or prostitution. The US Department of Labor has many publications on this specific issue.[40]

In order to do the right thing but also generate good publicity, companies can take an active approach to ethical issues. Reebok and Levi Strauss have done this by establishing standards that their contractors must follow, and they actively monitor results to ensure that standards are met.[41]

An increasing number of companies are addressing ethical issues. A recent survey of companies in 22 countries found that 78 percent of boards of directors were establishing ethical standards.[42] This is up significantly from 21 percent in 1987. The study also warns that regional differences can hinder effective implementation of any efforts.

Summary

The legal and political environment of global marketing is the set of governmental institutions, political parties, and organizations that are the expression of the people in the nations of the world. In particular, anyone engaged in global marketing should have an overall understanding of the importance of sovereignty to national governments. The political environment varies from country to country, and risk assessment is crucial. It is also important to understand a particular government's actions with respect to taxes, dilution of equity control, and expropriation.

The legal environment consists of laws, courts, attorneys, and legal customs and practices. The countries of the world can be broadly categorized in terms of common-law system or code (civil)-law system. The United States, United Kingdom, and the British

[39] Richard Adams, "Sanctions over Child Labor 'Can Backfire'," *Financial Times,* March 31, 1999, 4.

[40] U.S. Department of Labor, "The Apparel Industry and Codes of Conduct: A Solution to the International Child Labor Problem?" 1996.

[41] Philip Rosenzweig, "How Should Multinationals Set Global Workplace Standards?" Mastering Global Business Section of *Financial Times,* March 27, 1998, 11.

[42] "Global Ethic Codes," *The Wall Street Journal,* August 19, 1999, A1.

Commonwealth countries, which include Canada, Australia, New Zealand, the former British colonies in Africa, and India, are common-law countries; other countries are based on code law. Some of the most important legal issues pertain to establishment, jurisdiction, patents and trademarks, licensing, antitrust, and bribery. When legal conflicts arise companies can pursue the matter in court or use arbitration.

Corruption is a complex, global problem that depletes the economic, social, and environmental resources of a country and its citizens. Heightened awareness of the devastating costs of corruption in both the developed and developing nations of the world has facilitated efforts to combat it. Competition and short-term earnings pressure increase the temptation to engage in corrupt and other types of unethical behavior. The stakes are indeed very high: The impact of corruption scandals on global organizations have too often been the subject of sensational news stories during the past several years. Establishing a strategy in order to understand and confront the risks of corruption is a prerequisite to conducting business on a global scale.

The regulatory environment consists of agencies, both governmental and nongovernmental, that enforce laws or set guidelines for conducting business. Global marketing activities can be affected by a number of international or regional economic organizations; in Europe, for example, the EU makes laws governing member states. The WTO will have broad impact on global marketing activities in the years to come.

Although these three environments are complex, astute marketers plan ahead to avoid situations that might result in conflict, misunderstanding, or outright violation of national laws.

Discussion Questions

1. What is sovereignty? Why is it an important consideration in the political environment of global marketing?
2. The political risk scores for Taiwan and the United States were identical in June of 2011. Do you agree that these countries have an identical level of political risk? Why? Why not?
3. St. Ambrose said, "When you are in Rome live in the Roman style; when you are elsewhere live as they live elsewhere." Do you agree with his advice? Why? Why not?
4. Briefly describe some of the differences that relate to marketing between the legal environment of a country that embraces common law as opposed to a country that observes civil law.
5. Global marketers can avoid legal conflicts by understanding the reasons conflicts arise in the first place. Identify and describe several legal issues that relate to global commerce. What alternatives are available from a marketing perspective?
6. You are a sales representative of a multinational corporation traveling on business in West Africa. As you are leaving country X, the passport control officer at the airport tells you there will be a passport "processing" delay of one hour. You explain that your plane leaves in 30 minutes and the next plane out of the country does not leave for three days. You also explain how valuable your time is (at least $300 an hour) and that it is urgent that you catch the flight you have reserved. The official listens carefully to your appeal and then "suggests" that a contribution of $1,000 would definitely assure your passport clearance priority treatment, and considering how valuable your time is, it is quite a bargain.

   Would you comply with the "suggestion"? Why? Why not? If you would not comply, what would you do?

   If you comply with the suggestion, have you violated any laws? Explain.

   If the official requests $25, have you violated any laws?
7. "See you in court" is one way to respond when legal issues arise. What other approaches are possible?
8. If you were Nike, what would you do to prevent negative publicity regarding reports of unsafe factory conditions?

Suggested Readings

Albright, Katherine, and Grace Won. "Foreign Corrupt Practices Act." *American Criminal Law Review* (Spring 1993): 787.

Bagley, Jennifer M., Stephanie S. Glickman, and Elizabeth B. Wyatt. "Intellectual Property." *American Criminal Law Review,* 32 (Winter 1995): 457–479.

Chukwumerije, Okezie. *Choice of Law in International Commercial Arbitration.* Westport, CT: Quorum Books, 1994.

Clarke, Irvine III, Margaret Owens, and John B. Ford. "The Harmonization of Product Country Marking Statutes: Strategic Implications for International Marketers."

Journal of International Marketing, 7, no. 2 (1999): 81–103.

Dutta, Soumitra. "The Global Innovation Index 2011: Accelerating Growth and Development." INSEAD, 2011, www.globalinnovationindex.org/gii.

Epstein, M. J., and M. J. Roy. *Strategic Learning through Corporate Environmental Management: Implementing the ISO 14001 Standard.* INSEAD's Centre for the Management of Environmental Resources, 1997.

Fishbein, Bette K. *Germany, Garbage, and the Green Dot: Challenging the Throwaway Society.* New York: Inform, 1994.

Gillespie, Kate. "Middle East Response to the U.S. Foreign Corrupt Practices Act." *California Management Review,* 29 (1987): 9–31.

Graham, John L. "The Foreign Corrupt Practice Act: A New Perspective." *Journal of International Business Studies* (Winter 1984): 107–121.

Henisz, Witold J., and Bennet A. Zelner. "The Hidden Risks in Emerging Markets." *Harvard Business Review* (April 2010): 88–95.

Henry, Clement M., ed. "Special Issue: Islamic Banking." *Thunderbird International Business Review,* 41 (July–August and September–October 1999).

Jacoby, Neil H., Peter Nehemkis, and Richard Eells. *Bribery and Extortion in World Business.* New York: McMillan, 1977.

Katsh, Salem M., and Michael P. Dierks. "Globally, Trade Secrets Laws Are All Over the Map." *The National Law Journal,* 17 (May 8, 1995): C12–C14.

Krugman, Paul. *End This Depression Now!* New York: W. W. Norton & Company, 2012.

Nash, Marian Leich. "Contemporary Practice of the United States Relating to International Law." *American Journal of International Law,* 88 (October 1994): 719–765.

Ohmae, Kenichi. *The Borderless World.* New York: Harper Perennial, 1991.

Pines, Daniel. "Amending the Foreign Corrupt Practices Act to Include a Private Right of Action." *California Law Review* (January 1994): 185–229.

Reich, Robert B. "Government In Your Business." *Harvard Business Review* (July–August 2009): "94–99.

Sheng, Shibin, Kevin Zheng Zhou, and Julie Juan Li. "The Effects of Business and Political Ties on Firm Performance: Evidence from China." *Journal of Marketing,* 75, no.1 (January 2011).

Stiglitz, Joseph E. *Freefall: America, Free Markets, and the Sinking of the World Economy.* New York: W.W. Norton & Co., 2010.

Vogel, David. "The Globalization of Business Ethics: Why America Remains Distinctive." *California Management Review,* 35 (Fall 1992): 30–49.

Wilson, Ernest J. "How to Make a Region Innovative." *Strategy+Business* (Spring 2012): 20.

Zonis, Marvin, Dan Lefkovitz, and Sam Wilkin. *The Kimchi Matters: Global Business and Local Politics in a Crisis-Driven World.* B2B Books Agate Publishing, 2003.

VISIT THE WEBSITES

www.adb.org (Asian Development Bank)
www.eiu.com (Economist Intelligence Unit)
www.prsgroup.com (Political Risk Services)
www.beri.com (Business Environment Risk Intelligence)
www.icj-cij.org (International Court of Justice)
www.iccwbo.org (International Chamber of Commerce)
www.uncitral.org (United Nations Commission on International Trade Law)
www.adr.org (American Arbitration Association)

CHAPTER 4

The Global Cultural Environment[1]

I believe only in French culture, and regard everything else in Europe which calls itself "culture" as a misunderstanding. I do not even take the German kind into consideration.

—FRIEDRICH WILHELM NIETZSCHE, 1844–1900

I do not want my house to be walled in on all sides and my windows to be stuffed. I want the cultures of all the lands to be blown about my house as freely as possible. But I refuse to be blown off my feet by any.

—MOHANDAS K. "MAHATMA" GANDHI, 1869–1948

Learning Objectives

1. Describe the components of culture and society that affect global marketing (129–130).
2. Use Maslow's hierarchy of needs to explain cultural universals (131–132).
3. Compare and contrast cultural classification methods (134–136).
4. Discuss methods for improving cultural understanding and perception (138–143),
5. Explain the significance of environmental sensitivity to global marketing (148–150).
6. Discuss cross-cultural complications and possible solutions (152–153).

[1] This chapter was written by Professor Steven Burgess, Director and Professor of Marketing, Nelson Mandela Metropolitan University Business School, South Africa, and Warren J. Keegan. Copyright © 2012 Steven Burgess and Warren J. Keegan.

INTRODUCTION

The opening quote by the famous philosopher, Friedrich Nietzsche, is a reminder that culture has always been a source of disagreement and misunderstanding. What does Nietzsche mean when he says "culture"? As you will soon see, the meaning of culture to a global marketer is quite different than it was to Nietzsche, who is probably referring to art, literature, and perhaps even music in the preceding quote. All of these elements of culture are important, but as global marketers know, culture is about much more than art. The celebrated Indian spiritual and political leader, Mahatma Gandhi, refers to widely endorsed values and beliefs that guide one's actions in life. Culture comprises values, beliefs, habits, norms, roles, symbols, signs, and behaviors. It informs shared templates that people within groups use to interpret and respond to other people, their environment, and events in life and the institutions. When global marketers refer to culture, they refer to the formal and informal institutions in which cultural systems are preserved and communicated and the consumption-relevant behaviors through which culture is expressed.[2]

In Europe, where scones, croissants, and strudels have long been the pride of bakers and pastry chefs, trend-conscious consumers have started gobbling up American-style baked goods. It seems the Europeans are discovering what Americans have known all along: in addition to being tasty, brownies, muffins, and cookies are perfectly suited to on-the-go lifestyles that include snacking while traveling on the metro or riding a bicycle. Also, American baked goods have a shelf life of more than one day, unlike many traditional European baked goods such as fresh cream tarts. European bakers, many of whom regard pastries from across the Atlantic as inferior, had to make some adjustments to accommodate changing taste buds. As Bernard M. Schapiro of Millie's Foods Ltd. in Britain recalls, "It wasn't an easy sell. Here biscuits [cookies] are hard, and you don't find soft cookies. The perception was that it was underbaked."

American companies have also experienced culture shock. While British consumers snapped up soft, moist Otis Spunkmeyer muffins, the American company's managers soon discovered that the word *spunk* is slang for "semen" in Britain and other countries. After the disc jockey of a national radio show asked on the air, "Who's going to eat a product with a name like that?" the company sent him a free sample. The result was favorable publicity in the form of an on-air endorsement for the goodies. Now some bakeries that sell the muffins put stickers reading "American Muffin" over the offending word. In the final analysis, as Heather McEvoy of the Colorado Cookie Company points out, "A good pastry is a good pastry no matter where it comes from and no matter what country it's sold in. Any company making good pastries will have a market in Europe."

The warm reception in Europe for American baked goods shows that many products can achieve success outside the home-country cultural environment. This chapter focuses on the social and cultural forces that shape and affect individual and corporate behavior in the marketplace. The conceptual orientation of this chapter and this book is that the cultures of the world are characterized by both differences and similarities.

---

[2]For example, Steven Michael Burgess and Jan-Benedict E. M. Steenkamp, "Marketing Renaissance: Research in Emerging Markets Advances Marketing Science and Practice," *International Journal of Research in Marketing,* 23, no. 4 (2006); Cheryl Nakata and K. Sivakumar, "Instituting the Marketing Concept in a Multinational Setting: The Role of National Culture," *Journal of the Academy of Marketing Science,* 29, no. 3 (2001); P. Christopher Earley and Soon Ang, *Cultural Intelligence: Individual Interactions across Cultures* (Stanford, CA: Stanford University Press, 2003); Lismen L. M. Chan, Margaret A. Shaffer, and Ed Snape, "In Search of Sustained Competitive Advantage: The Impact of Organizational Culture, Competitive Strategy and Human Resource Management Practices on Firm Performance," in *International Journal of Human Resource Management* (Routledge, 2004).

Thus, the task of the global marketer is twofold. Marketers must be prepared to recognize and understand the differences between cultures and then incorporate this understanding into the marketing planning process so that appropriate strategies and marketing programs are adapted. At the same time, marketers should take advantage of shared cultural characteristics and avoid unneeded and costly adaptations of the marketing mix. Cultural similarities provide a basis for relatively standardized marketing strategies. Consider how global adoption of personal computers and mobile handheld devices has produced similarities in the style, format, and use of text and numbers across cultures.

Another fact about culture is that it constantly changes and evolves. At the beginning of the twentieth century, there was a culture of mistrust and ethnocentrism in Europe, which was a fundamental reason for the horror of World War I. At the beginning of the twenty-first century, the culture of Western Europe embraced the new European Union. Old suspicions and mistrust have been replaced with cooperation and integration. In the twenty-first century, the convergence of cultures could be enormously accelerated by the rapid expansion of the Internet and digitally enabled communications, information technology, and mobile telephony, including video and real-time photo sharing. Marketing communications including advertising, promotion, and entertainment as well as transactions have seen a radical shift to these mediums and platforms.

Global marketers must recognize and deal with the differences in the social and cultural environments of world markets. This chapter focuses on the important differences in world markets and the equally important similarities that express the fact of cultural universals. To help marketers better understand social and cultural dynamics in the global marketplace, several useful analytical approaches are explained. These include Maslow's hierarchy, Hofstede's cultural typology, the self-reference criterion, and environmental sensitivity. This chapter offers specific examples of the impact of culture and society on the marketing of both industrial and consumer products. The chapter ends with suggested solutions to cross-cultural difficulties and a review of cross-cultural training procedures currently being used in global companies.

DEFINING CULTURE

Culture as a subject has been studied by the anthropologists in depth since 17th century and has put forward several important understandings. However, one of the best understandings for the use of marketing practitioners came from Anthropologist Prof. Geert Hofstede when a comprehensive study was conducted by him during the period 1967 to 1973 at the global level. Prof Hofstede covered more than 70 countries to understand employee morale and cultural underpinnings. Later, he extended the same study to include more countries and published his understanding of culture in the form of a book.

According to him, "Culture is the collective programming of the mind which distinguishes the member of one group or category of people from another". Possibly, this one of the best definitions of culture for use of the marketing practitioners as it provides a very concise but easily understandable meaning. Cross cultural psychologist, Michael Bond provided another very comprehensive definition as follows.

> *Culture* is a shared system of beliefs (what is true); values (what is important); expectations, especially about scripted behavioral sequences (patterns of behavior); and behavior meanings (what is implied by engaging in a given action) developed by a group over time to provide the requirements of communal life (food and water, protection against the elements, security, belonging, social appreciation, and

> the exercise of one's skills) in a particular geographical niche. This shared system enhances communication of meaning and coordination of actions among a culture's members by reducing uncertainty and anxiety through making its members' behavior predictable, understandable, acceptable, and valuable.[3]

Culture includes both conscious and unconscious values, ideas, attitudes, and symbols that shape human behavior. Culture is transmitted from one generation to the next. In this sense, culture does not include one-time solutions to unique problems, or passing fads and styles.

In addition to agreeing that culture is learned, not innate, most anthropologists share two additional views. First, all facets of culture are interrelated: influence or change one aspect of a culture and everything else is affected. Second, because it is shared by the members of a group, culture defines the boundaries between different groups.[4]

Culture consists of learned responses to recurring situations. The earlier these responses are learned, the more difficult they are to change. Taste and preferences for food and drink, for example, represent learned responses that are highly variable from culture to culture and can have a major impact on consumer behavior. Preference for color is culturally influenced as well. For example, although green is a highly regarded color in Muslim countries, it is associated with disease in some Asian countries. White, usually associated with purity and cleanliness in the West, can signify death in Asian countries. Red is a popular color in most parts of the world (often associated with full flavor, passion, or virility); however, it is poorly received in some African countries.[5] Of course, there is no inherent attribute to any color of the spectrum; all associations and perceptions regarding color arise from culture.

Attitudes toward whole classes of products can also be a function of culture. For example, in the United States, consumers have a cultural predisposition for product innovations that have a "gadgetry" quality. Thus, the electric knife and can opener, the electric toothbrush, the Water-Pik (for cleaning between teeth before brushing), and a host of other "labor-saving" small appliances find ready market acceptance. There is unquestionably a smaller predisposition to purchase such products in other developed markets such as Europe.

This difference is a result of cultural differences. As we noted in the last chapter, income levels also influence consumer behavior and attitudes around the world. Indeed, a basic question that must be answered by marketers who want to understand or predict behavior is, "How much do social and cultural factors influence behavior independent of income levels?" Sometimes the influence is strong. For example, US companies introduced fluffy, frosted cake mixes in the United Kingdom where cake is eaten at tea time with the fingers rather than as a dessert with a fork. Green Giant Foods attempted to market corn in Europe where the prevailing attitude is that corn is a grain fed to hogs, not people. In both instances, cultural differences resulted in market failures.

Cultures evolve in response to ecological, economic, technological, and sociopolitical influences.[6] Cultural evolution can produce convergence and fragmentation. *Cultural convergence* occurs when cultures become more similar. Convergence toward

---

[3] Michael Harris Bond, "A Cultural-Psychological Model for Explaining Differences in Social Behavior: Positioning the Belief Construct," in *Culture and Behavior: The Ontario Symposium, Volume 10*, ed. Richard M. Sorrentino et al. (New York: Psychology Press, 2005).

[4] Edward T. Hall, *Beyond Culture* (Garden City, NY: Anchor Books, 1977), 16.

[5] Richard R. Still and John S. Hill, "Multinational Product Planning: A Meta Market Analysis," *International Marketing Review* (Spring 1985): 60.

[6] Dana L. Alden, Jan-Benedict E. M. Steenkamp, and Rajeev Batra, "Consumer Attitudes Toward Marketplace Globalization: Structure, Antecedents, and Consequences," *International Journal of Research in Marketing* 23, no. 3 (2006).

a global culture is promoted by factors such as globalized media, international travel, regional unification, standardized business processes and techniques, urbanization, and rising levels of formal education and literacy. Marketers can respond to cultural convergence with global or regional marketing strategies. Globally, the brand positioning of Coca-Cola and Levi Strauss emphasize youthful exuberance and excitement,[7] which is expressed in ways that are appropriate for regional cultures.

Cultural fragmentation occurs when population segments within a country diverge in culture. When cultures fragment, microcultures with different purchase and consumption preferences may emerge. This may be especially true in emerging markets, where rapid change typically contributes to cultural fragmentation. Emerging markets can be thought of as having two main segments.[8] In the *mass-market segment*, formal education and household income are low. Access to globalized media is relatively low. Culture emphasizes social connectedness and responsibilities that have been forged in generations of subsistence living. Letter writing is a popular way to stay in touch and maintain close social relationships. In the Philippines, Smart Communications appeals to this culturally motivated behavior by promoting its inexpensive SMS text-messaging service as a substitute for letter writing. The appeal of the SMS messaging is very different for the much smaller *urban-elite segment*. They have levels of formal education, household income, and living standards similar to those of high-income countries. Access to globalized media is higher and culture is more likely to be converging toward individual autonomy and independence. SMS messages provide a substitute for telephone calls.[9]

Nevertheless, the demand for convenience foods, luxury consumer products, electronic products, disposable products, and soft drinks in the United States, Europe, Asia, Africa, and the Middle East suggests that most consumer products have broad, almost universal, appeal. As communications continue to shrink the world, more and more products will be marketed and consumed globally. This implies that an important characteristic of culture—that it defines boundaries between people—will not limit the global reach of companies that want to extend their operations globally. This does not suggest, however, that these companies can ignore cultural factors. The fact that there is a global market for a product does not mean that you can approach the market in different countries identically. Cultural sensitivity to differences spells the difference between global success and failure.

If culture is a shared set of beliefs, values, expectations, and behaviors developed by a group, how does it affect an individual's behavior? Culture can also be thought of as having multiple layers, like an onion (see Figure 4-1).

The outside layer, *collective reality*, reflects the ecological, economic, and sociopolitical factors that determine the development of institutions within a culture and the core cultural ideas regarding what is good, what is moral, what is the self, and what is the group. Products can be symbols of individual or collective reality. *Sociopsychological processes* exert influence on the individual's reality at the next layer. These include formal and informal regulative and socioeconomic systems, customs, norms, practices, media, and reference group influences that reflect and promote the core ideas of society

---

[7] Youth may share cultural values around the world, see Dannie K. Kjelgaard and Søren Askegaard, "The Globalization of Youth Culture: The Global Youth Segment as Structures of Common Difference," *Journal of Consumer Research* 33 (September 2006).

[8] Rajeev Batra, "Marketing Issues and Challenges in Transitional Economies," *Journal of International Marketing* 5, no. 4 (1997).

[9] Steven Michael Burgess and Pfavai Nyajeka, "Market Orientation and Performance in Low-Income Countries: The Case of Zimbabwean Retailers," in *Advances in International Management*, José Antonio Rosa and Madhubalan Viswanathan, eds. (Elsevier, 2007); Rajeev Batra et al., "Effects of Brand Local and Nonlocal Origin on Consumer Attitudes in Developing Countries," *Journal of Consumer Psychology* 9, no. 2 (2000).

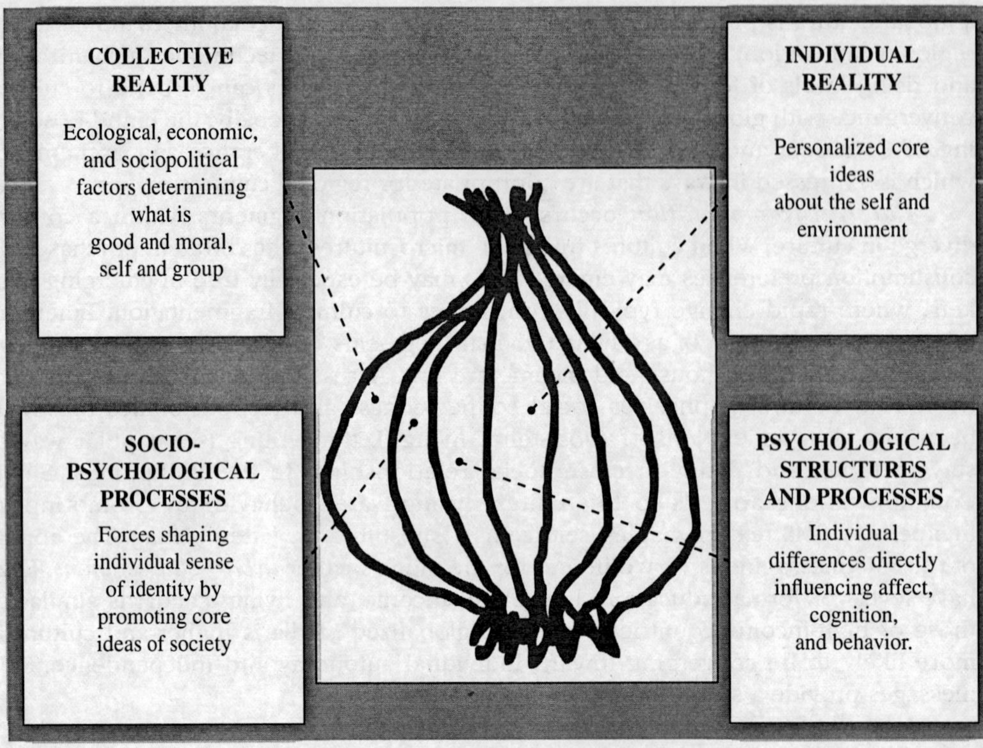

FIGURE 4-1 Culture Layers

and shape the individual's sense of identity. *Individual reality* is shaped by recurrent episodes in daily life, which personalize the core ideas communicated by the external world. Through a process of learning, individual reality helps shape psychological structures, such as needs, personality traits, values, attitudes, and beliefs that affect behavior by directing cognitive and hedonic processing and choices of appropriate behaviors. At the central layer, the individual's *psychological structures and processes* direct behavior.[10] Marketing strategies often relate to multiple layers of culture. For example, marketers of nutritional and nonprescription health-care products often attempt to stimulate consumption directly, with consumer marketing programs, and indirectly, through marketing activities targeting influential health-care professionals, educators, and government policy-makers.

Products, services, and marketing activities can play an important role in the creation and consumption of meaning in life.[11] Consumers evaluate two types of meaning when making purchase and consumption decisions. Consumers derive *utilitarian meaning* from products high in utilitarian value, which refers to a product's functional or physical qualities. They derive *hedonic meaning* from products high in hedonic value, which refers to the aesthetic and emotional properties and associations with personal, social, or cultural identity. Thus, consumer choices are part of a larger cultural process of creating and consuming meaning.

---

[10] These four layers are described by Alan Page Fiske et al., "The Cultural Matrix of Social Psychology," in *The Handbook of Social Psychology*, Daniel T. Gilbert, Susan T. Fiske, and Gardner Lindzey, eds. (Boston: McGraw-Hill, 1998).

[11] Søren Askegaard, Dannie Kjelgaard, and Eric J. Arnould, "Reflexive Culture's Consequences," in *Beyond Hofstede: Cultural Frameworks for Global Marketing and Management*, Cheryl A. Nakata, ed. (New York: Palgrave Macmillan, 2009).

Anthropologist Grant McCracken theorizes that meaning transfers *from the culturally constituted world to consumer goods* through advertising promotional communications, fashion systems, and word-of-mouth communication.[12] It is then transferred *from consumer goods to consumers*, often through consumer rituals. Rituals refer to expressive, symbolic behaviors, which are comprised of many activities that occur in a fixed, episodic sequence and often with formality, seriousness, and inner-intensity.[13] Consumers use *possession rituals* to display, discuss, reflect, or maintain consumer goods, for the purpose of extracting qualities associated with the object. Young, globally aware consumers proudly display the Abercrombie and Fitch brand on their clothing around the world, despite the fact that Abercrombie and Fitch marketing operations are limited to the United States, London, and two provinces in Canada. Premium price beverages enjoy higher market share in restaurants, nightclubs, and bars where consumers often display consumption of prestige beverage brands as part of a nonverbal communication to others. During possession rituals, brands may become integral parts of a consumer's identity.[14]

Constituents of Culture

Culture of any country is constituted by seven ingredients. They are (1) Religion (2) Values and Attitudes (3) Aesthetics (4) Social Organization (5) Material Culture (6) Language (7) Education.

RELIGION Religion is an important ingredient of cultural factor. It has strong influence on collective thinking of many people in the same identical way. The believers of the same religion worship together, read the same religious books, follow the same tradition etc., which allow them to have same behaviour in identical situation. Religion can strongly influence people's attitudes, values and behaviours at both the individual and societal levels. In this way people from same religion are expected to have the same cultural understanding.

VALUES AND ATTITUDES Human values are enduring beliefs which people hold for lifetime without allowing them to be challenged by other beliefs. People are so deeply engrossed in values that their actions and reactions in the social space would be identical.

AESTHETICS "Aesthetics" in general sense indicates towards a sense of appreciation of beauty that exist in a person. A group of people from same culture demonstrate a sense of appreciation for a thing, place and specific time in a year while people from other culture may not be able to appreciate those in the same way or with the same intensity.

SOCIAL ORGANIZATION Social organizations are representative of people's values and attitude. A group of people form a social organisation so that they can perform their respective roles assigned by the society. Hence the types and nature of social organisations varies from culture to culture. Social organization in a particular culture is formed by the people of the society so that members of society can carry out assigned social roles in line with the common mission that the society wants to achieve.

---

[12] See Grant McCracken, *Culture and Consumption: New Approaches to the Symbolic Character of Consumer Goods and Activities* (Bloomington, IN: Indiana University Press, 1988).

[13] Dennis W. Rook, "The Ritual Dimension of Consumer Behavior," *Journal of Consumer Research* 12, no. 3 (1985).

[14] For example, see Jennifer L. Aaker and Bernd H. Schmitt, "Culture-Dependent Assimilation and Differentiation of The Self: Preferences for Consumption Symbols in the United States and China," *Journal of Cross-Cultural Psychology* 32, no. 5 (2001).

MATERIAL CULTURE Refers to how people adopt and adapt to the technology in a material sense. The adoption of technology and adaptation of the same in different walks of life happens differently for different groups of people. People of same culture adopt and adapt technology in a similar way.

LANGUAGE The most important characteristics of culture is that it is learned, shared and interrelated. People from the same society learnt different facets of culture from other members. The learning, thereafter, are shared among the other members of the society and in this way people make the next generation understand the different facets of their culture. So generation after generation people of the same culture retain their uniqueness. This knowledge and understanding and the development process, is not unrelated but rather highly interrelated so that generations after generations, the cultural uniqueness is retained. In the process of learning and the sharing of common culture specific understanding, the language spoken by the people acts as the carrier. Therefore, the language spoken by the group of people of the same culture is the main carrier of culture.

EDUCATION Urge for education prevailing in a society or how the society encourages its people to be educated indicates values and belief prevailing in the society. As the time progresses, these values and beliefs spreads across the people living in the society and make the society unique with an identity as learning society. The society, therefore, would have its cultural identity and every person living in the society would learn in a similar way and behave in a particular fashion.

National Culture

The very characteristics of culture that it is learnt, shared and interrelated promotes national culture. People of a country are living within the four boundaries which are referred as international borders. The international borders have dampening effect on free and speedy flow of information. The speed and freeness that information has while flowing within a country naturally that speed and freeness information would not have while crossing international boundaries. Therefore, people living in a country learn in an identical way, share those learning with other countrymen more frequently, giving rise to a common set of values and beliefs. This process of learning and sharing continues for generations after generations constituting a national culture which is unique to a particular country. This paves way for development of national culture of a country which is evident from the fact that every country has its own national culture, and in accordance with that culture, citizens of that country behaves. For example, American culture promotes individualistic behaviour whereas Chinese culture promotes collectivist behaviour.

CULTURE AND GLOBAL BUSINESS

Since culture is a collective programming of human mind so it is important that marketers must understand the cultural underpinning of the prospective consumers before placing the product before them. How a consumer would think, develop perception, process information released by company led marketing communication, make a decision to buy a product or service depends upon the cultural influence. Since global marketers operate in different country markets so they must understand the cultural uniqueness of the prospective consumers living in the country (Table 4-1). Marketing is a people oriented subject and hence it is very important for the global marketers to understand culture led consumer behaviour. A good understanding of consumer behaviour would allow marketers to position the product for the particular segment. Full understanding of expected behaviour of targeted consumer in a culturally dictated way provides marketing advantage.

TABLE 4-1 Hofstede Index Value of 20 Countries with Low Masculinity Index

Sl. No.	Countries	Masculinity Index	Power Distance Index	Individualism index	Uncertainty Avoidance Index
1	Sweden	5	31	71	29
2	Norway	8	31	69	50
3	Iceland	10	30	60	50
4	Sri Lanka	10	80	35	45
5	Netherlands	14	38	80	53
6	Denmark	16	18	74	23
7	Slovenia	19	71	27	88
8	Costa Rica	21	35	15	86
9	Finland	26	33	63	59
10	Chile	28	63	23	86
11	Estonia	30	40	60	60
12	Portugal	31	63	27	100
13	Bhutan	32	94	52	28
14	Thailand	34	64	20	64
15	Russia	36	93	39	95
16	Guatemala	37	95	6	100
17	Suriname	37	85	47	92
18	Uruguay	38	61	36	100
19	South Korea	39	60	18	85
20	Bulgaria	40	70	30	85

Source: https://geert-hofstede.com/national-culture.html

The Search for Cultural Universals

An important quest for the global marketer is to discover cultural universals. A universal is a mode of behavior existing in all cultures. Universal aspects of the cultural environment represent opportunities for global marketers to standardize some or all elements of a marketing program. A partial list of cultural universals, taken from cultural anthropologist George P. Murdock's classic study, includes the following: athletic sports, body adornment, cooking, courtship, dancing, decorative art, education, ethics, etiquette, family feasting, food taboos, language, marriage, mealtime, medicine, mourning, music, property rights, religious rituals, residence rules, status differentiation, and trade.[15] The astute global marketer often discovers that much of the apparent cultural diversity in the world turns out to be different ways of accomplishing the same thing.

[15] George P. Murdock, "The Common Denominator of Culture," in *The Science of Man in the World Crisis*, Ralph Linton, ed. (New York: Columbia University Press, 1945), 145.

Music provides one example of how these universals apply to marketing. Music is part of all cultures, accepted as a form of artistic expression and source of entertainment. However, music is also an art form characterized by widely varying styles. Therefore, although background music can be used effectively in broadcast commercials, the type of music appropriate for a commercial in one part of the world may not be acceptable or effective in another part. A jingle might utilize a bossa nova rhythm for Latin America, a New Orleans jazz or rock rhythm for North America, and "high life" for Africa. Music, then, is a cultural universal that global marketers can adapt to cultural preferences in different countries or regions. It is no surprise that the music business is going global; global marketers in the business are always alert to the potential of extending a successful experience across national boundaries.

Increasing travel and digital communications mean that many national attitudes toward style in clothing, color, music, food, and drink are converging. The globalization of culture has been capitalized upon, and even significantly accelerated, by companies that have seized opportunities to find customers around the world.

Communication and Negotiation

Although English continues to grow in importance as the language of international travel and business, understanding and speaking the language of a country is an invaluable asset in understanding the country's culture. There is an often repeated maxim: You can buy in your home-country language, but you need to learn your customers' language to sell.

The ability to communicate in our own language is, as most of us have learned, not an easy task. Whenever languages and culture change, additional communication challenges will present themselves. For example, "yes" and "no" are used in an entirely different way in Japanese than in Western languages. This has caused much confusion and misunderstanding. In English, the answer "yes" or "no" to a question is based on whether the answer is affirmative or negative. In Japanese, this is not so. The answer "yes" or "no" may indicate whether or not the answer affirms or negates the question. For example, in Japanese the question, "Don't you like meat?" would be answered "yes" if the answer is negative, as in, "Yes, I don't like meat." The word *wakarimashita* means both "I understand" and "I agree." To avoid misunderstandings, Westerners must learn to distinguish which interpretation is correct in terms of the entire context of the conversation.

The challenges presented by nonverbal communication are perhaps even more formidable. For example, Westerners doing business in the Middle East must be careful not to reveal the soles of their shoes to hosts or pass documents with the left hand. In Japan, bowing is an important form of nonverbal communication that has many nuances. People who grow up in the West tend to be verbal, whereas those from the East are more nonverbal. Not surprisingly, there is a greater expectation in the East that people will pick up nonverbal cues and understand intuitively without being told.[16] Westerners must pay close attention not only to what they hear but also to what they see when conducting business in such cultures.

Social Behavior[17]

There are a number of social behaviors and comments that have different meanings in other cultures. For example, Americans generally consider it impolite to mound food on a plate, make noises when eating, and belch. However, some Chinese feel it is polite to take a portion of every food served and consider it evidence of satisfaction to belch.

---

[16] See Anthony C. diBenedetto, Miriko Tamate, and Rajan Chandran, "Developing Strategy for the Japanese Marketplace," *Journal of Advertising Research* (January–February 1992): 39–48.

[17] Adapted from Gary Bonvillian and William A. Nowlin, "Cultural Awareness: An Essential Element of Doing Business Abroad," *Business Horizons*, 37, no. 6 (November 1994): 44.

Other social behaviors, if not known, will place the international traveler at a disadvantage. For example, in Saudi Arabia, it is an insult to question a host about the health of his spouse. In Korea, both hands should be used when passing objects to another person. Also in Korea, formal introductions are very important. In both Japan and Korea, ranks and titles are expected to be used in addressing hosts. In the United States, there is not a clear rule on this behavior, except in select fields such as the armed forces or medicine. In Indonesia, it is considered rude to point at another person with a finger. However, one may point with the thumb or gesture with the chin.

When greeting someone, it is appropriate in most countries to shake hands. In some countries the greeting includes a handshake and more. In Japan, a handshake may be followed by a bow, going as low and lasting as long as that of the senior person. In Brazil, Korea, Indonesia, China, and Taiwan, a slight bow is also appropriate.

In some countries, the greeting involves more contact. For instance, in Venezuela, close friends greet each other with a full embrace and a hearty pat on the back; in Indonesia, a social kiss is in vogue, and a touching of first the right then the left cheek as one shakes hands. In Malaysia, close friends grasp with both hands; in South Africa, people traditionally shake hands, followed by a clench of each other's thumbs and another handshake.

In most countries, addressing someone as Mr., Mrs., Miss, or Ms. is acceptable, but this is certainly not universal. Monsieur, Madame, and Mademoiselle are preferred in France, Belgium, and Luxembourg, while Señor, Señora, and Señorita are the norm in Spain and Spanish-speaking Latin America. It is sometimes the case that conversation occurs as greetings are exchanged. Greetings when meeting vary from country to country. In Sweden, the greeting is "goddag"; in the United Kingdom it's "how do you do"; in Tanzania it is "jambo bwana" or "jambo mama"; and in Israel it is "shalom." In many countries, men do not shake hands with a woman unless she extends her hand first. In India, women, or a man and a woman, greet each other by placing the palms of their hands together and bowing slightly, and in Mexico simply by a slight bow. In some countries it is not advisable for men to touch or talk alone with a woman.

Religion as a Driver of Culture

Culture is shared, learnt and interrelated. Religion is one of the important drivers for culture to be shared amongst a group of people. Therefore, people of same religion can have certain types of attitudes, values and behaviors. Every religion periodically, observes certain rituals which are important carrier of cultural values. People participating in the rituals are expected to learn from each other about their values and share those with others of similar faith. In this way, it spreads across a large number of people from the same religious community. For example, people of Jewish community tend to be more innovative or people of Hindu community tend to be more liberal in accepting understanding of other religion. In this way, by cultural uniqueness, people living in the world can be divided into different cultural groups in accordance with their religion. There are about one hundred different religions across the countries of the world and dominant of them being Christianity, Islam, Hinduism, Buddhism and Judaism. Christians are 33.32% (of which Roman Catholics 16.99%, Protestants 5.78%, Orthodox 3.53%, Anglicans 1.25%), Muslims 21.01%, Hindus 13.26%, Buddhists 5.84%, Sikhs 0.35%, Jews 0.23%, Baha'is 0.12%, other religions 11.78%, non-religious 11.77%, atheists 2.32%[18]). Global marketers find it useful to track cultural values that emanates out of the religion of the different target customers. As values gives rise to attitude and attitude is responsible for human behavior, so marketer's intents to understand these culture backed behavior before devising marketing programme.

[18] The CIA Fact Sheet 2007 estimate.

For example, **McDonald's**, the American hamburger and fast food restaurant chain, well understood culture of Jewish people in the matter of food preference. The food can be non-kosher due to the presence of ingredients derived from non-kosher animals. The Jewish people do have a strong reservation towards non kosher foods. So, the company went for attracting Jewish people towards the 'Kosherfoods' for the followers that conform to the rules of the Jewish religion. Another Kentucky-based American company KFC, known for its range of chicken fillets and burgers, well understood the culture backed preference of Hindu community in terms of vegetarian foods. In a very smart move, the company unveiled a segregated vegetarian menu along with a strong marketing communication about its inclination to serve vegetarian offerings in India. It is in Hindu culture to purchase gold ornaments heavily a few days before the worshipping of goddess Kali as they believe that such act would bring prosperity to them. Gold ornaments marketers make their market offering in accordance with the preference of the Hindu women in India. The Indians, in general, like to purchase vehicle in religiously auspicious days and car companies take advantage of this belief by framing a numerable marketing events during these days. Different foreign automobile companies also ready their plan and release marketing communication to take advantage of culture backed behavior of Indian consumer.

Standardized Cultural Classifications

In global marketing, cultural analysis traditionally has focused on standardized cultural classification of countries based on values.[19] Strictly speaking, the dimensions on which countries are classified by Hofstede, Inglehart, Trompenaars, and Project Globe are derived from values, beliefs, norms, moral obligation duties, needs, desires, interests, identifications, wants, goals, preferences, pleasures, likes, interpretations of life events, and many other concepts. This is an historical artifact of early borrowing from sociology, where values can include "anything that is preferable."[20] However, studies showing strong links between values and consumer behavior draw on a psychological definition of values.[21] Beginning in the 1980s, social psychologists such as Rokeach and Schwartz began making rapid advances that stimulated extensive marketing research. Social psychologists define *values* as enduring, centrally held beliefs that pertain to goals in life (i.e., desirable end-states and modes of conduct), transcend specific objects and situations, and guide attention, comprehension, and the selection or evaluation of people, behavior, and events in life.[22]

As fundamental motives that cognitively transform human needs and core elements of personality, values are relevant to just about any behavior that interests marketers. In the consumer context, values affect every stage of the consumer decision process, including information processing.[23] In the organizational context, values

---

[19] Jan-Benedict E. M. Steenkamp, and Frenkel Ter Hofstede, "International Market Segmentation: Issues and Perspectives," *International Journal of Research in Marketing* 19, no. 3 (2002).

[20] Steven Hitlin and Jane Allyn Piliavin, "Values: Reviving a Dormant Concept," *Annual Review of Sociology* 30 (2004): 359–393; Robin M. Williams, "Change and Stability in Values and Values Systems: A Sociological Perspective," in *Understanding Human Values: Individual and Societal*, M. Rokeach, ed. (New York: Free Press, 1979), 15–44.

[21] Steven Michael Burgess, "Personal Values and Consumer Research: An Historical Perspective," in *Research in Marketing*, Jagdish N. Sheth, ed. (Greenwich, Connecticut: JAI Press, 1992).

[22] See Shalom H. Schwartz et al., "Extending the Cross-Cultural Validity of the Theory of Basic Human Values with a Different Method of Measurement," *Journal of Cross-Cultural Psychology* 32, no. 5 (2001); Shalom H. Schwartz, "Value Priorities and Behavior: Applying a Theory of Integrated Value Systems," in *The Psychology of Values: The Ontario Symposium*, C. Seligman, J. M. Olson, and M. P. Zanna, eds. (Hillsdale, NJ: Lawrence Erlbaum Associates, 1996).

[23] Reviewed by Burgess, "Personal Values and Consumer Research"; Wagner A. Kamakura and Jose Afonso Mazzon, "Value Segmentation: A Model for the Measurement of Values and Value Systems," *Journal of Consumer Research* 18 (September 1991).

relate to sources of guidance used when making sense of the world, rule of law, preferences for corporate governance, reward systems, and many other behaviors that influence marketing success.[24]

We now discuss several important cultural classification schemes that are used in marketing, discussing the cultural value orientations theory of Schwartz and the social axioms theory of Leung and Bond in greatest detail because of their firm grounding in theory and rigorous validation by collaborative research teams in many countries. We begin with Hofstede's seminal cultural theory.

Hall's Cultural Classification

Surely an attempt by anthropologist, Edward T. Hall, way back in 1960s, helped the cause of global marketers in understanding the cultural stereotypes of the different countries of the world. Hall made his understanding of culture well known when he published his book "Beyond Culture" during 1976. He came out with two general terms, "high context" and "low context" to differentiate the cultural stereotyping that exist in different countries of the world. According to him, high context countries are those where people are more closely knitted in the form of a society over a long period of time. They are culturally attuned to a type of behaviour which is not explicit but implicit because most members know what to do and what to think which derived out of a long term association in the form of a coherent society. Opposite to this are countries where low context culture prevails. Low context culture refers to those types of societies where people are not closely knitted and hence they require to spell out explicitly different motives behind their behaviour. For example, Japan, China, Korea, Arabic countries are high-context culture countries whereas USA, Germany, Sweden, etc., are low context culture countries.

Hofstede's National Culture Dimensions

Geert Hofstede proposed the first overarching theory of national culture and launched a rapidly expanding body of cross-cultural research.[25] Employed as research director, Hofstede collected data on 32 work goals (or values) from 116,000 IBM employees in more than 40 countries between 1967 and 1973.[26] Hofstede empirically identified four dimensions of work goals across national cultures,[27] later adding a fifth cultural dimension observed by Bond and his colleagues in China (see Table 4-2).[28]

---

[24] Julia Porter Liebeskind et al., "Social Networks, Learning, and Flexibility: Sourcing Scientific Knowledge in New Biotechnology Firms," *Organization Science* 7, no. 4 (1996); Shalom H. Schwartz, "A Theory of Cultural Values and Some Implications for Work," *Applied Psychology: An International Review* 48, no. 1 (1999); Peter B. Smith, Mark F. Peterson, and Shalom H. Schwartz, "Cultural Values, Source of Guidance, and Their Relevance to Managerial Behavior: A 47-Nation Study," *Journal of Cross-Cultural Psychology* 33, no. 2 (2002).

[25] Daphna Oyserman, Heather M. Coon, and Markus Kemmelmeier, "Rethinking Individualism and Collectivism: Evaluation of Theoretical Assumptions and Meta-Analyses," *Psychological Bulletin* 128, no. 1 (2002).

[26] Marieke de Mooij and Geert Hofstede, "Convergence and Divergence in Consumer Behavior: Implications for International Retailing," *Journal of Retailing* 78, no. 1 (2002).

[27] Geert Hofstede, *Culture's Consequences: International Differences in Work-Related Values*, 1st ed. (Newbury Park, CA: Sage Publications, 1980). Hofstede provides culture scores on his website at http://www.geert-hofstede.com/.

[28] The Chinese Culture Connection, "Chinese Values and the Search for Culture-Free Dimensions of Culture," *Journal of Cross-Cultural Psychology* 18, no. 2 (1987).

TABLE 4-2 Hofstede's Dimensions of National Culture[29]

Culture Dimension	Description
Power distance (high vs. low)	The extent to which less powerful individuals and groups accept unequal distribution of power in society. Represents inequality (more versus less), as defined by the less powerful. In high power-distance societies, inequality is expected by all. Paraphrasing Orwell, Hofstede contends that "all societies are unequal, but some are more unequal than others."
Individualism vs. Collectivism	The degree to which individuals are integrated into groups. Where individualism is high, individuals look after themselves and close others, such as their family. Where collectivism is high, people are integrated into strong, cohesive in-groups, often extended families that look after them and expect their unquestioning loyalty. In this sense, the word "collectivism" refers to any group and has no political meaning.
Masculinity vs. Femininity	The distribution of assertive/competitive roles versus modest/caring roles between genders. In masculine cultures, achievement and success are dominant values and performance is very important. In feminine cultures, caring for others and quality of life take precedence, status is not very important, and social relations are conducted in a humanistic manner.
Uncertainty avoidance (high vs. low)	The extent to which people feel threatened by, and try to avoid, uncertainty and ambiguity. Where uncertainty avoidance is high, societies typically employ strict laws and rules, safety and security measures, and dogmatic philosophical and religious beliefs to minimize uncertainty, and people typically show more emotion during social interactions. Where uncertainty avoidance is low, tolerance encourages people to show greater diversity in opinions and behavior and societies regulate behavior with far fewer rules. Innovation and entrepreneurship are higher. People typically show less emotion during interactions and are more contemplative.
Long-term vs. Short-term orientation	Derived from the teachings of the great Chinese philosopher Confucius, but applicable everywhere. Refers to a pragmatic, future-oriented perspective about achieving goals in life. Long-term orientation emphasizes thrift and perseverance. Short-term orientation emphasizes respect for tradition, fulfilling social obligations, and protecting one's public image.

Hofstede's work stimulated research into culture's consequences for consumer and organizational buyer behaviors. His cultural dimensions were soon linked to national differences in the diffusion of innovations; divergence in patterns of consumer behavior and consumption of products, such as automobiles, mineral water, and Internet services;[30] as well as to organizational commitment, transformational leadership, preferences for reward allocation and management styles, and organizational values.[31] Today, Hofstede's measures, data, and methodology are increasingly criticized for Western

[29] Adapted from Hofstede, *Culture's Consequences: Comparing Values, Behaviors, Institutions, and Organizations across Nations.*

[30] See Earley and Ang, *Cultural Intelligence: Individual Interactions across Cultures*; de Mooij and Hofstede, "Convergence and Divergence in Consumer Behavior: Implications for International Retailing."; Marieke de Mooij, "The Future Is Predictable for International Marketers: Converging Incomes Lead to Diverging Consumer Behaviour," *International Marketing Review* 17, no. 2 (2000); Dianne A. van Hemert, Fons J. R. van de Vijver, and Ype H. Poortinga, "Multilevel Models of Individuals and Cultures: Current State and Outlook," in *Multilevel Analysis of Individuals and Cultures*, Fons J. R. van de Vijver, Dianne A. van Hemert, and Ype H. Poortinga, eds. (New York: Lawrence Erlbaum Associates, 2008).

[31] For example, Michele J. Gelfand, Harry C. Triandis, and Darius K. S. Chan, "Individualism Versus Collectivism or versus Authoritarianism?" *European Journal of Social Psychology* 26, no. 3 (1996); Yilmaz Esmer, "Globalization, 'McDonaldization' and Values: Quo Vadis?" *Comparative Sociology* 5, no. 2/3 (2006); Katrijn Gielens and Marnik G. Dekimpe, "Do International Entry Decisions of Retail Chains Matter in the Long Run?" *International Journal of Research in Marketing* 18, no. 3 (2001); Daniel J. Flint, "Innovation, Symbolic Interaction, and Customer Valuing: Thoughts Stemming from a Service Dominant Logic of Marketing," *Marketing Theory* 6, no. 3 (2006); Mikael Sondergaard, "Research Note: Hofstede's Consequences: A Study of Reviews, Citations, and Replications," *Organization Studies* 15, no. 3 (1994).

cultural bias, reliance on unrepresentative samples, content and comprehensiveness of the cultural dimensions, and methodology.[32] Notwithstanding these criticisms, Hofstede is recognized for his seminal contribution to cultural research.

Project Globe

Building on Hofstede, Project GLOBE is a recent study of managerial values, which helps explain cultural effects in organizational structures and processes.[33] Using a theory-driven approach, a team of more than 170 collaborators in 62 countries collected data on societal culture, organizational culture, and organizational leadership from more than 17,000 managers. The nine culture-level dimensions partially overlap Hofstede, reflecting societal and organizational cultures, not dimensions of national culture (see Table 4-3). Project GLOBE illustrates cross-cultural research best practices and holds promise in the study of business-to-business marketing.[34]

Inglehart's World Values Survey

Political scientist, Ronald Inglehart, has orchestrated the *World Values Survey* (WVS) in five waves beginning in 1981.[35] He has collected "attitudes, values, and beliefs" data in more than 70 countries representing 80 percent of the world's population, which detail pervasive changes in what people want in life and what they believe.[36] Motivated by Inglehart's research on materialist and postmaterialist values, the WVS maintains an informative website with links to national cultural dimension scores, social and political attitudes and behaviors, survey data files, technical information, and even an online data analysis tool.[37] A sixth wave of research began in 2012.

---

[32] For recent commentaries on Hofstede's contribution and evaluations of his work, see Michael Harris Bond, "Reclaiming the Individual from Hofstede's Ecological Analysis—A 20-Year Odyssey: Comment on Oyserman et al. (2002)," *Psychological Bulletin* 128, no. 1 (2002); Mansour Javidan et al., "In the Eye of the Beholder: Cross Cultural Lessons in Leadership from Project GLOBE," *Academy of Management Perspectives* 20, no. 1 (2006): 67; Peter B. Smith, "Culture's Consequences: Something Old and Something New," *Human Relations* 55, no. 1 (2002); Harry C. Triandis, "The Many Dimensions of Culture," *Academy of Management Executive* 18, no. 1 (2004); Galit Ailon, "Mirror, Mirror on the Wall: Culture's Consequences in a Value Test of Its Own Design," *Academy of Management Review* 33, no. 4 (2008). See also Geert Hofstede, "What Did GLOBE Really Measure? Researchers' Minds Versus Respondents' Minds," *Journal of International Business Studies* 37, no. 6 (2006); Hofstede, "Dimensions Do Not Exist: A Reply to Brendan McSweeney," *Human Relations* 55, no. 11 (2002); and Ana Maria Soares, Minoo Farhangmehr, and Aviv Shoham, "Hofstede's Dimensions of Culture in International Marketing Studies," *Journal of Business Research* 60, no. 3 (2007): 277–284.

[33] Robert J. House et al., "Understanding Culture and Implied Leadership Theories Across the Globe: An Introduction to Project GLOBE," *Columbia Journal of World Business* (2002); Mansour Javidan and Robert J. House, "Cultural Acumen for the Global Manager: Lessons from Project GLOBE," *Organizational Dynamics* 29, no. 4 (2001).

[34] See Atilla Yaprak, "Culture Study in International Marketing: A Critical Review and Suggestions for Future Research," *International Marketing Review* 25, no. 2 (2008): 215–29. The research team reports extensive information about their research design, measurement instrument properties, and results in House et al., *Culture, Leadership, and Organizations;* Javidan et al., "In the Eye of the Beholder"; Hofstede, "What Did GLOBE Really Measure? Researchers' Minds Versus Respondents' Minds"; Mansour Javidan et al., "Conceptualizing and Measuring Cultures and Their Consequences: A Comparative Review of GLOBE's and Hofstede's Approaches," *Journal of International Business Studies* 37, no. 6 (2006). See also Robbert Maseland and André van Hoorn, "Explaining the Negative Correlation between Values and Practices: A Note on the Hofstede-Globe Debate," *Journal of International Business Studies* 40, no. 3 (2009).

[35] The project included the European Values Survey. When we refer to the WVS, we refer to both surveys.

[36] Christian Welzel, Ronald Inglehart, and Hans-Dieter Klingemann, "The Theory of Human Development: A Cross-Cultural Analysis," *European Journal of Political Research* 42 (2003).

[37] For more information, visit http://www.worldvaluessurvey.org/. See Ronald Inglehart, "Mapping Global Values," *Comparative Sociology* 5, no. 2–3 (2006); Ronald Inglehart and Wayne E. Baker, "Modernization, Cultural Change, and the Persistence of Traditional Values," *American Sociological Review* 65 (2000); Ronald Inglehart et al., eds., *Human Beliefs and Values: A Cross-Cultural Sourcebook Based on the 1999–2002 Values Surveys* (Mexico City: Siglio XXI, 2004); Ronald Inglehart and Christian Welzel, *Modernization, Cultural Change and Democracy: The Human Development Sequence* (Cambridge: Cambridge University Press, 2005).

TABLE 4-3 Project GLOBE Cultural Dimensions[38]

Cultural Dimension	Description
Power distance	The degree to which individuals in organizations or societies expect and agree that power should be distributed unequally, favoring those at higher levels.
Uncertainty avoidance	The extent to which members of an organization or society make efforts to avoid uncertainty, often by relying on established norms and behaviors.
Humane orientation	The degree to which individuals in organizations or societies encourage and reward individuals for fairness, altruism, generosity, caring, and kindness toward others.
Collectivism (institutional)	The degree to which organizational and societal institutional practices encourage and reward resource distribution and action by the collective, as opposed to the individual.
Collectivism (in-group)	The degree to which individuals express pride, loyalty, and cohesiveness in their collective (e.g., organizations, families, membership groups).
Assertiveness	The degree to which individuals in organizations or societies are assertive, confrontational, and aggressive in interpersonal relations.
Gender egalitarianism	The degree to which an organization or a society promotes gender equality and minimizes differences in gender roles.
Future orientation	The degree to which individuals in organizations or societies engage in future-oriented behaviors such as planning, investing in the future, and delaying individual or collective gratification.
Performance orientation	The degree to which an organization or society encourages and rewards group members for performance improvements and excellence.

Schwartz's Cultural Value Orientations

The social psychologist, Shalom Schwartz, has conducted the most important programmatic stream of values research in cross-cultural psychology.[39] Schwartz refined the values concept and proposed the first systematic theory on the content and structure of human values. He defines *values* as *desirable, trans-situational goals that vary in importance and serve as guiding principles in life.* Working with more than 100 collaborators, Schwartz proposed his new theory, developed new scales to measure values, validated their measurement properties rigorously, and empirically validated his theory in studies involving more than 200,000 subjects in some 70 countries located on every inhabited continent. He proposes a theory on values at the level of individuals and cultures. At the individual level, Schwartz identifies 10 motivational value types that can be employed in microcultural analysis. In this chapter, we focus on his culture-level theory.

[38] Adapted from Robert J. House et al, *Culture, Leadership, and Organizations: The GLOBE Study of 62 Societies* (Thousand Oaks, CA: Sage, 2004).

[39] Schwartz et al., "Extending the Cross-Cultural Validity of the Theory of Basic Human Values with a Different Method of Measurement"; Shalom H. Schwartz, "Are There Universal Aspects in the Content and Structure of Human Values?" *Journal of Social Issues* 50, no. 4 (1994); Shalom H. Schwartz, Sonia Roccas, and Lilach Sagiv, "Universals in the Content and Structure of Values: Theoretical Advances and Empirical Tests in 20 Countries," in *Advances in Experimental Social Psychology*, Mark P. Zanna, ed. (Orlando, FL: Academic Press, 1992).

To develop a theory on national culture, Schwartz began by considering three basic problems that confront all societies.[40] The first problem concerns the nature of the relation between the individual and the group. Are people autonomous entities expected to place their own interests first; or should they prioritize the interests of the social groups in which they are embedded? The second problem confronting all societies concerns ways of ensuring responsible behavior that preserves the social fabric. Should power, roles, and resources be distributed equally among members of societies who are socialized to voluntarily cooperate and show concern for others; or should unequal distribution of power be legitimized in hierarchical social institutions? The third problem concerns the relations of humankind to the natural and social world. Should people demonstrate mastery, changing and bending the world to their will in an effort to exploit it for group interests; or should they accept and harmoniously adapt to the contingent world?

These basic societal issues provide the foundation for the *content* aspect of the theory, which rests on three bipolar dimensions on which national cultures differ: autonomy vs. embeddedness, egalitarianism vs. hierarchy, and mastery vs. harmony. Schwartz derives seven value types which are detailed in Figure 4-2 and Table 4-4, distinguishing conceptually between intellectual (i.e., ideas and thoughts) and affective (i.e., feelings and emotions). National cultural orientations on these seven cultural values are presumed to arise over long periods of time, as societies respond to these

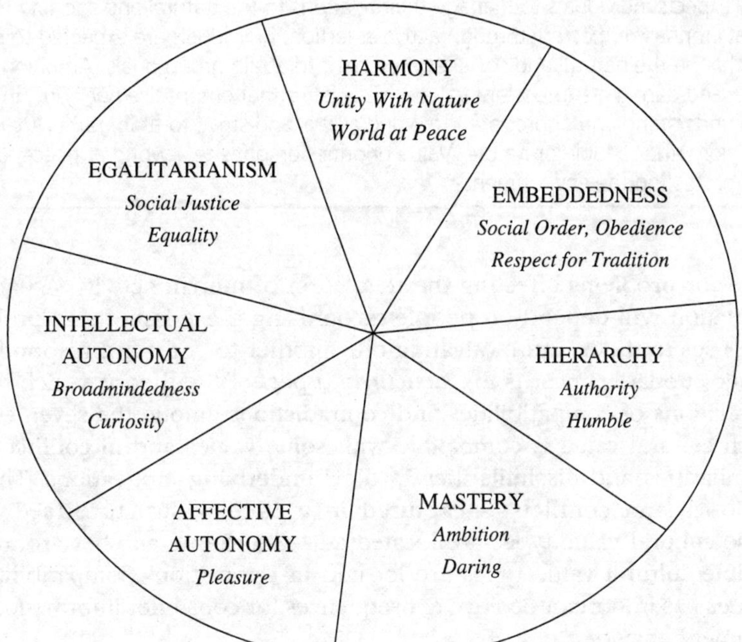

FIGURE 4-2 Prototypical Structure of Schwartz's National Cultural Value Dimensions

[40] Shalom H. Schwartz, "A Theory of Cultural Value Orientations: Explication and Applications," *Comparative Sociology* 5, no. 2–3 (2006); Schwartz, "Mapping and Interpreting Cultural Differences around the World," in *Comparing Cultures: Dimensions of Culture in a Comparative Perspective*, Henk Vinken, Joseph Soeters, and Peter Ester, eds. (Leiden, The Netherlands: Brill, 2004); Schwartz, "A Theory of Cultural Values and Some Implications for Work"; Shalom H. Schwartz and Anat Bardi, "Cross-Cultural Similarities in Value Hierarchies: Evidence and Implications" (Jerusalem: Hebrew University of Jerusalem, 1997); Shalom H. Schwartz and Lilach Sagiv, "Identifying Culture-Specifics in the Content and Structure of Values," *Journal of Cross-Cultural Psychology* 26, no. 1 (1995).

TABLE 4-4 Schwartz's National Culture Dimensions

Culture Dimension	Description
Autonomy vs. Embeddedness	How society determines the nature of the relation or the boundaries between the person and the group. In societies that emphasize *intellectual autonomy*, individuals are encouraged to be broad-minded, curious, and creative and pursue their own ideas and intellectual directions independently. Societies that emphasize *affective autonomy* encourage individuals to experience pleasure, excitement, novelty, and variation in life and to pursue affective positive experiences for themselves. Where *embeddedness* is emphasized, individuals are encouraged to respect social order and tradition and place importance on security, obedience, and wisdom. People view themselves as entities embedded in the collectivity. Their meaning in life comes largely through identification with the group, social relations, participating in a shared way of life, and striving toward its shared goals.
Egalitarianism vs. Hierarchy	How society induces individuals to consider the welfare of others, coordinate with them, manage their unavoidable interdependencies, and engage in the productive work necessary to preserve society. Where *egalitarianism* is emphasized, individuals are encouraged to recognize each other as equals who share basic interests as human beings. Society places importance on equality, social justice, responsibility, help, and honesty and socializes individuals to internalize a commitment to cooperate and be concerned about the welfare of others. In societies that emphasize *hierarchy*, individuals assume and expect unequal distribution of power, roles, and resources. Responsible, productive behavior is assured through hierarchical systems of ascribed roles. People are socialized to comply with the obligations and rules attached to roles in society and place importance on social power, authority, humility, and wealth.
Mastery vs. Harmony	How society expects individuals to manage their relations to the natural and social world. In societies that emphasize *mastery* through active assertion, individuals are expected to master, direct, and change the natural and social environment to attain group goals. Ambition, success, competence, and daring are important values. In societies that emphasize *harmony*, individuals are expected to understand and appreciate the world as it is and strive to fit in, rather than change, direct, or exploit other people or nature. Value priorities emphasize a world at peace, unity with nature, and protecting the environment.

basic issues or problems affecting the regulation of human activity. A particular society's orientation will depend on people recognizing these issues and problems, planning responses to them, and motivating one another to cope and respond.

A major update concerns the *structural aspect* of the theory, which describes the dynamic relations of compatibilities and contradictions among the seven cultural value types. Each cultural value is compatible with some values and in conflict with others, due to similarities and dissimilarities in their underlying motivations. This notion of compatibilities and conflicts is captured in a circular structure (see Figure 4-3). Compatible cultural value types are located adjacent to one another around the circle. Incompatible cultural value types are located in opposition. Compatibility with consumer values has important positive consequences for consumer information processing and consumer behavior.[41]

Value compatibilities and conflicts can be very helpful in choosing fundamental strategic approaches across countries and regions. An example is provided by the opposing cultural orientations of emerging markets and high-income Western

[41] James Agarwal, Naresh K. Malhotra, and Ruth N. Bolton, "A Cross-National and Cross-Cultural Approach to Global Market Segmentation: An Application Using Consumers' Perceived Service Quality," *Journal of International Marketing* 18, no. 3 (2010); Marieke de Mooij, *Consumer Behavior and Culture: Consequences for Global Marketing and Advertising*, 2nd ed. (Thousand Oaks, CA: Sage, 2011); Burgess, "Personal Values and Consumer Research."

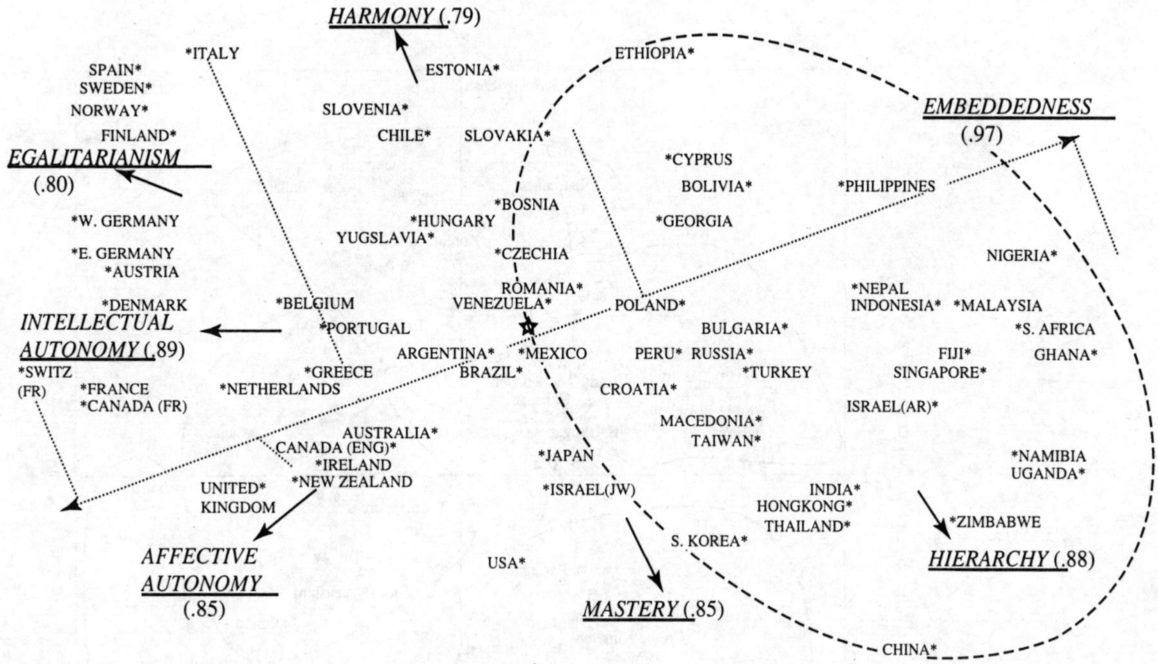

FIGURE 4-3 Co-Plot of 67 Countries on Schwartz's Cultural Orientations *Source:* Shalom H. Schwartz, "A Theory of Cultural Value Orientations: Explication and Applications," *Comparative* Sociology 5, no. 2/3 (2006): 156.

markets, which are apparent in Figure 4-4. Emerging-markets cultures emphasize embeddedness and hierarchy. These cultural orientations share the assumption that social rules and group obligations take precedence over personal aspirations or ideas. This promotes the importance of tradition, conformity, and maintaining social order. In contrast, Western European cultures emphasize autonomy and egalitarianism, which assume that individuals are responsible for their own actions and should make decisions based on their own personal understanding of the situation. These cultural orientations promote the importance of novelty, broadmindedness, creativity, curiosity, and change. These opposing cultural orientations relate to differences in fundamental motivations underlying consumer and organizational buyer behavior.

Applying the theory systematically across cultures has the potential for unlocking valuable behavioral insights, which can be reflected in a company's marketing mix across countries.[42] It provides a comprehensive and nearly universal set of cultural values for use in marketing activities such as segmentation, positioning, and designing advertising content. In Africa and Latin America, where embeddedness and hierarchy encourage compliance with social norms and traditions, Aspen Pharmacare's generic brands, for example, are positioned more as tried and trusted products than as less expensive alternatives or new and improved products. Similarly, an effective advertising strategy in the UK is likely to apply in countries with similar cultural orientations, such as Australia and New Zealand, but less likely to apply where countries have opposing cultural orientations, such as Bolivia or the Philippines.

---

[42] Michel Laroche, "Globalization, Culture, and Marketing Strategy: Introduction to the Special Issue," *Journal of Business Research* 64, no. 9 (2011).

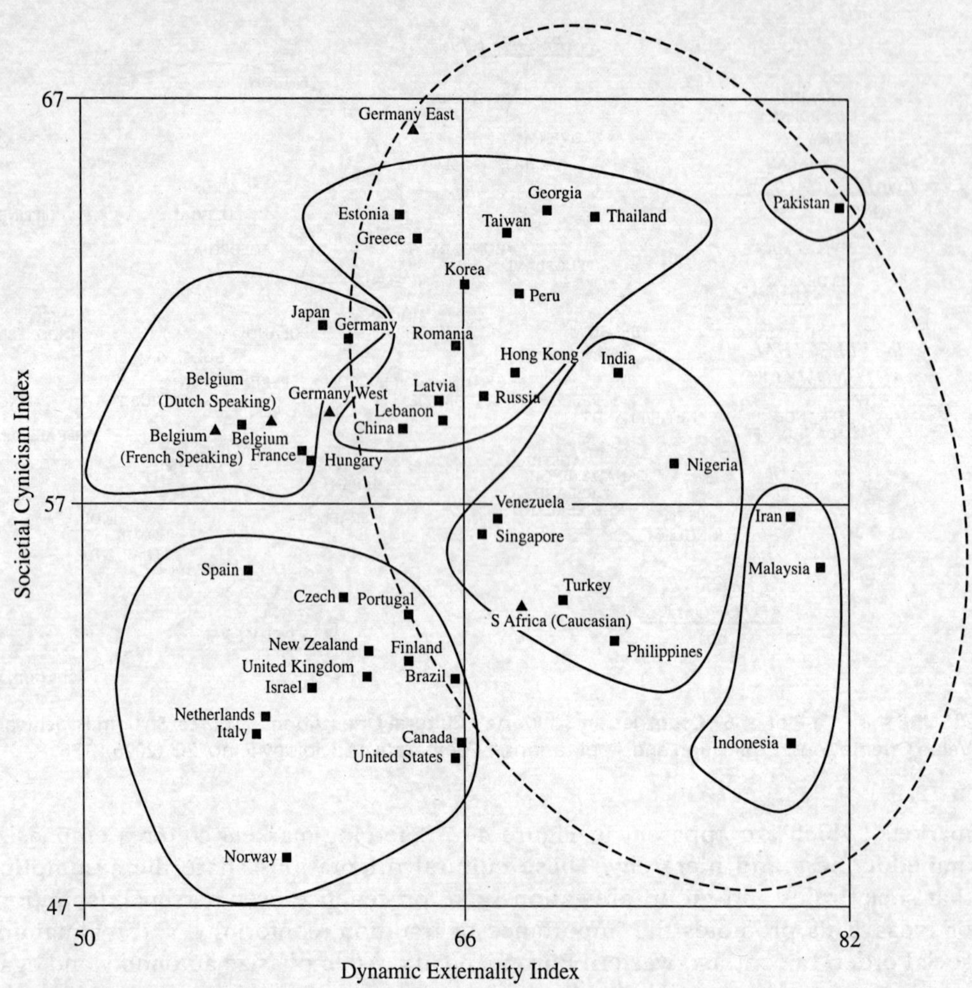

FIGURE 4-4 Co-Plot of 41 Countries on Cultural-Level Social Axioms *Source:* Adapted from Michael Harris Bond et al., "Culture-Level Dimensions of Social Axioms and Their Correlates across 41 Cultures," *Journal of Cross-Cultural Psychology*, 35, no. 5 (2004): 563.

Schwartz provides cultural orientation scores for many countries and seven world regions. Cultural correlations are provided with an encyclopedic array of socioeconomic variables that interest marketers, such as GNI per capita; life expectancy; educational attainment; measures of political institutions including democratization, rule of law, and shareholder rights; and population characteristics such as ethnic diversity, average family size, and gender equality.[43]

Leung and Bond's Social Axioms

So far, we have discussed standardized cultural classifications based on values. Culture is not limited to values. To broaden our understanding of culture, we need to explore new cultural constructs.[44] Social axioms are a new cultural construct that is the focus

[43] See Amir N. Licht, Chanan Goldschmidt, and Shalom H. Schwartz, "Culture, Law, and Corporate Governance," *International Review of Law and Economics* 25, no. 2 (2005); Licht, Goldschmidt, and Schwartz, "Culture Rules: The Foundations of the Rule of Law and Other Norms of Governance," *Journal of Comparative Economics* 35, no. 2 (2005); Schwartz, "A Theory of Cultural Value Orientations: Explication and Applications."

[44] For example, Eric J. Arnould and Jakki J. Mohr, "Dynamic Transformations for Base-of-the-Pyramid Market Clusters," *Journal of the Academy of Marketing Science* 33, no. 3 (2005); Peter B. Smith, "Nations, Cultures, and Individuals: New Perspectives and Old Dilemmas," *Journal of Cross-Cultural Psychology* 35, no. 1 (2004).

of a recent large-scale programmatic approach to cultural analysis in international business.[45] Research has already linked social axioms to more than 50 sociodemographic, psychographic, and organizational variables that are frequently used in market segmentation and has shown that social axioms add explanatory power over and above values in predicting human behavior.[46]

Social axioms are conceptualized as generalized expectancies that people hold about life and how it works. Learned during social interactions in daily life, social axioms express general beliefs about the relations of two concepts or entities. Statements such as "hard work is always rewarded," "every problem has a solution," and "power and status make people arrogant" are social axioms. Social axioms vary across individuals and cultures due to differences in life experiences, exposure to ecological factors, institutional influences, and other environmental influences and individual differences.

Leung and Bond have orchestrated the study of social axioms in 41 cultures. Cultural- and individual-level dimensions have been identified. The two cultural-level dimensions, *dynamic externality* and *societal cynicism*, are defined in Table 4-5. Five country clusters emerge within the 41 culture mapping (see Figure 4-4). The five individual-level dimensions, *reward for application*, *social complexity*, *fate control*, *religiosity*, and *social cynicism*, can be used to explore diversity within societies.[47] Social axioms are linked to important antecedents of market orientation and performance, including organizational citizenship behaviors, organizational commitment,

TABLE 4-5 Leung and Bond's Cultural Dimensions of Social Axioms[48]

Culture Dimension	Description
Dynamic externality	The degree to which societies are characterized by proaction in the face of external constraints. There is an outward-oriented, simplistic grappling with external forces that are construed to include fate and a supreme being. Characterized by engaged social systems in which individuals are mobilized psychologically to confront environmental difficulties and respond to expectations to succeed.
Societal cynicism	The degree to which societies are characterized by cognitive apprehension or assessment of the world confronting people. When societal cynicism is high, the world is believed to produce malignant outcomes. Individuals believe that the world is a dangerous place in which they are surrounded by powerful others who subject them to the depredations of willful and selfish individuals, groups, and institutions.

[45] Kwok Leung, Rabi S. Bhagat, Nancy R. Buchan, Miriam Erez, and Cristina B. Gibson, "Culture and International Business: Recent Advances and Their Implications for Future Research," *Journal of International Business Studies* 36, no. 4 (2005): 357–378.

[46] Michael Harris Bond et al., "Culture-Level Dimensions of Social Axioms and Their Correlates across 41 Cultures," *Journal of Cross-Cultural Psychology* 35, no. 5 (2004): 551; Kwok Leung et al., "Developing and Evaluating the Social Axioms Survey in Eleven Countries: Its Relationship with the Five-Factor Model of Personality," *Journal of Cross-Cultural Psychology*, 20(10), 1-25; Michael Harris Bond and Kwok Leung, "Cultural Mapping of Beliefs about the World and Their Application to a Social Psychology involving Culture: Futurescaping," in *Understanding Culture: Theory, Research, and Application*, Robert S. Wyer, Jr., Chi-yue Chiu, and Ying-yi Hong, eds. (New York: Psychology Press, 2009); Kwok Leung et al., "Social Axioms and Values: A Cross-Cultural Examination," *European Journal of Personality* 21, no. 2 (2007); Michael Harris Bond et al., "Combining Social Axioms with Values in Predicting Social Behaviors," *European Journal of Personality* 18, no. 3 (2004).

[47] Kwok Leung et al., "Social Axioms: The Search for Universal Dimensions of General Beliefs about How the World Functions," *Journal of Cross-Cultural Psychology* 33, no. 3 (2002); Leung et al., "Developing and Evaluating the Social Axioms Survey in Eleven Countries."

[48] Adapted from Michael Harris Bond et al., "Culture-Level Dimensions of Social Axioms and Their Correlates across 41 Cultures," *Journal of Cross-Cultural Psychology* 35, no. 5 (2004): 548–585.

conscientiousness in completion of tasks, and preferences for incentives, rewards, types of organizational structure, and styles of interdepartmental conflict resolution.[49]

Concept of Cultural Distance

In his research, Hofstede, (1980) measured the cultural pattern for countries through four dimensions like 'PowerDistance', 'Uncertainty Avoidance', 'Individualism' and 'Masculinity'. The two countries, when compared for these four cultural dimensions, allows the measurement of the cultural distance between these two countries by adding the absolute differences between the scores for the four dimensions in respect of comparing countries.

Kogut and Singh[50] came out with a technique for measuring cultural distance between countries. For cultural distance measurement, Kogut and Singh used Hofstede's four dimensions of culture, respective scores for the countries established by Hofstede.

Kogut and Singh's Cultural distance $=\sum_{t=1}^{4}\{(Iis - Iit)2/Vi\}/4$ where Cul^{d} is the cultural distance between country of origin, India (s), and target country, USA (t), (Iis-Iit) is the difference in scores of countries; s and t on characteristic i, and Vi is the variance on characteristic.

Consumer Ethnocentrism and Measurement

Ethnocentrism is the enduring belief retained by oneself that his or her own group is superior to others. This in-group bias does not allow the person or the persons belonging to the group to appreciate something good that exists with the other groups. Ethnocentric consumers of a country develop a bias towards the products whose country of origin is outside the home country. This may lead to a situation where, ethnocentric consumer may even reject a brand originated from countries other than home country, just on the basis of country of origin of the product or the brand. The level of ethnocentrism may vary from country to country. The global marketers must understand the level of ethnocentrism present in a country before extending the product or brand to a distant country. Shimp and Sharma (1987)[51],created Cetscale (Consumer Ethnocentrism Tendencies Scale) to measure the ethnocentric tendency of consumers towards products of foreign origin. The scale has 17 items questionnaire inventoried with a 7 point Likert-type questions.

BOX 4-1

Side Bar: Japan is Culturally Different

Power Distance:	Medium
Individualism/ Collectivism:	Collectivism
Masculinity:	High
Uncertainty Avoidance:	High

[49] Catherine T. Kwantes and Charlotte M. Karam, "Social Axioms and Organizational Behavior," in *Psychological Aspects of Social Axioms*, Kwok Leung and Michael Harris Bond, eds. (New York: Springer, 2009); Tobias Gress, "On the Nomological Relations of Culture and Market Orientation: The Case of the German and South African Automotive Industries," (University of Cape Town, 2009).

[50] Bruce Kogut & Harbir Singh, 1988. "The Effect of National Culture on the Choice of Entry Mode," Journal of International Business Studies, Palgrave Macmillan;Academy of International Business, vol. 19(3), pages 411–432, September.

[51] Shimp Terence A., and Subhash Sharma (1987), "Consumer Ethnocentrism: Construction and Validation of the CETSCALE," Journal of Marketing Research, 24 (August), 280–289.

1. Uncertainty Avoidance in Japan

According to Geert Hofstede's cultural dimensions, Uncertainty Avoidance is Japan's second most prominent cultural characteristic. Countries high in Uncertainty Avoidance, display such traits as strict laws, security measures, discomfort in unstructured situations, a tendency to shun ambiguity, and high emotional expression. Japan has a raw source of 92 in this cultural dimension.

2. Power Distance in Japan

Japanese culture is more attuned to accept, that a few people in the society have higher degree of power because of their social status. According to Geert Hofstede, Japan scored high on power distance dimension. It indicates that Japanese respects the people in the society having higher social status. Japanese workers are not required to be told what is expected out of them by their superiors but they are expected to work with extreme sincerity and respect the wisdom of the people who are holding higher status in the organization.

3. Collectivism and Japan

Japan scored very low on Hofstede's dimensions of individualism (46) and hence Japanese society is more collectivist in nature. They love to work as a group. They think that group will be able to provide better wisdom in case of any problem to the members of the group and that will be better than any advise coming from any outsiders. Japanese feel that when they are united as a group they stand to win and it is not a good idea to win something individually but it is always better to enjoy the winning collectively. So in the factory space, many difficult problems could be overcome and new process innovation could be effected in manufacturing because of team work.

4. Masculinity in Japan

Hofstede's research found that Japan was the world's most masculine society, with a rating of 95. So in the Japanese society, the masculine values were given priority over the feminine values. Workers are likely to spend more hours in factory by sacrificing family hours. They are ready to do any hard work if it means achievement in the business sense. Masculine society of the country allowed people to work very hard and increase the productivity of different companies so that Japanese companies are always at the top of the achievement score.

LIVING, WORKING, AND THRIVING IN DIFFERENT CULTURES

Living and working at the boundaries of cultures presents individuals with many interesting challenges and opportunities. *Acculturation* refers to a process of adapting to a foreign culture through continuous direct contact with it.[52] Acculturation does not require one to reject a home culture but rather to come to terms with the dominant logic of a foreign culture and its expectations for behavior. Individuals who cannot acculturate may experience *acculturative stress,*[53] which may manifest in complications such as anxiety, depression, and mood swings that diminish relationships with peers. Failing to adapt to a foreign culture can threaten the success of even the best-planned marketing strategies.

As we have seen, the reason cultural factors are a challenge to global marketers is that they are hidden from view. Because culture is learned behavior passed on from generation to generation, it is difficult for the inexperienced or untrained outsider to fathom. Becoming a global manager means learning how to let go of cultural assumptions.

[52] Lisa Penaloza and Mary C. Gilly, "Marketer Acculturation: The Changer and the Changed," *Journal of Marketing* 63, no. 3 (1999).

[53] John W. Berry, "Acculturation: Living Successfully in Two Cultures," *International Journal of Intercultural Relations* 29, no. 6 (2005).

Failure to do so will hinder accurate understanding of the meaning and significance of the statements and behaviors of business associates from a different culture.

Understanding the Complexity of Identity

Becoming more aware of your identity can be a good place to begin adapting life and work across cultures. Identity is complex, including personal and social identities that affect your perceptions of others and the ways you choose to respond to them and events in life.[54] *Personal identity* includes all the perceptions a person holds about "who I am as an individual who can be compared to others." *Social identity* includes all the perceptions a person holds about "who we are as members of emotionally important social groups" as well as the perceptions about "who I am in my relations and responsibilities to others."

The "minimal-group paradigm" experiments of French psychologist Henri Tajfel first brought social identity into prominence.[55] Tajfel observed that individuals categorized others into "in-groups" comprised of people similar to oneself and "out-groups" comprised of dissimilar people. His experiments showed that people evaluate and behave more favorably toward in-group members, even when people are placed in meaningless groups (e.g., greens and blues) just moments before they are observed. Social categorization is automatic and effortless, occurring as quickly as 55/1000s of a second in controlled laboratory experiments and often without an individual's awareness.[56]

People maintain a "digest of selves" (e.g., mother, friend, executive, Manchester United fan, plumber), which are situationally activated. Once activated, social identity is a lens through which people observe and categorize others based on their observable characteristics such as ethnicity, gender, age, home language, apparent religion, culture, and distinctive behaviors. Social identities are most likely to be activated when a person perceives meaningful behavioral differences between two or more groups, which include group members who are more similar to one another than members of other groups.[57] Magnetic resonance imaging shows that people acculturated to Western and Asian cultural identities activate different areas of their brains in response to Western or Asian situational cues.[58]

According to Tajfel, people strive universally to be part of positively evaluated in-groups, which marketers need to understand empathetically when interacting with people in a foreign culture. It is human nature to compare things to what one knows, and marketers often find themselves comparing a foreign culture to their own. People may even invite you to compare their culture to your home culture. Seasoned global marketers never fall into the trap of defending their home culture and politely avoid comparing cultures. Engaging in social comparison is likely to make someone feel that their group is less desirable than other groups. This is a threat to positive social identity.

---

[54] For an excellent review of social identity theory, see Marilynn B. Brewer and Rupert J. Brown, "Intergroup Relations," in *The Handbook of Social Psychology*, Daniel T. Gilbert, Susan T. Fiske, and Gardner Lindzey, eds. (Boston: McGraw-Hill, 1998).

[55] Henri Tajfel, *Differentiation between Social Groups: Studies in the Social Psychology of Intergroup Relations* (London: Academic Press, 1978), 63. Tajfel considered relational identity to be an aspect of social identity in his theory.

[56] Susan T. Fiske, "Stereotyping, Prejudice, and Discrimination," in *The Handbook of Social Psychology*, Daniel T. Gilbert, Susan T. Fiske, and Gardner Lindzey, eds. (New York: McGraw-Hill, 1998).54

[57] Henri Tajfel and John C. Turner, "The Social Identity Theory of Intergroup Behavior," in *Psychology of Intergroup Relations*, S. Worschel and W. G. Austin, eds. (Chicago: Nelson, 1986); Henri Tajfel, "Social Identity and Intergroup Behavior," *Social Science Information* 13, no. 2 (1974).

[58] Sik Hung Ng and Shihui Han, "The Bicultural Self and the Bicultural Brain," in *Understanding Culture: Theory, Research, and Application*, Robert S. Wyer, Chi-yue Chiu, and Ying-yi Hong, eds. (New York: Psychology Press, 2009).

When positive social identity is threatened, people employ three basic strategies. If group boundaries are permeable, they may move between groups (*social mobility*). In the global marketing contexts, social mobility strategies may cause associates within the company, its agents, distributors, or other important stakeholders to resign or give their allegiance to a competitive firm that does not evoke a perceived threat to positive social identity. If social mobility is not possible, people may respond to identity threats with *social creativity* (i.e., attempt to improve the desirability of group membership by associating groups with positive characteristics) or *social conflict* (i.e., actively challenge group desirability or overturn existing or imposed order). Social creativity or social conflict strategies may threaten harmonious relations within the company, distribution channel partners, or customers.

Astute global marketers consciously monitor others and themselves for signs of conscious or subconscious cultural defense. They are especially careful to respond to social creativity and social conflict strategies in a thoughtful way that is most likely to foster productive relations. Consulting trusted others, who are familiar with a foreign culture, can help a marketer respond appropriately.

To transcend ethnocentricity and cultural myopia, managers must make the effort to learn and internalize cultural differences. There are several guidelines that will improve the ability to learn about other cultures:

1. The beginning of wisdom is to accept that we will never fully understand ourselves or others. People are far too complex to be understood. As Carl Jung, the Swiss psychiatrist, observed, "There are no misunderstandings in nature…misunderstandings are found only in the realm of what we call understanding."[59]
2. Our perceptual systems are extremely limited. We "see" almost nothing. Our nervous systems are organized on the principle of negative feedback. That is, the only time our control system is brought into play is when input signals deviate from what we have learned to expect.
3. We spend most of our energy managing perceptual inputs.
4. When we do not understand the beliefs and values of a particular cultural system and society, things that we observe and experience may seem bizarre.
5. If we want to be effective in another culture, we must attempt to understand that culture's beliefs, motives, and values. This requires an open attitude that allows us to transcend perceptual limitations based on our own culture.

The Self-Reference Criterion and Perception

As we have shown, a person's perception of market needs is framed by his or her own cultural experience. A framework for systematically reducing perceptual blockage and distortion was developed by James Lee.[60] Lee termed the unconscious reference to one's own cultural values the *self-reference criterion,* or SRC. To address this problem and eliminate or reduce cultural myopia, he proposed a systematic four-step framework.

1. Define the problem or goal in terms of home-country cultural traits, habits, and norms.
2. Define the problem or goal in terms of the host culture, traits, habits, and norms. Make no value judgments.
3. Isolate the SRC influence and examine it carefully to see how it complicates the problem.

---

[59] Carl G. Jung, *Critique of Psychoanalysis*, Bollingen Series XX (Princeton, NJ: Princeton University Press, 1975), 228.

[60] James A. Lee, "Cultural Analysis in Overseas Operations," *Harvard Business Review* (March–April 1966): 106–114.

4. Redefine the problem without the SRC influence and solve for the host-country market situation.

The lesson that SRC teaches is that a vital, critical skill of the global marketer is unbiased perception, the ability to see what is so in a culture. Although this skill is as valuable at home as it is abroad, it is critical to the global marketer because of the widespread tendency toward ethnocentrism and use of the self-reference criterion. The SRC can be a powerfully negative force in global business, and forgetting to check for it can lead to misunderstanding and failure. While planning Euro Disney, chairman Michael Eisner and other company executives were blindsided by a lethal combination of their own prior success and ethnocentrism. Avoiding the SRC requires a person to suspend assumptions based on prior experience and success and be prepared to acquire new knowledge about human behavior and motivation.

Environmental Sensitivity

Environmental sensitivity is the extent to which products must be adapted to the culture-specific needs of different national markets. A useful approach is to view products on a continuum of environmental sensitivity. At one end of the continuum are

BOX 4-2

Side Bar: Cultural Understanding: Case of Germany

Power Distance:	35
Individualism:	67
Masculinity:	66
Uncertainty Avoidance:	65

1. Uncertainty avoidance and Germany

According to Geert Hofstede's cultural dimensions, uncertainty avoidance index is 65 which is considerably high, so Germans are not comfortable with ambiguity. They are comfortable while walking along the path which is straight and already proven. They believe in a structured rules in every walk of life.

2. Power Distance and Germany

According to Hofstede, the Power Distance Index is very low in Germany with 35. It indicates that Germans are not likely to show undue respect for somebody in the society who are not achievers. Even if the person is age -wise a senior, but the real respect can only come from achievement.

3. Collectivism and Germany

Germany scored relatively high in individualism index with a score of 67. Hence, Germans are individualistic in nature. They love hard work but not only as a group, they want to achieve success at the individual level also. Individualistic country characteristically shows inclination towards group work based on high target set for individual contribution in order to make group work to have synergistic effect. But at individual level people would like to maintain loose relationship.

4. Masculinity and Germany

Hofstede's research found that Germany has relatively high masculinity level with index score of 66. So, German society maintains considerable masculine values and German people love to cherish human achievements, success etc. High masculine value and high individualism index value together acts in way which makes German people highly ambitious and self-centered.

environmentally insensitive products that do not require significant adaptation to the environments of various world markets. At the other end of the continuum are products that are highly sensitive to different environmental factors. A company with environmentally insensitive products will spend relatively less time determining the specific and unique conditions of local markets because the product is basically universal. The greater a product's environmental sensitivity, the greater the need for managers to address country-specific economic, regulatory, technological, social, and cultural environmental conditions.

Independent of social class and income, culture is a significant influence on consumption behavior and durable goods ownership. Consumer products are more sensitive to cultural difference than industrial products. Hunger is a basic physiological need in Maslow's hierarchy; everyone needs to eat, but what we want to eat can be strongly influenced by culture. Evidence from the front lines of the marketing wars suggests that food is probably the most sensitive category of consumer products. CPC International failed to win popularity for Knorr dehydrated soups among Americans. The US soup market was dominated by Campbell Soup Company; 90 percent of the soup consumed by households was canned. Knorr was a Swiss company acquired by CPC that had a major share of the European prepared market in which bouillon and dehydrated soups accounted for 80 percent of consumer soup sales. Despite CPC's failure to change the soup-eating habits of Americans, the company went on to achieve success with Knorr as a sauce and gravy product in the United States.

At Campbell, by contrast, the figures are reversed: 64 percent of the soup, sauce, and beverage income is generated in the United States, and only 11 percent of income for the same category is from the rest of the world. When Campbell moved into global markets, it discovered that the attitude of homemakers toward food preparation is a cultural factor in marketing prepared foods. Recall that cooking was one of the identified cultural universals. However, cooking habits and customs vary from country to country. Campbell's research revealed that Italian housewives devoted approximately 4.5 hours per day to food preparation versus 1 hour a day spent by their US counterparts. The difference reflected cultural norms regarding the kitchen as well as the fact that a higher percentage of US women work outside the home. The differences, if anything, are increasing. The use of stoves in meal preparation in the United States has declined more than 30 percent since the 1990s, while a survey shows that over 80 percent of Italian men have a hot meal at home for lunch.

Campbell discovered a strongly negative opinion of convenience food in Italy. A panel of randomly selected Italian housewives was asked: "Would you want your son to marry a canned-soup user?" The response to this question was sobering: all but a small fraction of a percent of the respondents answered, "No." Increased incomes as well as product innovations may have an impact on Italian attitudes toward time and convenience, with a corresponding positive effect on the market for convenience foods.

Thirst also shows how needs differ from wants. Liquid intake is a universal physiological need. As is the case with food and cooking, however, the particular beverages people *want* to drink can be strongly influenced by culture. Coffee is a beverage category that illustrates the point. In the United Kingdom instant coffee has 90 percent of the total coffee market as compared with only 15 percent in Sweden. The other European countries fall between these two extreme points. Instant coffee's large share of the British market can be traced to the fact that, in the hot beverage category, Britain has historically been a nation of tea drinkers. Only in recent times have the British been persuaded to take up coffee drinking. Instant coffee is more like tea than ground coffee in its preparation. Not surprisingly, when the British did begin to drink coffee, they opted for instant since its preparation was compatible with past experience. Another reason for the popularity of instant coffee in Britain is the practice of drinking coffee with a large quantity of milk so that the coffee flavor is masked. Differences in the coffee flavor are thus hidden, so a "better cup" of coffee is not really important. In Sweden, on the other hand, coffee is the hot beverage of choice. Swedes consume coffee without large quantities of milk; therefore, the coffee flavor is not masked and brewed coffee is preferred.

Soft-drink consumption patterns also show conspicuous differences around the globe. Differences in soft-drink consumption are associated in part with much higher per capita consumption of other kinds of beverages in Europe. In France and Italy, for example, 30 to 40 times as much wine is consumed as in America on a per capita basis. The French also prefer mineral water to soft drinks; the converse is true in America, where soft-drink consumption surpasses that of water. Germany far exceeds the United States in per capita consumption of beer. Does culture alone account for the difference between the popularity of soft drinks in Western Europe and the United States? No. In fact, several variables—including culture—are responsible for the differences.

These variables include other beverages' relative price, quality and taste, advertising expenditure and effectiveness of the beverage companies, availability of products in various distribution channels, climatic conditions, and income levels, to name but a few. Accordingly, culture is an influencing rather than a determining factor. If a soft-drink marketer in Western Europe launches an aggressive marketing program (including lower prices, more intensive distribution, and heavy advertising), consumption can be expected to increase. However, it is also clear that any effort to convert Europeans to soft drinks will run up against cultural tradition, custom, and competition from widely available alternative beverages. Culture in this case is a restraining force, but it can be overcome.

The penetration of the US beverage market by bottled water producers is another excellent example of the impact of an effective creative strategy on a firmly entrenched cultural tradition. Prior to the 1980s, drinking bottled water was not an important part of US culture. The general attitude in the United States was, "Why pay for something that is free?" Source Perrier SA, the French bottled water firm, decided to take aim at the US market. It hired Bruce Nevin, an experienced American marketing executive, and gave him a free hand to formulate a creative strategy.

Nevin decided to reposition Perrier from an expensive imported bottled water to a competitively priced, low-calorie beverage in the soft-drink market. To back up this positioning, Nevin launched a major consumer advertising campaign, lowered prices, and moved the product from the gourmet section of the supermarket to the soft-drink section. The strategy boiled down to significant adjustment of three marketing mix elements: price, promotion, and place. Only the product was left unchanged.

The campaign succeeded beyond even the most optimistic expectations, essentially creating an entirely new market. The success of this strategy was rooted in two indisputable facts: Americans were ready for bottled water and the tactics were brilliantly executed. The results illustrate how the restraining force of culture can be changed by a creative marketing strategy grounded in market possibilities.[61]

One of the clearest and most painful instances of a failure of one culture to perceive another culture's motivations and behaviors dates back to the beginnings of World War II. Throughout the war and even to this day, the United States encountered great difficulties in attempting to understand the empire of Japan, its enemy. In response to the obstacles the United States faced, studies of Japanese culture were commissioned, focusing on Japan's history, tradition, national character, social life and customs, family, personality, and mind. The result is such great works as Benedict's *The Chrysanthemum*

---

[61] Charles Fishman, Message in a Bottle, July 1, 2007 at http://www.fastcompany.com/59971/message-bottle. (Accessed February 18, 2013).

and the Sword. Since the end of World War II, Japan has emerged as a leading competitor of the United States; thus, the body of studies and publications has continued to grow over the last 50 years, with the focus shifting somewhat from an emphasis on societal and individual values and motivations to business and corporate culture.

BOX 4-3

Side Bar: High-and Low-Context Cultures

Edward T. Hall has suggested the concept of high and low context as a way of understanding different cultural orientations.[62] In a low-context culture, messages are explicit; words carry most of the information in communication. In a high-context culture, less information is contained in the verbal part of a message. Much more information resides in the context of communication, including the background, associations, and basic values of the communicators. In general, high-context cultures function with much less legal paperwork than is deemed essential in low-context cultures. Japan, Saudi Arabia, and other high-context cultures place a great deal of emphasis on a person's values and position or place in society. In such cultures, a business loan is more likely to be based on who you are than on formal analysis of pro forma financial documents. In China, *guanxi* or *kuan-xie* is extremely important. *Guanxi* is roughly translated as "relationships," which take years to develop. In business and society, *guanxi* is even more important than laws. Chinning Chu quotes: "In China, it does not matter how many laws and how much righteousness are on your side, without Kuan-Xie, you have nothing. Even if you are outside the law and there is no righteousness to your position, if you have the right Kuan-Xie and Ho-Tai (backstage), you can do no wrong."[63] In a low-context culture such as the United States, Switzerland, or Germany, deals are made with much less information about the character, background, and values of the participants. Much more reliance is placed on the words and numbers in the loan application.

In a high-context culture, a person's word is his or her bond. There is less need to anticipate contingencies and provide for external legal sanctions because the culture emphasizes obligations and trust as important values. In these cultures, shared feelings of obligation and honor take the place of impersonal legal sanctions. This helps explain the importance of long and protracted negotiations that never seem to "get to the point." Part of the purpose of negotiating for a person from a high-context culture is to get to know the potential partner.

For example, competitive bidding may not be the best way to keep building costs down in a high-context culture. In a high-context culture, the job is given to the person who will do the best work and whom you can trust and control. In a low-context culture, one tries to make the specifications so precise that a builder is forced by the threat of legal sanction to do a good job. According to Hall, a builder in Japan is likely to say, "What has that piece of paper got to do with the situation? If we can't trust each other enough to go ahead without it, why bother?"

Table 4-6 summarizes some of the ways in which high- and low-context cultures differ.

MARKETING OF CULTURAL PRODUCTS

Cultural products are merchandises that are totally soaked in country specific culture. This includes various indigenous crafts, handcrafts, ethnic products, or handcrafted products created by the people of a country for generations. One important characteristics of the cultural product is that they are made with substantial use of hands and very little or no use of machines during the entire production

[62] See Hall, *Beyond Culture*, and Edward T. Hall, "How Cultures Collide," *Psychology Today* (July 1976): 66–97.
[63] Chin-ning Chu, *The Asian Mind Game* (New York: Rawson Associates, 1991), 199.

TABLE 4-6 High-and Low-Context Cultures

Factors/Dimensions	High Context	Low Context
Lawyers	Less important	Very important
A person's word	Is his or her bond	Is not to be relied on; "get it in writing"
Responsibility for organizational error	Taken by highest level	Pushed to lowest level
Space	People breathe on each other	People maintain a bubble of private space and resent intrusions
Time	Polychronic—everything in life must be dealt with in its own time	Monochronic—time is money. Linear—one thing at a time
Negotiations	Are lengthy—a major purpose is to allow the parties to get to know each other	Proceed quickly
Competitive bidding	Infrequent	Common
Country/regional examples	Japan, Middle East	United States, Northern Europe

process. The raw material for producing the cultural products are sourced locally and not even a single imported component is gone in to the production process is imported. More importantly, the producers use all cultural understanding only to produce the products so that the country's culture is recognisable by the consumers purchasing the products. International marketing of culture products are, therefore, supposed to be different than any other products because it involves market of country culture, in a sense, which could be substantially or totally unknown to the consumers of other countries. But yet, the marketers must make the consumers attracted towards the cultural products. Two options remains here for the international marketers; one, adaptation of the cultural product in accordance with the taste and preference of the foreign customers; two, standardised marketing where products are not at all adapted for a specific target market and thereby retaining the cultural uniqueness.

CROSS-CULTURAL COMPLICATIONS AND SUGGESTED SOLUTIONS

Local marketing activities are conducted in an ever-changing environment that blends economic, cultural, and social forces. Stepping out of the global perspective for a moment, we should acknowledge one thing: even when the parties to a commercial transaction belong to the *same* low-context society—America, for example—and the terms of the deal are spelled out "in black and white," different understandings of the respective obligations of the parties will often occur.

Business relationships between parties of *different* cultures and/or nationalities are subject to additional challenges. Parties from different countries may have trouble coming to contract terms because of differences in the laws governing their respective activities and problems of enforcement across international boundaries. No matter what is stated in a contract, taking another party to court for breach of contract will probably require a suit in the defendant's own home turf, which may be an insurmountable advantage for the home-country participant.

When a party from a high-context culture takes part in a business understanding, the proceedings are likely to be further complicated by very different beliefs about the significance of formal business understandings and the ongoing obligations of all parties. The business environment in many countries can be characterized by much complexity: natural and human-induced catastrophes, political problems, foreign exchange inconvertibility, widely fluctuating exchange rates, depressions, and changes in national economic priorities and tariff schedules. One cannot predict precisely how the most carefully laid plans will go awry, only that they will. Marketing executives and managers with dealings outside the home market must build mutual trust, rapport, and empathy with business contacts; all are required to sustain enduring relationships. Appointing a host-country national to a position as sales representative will not automatically guarantee success. If a corporation constantly shuffles its international staff, it risks impeding the formation of what we might call "high-context subcultures" between home office personnel and host nationals. This diminishes the company's chances of effectively dealing with the business crises that will inevitably occur.

Summary

Culture, a society's "programming of the mind," has both a pervasive and changing influence on each national market environment. Global marketers must recognize the influence of culture on all aspects of life including work habits and consumption of products. Human behavior is a function both of a person's own unique personality and that person's interaction with the collective forces of the particular society and culture in which he or she has lived.

Culture is a complex construct, which is multileveled, multilayered, and multidimensional. It is learned as it passes from generation to generation and slowly changes in response to changing environmental factors. Cultures are converging and fragmenting in response to contemporary forces of globalization. Products and services play a special role in creating, maintaining, and transmitting meaning within a culture.

When global marketers refer to culture, they include psychological factors such as values, beliefs, and social attitudes; sociological factors such as status, roles, and norms; and anthropological factors such as symbols, signs, and customs. These factors are the focus of cultural analysis. Cultural analysis helps global marketers choose appropriate marketing strategies and organizational structure and processes, helping improve profitability and reduce the risk of costly blunders.

Marketers employ two broad approaches to cultural analysis. They use standardized cultural classification to group countries where similar marketing strategies and appeals are likely to be effective. Cultural measurement scales and country scores are available from several sources. The theory-driven approaches of Schwartz and Leung and of Bond facilitate cultural analysis within and across countries. Hall's high- and low-context culture can be used to understand effective communication and negotiation styles across countries. Marketers also use approaches such as Maslow's hierarchy, Hofstede's typology, and the self-reference criterion to unlock clues about cultural differences and similarities. In addition, marketers use ethnographic and other nonsurvey approaches. These approaches provide rich insights that help explain cultures and their expressions, especially in marketplace behaviors within a particular culture.

Global marketing has played an important—even leading—role in influencing the rate of cultural change around the world. This is particularly true of food, but it includes virtually every industry, particularly entertainment, communications and consumer products. The Internet, digital communications, and global television and entertainment have changed how and what people learn about products. Soap and detergent manufacturers have changed washing habits, the electronics industry has changed entertainment patterns, clothing marketers have changed styles, and so on. Although culture can also affect characteristics of industrial products, it is more important as an influence on the marketing process, particularly in the way business is conducted.

Living and working across cultures can be challenging. Ethnocentrism arises as a universal and inevitable human attribute because most people know only their own culture and place themselves at the center of relations with all others beginning in their earliest years. Taking steps to understand the complexity of identity can help one recognize and avoid excessive self-referencing, which has been called the root cause of most international business problems. Acculturation can be smoothed by taking steps to improve one's social and cultural intelligence, which can help lower acculturative stress and affect the success of a well-planned and well-executed marketing strategy.

Discussion Questions

1. What is culture? Is there such a thing as a cultural universal or cultural universals? If your answer is affirmative, give an example of a cultural universal. If it is negative, explain why there is no such thing.
2. Can Hofstede's cultural typologies help marketers better understand cultures outside their home country? If your answer is yes, explain how, and if it is no, explain why not.
3. Explain the self-reference criterion. Go to the library and find examples of product failures that might have been avoided through the application of the SRC.
4. What is the difference between a low-context culture and a high-context culture? Give an example of a country that is an example of each type, and provide evidence for your answer. How does this apply to marketing?
5. Schwartz identifies embeddedness vs. autonomy, egalitarianism vs. hierarchy, and mastery vs. harmony as national cultural dimensions. In what way do national cultural dimensions affect marketing practices in your country?
6. What can global marketers do and what issues might they need to address in their marketing planning to launch a new product in a national market that traditionally resists change?
7. Take an element of the marketing mix and describe how cultural analysis and factors may impact its planning, execution, and design with respect to a new product launch.
8. With respect to global branding, are there elements of culture which need to be considered? If your answer is yes, what are they? If your answer is no, why not?

Suggested Readings

Abegglen, James C., and George Stalk, Jr. *Kaisha: The Japanese Corporation*. New York: Basic Books, Inc., 1985.

Agarwal, James, Naresh K. Malhotra, and Ruth N. Bolton. "A Cross-National and Cross-Cultural Approach to Global Market Segmentation: An Application Using Consumers' Perceived Service Quality." *Journal of International Marketing*, 18, no. 3 (September 2010): 18–40.

Alserhan, Baker Ahmad. *The Principles of Islamic Marketing*. Surrey, England: Grower Publishing Limited, 2011.

Bazerman, Max H., and Ann E. Tenbrunsel. "Ethical Breakdowns." *Harvard Business Review* (April 2011): 58–65.

Benedict, Ruth. *The Chrysanthemum and the Sword*. Rutland, VT: Charles E. Tuttle, 1972.

Benedict, Ruth. *Patterns of Culture*. Boston: Houghton Mifflin, 1959.

Corak, Miles. "Chasing the Same Dream, Climbing Different Ladders: Economic Mobility in the United States and Canada." Economic Mobility Project: An Initiative of The Pew Charitable Trusts. 2010.

Craig, C. Samuel, William H. Greene, and Susan P. Douglas. "Culture Matters: Consumer Acceptance of U.S. Firms in Foreign Markets." *Journal of International Marketing*, 13, no. 4 (December 2005): 80–103.

Dale, Peter N. *The Myth of Japanese Uniqueness*. New York: St. Martin's Press, 1986.

de Tocqueville, Alexis. *Democracy in America*. New York: New American Library, 1956.

Drolet Aimee, Norbert Schwarz, and Carolyn Yoon, eds. *The Aging Consumer: Perspectives from Psychology and Economics*. New York: Routledge, Taylor & Francis Group, Inc., 2010.

Dulek, Ronald E., John S. Fielden, and John S. Hill. "International Communications: An Executive Primer." *Business Horizons*, 34 (January–February 1991): 20–25.

Fields, George. *From Bonsai to Levi's*. New York: Mentor, New American Library, 1983, 1985.

Fields, George. *Gucci on the Ginza*. Tokyo and New York: Kodansha International, 1989.

Griffith, David A., Matthew B. Myers, and Michael G. Harvey. "An Investigation of National Cultures Influence on Relationship and Knowledge Resources in Interorganizational Relationships Between Japan and the United States." *Journal of International Marketing*, 14, no. 3 (September 2006): 33–63.

Hagen, E. *On the Theory of Social Change.* Homewood, IL: Dorsey Press, 1962.

Hall, Edward T. *Beyond Culture.* Garden City, NY: Anchor Press Doubleday, 1976.

Hall, Edward T., and Mildred Reed Hall. *Hidden Differences: Doing Business with the Japanese.* New York: Doubleday, 1990.

Hofstede, Geert. "Cultural Constraints in Management Theories." *Academy of Management Executive,* 7, no. 1 (1993): 81–93.

Hofstede, Geert, and Michael Harris Bond. "The Confucius Connection: From Cultural Roots to Economic Growth." *Organizational Dynamics* (Spring 1988): 5–21.

Hofstede, Geert, et al. "Measuring Organizational Cultures: A Qualitative and Quantitative Study Across Twenty Cases." *Administrative Science Quarterly* (June 1990): 286–317.

Homburg, Christian, Joseph P. Cannon, Harley Krohmer, and Ingo Kiedaisch. "Governance of International Business Relationships: A Cross-Cultural Study on Alternative Governance Modes." *Journal of International Marketing*, 17, no. 3 (September 2009): 1–20.

Jacobs, Laurence, et al. "Cross-Cultural Colour Comparisons: Global Marketers Beware!" *International Marketing Review*, 8, no. 3 (1991): 21–30.

Keh, Hean Tat, and Jin Sun. "The Complexities of Perceived Risk in Cross-Cultural Services Marketing." *Journal of International Marketing*, 16, no. 1 (March 2008): 120–146.

Lam, Desmond, Alvin Lee, and Richard Mizerski. "The Effects of Cultural Values in Word-of-Mouth Communication." *Journal of International Marketing*, 17, no. 3 (September 2009): 55–70.

Lee, Don Y., and Philip L. Dawes, "*Guanxi*, Trust, and Long-Term Orientation in Chinese Business Markets." *Journal of International Marketing,* 13, no. 2 (June 2005): 28–56.

Lin, Carolyn A. "Cultural Differences in Message Strategies: A Comparison between American and Japanese Commercials." *Journal of Advertising Research*, 33 (July–August 1993): 40–48

Madden, Thomas J., Kelly Hewett, and Martin S. Roth. "Managing Images in Different Cultures: A Cross National Study of Color Meanings and Preferences." *Journal of International Marketing* 8, no.1 (2000): 90–107.

McClelland, David. *The Achieving Society.* New York: Van Nostrand, 1961.

Moon, Tae Won, and Sang Park. "The Effect of Cultural Distance on International Marketing Strategy: A Comparison of Cultural Distance and Managerial Perception Measures." *Journal of Global Marketi*ng, 24, no. 1 (2011): 18–40.

Okazaki, Shintaro, Barbara Mueller, and Charles R. Taylor. "Global Consumer Culture Positioning: Testing Perceptions of Soft-Sell and Hard-Sell Advertising Appeals Between U.S. and Japanese Consumers." *Journal of International Marketing*, 18, no. 2 (June 2010): 20–34.

Ozdemir, Emre, and Kelly Hewett. "The Effect of Collectivism on the Importance of Relationship Quality and Service Quality for Behavioral Intentions: A Cross-National and Cross-Contextual Analysis." *Journal of International Marketing* 18, no. 1 (March 2010): 41–62.

Paul, Pallab, Abhijit Roy, and Kausiki Mukhopadhyay. "The Impact of Cultural Values on Marketing Ethical Norms: A Study in India and the United States." *Journal of International Marketing*, 14, no. 4 (December 2006): 28–56.

Pinker, Steven. *The Better Angels of our Nature: Why Violence Has Declined.* New York: Viking: The Penguin Group, 2011.

Reischauer, Edwin O. *The Japanese.* Cambridge, MA: The Belknap Press of Harvard University Press, 1977.

Sousa, Carlos M. P., and Frank Bradley. "Cultural Distance and Psychic Distance: Two Peas in a Pod?" *Journal of International Marketing*, 14, no. 1 (March 2006): 49–70.

Usunier, Jean-Claude, and Julie Anne Lee, *Marketing Across Cultures* (5th ed.). New York: Pearson Education Ltd., 2009.

Part III Analyzing and Targeting Global Market Opportunities

CHAPTER 5

Global Customers

One cannot simply assume that Indian consumers in 15 years will be just like Chinese ones today. One big difference is that Indians do not have the same preference for foreign brands that Chinese consumers show. That might change, but then again it might not. When Coca-Cola bought Thums Up, the leading Indian cola, it was planning to kill the brand. But Coke's local managers soon realised Indians preferred Thums Up. The big bosses at head office in Atlanta, who prefer their products to be the same everywhere, were aghast. But Coke now gives Thums Up plenty of shelf space next to its own bottles.

—PANKAJ GHEMAWAT. IESE BUSINESS SCHOOL, BARCELONA

The list of the world's ten largest economies may look quite different in 2050. The largest economies in the world (by GDP) may no longer be the richest (by income per capita), making strategic choices for firms more complex.

—DREAMING WITH BRICS: THE PATH TO 2050, GOLDMAN SACHS, 2003.

Learning Objectives

1. Summarize the characteristics of the world's major regional markets (159–174).

2. Discuss marketing challenges and opportunities in low-income countries (175–177).

3. Explain the significance of customer value in global marketing (177–178).

4. Describe the three key concepts of diffusion theory (178–181).

INTRODUCTION

In many ways, consumers around the world are becoming more alike. Almost everywhere in the world, one is never far from a fast-food restaurant, a cell phone, or an Internet connection. Several market segments, like the very wealthy, teenagers, and technocrats, even transcend national borders.

Yet, despite the decreasing importance of geography as a basis for distinguishing consumers, the average consumers are different around the world. As marketers in the clothing industry know, "Even underwear has national characteristics." Therefore, marketers must analyze up-to-date economic, demographic, and cultural information before either introducing new products or developing existing markets.

For the first time in history, there is the prospect of market opportunity in every world region. Today, over two-thirds of world income, as measured by exchange-rate comparisons of national income, is concentrated in the triad (the European Union, Japan, and North America, excluding Mexico). The rest of the world is now growing at a much faster and sustained rate than the triad, shifting the location of world opportunity to new market frontiers. The vanguard of this growth is in the BRIC-IT group of Brazil, Russia, India, China, Indonesia, and Turkey. They are the fast-growing countries of Asia, Europe, and Latin America. These countries are already major world markets, and will soon be joined by many of the smaller countries of Asia, Latin America, Europe, the Middle East, and Africa.

A glance at Tables 5-1 and 5-2 reveals that the average GDP per capita in the world today is almost $16,329, the world life expectancy at birth is 71.455 years, and the world average expenditure on education as % of total government expenditure stands at 14.25. This is a remarkable time in the world history: income, life expectancy, and educational level have reached new heights.

TABLE 5-1 List of Top 50 Countries by Gross Domestic Product (GDP) at Purchasing Power Parity Per Capita Prepared by International Monetary Fund (2016)

Rank	Country	Int. $
1	Qatar	1,29,727
2	Luxembourg	1,01,936
3	Macau SAR	96,148
4	Singapore	87,082
5	Brunei Darussalam	79,711
6	Kuwait	71,264
7	Ireland	69,375
8	Norway	69,296
9	United Arab Emirates	67,696
10	San Marino	64,443
11	Switzerland	59,376
12	Hong Kong SAR	58,095
13	United States	57,294
14	Saudi Arabia	54,078
15	Netherlands	50,846
16	Bahrain	50,303
17	Sweden	49,678
18	Australia	48,806
19	Germany	48,190

TABLE 5-1 Continued

Rank	Country	Int. $
20	Iceland	48,070
21	Austria	47,856
22	Taiwan	47,790
23	Denmark	46,603
24	Canada	46,240
25	Belgium	44,881
26	Oman	43,737
27	United Kingdom	42,514
28	France	42,384
29	Finland	41,813
30	Japan	38,894
31	Equatorial Guinea	38,699
32	Korea	37,948
33	Malta	37,891
34	Puerto Rico	37,723
35	New Zealand	37,108
36	Spain	36,451
37	Italy	36,313
38	Israel	34,834
39	Cyprus	34,387
40	Czech Republic	33,223
41	Slovenia	32,028
42	Trinidad and Tobago	31,934
43	Slovak Republic	31,182
44	Lithuania	29,882
45	Estonia	29,502
46	Portugal	28,515
47	Seychelles	28,148
48	Poland	27,715
49	Malaysia	27,234
50	Hungary	27,211

All figures are in current Geary–Khamis dollars, more commonly known as international dollars (Int$)*.

*a hypothetical unit of currency that has the same purchasing power parity that the U.S. dollar had in the United States at a given point in time (2000)

Source: https://en.wikipedia.org/wiki/List_of_countries_by_GDP_(PPP)_per_capita#cite_note-IMF_2015-4

TABLE 5-2 World Data

GDP World: 75,212,696 (million USD)

Population total: 7.4 billion. (Estimation, as of August 2016)

GDP per capita in the world: $16,329

GNI per capita, Atlas method (Current US$): 10510. 159

Urban population (% of total): 53.857 (2015)

Life Expectancy at birth, (year): 71.455 (2014)

CO2 emission (metric tonne per capita): 4.996 (2013)

Expenditure on education as % of total government expenditure (%): 14.253

Source: World Bank

Table 5-1 shows the rank of the top 50 countries of the world in purchasing power parity (PPP) a measure of national income that adjusts for local prices and consumption.

This chapter presents a broad overview of the markets of the world on a regional basis. The first half describes the characteristics of the major regional markets and includes an extended analysis of the Chinese, Indian, Russian, and Brazilian markets. The second half focuses on the processes through which buyers learn, evaluate, and adopt products and the factors that affect their decisions.

THE GLOBAL MARKETING PLAN

Each country in the world is sovereign and unique, but there are similarities among countries in the same region or in the same stage of development that make both the regional and the market stage approaches sound bases for marketing planning. In this chapter, the organization of material is around geographic regions. It could just as well be organized around stages of economic development from low to medium to high income.

REGIONAL MARKET CHARACTERISTICS

Defining regional markets is an exercise in clustering countries in order to maximize the similarities within clusters and differences between clusters. One approach to clustering is to rely on individual or group judgment regarding important or relevant criteria. Another method is to objectively identify the cluster criteria, weight them, and use tools that cluster countries based on the defined, weighted criteria. In the section that follows, national markets are clustered on the basis of geographic proximity, language, race, and religion. A brief description of each developing region and the high-income countries of Europe, North America, Australia, and New Zealand is presented. Brazil, Russia, India, China, Indonesia, and Turkey, the six largest rapidly growing emerging markets, referred to as BRIC-IT (Brick It), are also profiled.

As discussed in Chapter 2 on the Global Economic Environment, the World Bank has developed a classification system for countries: low income, middle income (divided into lower- and upper-middle income) and high income. Economies are divided according to 2011 GNI per capita, calculated using the World Bank Atlas method. The groups are low income, $1,025 or less; lower-middle income, $1,026–$4,035; upper-middle income, $4,036–$12,475; and high income, $12,476 or more. Classifications and data reported for geographic regions are for low-income and middle-income economies only. Low-income and middle-income economies are sometimes referred to as developing economies or less developed countries (LDCs). Taiwan, China, is included in high income. All GNI data in this chapter are from World Bank Data.[1]

European Union

The 27-country EU covers over 4 million km^2 and has 509 million inhabitants (2015)—the world's third largest population after China and India. By surface area, France is the biggest EU country and Malta the smallest. Economically it is now bigger than the United States, with a 2015 GNI of 19.597 Trillion. Operating as a single market, the EU is a major world trading power. The EU is seeking to sustain economic growth by investing in transport, energy, and research while minimizing the impact of further economic development on the environment. Language skills are becoming increasingly important, as globalization leads to more and more contact with people from other countries. The EU actively encourages the acquisition of language skills from an early age.

The countries of the European Union are among the most prosperous in the world, although income is unevenly distributed in the region. GDP per capita of Poland US $12,554 (2015) was only slightly more than one-fourth of Germany's $41,313. Even though there are differences in income, language, and culture, the old Europe of nation-states has been replaced by the European Union, which has adopted a common currency (the euro) and eliminated barriers to the movement of people, goods, and money within the EU. This is one of the great acheivements of the twentieth century and a demonstration of how people can work together peacefully to achieve common goals.

The objective of the EU member countries is to harmonize national laws and regulations so that goods, services, people, and money can flow freely across national boundaries. The 1992 Treaty of Maastricht was the seminal document that established the base for cooperation among the original 12 and all future members of the EU in such critical areas as foreign and defense policy, judicial and internal affairs, and in the creation of an economic and monetary union (including the adoption of a common currency). In the years that followed, the EU continued to grow, both geographically and economically, and the euro, which became the official currency of the region in 1999, has become a major world currency, second only to the US dollar. Figure 5-1 provides facts and figures and an affirmative argument for the euro.

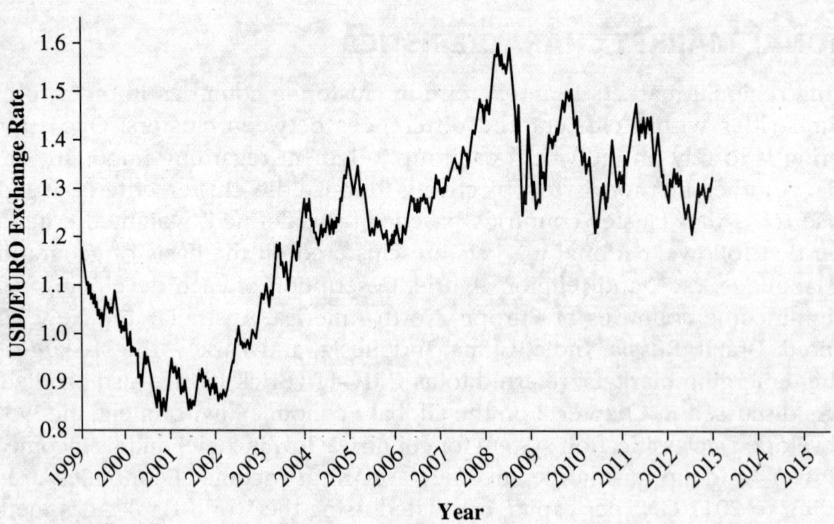

FIGURE 5-1 Euro–US Dollar Exchange Rate: 1999–2012

[1] http://data.worldbank.org/

In 2011, the EU faced one of the greatest challenges in its short history. As a result of the global financial crisis of 2008 and the soverign debt crisis triggered by the inability of Greece to meet payments due on its debt (Greek government expenditures without any debt service were 115% of revenues), the euro was at risk. The major European banks held Greek government debt which they incorrectly believed was a safe credit risk. In fact, the Greek debt was clearly certain to default unless the terms were renegotiated to recognize the Greece inablility to repay the debt on the issue terms. The Greek financial crisis spread fear, threatening Spain, Italy, and the entire European banking system. The one institution needed to meet the challenges of this crisis was a European Central Bank with the power to borrow and tax. Such an institution could ensure that any challenge to the euro would be met by soverign unlimited credit capacity. (The United States has such an institution, the US Treasury, which came to the rescue of the US financial system in the crisis of 1988.) However, the EU lacked this capacity. Any action required the agreement of each of the member countries. How this default is handled will determine the fate and future of the EU.

Only 60 percent of the EU population have adopted the euro. The United Kingdom, Denmark, and Sweden, for example, continue to keep their own currency. Norway, Iceland, and Switzerland have decided not to join at all, while othjer countries, including Turkey, have not been invited. Recent issues facing the EU include the roster of newer member countries, some of whom have to work much harder to reach and sustain standards required for admission, and the debate over issues ranging from the adoption of a Central Bank and a federal government with borrowing and taxing power to a federal EU Constitution and trade and immigration policies.

Table 5-3 summarizes the changes that are affecting marketers in this region. The marketing challenge is to develop strategies to take advantage of opportunities in one of the largest, most stable, and wealthiest markets in the world. Corporations must determine to what extent they can treat the region as one entity and how to change organizational structures to best take advantage of a unified Europe.

Russia

Back on its feet after years of economic struggles, Russia is beginning to fulfill its potential as one of the biggest, most promising markets in the world. Consumer confidence and consumer spending have been steadily rising and Russia's economy has been flourishing, buoyed by strong oil revenues and foreign direct investments. In the last few years, over 20 million Russians have been lifted out of poverty, thanks to the government's fiscally responsible policies and the continuous liberalization of the Russian market.[2]

A country of 144 million people and vast lands and natural resources, Russia represents a huge market that many companies are finally able and willing to pursue. On the industrial front, companies have been entering into the Russian market ready to rebuild its large, but badly outdated manufacturing base. Companies such as Intel Corp., Ford Motor Co., Toyota, Renault, and IKEA are already manufacturing in the country. These companies are not only investing in their own new facilities, they are also reviving old factories with their need for local suppliers. On the consumer side, the rising middle class in Russia has been quick to demand goods and services that put it on par with their Western counterparts, and foreign brands have been only too happy to oblige. With a per capita GDP of $9,092 in 2015, Russians across the country, not only in Moscow and a few of the other large cities, are now able to enjoy prosperity.

[2] Guy Chazan, "Lighting a Spark," *The Wall Street Journal*, March 13, 2007, A1.

TABLE 5-3 Marketing Strategies in the European Community

	Changes Affecting Strategies	Threats to Marketers' Planning	Management's Strategic Options
Product Strategies	Harmonization in product standards, testing, and certification process Common patenting and branding Harmonization in packaging, labeling, and processing requirements	Untimeliness of directives Rules of origin Local content rules Differences in marketing research	Consolidate production Obtain marketing economies Shift from brand to benefit segmentation Standardize packaging and labeling where possible
Pricing Strategies	More competitive environment Withdrawal of restrictions to foreign products Antimonopoly measures Widening of the public procurement market	Parallel importing Different taxation of goods Less freedom in setting transfer prices	Exploit different excise and value-added taxes Understand price elasticity of consumer demand High-margin products Introduce visible low-cost brand
Promotion Strategies	Common guidelines on TV broadcasting Deregulation of national broadcasting monopolies Uniform standards for TV commercials	Restrictions on alcohol and tobacco advertising Limits on foreign TV production Restrictions on alcohol and promotional techniques	Coordinate components of promotional mix Exploit advantage of pan-European media Position the product according to local markets
Distribution Strategies	Simplification of transit documents and procedures Elimination of customs formalities	Increase in distributors' margins Lack of direct-marketing infrastructure Restrictions in the use of computer databases	Consolidate manufacturing facilities Centralize distribution Develop nontraditional channels (direct marketing, telemarketing)

Source: G. Guido, "Implementing a Pan-European Marketing Strategy," *Long Range Planning* (October 1991): 32.

Not all developments in Russia are for the better, however. An economy that is still largely dependent on oil revenues, a continuous and entrenched corruption, and an increasingly autocratic political leadership that is quick to restrict free media and dissent still give many foreign investors pause. But the country's overall stability and largely untapped markets make it an enticing and profitable opportunity for large and small firms alike. Russia is well on its way to resuming its place as one of the leading economic and political powers in the world.

North America

The North American market, which includes the United States, Canada, and Mexico, is a distinctive world regional market. The United States' concentration of wealth and income in a single national economic and political environment presents unique marketing characteristics. With 357 million people,[3] a GDP of $19.6 trillion, and a per capita GNI of US$55,145 in 2015, North America offers a combination of high per capita income, large population, vast space, and plentiful natural resources.

[3] World bank data.

High product ownership levels are associated with a high income and relatively high receptivity to innovations and new ideas both in consumer and industrial products. The United States is the home country of more top global brands than any other country in the world (see Table 5-4). For example, US companies are the dominant producers in the computer, software, aerospace, entertainment, medical equipment, and jet engine industries. Foreign companies are attracted to this sizable market.

In 2015, The North American market and the EU had the total GDP ($19.6 trillion and 16.3 trillion respectively), which, at 35.9 trillion, was more than twice the GDP of the Japanese and Chinese markets ($15.12 trillion). Another distinctive feature is the relationship between business and government which provides relative freedom of entry and operations.[4] This results in greater opportunities for market access than is true in some other countries of the world. Elsewhere, closer partnerships between government and business often hamper the marketing efforts of foreign suppliers.

Canada, with a population of over 35 million, has a GDP of $1.55 trillion and a 2015 per capita GNI of $47,540. It is a market-oriented economy with a high-technology industry and highly skilled workforce. The country's economy has been more integrated with that of the United States and Mexico since the 1994 North American Free Trade Agreement (NAFTA). Today, exports represent almost half of Canada's GDP, most of them absorbed by the United States, to which it is the largest supplier of energy. The bulk of Canada's exports are unprocessed natural resources, which are vulnerable

TABLE 5-4 The Leading Brands of The World and American Dominance

Rank	Brand	Brand value in million USD (2012)	Brand value in million USD (2016)	Growth Rate	Industry	Countries covered	Origin country
1	Face book	5,421	32,593	56%	Internet	140	American
2	Amazon	18,625	50,338	28%	e commerce	180	American
3	LEGO	5,362 (2015)*	6,691	25%	Toy	70	Denmark
4	Nissan	4,969	11,066	22%	Automobile	200	Japan
5	Adobe	4,557	7,586	14%	Software	200	American
6	Starbucks	4,062	7,490	17%	Coffee	200	American
7	Zara	9,488	16,766	15%	Clothing	200	Spain
8	MINI	4,243 (2015)*	4,986	12%	Automobile	120	Britain
9	Porsche	5,149	9,537	16%	Automobile	200	Germany
10	Mercedes Benz	30,097	43,490	10%	Automobile	200	Germany
11	Huawei	4,313 (2013)*	5,835	11%	Telecommunication	200	China
12	Adidas	6,699	7,885	4%	Sports	200	Germany
13	Harmes	6,182	12,833	2%	Lifestyle Retail	160	French
14	PayPal	4,251 (2015)*	4,839	11%	Online money transfer	197	American
15	Audi	7,196	11,799	13%	Automobile	200	Germany

Source: http://interbrand.com/best-brands/best-global-brands/

Figures in the bracket pertains to the reference year

[4] There are many industries in the United States where the government has been captured by industries that it should be regulating (e.g., financial services, Wall Street, and pharmaceutical industries). For a description of the financial services capture of the the US government, see Simon Johnson and James Kwak, *13 Bankers: The Wall Street Takeover and the Next Financial Meltdown* (Pantheon Books, 2010).

to low-cost Latin American rivals. An effort is under way to develop innovation-based competitive advantages and maintain stability in the national health-care system. Life expectancy at birth in Canada is 81.96 years, as compared to 78.94 in the United States in 2015. Some experts believe that the country's health-care system, which offers universal coverage, provides better care at a lower cost than that in the United States. In 2006, spending on heath care in Canada was 10 percent of GDP as compared to 15.3 percent for the United States.

Over $500 billion in goods and services flow between Canada and the United States—the biggest trading relationship between any two nations. Americans have more invested in Canada than any other foreign land. Many American companies, including General Electric and IBM, use their Canadian operations as major global suppliers for some product lines. The auto market enables US automakers to gain greater economies of scale in North America.

Mexico had a population of 127 million, a GDP of $1.144 trillion, and GNI per capita of $9,710 in 2015. Since the formation of NAFTA, Mexico has been modernizing its infrastructure and the economy has been growing. Trade with the United States and Canada has tripled. Results have been so encouraging that Mexico has now entered into another 12 free trade agreements with countries in Latin America, Europe, and Asia that cover over 90 percent of its trade volume. Over 80 percent of Mexico's trade is with the United States (73.5%) and Canada (7.5%). Nevertheless, some problems persist. The per capita income in Mexico is less than one fifth that of the United States, and the gap between rich and poor remains very wide. This, in turn, feeds the persistent pattern of legal and illegal immigration from Mexico to its wealthier neighbors to the north. While filling an important need for a low-cost, manual labor force, the millions of economic refugees and workers who cross the borders from Mexico also fuel the debate over their legal, political, economic, and societal standing in their adopted country. From a marketing perspective, they also represent a large, underserved market that has distinct characteristics and economic dynamics.

Companies that want to manufacture in Mexico can set up wholly owned subsidiaries or joint ventures which often involve the creation of maquiladoras. The maquiladora shops are manufacturing, assembly, or processing plants where companies can import materials, components, and equipment duty free; assemble them using inexpensive local labor; and export them to the United States paying duty only on the value added in Mexico.

Asia-Pacific

From the booming hybrid economy of China to the myriad of developing countries in Southeast Asia and the rising star of India, Asia-Pacific is a patchwork of cultural, economic, social, and political systems. Only a regional or a country-specific approach allows an adequate look at the region's economic climate. However, one thing is clear: Asia-Pacific, due to its enormous population size and fast-growing economies, is a region that no marketer can afford to ignore. In fact, 10 of the 27 countries ranked as "emerging markets" by *The Economist*, due to their economic liberalization and potential for trade, are in Asia-Pacific.[5]

The five economic "tigers" of East Asia—Japan, South Korea, Taiwan, Singapore, and China—have forged the fastest industrial revolutions the world has ever seen. The first four are high-income nations, and the fifth, China, has a high-income market and economic segment which is larger that that of any of the other countries except Japan. Behind them are three countries—Thailand, Malaysia, and Indonesia—which are poised to repeat the gains of the first set of "tigers."

[5] Michigan State University (MSU-CIBER) Indexing Study, http://globaledge.msu.edu/ibrd/marketpot.asp.

CHINA With 1.381 billion people, almost 20 percent of the world's population, China is the most populated country in the world. It is also the fourth largest country in the world, with an area of 9.5 million square kilometers, which is just slightly smaller than the United States. In addition to its size, China is a rapidly developing economy that has been growing at approximately 10 percent annually over the last two decades. Over 90 percent of the population are Han Chinese, with other nationalities accounting for 8.5 percent. These facts are overwhelmingly attracting for global marketers. "Imagine if we just sold one package of X to every individual," is the motivating factor for many global companies' entry into this market.

GDP (nominal) in 2016 (estimated) $11.383 trillion based on the official exchange rate, overtaking Japan as the second largest country in the world. The per capita average is $8,239 (estimated for 2016) and varies widely from the coastal regions, where the highly industrialized provinces of Guangzhou and Shanghai are located, to the agricultural interior of the country. The economic increases are the result of a gradual conversion from a communist controlled command allocation economic system to a free-market system. The changes occuring in terms of consumer purchases among the growing number of families with increasing income are noteworthy. For example, the number of color television sets per 100 households went from an average of 17 in 1985 to 96 in 2008.

China was transformed during the era of Deng Xiaoping, who confronted the damage done by Mao's Cultural Revolution (1965–1976), when he became China's preeminent leader from 1978–1989 and again in 1992. When he stepped aside in 1992, he had fulfilled the aim of leaders in China for 150 years: He stregthened the country and enriched the Chinese people. The transformation that took place in the Deng era was shaped by the long and developed Chinese tradition, the scale and diversity of the Chinese society, the openness of the global system to share technology and management skills, the nature of the Chinese Communist Party, and the contributions of millions of creative and hard working people.[6] Figure 5-2 charts the history of the People's Republic of China to and including the Deng era.

China's largest trading partner is the United States, which absorbs over 20 percent of Chinese exports, followed by Hong Kong, Japan, South Korea, and Germany. In fact, China has become the biggest global supplier of consumer goods, producing 70 percent of the world's toys, 60 percent of its bicycles, and half of its shoes and microwave ovens, among other things. Its promise as a market is also beginning to materialize after many years of wishful thinking and patience by foreign companies. For example, China is Boeing's largest customer for commercial aircraft and Volkswagen's biggest foreign market for cars. In its own neighborhood, mainland China is the biggest market for South Korea, as is Greater China for the goods and services produced by virtually any other Asian nation.[7]

Marketers should remember, however, that approaching China as one large, unified market is wrought with dangers (refer Box 5-1). In fact, China is very similar to the European Union in terms of its subtle, but important, differences in culture, language, tastes, and economic development of its different regional markets. First, there are the differences between the urban, moneyed population in global cities such as Shanghai, Beijing, and Guagzhou and the interior of the country, which is much further behind in development. China's outdated transportation infrastructure and shaky commitment to scheduling also give Western marketers, used to "just-in-time" operations, quite a challenge when it comes to distribution and logistics. Then there are the gender

[6] Ezra F. Vogel, *Deng Xiaoping and the Transformation of China* (Cambridge, MA: The Belknap Press of Harvard University Press, 2011), 693.

[7] Oded Shenkar, *The Chinese Century* (Upper Saddle River, NJ: Wharton School Publishing, 2005), 2–7.

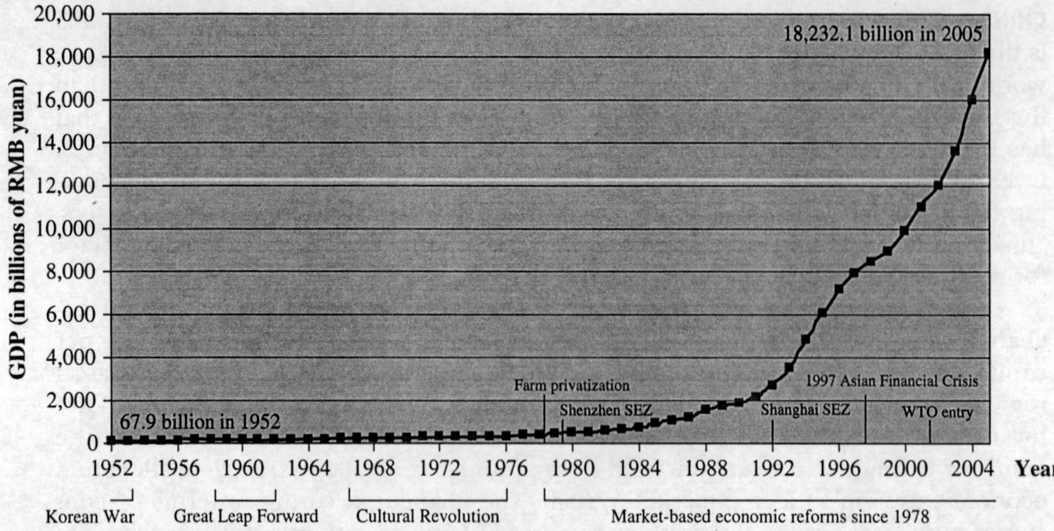

FIGURE 5-2 People's Republic of China's Nominal Gross Domestic Product (GDP) between 1952 and 2005
Source: http://en.wikipedia.org/wiki/File:Prc1952-2005gdp.gif.

differences. According to one experienced advertising agency executive, Chinese women in the field are more honest, flexible, and quicker learners than the men, but they may often be in short supply as bigger and better offers from competing agencies often sway even the most loyal professionals. Finally, there's the most important difference for marketers: Chinese consumers rely on advertising for different information, depending on their level of marketing sophistication. The Chinese middle class, which is quickly acquiring the needs and wants of its counterparts around the world, is more receptive to traditional product branding messages. The majority of the Chinese consumers, however, expect to learn more basic information about a product from its ads and labels. Thereore, localizing product packaging and marketing campaigns becomes as important as ever in China.[8]

JAPAN Population density and geographic isolation are the two crucial, immutable factors that cannot be overstated when discussing Japan as a world market. It is interesting that although Japan's territory occupies 0.28 percent of the world total, and its population of 127 (2015) million is about 2 percent of the world total, Japan's GDP (PPP) of $4.9 trillion is 8.5 percent of the world's GNP. Japan's 2016 per capita GDP totaled almost US$40,000. Recently, Japan's economy has begun to emerge from a prolonged slump, and the country's GDP growth was an encouraging 4 percent in 2010. This declined to an estimated –0.5 percent in 2011.[9]

Seventy-two percent of Japan's land area is mountainous. The residential area represents only 3 percent of the country's total land, and the industrial area is only 1.4 percent. Not surprisingly, land prices are among the highest in the world. Japan is experiencing an acute shortage of workers due to the steady decline in the birthrate since 1974. As a result, more women are entering the workforce and creating unprecedented changes in the marketplace as their affluence and independence grows. Smart Japanese and foreign companies alike are beginning to design products—from financial services to cell phones and makeup—that appeal to the single, professional,

[8] Anonymous, "Don't Think Local, Think Locals," *FDI: Foreign Direct Investment* (October–November 2006): 83.
[9] IMF Economic Outlook, September 2011

BOX 5-1

Side Bar: The Chuppies Are Here

The young, urban, and affluent Chinese professionals, or Chuppies as they are called, are still just a blip on marketers' radar screens, but they provide a telling example of the potential of the Chinese consumer market for the near future. For one, there's their size—50 million and growing by over 10 percent a year. Second, since they comprise the ranks of China's successful entrepreneurs, business leaders, or employees of predominantly foreign companies, they are quickly acquiring the tastes and attitudes of their Western colleagues. They own iPods, mobile phones, and credit cards. They dine out frequently and follow fashion trends. Unlike their parents, they are buying their own houses while young, staying single longer, traveling alone, and often booking their trips online. They prefer Bill Gates to Mao Zedong, invest in the stock market, and manage their "image." It is not only their attitude that has changed, they look different than their parents too. The hardships of the Cultural Revolution that mark older generations are not evident in those Chinese born after 1960, the "Lucky Generation." In fact, Chuppies under 30 look no different from Chinese professionals from other parts of the world.

However, a few significant differences remain between China's young consumers and their counterparts in Western countries. For example, Chuppies are extraordinary savers. Nearly half of them save at least 50 percent of their income. About a fifth prefer to live with their parents while saving for a house of their own. And a majority of them have no qualms about buying designer fakes.

Given that more and more of the original yuppies in the West are going to retire in the coming decades, are Chuppies going to become the new "model" consumers? Marketers are sure to follow this trend closely to find out.

Source: Robert Hsu, "The Chuppie Strategy," Phillips Investmet Resources, LLC newsletter to subscribers. See, for example, http://maravi.blogspot.com/2008/11/mailing-list-robert-shus-china-strategy.html (November 16, 2008), accessed December 20, 2012.

and financially flush Japanese female, who is much more likely than her mother to spend money on herself.[10]

Mastering the Japanese market takes flexibility, ambition, and a long-term commitment. Japan has changed from being a closed market to one that is just tough. The major barriers to entry in Japan are the nontariff barriers of expense, custom and tradition, practice, and preference. For example, buying or renting space for retail operations or any kind of operation is very expensive in Japan. The high cost of real estate has been a major financial obstacle to foreign automobile companies who need to create a dealer organization in Japan as part of a marketing strategy.

Any organization wishing to compete in Japan must be committed to providing top-quality products and services. In all cases, marketing strategies and plans must be tailored to Japanese tastes and practices. Countless visits and socializing with distributors are necessary to build trust. All competitors in Japan must understand the keiretsu system of tight-knit corporate alliances.

INDIA With a population of over 1.293 billion and an estimated total Nominal GDP of $2,25 trillion in 2016, India is the seventh largest economy in the world. India's per capita GDP (PPP) of $6,654 ranks the country 122nd in the world. GDP has been growing at more that 8 percent per year for the past decade. Some population experts

[10] David Turner, "Japan's Women Hit the Economic Radar," *Financial Times*, October 29, 2005, 19.

predict that India will overtake China, which had a one-child policy until recently, as the world's most populous country by the middle of the century. Income within the country is polarized. Almost 40 percent of the Indian population live close to or below the poverty line. But India also has a fast-growing population of middle- and upper-income consumers in cities such as Bangalore, the Indian Silicon Valley, where talented and computer-savvy young graduates are fueling the growth of the software industry in the country. Given this talent, the low salaries vis-à-vis high-income countries, and the availability of real-time communication links, many companies have sourced or opened offices in India for software development and export. India's software industry has been growing rapidly, and the electronics and IT industry accounted for a growing percentage of the country's exports.

Many believe that India has joined China as the other emerging economic giant in Asia. The Indians now compare themselves to China and closely observe China as a model of sustained high growth. Interestingly, the Chinese do not have a great interest in India. The comparisons that they are interested in are with the high-income countries of Europe and the Americas. However, there are some indications that India might have a difficult time keeping pace with China. From signs of rising inflation to dismal infrastructure, lacking public services and corruption, India is at least a decade behind China in development. Nevertheless, given India's enormous market size and its current relatively small but growing middle class, marketers should consider its potential and the opportunities presented in this underserved market.

INDONESIA Indonesia has a real growth rate of 6.1 percent and a GDP (PPP) of $3.010 trillion with a per capita GDP of $3,620 (Nominal, 2016 estimate). Purchasing power parity (PPP) GDP per capita was $11,633 (2016), which ranked 117th in the world in per capita PPP and 8th in the world in total PPP income. In the view of many experts, Indonesia is now approaching the growth stage of China two decades ago.

Indonesia is the second "I" in the BRIC-IT group of emerging markets. It is the most populous Islamic country in the world, the third most populous democracy in the world after India and the United States, and the fourth most populous country in the world after China, India, and the United States. The language of Indonesia is Bahasa Indonesia (literally "the language of Indonesia"). The Indonesian democracy has now completed three free and democratic elections and, in the view of many, is firmly rooted and established. The country is 86 percent Muslim, making it the largest muslim country in the world. It is notable that two of the countries in the BRIC-IT group are Islamic. Christians accout for 9 percent and Hindus 2 percent of the other religions in Indonesia, and the constitution guarantees freedom of religion.

The number of people in Indonesia who speak Bahasa Indonesia is approaching 100 percent, making it one of the most widely spoken languages in the world. Among the speakers of Bahasa Indonesian is President Barak Obama, who attended parochial and public schools in Indonesia before continuing his education in Hawaii. For readers who are interested in learning a new language, many people believe that Bahasa Indonesia is one of the easiest languages in the world to learn because of the many simplifications in the grammer, the phonetic spelling in the roman alphabet, the many words that are imported from other world languages, and the easy pronunciation.[11]

Indonesia is not only a populous country, it is a big country. It is the world's largest archipelagic state, spanning a distance of 5,000 kilometers (3,200 miles) from end to end. The total land area of Indonesia is three times larger than Texas.

[11] For information on how to learn Bahasa Indonesian see http://www.expat.or.id/info/bahasa.html.

BOX 5-2

Side Bar: Indonesia: A Necklace of Equatorial Emeralds[12]

Indonesia is often referred to as the world's largest archipelago, a name that aptly represents its 17,000 or so islands which span more than 5,000 km (around 3,200 miles) eastward from Sabang in northern Sumatra to Merauke in Irian Jaya. If you superimpose a map of Indonesia over one of Europe, you will find that it stretches from Ireland to Iran; compared to the United States, it covers the area from California to Bermuda. See Figure 5-3 for a map of Indonesia and Box 5-2 for country details.

There are eight major islands or island groups in this enormous chain. The largest landmasses consist of Sumatra, Java, Kalimantan (Borneo), Sulawesi (Celebes), and Irian Jaya (the western half of Papua New Guinea). The smaller islands fall into two main groups: the Molluccas to the northeast and the lesser Sunda chain east of Bali. Bali is a unique island, which for a number of reasons can be put into a class of its own.

Mountain lovers will find plenty to enjoy in Indonesia. A great volcano chain, the Bukit Barisan, runs the entire length of Sumatra. On the West Coast, the mountains fall abruptly to the sea, while to the east they ease gradually down to plains in a broad fringe of coastal mangroves. Vegetation-clad volcanoes also rise dramatically from the sea at Banda, Ternate, and Makian. Many of the volcanoes are still active, constantly smouldering and occasionally erupting violently, though geological stations monitor the active ones constantly and give warning if they are unsafe to climb. Mount Merapi in Central Java is a favorite for climbers, despite being one of the most active on the archipelago.

Mountain lakes are also abundant in dormant craters of many volcanoes, the most famous of these being Lake Toba in the northern highlands of Sumatra. This mountain lake covers an area four times the size of Singapore. In Kalimantan, waterborne transportation moves cargo and passengers up and down the major rivers: Mahakam, Barito, Kahayan, and Kapuas. The mountainous island of Flores is famous for its multicolored volcanic lakes, known as Keli Mutu. The three lakes are in a close group and range from dark red to turquoise.

Located between two distinct biogeographic groups—Asia and Australia—the flora and fauna of the archipelago is also quite idiosyncratic. Species found nowhere else on earth have flourished in certain areas, including the famous Komodo dragon on the island of the same name. Also in abundance are rare flowers, including exotic orchids, unusual insects, birds of paradise, and numerous indigenous spices such as clove, nutmeg, cinnamon, mace, and many more.

OCEANIA Australia and New Zealand are island economies in the Pacific region that were originally settled by Europeans. The two countries have a special relationship; however, there is no apparent desire in either country to merge governments. Although both countries cooperate closely in many areas, there are also many differences in outlook, culture, and character. Citizens of each country do move freely into the other. There are no barriers or border restrictions on trade between the two countries. The combined population is just over 38 million (2014, estimated). The income level in both countries is relatively high, with GDP per capita at approximately US$55,000 in Australia and US$33,000 in New Zealand.[13] The region accounts for almost 2 percent of global income.

Australia has a population of 22 million, a GDP of $1.2 trillion, a GDP per capita of $51,642, and ranks 17th in the world with a PPP GDP per capita of $47,318 (2015).

[12] http://www.indo.com/indonesia/archipelago.html and author visits and interviews.

[13] The World Factbook, CIA, 2015, https://www.cia.gov/library/publications/the-world-factbook/geos/nz.html.

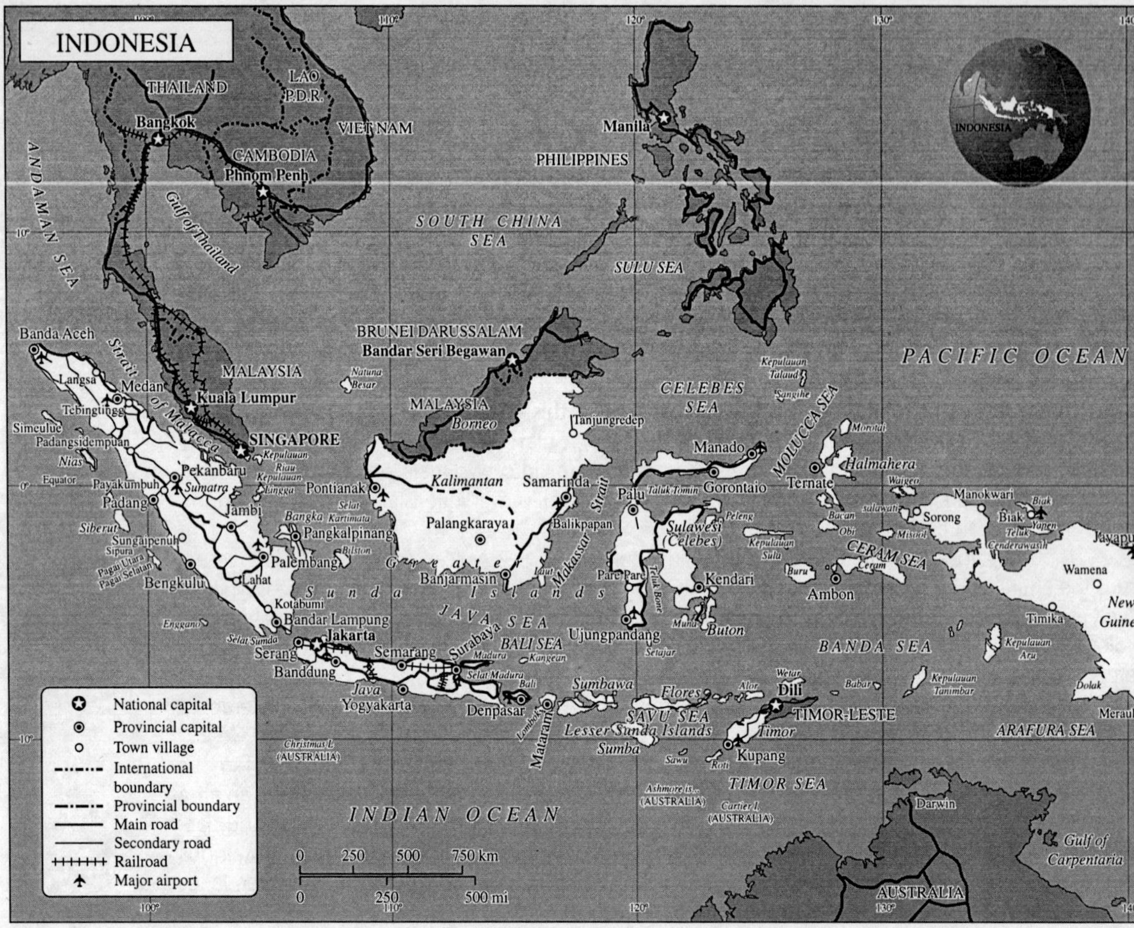

FIGURE 5-3 Indonesia: The World's Largest Archipelago, Most Populous Islamic Country, and Third Most Populated Country in the World. *Source:* http://www.nationsonline.org/oneworld/map/indonesia_map2.htm.

Australia is a very big island: the country's total area of 7.7 million square kilometers is slightly smaller the the contiguous 48 US states. The country's midsized but booming economy is very dependent on trading conditions in world markets for its major exports of low value-added agricultural and mineral products. The domestic marketing environment in Australia is characterized by product and marketing mix strategies comparable to those found in most developed markets. A major challenge facing all marketers in Australia is the fact that the eight major markets are widely dispersed across a vast continent. This presents distribution and communication considerations that tend to increase national marketing costs.

New Zealand is a small, developed country with a population of 4.2 million (2013 census) and a land area of 268,000 square kilometers, approximately the size of Japan, the United Kingdom, or Colorado. Only 40 years ago, the country had the world's third highest per capita GNP. The principal cause of the decline in the relative wealth of New Zealand was the country's failure to respond quickly enough to the decline in prices for agricultural commodities, which made up over 60 percent of its exports. In the last few years, the government has been successful in transforming the economy into a more technologically advanced and competitive one which depends on exports for about a third of its GDP.

Latin America and the Carribean

Latin America (South America and Central America) is a fast-growing region with 8.5 percent of the world's population. Average per capita GNI [Atlas method, current US$, World Bank, 2015] ranged from a high of $15,720 in Uruguay, followed by Chile with $14,100, Argentina with $12,460, Costa Rica with $10,400, Brazil with $9,870, and Mexico with $9,710. Latin America and the Caribbean region is home to more than 550 million people—a population greater than Europe or North America. The allure of the Latin American market has been its considerable size and huge resource base and now includes its fast-growing markets (refer Table 5-5).

After a decade of no growth, crippling inflation, increasing foreign debt, protectionism, and bloated government payrolls, the countries of Latin America have shown a startling change. Balanced budgets are a priority, and privatization is under way. All of the countries of Latin America now have democratically elected governments. Free markets, open economies, and deregulation have begun to replace the policies of the past, except in countries such as Bolivia and Venezuela, where the authoritarian regimes have not embraced open economies.

Most of Latin America is rapidly moving to eliminate barriers to trade and investment. In many countries, tariffs that sometimes reached as much as 100 percent or more have been lowered to 10 to 20 percent or less. Latin American countries have also focused on developing subregional common markets. These initiatives are now extending to North America as well.

Chile's export-driven success makes it a role model for the rest of Latin America. The world-class wines produced in Chile's vineyards enjoy favor among price-conscious consumers around the world, and Chilean sea bass, fruit, vegetables, and flowers can be found in markets in Europe, Asia, and North America. With inflation held below 5 percent, unemployment hovering at about 7 percent, and a modest budget surplus, Chile is pointing the way toward changes in economic thinking in other emerging markets. Chile also boasts an impressive record in privatization, and it pioneered debt-for-equity swaps as a way of retiring part of its foreign debt.

Latin American reforms show a broad shift away from the policy of protectionism toward recognition of the benefits of market forces and the advantages of participating fully in the global economy. Global corporations are watching developments closely. They are encouraged by import liberalization, the prospects for lower tariffs within subregional trading groups, and the potential for establishing more efficient regional production. However, major challenges are widespread corruption; a large informal economy, which accounts for a big portion of the GNP in some Latin American countries; and a wide income disparity between the poor majority and the rich elite.

TABLE 5-5 Latin America and The Caribbean[14]

GDP (current US$): 5.294 trillion
Population, total: 612,638,376
GNI per capita, Atlas method (current US$): $8,933
Urban population (% of total): 80%
Life expectancy at birth, (years): 74.94 (2015)
Environment CO2 emissions (metric tons per capita): 3.039 (2013)
Education—primary completion rate, total (% of relevant age group): 99.972%

[14] World Bank, 2015 data unless otherwise noted (http://data.worldbank.org/region/LAC).

TABLE 5-6 Brazil

Income level: Upper-middle income
GNI per capita: $9,850
Poverty headcount ratio at national poverty line (% of population): 7.4 (2014)
Life expectancy at birth (years): 74.40 (2014)
Literacy rate, adult total (% of people ages 15 and above): 92.587
Capital: Brasilia
External debt stocks (% of GNI): 31.302 (2015)
Improved sanitation facilities, urban (% of urban population with access): 82.8 (2015)
Unemployment, total (% of total labor force): 6.8 (2014)

BRAZIL Brazil, the largest country and economy in Latin America, is the "B" in BRIC-IT—(the six fast-growing developing countries of Brazil, Russia, India, China, Indonesia, and Turkey) that are expected to emerge as dominant economic powers in the next few decades (Table 5-6). With its large and well-developed industrial, services, mineral, and agricultural sectors, Brazil is beginning to move beyond some serious economic and monetary crises in the first years of this century. The country is finally catching up to its potential.

Brazil has a population of 194 million (2.9% of the world population), a GDP of 1.775 trillion (current US$, 2015), and an average GDP per capita of US$15,390 (PPP). Most analysts project that Brazil will continue its annual growth of 5 percent and that it is likely to surpass the GNP of Italy, France, and eventually Germany during the coming decades.[15]

The language of Brazil is Portuguese, which differs from European Portuguese. Portuguese and Spanish are closely related to the extent that there is mutual intelligibility. Both are part of what are know as West Iberian Romance languages.

Middle East and Africa

The Middle East and North Africa region encompasses 14 countries and has a total population of approximately 424 million, a GDP of $3.141 trillion, and an average annual GNI of $8,234.[16] The region has long been a batleground of rival religions, tribes, nations, and dynasties. In the view of many scholars, all of these conflicts, including the hostilities between Arabs and Israelis which have erupted since the creation of the Israeli nation, stem from the region's political inherentance: the arrangements, boundaries, unities, and divisions imposed on the region by the allies after The First World War.[17]

The majority of the population is Arab, followed by a large percentage of Persians and a small percentage of Israelis. Despite this apparent homogeneity, diversity exists within each country and within religious groups. The volatility that can be created by these strong ethnic and religious affiliations was apparent in the prolonged and violent clashes between Shiia and Sunni Muslims in Iraq after the fall of Saddam Hussein.

The winds of change have been growing in the Middle East and North Africa. A series of protests and demonstrations that began in 2010 has become known as

[15] Goldman Sachs, "Dreaming with BRICs: The Path to 2050," *Global Economics Paper #99* (2003): 3. http://www2.goldmansachs.com/insight/research/reports/99.pdf.

[16] World Development Indicators, World Bank, 2015.

[17] For an account of how the modern Middle East emerged from the Paris Treaty of 1919, see David Fromkin, *A Peace to End All Peace: The Fall of the Ottoman Empire and the Creation of the Modern Middle East* (New York: Henry Holt & Company, 1989).

the Arab Spring, even though not all participants in protests identify as Arab. It was triggered by the first protests that occurred in Tunisia in December 2010 following the self-immolation of Mohamed Bouazizi, a street vendor, in protest of police corruption and ill treatment. With the success of the protests in Tunisia, a wave of unrest struck Algeria, Jordan, Egypt, and Yemen, then spread to other countries. The largest, most organized demonstrations have often occurred on a "day of rage," usually Friday after noon prayers.

Governments have been overthrown in a growing number of countries including Tunisia; Egypt, where President Hosni Mubarak resigned ending his 30-year presidency; and Libya, where Muammar Gaddafi, the "leader" who ruled with absolute control over the government and the country for 42 years, was killed.

Business in the Middle East is driven by the price of oil. Seven of the countries have high oil revenue: Bahrain, Iraq, Iran, Kuwait, Oman, Qatar, and Saudi Arabia hold more than 75 percent of the free world's oil reserves. Oil revenues have widened the gap between poor and rich nations in the Middle East, and the disparities contribute to political and social instability in the area. At the same time, oil revenues allow authoritarian regimes to remain in power by providing unprecedented financial stipends to their citizens and essentially creating heavily subsidized welfare states that would not be able to sustain themselves once oil reserves are depleted. Saudi Arabia, a monarchy with 31 (2015) million people, has 25 percent of the world's known oil reserves.

The Middle East and North Africa region does not have a single societal type with a typical belief, behavior, and tradition. Each capital and major city in the region has a variety of social groups that can be differentiated on the basis of religion, social classes, educational fields, and degree of wealth. In general, Middle Easterners are warm, friendly, and clannish. Tribal pride and generosity toward guests are basic beliefs.

Connection is a key word in conducting business. Well-connected people find their progress is much faster. Bargaining is a Middle Eastern art, and the visiting businessman must be prepared for some old-fashioned haggling. Establishing a personal rapport, mutual trust, and respect are the most important factors leading to a successful business relationship. Decisions are usually not made by correspondence or telephone. The Arab businessperson does business with the individual, not with the company. Most social customs are based on the Arab male-dominated society. Women are usually not part of the business or entertainment scene for traditional Muslim Arabs.

The following conversation subjects should be avoided, as they are considered an invasion of privacy:

1. Avoid bringing up subjects of business before getting to know your Arab host. This is considered rude.
2. It is taboo to ask questions or make comments concerning a man's wife or female children.
3. Avoid pursuing the subjects of politics or religion.
4. Avoid any discussion of Israel.[18]

ISRAEL Israel is a high-income, technologically advanced, market-economy country in the Middle East with a population of 8.38 (2015) millon. It borders the Mediterranean Sea between Egypt and Lebanon, with a total area of 21,000 square kilometers, which is slightly larger than New Jersey. The GDP of Israel was $299.42 billion (current US$) in 2015, ranking it as the 56th largest country in the world. The GNI per capita is $35,770 (2015). Life expectancy at birth is 84.1 years, and the literacy rate is 97.1 percent (75th ranking in the world).

---

[18] Philip R. Harris and Robert T. Moran, *Managing Cultural Differences*, 3rd. ed. (Houston: Gulf Publishing Company, 1991), 506.

SUB-SAHARAN AFRICA A decade ago *The Economist* labeled Africa "the hopeless continent." The magazine has changed its mind. Over the past decade, profound changes have taken hold in Africa. Productivity is rising, trade is expanding, inflation has dropped, foreign debts have dropped, and budget deficits have declined. The current GDP growth rate is 3.013 percent (2015). The World Bank opines that Africa may be on the verge of an Asian-style takeoff.[19]

The African continent is an enormous land mass; the United States would fit into Africa about three and a half times. The continent is divided into three distinct areas: North Africa, the Republic of South Africa, and sub-Saharan Africa. The 48 countries of sub-Saharan Africa are located between the Sahara Desert in the north and the Zambezi River in the south. The sub-Saharan market is large, with over 1.001 billion people of which 37.74 percent are urban. The GDP is $1.59 trillion and the GNI per capita is $1,637 (2015). Two countries, Nigeria and South Africa, account for over two-thirds of sub-Saharan African GDP.

The Republic of South Africa is an upper-middle income country with a GDP of $314.6 billion in 2015, the second highest in the region, and one third of the sub-Saharan total GDP. The growh rate in 2015 was 1.3 percent. The population of 54.9 million lives in an area twice the size of Texas. GNI per capita, also the highest in the region, is $6080 (Atlas method, current (2015). South Africa suffers from some of the same problems as the rest of the continent: slow growth, big families, and low investment. The gold mines, which generate half of South Africa's exports, are winding down. Unemployment is close to 25 percent, and 50 percent of the population is below the poverty rate. Sanctions, official and unofficial, restricted South African growth for years. With the elimination of apartheid and the removal of sanctions in 1992, trade and tourism have improved. Foreign banks have started lending again. In sub-Saharan Africa, South Africa is an economic colossus with considerable promise and also significant political risk.

Nigeria is the largest nation of Africa with a population of 182.2 million in 2015 composed of more than 250 ethnic groups; the following are the most populous and politically influential: Hausa and Fulani, 29 percent; Yoruba, 21 percent; Igbo (Ibo), 18 percent; Ijaw, 10 percent; Kanuri, 4 percent; Ibibio, 3.5 percent; and Tiv, 2.5 percent. It is a lower-middle income country with a GDP (2015) of $480 billion, the largest in sub-Saharan Africa. Nigeria is one of the fastest growing countries in the world with a real growth rate of 6 percent in 2008, 7 percent in 2009, and 8.4 percent in 2010. But gone down to 2.65 percent during 2015. In spite of the fact that it is a major supplier of oil to the world, Nigeria's GNI per capita was $2,820 in 2015.

Oil-rich Nigeria has been politically unstable, corrupt, with inadequate infrastructure and weak macroeconomic management, but in 2008 the country launched economic reforms. Nigeria's former military rulers failed to diversify the economy away from its overdependence on the capital-intensive oil sector, which provides 95 percent of foreign exchange earnings and about 80 percent of budgetary revenues.The stability of Nigeria's general economic situation is highly dependent on the international oil market. Doing business in Nigeria has been difficult, to say the least: The country's government has been one of the most incompetent, inefficient, and corrupt in the world. However, Nigeria is currently experiencing its longest period of civilian rule since independence. The general elections of April 2007 marked the first civilian-to-civilian transfer of power in the country's history. Today, the people of Nigera report as one of the most optomistic nations in the world in international surveys.

[19] "The Sun Shines Bright," *The Economist*, December 3, 2011, 82.

BOX 5-3

Side Bar: In Africa, Mobile Phones Do the Work of Computers[20]

Technology leapfrogging by developing countries is nothing new these days. But in Africa, long ravished by war, poverty, corruption, and underdevelopment, the adoption of mobile phones instead of computers for business activities may represent one of the best examples of technological leapfrogging yet.

Mobile phone use has skyrocketed in Africa in recent years, with mobile phone ownership jumping from only 10 percent of the population in 1999 to 67 percent in 2015. Africa has about 1.13 billion people but an estimated more than 700 million SIM cards—often two or three per person for use with each network they use. Google indicates that in South Africa, 25 percent of searches during the week are via mobile technology. This percentage rises to 65 percent on weekends. More relaxed government regulation has spurred mobile usage through competitive offerings by global firms such as Virgin Mobile, Glo Mobile, and MTN. Today, wireless communications are an essential business tool. The Accra, Ghana–based TradeNet company plans to unveil a mobile-phone-enabled auction marketplace, reminiscent of eBay, for agricultural products in about a dozen west African countries. Trade at Hand, another mobile-phone-enabled marketplace, provides fruit and vegetable export price information in Burkima Faso and Mali, while the Senegali firm Manobi provides its subscribers with real-time prices for fish and agricultural products.

The challenge to marketing in the low-income markets of Africa is not to stimulate demand for products, but to identify the most important needs of the society and develop products that fit these needs. There is much opportunity for creativity in developing unique products that fit the needs of the people of the developing countries (see Box 5-3). An important social problem facing Africa today is its enormous disease burden. Africa is a continent ravaged by fatal diseases such as AIDS, malaria, and tuberculosis. These epidemics have cut the life expectancy in countries like Botswana, Lesotho, and Namibia to almost half that of the rest of the world, and wiped out over 20 percent of the population, leaving millions of orphaned children.[21] It is easy to see that one of the most pressing needs in these markets would be for low-cost, effective treatments for these devastating diseases.

MARKETING IN LOW-INCOME COUNTRIES

The shortage of goods and services is the central problem of transitioning economies and low-income countries. Marketing is a discipline that guides the process of identifying and fulfilling the needs and wants of people for goods and services. Clearly, marketing is urgently needed in LDCs.

Certain baseline characteristics present marketing challenges: (1) low per capita income ($4,000 and under), (2) high inflation (10 to 30 percent annually), (3) wide income distribution gap, (4) high levels of taxation, import duties, and other bureaucratic hurdles, (5) a lack of marketing awareness with the presence of a black market,

[20] "Buy, Cell, Hold," *The Economist*, January 27, 2007, 48; Toby Shapshak, "Africa Not Just a Mobile-First Contintent—It's Mobile Only," (October 24, 2012), accessed December 21, 2012, http://www.cnn.com/2012/10/04/tech/mobile/africa-mobile-opinion/index.html; Paul Bright, "Africa is Second Largest Phone Market," (November 21, 2011), accessed December 21, 2012, http://digitaljournal.com/article/314828; see also http://www.ictinagriculture.org/ictinag/sourcebook/module-3-mobile-devices-and-their-impact.

[21] Nadejda Ballard, *Globalization and Poverty* (Philadelphia: Chelsea House, 2006), 27.

(6) fragmented communications and distribution channels, and (7) inadequate distribution and logistics infrastructure.[22] Despite these difficulties, long-term opportunities can be nurtured. Today, Nike produces and sells only a small portion of its output in China; but when the firm refers to China as a "two-billion-foot market," it clearly has the future in mind. Greater competitive pressures will force firms to reevaluate their strategies and look for new markets in low-income countries. Even some fast-growing low-income countries are initiating business in countries that lag behind them. Emerging markets can be lost through indifference and preemptive foreign competition.

However, these markets can not only be profitable for companies but also catalysts of innovation. Consider the "$100 laptop," now officially named XO, which was developed by the nonprofit organization One Laptop Per Child (OLPC). In the effort to make a cheap, rugged, and simple laptop that can be distributed to children in poor and developing countries, the product designers and technical experts developed a number of innovative solutions such as a bright screen visible even in direct sunlight, a completely new interface design, the ability to power the computer manually, and an Internet connection that is ready to go "out of the box."[23] While the immediate benefits of this new product will be felt mostly in developing countries, such as Brazil and Thailand, which have ordered millions of these laptops,[24] the technological innovations can eventually be adopted into many products marketed in the developed world as well.

In deciding whether to enter a low-income market, one study suggested the following:

- Look beyond per capita GNP. The per capita figures may hide the existence of a sizable middle-class in that market. India, for example, has a huge middle-class market that is hidden by the country's average statistics.
- Consider low-income countries collectively rather than singly. One market may not be appealing; however, there may be broader possibilities with neighboring countries.
- Weigh the benefits and costs of being the first firm to offer a product or service in a developing market. Governments in these countries often bestow tax subsidies or other special treatment on companies that set up operations. Entering a successful developing country is an opportunity to get in on the ground floor of a significant market opportunity.
- Set realistic deadlines for results. Due to different legal, political, or social forces, events may move slowly.[25]

Despite the serious economic difficulties now facing developing countries in Asia, Latin America, and Africa, many of these nations will evolve into attractive markets. Marketing's role in these countries is to focus resources on the task of creating and delivering products that best serve the needs of the people. Basic marketing concepts can be applied so that products are designed that fit the needs and incomes of the market. Appropriate marketing communications techniques can also be applied to accelerate acceptance of these products. Marketing can be the link that relates resources to opportunity and facilitates need satisfaction on the consumer's terms. In fact, in his influential book *The Fortune at the Bottom of the Pyramid*, the

[22] Rajeev Batra, "Executive Insights: Marketing Issues and Challenges in Transitional Economies," *Journal of International Marketing*, 5, no. 4 (1997): 95–114.

[23] James Surowiecki, "Philanthropy's New Prototype," *Technology Review* (November 13, 2006).

[24] Steve Hamm, "Meet Sugar, the Face of the $100 Laptop and a Quantum Leap in Design," Inside Innovation, a *Businessweek* supplement, March 2007, 26–27.

[25] Donald G. Halper and H. Chang Moon, "Striving for First-Rate Markets in Third-World Nations," *Management Review* (May 1990): 20–21.

university professor and author the late C.K. Prahalad asserted that these developing markets provide one of the biggest opportunities for companies currently. The 4 billion people in the world today who live on less than $2 a day represent tomorrow's 4 billion consumers if only they are offered the right products. Surprisingly, marketers control many of the factors that can make these products a reality and thus create the "capacity to consume" in these previously ignored target markets. According to the book's author, the three basic principles for developing such products are based on the three A's:[26]

Affordability: Whether by designing smaller packets of shampoo, tea, matches, etc., or by devising innovative purchasing schemes that allow poor people to pay in smaller increments, marketers can develop products that are affordable for this market segment without being inferior in quality or efficacy.

Access: By making their products available where the poor live and during the hours when they are not at work, marketers can take advantage of the distribution channels that will put their products within the reach of these consumers.

Availability: The poor shop when and where they have cash in their hands. Therefore, by making their products easily available at more locations marketers can increase their sales and market share at the "bottom of the pyramid" (BOP).

Developing markets in developing countries by designing products and services that fit the poor's special needs and purchasing patterns can mean opportunities not only for the underprivileged but also for the companies that are serving these markets.

GLOBAL BUYERS

Each buyer is unique; however, all buyers go through a similar process in making a purchase decision. Thus, although buyers in different countries and world regions will go through a similar process in making their purchase decisions, they will make different purchases since they will respond to the unique economic, social and cultural, political and governmental, environmental, competitive, and personal factors that influence buyer decisions.

Customer Value and the Value Equation

For any organization operating anywhere in the world, the essence of marketing is to surpass the competition at the task of creating perceived value for customers. The value equation is a guide to this task:

$$V = B/P$$

where

V = value

B = benefits

P = price

The marketing mix is integral to the equation because value is created by the Four Ps: product, price, promotion, and place (distribution). Value for a customer can be increased in two basic ways: improve and/or expand the benefits of the product or service. Value can be improved for the consumer by reducing or bundling price. (With certain categories of differentiated goods, including designer clothing and other

[26] C.K. Prahalad, *The Fortune at the Bottom of the Pyramid* (Upper Saddle River, NJ: Pearson Education, 2002). Accessed online at http://www.whartonsp.com/articles/article.asp?p=389714&seqNum=4&rl=1.

luxury products, higher price is associated with increased value.) Companies using price as a competitive weapon may enjoy an ample supply of low-wage labor or access to cheap raw materials. Companies can also reduce prices if costs are low due to efficiencies in manufacturing. If a company is able to offer both superior product, distribution, or promotion benefits and lower prices relative to the competition, it enjoys an extremely advantageous position. This is precisely how Japanese automakers made significant gains in the American market in the 1980s. They offered cars that were higher in quality and lower in price than those made by Chrysler, Ford, and General Motors. However, to become a market success, a product must also come up to a threshold of acceptable quality.

The second round of new entrants to the US market are the Korean automakers who have, like the Japanese before them, offered cars with a lower price but with a level of quality that aims to be as good as or better than that of the competition. Korean cars suffered from an early reputation for poor quality, but have since established themselves as competitors in the US market.

The upside of the value equation is that when a company's perceived value is high, it can charge more than the competition for the same product. Toyota and General Motors (GM) produced the Toyota Corolla and the GM Prizm in a joint venture in California. Identical cars got Toyota and GM nameplates at the end of the assembly line. The Toyota Corolla sold for $1,000 more than the GM Prizms because of the greater perceived value of a Toyota. This was in part a perception about the quality of the product based on the brand equity, and in part based on the perceived value of the Toyota dealer organization versus that of the Chevrolet dealer organization. The perception was so powerful that stories of the superior quality of the Corolla versus the Prizm were not uncommon in the United States. This is a dramatic example of the power of brand equity on perceptions of quality.

The bottom line on the value equation is that you can succeed in a market only if you have perceived value that is equal to or greater than that of your competitors. If you are new and unknown, your best entry strategy is to enter the market with an offer that customers will find hard to refuse: Offer quality and features that equal or exceed that of your competition at a lower price. The price will get your prospect's attention, and the quality and features will keep it. Over time, as you become known, you can raise your prices to a level that is consistent with your perceived value.

Diffusion Theory[27]

The process that buyers go through is summarized in diffusion theory, a marketing universal. Hundreds of studies have described the process by which an individual adopts a new idea. Sociologist Everett Rogers reviewed these studies and discovered a pattern of remarkably similar findings. In his book, *Diffusion of Innovations*, Rogers distilled the research into three concepts that are extremely useful to global marketers: the adoption process, characteristics of innovations, and adopter categories.

An innovation is something new. When applied to a product, new can mean different things. In an absolute sense, once a product has been introduced anywhere in the world, it is no longer an innovation because it is no longer new to the world. Relatively speaking, however, a product already introduced in one market may be an innovation elsewhere because it is new and different for the market being targeted. Global marketing often entails just such product introductions. Managers find themselves marketing products that may be, simultaneously, innovations in some markets and mature or declining products in other markets.

---

[27] This section draws from Everett M. Rogers, *Diffusion of Innovations* (New York: Free Press, 1962).

THE ADOPTION PROCESS One of the basic elements of Rogers' diffusion theory is the concept of an adoption process—the mental stages through which an individual passes from the time of his or her first knowledge of an innovation to the time of product adoption or purchase. Rogers suggests that an individual passes through five different stages in proceeding from first knowledge of a product to the final adoption or purchase of that product:

1. **Awareness.** In the first stage, the customer becomes aware for the first time of the product or innovation. Studies have shown that at this stage impersonal sources of information such as mass media advertising are most important. An important early communication objective in global marketing is to create awareness of a new product through general exposure to advertising messages.
2. **Interest.** During this stage, the customer is interested enough to learn more. The customer has focused his or her attention on communications relating to the product and will engage in research activities to seek out additional information.
3. **Evaluation.** In this stage, the individual mentally assesses the product's benefits in relation to present and anticipated future needs and, based on this judgment, decides whether or not to try it.
4. **Trial.** Most customers will not purchase expensive products without the "hands-on" experience marketers call trial. A good example of a product trial that does not involve purchase is the automobile test drive. For health-care products and other inexpensive consumer packaged goods, trial often involves actual purchase. Marketers frequently induce trial by distributing free samples. For inexpensive products, an initial single purchase is defined as trial.
5. **Adoption.** At this point, the individual either makes an initial purchase (in the case of the more expensive product) or continues to purchase—adopts and exhibits brand loyalty to—the less expensive product. Studies show that, as a person moves from evaluation through trial to adoption, personal sources of information are more important than impersonal sources. It is during these stages that sales representatives and word of mouth become major persuasive forces affecting the decision to buy.

CHARACTERISTICS OF INNOVATIONS In addition to describing the product adoption process, Rogers also identifies five major factors affecting the rate at which innovations are adopted:

1. **Relative advantage.** How does a new product compare with existing products or methods in the eyes of customers? The perceived relative advantage of a new product versus existing products is a major influence on the rate of adoption. If a product has a substantial relative advantage vis-à-vis the competition, it is likely to gain quick acceptance. When high-definition TVs were first introduced in the 1990s, industry observers predicted that only true couch potatoes would care enough to purchase them. However, the picture advantages of HDTVs were obvious to the mass market; as prices for HDTVs plummet, the old cathode ray televisions are facing virtual extinction in less than a decade.

   However, many innovations have unsuccessfully challenged the dominance of category-leading products. A rule of thumb for venture investors in innovations is that the innovation must be at least 10 times better than the established product in order to succeed in an existing category.

2. **Compatibility.** This refers to the extent to which a product is consistent with existing values and past experiences of adopters. The history of innovations in international marketing is replete with failures caused by the lack of compatibility of new products in the target market. For example, the first consumer video cassette recorder (VCR), the Sony Betamax, ultimately failed because it could record for only one hour. Most buyers wanted to record movies and sports events; they shunned the Betamax in favor of VHS-format VCRs that could record four hours of programming.
3. **Complexity.** This is the degree to which an innovation or new product is difficult to understand and use. Product complexity is a factor that can slow down the rate of adoption, particularly in developing-country markets with low rates of literacy. Dozens of global companies are developing new, interactive, multimedia consumer electronics products. Complexity is a key design issue; it is a standing joke that in most households, most electronics are underused because users do not know how to take advantage of all features. To achieve mass success, new products will have to be as simple as pushing a button.
4. **Divisibility.** Can a product be tried and used on a limited basis without great expense? Wide discrepancies in income levels around the globe result in major differences in preferred purchase quantities, serving sizes, and product portions. CPC International's Hellmann's mayonnaise was simply not selling in US-sized jars in Latin America. Sales took off after the company placed the mayonnaise in small plastic packets. The plastic packets were within the food budgets of local consumers, and they required no refrigeration—another plus.
5. **Communicability.** This is the degree to which benefits of an innovation or the value of a product may be communicated to a potential market.

ADOPTER CATEGORIES Adopter categories are classifications of individuals within a market on the basis of their innovativeness. The hundreds of studies of the diffusion of innovation demonstrate that adoption is a social phenomenon that is characterized by normal distributions, as shown in Figure 5-4.

Five categories have been assigned to the segments of this normal distribution. The first 2.5 percent of people to purchase a product are defined as innovators. The next 13.5 percent are defined as early adopters, the next 34 percent as the early majority, the next 34 percent as the late majority, and the final 16 percent as laggards. Studies show that innovators tend to be venturesome, more cosmopolitan in their social relationships, and wealthier than those who adopt later. Early adopters are the most influential people in their communities, even more than the innovators. Thus, the early adopters are a critical group in the adoption process, and they have a great influence on the majority, who make up the bulk of the adopters of any product. Several characteristics of

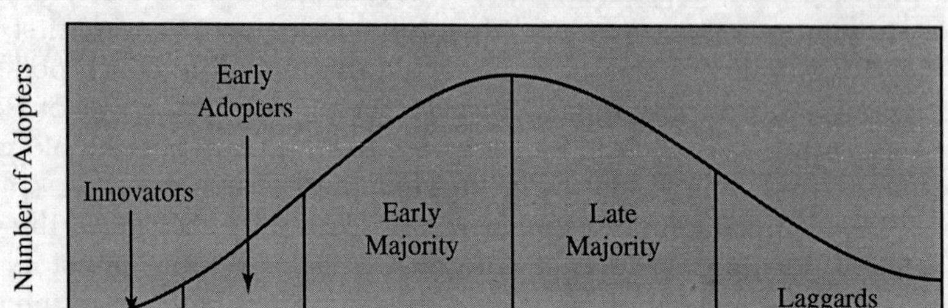

FIGURE 5-4 Adopter Categories

early adopters stand out. First, they tend to be younger, have higher social status, and are in a more favorable financial position than later adopters. They must be responsive to mass-media information sources and must learn about innovations from these sources because they cannot simply copy the behavior of earlier adopters.

One of the major reasons for the normal distribution of adopter categories is the interaction effect, that is, the process through which individuals who have adopted an innovation influence others. Adoption of a new idea or product is the result of human interaction in a social system. Today, with the spread of mobile phones and the rise of user-generated content on the web (UGC), early adopters and influencers have more ways than ever to communicate with their social circle and the world at large. Blogs, podcasts, websites, and all other interactive tools available through Web 2.0 technologies make such interactions exceedingly simple.

From the point of view of the marketing manager, steps taken to persuade innovators and early adopters to purchase a product are critical. These groups must make the first move and are the basis for the eventual penetration of a product into a new market because, over time, the majority copy their behavior.

DIFFUSION OF INNOVATIONS IN PACIFIC RIM COUNTRIES In a cross-national comparison of the United States, Japan, South Korea, and Taiwan, researchers have presented evidence that different country characteristics—in particular, culture and communication patterns—affect diffusion processes for room air conditioners, washing machines, and calculators.[28] Proceeding from the observation that Japan, South Korea, and Taiwan are high-context cultures with relatively homogeneous populations whereas the United States is a low-context, heterogeneous culture, Takada and Jain surmised that faster rates of diffusion would be found in Asia compared with the United States. A second hypothesis supported by the research was that adoption would proceed more quickly in markets in which innovations were introduced relatively late. Presumably, the lag time would give potential consumers more opportunity to assess the relative advantages, compatibility, and other product attributes. Takada and Jain's research has important marketing implications. They conclude that if a marketing manager plans to enter the fast-growing markets of Asia or other regions with products that have proved to be successful in high-income markets, the product's diffusion processes are likely to be much faster than in the home market.

Summary

Perhaps the most striking fact about world markets and buyers is that, for the first time in modern history, the entire world is growing. According to World Bank estimates, every world region, including Africa, will continue to grow, and for the most part the developing countries will grow faster than the rich countries.

There are various ways of dividing the countries of the world into different regional markets. In effect, defining regional markets is an exercise in clustering countries so that similarities within clusters and differences between clusters will be maximized.

The shortage of goods and services is the central problem of transitioning economies and low-income countries. While these countries may pose certain challenges for marketers, they represent potentially attractive markets for many consumer product companies. Marketers should apply basic marketing concepts to ensure that products are designed that fit the needs and incomes of these markets.

All buyers go through a similar process in making a purchase decision; however, they will make different purchases since they will respond to the unique

[28] Hirokazu Takada and Dipak Jain, "Cross-National Analysis of Diffusion of Consumer Durable Goods in Pacific Rim Countries," *Journal of Marketing*, 55 (April 1991): 48–53.

economic, social and cultural, political and governmental, environmental, competitive, and personal factors that influence buyer decisions. The process that buyers go through is summarized in diffusion theory, a marketing universal. The pattern by which an individual adopts a new idea, described by sociologist Everett Rogers, comprises three concepts that are extremely useful to global marketers: the adoption process, characteristics of innovations, and adopter categories.

CLOSING CASE—BORDERLESS BRAND LAUNCH: IS IT BETTER?[29]

The Italian denim brand 55DSL, a spin-off company from the much larger Diesel brand, needed to do something big in order to attract the coveted 15-to-25-year olds who are the target audience for their high-end denim products. The company decided to go global with its marketing campaign, despite its limited budget, tight deadlines, and virtually no name recognition in their most coveted market—the United States. 55DSL conceived a campaign that recruited two "junior lucky bastards" via posters, classified ads, and Monster.com banner ads. Chosen from 900 applicants from over 100 countries, the two winners, from the United Kingdom and France, embarked on a 55-day, 17-stop trip around the world. Along the way, they posted videos of their adventures online showing how they were "living at least 55 seconds a day" at the different locations they visited.

The strategy relied on PR campaign tactics, word-of-mouth, and online viral marketing to generate interest in the brand. They were not disappointed: the trip generated 480 million impressions (including TV, blog coverage, and video views), 135 print articles worldwide, nearly 400,000 unique visitors to the "Junior Lucky Bastard" webpage, and over 300,000 blog links. However, a direct jump in sales could not be detected, despite all the exposure and the publicity campaign in six countries—Japan, United States, and four European countries. At the end of the day, company executives were left wondering: was the worldwide exposure to 400,000 potential buyers worth it?

Discussion Questions

1. What are the major characteristics of the world's regional markets?
2. Which region is the fastest growing? Why?
3. What is the significance of the value equation for global marketers?
4. Do you agree with James Fallows' characterization of the "Asian model" in the opening chapter quote? Is it possible to achieve high income levels without political democracy?

Experiential Exercise: The Global Marketing Plan

Each country in the world is sovereign and unique, but there are similarities among countries in the same region or in countries at the same stage of development that make both the regional and the market stage approaches sound bases for marketing planning. In this chapter, the organization of material is around geographic regions. It could just as well be organized around stages of economic development. It is important for marketers to have a broad overview of the nature of world regions so that they will not make serious oversights in developing the marketing plan. Pick an internationalizing company of your country and develop a marketing plan for a specific region (e.g., EU, North America, or Africa). Then, develop a more detailed plan for a specific country within that region that represents a different stage of development within that region (e.g., Romania, Mexico, or Yemen, respectively).

Application Exercises

1. View The Global Risks Report 2016 (11th Edition) published by the World Economic Forum : http://www3.weforum.org/docs/Media/TheGlobalRisksReport2016.pdf

   Discuss how marketers can leverage these findings for their own strategic international marketing plans.
2. Based on the information about India, develop a market entry plan for a hypothetical wine label from Spain that is looking to enter the Indian market.

[29] Michael Fielding, "Worldwide Brand Release," *Marketing News*, March 15, 2007, 7.

Suggested Readings

Cayla, Julien, and Eric J. Amould. "A Cultural Approach to Branding in the Global Marketplace. " *Journal of International Marketing*, 16, no. 4 (December 2008): 86–112.

Cleveland, Mark, Michel Laroche, and Nicolas Papadopoulos. "Cosmopolitanism, Consumer Ethnocentrism, and Materialism: An Eight County Study of Antecedents and Outcomes." *Journal of International Marketing,* 17, no. 1 (March 2009): 116–146.

Flatters, Paul, and Michael Willmott. "Understanding the Post Recession Consumer." *Harvard Business Review* (July–August 2009): 106–112.

Gaddis, John Lewis. *George F. Kennan: An American Life.* New York: The Penguin Press, 2011.

Ghemawat, Pankaj. "The Cosmopolitan Corporation." *Harvard Business Review* (May 2011): 92–99.

Nijssen, Edwin J., and Susan P. Douglas. "Consumer World-Mindedness, Social-Mindedness and Store Image." *Journal of International Marketing*, 16, no. 3 (September 2008): 84–107.

Nunes, Paul F., Brian A. Johnson, and R. Timothy S. Breene. "Selling to the Moneyed Masses." *Harvard Business Review* (July–August 2004): 95–104.

Ohmae, Kenichi. The *End of the Nation State: The Rise of Regional Economies*. New York: Free Press, 1995.

Okazaki, Shintaro, Barbara Mueller, and Charles R. Taylor. "Global Consumer Culture Positioning: Testing Perceptions of Soft-Sell and Hard-Sell Advertising Appeals Between U.S. and Japanese Consumers." *Journal of International Marketing*, 18, no. 2 (June 2010): 20–34.

Ozsomer, Aysegul, and Selin Altaras. "Global Brand Purchase Likelihood: A Critical Synthesis and an Integrated Conceptual Framework." *Journal of International Marketing*, 16, no. 4 (December 2008): 1–28.

Shaw, Colin. *The DNA of Customer Experience: How Emotions Drive Value.* New York: Palgrave MacMillan, 2007.

Steenkamp, Jan-Benedict E. M., Frenkel ter Hofstede, and Michel Wedel. "A Cross-National Investigation into the Individual and National Cultural Antecedents of Consumer Innovativeness." *Journal of Marketing*, 63, no. 2 (1999): 55–69.

Strizhakova, Yuliya, Robin A. Coulter, and Linda L. Price. "Branded Products as a Passport to Global Citizenship: Perspectives from Developed and Developing Countries." *Journal of International Marketing*, 16, no. 4 (December 2008): 57–85.

Sunje, Aziz. "Selling to Newly Emerging Markets." *Journal of International Marketing*, 7, no. 2 (1999): 93–96.

Tellis, Gerard J., Eden Yin, and Simon Bell. "Global Consumer Innovativeness: Cross-Country Differences and Demographic Commonalities." *Journal of International Marketing*, 17, no. 2 (June 2009): 1–22.

Tyler, Gus. "The Nation-State vs. the Global Economy." *Challenge*, 36 (March 1993): 26–32.

Vogel, Ezra F. *Deng Xiaoping and the Transformation of China.* Cambridge, MA: The Belknap Press of Harvard University Press, 2011.

World Factbook, Washington, DC: Central Intelligence Agency of U.S. Government.

Yergin, Daniel, and Thane Gustafson. *Russia 2010 and What It Means for the World.* New York: Vintage Books, 1995.

CHAPTER 6

Global Marketing Information Systems and Research

To survive in this new globally competitive world, we had to modernize. Information technology is the glue for everything we do.

—JAMES WOGSLAND *Former Vice Chairman, Caterpillar*

Nothing changes more constantly than the past; for the past that influences our lives does not consist of what happened, but of what men believe happened.

—GERALD W. JOHNSON *American Heroes and Hero-Worship* (NY: HARPER, 1943)

Learning Objectives

1. Describe the purpose and components of global marketing information systems (187–188).
2. Distinguish between the surveillance and search modes of scanning (189–191).
3. Discuss the sources of market information (191–193).
4. Explain the steps of the formal marketing research process (196–206).
5. Describe the challenges and benefits of global marketing research (201–203).
6. Discuss the role of global marketing research in the decision-making process (206–209).

INTRODUCTION

Information, or useful data, is the raw material of executive action. The global marketer is faced with a dual problem in acquiring the information needed for decision making (refer Box 6-1). In high-income countries, the amount of information available far exceeds the absorptive capacity of an individual or an

BOX 6-1

Side Bar: Market Research in India Is Challenging

Today, India is on every multinational's radar, and there is an increasing trend towards formulating an India-specific strategy. The trillion dollar plus Indian GDP in purchasing power parity terms (PPP) is now ranked fourth place, and with 40 percent of the population under the age of 15 years, the future is increasingly looking more promising for India.

One uniform strategy cannot be adopted for the Indian market. India is more of a continent than a country, with its numerous religions, languages, dialects, customs, and traditions. Spread across 29 states and 6 union territories, this market of a billion people is something that needs to be well researched and understood before creating an entry strategy. Following are some of the most important challenges when doing market research in India:

- One of the largest drawbacks in India is the lack of secondary data in the public domain. Certain countries like China are better documented. The information that is available is either outdated or is highly fragmented, with no single authoritative source. For example, the latest government census data available is for 2001.
- Company data may be maintained in hard copy, but the digitization process is only a recent phenomenon and progress is slow. This can be prominently seen in dealings with the Registrar of Companies (RoC). Individual RoC offices have different levels of digitization, making it extremely difficult to get similar data for companies across India.
- Although English is the most prevalent business language, consumer insights may well not be covered in English alone. There are 10 major languages that are spoken, and they have to be considered while covering the market. There are also challenges in the translation of questionnaires as well as their responses.
- Culturally, too, there is a challenge in the interviewing process. For example, when there's a group discussion scheduled, there are bound to be drop-outs or delays at the last minute. Therefore, the sample size of respondents to be taken should be almost double that of the successful numbers intended. In the case of high net-worth individuals or senior personnel, additional gestures, such as personally escorting them, will ensure that there is participation and cooperation.
- There is a difference between attracting respondents in large cities versus smaller ones. The respondents in smaller cities tend to be more cooperative and willing compared to those from larger cities where incentives are almost a must for participation.
- Use of technology enablers to streamline the research process. Computer-aided telephonic interviewing (CATI), which is pretty popular internationally for fast turnaround and cost minimization, has its limitations in an Indian context. This could be attributed to the lack of penetration of phone lines across the strata of society and also to the cultural lack of interest in answering the phone. So, CATI is seen to be effective only in the more affluent areas, which constitute around 10 percent of the country.
- Business respondents (business customers, channel members, suppliers, business partners) have an inherent tendency to be suspicious of giving interviews and sharing information. They tend to respond either vaguely or provide responses that do not necessarily reflect reality in the market; therefore, it is imperative that cross-checks are done.

In conclusion, there are a few golden rules to succeed with market research in India:

- Use multiple data collection sources to validate and strengthen hypotheses about market characteristics.
- Hire locally experienced personnel or choose a local partner for the practical research tasks.

Source: Adapted from K. Ramamurthy and A. Naikare, "Analyzing the Indian Market," in *Global Market Briefings: Doing Business with India,* 2nd Edition, Roderick Millar, ed. (Great Britain: GMB Publishing Ltd., 2007); see also Country Report, 2011 India, Economist Intelligence Unit Limited, UK at http://wikileaks.org/gifiles/attach/14/14011_EIU%20India%20Report%20Nov%202011.pdf.

organization. The information problem is superabundance, not scarcity. Although advanced countries all over the world are in the middle of an information explosion, there is less information available on the market characteristics of less developed countries.

Thus, the global marketer is faced with the problem of information abundance and information scarcity. The global marketer must know where to go to obtain information, the subject areas that should be covered, and the different ways that information can be acquired. Acquired information must be processed in an efficient and useful way. The technical term for the process of information acquisition is *scanning*. This chapter presents an information acquisition model for global marketing as well as an outline of the global marketing research process. The chapter concludes with a discussion of how to manage the marketing information collection system and the marketing research effort.

When managed correctly, the insights collected through marketing research can yield valuable insights for a company. For example, by monitoring its loyalty card data and combining that with survey research on products that were not popular at some of its stores, the European grocer Tesco was able to find out why young mothers were not buying baby products at certain stores: they perceived pharmacies as more trustworthy sources. In response, Tesco launched BabyClub, a program that provides expert advice and baby product discounts to that consumer segment. As a result, baby product sales at Tesco jumped by 8 percent in the first two years of the program.[1]

RESEARCH REQUIREMENTS IN INTERNATIONAL MARKETING

An international company steps out to a new foreign country environment where many issues regarding doing the business are unknown. In case of sequential process of entry like from exporting to establishing own subsidiaries, the concerned company progressively collects information about doing business. However, advance information about the foreign country, irrespective of mode of entry always helps an entrant company to be strategic. Therefore, information/data about the destination country in a structured way and through a right research framework allows the entrant company to take conscious business decisions. Depending on the extent of involvement of the entrant company in the foreign market the researchable issues could be varied where some are trivial and others are of vary substantial nature. However, based on commonality in terms of their position in business areas, they essentially can be as under:

Foreign market competition related issues

- Market the potential of the products offered to the host country consumers.
- Level of market competition the products on offer would face.
- Host country macro environment and its stability.
- Business risk in terms of political, economical, etc., in the host country.
- Locally grown products and their market dominance.
- Government restrictions on foreign companies.

Initial start up issues in foreign environment

- Effect of organization specific advantage like brand and other unique capabilities in the host country market competition.
- Brand building effort and brand image transferability to the host country environment.

[1] John E. Forsyth, Nicolò Galante, and Todd Guild, "Capitalizing on Customer Insights," *The McKinsey Quarterly,* 3 (2006): 43–53.

- Level of financial resource requirements to start foreign operation.
- Compatibility of home country managerial experience in host country market.

Mandatory requirement issues

- Laws/regulations of the host country governing the product specification.
- Country specific product and quality standards.
- Packaging norms and standards in the destination country.
- Environment regulations and standards.
- Labeling requirements and standards.
- Production process standard in the destination country.
- Advertising regulations/ legal restrictions.

Host country culture related issues

- Basic country culture and its impact on people's behavior in general.
- Impact of country culture on consumer behavior.
- Society influence on buying and decision making.
- Material culture of the foreign country population.
- Culture effect on distribution channel intermediary behavior.
- Technology environment in the host country.
- Effect of cultural norms on marketing communication.

Marketing mix related issues

- Complete profiling of the targeted consumer segments.
- Discretionary product modification requirements.
- Perception mapping of the target segment about the product to be marketed.
- Distribution channel options in the target country and channel structure.
- Nature of media availability in the target country and their effectiveness.
- Pricing strategy of the competitors and impact of price on the demand of product.
- Sales and merchandising strategy.

OVERVIEW OF GLOBAL MARKETING INFORMATION SYSTEMS

The purpose of a marketing information system (MIS) is to provide managers and other decision makers with a continuous flow of information about markets, customers, competitors, and company operations. An MIS should provide a means for gathering, analyzing, classifying, storing, retrieving, and reporting relevant data about customers, markets, channels, sales, and competitors (refer Box 6.2). A company's MIS should also cover important aspects of a company's external environment. For example, companies in any industry need to pay close attention to government regulations, mergers, acquisitions, and alliances. As suggested by the quote from James Wogsland of Caterpillar at the beginning of this chapter, global competition intensifies the need for an effective MIS. In addition to Caterpillar, Toyota, ABB, Federal Express, Grand Metropolitan PLC, Ford, and Texas Instruments are among the companies with global operations that have invested in sophisticated systems networks to improve intracompany information sharing.

Poor operating results can often be traced to insufficient data and information about events both inside and outside the company. For example, when a new management team was installed at the American unit of Adidas AG, the German-headquartered athletic shoe marketer, data was not even available on normal inventory turnover rates. A new reporting system revealed that archrivals Reebok and Nike turned inventories five times per year, compared with twice a year at Adidas. This information was used to tighten the marketing focus on the best-selling Adidas products. Perry Ellis International's use of MIS as a strategic competitive tool is described in the Side Bar on the following page.

Indeed, it is no easy task to organize, implement, and monitor global marketing information and research strategies and programs. Moreover, these are not simply marketing issues; they are organizational imperatives. These tasks must be coordinated in a coherent manner that contributes to the overall strategic direction of the organization. The MIS and research function must provide relevant information in a timely, cost-efficient, and actionable manner.

The past few years have seen dramatic changes in worldwide political and economic events. Increased global economic integration between countries, the emergence of new markets, volatile currency exchange rates, and other factors are driving the demand for access to credible worldwide business and political information. Today's economic and political environments require worldwide news information on a daily basis. Geocentric global companies generally have intelligence systems that meet these challenges. Typically, the strategic planning or market research departments staff these systems. They distribute information to senior management and to managers throughout the organization.

BOX 6-2

Side Bar: Perry Ellis Deploys a Valuable Tool for Growth and Integration

Delivering products based on customers' needs, growing its stores, and integrating its brick-and-mortar operations with its e-commerce business were three of the main goals for Perry Ellis International, Inc., a Miami-based fashion house that manages a portfolio of 27 established brands such as Perry Ellis, Nike Swim, and Jantzen. The company sells its products at 12,500 locations, including its own boutiques and luxury department stores such as Nordstrom and Neiman Marcus in the United States.

Maintaining relevancy in the fast-moving fashion industry across so many brands and so many channels of distribution requires paying close attention to customers' needs and tastes, according to Perry Ellis CIO, Luis Paez. "We do this by mining point-of-sale data collected from each location. We also use Geographic Information System [GIS] software and custom programs to predict trends and analyze POS [point-of-sale] down to the SKU [stock keeping unit] at store level," he says, adding, "These strategies enable us to target the right product to the right market."

Using specialized software from Oracle Corp., Perry Ellis is able to filter POS data and import it into another software module that calculates markdown recommendations and almost immediately sends these back to the retail stores. This process reduces unnecessary markdowns and increases sales at the same time. Most importantly, the same system can be integrated into the company's new online stores, where it will help calculate demand and design promotions in direct response to trends seen in its customers' purchasing behavior. Thus, a single stream of customer data can be used across the organization to plan marketing and pricing strategies almost in real time—a much needed competitive edge in the crowded fashion retail industry.

Source: Deena M. Amato-McCoy, "Perry Ellis' IT Priorities," *Chain Store Age* 83, no. 2 (February 2007): 33. See also "Global POS Software Market 2011-2105," (June 2012), accessed December 26, 2012, http://www.reportlinker.com/p0463538-summary/Global-POS-Software-Market.html; Rosemary Peavler, "What are Point of Sales Systems for Inventory Management," About.com Money–Business Finance, accessed December 26, 2012, http://bizfinance.about.com/od/inventory/f/what-are-point-of-sales-systems-for-inventory-management.htm.

A more detailed discussion of the workings of an intracompany MIS is beyond the scope of this book. The discussion that follows focuses on the subject agenda, scanning modes, and information sources characteristic of a global information system that is oriented toward the external environment.

Information Subject Agenda

A starting point for a global MIS is a list of subjects about which information is desired. The resulting "subject agenda" should be tailored to the specific needs and objectives of the company. The general framework suggested in Table 6-1 consists of six broad information areas. The framework satisfies two essential criteria. First, it comprises all the information subject areas relevant to a company with global operations. Second, the categories in the framework are mutually exclusive: any kind of information encompassed by the framework can be correctly placed in one and only one category. The basic elements of the external environment outlined in the last four chapters—economic, social/cultural, legal/regulatory, and financial—will undoubtedly be on the information agenda of most companies, as shown in the table.

Scanning Modes: Surveillance (viewing and monitoring) and Search (investigation and research)

Once the subject agenda has been determined, the next step is the actual collection of information. This can be accomplished using either surveillance or search.

In the surveillance mode, the marketer engages in informal information gathering. Globally oriented marketers are constantly on the lookout for information about potential opportunities and threats in various parts of the world. They want to know everything about the industry, the business, the marketplace, and consumers. This passion shows up in the way they stay alert for clues, rumors, nuggets of information, and insights from other people's experiences. Browsing through newspapers and magazines and surfing the Internet is one way to ensure exposure to information on a regular basis. Global marketers may also develop a habit of watching news programs from around the world via the web, cable, or satellite. This type of general exposure to information is known as *viewing*. If a particular news story has special relevance for a company—for example, entry of a new player into a global industry, say Samsung, into automobiles—marketers in the automobile and related industries and all competitors of Samsung will pay special attention, tracking the story as it develops. This is known as **monitoring**.

TABLE 6-1 Six Subject Agenda Categories for a Global Business Intelligence System

Category	Coverage
1. Markets	Demand estimates, consumer behavior, products, channels, communication media availability and cost, market responsiveness
2. Competition	Corporate, business, and functional strategies and plans
3. Foreign exchange	Balance of payments, interest rates, attractiveness of country currency, expectations of analysts
4. Prescriptive information	Laws, regulations, rulings concerning taxes, earnings, dividends in both host countries and home country
5. Resource information	Availability of human, financial, information, and physical resources
6. General conditions	Overall review of sociocultural, political, technological environments

The search mode is characterized by more formal activity. Search is characterized by the deliberate seeking out of specific information. Search often involves *investigation*, a relatively limited and informal type of search. Investigation often involves seeking out books or articles in trade publications or searching the Internet on a particular topic or issue. Search may also consist of **research**, a formally organized effort to acquire specific information for a specific purpose. This type of formal, organized research is described later in the chapter.

One study found that nearly 75 percent of the information acquired by headquarters executives at US global companies comes from surveillance as opposed to search. However, the viewing mode generated only 13 percent of important external information, whereas monitoring generated 60 percent. Two factors contribute to the paucity of information generated by viewing. One is the limited extent to which executives are exposed to information that is not included in a clearly defined subject agenda. The other is the limited receptivity of the typical executive to information outside this agenda. Every executive limits his or her exposure to information that will not have a high probability of being relevant to the job or company. This explains the increasing popularity of features such as customizable information filters and electronic agents at information portals like MSN and Google and the rise of Really Simple Syndication (RSS) tools called "aggregators" or feed readers. This is rational: a person can absorb only a minute fraction of the data available to him or her. Exposure to and retention of information stimuli must be selective.

Nevertheless, it is vital that the organization as a whole be receptive to information not explicitly recognized as important. To be effective, a scanning system must ensure that the organization is viewing areas where developments that could be important to the company might occur. Innovations in information technology have increased the speed with which information is transmitted and simultaneously shortened the life of its usefulness to the company. Advances in technology have also placed new demands on global firms in terms of shrinking reaction times to acquired information. In some instances, the creation of a full-time scanning unit with responsibility for guiding and stimulating the process of acquiring and disseminating strategic information may be advisable.

Of all the changes in recent years affecting the availability of information, perhaps none is more apparent than the explosion of documentary and electronic information. An overabundance of information has created a major problem for anyone attempting to stay abreast of key developments in multiple national markets. Today, executives are overwhelmed with documentary information. However, too few companies employ a formal system for coordinating scanning activities. This situation results in considerable duplication of effort. For example, it is not uncommon for members of an entire management group to read a single publication covering a particular subject area despite the fact that several other excellent publications covering the same area may be available. The best way to identify unnecessary duplication is to carry out an audit of reading activity by asking each person involved to list the publications he or she reads regularly. A consolidation of the lists will reveal the surveillance coverage. Often, the scope of the group will be limited to a handful of publications to the exclusion of other worthwhile ones. A good remedy for this situation is consultation with outside experts regarding the availability and quality of publications in relevant fields or subject areas. Also, new technological tools are at hand to help marketers. Data management programs, specialized software tools for data mining, text retrieval and classification, patent searching, webpage tracking, and Internet monitoring are becoming more and more popular at leading firms in highly competitive industries (e.g., pharmaceuticals, computer technology, telecommunications, defense, and aerospace). They also make it much easier for executives to cover a wider array of media sources, hone in on the most pertinent information for their company, and share that information across the organization.

Overall, then, the global organization is faced with the following needs:

- An efficient, effective system that will scan and digest published sources and technical journals in the headquarters country as well as all countries in which the company has operations or customers.
- Daily scanning, translating, digesting, abstracting, and electronic input of information into a market intelligence system.
- Expanding information coverage to other regions of the world.

SOURCES OF MARKET INFORMATION

Human Sources

Although scanning is a vital source of information, research has shown that headquarters executives of global companies obtain as much as two-thirds of the information they need from personal sources. A great deal of external information comes from executives based abroad in company subsidiaries, affiliates, and branches. These executives are likely to have established communication with distributors, consumers, customers, suppliers, and government officials. Indeed, a striking feature of the global corporation—and a major source of competitive strength—is the role executives abroad play in acquiring and disseminating information about the world environment. Headquarters executives generally acknowledge that company executives overseas are the people who know best what is going on in their areas. The following is a typical comment by headquarters executives:

> Our principal sources are internal. We have a very well-informed and capable overseas group. The local people have a double advantage: they know the local scene and they know our business; therefore, they are an excellent source. They know what we are interested in learning, and because of their local knowledge they are able to effectively cover available information from all sources.

The information issue exposes one of the key weaknesses of a domestic company: although more attractive opportunities may be present outside existing areas of operation, they will likely go unnoticed by inside sources in a domestic company because the scanning horizon tends to end at the home-country border. Similarly, a company with only limited geographical operations may be at risk because internal sources abroad tend to scan only information about their own countries or region.

Other important information sources are friends, acquaintances, professional colleagues, consultants, and prospective new employees. The latter are particularly important if they have worked for competitors. Sometimes, information-related ethical and legal issues arise when a person changes jobs. When a Canadian employee of Mattel Inc. (maker of the Barbie doll) allegedly copied internal company documents on a portable storage device and soon after went to work for the toy company's rival MGA Entertainment (maker of the Bratz dolls), Mattel wasted no time filing a lawsuit against MGA for stolen trade secrets.[2] Professional organizations, networking groups, trade shows, and other business forums also provide ample opportunities to "take the pulse" of an industry, competitor, or target market by talking to colleagues.

---

[2] Christopher Palmeri, "Totally Teed-Off Barbie," *BusinessWeek*, December 18, 2006: 13.

And, once again, today's technology can make those connections easier than ever. Business-related social networking sites such as LinkedIn and Spoke offer many ways to connect online with people in the same industry, position, or of similar professional interests.

It is hard to overstate the importance of travel and contact for building rapport and personal relationships. Moreover, one study found that three-quarters of the information acquired from human sources is gained in face-to-face conversation. Why? Some information is too sensitive to transmit in any other way. For example, highly placed government employees could find their careers compromised if they are identified as information sources. In such cases, the most secure way of transmitting information is face-to-face rather than in writing. Information that includes estimates of future developments or even appraisals of the significance of current happenings is often considered too uncertain to commit to writing. Commenting on this point, one executive said the following:

> People are reluctant to commit themselves in writing to highly "iffy" things. They are not cowards or overly cautious; they simply know that you are bound to be wrong in trying to predict the future, and they prefer to not have their names associated with documents that will someday look foolish.

The great importance of face-to-face communication lies also in the dynamics of personal interaction. Personal contact provides an occasion for executives to get together for a long enough time to permit communication in some depth. Face-to-face discussion also exposes highly significant forms of nonverbal communication, as discussed in Chapter 4. One executive described the value of face-to-face contact in the following terms:

> If you really want to find out about an area, you must see people personally. There is no comparison between written reports and actually sitting down with someone and talking. A personal meeting is worth a thousand written reports.

Today face-to-face is often screen-to-screen. Businesses and market researchers alike have been flocking to videoconferencing, an increasingly viable substitute to in-person meetings. With the continuously improving quality of images and the increasing bandwidth availability, connecting online with colleagues, customers, or focus groups halfway across the world is easier—and more lifelike—than ever.

Documentary Sources

One of the most important developments in global marketing research is the extraordinary expansion in the quantity and quality of documentary sources of information. The information explosion is an explosion in the availability of documentary information not only in print but increasingly online and on the Internet and the intranet for company-restricted information. The two broad categories of documentary information are published public information and unpublished private documents. The former is available on the Internet, and the latter is available on the intranet or company password-restricted-access networks created by organizations for their own employees.

The vast quantities of published documentary information that are available create a unique challenge: How can you find the exact information you want? One of the fast-growing industries in the world is companies that gather, analyze, and organize data from multiple sources, which they then make available to clients.

Internet Sources

The range and depth of information available on the Internet is vast and growing every day. Companies, governments, nongovernmental organizations, market research firms, data assemblers and packagers, security analysts, news gathering organizations, universities, and university faculty, to mention just a few, are all sources that can be accessed online. The Internet is a unique information source. It combines the three basic information source types: human, documentary (published and private), and direct perception. And, being still a relatively young technology, the Internet continues to stimulate the introduction of new information and communication tools almost on a monthly basis. Whether it's instant messaging, Voice over Internet Protocol(VoIP) telephony, blogs, podcasts, or file sharing—these tools represent an ever-increasing array of new ways to search, monitor, and acquire information, often in more than one medium (text, video, music, images, etc.).

A number of electronic resources have been developed in recent years, as seen in the sample list compiled in Table 6-2.

CREATING BUSINESS VALUE THROUGH SOCIAL MEDIA ANALYTICS The worldwide social network community now consists of more than 1.2 billion people. Facebook's current 500 million users, if they were a country, would be the third largest behind China and India. Of the 4 billion people worldwide who use cell phones, 450 million have full access to the web on their phones. Many companies have adopted consumer social media to facilitate online customer interactions which, when monitored, provide an often less costly and new platform for gleaning insights into customer behavior, sentiment, choices, and company–customer relationships.[3]

TABLE 6-2 Industry and Marketing Information Sources on the Web

Industry Resources	Market Research Resources
Cole Library Rensselaer at Hartford www.ewp.rpi.edu/hartford/library/index.html	Guide to Market Research on the Web www.knowthis.com
US International Trade Administration www.ita.doc.gov	Alacra www.alacra.com
Valuation Resources www.valuationresources.com	ECNext Knowledge Center www.ecnext.com/commercial/knowledgecenter.shtml
Industrial Reports www.census.gov/manufacturing/cir/index.html	Market Research.com www.marketresearch.com
First Research Industry Profiles www.1stresearch.com	OneSource www.onesource.com
Hoover's www.hoovers.com	Profound www.profound.com
Standard & Poor's Industry Surveys www.netadvantage.standardandpoors.com	

Source: Cynthia Shamel, Introduction to Online Market & Industry Research, Cincinnati: Thomson Texere, 2004.

[3] Jacques Bughin, Michael Chui, and James Manyika, "Capturing Business Value with Social Technologies," *The McKinsey Quarterly,* (November 2012), accessed December 12, 2012, https://www.mckinseyquarterly.com/Capturing_business_value_with_social_technologies_3029.

Companies can obtain important and actionable data from wide-ranging online communities at significantly reduced cost as compared to traditional marketing research. Companies also seek increased effectiveness of advertising expenditures with social media.[4]

Social media facilitates virtual conversations. Measuring the impact of social media is moving beyond counting "clicks" toward measuring influence, participation, engagement, and excitement. Social media monitoring tools have the potential to provide rich data to reveal important information about customers in order to customize both the digital experience and on- and off-line purchasing behavior and decision making. Although companies create Facebook pages and Twitter feeds, many do not have a comprehensive understanding of how social media influences consumer product and brand awareness, drives sales and profitability, and builds loyalty across platforms, diverse communities, and over shorter or longer periods of time.[5]

Social media has the potential to reach consumers and influence purchasing behavior and brand awareness. With respect to these opportunities, four primary functions have been identified. These include monitoring, responding, amplifying, and influencing consumer purchase behavior.[6] Understanding how social media influences consumer behavior through measureable results assists the global marketer's ability to use social media to engage with the customer, whether the goal is to create "buzz" and interest in an offering, learn from customers about what they need and want, mitigate negative word-of-mouth, or target consumers with location-specific deals. There is no one-size-fits-all approach to social media and digital measurement. Measuring social initiatives as part of a formalized process of marketing research is the basis for making data-driven decisions.

Web Analytics: Clouds, Big Data, and Smart Assets[7]

Cloud computing, wireless technology, embedded chips, and tracking devices raise important questions for marketers about how to best utilize and capture ever-expanding data from multiple sources. Social media monitoring tools and analytics packages can produce rich data sets to fine-tune e-mail communications, personalize the web experience, or create digital advertisements. The term "big data" is used to describe the growing size of data banks so large that they require more sophisticated analytical tools than traditionally smaller data banks.[8]

Digital marketers should understand real-time intelligence-gathering tools that analyze customers' online activities. What are customers actually seeing and responding to and what they are saying? One of the UK's top grocery chains, Tesco, gathers transaction data on its millions of customers through its loyalty card program, using the data to target new business opportunities and inform decisions on pricing, promotion, and shelf allocation.[9] Fresh Direct, an online grocer, analyzes online data to immediately adjust pricing and promotions based on data feeds from online transactions, website traffic, and

---

[4] Ibid.

[5] Roxanne Divol, David Edelman, and Hugo Sarrazin, "Demystifying Social Media," *The McKinsey Quarterly* (April 2012), accessed January 23, 2013, https://www.mckinseyquarterly.com/Demystifying_social_media_2958.

[6] Ibid.

[7] Jacques Bughin, Michael Chui, and James Manyika, "Clouds, Big Data, and Smart Assets: Ten Tech-Enabled Business Trends to Watch," *The McKinsey Quarterly* (August 2010), accessed May 8, 2012, https://www.mckinseyquarterly.com/Capturing_business_value_with_social_technologies_3029.

[8] Brad Terrell, "Big Data: What Marketers Need to Know," ClickZ online newsletter, (April 17, 2012), accessed April 17, 2012, http://www.clickz.com/clickz/column/2167777/-marketers.

[9] Ibid.

face-to-face customer service interactions captured by brick and mortar staff.[10] Many firms, including Ford Motor, Cisco, and PepsiCo, analyze social media to measure the impact of marketing campaigns and assess how consumer brand sentiment is changing.

The combination of big data, cloud computing, unprecedented capabilities of combining data from a myriad of sources, as well as the algorithms that enable understanding, has given rise to the concept and application of "convergence analytics."[11] The use of advanced data gathering and data analysis can be used by marketers to gain new insights into consumer behavior.

In a recent study, 71 percent of marketing executives surveyed reported that data-driven customer insights will be very or extremely important to their firm's competitiveness over the next two to four years.[12] Companies report they must grow their technology infrastructure, expand analytical skills and talent, adjust organizational structures across business unit boundaries, create processes that impose new operational discipline, and rebalance roles of more traditional media content creation with digital initiatives.[13] In fact, the cost of marketing analytic technology in some industries is greater than the spending by IT departments. This fact highlights the continuing truth that the marketers are the primary owners and users of data for delivering customer insight and relevance to the organization.[14]

Despite the new technology environment where capabilities for capturing and analyzing information is more widely available than in the past, some things never change. Marketers have always been the primary users of data to connect customers with experiences and purchase opportunities. Social media, web analytics, and big data must be aligned with business objectives, and objectives need to address the major problems and opportunities the business faces.

An example of new analytics and big data is online survey research. It is now possible to conduct test/control double-blind studies that can address national markets (from broad to niche) defined both demographically and psychographically on any marketing issue or question, with samples that are large enough to get results at a 95 percent confidence level. Once the survey is designed, the results are normally available within 24 hours and the cost of such a study is dramatically lower that it was when interviews were conducted by traditional methods including mail, telephone, and mall intercept interviews.

Direct Perception

Direct sensory perception provides a vital background for the information that comes from human and documentary sources. Direct perception gets all the senses involved. It means seeing, feeling, hearing, smelling, or tasting for oneself to find out what is going on in a particular country, rather than getting secondhand information by hearing or reading about a particular issue. Some information is easily available from other sources but requires sensory experience to sink in.

---

[10] Ibid.

[11] Andrew Edwards, "The Dawn of Convergence Analytics," ClickZ, an online newsletter (December 17, 2012), accessed August 13, 2012, http://www.clickz.com/clickz/column/2198207/the-dawn-of-convergence-analytics.

[12] "Marketing & Sales Practice: What Marketers Say About Working Online," McKinsey Global Survey Results, *McKinsey Quarterly* (November 2011), accessed November 29, 2011, https://www.mckinseyquarterly.com/What_marketers_say_about_working_online_McKinsey_Global_Survey_results_2892.

[13] David C. Edelman, "Four Ways to Get More Value from Digital Marketing," *McKinsey Quarterly* (March 2010), accessed April 17, 2010, https://www.mckinseyquarterly.com/Four_ways_to_get_more_value_from_digital_marketing_2556.

[14] Stephanie Miller, "Big Data and the Marketing Organization," ClickZ, an online newsletter (October 1, 2012), accessed October 1, 2012, http://www.clickz.com/clickz/column/2213370/big-data-and-the-marketing-organization.

Often, the background information or context one gets from observing a situation can help fill in the "big picture." For example, after spending much time in Japan, the chief executive of a small US company that manufactures an electronic device for controlling corrosion managed to book several orders for the device. Following an initial burst of success, Japanese orders dropped off; for one thing, the executive was told the packaging was too plain. "We couldn't understand why we needed a five-color label and a custom-made box for this device, which goes under the hood of a car or in the boiler room of a utility company," the executive said. While waiting for the bullet train in Japan one day, the executive's local distributor purchased a cheap watch at the station and had it elegantly wrapped. The distributor asked the American executive to guess the value of the watch based on the packaging. Despite everything he had heard and read about the Japanese obsession with quality, it was the first time the American understood that in Japan, "a book is judged by the cover." As a result, the company revamped its packaging, seeing to such details as ensuring that strips of tape used to seal the boxes were cut to precisely the same length. On a more personal level, face-to-face communications with overseas clients or partners allows marketers to observe many of the nonverbal cues that provide a deeper understanding of how they react to one's product, advertising campaign, or price label, for example. Much of the message content in any conversation is delivered by facial expressions, body language, tone, and other nonverbal signs. To marketers, this unfiltered, direct source of information is just as valuable as any formal marketing research.

As these examples show, cultural and language differences require firsthand visits to important markets to "get the lay of the land." Travel should be seen not only as a tool for management control of existing operations but also as a vital and indispensable tool in information scanning.

FORMAL MARKETING RESEARCH

Information is a critical ingredient in formulating and implementing a successful marketing strategy. As described earlier in the chapter, an MIS should produce a continuous flow of information. Marketing research, on the other hand, is the project-specific, systematic gathering of data in the search scanning mode. There are two ways to conduct marketing research. One is to design and implement a study with in-house staff. The other is to use an outside firm specializing in marketing research. The importance of the global market to research firms has increased considerably in recent years. In 2016, most of the world's largest 25 marketing, advertising, public opinion and research conglomerates were international with 37.1% of their combined revenues coming from countries outside their home market as shown in Table 6-3.[15] The globalization and boundary breaking of the industry continues, particularly among the Global Top 25. The average number of countries in which a Global Top 25 company has an office or a subsidiary is 27 countries. These numbers include more outreach to and establishment of offices in emerging research markets in Africa, the Middle East, Southeast Asia and South and Central America. Only 1 of the top 25 global firms, Video Research Ltd. in the Japan and has for practical purposes, no revenue from outside their home country.[16] The 25 largest global companies in terms of total revenue are shown in Table 6-3 for 2016.

The process of collecting data and converting it into useful information can be divided into five basic steps: identifying the research problem, developing a research plan, collecting data, analyzing data, and presenting the research findings. Each step is discussed below.

---

[15] https://www.ama.org/publications/MarketingNews/Pages/2016-top-25-marketing-research-firms.aspx.
[16] Ibid.

TABLE 6-3 The Top 25 Research Company Revenue and Spread During 2016

		2016 Global Revenue in Billion USD	% Global Revenue From Outside Home Country in %	Parent Country
1	Nielsen	6.2	41.6	USA
2	Kantar	3.7	79.7	UK
3	IMS Health Inc.	2.9	61.4	USA
4	Ipsos SA	2	93.1	France
5	GfK SE	1.7	75.3	Germany
6	IRI	0.981	38.3	USA
7	dunnhumby	0.971	61.7	UK
8	Westat	0.51	3.6	USA
9	INTAGE Holdings Inc.	0.376	8.2	Japan
10	ComScore	0.369	27.3	USA
11	Wood Mackenzie	0.365	58.1	UK
12	The NPD Group	0.307	24.9	USA
13	MACROMILL Inc.	0.296	30.7	Japan
14	J.D. Power	0.247	33.8	USA
15	ICF International	0.219	29.5	USA
16	Video Research Ltd.	0.182	0	Japan
17	Decision Resources Group	0.168	28.1	USA
18	MaritzCX	0.152	26.5	USA
19	Abt SRBI	0.124	4.1	USA
20	YouGov	0.123	71.8	UK
21	ORC International	0.122	31.8	USA
22	Lieberman Research Worldwide	0.12	30.9	USA
23	Rentrak	0.116	15	USA
24	Médiamétrie	0.105	10.1	France
25	Cello Health	0.097	42	UK
Global average for 25 top companies			37.1	

Step 1: Identify the Research Problem

The following story illustrates the first step in the formal marketing research process.

The vice presidents of finance and marketing of a shoe company were traveling around the world to estimate the market potential for their products. They arrived in a very poor country and both immediately noticed that none of the local citizens were wearing shoes. The finance vice president said, "We might as well get back on the plane. There is no market for shoes in this country." The vice president of marketing replied, "What an opportunity! Everyone in this country is a potential customer!"

The potential market for shoes was enormous in the eyes of the marketing executive. To formally confirm his instinct, some research would be required. As this story shows, research is often undertaken after a problem or opportunity has presented itself. Perhaps a competitor is making inroads in one or more important markets around the world, or, as in the story recounted above, a company may wish to determine whether a particular country or regional market provides good growth potential. It is a truism of market research that "a problem well defined is a problem half solved." Thus, regardless of what situation sets the research effort in motion, the first two questions a marketer should ask are, "What information do I need?" and "Why do I need this information?"

The research problem often involves assessing the nature of the market opportunity. This, in turn, depends in part on whether the market that is the focus of the research effort can be classified as existing or potential. Existing markets are those in which customer needs are already being served by one or more companies. In many countries, data about the size of existing markets—in terms of dollar volume and unit sales—are readily available. Information Resources Inc. and Nielsen, among others, compile exhaustive amounts of data about sales in various product categories worldwide. In countries in which such data are not available, a company focusing on existing markets must first estimate the market size, the level of demand, or the rate of product purchase or consumption. A second research objective in existing markets may be assessment of the company's overall competitiveness in terms of product appeal, price, distribution, and promotional coverage and effectiveness. Researchers may be able to pinpoint a weakness in the competitor's product or identify an unserved market segment.

LATENT VERSUS INCIPIENT MARKETS Potential markets can be further subdivided into latent and incipient markets. A latent market is, in essence, an undiscovered segment. It is a market in which demand would materialize if an appropriate product were made available. In a latent market, demand is zero before the product is offered. In the case of existing markets, the main research challenge is to understand the extent to which competition fully meets customer needs. With latent markets, initial success is not based on a company's competitiveness. Rather, it depends on the prime-mover advantage—a company's ability to uncover the opportunity and launch a marketing program that taps the latent demand. Sometimes traditional marketing research is not an effective means for doing this. In fact, many products that are ubiquitous today would not have been developed if market research was the only way to measure demand.

Imagine how consumers would have responded to survey questions that asked: "Would you buy a smaller Walkman that costs upwards of US$100?" or "Would you buy used items from strangers who require payment up front and live far away?" The iPod, iPad, iTunes and Apple Store, and eBay and Facebook, as we know them today, would never have been born if the only source of information about markets was marketing research. Steve Jobs, arguably the greatest business innovator of the last half century, never relied upon marketing research to determine what to offer customers. He knew what customers wanted. Mark Zuckerberg, *Time* Magazine's Person of the Year in 2010, also knows what his customers want. He created a network of more than 750 million active users. Fifty percent of active users log on to Facebook in any given day; the average user has 130 friends, and users spend over 700 billion minutes per month on Facebook. By focusing on the benefits provided by new products rather than the markets for them, entrepreneurial companies like Apple and Facebook gain the freedom to innovate and the market shares that come with first-mover advantage.

Incipient demand is demand that will emerge if a particular economic, technological, political, or sociocultural trend continues. If a company offers a product to meet incipient demand before the trends have taken root, it will have little market response. After the trends have had a chance to unfold, the incipient demand will become latent, and later existing, demand. This can be illustrated by the impact of smaller family size on demand for supermarkets and other retail stores in India. As the traditional household size shrinks and the time spent at work grows, the demand for retail outlets also rises. Therefore, if a company can predict a country's future rate of growth, it can also

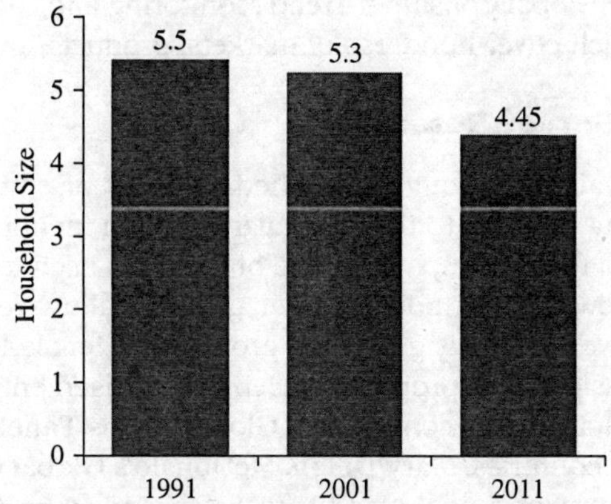

FIGURE 6-1 Family Size in India

predict the growth rate of its products for that market. Figure 6-1 illustrates the family size reduction over the years in India.

Step 2: Develop a Research Plan

After defining the problem to be studied or the question to be answered, the marketer must address a new set of questions. What is this information worth to me in dollars (or yen, euros, etc.)? What will we gain by collecting this data? What would be the cost of not getting the data that could be converted into useful information? Research requires the investment of both money and managerial time, and it is necessary to perform a cost–benefit analysis before proceeding further.

In some instances, a company may pursue the same course of action no matter what the research reveals. Even when more information is needed to ensure a high-quality decision, a realistic estimate of a formal study may reveal that the cost to perform research is simply too high. As discussed in the next section, a great deal of potentially useful data already exists; utilizing such data instead of commissioning a major study can result in significant savings. In any event, methodologies, budgets, and time parameters are all spelled out during the planning step. Only when the plan is completed should the next step be undertaken.

Step 3: Collecting Data

Are data available in company files, a library, industry or trade journals, or online? When is the information needed? Marketers must address these issues as they proceed to the data collection step of the research. Using readily available data saves both money and time. A formal market study can cost hundreds of thousands of dollars and take many months to complete.

SECONDARY DATA A low-cost approach to marketing research and data collection begins with desk research. Personal files, company or public libraries, online databases, government census records, and trade associations are just a few of the data sources that can be tapped with minimal effort and cost. Data from these sources already exist. Such data are known as secondary data because they were not gathered for the specific project at hand. Syndicated studies published by research companies are another source of secondary data and information. The Cambridge Information Group publishes Findex, a directory of more than 13,000 reports and studies covering 90 industries. The Economist Intelligence Unit's EIU Country Data is another valuable source of information both in print and online. Other online examples are the databases published by Euromonitor International, including those on the Global Consumer Trend Monitoring and Global Market Information Database (GMID), which cover hundreds of markets, products, and consumer trends.

Primary Data and Survey Research

When data are not available through published statistics or studies, direct collection is necessary. Primary data pertains to the particular problem identified in step 1. Survey research, interviews, and focus groups are some of the tools used to collect primary market data. Personal interviews—with individuals or groups—allow researchers to ask "why" and then explore answers. A focus group is a group interview led by a trained moderator who facilitates discussion of a product concept, advertisement, social trend, or other topic. For example, McDonald's convened a Global Moms Panel recently, comprised of nine mothers from six countries. Mary Dillon, McDonald's Global Chief Marketing Officer, explained that the company's goal was to "to listen and learn from our Global Moms Panel with the goal of providing the best possible experience for families in our restaurants around the world. We want to become the best ally we can for moms and a true partner in the well-being of families everywhere."[17] Intended to focus on topics such as healthy lifestyle initiatives, restaurant communications, and children's well-being, the panel's input will likely help McDonald's develop new products and marketing campaigns that combat reports that its food contributes to obesity and other health problems.

Survey research often involves obtaining data from customers or some other designated group by means of a questionnaire. Surveys can be designed to generate quantitative data ("How often would you buy?"), qualitative data ("Why would you buy?"), or both. Survey research generally involves administering a questionnaire by mail, by telephone, in person, or, increasingly, online (see Box 6-3 entitled "The Rise of Online Survey Research"). Many good marketing research textbooks provide details on questionnaire design and administration. A good questionnaire has three main characteristics:

1. It is simple.
2. It is easy for respondents to answer and for the interviewer to record.
3. It keeps the interview to the point and obtains desired information.

BOX 6-3

Side Bar: The Rise of Online Survey Research[18]

Online research has been used in savvy research markets with high Internet penetration for close to two decades. During that time, many lessons have been learned about when to use online research. The global Internet landscape has also changed dramatically over the past decade, with a steady increase in Internet usage in developed countries as well as many developing markets. Today, online research is available in over 150 countries.

Most of the large, successful consumer products firms (as well as those in almost every other field) are using online research. It is important to evaluate the advantages and disadvantages of online research when deciding on a data collection method.

[17] McDonald's Press Release, "McDonald's Announces Global Moms Panel," May 9, 2006, http://www.mcdonalds.com/corp/news/corppr/2006/corp_05162006.html.

[18] Author interview, Mark Keegan and Anthony Donato, Keegan & Company, Rye, NY. 2012. "Are Online Surveys As Accurate As Offline Surveys?," February 26, 2013, http://kr.en.nielsen.com/pubs/2005_q1_ap_surveys.shtml.

Benefits of Online Research

The primary advantages of online surveys versus phone or field surveys:

- Online surveys eliminate interviewer bias: interviewers can have different effects on respondents' answers based on a variety of factors—for example, whether they are male or female, cheerful or stern, fast or slow, etc. Online research eliminates such variations.
- Online data collection is usually lower cost: Internet surveys present potential respondents with pop-ups on websites or e-mailed invitations which direct respondents to a questionnaire. This eliminates the need for one-on-one recruiting over the phone or in person, a time consuming and therefore costly process.
- Faster fieldwork: interviewers can only speak to one person at a time, while hundreds of online respondents can all answer at the same time.
- Accuracy: online respondents can read the questions and possible responses themselves, resulting in a greater level of comprehension and higher quality responses.
- Improved recall: online respondents do not feel pressured into giving quick answers so they are likely to think of more to say, name more brands, etc., before moving on to the next question. Respondents being interviewed by an interviewer feel more pressure to answer or move on because the interviewer is waiting.
- Pictures, sound clips, and video clips can be included in online surveys: this enables online research to do as much as face-to-face research at a lower cost and with a much greater geographical spread.
- Easier to target lower incidence populations: relatively difficult-to-reach respondents (such as doctors or users of a certain brand) can be targeted through specialized panels or larger e-mail approaches.
- Research panel providers are committed to maintaining panel "health" to insure that panel members are providing reliable and truthful answers to questions.

Disadvantages of Online Research

The primary disadvantages of online surveys compared to phone or field surveys:

- The researcher is unable to explain questions: if a respondent does not understand a question, an online survey cannot clarify like a telephone or field interviewer can. This problem can be minimized by ensuring that questions are clear and concise.
- The researcher cannot ask follow-up questions: an online survey cannot ask a specific respondent to clarify their answer if it does not make sense or if it goes off on a tangent. This potential disadvantage can be eliminated by carefully worded questions.

Primary Research Benefits and Problems

Primary research is a very sought after research for many international marketing companies. Through the primary research, the companies ascertain and develop understanding for some very purpose-specific causes and desires to arrive at more realistic understanding on business issues. For example, Mahindra & Mahindra wanted to introduce its flagship sports utility vehicle, 'Scorpio', in United States of America. After all the preparation to launch the vehicle, the company was in a dilemma about the pricing of the product in the competitive US market. The company launched a primary research and collected primary data from target consumers about their willingness to pay for the Indian made automobile. Here, the company used a technique of direct interaction with respondents in the foreign country without a questionnaire developed for the specific purpose. The company can also use structured questionnaire to illicit information from the targeted respondents. Also for the purpose of primary research other techniques like mail survey, focus group discussions, etc. are also used. There are various benefits of primary research as stated under.

- The primary research provides data which are very specific and current.
- Allows the researcher to have a close feel of the situation under research.
- The research can instil a sense of seriousness amongst the respondents.
- Primary research are undertaken for a specific purpose so the result of the research are more usable and to the point.

However, there are some problems associated with primary research:

- In international marketing, primary research is conducted in another country so primary data collection through this method is comparatively more difficult, time consuming, and expensive.
- The less costly primary research data collected through mail survey usually suffers from poor response rate.
- In the case of direct questionnaire survey in a foreign country, the foreign respondents may not be willing to participate in an interview session.
- Cultural differences may not allow the researcher to exactly understand the feeling of the respondents. Hesitancy of the respondents while confronting a foreigner is another issue noticed in case of countries with high-context culture.
- A researcher with low-context cultural background will often fail to understand and appreciate this very cultural issue, which may distort the information flow.

SAMPLING Sampling is the selection of a subset or group from a population that is representative of the entire population. The two basic sampling methods in use today are probabilistic and nonprobabilistic sampling. In a probabilistic sample, each unit chosen has a known chance of being included in the sample. In a random sample, which is one type of probabilistic sample, each unit has an equal chance of being selected. The results of a probabilistic sample can be projected to the entire population with statistical reliability.

The results of a nonprobabilistic sample cannot be projected with statistical reliability. For example, a quota sample is the selection of the proportions that are known to exist in the universe. Because the units that are selected in a quota sample do not have an equal or even a known chance of being selected, the results of a quota sample cannot be projected with any statistical reliability to the universe. However, if there are no reasons to expect that the quota is significantly different from the universe, then it is assumed that the sample will be representative of other characteristics. Thus, only the random or probabilistic sample produces results of statistically measurable accuracy. This is the major advantage of a probability sample. The disadvantage of a probability sample is the difficulty of selecting elements from the universe on a random or probability basis. The quota sample does not require selection on a probability basis and is, therefore, much easier to implement. Its main disadvantage is the possible bias that may exist in the sample because of inaccurate prior assumptions concerning population or because of unknown bias in selection of cases by field workers.

Three key characteristics of a probability sample determine the sample size:

1. The permissible sampling error that can be allowed (e).
2. The desired confidence in the sample results. In a statistical sense, the confidence is expressed in terms of the number of chances in 100 tries that the results obtained could be due to chance. Confidence is usually desired at the 99 percent level and is expressed as three standard errors (t).
3. The amount of variation in the characteristic being measured. This is known as the standard deviation (s).

The formula for sample size is

$$n = \frac{(t^2)(s^2)}{e^2}$$

where

n = sample size

t = confidence limit expressed in standard errors (three standard errors = 99 percent confidence)

s = standard deviation

e = error limit

The important characteristic of this formula from the point of view of international marketers is that the sample size, n, is not a function of the size of the universe. Thus, a probability sample in Tanzania requires the same sample size as one in the United States if the standard deviation in the two populations is the same. This fact underlines the scale economies of marketing research in larger markets.

A quota sample is designed by taking known characteristics of the universe and including respondents in the sample in the same proportion as they occur in the known characteristic universe. For example, population may be divided in six categories according to income as follows:

Percent of population	10%	15%	25%	25%	15%	10%
Earnings per month	0–10	11–20	21–40	41–60	61–70	71–100

If it is assumed that income is the characteristic that adequately differentiates the population for study purposes, then a quota sample would include respondents of different income levels in the same proportion as they occur in the population, that is, 15 percent with monthly earnings from 11 to 20, and so on.

The results of a nonprobability sample cannot be projected with statistical reliability. One form of nonprobability sample is a convenience sample. As the name implies, researchers select people who are easy to reach. For example, in one study comparing consumer shopping attitudes in the United States, Jordan, Singapore, and Turkey, data for the latter three countries were gathered from convenience samples recruited by an acquaintance of the researcher. While data gathered in this way are not subject to statistical inference, they may be adequate to address the problem defined in step 1. In this study, for example, the researchers were able to identify a clear trend toward cultural convergence in shopping attitudes and customs that cut across modern industrial countries, emerging industrial countries, and developing countries.

Step 4: Analyze Research Data

DEMAND PATTERN ANALYSIS Industrial growth patterns provide an insight into market demand. Because they generally reveal consumption patterns, production patterns are helpful in assessing market opportunities. Additionally, trends in manufacturing production indicate potential markets for companies that supply manufacturing inputs. At the early stages of growth in a country, when per capita incomes are low, manufacturing centers on such necessities as food and beverages, textiles, and other forms of light industry. As incomes rise, the relative importance of these industries declines as heavy industry begins to develop. As incomes continue to rise, service industries rise to overtake manufacturing in importance.

INCOME ELASTICITY MEASUREMENTS Income elasticity describes the relationship between demand for a good and changes in income. Income elasticity studies of consumer products show that necessities such as food and clothing are characterized by inelastic demand. Stated differently, expenditures on products in these categories increase but at a slower percentage rate than do increases in income. This is the corollary of Engel's law, which states that as incomes rise, smaller proportions of total income are spent on food. Demand for durable consumer goods such as furniture and appliances tends to be income elastic, increasing relatively faster than increases in income.

MARKET ESTIMATION BY ANALOGY Estimating market size with available data presents challenging analytic tasks. When data are unavailable, as is frequently the case in both less developed and industrialized countries, resourceful techniques are required. One resourceful technique is estimation by analogy. There are two ways to use this technique. One way is to make cross-sectional comparisons and the other is to displace a time series in time. The first method, cross-sectional comparisons, amounts simply to positing the assumption that there is an analogy between the relationship of a factor and demand for a particular product or commodity in two countries. This can best be explained as follows:

Let

X_A = demand for product *X* in country *A*
Y_A = factor that correlates with demand for product *X* in country *A*, data from country *A*
X_B = demand for product *X* in country *B*
Y_B = factor that correlates with demand for product *X* in country *A*, data from country *B*

If we assume that

$$\frac{X_A}{Y_A} = \frac{X_B}{Y_B}$$

and if X_A, Y_A, and Y_B are known, we can solve for X_B as follows:

$$X_B = \frac{(X_A)(Y_B)}{Y_A}$$

Basically, estimation by analogy amounts to the use of a single-factor index with a correlation value obtained from one country applied to a target market. This is a very simple method of analysis, but in many cases it is an extremely useful, rough estimating device whenever data are available in at least one potentially analogous market for product sales of consumption and a single correlation factor.

Displacing time is a useful method of market analysis when data are available for two markets at different levels of development. This method is based on the assumption that an analogy between markets exists in different time periods or, put another way, that the markets in question are going through the same stages of market development. The method amounts to assuming that the demand level for product *X* in country *A* in time period 1 was at the same stage as demand in time period 2 in country *B*. This can be illustrated as follows:

Let

X_{A1} = demand for product *X* in country *A* during time period 1
Y_{A1} = factor associated with demand for product *X* in country *A* during time period 1
X_{B2} = demand for product *X* in country *B* during time period 2

Y_{B2} = factor or factors correlating with demand for product X in country A and data from country B for time period 2

Assume that

$$\frac{X_{A1}}{Y_{A1}} = \frac{X_{B2}}{Y_{B2}}$$

If X_{A1}, Y_{A1}, and Y_{B2} are known, we can solve for X_{B2} as follows:

$$X_B = \frac{(X_{A1})(Y_{B2})}{Y_{A1}}$$

The time displacement method requires a marketer to estimate when two markets are at similar stages of development. For example, the market for disposable cameras in Russia in the mid-2000s might be comparable to the disposable camera market in the United States in the mid-1990s. By obtaining data on the factors associated with demand for digital cameras in the United States in 1995 and in Russia in 2004, as well as actual US demand in 1995, one could estimate potential in Russia at the present time. However, because digital audio players, or MP3 players, for example, were not available in the United States in the mid-1990s, this analogy is seriously flawed. Indeed, for many digital and Internet-based products and services, there is no market today that is analogous to markets anywhere in the world in the 1980s and 1990s because the competing technologies of today were not available then.

Several issues should be kept in mind in using estimation by analogy.

1. Are the two countries for which the analogy is assumed really similar? To answer this question with regard to a consumer product, the analyst must understand the similarities and differences in the cultural systems in the two countries. If the market for an industrial product is under study, an understanding of the respective national technology bases is required.
2. Have technological and social developments resulted in a situation in which demand for a particular product or commodity will leapfrog previous patterns, skipping entire growth patterns that occurred in more developed countries? For example, cell phone sales in Eastern Europe and Africa leapfrogged the pattern of sales in the United States, where most people had landline phones first.
3. If there are differences among the availability, price, quality, and other variables associated with the product in the two markets, potential demand in a target market will not develop into actual sales of a product because the market conditions are not comparable.

COMPARATIVE ANALYSIS One of the unique opportunities in global marketing analysis is to conduct comparisons of market potential and marketing performance in different country markets at the same point in time. One form of comparative analysis is the intracompany cross-national comparison. For example, general market conditions in country X (as measured by income or stage of industrialization) may be similar to those in country Y. If there is a significant discrepancy between per capita sales of a given product in the two countries, the marketer might reasonably wonder about it and determine what actions need to be taken. When the CEO of Kodak, a world leader in the color film business, asked for a review of market share in color film on a country-by-country basis, he was shocked to learn that Kodak's market share in Japan was only 7 percent compared with 40 percent in most other countries. The situation prompted him to lodge a petition with the US Trade Representative seeking removal of alleged anticompetitive barriers in Japan. There is a lesson from this story: Kodak was asleep at the wheel as a corporation. They were surprised to learn of their position in Japan, and they were equally surprised when digital imaging destroyed the chemical film market. Today, Kodak is in bankruptcy.

CLUSTER ANALYSIS The objective of cluster analysis is to group variables into clusters that maximize within-group similarities and between-group differences. Cluster analysis is well suited to global marketing research because similarities and differences can be established between local, national, and regional markets of the world.

Step 5: Present the Findings

The report based on the marketing research must be useful to managers as input to the decision-making process. Whether the report is presented in written form, orally, or electronically, it must relate clearly to the problem or opportunity identified in step 1. Most managers are uncomfortable with research jargon and complex quantitative analysis. Results should be clearly stated and provide a basis for managerial action; otherwise, the report may end up on the shelf where it will gather dust and serve as a reminder of wasted time and money. As the data provided by a corporate information system and marketing research become increasingly available on a worldwide basis, it becomes possible to analyze marketing expenditure effectiveness across national boundaries. Managers can then decide where they are achieving the greatest marginal effectiveness for their marketing expenditures and can adjust expenditures accordingly.

LINKING GLOBAL MARKETING RESEARCH TO THE DECISION-MAKING PROCESS

Global marketing research should be linked to the decision-making process within the firm. The recognition that a situation requires action is the initiating factor in the decision-making process.

Even though most firms recognize the need for domestic marketing research, this need is often less recognized for global markets. Often decisions concerning entry into and expansion in global markets and the selection and appointment of distributors are made after a subjective assessment of the situation. The research done is frequently less rigorous than it could be. Furthermore, once a company has entered a global market, it may fail to conduct ongoing research of new markets.

A major reason that firms are reluctant to engage in global marketing research is a lack of sensitivity to cross-cultural customer tastes and preferences.

Table 6-4 summarizes the five stages of the global marketing investment decision. As can be seen, both internal (firm-specific) and external (market) data are needed at each stage of the decision process. The task of a firm's global information system to provide objective data to support the global decision makers for marketing decisions is often forgotten.

Headquarters Control of Global Marketing Research

An important issue for the global company is where to locate control of the organization's research capability. The difference between a multinational, polycentric company and a global, geocentric company on this issue is significant. In the multinational company, responsibility for research is delegated to the operating subsidiary. The global company delegates responsibility for research to operating subsidiaries but retains overall responsibility and control of research as a headquarters function. In practice, this means that the global company will, as in the PepsiCo example, ensure that research is designed and executed so as to yield comparable data.

TABLE 6-4 The Global Marketing Investment Decision

Decision	Information Needed
1. Deciding whether, where, and when to grow	Assessment of global market opportunities (global demand) for the firm's products Commitment of management to globalize Competitiveness of the firm compared to local and international competitors Where to allocate resources in the world
2. Deciding which markets to enter	Ranking of world markets according to market potential of countries/regions Local competition Political risks Trade barriers Cultural, political, and geographic distance to potential market
3. Deciding how to enter foreign markets	Nature of the product (standard versus complex product) Size of markets/segments Behavior of potential intermediaries Behavior of local competition Transport costs Government requirements With or without partners
4. Designing the global marketing program	Customer needs and wants Competitive strengths and weaknesses Available distribution channels Media and promotional channels
5.Implementing and controlling the global marketing program	Strategy for entry and growth Country and regional selection and weight Wholly owned subsidiary vs. partners Integrating country operations into the global business

Comparability requires that scales, questions, and research methodology be standardized. To achieve this, the company must inject a level of control and review of marketing research at the global level. The director of worldwide marketing research must respond to local conditions as he or she searches for a research program that can be implemented on a global basis. It is most likely that the marketing director will end up with a number of marketing programs tailored to clusters of countries that exhibit within-group similarities.

The director of worldwide research should not simply direct the efforts of country research managers. His or her job is to ensure that the corporation achieves maximum results worldwide from the total allocation of its research resources. Achieving this requires that personnel in each country are aware of research being carried out in the rest of the world and involved in influencing the design of their own in-country research as well as the overall research program. Ultimately, the director of worldwide research must be responsible for the overall research design and program. It is his or her job to take inputs from the entire world and produce a coordinated research strategy that generates the information needed to achieve global sales and profit objectives.

BOX 6-4

Side Bar: Beware of Misleading Secondary Data!

Myanmar is one of the most isolated countries of the world. This country remained under military rule up to 2011, which took it away from the mainframe of world business. After US banned all goods and services trade with Myanmar, and placed a freeze order on extending financial services to Burma along with imposed visa restrictions on Myanmar officials, further took away the country from the world map. Under the military rule, the country underwent a population census way back in1983 and thereafter it took about 30 years to place the census machinery back to carry out a full-fledged population census with the support of several other countries. In between, the world of business was in a state of confusion as to the demographic structure of the countries which for them was absolutely important in deciding the marketing strategy. Interestingly, the Myanmar Department of Labour came out with a result of a population census type of survey result during 2010. This survey estimated the population of Myanmar to be close to 60 million. However, during that year, United Nations Population Division (UNPD) estimated the population of Myanmar which did not match with the official figure. UNDP actually projected about 12 million people less than the official estimate of the country which was quite a significant number for a small country like Myanmar. In addition, the United Nations Population Fund (UNPF) released few facts about some important parameters connected with socio economic development of the country. According to UNPF, the maternal mortality rate per 100,000 births for Myanmar was 240 during 2010. It further added that under the age of 5, mortality rate was 73 per 1,000 births and lifetime risk of death for pregnant women was 1 in 180. According to the United Nations Children's Fund (UNICEF), Myanmar had the 4th highest child mortality rate in the world.[19] There was a widespread speculation that the country's official estimate did not want to project some of the vital figure connected to demographic profile like life expectancy or child mortality rate. The confusion about data mismatch was not only confined to demographic profiling of the country but was extended to the economic parameters also. Many economic experts felt that GDP growth rate as well as GDP per capita figures were grossly exaggerated during the military regime to show the country's economic condition in a brighter state. Even some foreign experts reported an alarming inflation rate that prevailed in the country but was not reported by the military government. Most damaging for international business community was the real currency exchange rate between the local currency Kyat and US dollar. During the year 1994-95, the official currency exchange rate announced was 1 USD= 6 Kyat, and accordingly the GDP per capita calculated turned out to be 222.5 USD, which allowed the country to come out of the tag of 'least developing country'. During that time, United Nation's bench mark rate was below 200 USD for the least developing country status. External agencies vehemently criticised the artificially created exchange rate when actually the unofficial exchange rate was 1 USD = 120 Kyat[20]. International businesses were in an utter state of confusion when analysing using secondary data of the country. The Central Statistical Organisation, the wing for dissemination of government published the data which in several ways contradicted the data published by the reputed and established agencies like Economic Intelligence Unit. The net result was in terms of reduced dependency on the use of secondary data by the international business community while assessing the investment attractiveness of Myanmar.

[19] Burma has second highest child mortality rate in Asia," Irrawaddy, January 27, 2008, at http://irrawaddy.org/article.php?art_id=10027

[20] The Ministry of National Planning and Development, The Union of Myanmar, *Review of the Financial, Economic and Social Conditions for 1994/95* (Yangon: Ministry of National Planning and Development, 1995), p. 11.

BOX 6-5

Side Bar: Market Research in China

It is easy to understand the allure of the vast Chinese market on a grand scale, but conducting market research to specifically pinpoint the opportunities is a different matter. Collecting reliable and timely information that can aid in the development of marketing strategies is often not easy. Marketers are often forced to depend on secondary data that may not be reliable because it is often collected by politically biased regional and local authorities. The differences in economic development, purchasing power, and cultural factors correspond to differences in consumer behavior across China's regions, complicating primary data collection. Underdeveloped infrastructure and the sheer enormity and diversity of the market make it hard to identify, select, and interview representative samples for survey research. Furthermore, questionnaire development and measurement are challenging when many concepts widely used in Western market research are unknown in China and hard to translate linguistically and culturally. Other cultural and social factors, such as the reluctance of many consumers to provide open feedback and government controls on data collection, further contribute to the problem. Add to it various protectionist practices on national, regional, and local levels; a complex and unreliable legal system; and the need to develop personal relationships, and one can see why market research in China is reserved for the true pioneers.

Sources: Peter G. P. Walters and Saeed Samiee, "Marketing Strategy in Emerging Markets: The Case of China," *Journal of International Marketing*, 11, no. 1 (2003): 97–106; Michael Fielding, "Special Delivery," *Marketing News*, February 1, 2007: 13.

The Marketing Information System as a Strategic Asset

The advent of the global enterprise means that boundaries between the firm and the outside world are dissolving. Marketing has historically been responsible for managing many of the relationships across that boundary. The boundary between marketing and other functions is also dissolving, implying that the traditional notion of marketing as a distinct functional area within the firm is giving way to a new model.

The process of marketing decision making is also changing. This is due largely to the changing role of information: information has switched from a support tool to a wealth-generating, strategic asset for marketers. However, the "democratization" of information—its availability on the Internet and other free and easily accessible sources—has shifted the control over the marketing fate of a product or company from the marketers to the consumers. Today, international marketers have to scan and monitor not only what competitors are doing, but also what kind of information bloggers post about your product for their audience, what YouTube.com video features it, and what rating it gets on consumer review sites such as Epinions.com.

Dell recently experienced the impact of the empowered consumer. One popular blogger's "Dell Hell" posts about his negative experiences with the computer-maker's customer service department garnered thousands of page views, links to other blogs, chatter in customer forums, and wide media coverage. The resulting backlash and damage to Dell's brand and bottom line were eloquently summed in Chris Anderson's book *The Long Tail*:

> Dell spends hundreds of millions each year on promoting its quality and customer service, but if you Google "Dell hell," you'll get 55,000 pages of results.

> Even the word "Dell" returns customer complaints by the second page of results. The same inversion of power is now changing the marketing game for everything from individual products to people. The collective now controls the message.[21]

Information intensity in the firm impacts market attractiveness, competitive position, and organizational structure. The greater a company's information intensity, the more the traditional product/market boundaries shift. In essence, companies increasingly face new sources of competition from other firms in historically noncompetitive industries, particularly if those firms are also information intensive. The most obvious and dramatic example is the emergence of the superindustry, combining telecommunications, computers, financial services, and retailing into what is essentially an information industry. Such diverse firms as AT&T, IBM, Google, and Apple now find themselves in direct competition with each other. The new competition reflects a natural extension and redefinition of traditional product lines and marketing activities. Today, when a company speaks of value added, it is less likely to be referring to unique product features. Rather, the emphasis is on the information exchanged as part of customer transactions—much of which cuts across traditional product lines.

CASE 6-1

Marketing of Automobile Parts in Africa: International Marketing Research Requirements for Indian companies[22]

It is said that Africa will be the future destination of the global companies. It is really happening as demand of products and services are increasing with time in the continent. Many African countries are moving fast in the path of economic development which resulted in an increased demand for various types of machineries, automobiles, lubricants, spare parts, and other mechanical goods and accessories. Africa shelters more than one billion people and by 2025, as per estimate of Department of Economic and Social Affairs, Population Division, United Nations, the population will more than double to 2.3 billion by 2050. Different countries in Africa are facing huge rural- urban migration problem because jobs are created in the urban areas and cities. Therefore, it is not difficult to understand that presently nearly 40 percent of its population lives in urban areas and cities. The railway system has not been vast enough and also not been well networked across the cities and towns except for the southern African network. Though a lot of attention has been given presently on improving railway network in the entire continent but surely it would take time to position it as a viable alternative to the road transport. So the entire pressure of transportation is on the road transport.

According to OICA (Organisation Internationale des Constructeurs d'Automobiles), motorization rate i.e. number of motor vehicles per thousand population was 43 during 2013 and increased to 44 during 2014. This may be regarded as marginal increase, but some of the countries in Africa are moving very fast in terms of motorisation rate shooting over 100 as shown in the Table 6-5 below. Libya has the highest motorisation rate of 416 during 2014 followed by Congo (405), South Africa (180),Mauritius (172), Botswana (155), Tunisia (125) and Morocco (101).

The requirement of automobile and absence of big automobile production house in Africa was noted by the automobile dealers located at Dubai and the entire UAE has long been taking advantage of those opportunities. Dubai is a place where the major suppliers of automobile and automobile

[21] Chris Anderson, *The Long Tail*, New York: Hyperion, 2006: 99.

[22] OICA vehicle in use data for Africa available at http://www.oica.net/category/vehicles-in-use/

TABLE 6-5 Increase in Motorisation Rate in Africa

	2010	2011	2012	2013	2014	Motorisation rate, 2013	Motorisation rate, 2014
Africa	35,887	37,249	39,002	40,644	42,511	43	44
Botswana	297	300	310	330	340	152	155
Congo	1,631	1,669	1,723	1,760	1,830	401	405
Libya	2,122	2,229	2,352	2,480	2,610	395	416
Mauritius	170	180	191	205	220	162	172
Morocco	2,760	2,920	3,088	3,248	3,397	98	101
South Africa	8,472	8,794	9,168	9,319	9,600	176	180
Tunisia	1,259	1,269	1,279	1,330	1,390	121	125

Adapted from OICA vehicle in use data for Africa available at http://www.oica.net/category/vehicles-in-use/, as accessed on 10 January 2017 at 12pm.

spare parts are located. Though there was temporary depression in the economy of the Gulf region but the interest of automobile exporters of Gulf region was not to be subdued. However, the Gulf exporters are facing stiff competition in the African market as demand for quality spare parts has increased to a great extent. Other developing countries are also looking in the opportunities and resorted to brisk exporting of spare parts to African country. Mr. Ranjan, Chairman of the Adityapur auto cluster was emphasising this moot point in the meeting organised by Engineering Export Promotion Council (EEPC) of India. The meeting took place in the conference hall of Adityapur Auto Cluster in order to enhance the export of auto spare parts from Adityapur Cluster to African countries. Adityapur Auto Cluster (AAC) came into existence to develop the Industrial Infrastructure facilities in Adityapur Industrial Area, with the support of Government of India and Government of Jharkhand. CEOs of several small auto companies, participating in the meeting were very much interested to grab the export marketing opportunities in Africa but found that before they can actually jump in to the actual exporting, they require more information. Based on the requirements of different CEOs the following Export Research Plan were formulated.

KEY QUESTIONS

Exporting of auto spare parts required full understanding of the African spare parts market. More importantly, a product – country matching is required where each company can understand which of the African countries would become a perfect match as the destination of the products presently produced by them. In additions, the companies are required to understand the annual demand for the products, price, import duty, ease of exporting, possible buyers etc. After, a thorough deliberation it was decided to install market research with the following research questions.

The critical research questions were:

- Who are the top 10 target country markets in Africa for exporting automobile spare parts?
- Who are the competitors in the target markets?
- What is the present position Indian spare parts export to the African countries?
- Whether the demand of auto spare parts is increasing in all the African countries? Which African countries are more promising?
- How much of the export market share is presently occupied by the Gulf countries.
- What is the freight cost from Haldia Port or Paradip Port to Port Luanda (Angola) or Port Tanger(Morocco), or Port Mombasa (Kenya).
- What are the tariff structures of the important countries for various auto spare parts?
- What are the economic partnership agreements (EPAs) existing in Africa with present suppliers of spare part and tariff concession granted?
- What are the documents, required by the importers of selected African countries where export opportunity exist, while importing from India?
- Who could be the possible importing companies located in African countries for Indian Exporters?

RESEARCH OBJECTIVES

Based on the above research questions the following are the objectives of the research:

1. To understand different types of automobile spare parts being produced by the different manufactures located in Adityapur auto cluster and assess their comparative advantage in the international markets.
2. To indentify the potential African countries for export of automobile spare parts from Adityapur auto cluster.
3. To understand the competitive position of Indian automobile spare parts in African markets.
4. To understand the role of tariff as barrier to export to the African countries.
5. To understand the impact of tariff concession, granted by the African countries to the economic partners, on Indian export possibilities.
6. To understand the impact of non tariff barriers on Indian export arising out of not non-regular documentation requirements.
7. To understand the impact of freight charges and import duty on the product pricing for African markets.
8. To list out top 10 African countries in terms of attractiveness for Indian automobile spare parts and indentify the possible importers from those countries.

METHODOLOGY

1. Understand the products i.e. different types of automobile spare parts being produced by the different manufactures located in Adityapur auto cluster through primary survey and assess their comparative advantages through RCA (revealed comparative analysis) through secondary analysis.
2. Isolate the products having RCA > 1 and establish the trend of import of those products by the African countries.
3. List out the growth based African country having substantial import demand with increasing trend for the past five years.
4. Understand the countries now exporting to the growth countries and rank them in order of intensity.
5. Understand the competitive position of India in the above rank.
6. Sort out top ten opportune countries based on the above analysis where presently India figures within top ten exporters.
7. Execute tariff analysis for the above opportune countries and make a tariff profile for the opportune countries.
8. Analyze the nature of economic partnership agreement executed by the opportune countries and list of the import tariff concession granted by the opportune countries. Identify these countries if they are present in the top ten competitor countries for India.
9. Understand the import documents that are required by the opportune countries while importing the products like automobile spare parts and identify those countries requiring non regular import documents.
10. Understand the freight charges that are usually charged by the liners while carrying products from major Indian ports to major African ports.
11. Sort the opportune countries based on the finding arrived at step 7, 8 and 9 to arrive at a new ranking of the opportune countries in terms of attractiveness to the exporters.
12. Conduct internet based research and identify the buyers of the automobile products located in Africa.
13. Find out a suitable export price for the automobile spare parts at which they can be offered to the borrowers based on cost of sale, freight charges, and import duty.

DATA SOURCES

Both secondary and primary data will be utilized for carrying out the research.

OUTCOME OF THE RESEARCH

Export marketing Strategy for the Adityapur automobile cluster to African countries.

CONCLUSION

The research analysis is going to give a detailed research based understanding to the manufactures of automobile spare parts for exporting products to African country markets.

Case Questions

1. Evaluate the merits and demerits of the research plan.
2. Execute the research as per the stated methodology with the help of secondary trade data sources like www.trademap.org or wits.worldbank.org and present in the class.

Summary

Information is one of the most basic ingredients of a successful marketing strategy. The global marketer must scan the world for information about opportunities and threats and make information available via a management information system. Scanning can be accomplished by keeping in touch with an area of interest through surveillance or by actively seeking out information by means of search. Information can be obtained from human and documentary sources or from direct perception.

Formal research is often required before decisions can be made regarding specific problems or opportunities. After developing a research plan, data are collected using either primary or secondary sources. A number of techniques are available for analyzing data, including demand pattern analysis, income elasticity measurements, estimation by analogy, comparative analysis, and cluster analysis. Research findings must be presented clearly to facilitate decision making.

Global marketing research presents a number of challenges. One is the simple fact that research on a number of markets may be required, some of which are so small that only modest research expenditures can be made. Secondary data from some countries may be distorted; also, comparability may be an issue. A final issue is how much control headquarters will have over research and the overall management of the organization's information system.

Discussion Questions

1. What is the major source of information for headquarters executives of global companies?
2. What are the different modes of information acquisition? Which is the most important for gathering strategic information?
3. Assume that you have been asked by the president of your organization to devise a systematic approach to scanning. The president does not want to be surprised by major market or competitive developments. What would you recommend?
4. Outline the basic steps of the marketing research process.
5. What is the difference between existing, latent, and incipient demand? How might these differences affect the design of a marketing research project?
6. Describe some of the analytical techniques used by global marketers. When is it appropriate to use each technique?

Application Exercises

1. Visit www.acnielsen.com and pick one consumer report from the "Trends and Insights" section. Based on the findings reported, recommend a strategy for entering a new geographic market with a specific product category. Justify your recommendations.
2. The midsized consumer products company that you work for has decided to expand into China. As the marketing manager, you were tasked with hiring a market research firm to conduct primary research to help you determine which of your product lines you should first offer in this new market. Formulate the research problem that you face and the questions you would like answers to at the end of the research project.

Suggested Readings

Cavusgil, S. Tamer. "Qualitative Insights into Company Experiences in International Marketing Research." *Journal of Business and Industrial Marketing* (Summer 1987): 41–54.

Czinkota, M. R., and I. A. Ronkainen. "Market Research for Your Export Operations, Part I." *International Trade Forum,* 3 (1994): 22–33.

Davenport, Thomas H., Leandro Dalle Mule, and John Lucker. "Know What Your Customers Want Before They Do." *Harvard Business Review* (December 2011): 84–92.

Douglas, Susan P., and C. Samuel Craig. "On Improving the Conceptual Foundations of International Marketing Research." *Journal of International Marketing*, 14, no. 1 (March 2006): 1–22.

Douglas, Susan P., C. Samuel Craig, and Warren J. Keegan. "Approaches to Assessing International Marketing Opportunities for Small- and Medium-Sized Companies." *Columbia Journal of World Business* (Fall 1982): 2–30.

Green, Robert, and Eric Langeard. "A Cross-National Comparison of Consumer Habits and Innovator Characteristics." *Journal of Marketing* (July 1975): 34–41.

Keegan, Warren J. "Multinational Scanning," Administrative Science Quarterly (September 1974), 411-21.

Keegan, Warren J. "Scanning the International Business Environment: A Study of the Informational Acquisition Process." Doctoral Dissertation, Harvard Business School, 1967.

Lindberg, Bertil C. "International Comparison of Growth in Demand for a New Durable Consumer Product." *Journal of Marketing Research* (August 1982): 364–371.

MacDonald, Emma, Hugh N. Wilson, and Umut Konus. "Better Customer Insight—In Real Time." *Harvard Business Review* (September 2012): 102–108.

Mauboussin, Michael J. "The True Measure of Success." *Harvard Business Review* (October 2012): 46–56.

Meer, David. "A New Way to Gain Customer Insights." *Strategy+Business* (Spring 2012): 16.

Moyer, Reed. "International Market Analysis." *Journal of Marketing Research* (November 1968): 353–360.

Sarstedt, Marko. *Measurement and Research Methods in International Marketing*. Birgley, UK: Emerald Group Publishing Limited, 2011.

Steenkamp, Jan-Benedict E. M. "Assessing Measurement Invariance in Cross-National Consumer Research." *Journal of Consumer Research,* 25, no. 1 (1998): 78–91.

Vogel, R. H. "Uses of Managerial Perceptions in Clustering Countries." *Journal of International Business Studies* (Spring 1976): 91–100.

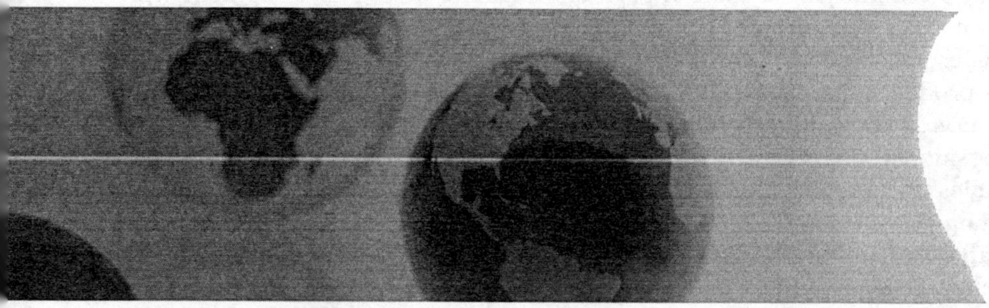

CHAPTER

7

Segmentation, Targeting, and Positioning

What is reasonable is real; that which is real is reasonable.

—GEORG WILHELM FRIEDRICH HEGEL *Philosophy of Right* (1821)

Learning Objectives

1. Understand the concepts of segmentation, targeting and positioning and their importance as global marketing tools. (216–218).
2. Describe the common attributes used to segment world markets. (219–224).
3. Identify the major criteria for targeting world market opportunities and selecting a target market strategy (229–230).
4. Describe the importance of product positioning and identify the major global product positioning strategies. (231–233).

INTRODUCTION

Segmentation, targeting, and positioning are three of the most powerful tools available to the marketer. A *market segment* is a subset of a larger market of people or organizations who will respond similarly to a marketing mix. A market segment meets the following criteria: it is distinct from other segments (different segments have different needs), it is homogeneous within the segment (exhibits common needs), it responds similarly to a market stimulus, and it can be reached by a market mix. Members of a market segment are similar to one another and different than those who are not members of the segment.

Targeting is identifying a market segment and addressing that segment with a marketing mix tailored to meet the needs, wants, and resources of the segment. Positioning is establishing a place in the mind of customers. Positioning defines the position of a product or company in the mind of the customer. For example, automobiles are positioned according to body style, price, and performance. Auto companies/brands are positioned according to segment: economy versus luxury, for example.

Companies and organizations face unique challenges in segmenting, targeting, and positioning products and services globally. The challenge is to ensure that segmentation, targeting, and positioning are correct globally and for each country or market. Because markets are different, many companies do not have globally consistent market targets and positioning. For example, Mercedes is positioned as a luxury car globally, but in Europe it is also positioned as a taxi. Globally, McDonald's is positioned as a fast-food outlet, but in Indonesia and many other lower-income countries it is more of a sit-down restaurant.

TASK OF INTERNATIONAL MARKET SEGMENTING

It is understandable that any marketers, be it domestic or international, cannot create customer value for all the people living in a geographic territory with equal intensity. It is not simply possible that a single marketing mix strategy of a company would be fitted rightly in-to the requirements of all the people living in a country. Different people have different functional, experiential and social needs. Functional need wise, people can vary widely. The need is the desire that a consumer likes to have fulfilled out of use of the product which has been selected for purchase. Functional need is connected with product features provided by the manufactures which are expected to fulfil the desire of consumers in terms of effectiveness, durability, speed, ease-of-use, and cost savings while in use. A group of consumers in India may have the functional need to have a car which is extremely fuel efficient but another group of consumers may not be so concerned with fuel efficiency but in need of a car which is highly durable. Likewise experiential need wise customer may be widely different. Experiential needs are related to consumer's feelings for the product while in use. The product features may be responsible for creating a stimulus in a consumer which led to feeling of pleasure or displeasure. Different types of consumers are expected to have different feelings when exposed to same set of stimulus emanating out of a same set of product features. Socially also, consumers are likely to vary widely. Different people want to derive different types of social accomplishment out of use of a product. Consumers desire to use the product's extrinsic features to earn social status in a society. In this respect also, same set of product's external features would lead to general different social benefits to different consumers.

The strategic process through which a company decides a group of consumers having identical set of needs for whom it will create products or services and develop marketing communication plans, so that a close association could be build up between the targeted group and a company's marketing offers is known an exercise of segmenting, targeting and position. This is also popularly known as STP model in the parlance of marketing.

The segment

So in order to create customer value uniquely, it is essential that marketing mix devised by a company must have a fairly known segment consisting of sizable prospective consumers. The prospective population in the segment is comprised of a group of people, which have no differentiation between them and likely to react to the marketing stimuli emanating from the marketing mix strategy adopted by a company. The segment of prospective consumers defined by their educational status, age, income, psychological orientation etc is very useful for a company as because a detailed understanding of the segment is possible and therefore the company can decide the right marketing mix for the segment with expectation of creating customer value in a pre-planned way.

The target

Once the segment is known in terms of characteristics and desires, it is easy for the company to target the specific set of prospective consumers rather that targeting an unknown population. Henceforth the company can understand the size of the market in terms of population which it is supposed to cater with its products and services. Once the company can quantify the market size it is also possible to understand precisely the revenue size which the company desires to generate out of its presence in the market. The target, therefore, can provide to set revenue target to the company which can be monitored to assess its performance time to time.

Positioning

Since the target is known the next plan of action of a company should be to hit the bull's eye by positioning its marketing mix according to the requirement of the segment. How accurately the company can design its marketing mix depends on how efficiently it understood the needs of the segment. The process of understanding the segment needs and marshalling all its marketing communications tools, as deemed fit, to let the prospective consumers in the target segment know about the presence of a product or service which can accurately fulfil their needs and thereby creating a tie between company and consumer. The more cemented is the tie between the company and segment consumers the more effective is the positioning effort of the company.

STP in International Context

An international company would also like to take advantage of STP model (refer Figure 7-1) so that it can be close to the targeted customer in a pre-defined way. The problem encountered by the company is identification of the cross country segment having homogeneity in terms of need. As the countries are different in terms of economic status, socio cultural underpinning, political ideologies and legal frameworks, so it requires a good amount of research effort to identify the segments across countries

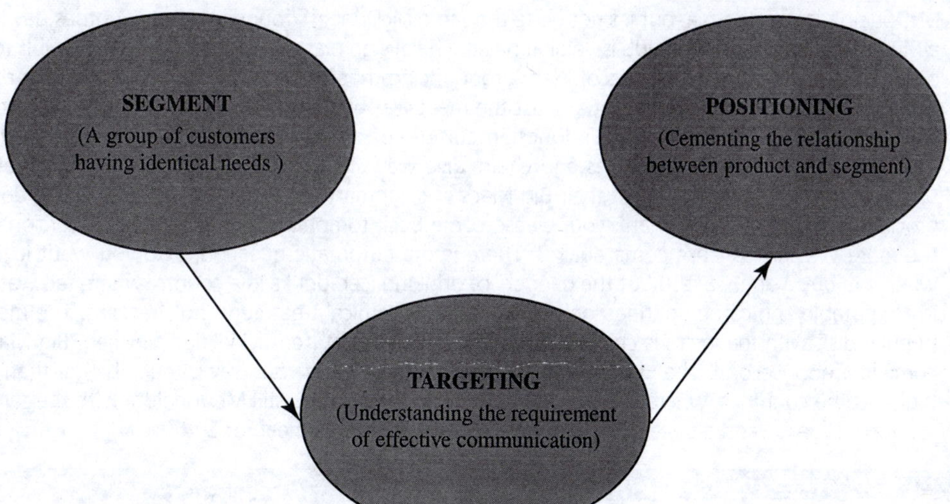

FIGURE 7-1 The STP Diagram

which are substantially similar in terms of needs. The international marketing research is not only a costly affair for companies but also requires quite good understanding of research process. Even if cross country segments are identified and are found to be of desired size worth targeting then the next problem comes in terms of positioning. The marketing communication unleashed by the company may not be tenable in all the countries targeted because of different advertising regulations in place in different countries. The prevailing country specific socio-cultural environment may not also allow the effect of the marketing communications to be felt uniformly by the different target groups living in different countries. Therefore, it is wise to take up the task of international market segmentation keeping in mind that three types of segments are possible in international markets:

UNIQUE SEGMENTS These segments are country specific. In each country there will be some segments where consumers pertaining to the segment have unique need and these needs are highly connected with the country's culture.

REGIONAL SEGMENT These cross country segments exist because the countries in regional set up have developed various commonalities because of co-existence for a longer period of time. Some regional characteristics were strong enough to permeate across the international borders even if they are very rigid. As a result there exist a group of prospective customers spanning across the countries of a region having similarity of needs and preferences.

GLOBAL SEGMENT This segment has presence in many countries of the world and prospective consumers transcend many national boundaries but have similar needs and preferences. For example, after World War, the baby boomers, irrespective of country of their origin, demonstrated to have same needs and preferences. Some market research company, in the latter period, identified some global segment like fast adopters of the product, ultra-rich, aspirators etc.

BOX 7-1

Side Bar: McDonald Found Its Unique Segment![1]

McDonald's is in Indonesia, but it's not quite the same McDonald's found in other countries. Java is a Muslim island, and McDonald's is halal: it has the halal sign plastered on its food, on its publicity, on the certificate from the leaders of Islam pronouncing that McDonald's might be lacking in nutrition and redeeming qualities, but at least the meat was bled properly. Then there's McDonald's chili sauce——an essential part of Indonesian cuisine, of course—and the McRice meal. In the center of the restaurant, the tables and chairs give way to six-inch-high tables and floor mats, so those who so desire it can eat their Big Macs in customary comfort. The sign above the door proclaims, in Indonesian, "Thank you, please come back tomorrow," a far less subtle version of the more Western "Please come again." There is the automatic question, "Do you want ice?" when you buy a drink, a result of the dangers of drinking iced drinks in a country where tap water is not potable and can be purified only by boiling or chemical treatment, not freezing. The most popular dish with the locals is chicken, cooked just like it is at Kentucky Fried Chicken. Big Macs come in a poor second. The number of staff ready to take away your tray is much bigger than in high-income countries, where labor costs are much higher. But it's still McDonald's, with the same wonderful fries. . . and a price that's Indonesian, with a Big Mac meal for $1.50.

[1]Author interviews and Mark Moxon, http://www.moxon.net/indonesia/mcdonalds_indonesian_style.html.

GLOBAL MARKET SEGMENTATION

Market segmentation is the process of subdividing a market into distinct subsets of customers that behave in the same way or have similar needs. Each subset may conceivably be chosen as a market target to be reached with a distinctive marketing strategy. The process begins with a basis of segmentation—a product-specific factor that reflects differences in customers' requirements or responsiveness to marketing variables (possibilities are purchase behavior, usage, benefits sought, intentions, preference, or loyalty).[2]

Global market segmentation is the process of dividing the world market into subsets of customers that behave in the same way or have similar needs. As one author put it, it is "the process of identifying specific segments—whether they be country groups or individual consumer groups—of potential customers with homogeneous attributes who are likely to exhibit similar buying behavior."[3] Interest in global market segmentation dates back several decades. In the late 1960s, one observer suggested that the European market could be divided into three broad categories—international sophisticate, semisophisticate, and provincial—solely on the basis of consumers' presumed receptivity to a common advertising approach.[4] Another writer suggested that some themes (e.g., the desire to be beautiful, the desire to be healthy and free of pain, the love of mother and child) were universal and could be used in advertising around the globe.[5]

In the 1980s, Professor Theodore Levitt advanced the thesis that consumers in different countries increasingly seek variety and that the same new segments are likely to show up in multiple national markets. Thus, ethnic or regional foods such as sushi, Greek salad, or hamburgers might be in demand anywhere in the world. Levitt described this trend as the "pluralization of consumption" and "segment simultaneity" that provides an opportunity for marketers to pursue a segment on a global scale.[6]

Today, global companies (and the advertising agencies that serve them) are likely to segment world markets according to one or more key criteria: geography, demographics (including national income and size of population), psychographics (values, attitudes, and lifestyles), behavioral characteristics, and benefits sought. It is also possible to cluster different national markets in terms of their environments (e.g., the presence or absence of government regulation in a particular industry) to establish groupings. Another powerful tool for global segmentation is horizontal segmentation by user category. This is the identification of users by category globally, not nationally or regionally.

BOX 7-2

Side Bar: Rural Rich as Segment in India

People Research on Indian Consumer Economy or the acronym, PRICE, made a wonderful research on Indian economy to understand some very important economic facts. Its ICE 360° survey conducted during 2016 covered 61,000 representative households spread across India. From this

continued

[2]Peter D. Bennett, ed., *Dictionary of Marketing Terms,* 2nd ed. (Chicago: American Marketing Association, 1995), 165–166.

[3]Salah S. Hassan and Lea Prevel Katsanis, "Identification of Global Consumer Segments: A Behavioral Framework," *Journal of International Consumer Marketing,* 3, no. 2 (1992): 17.

[4]John K. Ryans, Jr., "Is It Too Soon to Put a Tiger in Every Tank?" *Columbia Journal of World Business* (March–April 1969): 73.

[5]Arthur C. Fatt, "The Danger of 'Local' International Advertising," *Journal of Marketing* (January 1967).

[6]Theodore Levitt, "The Globalization of Markets," *Harvard Business Review* (May–June 1983): 92–102.

survey it was revealed that top 12000 households (20 percent) had annual per capita disposable income (adjusted) of ₹168179. Whereas, the per capita disposable income of the bottom 20 percent households had their per capita disposable income (adjusted) of 74929. Just below the top quintile there was the second best quintile where the per capita disposable income (adjusted) was 82817. So it can be said that, out of 61000 respondent household the top two quintile had the disposition income range per capita from ₹82817 to ₹168179. In this representative households of 61000, covered by PRICE survey, there were 25000 (41%) rural households representing the characteristics of rural India. Interestingly, in the top two quintiles there were any trace of these 25000 respondents. Most of these 41 percent respondents household fell in to bottom two quintiles where disposable income ranges from ₹26009 to ₹40647 as theirs disposable per capita income (adjusted). The survey divided the rural India into different clusters: "developed rural", "emerging rural", and "underdeveloped rural" based on development parameters. For example, "developed rural" included districts like Bathinda (Punjab) and Kangra (Himachal Pradesh). Emerging rural category represented by the districts like Latur (Maharashtra) and Kamrup (Assam) and the last category of 'under developed rural 'represented by Kalahandi (Odisha) and Bastar (Chhattisgarh). The survey of PRICE developed a rosy picture for the 'developed rural' cluster. This 'developed rural' households had the average income and average consumption expenditure roughly equivalent to the households living in niche cities (cities with population 1-2.5 million) of India. This survey reveals that this 'developed rural' could be a destination of the multinational company for marketing their products because the difference between cities and rural are the most minimum here in terms of household income and expenditure.

Source: http://www.ice360.in/en/projects/what-are-ice-360-surveys/upcoming-survey-ice360o-2016 and http://www.livemint.com/Politics/VqSawm4kzDAChnUPwwNb4I/Middle-India-is-still-some-way-off-from-being-middle-class.html.

Geographic Segmentation

Geographic segmentation is dividing the world into geographic subsets. The advantage of geography is proximity: markets in geographic segments are closer to each other and easier to visit on the same trip or call on during the same time window. Geographic segmentation also has major limitations: the mere fact that markets are in the same geographic region does not mean that they are similar. Japan and Vietnam are both in East Asia, but one is a high-income, postindustrial society and the other is an emerging, less developed, preindustrial society. The differences in the markets in these two countries overwhelm their similarities. Simon, in his sample of "hidden champions," found that geography was ranked lowest as a basis for market segmentation (see Figure 7-2).

FIGURE 7-2 Importance of Market Definition Criteria

Source: Hermann Simon, *Hidden Champions: Lessons from 500 of the World's Best Unknown Companies* (Boston, MA: Harvard Business School Press, 1996), p. 45. Copyright © 1996 by Harvard Business School Publishing Corporation. Reprinted by permission of Harvard Business School Press.

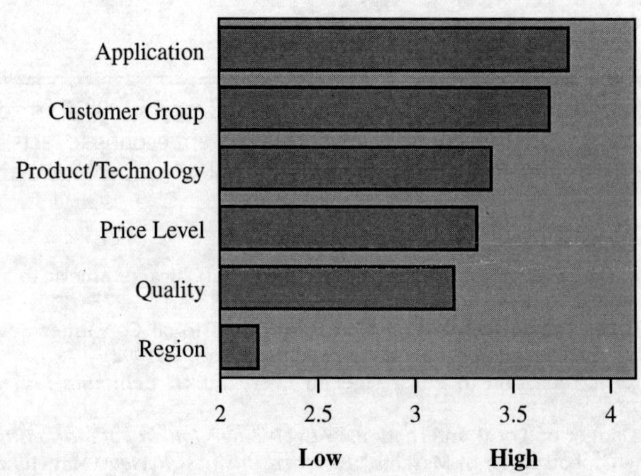

Demographic Segmentation

Demographic segmentation is based on measurable characteristics of populations such as age, gender, income, education, and occupation. A number of demographic trends—aging population, fewer children, more women working outside the home, and higher incomes and living standards—suggest the emergence of global segments.

For most consumer and industrial products, national income is the single most important segmentation variable and indicator of market potential. Annual per capita income varies widely in world markets, from a low of $140 in Burundi to a high of $110,000 in Luxembourg. The World Bank segments countries into high income, upper-middle income, lower-middle income, and low income.

The US market, with per capita income of $46,350, more than $14 trillion in 2008 national income, and a population of more than 300 million people, is enormous. Little wonder, then, that Americans are a favorite target market! Despite having comparable per capita incomes, other industrialized countries are nevertheless quite small in terms of total annual income. In Sweden, for example, per capita gross domestic product (GDP) is $52,000; however, Sweden's smaller population of 9 million means that annual national income is about $500 billion. Over 70 percent of world income is located in the Triad. Thus, by segmenting in terms of a single demographic variable—income—a company could reach the most affluent markets by targeting three regions: the European Union, North America, and Japan.

Many global companies also realize that for products with a low enough price—for example, soft drinks—population is a more important segmentation variable than income. Thus, China and India, with respective populations of 1.3 billion and 1.2 billion, represent key target markets, and even the low-income countries of the world are attractive target markets. Segmenting decisions can be complicated by the fact that the average per capita national income figures, such as those cited previously for China and India, are averages. There are also large, fast-growing, high-income segments in both of these countries. In India, for example, 100 million people can be classified as "upper-middle class," with average incomes of more than $1,400. Pinning down a demographic segment may require additional information; India's middle class has been estimated to be as low as a few million and as high as 250 million to 300 million people. If *middle class* is defined as "persons who own a refrigerator," the figure would be 30 million people. If television ownership were used as a benchmark, the middle class would be 100 million to 125 million people.[7] The important lesson for global marketers is to beware of the misleading effect of averages; they can distort the true market conditions in emerging markets.

Note also that the average income figures quoted here do not reflect the standard of living in these countries. In order to really understand the standard of living in a country, it is necessary to determine the purchasing power of the local currency. In low-income countries, the actual purchasing power of the local currency is much higher than that implied by exchange values. In India, for example, the authors' colleague recently returned from a trip during which he received a slight cut on his forehead from a taxi trunk lid. He decided to visit a doctor to get a tetanus shot and, because he knew that malaria was a hazard in India, he requested a prescription and a one-month supply of malaria pills. He did this, and the bill from the doctor for the shot, the pills, and the prescription was 30 rupees, or US $1.00.

Age is another useful demographic variable. One global segment based on demographics is global teenagers—young people between the ages of 12 and 19. Teens, by

---

[7] John Bussey, "India's Market Reform Requires Perspective," *The Wall Street Journal,* May 8, 1994, A1. See also Miriam Jordan, "In India, Luxury Is Within Reach of Many," *The Wall Street Journal,* October 17, 1995, A1.

virtue of their interest in fashion, music, and a youthful lifestyle, exhibit consumption behavior that is remarkably consistent across borders. Young consumers may not yet have conformed to cultural norms—indeed, they may be rebelling against them. This fact, combined with shared universal needs, desires, and fantasies (for name brands, novelty, entertainment, and trendy and image-oriented products), make it possible to reach the global teen segment with a unified marketing program. This segment is attractive both in terms of its size (about 1.3 billion) and its multibillion-dollar purchasing power. Coca-Cola, Benetton, Swatch, and Sony are some of the companies pursuing the global teenage segment. The global telecommunications revolution is a critical driving force behind the emergence of this segment. Global media such as MTV are perfect vehicles for reaching this segment. Satellites such as AsiaSat I are beaming Western programming and commercials to millions of viewers in China, India, and other countries.

Another global segment is the so-called elite: older, more affluent consumers who are well traveled and have the money to spend on prestigious products with an image of exclusivity. This segment's needs and wants are spread over various product categories: durable goods (luxury automobiles), nondurables (upscale beverages such as rare wines and champagne), and financial services (American Express gold and platinum cards). Technological change in telecommunications makes it easier to reach the global elite segment. Global telemarketing is a viable option today as AT&T International 800 services are available in more than 40 countries. Increased reliance on catalog marketing by upscale retailers such as Harrods, Laura Ashley, and Ferragamo has also yielded impressive results.

BOX 7-3

Side Bar: Emerging Market Segment in India!

For international marketers it is important not only to identify a growing segment of prospective consumers but they should be able to describe them correctly in terms of its size, homogeneity, accessibility, exploitability and country spread. Recently Economic Intelligence Unit (EIU) reported a growing segment in the world and termed it as NWB (New wealth builders). The NWB segment description is as below:

- Hardworking persons, both man and women.
- They are self-made not dependent on inherited wealth.
- Out of own effort they have made wealth between $1,00,000 and within $2 million and still growing.
- They could be professionals or entrepreneurs.
- Psychologically they are strong and hate stereotyping.
- They have a high degree of aspiration but also believe in hard work.

As per EIU Survey of 1552 individuals across 30 countries of the world, who met the above segment criteria, the segment is unique in terms of lifestyle, taste, choice and preference. As per forecast of EIU the segment is likely to grow further. Of course the growth of the NWBs is not the same across all the countries of world. The average growth of NWB households through 2020, as forecasted by EIU, put India on the top with 47 percent CAGR followed by countries like Indonesia (41%), Vietnam (35%), and Thailand (24%). Clearly, therefore, in the years to come Asian countries like India, Vietnam, Thailand, and Indonesia will be the abode of the NWBs. If we look at the growth rate of NWBs in the different regions of the world then Asia is just marginally out paced by Latin America. While average growth in number of NWB households between 2014-2020 is

continued

11.1% for Latin America, but the same 10.1% for Asia Pacific, 9.0% for Russia & Central Eastern Europe, 2.5 percent for Western Europe and 2 percent for North America. Country wise various erstwhile rich countries came as laggard in term of growing ground for the NWBs. For example, Singapore predicted to have average growth rate of -0.3% percent followed by Argentina -0.8%.

The above discussion shows that the international marketers seem to have new growing global segment in terms of NWBs. The segment is global and well spread across the countries of the world. The uniqueness of this growing segment is required to be understood more in details so that marketers can produce and place right product for the right segment.

Adapted from Spotlight on the New Wealth Builders, Report of Economist Intelligence Unit (EIU) and sponsored by Citi, avaialble at https://www.eiuperspectives.economist.com/sites/default/files/TheEIU_spotlight_new_wealth_builders.pdf, as accessed on 10 January 2017 at 12pm.

Psychographic Segmentation

Psychographic segmentation involves grouping people in terms of their attitudes, values, and lifestyles. Data are obtained from questionnaires that require respondents to indicate the extent to which they agree or disagree with a series of statements. In the United States, psychographics is primarily associated with SRI International, a market research organization whose original VALS and updated VALS 2 analyses of US consumers are widely known.

Porsche AG, the German sports-car maker, turned to psychographics after watching worldwide sales decline from 50,000 units in 1986 to about 14,000 in 1993. Its US subsidiary, Porsche Cars North America, already had a clear demographic profile of its customers: 40+-year-old male college graduates whose annual income exceeded $200,000. A psychographic study showed that, demographics aside, Porsche buyers could be divided into five distinct categories (see Table 7-1). Top Guns, for example, buy Porsches and expect to be noticed; for Proud Patrons and Fantasists, on the other hand, such conspicuous consumption is irrelevant. Porsche used the profiles to develop advertising tailored to each type. Notes Richard Ford, Porsche vice president of sales and marketing, "We were selling to people whose profiles were diametrically opposed. You wouldn't want to tell an elitist how good he looks in the car or how fast he could go." Results have been promising; Porsche's US sales improved nearly 50 percent in 1994.[8]

TABLE 7-1 Psychographic Profiles of Porsche's American Customers

Category	% of All Owners	Description
Top Guns	27%	Driven and ambitious; care about power and control; expect to be noticed
Elitists	24%	Old money; a car—even an expensive one—is just a car, not an extension of one's personality
Proud Patrons	23%	Ownership is what counts; a car is a trophy, a reward for working hard; being noticed doesn't matter
Bon Vivants	17%	Cosmopolitan jet setters and thrill seekers; car heightens excitement
Fantasists	9%	Car represents a form of escape; don't care about impressing others; may even feel guilty about owning car

[8]Alex Taylor III, "Porsche Slices Up Its Buyers," *Fortune,* January 16, 1995, 24.

One early application of psychographics outside the United States focused on value orientations of consumers in the United Kingdom, France, and Germany. Although the study was limited in scope, the researcher concluded that "the underlying values structures in each country appeared to bear sufficient similarity to warrant a common overall communications strategy."[9] SRI International has recently conducted psychographic analyses of the Japanese market; broader-scope studies have been undertaken by several global advertising agencies, including Backer, Spielvogel & Bates Worldwide (BSB); D'Arcy Masius Benton & Bowles (DMBB); and Young & Rubicam (Y&R).[10] These analyses offer a detailed understanding of various segments, including the global teenager and global elite discussed earlier in the chapter.

BOX 7-4

Side Bar: "Khadi Mark" Gaining Momentum!

The word 'khadi' has different connotations in India. It is connected symbolically with the independence movement launch by the father of the country, Mohandas Karamchand Gandhi. The cloth, ' khadi', represents an ideology of self-reliance of the people of India. During pre-independence period, the khadi movement aimed at boycotting foreign goods and promoting Indian goods for self reliance. Therefore, from 1920s, the word khadi evokes a feeling of patriotism, self reliant, simple living high thinking and 'ahinsa' (nonviolence). Khadi clothes are made from hand woven cotton and production of such clothes takes place mostly in rural India. In a country like India, majority of its population lives in rural India and hence an economically strong India means rural economy is also strong where there are products produced with pan India acceptance. But how can this be possible without a strong brand. It would be highly desired therefore to provide unique brand identity to 'Khadi' in India. Indian textile market is very competitive where big national and international players are fighting a hard battle to retain their market share. Brand positioning in a competitive market requires a comprehensive understanding of these basic seven tenets of brand building exercise. The brand 'Khadi' has followed them successfully as it is revealed below.

1. Relevance: It is required to focus on the benefits that 'Khadi' can provide to the target group by reflecting the character of the product. To this extent, 'Khadi Mark', was created and marketing communication was released to promote the products intimate relation with the rural economy.
2. Clarity: It requires the target group to understand the brand without ambiguity. Khadi has been positioned in India over the years to represent a handmade and made in India product to represent country's rural economy and its evolving nature.
3. Distinctiveness: Ever since India got independence, 'Khadi' has been maintaining its distinctiveness in the minds of the targeted segment and even beyond. 'Khadi' is not just a cloth or apparel product but it the national pride.
4. Coherence: Since independence 'khadi' is strongly associated with the torturous freedom movement. Its tag line "being a true Gandhian" provided the brand a unified voice.
5. Commitment: From 1947 to till date India remained committed to retain "Khadi" as India's pride originating from rural India. The successive governments in India patronised the movement which is now very strong and stable.

continued

9Alfred S. Boote, "Psychographic Segmentation in Europe," *Journal of Advertising Research,* 22, no. 6, (December 1982–January 1983): 25.

10The following discussion is adapted from Rebecca Piirto, *Beyond Mind Games: The Marketing Power of Psychographics* (Ithaca, NY: American Demographics Books, 1991).

6. Patience: "Khadi " is as old as the independence of India. Over the years the brand has been nurtured with unified voice.
7. Courage: 'Khadi' started its journey in India as only cloth to wear for a patriotic Indian during pre and post-independence. As the days progresses "Khadi" had to compete with various national and international brand. Since liberalisation of Indian economy it faced more fierce competition from several reputed foreign brands. However, "Khadi" maintained its courage and proceeded in its own laid down path.

BACKER SPIELVOGEL & BATES'S GLOBAL SCAN Global Scan encompassed 18 countries, mostly located in the Triad. To identify attitudes that could help explain and predict purchase behavior for different product categories, researchers studied consumer attitudes and values, as well as media viewership/readership, buying patterns, and product use. The survey attempted to identify both country-specific and global attitudinal attributes; sample statements are "The harder you push, the farther you get," and "I never have enough time or money." Combining all the country data yielded a segmentation study known as Target Scan, a description of five global psychographic segments that BSB claimed represent 95 percent of the adult populations in the 18 countries surveyed (see Figure 7-3). BSB labeled the segments as Strivers, Achievers, Pressured, Traditionals, and Adapters.

Strivers (26 percent). This segment consists of young people with a median age of 31 who live hectic, on-the-go lives. Driven to achieve success, they are materialistic pleasure seekers for whom time and money are in short supply.

Achievers (22 percent). Older than the Strivers, the affluent, assertive Achievers are upwardly mobile and already have attained a good measure of success. Achievers are status-conscious consumers for whom quality is important.

Pressured (13 percent). The Pressured segment, largely comprised of women, cuts across age groups and is characterized by constant financial and family pressures. Life's problems overwhelm the members of this segment.

Traditionals (16 percent). This segment is "rooted to the past" and clings to the country's heritage and cultural values.

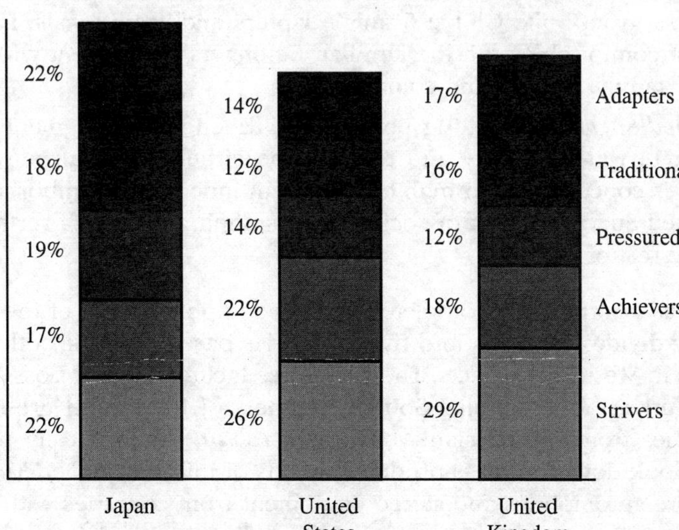

FIGURE 7-3 BSB's Global Scan Segmentation Study

Adapters (18 percent). This segment is composed of older people who are content with their lives and who manage to maintain their values while keeping open minds when faced with change.

Global Scan is a tool for identifying consumer similarities across national boundaries, as well as highlighting differences between segments in different countries. For example, in the United States, baby boomers help swell the ranks of Strivers and Achievers to nearly half the population. In Germany, on the other hand, the Striver segment is older and comprises a smaller proportion of the population. Global Scan has also pinpointed important differences between Americans and Canadians, who are part of the same geographic segment of North America.

Similarly, Global Scan revealed marked differences between the circumstances in which Strivers find themselves in different countries. In the United States, Strivers are chronically short of both time and money, whereas Japanese Strivers have ample monetary resources. These differences translate directly into different preferences: US Strivers buy cars that are fun, stylish, and represent a good value; Japanese Strivers view cars as an extension of their homes and will accessorize them with lavish features—curtains and high-end stereo systems, for example. This implies that different advertising appeals would be necessary when targeting Strivers in the two countries.

D'ARCY MASIUS BENTON & BOWLES'S EUROCONSUMER STUDY DMBB's research team focused on Europe and produced a 15-country study titled "The Euroconsumer: Marketing Myth or Cultural Certainty?" The researchers identified four lifestyle groups: Successful Idealists, Affluent Materialists, Comfortable Belongers, and Disaffected Survivors. The first two groups represent the elite, the latter two represent mainstream European consumers.

Successful Idealists. Comprising from 5 to 20 percent of the population, this segment consists of persons who have achieved professional and material success while maintaining commitment to abstract or socially responsible ideals.

Affluent Materialists. These status-conscious "up-and-comers," many of whom are business professionals, use conspicuous consumption to communicate their success to others.

Comfortable Belongers. Comprising one quarter to one half of a country's population, this group, like Global Scan's Adapters and Traditionals, is conservative and most comfortable with the familiar. Belongers are content with the comfort of home, family, friends, and community.

Disaffected Survivors. Lacking power and affluence, this segment harbors little hope for upward mobility and tends to be either resentful or resigned. This segment is concentrated in high-crime, urban inner-city neighborhoods. Despite Disaffected Survivors' lack of societal status, their attitudes nevertheless tend to affect the rest of society.

DMBB has also recently completed a psychographic profile of the Russian market. The study divides Russians into five categories based on their outlook, behavior, and openness to Western products. The categories include *kuptsy,* Cossacks, students, business executives, and "Russian Souls." Members of the largest group, the *kuptsy* (the label comes from the Russian word for *merchant*), theoretically prefer Russian products but look down on mass-produced goods of inferior quality. *Kuptsy* are most likely to admire automobiles and stereo equipment from countries with good reputations for engineering, such as Germany and Scandinavia. Nigel Clarke, the author of the study, notes that segmentation and targeting are appropriate in Russia, despite the

TABLE 7-2 Y&R's 4Cs

Attitudes	Work	Lifestyle	Purchase Behavior
Resigned Poor			
Unhappy	Labor	Shut-in	Staples
Distrustful	Unskilled	Television	Price
Struggling Poor			
Unhappy	Labor	Sports	Price
Dissatisfied	Craftsmen	Television	Discount stores
Mainstreamers			
Happy	Craftsmen	Family	Habit
Belong	Teaching	Gardening	Brand loyal
Aspirers			
Unhappy	Sales	Trendy sports	Conspicuous consumption
Ambitious	White collar	Fashion magazines	Credit
Succeeders			
Happy	Managerial	Travel	Luxury
Industrious	Professional	Dining out	Quality
Transitionals			
Rebellious	Student	Arts/crafts	Impulse
Liberal	Health field	Special-interest magazines	Unique products
Reformers			
Inner growth	Professional	Reading	Ecology
Improve world	Entrepreneur	Cultural events	Homemade/grown

fact that its broad consumer market is still in its infancy. "If you're dealing with a market as different as Russia is, even if you want to go 'broad,' it's best to think: 'Which group would go most for my brand? Where is my natural center of gravity?' "[11]

YOUNG & RUBICAM'S CROSS-CULTURAL CONSUMER CHARACTERIZATIONS (4Cs) Young & Rubicam's 4Cs is a 20-country psychographic segmentation study focusing on goals, motivations, and values that help to determine consumer choice. The research is based on the assumption that "there are underlying psychological processes involved in human behavior that are culture-free and so basic that they can be found all over the globe."[12]

Three overall groupings can be further subdivided into a total of seven segments: Constrained (Resigned Poor and Struggling Poor), Middle Majority (Mainstreamers, Aspirers, and Succeeders), and Innovators (Transitionals and Reformers). The goals, motivations, and values of these segments range from "survival," "given up," and "subsistence" (Resigned Poor) to "social betterment," "social conscience," and "social altruism" (Reformers). Table 7-2 shows some of the attitudinal, work, lifestyle, and purchase behavior characteristics of the seven groups.

Combining the 4Cs data for a particular country with other data permits Y&R to predict product and category purchase behavior for the various segments. Yet, as noted previously in the discussion of Global Scan in the chapter, marketers at global companies that are Y&R clients are cautioned not to assume that they can

[11]Stuart Elliot, "Figuring Out the Russian Consumer," *The New York Times,* April 1, 1992, C1, C19.
[12]Piirto, *Beyond Mind Games,* 161.

develop one strategy or one commercial to be used to reach a particular segment across cultures. As a Y&R staffer notes, "As you get closer to the executional level, you need to be acutely sensitive to cultural differences. But at the origin, it's of enormous benefit to be able to think about people who share common values across cultures."[13]

Behavior Segmentation

Behavior segmentation focuses on whether people buy and use a product, as well as how often and how much they use it. Consumers can be categorized in terms of usage rates—for example, heavy, medium, light, and nonuser. Consumers can also be segmented according to user status: potential users, nonusers, ex-users, regulars, first-timers, and users of competitors' products. Although bottled water may be considered a luxury product in some high-income markets, Nestlé is marketing bottled water in Pakistan where there is a huge market of nonusers who, despite their low income, are willing to pay 18 rupees a bottle for clean water because of the widespread presence of arsenic poisoning in well water and the pollution of surface water. Tobacco companies are targeting China because the Chinese are heavy smokers.

Financial institutions have to consider many different pieces of information regarding consumer behavior toward saving and spending money. Japan has the highest number of cash dispensers, 1,115 per 1 million population, followed by Switzerland, Canada, and the United States where the average is slightly higher than 600. The average dollar amount withdrawn also varies considerably. In Japan, the average withdrawal is \$289. This is followed by Switzerland at \$187 and Italy at \$185. The United States is far down the list with \$68 as the average withdrawal. Japanese people tend to carry around a lot more cash than people in other countries.[14]

Benefit Segmentation

Global benefit segmentation focuses on the numerator of the value equation—the B in $V = B/P$. This approach can achieve excellent results by virtue of marketers' superior understanding of the problem a product solves or the benefit it offers, regardless of geography. For example, Nestlé discovered that cat owners' attitudes toward feeding their pets are the same everywhere. In response, a pan-European campaign was created for Friskies dry cat food. The appeal was that dry cat food better suits a cat's universally recognized independent nature.

Vertical Versus Horizontal Segmentation

Vertical segmentation is based on product category or modality and price points. For example, in medical imaging there is x-ray, computed axial tomography (CAT) scan, magnetic resonance imaging (MRI), and so on. Each modality has its own price points. These price points were the traditional way of segmenting the medical imaging market. One company decided to take a different approach and segment the same market by the health care delivery system: national research and teaching hospitals, government hospitals, and so on. It then rolled out a campaign that was regional, national, and finally global, which was tailored for each different type of health care delivery. This horizontal segmentation approach worked as well in markets outside the home-country launch market as it did in the home country.[15]

---

[13]Ibid., 165.

[14]"Holes in the Wall," *The Economist*, March 6, 1999, 99.

[15]Interview with Nicholas F. Rossiello, Vice President Marketing and Sales, AFP Imaging Corporation, Elmsford, NY, October 30, 1996.

BOX 7-5

Side Bar: Harry Potter Clicked Right Segment in China!

Harry potter books own the tag of a grand global marketing miracle. The product i.e. the book itself was excellent when it came out of the very able hands of JK Rowling. The first book of Harry Potter came out during 1997 and it hasn't looked back since. Uptill 2016, nine Harry potter books have been written and published and all sold like hotcakes across the the world by braking the traditionally talked about cultural, political, and legal barriers. By 2013 it created a world record, when a single writer's book registered a sales figure of above 400 million in all over the world. Though the book was mainly written targeting the young children, but adults also took interest in Harry Potter books. In order to capture market in countries where English is not the main language, the book has been carefully translated into 73 local languages.

British author J.K. Rowling, can be proud of the fact that Harry Potter books crossed 1.3 million books sales in China which made it one of the most read books in the populous country. In the initial years when the Harry Potter book was in turmoil regarding the translation issues, untenable plot of wizardry etc; no one thought that the book is going to attain this magical milestone by dwarfing the history of sales of western books in China. The screening of Harry Potter movies actually made the Chinese student break the slumber and made them fond of Harry potter. Internationally, researchers found that there was not much different between boys and girls in terms of their addiction towards reading Harry Potter books. They almost equally liked the fantasy factors ingrained in the books as much as they liked the humours. The combination of fantasy and humour made the reading a fun for students. The Chinese children literature was devoid of these two mixture for a long period of time as they were mainly focusing on ancient Chinese mythology dealing with excitement but devoid of the right punch of humour. This segment was useful for Harry potter marketing company who put the right product for the right segment.

Adapted from China Internet Information Center available at http://www.china.org.cn/english/13667.htm, as accessed on 10 January 2017 at 12pm; China Daily dated 07/26/2001 available at http://www.china.org.cn/english/2001/Jul/16607.htm, as accessed on 10 January 2017 at 12pm.

GLOBAL TARGETING

As discussed earlier in the chapter, segmenting is the process by which marketers identify groups of consumers with similar wants and needs. Targeting is the act of evaluating and comparing the identified groups and then selecting one or more of them as the prospect(s) with the highest potential. A marketing mix is then devised that will provide the organization with the best return on sales while simultaneously creating the maximum amount of value to consumers.

Criteria for Targeting

The three basic criteria for assessing opportunity in global target markets are the same as in single-country targeting: current size of the segment and anticipated growth potential, competition, and compatibility with the company's overall objectives and the feasibility of successfully reaching a designated target.

CURRENT SEGMENT SIZE AND GROWTH POTENTIAL Is the market segment currently large enough that it presents a company with the opportunity to make a profit? If it is not large enough or profitable enough today, does it have high growth potential so that it is attractive in terms of a company's long-term strategy? Indeed, one of the advantages of targeting a market segment globally is that, whereas the segment in a single-country market might be too small, even a narrow segment can be served profitably with a standardized product if the segment exists in several countries.[16] The billion-plus members of the global "MTV Generation" constitute a huge market that, by virtue of its size, is extremely attractive to many companies.

China represents an individual geographic market that offers attractive opportunities in many industries. Consider the growth opportunity in financial services, for example. There are currently only about 3 million credit cards in circulation, mostly used by businesses. Low product saturation levels are also found for personal computers; there is one computer for every 1,250 people. The ratio in the United States is approaching one computer for every two people. The opportunity for automobile manufacturers is even greater. China has 1.2 million passenger cars, one car for every 20,000 Chinese. Even with the market in China growing at an annual rate of 33 percent, a tremendous potential market still exists.

POTENTIAL COMPETITION A market or market segment characterized by strong competition may be a segment to avoid or one in which to utilize a different strategy. Often a local brand may present competition to the entering multinational. In Peru, Inca Kola is as popular as Coca-Cola. In India, Thumbs Cola is a major brand. In the Siberian city of Krasnoyarsk, Crazy Cola has a 48 percent share of the market.[17] The global might try more or different promotions or may acquire the local company or form an alliance with it.

Kodak vs. Fuji in film is a story of a company who failed to recognize that it was engaged in a battle for a market that was on a glide path to extinction. Kodak's strategy is an example of fighting the wrong battles and losing the war. Both companies focused on competition in the market for film when they should have been focusing on how to survive and prosper in a world of digital cameras. Kodak was in the 1990's the undisputed leader in the US color film market. Fuji launched a competitive offensive in the US and also attacked Kodak in Europe, where Kodak had almost half of the color film market. Kodak responded by attacking Fuji in Japan. These expensive battles resulted in minor share of market shifts. For example, Kodak spent over a billion US dollars to gain a few share points increase in the Japanese Market. Fast forward to January 2012: Kodak filed for Chapter 11 bankruptcy protection and announced that it would exit the digital camera business. In January 2013, a court approved a plan to emerge from Bankruptcy.

COMPATIBILITY AND FEASIBILITY If a global target market is judged to be large enough, and if strong competitors are either absent or not deemed to represent insurmountable obstacles, then the final consideration is whether a company can and should target that market. In many cases, reaching global market segments requires considerable resources, such as expenditures for distribution and travel by company personnel. Another question is whether the pursuit of a particular segment is compatible with the company's overall goals and established sources of competitive advantage. Although Pepsi was firmly entrenched in the Russian market, having entered in 1972, Coke waited 15 years to make its first move in Russia and waited 20 years before it decided to make major investments. At the time of Coke's entry, Pepsi had 100 percent of the Russian cola market. This would appear to be a difficult position to challenge, but because of the size of the Coke investment and the skillful execution of its investment moves in Russia, by 1996 Coke's market share had reached 50 percent.[18]

---

[16]Michael E. Porter, "The Strategic Role of International Marketing," *The Journal of Consumer Marketing,* 3, no. 2 (Spring 1986): 21.

[17]Betsy McKay, "Siberian Soft Drink Queen Outmarkets Coke and Pepsi," *The Wall Street Journal,* August 23, 1999, B1.

[18]Interview with Oleg Smirnoff, former marketing manager, PepsiCola International, New York, October 31, 1996.

BOX 7-6

Side Bar: Where is the TATA Nano Segment?

In India, marketing failure of TATA Nano is a much talked about topic. It all started with much hype about this USD 2000 car and market speculators located in India predicted a grand success considering the poor affordability of bulk section prospective consumers living in rural India. The pundits, knowing Indian market well also predicted that the market will extend from rural market to the low and medium income population the country living in urban area. Finally the date came during 2008 when the company for the first time allowed Indian consumers to have a look in the car priced at 2500 USD, a hike of only 500 USD which was attributed to the rising cost of various inputs that had gone in manufacturing the car. The possible segment for the car was decided in the following way

- The lower and middle class income group living in rural or urban area.
- Family with possession of 2-wheeler.
- The prospective consumers have the aspiration to buy four wheelers but could not afford it.
- The prospective consumers desire economic efficiency hence select cars with low fuel cost.
- The prospective consumers felt the need of a car as a matter of convenience and not as status symbol.
- The prospective consumers had occasions when felt the need for an automobile which can carry entire family.

Rough pre launch estimate had shown that the described segment characteristic was very common not only in rural India but as well as in many B class cities. Hence the production capacity of the plant was kept at plant's annual production capacity of 2.5 lakh cars. Accordingly the company printed over 20 lakh booking forms and expected bookings to be more than 5 lakh which could be met on staggering basis.

But alas! The car made commercial beginning during March 2009 and Tata Motors could just manage to sell 1.75 lakh Nanos in the first two years of operation which was completely unexpected for the company. What went wrong? The segment still existed in India with its overwhelming size but the car bookings were not picking up. A deeper analysis had shown a mismatch between marketing plan of Nano and segment need and aspiration. In India, particularly in the low income segment, buying a car was a life time event with lot of involvement. The car owner also used to get social benefits as the society around perceived the person as blessed. On the contrary to segment expectation, the company came out with marketing communication projecting the car to be the "Cheapest Car". Usually in India, taking consideration of the high power distance status of Indian society, the automobile company usually take help of a celebrity to publicize a car during the launch period and thereafter as well, to provide the "social status" punch in the minds of the prospective consumers. Tata Nano did not have celebrity endorsement while launching but relied highly on the low price factor to drive the sales. Altogether, it seemed that there was a great disconnect between the product and the need and aspiration of the targeted segment.

GLOBAL PRODUCT POSITIONING

Positioning is the location of your product in the mind of your customer. Thus, one of the most powerful tools of marketing is not something that a marketer can do to the product or to any element of the marketing mix: positioning is what happens in the mind of the customer. The position that a product occupies in the mind of a customer depends on a host of variables, many of which are controlled by the marketer.

After the global market has been segmented and one or more segments have been targeted, it is essential to plan a way to reach the target(s). To achieve this task, marketers use positioning. In today's global market environment, many companies find it increasingly important to have a unified global positioning strategy. For example, Chase Manhattan Bank launched a $75 million global advertising campaign geared to the theme "profit from experience." According to Aubrey Hawes, a vice president and corporate director of marketing for the bank, Chase's business and private banking clients "span the globe and travel the globe. They can only know one Chase in their minds, so why should we try to confuse them?"

Can global positioning work for all products? One study suggests that global positioning is most effective for product categories that approach either end of a "high-touch/high-tech" continuum.[19] Both ends of the continuum are characterized by high levels of customer involvement and by a shared "language" among consumers.

High-Tech Positioning

Personal computers, video and stereo equipment, and automobiles are examples of product categories in which high-tech positioning has proven effective. Such products are frequently purchased on the basis of concrete product features, although image may also be important. Buyers typically already possess or wish to acquire considerable technical information. High-tech products may be divided into three categories: technical products, special-interest products, and demonstrable products.

TECHNICAL PRODUCTS Computers, chemicals, tires, and financial services are just a sample of the product categories whose buyers have specialized needs, require a great deal of product information, and share a common "language." Computer buyers in Russia and the United States are equally knowledgeable about microprocessors, 20-gigabyte hard drives, modems, and RAM (random access memory). Marketing communications for high-tech products should be informative and emphasize features.

SPECIAL-INTEREST PRODUCTS Although less technical and more leisure or recreation oriented, special-interest products also are characterized by a shared experience and high involvement among users. Again, the common language and symbols associated with such products can transcend language and cultural barriers. Fuji bicycles, Adidas sports equipment, and Canon cameras are examples of successful global special-interest products.

High-Touch Positioning

Marketing of high-touch products requires less emphasis on specialized information and more emphasis on image. Like high-tech products, however, high-touch categories are highly involving for consumers. Buyers of high-touch products also share a common language and set of symbols relating to themes of wealth, materialism, and romance. The three categories of high-touch products are products that solve a common problem, global-village products, and products with a universal theme.

PRODUCTS THAT SOLVE A COMMON PROBLEM At the other end of the price spectrum from high tech, products in this category provide benefits linked to "life's little moments." Ads that show friends talking over a cup of coffee in a café or quenching thirst with a soft drink during a day at the beach put the product at the center of everyday life and communicate the benefit offered in a way that is understood worldwide.

GLOBAL-VILLAGE PRODUCTS Chanel fragrances, designer fashions, mineral water, and pizza are all examples of products whose positioning is strongly cosmopolitan in

---

[19]See Teresa J. Domzal and Lynette Unger, "Emerging Positioning Strategies in Global Marketing," *Journal of Consumer Marketing,* 4, no. 4 (Fall 1987): 26–27.

nature. Fragrances and fashions have traveled as a result of growing worldwide interest in high-quality, highly visible, high-priced products that often enhance social status. However, the lower-priced food products just mentioned show that the global-village category encompasses a broad price spectrum.

In global markets, products may have a global appeal by virtue of their country of origin. The "American-ness" of Levi's, Marlboro, and Harley-Davidson enhances their appeal to cosmopolitans around the world. In consumer electronics, Sony is a name synonymous with vaunted Japanese quality; in automobiles, Mercedes is the embodiment of legendary German engineering.

PRODUCTS WITH UNIVERSAL THEMES As noted earlier in the chapter, some advertising themes and product appeals are thought to be basic enough that they are truly transnational. Additional themes are materialism (keyed to images of well-being or status), heroism (themes include rugged individuals or self-sacrifice), play (leisure/recreation), and procreation (images of courtship and romance).

It should be noted that some products can be positioned in more than one way, within either the high-tech or high-touch poles of the continuum. A BMW car, for example, could simultaneously be classified as technical and special interest. To reinforce the high-touch aspect, BMW publishes *BMW Magazine* for BMW owners. In addition to articles on the technical characteristics of the car, the magazine has lifestyle articles and advertisements for luxury products such as expensive watches and jewelry.

CASE 7-1

Positioning Dairy Milk as a Compelling Alternative to Traditional Indian Sweets as Dessert[20]

John Cadbury founded the Cadbury Company in England during 1824 and thereafter the surname of the founder almost became a synonym for chocolate in the world. The journey of Cadbury which started from Birmingham, England was unstoppable and soon it started spreading in different countries of the world irrespective of the fact whether it is a traditional chocolate loving country or not. Switzerland, which traditionally is known for its love for chocolate and preference for chocolate consumption was also increasing with time. During 2014 the chocolate consumption per capita for Switzerland stood at 19.8 pounds followed by Germany (17.4), Ireland (16.3), United Kingdom (16.3), Norway (14.6), Sweden (11.9), Australia (10.8), Netherland (10.4), United State (9.5), and France (9.3).

India traditionally was not known as a chocolate consuming country in the world like many other third world countries. Interestingly, some pundits found high correlation between chocolate consumption rate of a country per capita and GDP per capita status of the country. High GDP per capita countries are the most chocolate consuming countries of the world. As it is evident from the Table 7-3, that countries who had high GDP per capita in the range of 39000 to 61000 USD are the top ten chocolate producing countries. Interestingly, the top ten countries are also mostly the European countries. So going by this benchmark Indians are not likely to be chocolate

[20] More information on Cadbury campain in India are available at websites (1) http://www.livemint.com/Consumer/jQgsAxOYWsrX0ReTbMwUZJ/Cadbury-launches-new-ad-for-Diwali.html (2) https://archive.tehelka.com/story_main52.asp?filename=Fw260512Celebration.asp (3) https://www.telegraphindia.com/1160710/jsp/7days/story_95758.jsp (4) http://onlinechocolatesstore.blogspot.in/2012/03/cadbury-celebrations.html (5) http://www.livemint.com/Opinion/hVDgxYVNCozGAEQeLwwWYN/An-excuse-to-consume.html (6) http://in.mondelezinternational.com/brand-family

TABLE 7-3 Top Ten Chocolate Consuming Countries of the World

	Country	Pounds of chocolate consumption per capita each year (2014)	GDP per capita in USD (2015)	Continent of the country
1	Switzerland	19.8	60535	Europe
2	Germany	17.4	47268	Europe
3	Ireland	16.3	54654	Europe
4	United Kingdom	16.3	41325	Europe
5	Norway	14.6	61472	Europe
6	Sweden	11.9	46420	Europe
7	Australia	10.8	45514	Australia
8	Netherland	10.4	48459	Europe
9	United States	9.5	55837	North America
10	France	9.3	39678	Europe
11	India	0.26	6020	Asia

Adapted from https://www.statista.com/chart/3668/the-worlds-biggest-chocolate-consumers/, as accessed on 10 January 2017 at 12pm; (GDP data put in the same table IMF GDP) http://www.imf.org/en/data, as accessed on 10 January 2017 at 12pm.

loving and consuming country. John Cadbury therefore, had to face two types of barriers while internationalising in different countries of the world. The European rich countries are hugely competitive as other famous chocolate brands like Godiva, Lindt & Sprungli,, Patchi etc. were dominating those markets. In countries like India, for Cadbury it was not the severity of competition but Cadbury had to fight in a new front altogether. The people living in India they were not avid consumer of chocolates. The important reasons were:

- High cost of milk based chocolates and limited availability.
- Society accepted that chocolates were for children only, society customs puts the tag "childish" when an adult developed habit of consuming chocolates.
- Indians were are not exposed to different variety of chocolates available at the global level.
- Indian sweets were more accepted in the society and chocolates were never considered as a candidate for replacement.
- Traditionally, India is not known for great inclination for chocolate.

Therefore, during initial internationalisation period, the Cadbury company did not consider India as a country of not immediate but distant prospect. So it did not have any manufacturing facility in the beginning but used to be present in Indian market through limited export. The product had limited distribution in cities like Mumbai and Kolkata. As the company felt that in the long run India could be a huge market because of its population and prospect of economic development, the company took up three important tasks. Firstly, Cadbury attempted to develop its production capabilities. It added manufacturing facilities one by one in different strategic locations like Thane (Maharastra), Induri (Pune) and Malanpur (Gwalior), Bangalore and Baddi (Himachal Pradesh). Secondly, it did not lose sight of raw material availability in India and hence since 1965 it actively worked with Indian farmers for cocoa cultivation. It also linked up with Kerala Agriculture University and planned long term joint research for quality cocoa cultivation in the country and yield high cocoa. Thirdly, Cadbury went on to take up the most important task of category development as India was not an established market for chocolate, neither sweet nor bitter. Milk chocolate was just at the initial stage of category life cycle and bitter chocolate category had yet to take birth.

Cadbury made a very humble journey in India towards category development. The market for the milk based chocolates was very small. The product was only purchased by the urban rich to be consumed by the children only. The chocolate consuming adult population was almost non-existent. The frequency of purchase of milk chocolate like Cadbury was also very low as this was used only as gift item during occasions like birthday etc. In order to establish a sustainable market for Cadbury product it launched few land mark marketing campaigns.

1990 Campaign

During early 1990s the usual perception about Cadbury Diary Milk was that it could only be purchased by parents to express true love for their children. Actually, the communication taglines like 'Sometimes Cadbury's can say it better than words' or 'Nothing but the best will do' were also supportive to the cause of building up a niche market segment for milk chocolates. It was very difficult for the milk chocolates to break the shackles as the adult population continued to perceive that consuming chocolates almost intruded in to the territory reserved for the younger generation.

1997 Campaign

Cadbury campaign for the first time came out of the image 'only for children' and dared to lure adult population to enlarge the market size. The Cadbury celebrations campaign journey began in 1997 with Cadbury attempting to introduce the celebrations range of chocolates as a typical gift for a festive occasion instead of usual clothes or sweets. 'Diwali Ki Meethi Shubhkaamnaaye' campaign was purposefully unleased so that adult population could be lured to gift chocolates to their loving ones irrespective of age.

2000 Campaign

In 2000, Cadbury wanted to increase the frequency of use and positioned for all purpose gift items. It released a new campaign like 'Rakhi Par Ek Meetha Sa Uphar' which compelled Indian consumers to needle with the idea of gifting their near and dear ones delicious chocolates in place of traditional sweets. In quick succession it came up with similar campaigns like 'Har Pal Bane Ek Utsav', 'Rishtey Pakne Do', 'Aankhon Se Chakne Do' to cement the belief that Cadbury chocolates could be alternative to traditional gifts during the celebration of Indian festival like 'Raksha Bandhan'.

2004 Campaign

The 2004 Celebrations commercials starring the most popular Bollywood hero Amitabh Bachchan was a grand success. Amitabh Bachchan was still remembered for his friendship role and hence the cementing friendship with Cadbury chocolate was accepted as idea by general people also. The tagline 'Aisi Mithaas Jo Dosti Banaye Khaas' as such came to a grand success.

2009 Campaign

The, 'Iss Diwali Aap Kisse Khush Karenge?' campaign tried to utilise the festive mood of Diwali celebration. The festive mood of people allowed them to be close to each other and a total atmosphere of fun and celebration prevailed in India. The company was successful in placing Cadbury chocolates as a gift item amongst people irrespective of their age.

2010 Campaign

With the taglines "Shubh Aarambh" (auspicious beginnings), Cadbury wanted to have a reversal in its campaign. Instead the previous campaigns related to celebration happy occasion over chocolates the new campaign provoked people to start happy occasions after consuming the chocolate.

2011 Campaign

Cadbury carefully noted one unique aspect in the matter of competition in India which possibly it did not face in any other country. Indian sweets were really posing a threat for further expansion of chocolate market in India. Culturally, sweets made of milk were much closer to the Indians than milk based chocolates. Indians were culturally very attached to sweet meats and hence it looked almost impossible to replace sweets with meats. But it was almost a compulsion for Cadbury to take Indian sweets head on. It released 'Kuch meetha ho jaye' campaign to allure Indians to use Cadbury in places where otherwise traditional sweets would have been used

CADBURY INDIA BRANDS

Cadbury India has different products in the different brands.

Chocolates

The manufactures of Cadbury India in the chocolates brand are:

Cadbury Dairy Milk Its journey in India began in the year 1948. Other than the most popular Cadbury Dairy Milk, there are other variants in the brand as Fruit & Nut, Crackle, Roast Almond, Cadbury Dairy Milk Wowie, and Cadbury Dairy Milk 2 in 1.

5 Star This chocolate bar was launched in 1969. It is the second largest chocolate brand after Cadbury Dairy Milk with a market share of 14%. Cadbury 5 Star Crunchy and Cadbury 5 Star Fruit and Nut are the variants in this brand.

Perk Cadbury Perk was launched in 1996. The brands launched later are Perk XL and Perk XXL.

Celebrations Cadbury Celebrations brand was launched with a target of replacing the conventional gift items as sweets etc on occasions like Diwali, Rakhi etc.

Éclairs The Cadbury Dairy Milk Éclairs is one of the most popular brands in the Éclairs category. The newly launched brand in this category is the Cadbury Éclairs Rich Brownie.

Gems This brand was launched in 1968 and is one of the most popular brands among the kids.

Beverages

Cadbury Bournvita It was launched in India in 1948. It is one of the oldest brands in the category of Malt Based food.

Bournvita's Li'l Champs: This is an ideal milk additive product for the children launched in 2008 with key ingredients for proper growth as DHA, whey protein etc.

Candy

Halls Halls was included in the Cadbury Brand in the year 2003 as a part of the global unification with Adams Confectionery.

Biscuits

Oreo It was launched globally in the year 1912. It was launched in the Indian market in 2011.

Gum

Bubbaloo This gum with a bubbly taste was launched in India in the year 2007.

Case Questions

1. How much Cadburi has been successful in penetrating Indian market?
2. Evaluate the segmentation, targeting and positioning efforts of the company.

Summary

The global environment must be analyzed before a company pursues expansion into new geographic markets. Through global market segmentation, the similarities and differences of potential buying customers can be identified and grouped. Demographics, psychographics, behavioral characteristics, and benefits sought are common attributes used to segment world markets. After marketers have identified segments, the next step is targeting. The identified groups are evaluated and compared; the prospect(s) with the greatest potential is selected from among them. The groups are evaluated on the basis of several factors: segment size and growth potential, competition, and compatibility and feasibility. After evaluating the identified segments, marketers must decide on an appropriate targeting strategy. The three basic categories of global target marketing strategies are standardized marketing, concentrated marketing, and differentiated marketing. Finally, companies must plan a way to reach their chosen target market(s) by determining the best positioning for their product offerings. Here, marketers devise an appropriate marketing mix to fix the product in the mind of the potential buyers in the target market. High-tech and high-touch positioning are two strategies that can work well for a global product.

Discussion Questions

1. What is a global market segment? Pick a market that you know something about and describe the global segments for this market.
2. Identify the major geographic and demographic segments in global markets.
3. What is positioning? Why is it an important tool for the global marketer?
4. Some marketing experts believe that positioning should be the fifth P of the four P's of marketing. Do your agree? Why? Why not?
5. Amazon.com has been an early winner in the online book business. Which market segments has Amazon.com served? Are the Amazon.com target market segments in the United States and the rest of the world identical?
6. Smoking is on the decline in high-income countries where the combination of higher life expectancy, education, income, and legal action has created a powerful antismoking campaign. Global tobacco companies are shifting their focus from high-income to emerging markets where the combination of rising income and the absence of antismoking campaigns is leading to ever-increasing demand for cigarettes. Is this shift in focus by the global tobacco companies ethical? What, if anything, should residents in high-income countries do about the rise in smoking in emerging markets?

Suggested Readings

Agarwal, James, Naresh K. Malhotra, and Ruth N. Bolton. "A Cross-National and Cross-Cultural Approach to Global Market Segmentation: An Application Using Consumers' Perceived Service Quality." *Journal of International Marketing*, 18, no. 3 (September 2010): 18–40.

Chu, Michael, and Djordjija Petkoski, "Segmenting the Base of the Pyramid," *Harvard Business Review* (June 2011): 113–117.

Green, Paul E., and Abba M. Krieger. "Segmenting Markets with Conjoint Analysis." *Journal of Marketing*, 55, no. 4 (October 1991): 20–31.

Hout, Thomas, Michael E. Porter, and Eileen Rudden. "How Global Companies Win Out." *Harvard Business Review* (September–October 1982): 98–108.

Nijssen, Edwin J., and Susan P. Douglas. "Consumer World-Mindedness and Attitudes Toward Product Positioning in Advertising: An Examination of Global Versus Foreign Versus Local Positioning." *Journal of International Marketing*, 19, no. 3 (September 2011) 113–133.

Piirto, Rebecca. *Beyond Mind Games: The Marketing Power of Psychographics.* Ithaca, NY: American Demographics Books, 1991.

Quelch, John A., and Katherine E. Jocz. "How To Market In A Downturn." *Harvard Business Review* (April 2009): 52–62.

Rangan, V. Kasturi, Michael Chu, and Djordjija Petkoski. "Segmenting the Base of the Pyramid." *Harvard Business Review* (June 2011): 113–117.

Taylor, Gabriela. *Targeting Your Market (Marketing Across Generations, Cultures and Gender).* CreateSpace Independent Publishing Platform, 2012.

Taylor, William. "Message and Muscle: An Interview with Swatch Titan Nicolas Hayek." *Harvard Business Review*, 71 (March–April 1993): 99–110.

Ter Hofstede, Frenkel, Jan-Benedict E. M. Steenkamp, and Michel Wedel. "International Market Segmentation Based on Consumer-Product Relations." *Journal of Marketing Research*, 36, no. 1 (1999): 1–17.

Trout, Jack, and Steve Rivkin. *The New Positioning: The Latest on the World's #1 Business Strategy.* New York: McGraw-Hill, 1996.

Womack, James P., Daniel T. Jones, and Daniel Roos. *The Machine That Changed the World.* New York: HarperCollins, 1990.

Part IV Global Marketing Strategy

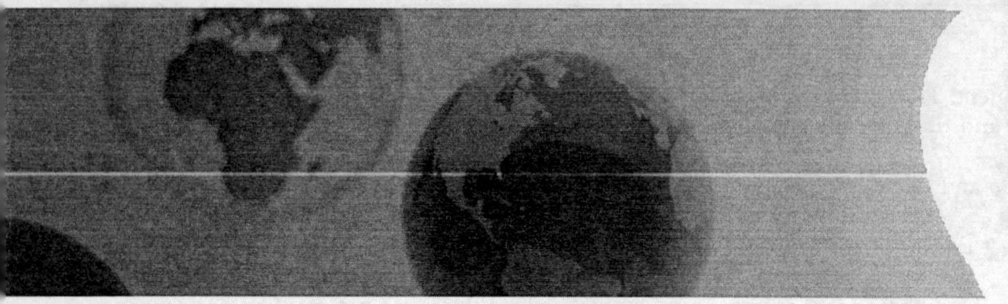

CHAPTER 8

Global Entry and Expansion Strategies

I don't look to jump over 7-foot bars: I look around for 1-foot bars that I can step over.

—Warren Buffett[1], (The Most Successful Investor in History), 1930

Learning Objectives

1. Identify the decision criteria for global market entry (242–246).
2. Describe the process of selecting an export market (247–249).
3. Compare and contrast global market entry methods (251–257).
4. Discuss global market expansion strategies (257–259).

INTRODUCTION

When a company decides to expand internationally, it faces a host of decisions. The most basic is making the decision that entering international markets is in the best interest of the company. This is followed by a series of considerations. Which countries should it enter and in what sequence? What criteria should be used to select entry markets: proximity, stage of development, geographic region, cultural and linguistic criteria, the competitive situation, or other factors? How should it enter new markets: export sourcing from the home country, the use of independent agents and distributors in target markets, or an investment in company-owned and managed operations? Should the new market be supplied with imported product from the home market or third countries or locally manufactured? And should the offering be customized to meet local demand or be standardized across markets? These options are not mutually exclusive and can be combined to improve both market access and a firm's competitive position. The entire decision process can be framed by understanding the evolution of companies operating across borders, from domestic/ethnocentric organizations to transnational/geocentric operations. This chapter addresses key issues that global managers face and strategic alternatives a company must consider to begin or expand their share of world markets.

[1] Born August 30, 1930, Omaha, Nebraska. Buffet is an investor, businessman, and philanthropist. Known as the "Oracle of Omaha."

A good example of the management decision process is the entry of International Paper Company's consumer packaging division into Asian beverage markets (see Box 8-1). Despite its global-sounding name, International Paper (IP) was primarily focused on markets in North America. It is instructive to look at the "why" behind IP's strategic moves—exporting to some countries and investing in "green-field" subsidiaries in others.

BOX 8-1

Side Bar: International Paper Company's International Expansion[2]

The major challenges faced by IP illustrate the breadth of issues that managers need to think through before "going international." Economies of scale, specialization, and first-mover advantage led IP to invest in "global scale" primary paper mills. The mills, coupled with IP's vertically integrated access to timberlands and efficient logistics infrastructure, created a competitive advantage. IP's primary mills were sized to serve the market needs of its regional US converting plants (those that "convert" large roll-stock into the actual cartons used by dairy and juice processors). In addition, they had available capacity to produce and export commodity roll-stock to modern paper converters in Europe and Japan. IP's principal markets represent the same Triad countries discussed earlier.

As markets evolved, and despite its strong competitive cost position, IP's home market paper operations were put in jeopardy by a growing use of the now ubiquitous plastic gallon milk jug. Consumers that had once purchased milk in quarts and half-gallons increasingly began to buy milk by the gallon. Plastic jugs presented a lower cost and more convenient option to milk processors than traditional paper. Today, plastic jugs have all but replaced the paper gallon carton and they continue to take share from the half-gallon paper carton (though not in the high-margin juice and juice-drink category where paper's superior printability and "billboarding" retain a marketing advantage over plastic). With the loss of market volumes to plastic, International Paper's primary paper mills (those that produced giant rolls of bleached paperboard that other facilities then cut, printed, and "converted" into specialty-sized cartons) began operating below design efficiency levels, a critical underutilization of large fixed-capital assets. The plastic jug's success in taking share from paper put the primary mills' low-cost position and profitability in jeopardy. To preserve economies of scale, International Paper had to expand its presence offshore to compensate for its eroding domestic volumes. "Going international" and generating increased export volumes would not only help return the primary mills to efficient scale, but offshore volumes would concurrently improve the allocation of fixed costs per unit thereby preserving profitability. With its global focus, IP moved beyond "passive" exporting of commodity paperboard to regional paper companies in Europe and Japan. IP became actively involved in the "growing" consumer demand for modern paper packaging in Asian markets not only by commodity sales of bulk roll-stock, but also by capturing healthy "value-added" margins in-selling finished cartons directly to local beverage companies. IP had to "forward integrate" and establish production inside major Asian markets to meet the demand for high-quality, ready-to-fill printed cartons. IP assembled a team of international marketers to implement its strategy and set up regional support staff to provide local dairy and juice processors with technical assistance and in-country consumer marketing support.

Going international for IP was a result of the combination of a domestic competitive challenge and the pull of market opportunities beyond the home market to diversify the firm's geographic and market opportunities, Far too many companies fail to appreciate the range of strategic options open to them and, therefore, employ only one strategy—often to their disadvantage. Some companies also do not appreciate how truly competitive markets are or consider the strategy alternatives that are simultaneously open to their competitors. To expand revenues in the burgeoning markets of Asia, International Paper wisely utilized a blend of strategies. These decisions were affected by issues of investment and control as well as the company's overall attitude toward risk.

---

[2] A. D. Chandler, Jr., *Scale and Scope* (Boston: Harvard University Press, 1990); E. Helpman and P. Krugman, *Market Structure and Foreign Trade* (Boston: Massachusetts Institute of Technology, 1985); P. Krugman, *The Conscience of a Liberal* (New York: W.W. Norton & Company, Inc., 2008).

SYSTEMATIC SELECTION OF COUNTRY FOR SUBSIDIARY ESTABLISHMENT

It is natural that the growth oriented companies will be entering in-to a new country market for market expansion. A company who is yet to be internationalised will look for its first country to establish business while a company who is, say, already internationalised in fifty countries will look for fifty-one country market for internationalisation. How do companies select their country market for international expansion? There are cases where wrong selection of a country market led a company to loss huge investment which could not be recovered later. In 2009, Mahindra Mahindra (M&M), the Indian automobile giant, selected USA to enter and market its flagship sport utility vehicle (SUV) 'Scorpio', in that country. The question arises as to why USA was selected? Why not some other country like Italy or Germany? Was any process of market selection installed before selecting and deciding to enter in to USA? The end result in case of M&M, was not good for the company as it could not successfully market its product there due to several reasons like difference of taste, choice , preferences of US consumers. In addition the Indian company had to face strict pollution control norms in USA which was again much stringent that its home country India. The Indian switch gear manufacturer Larsen and Toubro (L&T), entered Wuxi province of China and made equity investment to do business in that country. But the company could not fulfil its marketing ambition there and had to return back to its own country empty handed, primarily showing competitive reasons. Indian company, Kajaria Tiles, selected Ethiopia to make equity investment and to open up its subsidiary there but had to face a great deal of marketing problems. All these examples demonstrate the need of systematic market selection of a country market out of 220 country markets while entering a new market. Historically, international businesses have shown inclination to select country market based on convenience. For example the Dutch liquor company Heineken decided to enter Congo in Africa simply because of convenience, as another Dutch brewer wanted to sell off its breweries to Heineken. The Japanese companies at least were better that Heineken in terms of market selection process as they always followed a single criterion for international market selection. Japanese companies went on in bargaining out a better deal with respective country government in the matter of equity investment in that country and the country's government acceded to their demand figured out in the shortlisted country market for entry.

Experts in international business have been advocating a concept of systematic selection of country market rather than **adhoc** market selection process in order to ensure better chance of marketing success in a foreign land. Systematic selection of international market entails a detailed selection methodology to be placed, which actually selects one or a few country markets. This methodology uses objective criteria and data, both primary and secondary, to validate those set criteria and through a process arrives at the destination i.e. one selected country market or a few selected country markets for consideration as a possible country to enter.

Objectives of International Market Selection

A decision to finally commit resource for international expansion is a major decision where both risk and opportunities are involved. A company must have a firm objective for market expansion spelled out without ambiguity to set the ball rolling. For example, Coromandel International Limited, India's second largest Phosphatic fertilizer player, in the business segments of Fertilizers, Specialty Nutrients, Crop Protection and Retail; desired to be the market leader internationally so that more than fifty percent of revenue is earned from foreign operation in the next five years of business operation. This objective of the company was adequately integrated with the overall corporate strategy of the company hence everyone in the company could be geared up to the fulfilment of the objective. The various objectives of an internationalizing company may be as listed below:

GROWTH the company wants to grow and domestic market is not sufficiently providing the market to have the desired growth. Many Swedish companies had growth as objective while internationalising. Sweden as a market is not big enough as households are small in terms of persons. Small domestic market may not provide the growth envisaged by the company.

MARKET PENETRATION a country market where market is still not explored up to its potential, provides wonderful scope for an international company to enter. There were mobile companies in Africa but Bharti airtel found African countries as potential countries to enter and get marketing benefit out of the untapped potential.

COST REDUCTION In a competitive market it is very much essential that products have pricing flexibility to tide over difficult situation. Several countries in the world are welcoming manufacturing companies to set up subsidiaries in designated "industrial zones' or 'special economic zones" or "free trade zones" to take advantages in terms of nearness to raw material, lower logistic costs, export etc. Companies in order to leverage the beneficial cost situation are resorting to internationalisation and set up business in strategically located countries of the world.

USE OF TECHNOLOGY COMPETENCE Technology competence leads to internationalization which is almost automatic. Tetra Pak, the Swedish company, now markets its product in 170 countries of the world. Rapid Innovations in Tetra Pak leading to development of new products and services was the most important driving force behind fast internationalisation of the company. Newness in the products or services brought about by technology competence allows to have an easy marketability in different countries which is well supported by demand situation created by consumers' aspiration.

ACHIEVING ECONOMIES OF SCALE Desperation in achieving economies of scale, pushes companies to extend business crossborder. The best example in the instant case has been the semiconductor businesses. Characteristically, semiconductor businesses are very capital intensive with a high amount of fixed costs associated with its production. Therefore, to achieve breakeven it requires a larger sales volume which can only come when different country markets are invaded.

TAX ADMINISTRATION Different countries have different tax laws and according to that the corporates are taxed. Some countries provide liberal relaxation to the corporates in terms of tax rates, profit repatriation norms which encourages international businesses to set up their businesses in those countries and do business there.

SATURATED MARKET CONDITION An excellent example of this objective was demonstrated by the Bharti Airtel, the telecommunication company of India, while extending its business to different countries in Africa. Airtel Africa, subsidiary of Airtel, was created during 2010 to enter seventeen African countries when the level of competition in Indian market was cut throat which was resulting in thin margin of profit. Gerber baby food company of USA, was forced to take its business out of USA and go for other country markets when the domestic market for baby food was found getting highly saturated because of entry of newer companies in to the market and demand shrinkage due to less number of babies taking birth in the country.

COMPETITIVE PRESSURE Another objective to internationalize business activities is to avoid acute competitive pressure in domestic market. This can be achieved by a decentralization of manufacturing and marketing activities through the establishment of different country subsidiaries.

Variables Intervening Market Selection

Different countries provide different marketing environment. A company requires to consider different environmental variables in order to understand suitability of a particular country for doing business. The following are the usual environmental variables that are required to be considered for selecting country markets for entry.

ECONOMIC VARIABLES Economic variables are important as these allow economic stability in the country. The overall economic environment of a country can be assessed by considering the following factors relevant to a particular country.

1. Overall level of development of the economic growth
2. GNP and GDP per capita
3. Contribution of industrial sector to the GDP of the country
4. Currency volatility & controls
5. Inflation rate
6. Openness to foreign trade
7. Balance of payments
8. Per capita distribution & Disposable income
9. Monetary inflation patterns
10. Income inequality status.

SOCIAL/CULTURAL VARIABLES The socio cultural variables are important because of the fact that consumers' behaviour is strongly connected with the cultural underpinning of the country. Since marketers want to know the possible consumer behaviour in advance to decide the marketing mix programmes, so before entry, the entrant company must understand the following socio cultural variables in respect of the targeted country.

1. Literacy rate
2. Educational level
3. Existence of middle class
4. Similarities and differences in relation to home market
5. Language
6. Cultural considerations like power distance and individualism present in the society
7. Religious bias
8. Entrepreneurial acumen
9. Prevalence of cultural taboos
10. Outlook towards foreign business.

POLITICAL-ENVIRONMENT RELATED VARIABLES The political situations in different countries are different. However, prevailing political system has its direct impact on the foreign businesses operating there. The whims of political leaders in power may jeopardise the business ambition of a foreign company. Therefore, it is imperative to understand the political situation of the country before entry through understanding of the following variables about the targeted country.

1. System of government
2. Political stability and continuity
3. Ideological orientation of the present and past government
4. Government involvement in business
5. Government restriction in communications
6. Inclination of government towards bilateral trade agreements
7. Developmental priorities
8. Terrorist activities
9. Present and past cases of nationalisation or confiscation
10. Pressure groups and government support
11. Strength of opposition political parties
12. Political risk perception of the experts about the country
13. Ease of entry.

DEMOGRAPHIC/PHYSICAL ENVIRONMENT Various demographic and physical environment related variables can effect doing business in a foreign country. A populous country may provide marketing and growth opportunities which possibly a sparsely populated country cannot. Understanding demographic uniqueness of a country may help the entrant company to assess applicability of its present marketing strategy in the targeted country. The following variables in this category, therefore, are important to be understood in respect of targeted country before entry.

1. Population size, growth, density
2. Urban and rural divide
3. Climate and variations
4. Port infrastructure and efficiency
5. Demographic uniqueness
6. Physical distribution efficiency
7. Natural resources
8. Communication network
9. Efficiency of customs and border clearance.

TECHNOLOGY ENVIRONMENT Technology environment relates to how a country perceives and welcomes technological development in different fields and consciously makes efforts not only to bring latest technology to the country but also makes efforts to put it in to use in practical purposes. In this respect, the countries are differently placed. The technological environment prevailing in a country is different than another country and this difference is important for an entrant company to understand before entry. The following variables must be kept in mind:

1. Internet penetration rate
2. R&D activities and institution
3. Patent obtained and filed
4. Use of internet bases social apps
5. Universities with global ranks.

SME's Market Selection Process

Small and Medium Enterprises (SME) sector have always been very important for the countries, both developed and developing. In countries where SMEs emerged as a highly vibrant and dynamic sector, there the economy as whole is benefited in terms of economic development and employment generation. In addition, these SME sector companies are the driver of internationalisation. The method through which these

SMEs select their country market, therefore, is a matter of importance for policymakers of any country. In India, SME sector is very vibrant and responsible for more than 6,000 products production, contribution of about 8% to GDP, 45% to the total manufacturing output and 40% to the exports from the country. The SMEs' international market section has the following characteristics.

NEIGHBOURING COUNTRY ORIENTATION The range of country markets for entry consideration often is limited to the neighbouring country markets of the SMEs. Usually, the SMEs have more information about business opportunities that exist in the neighbouring country. They also find it safe to start the internationalisation process by entering in business in neighbouring countries because of perceived similarity of doing business parameters with domestic market. Low geographical distance allow SMEs to manage business with headquarter located in domestic country. Frequent visits to the neighbouring country markets are also possible and that too at a comparatively low expenditure.

EXTERNAL STIMULUS ORIENTATION For many SMEs the internationalisation actions are due to an external stimulus and hence reactive in nature. The stimuli may come from a relative or a friend, government sponsored export promotion organisations etc that motivate the SME to get involved in exploring distant country market. The SMEs may simply react to the situation not by design but by the pressure of the circumstances which unfolds around them in a sequential manner.

SUPPLIER-BUYER RELATIONSHIP ORIENTATION The big brand companies of the world actively scout for suppliers of intermediary products or raw materials in low cost countries. This allows them to reduce the overall cost of the finished product and enjoy pricing flexibility. In most of the cases, the big brand companies prefer to develop supplier- buyer relationship with the SMEs so that the smaller suppliers are exactly in tune with the requirements of the big companies. The SMEs also proactively get involved in the relationship development process as they find a readymade buyer of the product produced and also a psychological satisfaction being attached to a big name in the world of business.

ENTRY AND EXPANSION DECISIONS AND ALTERNATIVES

The first issue that an expanding firm must address is whether to serve a market via sourcing from the home country, in the market country, or a third country—or use a combination of the three. In some countries, this is not a management issue—local production may be required by national policies, thus any foreign company wishing to enter that market must invest and produce locally. However, in most countries, local production is not mandatory—so a company needs a global sourcing strategy which will best strengthen its competitive position in the country.

The trade-offs for local versus regional or global production can include cost, quality, delivery, and customer value. Local costs will include labor, materials, capital, land, and transportation. Scale economies are an important factor in determining cost: for every product, there is some minimum volume required to justify the investment required to establish a product site. Logistics is another important factor to consider. If an exporter's product is heavy, transportation costs will be greater and provide an incentive to locate production closer to the customer. If products are heavy with a low value-to-weight ratio (for example, lumber or raw materials), the relative cost of transportation over long distances will account for a large percentage of a product's cost. On the other hand, if there is a high value-to-weight ratio, the transportation cost/unit

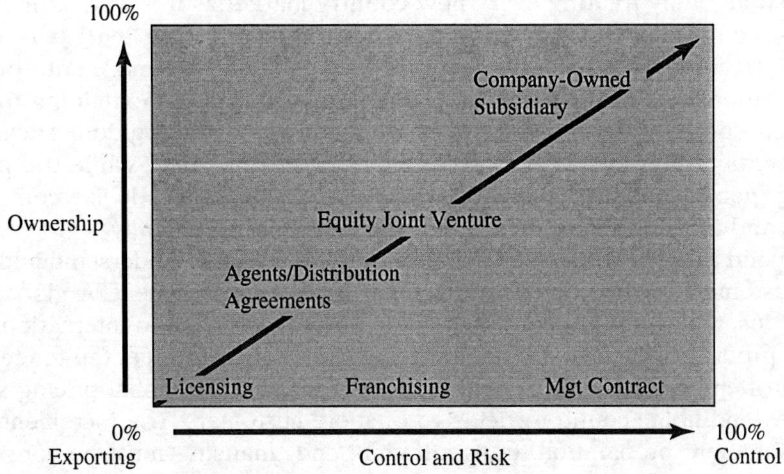

FIGURE 8-1 Ownership, Control, and Risk

will be low and, assuming limited barriers to trade, allow a firm to choose optimal locations for global production. Even with high-cost transportation (air versus ocean freight), concentrating production in global-scaled manufacturing plants may be optimal if transportation costs are more than offset by factor costs and economies of scale resulting from spreading fixed costs over increased production runs. It is worth noting that while airfreight may be high-profile, 90 percent of internationally traded goods are shipped by sea. Maritime transport continues to be one of the most carbon-efficient and "green" modes of transport.[3]

It is important to recognize that, from a market and service perspective, there may be value and competitive advantage in being physically near one's customers. This could tip the balance for in-country sourcing even if there are potential savings in importing product from outside the country.

Once a company decides the best way to serve a market's needs is via local in-country production, it faces the options of buying, building, or renting its own manufacturing plant—or cooperating with a local manufacturer in an arrangement called contract manufacturing. As with production decisions, modes-of-entry choices are seldom simple. Studies have shown that these choices are rarely the result of a single precise and unambiguous decision, but rather they are made as a result of an accumulation of factors, initiatives, explorations, and events that gradually build momentum and indicate the direction the firm should take. While one might assume that economic and political issues are the main drivers, studies have found that most often human influences and organizational factors are of major importance.[4] Uncertainty and risk in these areas are seen as key factors as a company's decisions move in a "northeasterly" direction (in Figure 8-1) toward more ownership and control.

"Going Global" Decision Criteria

A domestic company can "go global" simply by responding to an unsolicited order. A firm may respond but still operate in "selling mode" by simply quoting off a price-list. A more enterprising firm—one that makes a true commitment to operating in

---

[3] World Trade Organization, news release, May, 26, 2009.

[4] See, for example, Y. Aharoni, "The Foreign Investment Decision Process," Wiley Periodicals Inc., 1966, republished online in 2007, *The International Executive*, 8, no. 13–14, doi: 10.1002/tie.5060080407.

the global arena by treating every new country market as if it were a home-country market—would view such an inquiry as an opportunity for market research and revenue stream growth through geographic expansion. The more enterprising firm will also appreciate the role that global markets can play in extending the product life cycle, especially if its product sales are mature or declining domestically in light of competitive offerings or new technology platforms. Also, while the probability of going global does increase with a firm's size, small and midsize companies can succeed and indeed ensure their survival by expanding globally.

Beyond simply taking orders, global marketers seek to understand and approach target customers in the context of the total market environment. A global marketer does not just take a domestic product "as is" and simply sell it to international customers. The product offered in the home market is modified to meet the range of preferences in often diverse, international markets. For example, global pricing should not merely extend home-country pricing to offshore customers. The incremental costs of export shipment preparation, transportation, and financing must be considered but cannot simply be added on in determining foreign market prices. In other words, pricing should be "to market" and not set at an arbitrary level decided by internal cost accounting. As with pricing, the global marketer will also develop and implement strategies for communications and messaging along with distribution—all tailored to the target market's economic, social, cultural, regulatory, and competitive environment.

The decision to expand globally should be based on a number of criteria, including potential market size, competitor activities, and overall marketing mix issues such as price, distribution, and promotion. The next step is the choice of target export markets.

Choosing country and target markets is a key task in formulating a global marketing strategy. The selection criteria include the following key factors:

1. Market entry potential is an estimate that includes the target market size and an estimate of the company's competitive strength in the market. It is quite possible that a smaller market (B) could offer greater potential than a larger market (A) because of the company's greater competitive strength in market B.
2. Market growth potential. Again, market (B) with a higher growth potential might offer greater potential than the larger market (A) with lower growth potential.
3. Market/country impact on the overall competitiveness. If successful entry into a country/target market will result in a significant increase in competitive strength and advantage, there is a compelling case to enter a market where the company does not have a competitive advantage. In order to succeed, the company will need to develop new capabilities and products which will reposition it as a global competitor. In other words, don't just look for low-hanging fruit: consider the difficult-to-reach fruit; it may be the key to long-term success.

   Which markets should be considered and in what order? For companies that are just getting started, one strategy is to target the low-hanging fruit: countries that offer the prospect of easier entry because of lower barriers. Barriers to entry of any market include tariff and nontariff barriers (NTBs). NTBs include bribery and corruption, lack of transparency, absence of a legal system and rule of law, absence of a level playing field, or institutional preferences for local versus foreign investors.
4. Another factor is proximity, language, and cultural "distance." Thus, for an EU country, the lowest hanging fruit may be other EU members. For a US company, Canada and Mexico are the lowest hanging fruit on the tree. For Japan and Korea, China is not only a huge market, it is also nearby. After a company picks the low-hanging fruit, it needs to then consider its global marketing strategy. If the company's goal is to compete in the global market, it must develop a strategy

for entry into all of the world's key markets. The question is not only which markets are attractive and easy to enter but which markets should be part of a company's global marketing strategy. This is the focus of Chapter 9.

EXPORTING AND EXPORT SOURCING

Implicit in any form of exporting is the fact that the firm is supplying the foreign market from domestic or third-country manufacturing facilities. Intermediate entry modes into new foreign markets are different from exporting. They are generally viewed as vehicles for the transfer of knowledge and skills between partners and normally involve shared ownership and control to varying degrees. Intermediate modes of entry include contractual agreements such as licensing and franchising. These arrangements are normally long term and are designed to transfer knowledge, skill base, or property rights to firms in foreign markets including technical or marketing advice and assistance, manufacturing processes, patents, copyrights, trademarks, and brand names. Exporting is increasingly important to the world economy. Today, almost 31 percent of the world's output of goods and services cross a national border. That is up 10 percentage points from the mid-1990s and double the preglobalization ratio of the mid-1970s.[5] Country exports as a percentage of GDP depend upon country size, competitiveness, and relationship to the world economy. Germany has export levels that represent almost half of its GDP. Taiwan relies on exports for 70 percent of its GDP. In comparison, exports account for just 11 percent of the US GDP.[6]

There is a difference between "export selling" and "export marketing." Export selling involves minimal tailoring of the Four Ps of the marketing mix to meet the needs of an offshore customer. The only marketing mix element that significantly differs in "export selling" is "place"—that is, the country where the product is sold and the logistics of getting it there. This selling approach can work for some products and services—specifically those that are unique or for which there is minimal international competition. Companies that are new to exporting may initially experience some success with this model. However, such an approach and managerial mind-set is increasingly inappropriate and ineffective. As companies mature and understand the global marketplace, and as global competitors enter the arena from home markets large and small, success requires that managers engage in true export marketing by tailoring the marketing mix elements of price, product, and promotion to local market demands. Exporting is often the first step for a company that is going global. However, there are other options including licensing, franchising, joint ventures, direct investment, and the "born global" start-up.

The extent of in-country presence in a target country market can affect perceived customer value. Local manufacturing employment can in many industries increase competitive advantage with customers and governments who value a company's contribution to jobs and employment in the host country. In-country activity which creates jobs is an example of the shared value discussed in Chapter 16, the Future of Global Marketing. When a company creates good jobs, it becomes more than a source of products and services; it is also an enterprise that contributes to society. It is no longer just a "foreign" company. It is a local company that is part of a global company.

With the rise of globalization, the country of origin of a product is less important—more and more companies have created brands that deliver the brand promise with sourcing outside of the home country of the brand owner. When a consumer or

[5] Stephen Roach, Chief Economist, Morgan Stanley, as quoted in David R. Francis, "World Trade Faces a Big Chill," *The Christian Science Monitor*, April, 23, 2007.

[6] US Department of Commerce, National Exports Initiative, February 4, 2010.

customer buys a Sony, Toyota, VW, or Apple product, they are buying the brand. They don't know where the product is made. What they believe is the brand promise: the reason they believe in the promise is because the brand owner has delivered on its promise. Global companies benefit from leveraging their brands' equity and educating overseas customers on the value and quality benefits that their global brand represents. The brand itself is more important than the country of manufacture. Globally diversified companies often source products in multiple locations and customers increasingly trust the quality of the brand and care less or not at all about the country of origin.

ORGANIZING FOR EXPORT SOURCING

Companies interested in serving global markets have foundational decisions to make, including how to organize operations in both the home country and the rest of the world (ROW). Home-country issues involve deciding whether to work with an external firm that specializes in exporting to a geographic area or handling a specific range of products—or whether the firm should look to assign and develop export responsibility within the company. The Box 8-2 has been provided which describes the entities a firm may choose to work with if the firm chooses not to develop internal expertise.

IN-HOUSE EXPORT ORGANIZATION Most companies handle export operations in-house. This should be the long-term goal of any globally-oriented firm. In a small firm, such responsibilities may be incorporated into an existing employee's domestic job description. An obvious advantage of this low-cost approach is that it requires no additional personnel. However, this can only work effectively if the domestic employee is thoroughly competent in terms of product and customer knowledge, and if the export target market has customer characteristics similar to the familiar domestic market. Strategically-minded firms will determine that they need a dedicated and skilled staff to handle and grow exports. Export responsibilities can also be handled by separate divisions in a firm or within a specific export-oriented organizational structure.

BOX 8-2

Side Bar: External Independent Export Organizations

If a firm is small or chooses not to perform its own export marketing and promotion, there are export service providers that can help. These include export trading companies (ETCs), export management companies (EMCs), export merchants, export brokers, manufacturers' export representatives, and export distributors. An EMC is often retained by several companies that lack export experience and acts as their export departments. EMCs can perform a variety of services, including marketing research, channel selection, financing, shipping arrangements, and documentation. According to one survey of US-based EMCs, the most important activities for export success are gathering marketing information, communicating with markets, setting prices, and ensuring parts availability. The same survey ranked export activities in terms of degree of difficulty; analyzing political risk, sales force management, setting pricing, and obtaining financial information were deemed most difficult to accomplish. One of the study's conclusions was that the US government should do a better job of helping EMCs and their clients analyze the political risk associated with foreign markets.[7]

[7] Donald G. Howard, "The Role of Export Management Companies in Global Partners Capital Investment Marketing," *Journal of Global Marketing,* 8, no. 1 (1994): 95–110.

A critical step in export success is for a company to interview and then select a Foreign Freight Forwarder (we'll just use the term "Forwarder"). This is a highly specialized outside company that acts almost as an extension of the organization—over time, an almost organic relationship between the firm and its Forwarder will develop. Export traffic and documentation is complex and a Forwarder handles this vital work on behalf of the firm, which removes much of the stress of operating internationally. Forwarders, essentially, are retained to handle a firm's logistics and documentation needs.

ORGANIZING INSIDE THE TARGET MARKET COUNTRY A firm also must decide how best to manage in-market sales representation and product distribution. A basic question is: Should a firm use direct market representation (using its own professional staff) or be represented by a third-party intermediary?

a) **Direct Representation.** The major advantages of direct representation in a market are control and communication. Direct representation means that decisions on market development, resource allocation, and pricing can be implemented unilaterally. Moreover, when a product is new-to-market, special efforts are necessary to induce trial and support follow-on sales. Direct representation helps ensure that these efforts are closely managed and will optimize the firm's investment. The other great advantage of direct representation is that it provides immediate feedback and information from the market. Such feedback can vastly improve export marketing decisions on product, price, communications, and distribution—enabling improved tailoring of the marketing offer for increased sales.

   Direct representation does not necessarily mean the exporter sells directly to the end-user. Most sales are in fact B2B and involve selling to wholesalers, retailers, or manufacturers that incorporate the exporters' materials/components into their finished product. A disadvantage of direct representation is the cost of maintaining a capable sales/marketing staff in the overseas market or region. The ongoing costs of keeping such global staff "in the field" compared to domestic sales are significant. Such direct representatives may be local hires or "road warriors" from the exporter's home country or, if the market potential is significant, an expatriate manager permanently residing in-country.

b) **Independent Representation.** In many markets, it is not feasible to establish direct representation, since low sales volumes may not justify the cost. This depends less upon the size of the country than upon the size of the specific market opportunity within that market. As significant sales volumes are required to justify the costs of direct representation, the use of an independent agency or distributor can be an effective means of accessing a market. In this case, finding a capable and trustworthy agent and/or distributor will be the key to a firm's export success.

   Independent representatives or distributors (sometimes called "value-added resellers") often handle a range of products for several companies—there is often simply not enough volume or incentive for independents to invest in representing a single company or product line.

From a management perspective, the selected local agent should not also represent a firm's competitors (refer Box 8-3). However, an agent with "complementary" product lines to a firm's export offerings should be embraced as they can provide marketing synergies. For example, even though International Paper has a global presence and skilled international managers, the company entered into agreements with local agents in Singapore, Malaysia, and Thailand. These agents, in addition to promoting IP's packaging, also represented the manufacturers of sophisticated carton-filling equipment that would "form-fill-seal" the IP cartons. These complementary offerings provided an attractive single-source marking approach, one that was appreciated by

BOX 8-3

Side Bar: A Word of Caution

Marketers should perform careful due diligence on any prospective agent or representative and not rush to embrace any local company—interview several and thoroughly check their local reputation and industry knowledge. In developing markets, a key criteria for an export manager is the level of personal friendships and connections that a local agent or representative has with local industry leaders and government officials. Much more than in the "low-context" business environment of Europe and North America, business relations in a developing market (or an NIC, a newly industrialized country) are "high-context" and owners of in-country firms are more apt to do business with those with whom they have a long-standing personal rapport.

Having a local agent represent your company is a natural and common evolutionary step in export development. Agents provide expertise in understanding the local industry and the cultural and legal environment, plus they will have connections inside key government agencies that can assist shipment documentation, local logistics, and customs clearance. The local agent or representative also keeps track of customer marketing needs, keeps an eye on client inventories, and provides valuable market guidance and feedback to the exporter. While using agents is often the correct and necessary step in entering and growing a market, managers should nonetheless be very sure to understand the legal ramifications of entering into an agency agreement. If an agency turns out to be nonproductive or the market grows to the point that direct representation is justified and the agent is no longer needed, an agreement that anticipates this situation can ensure that termination will not be difficult, time-consuming, and costly, which it can be if the agreement has not considered terms of termination.

beverage processors. The choice of whether to use an agent or a distributor for market entry depends upon the specific product and market—there is no firm rule. Agents add channel value in handling import/export sales with a limited number of customers. However, while agents assist with invoice collections, they do not take title to the goods. Distributors, on the other hand, add channel value where there are hundreds (if not thousands) of customers—such as retail outlets. Distributors take title, add their margin, and resell to the trade. Using distributors provides additional value as exporters are paid directly by distributors and therefore the exporter doesn't have to "chase" end-user receivables in offshore markets (refer Box 8-4).

BOX 8-4

Side Bar: Yellow Tail Enters The United States—The Distributor Model

What started as a small family winery in the Australian "outback" has become the leading imported wine in the United States. In 1997, John Casella of Casella Wines in New South Wales, Australia, was looking for a way to enter the lucrative US wine market, a market already "saturated" with over 6,500 competing labels. Casella knew his company didn't have the staff, resources, or scale to enter the American market directly. Finding a reputable distributor with a deep understanding of the US market was thus imperative. In the same year, William J. Deutsch & Sons, an experienced wine distributor based in White Plains, New York, was looking to add an Australian wine label to

continued

its portfolio. The distributor's principal, Bill Deutsch, approached the Australian Trade Commission for assistance in identifying prospective exporters. At the same time, Casella Wines was asking its own government for assistance, and the Australian Trade Commission made the connection. Bill Deutsch and John Casella then agreed to meet at a trade show in San Francisco and, as Bill Deutsch says, "It was a perfect match." The first export shipment of Casella wine arrived in 1999. However, there were immediate quality issues with out-of-spec corks and W.J. Deutsch had trouble moving the stock. However, in an important demonstration of support, Bill Deutsch agreed to work through the problems and continue the relationship. After thinking through the next steps and with marketing input from Bill Deutsch and Casella's marketing director, Casella Wines developed an easy-drinking wine and positioned it as an approachable social drink with an image intended to resonate with America's affection for the iconic laid-back Australian culture. The new wine, under the [yellow tail] label, was targeted to the largely uncontested segment between low-end jug wines and premium wines. The plan was that jug-wine drinkers could be induced to trade up to the very drinkable wine, while premium wine drinkers would trade down to the good quality but value-priced [yellow tail]. The strategy succeeded well beyond Casella Wines' or W.J. Deutsch's expectations; shipments grew from an initial trial of 60,000 cases in 2001 to over 8 million cases annually. In what has now become a template for other wine distributors, W.J. Deutsch negotiated a 50 percent ownership of the [yellow tail] label in the US market. Such joint ownership helps to ensure that both parties remain committed to a long-term collaboration.

Far beyond expectations, the sales of [yellow tail] grew faster than planned and created a severe strain on Casella wines' ability to meet demand. A key issue in the success or failure of a product launch is consistency and continuity of supply. Casella was in danger of "losing the market" and needed to rapidly ramp up production and its wine shipments. As with most startups, they were perennially short of cash and urgently needed more capital equipment and operating funds but were unable to secure sufficient bank credit lines to grow the business. On the other side of the Pacific, the W.J. Deutsch company was not in a position to provide the cash. In effect, Casella's limited cash was tied-up in its product transiting the Pacific and in the 90-day payment terms agreed to by the parties. To manage this early challenge, W.J. Deutsch worked with a bank and arranged for an unusual form of b/a, known as a *clean banker's acceptance*. With this structure, Casella's 90-day drafts were "accepted" by W.J. Deutsch's US bank, which could then be immediately discounted by Casella wines and the cash used back in Australia. Without this flexibility, the market growth of [yellow tail] would have stumbled.

Licensing

Licensing is a contractual arrangement where one company (the licensor) provides technology, know-how, patents, or a successful brand to another company (the licensee) in exchange for a licensing fee and an ongoing royalty stream that is based upon a negotiated percentage of the licensee's sales that use the licensed technology. Licensing can be an appealing form of global market entry. A company can use licensing agreements with a foreign firm to supplement its domestic bottom line with almost no capital or marketing costs. Over the life of the license agreement, licensing can offer an attractive return on a firm's prior investment in patents and know-how, providing the licensee adheres to the contract.

Licensing may seem to offer low financial or market exposure—but there are risks. One disadvantage of licensing is that it limits the licensor's direct involvement with the overseas market and the final end-user's needs or desires. A license may also limit a firm's upside profits from prospective in-market expansion or overseas manufacturing. There is also the risk that while the license agreement is in force, the licensee will fully absorb the technology and know-how of the licensor, develop its own independent abilities, and become globally competitive even as a direct competitor of the licensor—not just in their country, but in the original licensor's own home market. An example of this is the recent US $1.5 billion sale and installation of advanced wind turbines in Texas. The provider was the Chinese firm Shenyang Power Group, utilizing technology licensed to it by the General Electric Company. General Electric, for short-term financial gain as a licensor, helped establish a foreign competitor (GE also sells wind turbines) that would then go on to install the largest wind farm in the United States, GE's home market.[8] The implications are significant, as this large project will give Shenyang Power Group sufficient specialized experience and scale economies to compete anywhere in the world. An additional note is that the West Texas installation received very beneficial project financing from the Export-Import Bank of China, which, as a banking arm of the Chinese government, plays an active role in that nation's competitiveness via supporting and encouraging nascent technologies and industries and providing the basis for scale and first-mover advantage.

The principal disadvantage of licensing is that it can be a very limited form of participation. When licensing technology or know-how, what a company does not know can put it at risk. Potential returns from marketing and manufacturing may be lost, and the agreement may have a short life if the licensee develops its own know-how and capability to stay abreast of technology in the licensed product area. Even more distressing, licensees have a troublesome way of turning themselves into competitors or industry leaders. This is especially true because licensing enables a company to borrow—leverage and exploit—another company's resources.

Licensing can improve the net cash flow position of the licensee but may result in lower profits in the long term. Technology licensing, for example, allows a positive cash flow earlier since a firm can have its products to market sooner with technology requirements in place. Licensing often also means less up-front development costs. In the technology sector, for example, firms not only profit from their intellectual property and patents but increase profitability by licensing to others, including their competitors. Technology licensing may in fact be a strategic move by firms facing competition in the marketplace; competitors not only compete in the products market but also in the technology market. Stronger patents raise barriers against imitation by rivals; however, they may also increase competition in the licensing of technology.

Franchising

Franchises are a variation on licensing and fall into several categories. These include manufacturer-sponsored franchises (such as a Ford or Honda independent dealership) and service-firm-sponsored retail franchises (such as Jiffy-Lube or Pizza Hut). Franchises are a growing part of the world economy[9] and can be expected to continue to be a highly utilized model for international growth into new markets for service firms such McDonald's and KFC (refer Box 8-5). Franchising is a contractual arrangement where a company, the *franchis<u>or</u>*, sells the rights to its brand, logo and business model to a *franchis<u>ee</u>* to establish a new company in a specific territory or market. Typically, the franchisor also receives an ongoing fee (a specific percentage of the franchisee's revenues). The fees or royalties go toward ongoing operational support, R&D, marketing programs, and profit back to the franchisor. Franchising has proven to be a successful business model for several reasons. Both parties have a mutual interest in the success of the franchise. The franchisor's business model and management processes are proven. The franchisor's logo and brand identity are well known. Franchisees are local entrepreneurs who have placed their own investment capital at risk and, being local, bring a better understanding of the local market opportunities

---

[8] Rebecca Smith, "Chinese-Made Turbines Will Fill Texas Wind Farm," *The Wall Street Journal*, October 30, 2009.

[9] See "Quick Franchise, Franchising, Facts and Statistics," See for example, http://www.link2franchises.com/franchise-statistics. (Accessed March 3, 2013).

and constraints as well as governmental players than any distant corporate entity. The franchisee receives support via the transfer of business processes, staff, and management training. Also, being part of a proven association, the franchisee has greater access to bank loans and credit lines than other start-up companies. Finally, a franchise system with hundreds of franchisees benefits from far greater economies of scale in procurement, logistics, and advertising than a stand-alone firm.

The international growth of franchises has been one of the hallmarks of globalization. SUBWAY began as small deli operation in Connecticut and began selling franchises in 1974. By 2010, there were over 33,000 SUBWAY restaurants globally—30 percent outside the United States across 90 countries.

BOX 8-5

Side Bar: KFC Enters China—The Franchise Model

When China reengaged with the world in the 1980s, its economy grew at unprecedented double-digit rates—driven by export trade and enabled by abundant inexpensive labor. As the Chinese economy matured, more value-added products were produced, providing greater profits to China's growing cadre of entrepreneurs. The global demand for Chinese products increased exporter margins and workers' wages. Recently, China's coastal cities have faced a tightening supply of qualified workers, labor rates have risen, and a nascent "middle-class" is gaining significant ground. As the wages of labor increased, so too did the ability of workers to afford "international-quality" consumer goods. When Chinese have disposable income, one of the immediate lifestyle changes is to move "up-market" in food consumption. Accordingly, diet in urban centers is changing from grains and vegetables to a greater consumption of pork and poultry.

The management of KFC recognized this evolving market opportunity and in 1987 established the first fast-food restaurant in China. KFC's sister brand, Pizza Hut, followed in 1990. In 1992, KFC introduced the entrepreneurial concept of franchising to China. The success of this market and consumer-driven business model has been spectacular. By 2010, there were 2,600 KFC restaurants in 550 cities across China—with a new restaurant opening nearly every day. KFC is part of a family of franchise brands operated by Louisville-based Yum! Brands. These include Pizza Hut, Taco Bell, Long John Silver, and A&W. Globally, 80 percent of the Yum!-branded stores are owned by independent franchise operators—the entrepreneurial drivers of this transformative business model.

During the initial years of the China launch, KFC went to market with a mix of both traditional franchises and company-owned restaurants (the majority being company-owned). One rationale for this mix was that China's infrastructure was not well developed and, therefore, direct management could help ensure both marketing and quality control during the key market-entry phase. This control would also speed the drive to rapidly develop the food service category in China, and so secure for KFC the benefits of being first to market. Geographic expansion was based upon "saturating" markets in sequence—an initial focus on first-tier cities, then second-tier cities, then third-tier, etc. Regional KFC managers were encouraged to localize menus and focus on food innovation—all part of tailoring offerings to local needs, yet all under the umbrella and cachet of a global brand. Yum! Brands Senior Vice President Joaquin Pelaez comments, "The Chinese consumer loves Western brands because they trust Western brands. KFC is the most recognizable brand in China . . . a foreign brand with a Chinese heart."[10]

Both KFC and Pizza Hut had first-mover advantage—not only with selling into largely uncontested markets, but also tactically. Early on, they secured high-traffic real estate to position themselves for the anticipated rise in consumer affluence. This early decision to own the best retail locations has preempted competitor expansion. McDonald's entered China three years behind KFC. They were not as aggressive in entering the market and today have only a third of Yum!

[10] J. Pelaez's address to the Alltech Symposium (May 2010).

Brand's market presence. KFC's success vis-à-vis McDonald's also has cultural roots. The Chinese diet has the tradition of consuming poultry, so a foreign menu based on chicken is more easily accepted. In contrast, ground-up meat patties are not familiar to the Chinese diet—building an appreciation for Western-style burgers requires a longer time line.

At a KFC restaurant opening, local consumers immediately appreciate the friendly, non-governmental, nonbureaucratic customer service provided by KFC—an important perceived attribute—and internally, management has built a culture around the term, "Yum! Customer Mania." A further point of distinction is KFC's very visible and well promoted focus on food safety (something often taken for granted in the West, but not in China). KFC's China management is truly local, yet the international branding, staff training, and quality control are world class and continue to generate strong customer preference. By 2010, China was generating US$4 billion in sales and had become a major source of operating profits within Yum!'s global system of 37,000 restaurants across 100 countries.

Product Sourcing

Product sourcing refers to the company and country source of product. Few companies make all of the components of the products they offer. An increasing number of companies do not manufacture any of their product's components. Nike doesn't produce any athletic shoes and it does not own any manufacturing facilities. All its shoes are sourced from factories located in emerging countries, primarily in Asia. Apple products are designed in California and manufactured and assembled in the rest of the world. Benetton and IKEA rely on a network of suppliers.

There are no simple rules to guide sourcing decisions. There are six issues that should be taken into account in any sourcing decision (they are naturally similar to the issues facing exporters):

1. Factor quality, costs, and terms of sale
2. Logistics (time line to fill and deliver orders plus transportation costs)
3. Source-country infrastructure (roads, ports, rail, utilities, customs administration)
4. Political risk (government stability, history, and continuity)
5. Source-market constraints (outbound restrictions, taxes, and fees)
6. Currency availability, stability, convertibility

Product sourcing by contract manufacturing offers a number of advantages, especially to a global enterprise whose strength lies in marketing and distribution such as Nike and Dell. Contract manufacturing enables a firm to develop and control R&D, marketing, distribution, sales, and service in global markets. However, it is necessary to control product quality to meet both international, local, and company standards. Issues surrounding product warranties, production capacities, and timing of delivery are among the many issues to be dealt with in a contract manufacturing agreement.

Investment: Joint Venture and FDI

After companies gain experience outside their home country through exporting or licensing or an in-country distributor, management may look for a deeper level of participation in global markets. A joint venture (JV) with a local partner is a more extensive form of participation in a foreign market than either exporting or licensing. A JV is collaboration between two or more firms on a specific project to serve one or more markets. This often takes the form of an equity investment (sometimes called an equity-joint-venture or EJV) between two companies in the creation of a third company. The "parent" companies remain independent but commit resources to support the new entity. The advantages of this strategy include the sharing of risk and the ability to combine different, hopefully complementary, strengths—for example, a mix of marketing with manufacturing expertise. A JV partner might have in-depth knowledge of a local market, an extensive distribution system, or access to low-cost labor or raw materials (see Box 8-6). The other partner might be a foreign firm with a global brand or process knowledge and technology. Firms with limited capital resources might seek partners to jointly finance projects. Also, a JV may be the only way to enter a country if the government awards business routinely to local companies or if there are laws that prohibit foreign-controlled firms but do allow JVs. Proceeding with either a JV or a "wholly-owned" enterprise, the new company can accrue market advantages through closer relations with customers, provide improved customer service and technical support, and serve customers with much shorter order and delivery lead-times via local production.

In each market, the decision whether to position oneself in a JV or as a wholly-owned enterprise must be decided on the merits. Managers must be clear on what each partner brings to the table. Also, managers need to ascertain the interests and capabilities of the prospective partners going forward. JVs can be hard to sustain. Partners may have different capabilities, resources, objectives, and differences in managerial styles. These differences can present significant challenges, as was seen in the clash of corporate cultures between Germany's Daimler-Benz and America's Chrysler—which contributed significantly to that venture's failure.

Each decision is market specific. For example, the government of the People's Republic of China (PRC) often favors joint ventures over a "wholly foreign-owned enterprise" (WFOE). JVs facilitate the transfer of foreign technologies, know-how, and modern business processes. Similar to what was noted earlier in the chapter with licensing, a dynamic JV partner can evolve into a strong competitor. A further push to the joint-venture model in the PRC is that, in contrast to a JV, a WFOE may well lack the necessary *guanxi* (trade and governmental connections) to succeed.

In an EJV, partners share the profits, the risks, and control. An investor should not underestimate the significant management time required to handle the many issues associated with working with a JV partner. Given that control is shared, success will depend upon the caliber of executive leadership of the new enterprise. By comparison, management of a "majority-owned" or "wholly-owned" enterprise will not face the ongoing issues of control, authority, and strategic direction of the JV entity. Companies with wholly-owned affiliates/subsidiaries have full control over operations, marketing, financial strategies and investment, structure, human resources, and overall strategic direction.

BOX 8-6

Side Bar: Tropicana Enters The Japanese Market

In addition to its dominant domestic position in the United States, Tropicana is a familiar brand internationally; Tropicana's first not-from-concentrate exports were to France in 1966. However, it was not until 1991 that Tropicana found a way to enter Japan—among the world's largest and most affluent economies, but one of the most difficult markets to access. In Japan, unlike North America and Europe, packaged juice is required to carry a 14-day date-code for its shelf life. This rule was based upon historic practices for date-coding milk after the war. Ocean shipping times between the United States and Japan simply could not accommodate the 14-day sales window. To sell in Japan, Tropicana management had to address four key in-market issues:

- Bulk chilled and frozen juice needed to be imported, processed, packaged, and date-coded.
- In-country distribution needed to be secured.
- Ongoing quality control (QC) needed to be assured on both sides of the Pacific.
- Culturally sensitive marketing and brand-management needed to be established.

Collaboration with an established local firm is a frequent approach by global companies entering the Japanese market, as trying to set up an independent operation in Japan is culturally problematic. Additionally, product distribution in Japan is an arcane, multitiered process based upon long-standing company and personal relationships. In 1988, ten years before its acquisition by PepsiCo, Tropicana was part of the Seagram Company, the largest distiller of alcoholic beverages in the world. Seagram had a joint venture (JV) with the Japanese brewer Kirin, a marketer of premium brands of alcohol and spirits. Management judged that the JV relationship (Kirin-Seagram) could be leveraged to introduce the premium juice brand Tropicana in Japan. To manage the market access issues, a new JV was formed between Tropicana and Kirin Beverage Corporation (the soft drink arm of the Kirin conglomerate). Tropicana had the globally recognized product, brand-management, marketing know-how, and process and quality control expertise. Kirin had capable in-country staff, proven distribution channels, and long-standing trade and operational contacts throughout Japan. The resulting JV was a 50:50 partnership, with all marketing, advertising, and operational costs shared equally; profits were shared via a complex transfer pricing mechanism.

Chilled bulk juice is today imported by the logistics arm of Kirin Beverage. These bulk shipments are then delivered to dairy and beverage plants across Japan for processing and packaging. The plants are "contract-packers" (often processors with excess capacity) with whom the Kirin production arm contracts to process and package the juice. Contract-packers are paid for this service, but do not take title to the product. Tropicana assures QC of all the citrus juices and related by-products such as pulp, and shares its proprietary process technology for Pure Premium juice. It should be noted that juice can be processed and the cartons formed-filled-sealed on the same stainless steel equipment as milk—accordingly, the JV benefits from in-place "swing capacity" at Japan's dairies. After contract-packing, the retail juice is sold at an agreed-upon-transfer price by the JV to Kirin Beverage (the JV's only customer). Kirin Beverage would then add its distributor markup as it sells the finished product into the trade.

Marketing managers should appreciate the value of "speed-to-market," and the prospect for such a key competitive benefit should always be pursued. A firm with "first-mover advantage" can establish a market presence that enables the associated cost advantage of scale economies, while follow-on competitors are often faced with extended periods before reaching profitable scale.

The contract-packers also benefit from the arrangement as the additional throughput enables them to better cover the heavy fixed capital costs of their productive assets.

Up to this point, Tropicana had addressed three of the four critical issues for success in Japan. And while going to market in Japan with a major player like Kirin was foundational, ultimate success would depend upon the competence of the JV's senior management. This is a central point and one of the underlying themes of this text. As previously noted in the chapter, a JV presents major management challenges—and evermore so in Japan, where one must understand and navigate a complex and often opaque business culture. The JV not only needed a bilingual manager, but one that could understand both Japanese and American worldviews, act as a bridge between two diverse corporate cultures, keep all sides focused and collaborating in the right direction, and—at the same time—be responsible for quality brand management, product development, and consumer education. With the key commercial factors in place, the first cartons of Tropicana from concentrate juice entered the market under the Kirin-Tropicana Inc. company name in 1991. Tropicana Pure Premium followed in 1992. The Tropicana rollout was a success and the brand with its "American cachet" (brilliantly reinforced at times with such iconic music as "*in the summertime when the weather is fine*..." by the band Mungo Jerry) continues to hold a leading share in one of the world's most competitive and quality-conscious markets.

Ownership/Investment

The desire for control and ownership of operations outside the home country drives the decision to make a Foreign Direct Investment (FDI). This can be a green-field investment or the acquisition of plant, equipment, or other assets outside the home country. By definition, direct investment presumes the investor has control or significant influence over the investment, compared to a portfolio investment, where the investor has a passive role without significant influence or management control. An operational definition of direct investment is ownership of at least 20 percent of the equity of a company.

The most extensive form of participation in global markets is 100 percent ownership of a foreign subsidiary—which, again, may be achieved by start-up or acquisition. Such ownership requires a significant commitment of capital and managerial effort and offers the fullest level of market participation. Companies here move beyond accessing a market via exports and a local agent to direct investment and ownership and so achieve faster expansion, greater control, and higher profits. Acquisitions require due diligence. Local firms are known to falsify their balance sheets for tax reasons, and sellers may conceal off-balance-sheet liabilities, verbal barter agreements, and commitments associated with governmental favors. It is also not uncommon to have signage changed on a facility the day before a foreign partner arrives for a tour or a signing ceremony.[11] Beyond equity deals, even the straight purchase of assets can be problematic. A foreign firm will need a registered legal entity that is allowed to accept the assets—and in some cases, assets are simply not transferrable under local law. The benefit of an acquisition is that it is instantaneous and sometimes a less expensive approach to market entry (than a green-field) and has the advantage of avoiding communication and conflict-of-interest problems that may arise with the joint venture model. Nonetheless, acquisitions still present the demanding and challenging task of integrating the acquired company into a firm's worldwide organization.

Several of the advantages of the JV model also apply to wholly-owned subsidiaries, including access to markets and avoidance of tariff or quota barriers. Like joint ventures, ownership enables the transfer of new technology, experience, and manufacturing know-how to a new national market. The wholly-owned investment combines control and ownership. Both risk and reward go 100 percent to the owner. This not only requires greater financial investment, it also requires a major commitment of managerial time and energy. The decision to invest abroad—whether by expansion or acquisition—can clash with short-term profitability goals and present significant financial exposure to the parent company. The upside of this approach is the opportunity to move towards becoming an integrated global corporation with all of the strengths and advantages that this brings. The global corporation is described in Chapter 14.

THEORIES OF INTERNATIONALISATION

How a domestic company internationalizes has always been a matter of great curiosity amongst the researchers who were active in the field of international business. It became an interesting area of research when companies of some country went for internationalization faster than the companies of other countries. As international businesses can contribute to the national economic development, so the country's

[11] James Boyle and Matthew Winter, "A Different Toolbox for M&A Due Diligence in China," *Thunderbird International Business Review*, 51 (February 2010).

authorities were also actively promoting such research. The researchers carried out research on this unique aspect over a long period of time and empirically established their understanding in the form of theory. They are:

1. Process approach
2. The transaction cost approach
3. The eclectic paradigm
4. International Networks approach.

Process Approach or Uppsala Model of Internationalization

The process approach is also popularly known as the Scandinavian stage model or stage model of internationalization focusing on the small and medium enterprises (SMEs). Two professors of Uppsala University, namely Johanson and Valne, studied the internationalization of Swedish SMEs and came out with the following understanding.

1. The theory is also known as a gradual incremental approach as these two Swedish professors found that in case of SMEs the internationalization is not straightforward but they enter foreign market in an incremental fashion. SMEs first enter a foreign neighboring country market with low risk export mode i.e. export.
2. The SME is then likely to expand its business in another foreign country with time as knowledge about the country is known more while doing business with that country. As the company gets acquainted with language, culture, political system etc of the country there will be an urge to exploit more business opportunities and hence switchover from simple exporting to setting up of a foreign subsidiary will happen.

The Transaction Cost Approach of Internationalization

The transaction cost can metaphorically be described as 'friction' between a buyer and a seller. A seller in India may experience friction (transaction cost) while exporting product to a buyer located in Bangladesh. The friction took place because of the fact that the Bangladeshi buyer was not abiding by the terms of contract which mutually they agreed upon while initiating the cross border transaction. As a result the Indian seller was losing profit in the Bangladesh market and hence had to look for other alternative buyers. It led to more spending in terms of search and information cost. Bargaining costs also crept in as new possible buyer is required to be within the agreeable terms and conditions of the Indian exporter. Therefore, it can be said that these costs to the sellers like search cost, information costs, monitoring cost and enforcement costs etc were due to the 'friction' between the buyer and seller. Had there been no friction between the Bangladeshi buyer and Indian seller there would have been no 'extra cost' or so to say transaction cost. The quantum of transaction cost also influences internationalization of the companies. If transaction cost is considerably high then the Indian seller may think of opening its own sales subsidiary in Bangladesh. The transaction cost approach, therefore, makes transaction cost as a pivot, which ultimately decides the internationalization process of an internationalizing company.

The Eclectic Theory or OLI Approach

John Dunning[12], added a new dimension to the understanding when he underlined a three factor theory best known as Dunning's eclectic paradigm which portrays a matrix of three advantages like Firm-specific advantages (FSA), Country-specific advantages

---

[12]Dunning, J.H.: "Trade, Location of Economic Activity and the MNE: A Search for an Eclectic Approach", in B. Ohlin et al. (eds): The International Allocation of Economic Activity, Macmillian, London 1977.

(CSA), Internalization-specific advantages (ISA). Firm-specific advantages (FSA), are those advantages which a firm enjoys in a competitive market because of big brand name, technology competence, and operational excellence. Country-specific advantages (CSA), are those advantages like availability of skilled man power, low cost raw material, advanced R&D institution etc which a country enjoys. Internalization-specific advantages (ISA), are those advantages which a firm enjoys because of possession of exploiting capacity of country-specific advantages of a distant country by its own. The eclectic theory states that when a company possesses only FSA it would look for internationalization through export only. It also states that when the company also possesses CSA then it would look for internationalization through joint venture and if all the three types of advantages (FSA, CSA and ISA) are with the company then wholly owned subsidiary would be preferred to be set up in the foreign country.

STAGES OF DEVELOPMENT MODEL

Bartlett and Ghoshal trace the development of MNCs as they moved from early motivations such as seeking key suppliers, low cost factors of production (i.e., cheap labor), and new markets, to pursuit of more sophisticated objectives such as scale economies, global learning, and competitive positioning. Their work also provides insight into the evolution of companies through five stages of development in international markets. Table 8-1 shows the stages in the evolution of the global corporation, from domestic to international, multinational, global, and transnational. This closely parallels the discussion in Chapter 1, where companies evolved from ethnocentric (domestic) to geocentric (transnational). As discussed in previous chapters, the differences between the stages can be quite significant. Unfortunately, there is little general agreement about the usage of each term. The terminology suggested here conforms to current usage by leading scholars. However, it should be noted that executives, journalists, and others who are not familiar with the scholarly literature may use the terms in quite different ways.

Bartlett and Ghoshal provide an excellent discussion of three industries—branded packaged goods, consumer electronics, and telecommunications switching—in which individual competitors have exemplified the different stages at various times in their corporate histories. For example, P&G, General Electric (GE), and Ericsson were Stage 2 international companies. For many years, Unilever, Philips, and International Telephone and Telegraph (ITT) were Stage 3 multinationals. The Stage 4 global companies included in the study were all from Japan: Kao, Matsushita, and NEC.[13]

TABLE 8-1 Stages of Development of the Transnational Corporation

1. Domestic
2. International
3. Multinational
4. Global
5. Transnational

[13] See Christopher A. Bartlett and Sumantra Ghoshal, *Managing Across Borders: The Transnational Solution* (Boston: Harvard Business School Press, 1989).

TABLE 8-2 Stages of Development I

Stage and Company	1 Domestic	2 International	3 Multinational	4 Global	5 Transnational
Strategy	Domestic	International	Multidomestic	Global	Global
Model	NA	Coordinated federation	Decentralized federation	Centralized hub	Integrated network
View of world	Home country	Extension markets	National markets	Global markets or resources	Global markets and resources
Orientation	Ethnocentric	Ethnocentric	Polycentric	Mixed	Geocentric

NA = not available.

As you can see in Table 8-2, orientation does not change as a company moves from domestic to international. The difference between the domestic and the international company is that the international is doing business in many countries. Like the domestic company, it is ethnocentric and home-country oriented. However, the Stage 2 international company sees extension market opportunities outside the home country and extends marketing programs to exploit those opportunities. The first change in orientation occurs as a company moves to Stage 3, multinational. At this point, its orientation shifts from ethnocentric to polycentric. The difference is quite important. The Stage 2 ethnocentric company seeks to extend its products and practices to foreign countries. It sees similarities outside the home country but is relatively blind to differences. The Stage 3 multinational is the opposite: it sees the differences and is relatively blind to similarities. The focus of the Stage 3 multinational is on adapting to what is different in a country. Figure 8-2 outlines the different orientations of management.

The Stage 4 global company is a limited form of the transnational. Management's orientation is either on global markets or global resources but not on both. For

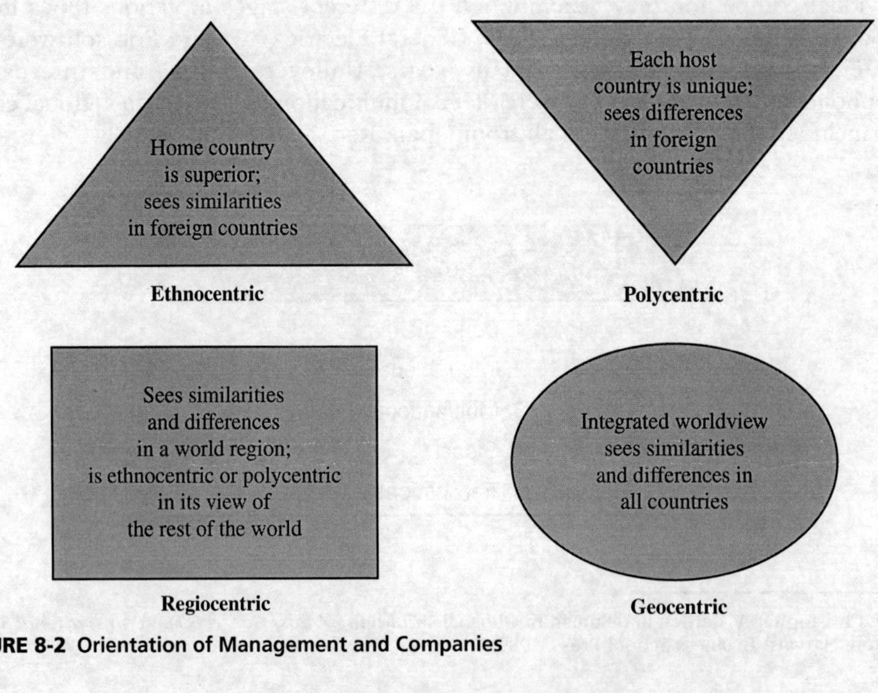

FIGURE 8-2 Orientation of Management and Companies

TABLE 8-3 Stages of Development II

Stage and Company	Organization Characteristics 1 Domestic	2 International	3 Multinational	4 Global	5 Transnational
Key assets	Located in home country	Core centralized other dispersed	Decentralized and self-sufficient dispersed	Concentrated in home country except marketing (e.g. Harley Davidson) or production (e.g. Apple)	Dispersed interdependent and specialized sourcing
Role of country units	Single country	Adapting and leveraging competencies	Exploiting local opportunities	Marketing or sourcing	Contributions to company worldwide
Knowledge	Home country	Created at center and transferred	Retained within operating units	Marketing or sourcing developed jointly and shared	All functions developed jointly and shared

example, Harley-Davidson is focused on global markets but not on global resources. The company has no interest in conducting R&D, design, engineering, or manufacturing outside of the United States. Until recently, the same was true for BMW and Mercedes. Both companies marketed globally but limited R&D, engineering, design, and manufacturing activity to Germany. Mercedes now plans to double its purchases from outside suppliers and to build more than 10 percent of its vehicles outside Germany. Notes Mercedes chairman, Helmut Werner, "The fundamental problem of German exports is that we are producing in a country with a hard currency and selling in countries with soft currencies."[14] When a company moves from Stage 4 to Stage 5, its orientation encompasses both global markets and global resources.

Table 8-3 illustrates some of the other differences in companies at the different stages. Special mention must be made of some of the distinctive qualities of Stage 4 companies that pursue integrated global strategies. Key assets are dispersed, specialized, and interdependent. A transnational automobile company—Toyota, for example—makes engines and transmissions in various countries and ships these components to assembly plants located in each of the world regions. Specialized design labs might be located in different countries and work together on the same project. The role of country units changes dramatically as a company moves across the stages of development. In the Stage 2 international company, the role of the country unit is to adapt and leverage the competence of the parent or home-country unit. In the Stage 5 transnational, the role of each country is to contribute to the company worldwide. In the international and multinational, the responsibility of the marketing organization is to realize the potential of the individual national markets. In the transnational, the responsibility of the marketing unit is to realize the potential of the national market and, if possible, to contribute to the success of marketing efforts worldwide by sharing successful innovations and ideas with the entire.

[14] Audrey Choi, "For Mercedes, Going Global Means Being Less German," *The Wall Street Journal*, April 27, 1995, B4.

TABLE 8-4 Stages of Development III

Strengths at Each Level
International
Ability to exploit the parent company's knowledge and capabilities through worldwide diffusion of products
Multinational
Flexible ability to respond to national differences
Global
Global market or supplier reach, which leverages the home-country organization, skills, and resources
Transnational
Combines the strengths of each of the preceding stages in an integrated network, which leverages worldwide learning and experience

As shown in Table 8-4 each of the stages has its strengths. The international company's strength is its ability to exploit the parent company's knowledge and capabilities outside the home country. In the telecommunications industry, Ericsson gained a competitive edge over NEC and ITT by pursuing this approach. The multinational's strength is its ability to adapt and respond to national differences. Unilever's local responsiveness was well-suited to the packaged goods industry. Thus, in many markets, the company outperformed both Kao and P&G. The global company leverages internal skills and resources by taking advantage of global markets or global resources. In consumer electronics, Matsushita's ability to serve global markets from world-scale plants caused great woes for Philips and GE. (In fact, GE's Jack Welch decided to exit the business altogether.)[15] The transnational combines the strengths of each of the earlier stages by serving global markets using global resources and leveraging global learning and experience.

In Stage 3, the most frequently preferred sourcing arrangement is local manufacture. In Stage 5, product sourcing is based on an analysis that takes into account cost, delivery, and all other factors affecting competitiveness and profitability. This analysis produces a sourcing plan that maximizes both competitive effectiveness and profitability. When a company is in Stage 2, key jobs go to home-country nationals in both the subsidiaries and the headquarters. In Stage 3, key jobs in host countries go to country nationals, whereas headquarters management positions are usually held by home-country nationals. In Stage 5, the best person is selected for all management positions regardless of nationality. Research and development (R&D) in Stage 2 is conducted in the home country; in Stage 3, R&D becomes decentralized and fragmented. By the time a company reaches Stage 5, research is part of an integrated worldwide R&D plan and is typically decentralized. The transnational company in Stage 5 can take advantage of resources as well as respond to local aspirations to produce a worldwide decentralized R&D program.

[15] For an excellent in-depth treatment of GE, see Noel Tichy and Stratford Sherman, *Control Your Destiny or Someone Else Will* (New York: HarperBusiness, 1994).

CASE 8-1

The Internationalization of ONGC Business and Entry Modes

ONGC Videsh Ltd or simply OVL is a wholly owned subsidiary of the Oil and Natural Gas Corporation (ONGC) Limited. ONGC operates its international operations through an arm called ONGC Videsh Limited, since 1996. ONGC started off with its international ventures in the year 1988 with its first property acquisition at Vietnam. This was followed by a lull for nearly 12 years and then during 2000 it entered the neighbouring country of Myanmar. Up to 2008 it entered in-to eighteen countries which are located in different regions (refer Table 8-5 and 8-6). The international market for ONGC can be grouped geographically as (a) Sub Saharan countries, (b) developed markets like USA, Russia, Australia, (c) Middle East regions: Iran, Iraq, Afghanistan, (d) South East Asian regions like Myanmar, Vietnam, Cambodia and Bangladesh and (e) Other markets like Ecuador, Cuba, Zimbabwe, Columbia.

The objectives behind internationalisation were threefold:

1. **Domestic Demand Conditions** India was spending huge amounts of foreign exchange for importing crude oil. Oil is, therefore, a key element of the import list of the country. Moreover, the International energy agency (IEA), projected that with the ongoing development efforts, the country is going to import more in the coming years.
2. **Foreign Exchange Crisis** As dollar—Rupee exchange rates were volatile with every increase in the dollar price of the crude, this situation is further aggravated. So more resource sourced from outside would reduced the pressure on valuable foreign exchange of the country.
3. ONGC was interested to take advantage of the ongoing liberalisation policy of India and go

TABLE 8-5 OVL Internationalisation Till 2008

Sl no	Country	Years of entry	No of Projects
1	Vietnam	1988	3
2	Myanmar	2000	5
3	Iraq	2000	1
4	Russia	2001	1
5	Iran	2002	1
6	Libya	2002	3
7	Sudan	2003	4
8	Syria	2004	2
9	Nigeria Sao Tome & Principe, JDZ	2005	1
10	Qatar	2005	1
11	Egypt	2005	2
12	Cuba	2005	2
13	Nigeria	2005	2
14	Brazil	2006	3
15	Columbia	2006	4
16	Congo	2006	1
17	Turkmenistan	2008	1
18	Venezuela	2008	1

TABLE 8-6 Details of Market Participation of OVL up to 31st March, 2008

Sr. No	Name of the Project and Country of Operation	OVL's Participating Share (%)	Other Consortium Members
1	Block–06.1, Project, Vietnam, Offshore	45	British Petroleum–35% Petro Vietnam–20%
2	Sakhalin 1, Project Offshore	20	Exxon Mobil–30% SODECO–30% SMNG–11.5% RN Astra–8.5%
3	Block 5A Project, Sudan Onshore	24.125	Petronas–67.875 % Sudapet–8%
4	Block A1 Project, Myanmar Offshore	20	Daewoo–60% KOGAS–10% GAIL–10%
5	Block A3 Project, Myanmar Offshore	20	Daewoo–60% KOGAS–10% GAIL–10%
6	Farsi Block Project, Iran Ofshore	40	IOC–40% OIL–20%
7	Block NC -188 & NC-189 Project, Libya, Onshore	49	TPOC -51%
8	Block XXIV Project, Syria, Onshore	60	IPR–40%
9	Block 5B Project, Sudan Onshore	23.5	Pertronas–39% Lundin–24.5% Sudapet–13%
10	Block 6 North Ramadan Project, Egypt Offshore	70	IPR Red SEA–30%
11	Block 25-29, 35 (Part) & 36 Project, Cuba Offshore	30	Repsol YPF–40% Hydro–30%
12	Khartoum–Port Sudan Pipeline Project Sudan	90	Oil–10%
13	Block NEMED, Egypt Offshore	33	Shell -51% Petronas–16%
14	Block RC-8 Columbia offshore	40	Ecopetrol–40% Petrobas–20%
15	Block RC-9 Columbia offshore	50	Ecopetrol–50%
16	Block RC-10 Columbia offshore	50	Ecopetrol–50%
17	MTPN Block, Congo Offshore	20	ENI–40% Exxon–40%

outside of the country for exploration of oil resources.

Market entry Strategies followed by OVL

The different entry strategies used by OVL, for internationalisation of its activities are: Acquisitions, Joint ventures, Turnkey operations and Special arrangements

Acquisitions

A cash rich company like ONGC finds that acquisition is one of the modes by which it can seek to buy out stakes of other companies in the international market. This is perhaps the fastest way to expand the market. ONGC was under pressure to increase its strategic reserve and with the domestic reserve acreage saturation and production from existing reserves; the company began to acquire stakes of other oil companies strategically. A Canadian company, Talisman, was interested to quit Sudan oil field by selling its stake to other companies. However the law of the Sudanese law did not allow a single foreign company to hold 40 % stake in any oil field. OVL outrightly purchased 25 percent stake of the company while CNPC, of China took 40% and Petronas, of Malaysia took 30%. The balance 5 percent share was taken over by the Sudanese oil company.

Joint venture route

Joint venture as an entry mode is preferred by OVL in majority cases of international entry. From 1998 to 2008, altogether 17 cases of JV mode of entry was adopted by the company. The joint venture route was used by the company because most of the oil fields are in the geographically remote locations where it may not be possible to operate oil fields alone. It was also required to develop partnership or alliance with other related companies for crude transfer, as most of the explorations took place far away from crude refining facilities. In absence of a partner in the form of JV, it could have been possible that OVL had to sell crude oil to US or to Japanese companies at a distress rate and thereby jeopardising the benefits of international entry. The joint venture route reduced this risk as OVL could sell its share to JV partners like Exxon, USA or to Sodeco, Japan as and when needed. In addition, the oil sector in almost all the countries of JV was not very much well regulated but politically charged up. For example in Russian oil fields, politically backed struggle for control of Russia's booming oil sector was common. Similarly, most sub Saharan countries were very much politically unstable and a civil war like situation was prevalent in Sudan. To mitigate the risk, a joint venture with companies from 3 to 4 countries was preferred to reduce the political risk or face eventualities in case of a change in the government leading to radical changes in business conditions.

Turnkey operations

Zimbabwe as a country has limited oil resources but is rich in coal, which could not be mined. The country, because of its traditional linkages with India wanted OVL to undertake turnkey projects in the field of coal bed methane. The task on OVL was to execute all the development as well as commercial exploitation of the CBM in Zimbabwe. OVL was one of the few companies of the world who was equipped with the requisite technology besides USA and Japan. Similar turnkey operation OVL accepted in Sudan also. OVL and ONGC took up turnkey contracts for revamping and upgradation of Sudan refinery and also laying of Gas and Oil pipeline in Sudan and in Myanmar.

Special arrangements

The local laws of Iran did not allow a non-state owner ship of oil fields. However Iranian government was interested in developing the oil fields with assistance from friendly countries like India in the back drop of US sanction. The Government of Iran proposed a mechanism by which ONGC could invest in the development activities and receive a certain fixed return on investment in terms of oil. This may be perceived as an investment wherein the returns are not connected to the prevailing oil prices but a mechanism to mitigate/distribute the risk involved in the oil business. Iran, being geographically closer to India, received from Iran, oil could be shipped to India for consumption.

Case Questions

1. Visit the website http://www.ongcvidesh.com/assets/ and list out entry modes of the company OVL in the recent years.
2. Justify the entry modes in the backdrop of theories of internationalization.

Summary

Companies can choose from among a wide range of alternatives when deciding how to participate in markets around the world. Exporting, licensing, joint ventures, and ownership by acquisition or direct investment expansion each offer distinct advantages and disadvantages. The choice depends first on the strategy of the firm and then on the mix of resources, competencies, and available alternatives. Exporting can help a company build volume and achieve scale economies. If a country's currency is weak relative to currencies of trading partners, export sales are especially advantaged. Licensing is a good strategy for increasing the bottom line with little investment; it can be a good choice for a company with advanced technology or a strong brand image. Joint ventures, the third strategic alternative, offer companies the opportunity to share risk and combine value-chain strengths. Companies considering joint ventures must plan carefully and communicate with partners to avoid "divorce." Ensure that if there must be a "divorce," that it will be a good divorce and not a costly mistake. Ownership, through start-up or acquisition, can require a major commitment of resources. Acquisitions can offer the benefits of full control and an opportunity to blend technologies, and green-field expansion offers great advantage to the firm that has the resources and capabilities to expand in this way.

Sourcing from a local or third-country supplier allows a company to enter new markets without investing in additional production capacity. Close cooperation with an overseas distributor can provide market access and market feedback. Licensing is a strategy to monetize intellectual property, know-how, and brand equity with minimal investment. It can be a good choice for a company with advanced technology or a strong brand image. Franchises can take a proven domestic business model overseas with rapid global penetration. Joint ventures offer companies the opportunity to share risk and combine value-chain strengths—but also require a long-term management commitment and careful planning and communication between the venture partners. Direct ownership, through a start-up or acquisition, similarly requires a major commitment of resources, both capital and managerial.

Market expansion strategies can be developed in matrix form to assist managers in thinking through the various alternatives. The options include country and market concentration, country concentration and market diversification, country diversification and market concentration, and country and market diversification. The preferred expansion strategy will depend upon a company's stage of development. An international company will use exporting and licensing to exploit headquarter knowledge through worldwide diffusion of products. Multinational companies can respond to local opportunities via acquisitions and green-field manufacturing start-ups. Globally diversified companies can export products around the globe from world-scale plants and benefit from a wealth of diverse intellectual capital.

In choosing global markets, companies must assess market potential, market access, shipping costs, competition, product fit, and service requirements. It is essential to visit a potential market before developing an entry and expansion strategy. Nothing compares to what can be learned on the ground and nothing compares to face-to-face discussions and negotiations.

Discussion Questions

1. Why should a company consider expanding globally?
2. What are the alternative tools or strategies for expanding globally? What are the major advantages and disadvantages of each strategy?
3. You work for a specialty process-control manufacturer in Indiana. The president comes to you with a license offer from a Chinese conglomerate. In return for sharing your company's patents and process know-how, the Chinese company is offering to pay a license fee of 5 percent of the ex-factory price of all products sold under license. The president asks for your advice. What would you tell her?
4. What criteria should be assessed when evaluating potential global markets?
5. Why would a firm consider forming a partnership with a competitor? What are some examples of this being beneficial or destructive? In what industries has this proved successful?
6. Why is there no "ideal" market entry strategy?

Suggested Readings

Baghai, Mehrdad, Sven Smit, and Patrick Viguerie. "Is Your Growth Strategy Flying Blind." *Harvard Business Review* (May 2009): 86–96.

Cavusgil, S. Tamer, Shaoming Zou, and G. M. Naidu. "Product and Promotion Adaptation in Export Ventures: An Empirical Investigation." *Journal of International Business Studies,* 24, no. 3 (Third Quarter 1993): 449–464.

Chironga, Mutsa, Acha Leke, Susan Lund, and Arend van Wamelen. "Cracking the Next Growth Market: Africa." *Harvard Business Review* (May 2011): 117–122.

Etgar, Michael, and Dalia Rachman-Moore. "Geographical Expansion by International Retailers: A Study of Proximate Markets and Global Expansion Strategies." *Journal of Global Marketing*, 23, no. 1 (2010): 5–15.

Eyring, Matthew J., Mark W. Johnson, and Hari Nair. "New Business Models in Emerging Markets." *Harvard Business Review* (January–February 2011): 89–95.

Freeman, Susan, Ron Edwards, and Bill Schroder. "How Smaller Born-Global Firms Use Networks and Alliances to Overcome Constraints to Rapid Internationalization." *Journal of International Marketing*, 14, no. 3 (2006).

Hamel, Gary, and C. K. Prahalad. "Do You Really Have a Global Strategy?" *Harvard Business Review* (July–August 1985): 139–148.

Hortinha, Paula, Carmen Lages, and Luis Filipe Lages. "The Trade-Off Between Customer and Technology Orientations: Impact on Innovation Capabilities and Export Performance." *Journal of International Marketing*, 19, no. 3 (September 2011).

Hultman, Magnus, Matthew J. Robson, and Constantine S. Katsikeas. "Export Product Strategy Fit and Performance: An Empirical Investigation." *Journal of International Marketing*, 17, no. 4 (December 2009): 24–46.

Kogut, Bruce. "Designing Global Strategies: Comparative and Competitive Value-Added Chains." *Sloan Management Review* (Summer 1985): 17–27.

Mayrhofer, Ulrike. "International Market Entry: Does the Home Country Affect Entry-Mode Decisions?" *Journal of International Marketing*, 12, no. 4 (December 2004): 71–96.

Ojala, Arto, and Pasi Tyvainen. "Market Entry and Priority of Small and Medium-Sized Enterprises in the Software Industry: An Empirical Analysis of Cultural Distance, Geographic Distance, and Market Size." *Journal of International Marketing*, 15, no. 3 (September 2007): 123–149.

Perlmutter, Howard V., and David A. Heenan. "How Multinational Should Your Top Managers Be?" *Harvard Business Review* (November–December 1974): 121–132.

Prahalad, C. K., and Hrishi Bhattacharyya. "How to Be a Truly Global Company." *Strategy+Business*, 64 (Autumn 2011): 54–61.

Raval, Dinker, and Bala Subramanian. "Product Cycle and International Product Life Cycle: Economic and Marketing Perspectives." *Business Journal*, 12, nos. 1 and 2 (1997): 48–51.

Robertson, Thomas S. "How to Reduce Market Penetration Cycle Times." *Sloan Management Review* (Fall 1993): 87–96.

Sanchez-Peinado, Esther, Jose Pla-Barber, and Louis Hébert. "Strategic Variables That Influence Entry Mode Choice in Service Firms." *Journal of International Marketing*, 15, no. 1 (March 2007): 67–91.

Sibanda, Khutula, Ronel Erwee, and Eric Ng. "Factors That Distinguish Proactive Versus Reactive Exporters: Decisions by Export Firms in a Developing Country." *Journal of Global Marketing*, 24, no. 1 (2011): 69–84.

Solberg, Carl Arthur. "Educator Insights: Standardization or Adaptation of the International Marketing Mix." *Journal of International Marketing*, 8, no. 1 (2000): 78–98.

Sousa, Carols M. P., Ruzo Emilio, and Fernando Losada. "The Key Role of Managers' Values in Exporting: Influence on Customer Responsiveness and Export Performance." *Journal of International Marketing*, 18, no. 2 (June 2010): 1–19.

Tan, Qun, and Carlos M.P. Sousa. "Research on Export Pricing: Still Moving Toward Maturity." *Journal of International Marketing*, 19, no. 3 (September 2011).

Tse, Edward, John Jullens, and Bill Russo. "China's Mid-Market Innovators." *Strategy + Business* (Summer 2012): 32–36.

Uzama, Austin. "A Critical Review of Market Entry Selection and Expansion Into Japan's Market." *Journal of Global Marketing*, 22, no. 4 (2009): 279–298.

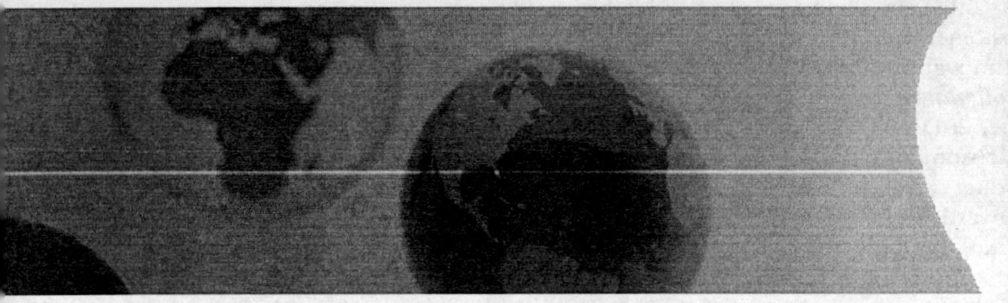

CHAPTER 9

Competitive Analysis and Strategy

The best strategy is always to be very strong, first generally then at the decisive point.... there is no more imperative and no simpler law for strategy than to keep the forces concentrated.

—CARL VON CLAUSEWITZ, 1780–1831

Vom Kriege, *Book III, Chapter XI, "Assembly of Forces in Space" (1832–1837)*

People think focus means saying yes to the thing you've got to focus on. But that's not what it means at all. It means saying no to the hundred other good ideas.... waves of technology, you can see them way before they happen, and you just have to choose wisely which ones you're going to surf.

—STEVE JOBS, 1955–2011

2008 Fortune Magazine Interview[1]

Learning Objectives

1. Define strategy (271–272).
2. Describe the forces that influence industry competition (272–276).
3. Discuss the causes and effects of global competition and national competitive advantage (276–277).
4. Differentiate between broad market and narrow target strategies (287–289).
5. Describe the three classifications for strategic positions (289–291).
6. Explain how strategic intent facilitates competitive innovation (291–293).
7. Discuss the theory of hypercompetition (294).

[1] http://money.cnn.com/galleries/2008/fortune/0803/gallery.jobsqna.fortune/index.html

BOX 9-1

IKEA—Creating Unique Value

From its home base in Sweden, IKEA has become the world's largest furniture retailer doing $30 billion in annual sales in 2010. With more than 300 stores in 37 countries, the company's success reflects founder Ingvar Kamprad's vision of selling a wide range of stylish, functional home furnishings at prices so low that the majority of people can afford to buy them. The store exteriors are painted bright blue and yellow—Sweden's national colors. Shoppers view furniture on the main floor in scores of realistic settings arranged throughout cavernous showrooms. In a departure from standard industry practice, IKEA's furniture bears names such as "Ivar" and "Sten" instead of model numbers. At IKEA, shopping is very much a self-service activity; after browsing and writing down the names of desired items, shoppers pick up their furniture on the lower level. There they find boxes containing the furniture in kit form; one of the cornerstones of IKEA's strategy is having customers take their purchases home in their own vehicles and assemble the furniture themselves. The lower level of a typical IKEA store also contains a restaurant, a grocery store called the Swede Shop, a supervised play area for children, and a baby care room.

The bottom line for IKEA is that the company creates a unique value for customers: instead of salespeople, a limited number of display items, and a catalog from which to order, IKEA offers informative displays and product information for everything it sells. In a traditional furniture store, you place an order and wait weeks or months for delivery. At IKEA, you make a purchase and take it with you. Traditional furniture is assembled and ready to use. IKEA furniture is sold in kit form ready to assemble. The traditional store offers salespeople or consultants, assembled and ready-to-use product, delivery, and higher prices. IKEA offers rock-bottom prices.

IKEA is focused on the young customer or the young at heart: the core market is the customer with a limited budget who appreciates IKEA's product line, displays, and prices. Because IKEA knows the needs and wants of this market segment, it has been successful in serving customers not only in Sweden where the company was founded but also globally. IKEA's success in crossing borders has been instrumental in changing furniture retailing from a multidomestic industry to a global one.

INTRODUCTION

What is strategy? Karl von Clausewitz answered this question in his famous book Vom Krieg (On War). His answer: "The best strategy is always to be very strong, first generally then at the decisive point....there is no more imperative and no simpler law for strategy than to keep the forces concentrated." Strength and determining the decisive point is critical to strategic advantage in war and peace. Identifying that point and achieving an advantage at that point is a critical element in strategic success. Von Clausewitz underlines the great law of strategy: *keep the forces concentrated.* Steve Jobs demonstrated power, strength, and concentration and led Apple to the greatest recovery in the history of business. Apple today is one of the most valuable companies in the world: a position of strength that is based on Apple's ability to deliver unique value with its iPod, iPhone, iPad, Macintosh computers, software, and the online and brick-and-mortar Apple Stores.

Every industry and product class has its decisive points. In automobiles, it is generally performance and overall quality, and the decisive point is fit, finish, feel and styling, and the sales and service network. The component parts of a BMW cost 2 percent more than a comparable Chevrolet, but the BMW, a global brand, sells for a 30 percent price premium over the Chevrolet, a national brand. The premium is based on the value of the BMW's great general strength as an automobile company in the

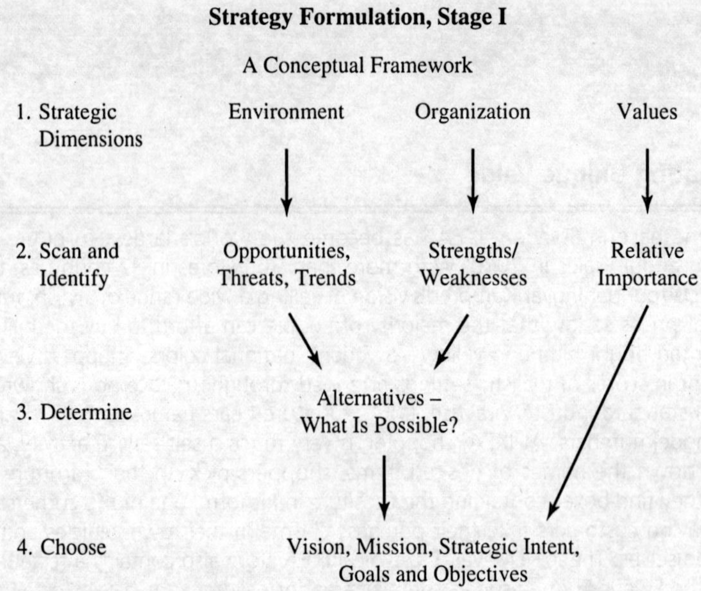

FIGURE 9-1 Strategy Formulation, Stage I

luxury segment of the automobile market and its strength at the decisive points of that market. The decisive points for BMW's market include the compact, small, midsize, and large sedans, coupes, convertibles, SUVs, and station wagons, brand image and equity, and its dealer sales and service network.

As shown in Figure 9-1, strategy formulation is based on three dimensions or domains: the environment, the organization, and values. It begins with the three steps of identifying opportunities, threats and trends in the environment, strengths and weaknesses in the organization, and the relative importance of values. With the identification and analysis of these elements, a determination can be made of what is possible. The forth step in the process is to formulate and choose a vision, mission, strategic intent, and specific goals and objectives.

The process continues as shown in Figure 9-2 with building core competencies, formulating strategic plans and integrated business plans, implementing the plans,

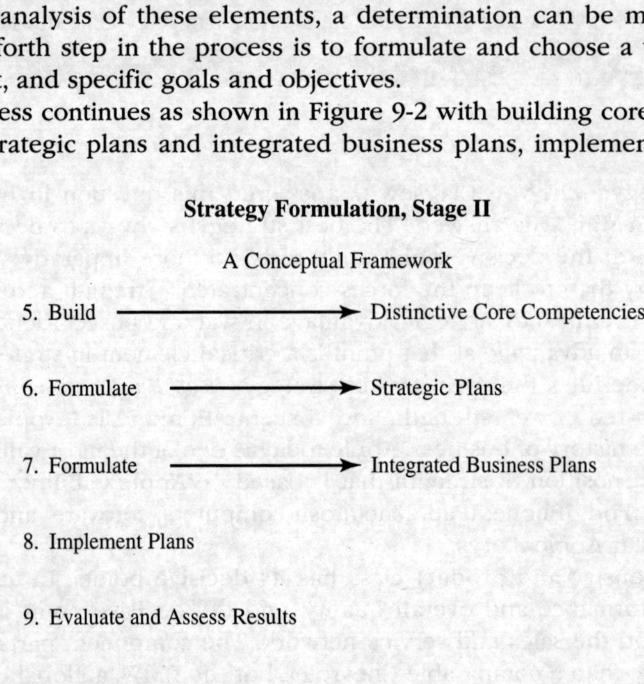

FIGURE 9-2 Strategy Formulation, Stage II

evaluating and assessing the results, and going back to steps 1–4 continuing the process of tracking and assessing the status of environment, organization, and values.

STRATEGY DEFINED

There are many definitions of strategy. Alfred Chandler offered an early definition for business:

> The determination of the basic long-term goals and objectives of an enterprise, and the adoption of courses of action and the allocation of resources necessary for carrying out these goals.[2]

Kenneth Andrews, in *The Concept of Corporate Strategy,* expanded Chandler's definition to include defining the business that the company is in and the kind of company that it is to be.

> Strategy is the pattern of objectives, purposes, or goals and the major policies and plans for achieving these goals, stated in such a way as to define what business the company is in or is to be in and the kind of company it is or is to be.

Strategy can be defined as a concerted and coordinated set of activities designed to achieve a goal or objective. The goal of every business should be to create unique value and achieve a competitive advantage. In competitive markets, strategy is driven by competition. One objective of strategy is to win competitive battles and achieve a sustainable competitive advantage. Business strategy is integrated action in pursuit of competitive advantage. Put most simply, it is the art of creating value. Although strategy can be defined, there is often little agreement on the best strategy for a given competitive situation.

According to Michael E. Porter of Harvard University, a leading theorist of competitive strategy, winning strategies are either choosing different activities than competitors or different and better execution of the same activities as competitors. He also believes that companies need to develop strategies that bring business and society together in a way that is mutually beneficial. In many countries, the success of business has been at the expense of the well-being of society. Companies are trapped in an outdated approach to value creation where value is narrowly defined as short-term financial performance. An example of this is the practice of shifting activities to locations with lower wages as a solution to competitive challenges. This practice simultaneously weakens the company and the community. The community loses jobs and income and the company gets a temporary advantage that is far from sustainable.

> *"The solution to this problem lies in the principle of shared value, which involves creating economic value in a way that also creates value for society by addressing its needs and challenges. Businesses must reconnect company success with social progress. Shared value is not social responsibility, philanthropy, or even sustainability, but a new way to achieve economic success."*[3]

---

[2] Alfred Chandler, *Strategy and Structure: Chapters in the History of American Industrial Enterprise* (Cambridge: Massachusetts Institute of Technology, 1962): 13.

[3] Michael E. Porter and Mark R. Kramer, "Creating Shared Value," *Harvard Business Review* (January–February 2011): 64.

Hambrick and Fredrickson define strategy in terms its basic elements and in terms of the context of strategy. Strategy is the whole, not the parts. The bigger, coherent whole is achieved not by following a sequential process as prescribed in textbooks (e.g., SWOT analysis), but by achieving a "robust consistency among the elements of the strategy itself."

The five elements of a strategy as defined by Hambrick and Fredrickson are

- Arenas—where
- Vehicles—what and how
- Differentiators—what is the competitive advantage
- Staging—sequence of actions
- Economic logic—the financial returns.

The IKEA example above illustrates the elements of strategy from a global marketing perspective:

- Arenas—IKEA focuses on growth in urban areas where the aspiring middle class is attracted to and can afford their products.
- Vehicles—The approach is fairly uniform across markets: a large, centrally-located building with a broad range of affordable, stylish furniture and fixtures to take home.
- Differentiators—The competitive advantage is style, affordability, and instant gratification (plus Swedish meatballs at a very good price!).
- Staging—IKEA starts with a single location in a new country and then gradually expands outward from that base.
- Economic logic—The economic logic works through control over the product and delivery approach (none of the stores are franchised) and global economies of scale in production.

Arenas, the "where" in the strategy elements above, are of particular concern for global marketing strategists. An overseas location can be (1) a source for products or services as part of the global value chain, and/or (2) a market for existing or new products and services, and/or (3) a source of technology and innovation for existing or new markets.

Strategy formulation is based on strategic analysis that leads to choices of activities. We start with competitive analysis at the industry level and follow to the national level.

The essence of global marketing strategy is in successfully relating the strengths of an organization to its environment. As the horizons of marketers have expanded from domestic to global markets, so too have the horizons of competitors. The reality in almost every industry today—including home furnishings—is global competition. This fact of life puts an organization under increasing pressure to master techniques for conducting industry analysis, competitor analysis, understanding competitive advantage at both the industry and national levels, and developing and maintaining competitive advantage. These topics are covered in detail in this chapter.

INDUSTRY ANALYSIS FORCES INFLUENCING COMPETITION

A useful way of gaining insight into the nature of competition is through industry analysis. As a working definition, an industry can be defined as a group of firms that produce products that are close substitutes for each other. In any industry, competition works to drive down the rate of return on invested capital toward the rate that would be earned in the economist's perfectly competitive industry. Rates of return that are greater than this so-called competitive rate will stimulate an inflow of capital

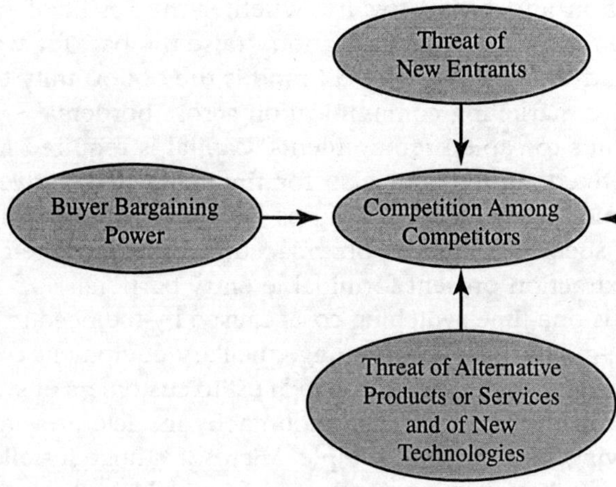

FIGURE 9-3 Forces Influencing Competition in an Industry

either from new entrants or from existing competitors making additional investment. Rates of return below this competitive rate will result in withdrawal from the industry and a decline in the levels of activity and competition.

Five Forces

Michael Porter identifies five forces influencing competition in an industry (see Figure 9-3): the threat of new entrants, the threat of substitute products or services, the bargaining power of suppliers, the bargaining power of buyers, and the competitive rivalry between current members of the industry. In industries such as soft drinks, pharmaceuticals, and cosmetics, a favorable combination of the five forces has resulted in attractive returns for competitors. However, pressure from any of the forces can reduce or limit profitability, as evidenced by the recent fortunes of some competitors in the personal computer (PC) and semiconductor industries. A discussion of each of the five forces follows.

THREAT OF NEW ENTRANTS New entrants to an industry bring new capacity, a desire to gain market share and position, and, very often, new approaches to serving customer needs. The decision to become a new entrant in an industry is often accompanied by a major commitment of resources. New players push prices downward and squeeze margins, resulting in reduced industry profitability. Porter describes eight major sources of barriers to entry, the presence or absence of which determines the extent of the threat of new industry entrants.[4]

The first barrier, economies of scale, refers to the decline in per unit product costs as the absolute volume of production per period increases. Although the concept of scale economies is frequently associated with manufacturing, it is also applicable to research and development (R&D), general administration, marketing, and other business functions. Honda's efficiency at engine R&D, for example, results from the wide range of products it produces that feature gasoline-powered engines. When existing firms in an industry achieve significant economies of scale, it becomes difficult for potential new entrants to be competitive.

Product differentiation, the second major entry barrier, is the extent of a product's perceived uniqueness—in other words, whether or not it is a commodity. High

[4] Michael E. Porter, *Competitive Strategy* (New York: Free Press, 1980): 7–33.

levels of product differentiation and brand loyalty, whether the result of physical product attributes or effective marketing communication, "raise the bar" for would-be industry entrants. One of the advantages of a global brand is the opportunity to leverage differentiation and effective marketing communication across borders.

A third entry barrier relates to capital requirements. Capital is required not only for manufacturing facilities (fixed capital) but also for financing R&D, advertising, field sales and service, customer credit, and inventories (working capital). The enormous capital requirements in such industries as pharmaceuticals, mainframe computers, chemicals, and mineral extraction present formidable entry barriers.

A fourth barrier to entry is one-time switching costs caused by the need to change suppliers and products. These might include retraining, ancillary equipment costs, the cost of evaluating a new source, and so on. The perceived cost to customers of switching to a new competitor's product may present an insurmountable obstacle preventing industry newcomers from achieving success. For example, Microsoft's huge installed base of computer operating systems and applications presents a formidable entry barrier.

A fifth barrier to entry is access to distribution channels. To the extent that channels are full, expensive to enter, or unavailable, the cost of entry is substantially increased because a new entrant must create and establish new channels. Global companies encounter this barrier in every new market. This is not a so-called nontariff barrier, or a barrier designed to discriminate against foreign firms—it applies to *any* firm, domestic or foreign, seeking market entry.

Government policy is frequently a major entry barrier. In some cases, the government will restrict competitive entry. This is true in a number of industries, especially those in the low, lower-middle, and upper-middle income countries that have been designated as national industries by their respective governments. Japan's postwar industrialization strategy was based on a policy of preserving and protecting national industries in their development and growth phases. In many cases, the Japanese companies in these protected industries have gone on to become major world competitors in their industries. Komatsu, for example, was a weak local company when Caterpillar announced its interest in entering the Japanese market. Komatsu was given two years of protection by the Japanese government, and today it is the number-two earth-moving equipment company in the world. China is following a policy today of requiring foreign investors in many industries to join with local partners in their Chinese investments.

Established firms may also enjoy cost advantages independent of the scale economies that present barriers to entry. Access to raw materials, favorable locations, and government subsidies are several examples.

Finally, expected competitor response can be a major entry barrier. If new entrants expect existing competitors to respond strongly to entry, their expectations about the rewards of entry will certainly be affected. A potential competitor's belief that entry into an industry or market will be an unpleasant experience may serve as a strong deterrent. Bruce Henderson, former president of the Boston Consulting Group, used the term *brinkmanship* to describe a recommended approach for deterring competitive entry. Brinkmanship occurs when industry leaders convince potential competitors that any market entry effort will be countered with vigorous and unpleasant responses.

THREAT OF SUBSTITUTE PRODUCTS A second force influencing competition in an industry is the threat of substitute products. The availability of substitute products places limits on the prices market leaders can charge in an industry; high prices may induce buyers to switch to the substitute.

For example, Barnes & Noble watched the upstart Amazon.com create a new product: the online bookstore. Customers could now order from millions of books and have them delivered to their doors in a matter of days. For a segment of the book market, local bookstores with only a few thousand books and a Starbucks Coffee facility were not necessary. Since it went online in 1995, Amazon.com has grown to over $35 billion in total revenue, expanded its product line into everything from CDs and videos to clothing, electronics, food, health and personal care, and pet and drug supplies, to name just a few areas. Amazon.com is growing at the rate of 40 to 50 percent per annum, while brick-and-mortar book retailers have either closed (Borders) or are struggling to survive in a market that is shifting to digital as opposed to print distribution (Barnes & Noble). The virtual bookstore continues to replace the traditional format.

BARGAINING POWER OF SUPPLIERS If suppliers have enough leverage over industry firms, they can raise prices high enough to significantly influence the profitability of the industry. Several factors influence supplier bargaining power:

1. Suppliers will have the advantage if they are large and relatively few in number.
2. When the suppliers' products or services are important inputs to user firms, are highly differentiated, or carry switching costs, the suppliers will have considerable leverage over buyers.
3. Suppliers will also enjoy bargaining power if their business is not threatened by alternative products.
4. The willingness and ability of suppliers to develop their own products and brand names if they are unable to get satisfactory terms from industry buyers will influence their power.

A good example of the bargaining power of suppliers is OPEC, which can influence the price of oil and refined product by limiting production. In the 1970s and again in 2000 and 2011, gasoline prices increased rapidly in response to limited supplies and growing demand. Since there is no alternative, customers are forced to pay the higher prices.

BARGAINING POWER OF BUYERS The ultimate aim of industrial customers is to pay the lowest possible price to obtain the products or services that they use as inputs. Usually, therefore, the buyers' best interests are served if they can drive down profitability in the supplier industry. The following are conditions under which buyers can exert power over suppliers:

1. When they purchase in such large quantities that supplier firms depend on the buyers' business for survival.
2. When the supplier's products are viewed as commodities—that is, as standard or undifferentiated—buyers are likely to bargain hard for low prices because many supplier firms can meet their needs.
3. When the supplier industry's products or services represent a significant portion of the buying firms' costs.
4. When the buyer is willing to achieve backward vertical integration.

RIVALRY AMONG COMPETITORS Rivalry among firms refers to all the actions taken by firms in the industry to improve their positions and gain advantage over each other. Rivalry manifests itself in price competition, advertising battles, product positioning, and attempts at differentiation. To the extent that rivalry among firms forces companies to innovate and/or rationalize costs, it can be a positive force. To the extent that it drives down prices and, therefore, profitability, it creates instability and negatively influences the attractiveness of the industry. Several factors can create intense rivalry:

1. Once an industry becomes mature, firms focus on market share and how it can be gained at the expense of others.

2. Industries characterized by high fixed costs are always under pressure to keep production at full capacity to cover the fixed costs. Once the industry accumulates excess capacity, the drive to fill capacity will push prices—and profitability—down.
3. A lack of differentiation or an absence of switching costs encourages buyers to treat the products or services as commodities and shop for the best prices. Again, there is downward pressure on prices and profitability.
4. Firms with high strategic stakes in achieving success in an industry generally are destabilizing because they may be willing to accept unreasonably low profit margins to establish themselves, hold position, or expand.

GLOBAL COMPETITION AND NATIONAL COMPETITIVE ADVANTAGE[5]

An inevitable consequence of the expansion of global marketing activity is the growth of competition on a global basis. In industry after industry, global competition is a critical factor affecting success. In some industries, global companies have virtually excluded all other companies from their markets. An example is the detergent industry, in which three companies—Colgate, Unilever, and Procter & Gamble (P&G)—dominate an increasing number of detergent markets worldwide, including Latin America and the Pacific Rim. Because many companies can make a quality detergent, global brand-name muscle and marketing skills have become the sources of global competitive advantage that overwhelm local competition in market after market.[6]

Based on recent changes in the way business is done around the world, Michael Porter urges global companies not to lose sight of "local things—knowledge, relationships, and motivation that distant rivals cannot match."[7] (See discussion under "Related and Supporting Industries" later in this chapter.)

The automobile industry has also become fiercely competitive on a global basis. Part of the reason for the initial success of foreign automakers in the United States was the reluctance or inability of US manufacturers to design and manufacture high-quality, inexpensive small cars. The resistance of US manufacturers was based on the economics of car production: the bigger the car, the higher the list price. Under this formula, small cars meant smaller unit profits. Therefore, US manufacturers resisted the growing preference of US customers for smaller cars—a classic case of ethnocentrism and marketing myopia. Meanwhile, European, Japanese, and Korean manufacturers' product lines have always included cars smaller than those made in the United States. In Europe and Asia, market conditions were much different than in America: less space, high taxes on engine displacement and fuel, and greater market interest in functional design and engineering innovations. First Volkswagen and then Japanese automakers such as Nissan and Toyota discovered a growing demand for their cars in the US market. It is noteworthy that many significant innovations and technical advances—including radial tires, antilock brakes, and fuel injection—also came from Europe and Japan. Airbags are a notable exception.

Another major innovation in the auto industry, which has since spread to all industries, is the revolutionary innovation of lean manufacturing first introduced at Toyota. This radically different way of designing and building an automobile dramatically reduced

---

[5] This section draws heavily on Michael E. Porter, *The Competitive Advantage of Nations* (New York: Free Press, 1990), 179–273.

[6] See Joseph Kahn, "Cleaning Up: P&G Viewed China as a National Market and Is Conquering It," *The Wall Street Journal*, September 12, 1995: A1, A6.

[7] Michael E. Porter, "Clusters and the New Economics of Competition," *Harvard Business Review*, 76, no. 6 (November–December 1998): 77–90.

costs and increased quality. Lean manufacturing was invented in Japan and gave the Japanese automobile companies a knockout advantage in world markets: lower costs and higher quality. Indeed, lean manufacturing has replaced mass production in the same way that mass production replaced craft production, and for the same reasons: it raised the bar on quality and dramatically reduced costs. Today, companies that have not mastered the art and science of lean manufacturing are no longer in the auto business.

The effect of global competition has been highly beneficial to consumers around the world. In the two examples cited—detergents and automobiles—consumers have benefited. In Central America, detergent prices have fallen and quality has risen as a result of global competition. In the United States, for example, foreign companies have provided consumers with the automobile products, performance, and price characteristics they wanted. If smaller, lower-priced imported cars had not been available, it is unlikely that Detroit manufacturers would have provided a comparable product as quickly. What is true for automobiles in the United States is true for every product class around the world. Global competition expands the range of products and increases the likelihood that consumers will get what they want.

The downside of global competition is its impact on the producers of goods and services. When a company offers consumers in other countries a better product at a lower price, this company takes customers away from domestic suppliers. Unless the domestic supplier can create new values and find new customers, the jobs and livelihoods of the domestic supplier's employees are threatened. The social effects of these influences often prompt political responses that destabilize the business environment. Both business and government policy makers are trying to better understand the factors that make a specific nation a better (or worse) place for a company in a specific industry. Businesses want to understand how to choose locations for their activities that give them a competitive advantage. Governments want to know whether they should intervene in the business environment and, if so, how.

The following section addresses a number of questions. Why is a particular nation a good home base for specific industries? Why, for example, is the United States the home base for the leading competitors in PCs, software, credit cards, and movies? Why is Germany the home of so many world leaders in printing presses, chemicals, and luxury cars? Why are so many leading pharmaceutical, chocolate/confectionery, and trading companies located in Switzerland? Why are the world leaders in consumer electronics based in Japan?

According to Porter, the presence or absence of particular attributes in individual countries influences industry development. Porter describes these attributes—factor conditions, demand conditions, related and supporting industry, and firm structure and rivalry—in terms of a national diamond (see Figure 9-4). The diamond shapes the environment in which firms compete in their global industries.

Factor Conditions

The phrase *factor conditions* refers to a country's endowment of resources. Factor resources may have been created or inherited and are divided into five categories: human, physical, knowledge, capital, and infrastructure.

HUMAN RESOURCES The quantity of workers available, the skills possessed by these workers, wage levels, and the overall work ethic of the workforce together constitute a nation's human resource factors. Countries with a plentiful supply of low-wage labor have an obvious advantage in the current production of labor-intensive products; however, in most manufacturing industries of the developed world, the cost of manual labor is rapidly becoming a smaller and smaller factor. Presently, labor averages about

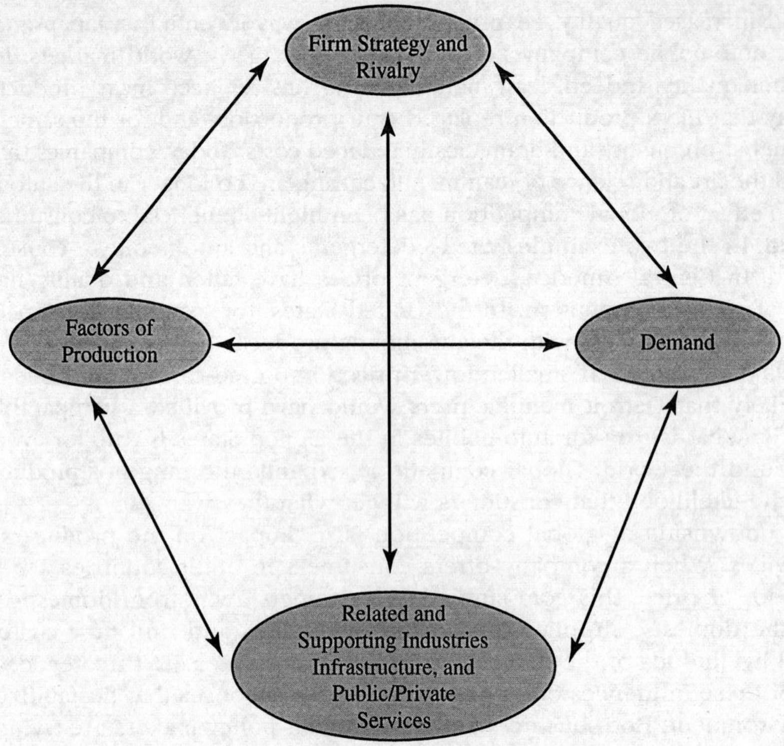

FIGURE 9-4 Determinants of Nations' Competitive Advantage

one-eighth or less of total costs.[8] Any cost advantage will disappear if wages increase and production moves to another country. However, low-wage countries may be at a disadvantage when it comes to the production of sophisticated products requiring highly skilled workers capable of working without extensive supervision.

PHYSICAL RESOURCES The availability, quantity, quality, and cost of land, water, minerals, and other natural resources determine a country's physical resources. A country's size and location are also included in this category because proximity to markets and sources of supply, as well as transportation costs, are strategic considerations. These factors are obviously important advantages or disadvantages to industries dependent on natural resources.

KNOWLEDGE RESOURCES The availability within a nation of a significant population with scientific, technical, and market-related knowledge means a nation is endowed with knowledge resources. The presence of these factors is usually a function of the educational orientation of the society as well as the number of research facilities and universities—both government and private—operating in the country. These factors are important to success in sophisticated products and services and to doing business in sophisticated markets. This factor relates directly to Germany's leadership in chemicals; for some 150 years, Germany has been home to top university chemistry programs, advanced scientific journals, and apprenticeship programs.

CAPITAL RESOURCES Countries vary in the availability, amount, cost, and types of capital available to the country's industries. The nation's savings rate, interest rates,

[8] Peter F. Drucker, *Management Challenges for the 21st Century* (New York: HarperBusiness, 1999): 99.

tax laws, and government deficits all affect the availability of capital. The advantage to industries with low capital costs versus those located in nations with relatively high costs is sometimes decisive. Firms paying high capital costs are frequently unable to stay in a market in which the competition comes from a nation with low capital costs. The firms with the low cost of capital can keep their prices low and force the firms paying high costs to either accept low returns on investment or leave the industry. The globalization of world capital markets is changing the manner in which capital is deployed. Investors can now send their capital to nations or markets with the best risk/return profile. Global firms will increasingly be following capital to the best places rather than operating in nations where capital is scarce or expensive.

INFRASTRUCTURE RESOURCES Infrastructure includes a nation's banking system, health-care system, transportation system, and communications system, as well as the availability and cost of using these systems. More sophisticated industries are more dependent on advanced infrastructures for success.

Basic Versus Advanced Factors

Factors can be further classified as either basic factors, such as natural resources and labor, or advanced factors, such as highly educated personnel and modern data communications infrastructure. Basic factors do not lead to sustainable international competitive advantage. For example, cheap labor is a transient national advantage that erodes as a nation's economy improves and average national income increases relative to other countries. Advanced factors, which lead to sustainable competitive advantage, are scarcer and require sustained investment. For example, the existence of a labor force of trained artisans offers Italy a basis of sustained competitive advantage in the Italian tile industry.

Generalized Versus Specialized Factors

Another categorization of factors differentiates between generalized factors, such as a suitable highway system, and specialized factors, such as focused educational systems. Generalized factors are precedents required for competitive advantage; however, sustainable advantage requires the development of specialized factors. For example, the competitive advantage of the Japanese robotics industry is fueled by extensive university robotics courses and programs that graduate skilled robotics trainees of the highest caliber.

Competitive advantage may also be created indirectly by nations that have selective factor disadvantages. For example, the absence of suitable labor may force firms to develop forms of mechanization that give the nation's firms an advantage. Scarcity of raw materials may motivate firms to develop new materials. For example, Japan, faced with scarce raw materials, developed an industrial ceramics industry that leads the world in innovation.

Demand Conditions

The nature of home-market demand conditions for the firm's or industry's products and services is important because it determines the rate and nature of improvement and innovation by the firms in the nation. These are the factors that either train firms for world-class competition or fail to adequately prepare them to compete in the global marketplace. Three characteristics of home demand are particularly important to the creation of competitive advantage: (1) the composition of home demand, (2) the size and pattern of growth of home demand, and (3) the means by which a nation's home demand pulls the nation's products and services into foreign markets.

The composition of home demand determines how firms perceive, interpret, and respond to buyer needs. Competitive advantage can be achieved when the home demand sets the quality standard and gives local firms a better picture of buyer needs, at an earlier time, than is available to foreign rivals. This advantage is enhanced when home buyers pressure the nation's firms to innovate quickly and frequently. The basis for advantage is the fact that the nation's firms can stay ahead of the market when firms are more sensitive to and more responsive to home demand and when that demand, in turn, reflects or anticipates world demand.

The size and pattern of growth of home demand are important only if the composition of the home demand is sophisticated and anticipates foreign demand. Large home markets offer opportunities to achieve economies of scale and learn while dealing with familiar, comfortable markets. There is less apprehension about investing in large-scale production facilities and expensive R&D programs when the home market is sufficient to absorb the increased capacity. If the home demand accurately reflects or anticipates foreign demand, and if the firms do not become content with serving the home market, the existence of large-scale facilities and programs will be an advantage in global competition.

Rapid home-market growth is another incentive to invest in and adopt new technologies faster, and to build large, efficient facilities. The best example of this is Japan, where rapid home-market growth provided the incentive for Japanese firms to invest heavily in modern, automated facilities. Early home demand, especially if it anticipates international demand, gives local firms the advantage of getting established in an industry sooner than foreign rivals. Equally important is early market saturation, which puts pressure on a company to expand into international markets and innovate. Market saturation is especially important if it coincides with rapid growth in foreign markets.

The means by which a nation's products and services are pushed or pulled into foreign countries is the third aspect of demand conditions. The issue here is whether a nation's people and businesses go abroad and then demand the nation's products and services in those second countries. For example, when the US auto companies set up operations in foreign countries, the US auto parts industry followed. The same is true for the Japanese auto industry. When the Japanese auto companies set up operations in the United States, Japanese parts suppliers followed their customers. Similarly, when overseas demand for the services of US engineering firms skyrocketed after World War II, those firms in turn established demand for US heavy construction equipment. This provided an impetus for Caterpillar to establish foreign operations.

A related issue is whether foreigners come to a nation for training, pleasure, business, or research. After returning home, they are likely to demand the products and services with which they became familiar while abroad. Similar effects can result from professional, scientific, and political relationships between nations. Those involved in the relationships begin to demand the products and services of the recognized leaders.

It is the interplay of demand conditions that contributes to competitive advantage. Of special importance are those conditions that lead to initial and continuing incentives to invest and innovate and to continuing competition in increasingly sophisticated markets.

Related and Supporting Industries

A nation has an advantage when it is home to internationally competitive industries in fields that are related to, or in direct support of, other industries. Internationally competitive supplier industries provide inputs to downstream industries that are likely to be internationally competitive in terms of technological innovation, price, and quality. Access is a function of proximity, both in terms of physical distance and cultural similarity. It is not the inputs themselves that give advantage. It is the contact and coordination with the suppliers that allow the firm the opportunity to structure the value chain so that linkages with suppliers are optimized. These opportunities may not be available to foreign firms.

Similar advantages accrue when there are internationally competitive and related industries in a nation that coordinate and share value-chain activities. These centers of competitive advantage are known as *clusters*. Clusters are geographic concentrations of interconnected companies and institutions in a particular field, which constitute a critical mass. Opportunities for sharing between computer hardware manufacturers and software developers provide a clear example of clusters. Related industries also create pull-through opportunities as described earlier in the chapter. Sales of US computers abroad have created demand for software from Microsoft and other US companies. Porter notes that the development of the Swiss pharmaceuticals industry can be attributed, in part, to Switzerland's large synthetic dye industry; the discovery of the therapeutic effects of dyes, in turn, led to the development of pharmaceutical companies.[9]

Other clusters are the leather fashion industry in Italy; chemicals, home appliances, and household furniture in Germany; wood products in Portugal; and flower growing in the Netherlands. Multinational companies such as Nestlé are incorporating this concept when establishing locations for their various businesses. They have relocated their headquarters for bottled water to France and moved the Rowntree Mackintosh confectionery division to York, England.

Firm Strategy, Structure, and Rivalry

Differences in management styles, organizational skills, and strategic perspectives create advantages and disadvantages for firms competing in different types of industries, as do differences in the intensity of domestic rivalry. In Germany, for example, company structure and management style tend to be hierarchical. Managers tend to come from technical backgrounds and to be most successful when dealing with industries that demand highly disciplined structures, such as chemicals and precision machinery. Italian firms, however, tend to look like, and be run like, small family businesses that stress customized rather than standardized products, niche markets, and substantial flexibility in meeting market demands.

Capital markets and attitudes toward investments are important components of national environments. For example, the majority of shares of US publicly held companies are owned by institutional investors such as mutual funds and pension plans. These investors will buy and sell shares to reduce risk and increase return rather than get involved in an individual company's operations. These very mobile investors drive managers to operate with a short-term focus on quarterly and annual results. This fluid capital market structure will provide funds for new growth industries and rapidly expanding markets in which there are expectations of early returns. On the other hand, US capital markets do not encourage more mature industries in which return on investment is lower and patient searching for innovations is required. Many other countries have an opposite orientation. For example, in Japan, banks are allowed to take equity stakes in the companies to which they loan money and provide other profitable banking services. These banks take a longer-term view than stock markets and are less concerned about short-term results.

Perhaps the most powerful influence on competitive advantage comes from domestic rivalry. Domestic rivalry keeps an industry dynamic and creates continual pressure to improve and innovate. Local rivalry forces firms to develop new products, improve existing ones, lower costs and prices, develop new technologies, and improve

[9] Porter, "Clusters and the New Economics of Competition," 77–90.

quality and service. Rivalry with foreign firms lacks this intensity. Domestic rivals have to fight each other not just for market share but also for employee talent, R&D breakthroughs, and prestige in the home market. Eventually, strong domestic rivalry will push firms to seek international markets to support expansions in scale and R&D investments, as Japan amply demonstrates. The absence of significant domestic rivalry will create complacency in the home firms and eventually cause them to become noncompetitive in the world markets.

It is not the number of domestic rivals that is important; rather, it is the intensity of the competition and the quality of the competitors that make the difference. It is also important that there be a fairly high rate of new business formations to create new competitors and safeguard against the older companies becoming comfortable with their market positions and products and services. As noted earlier in the chapter in the discussion of the forces shaping industry competition, new entrants bring new perspectives and new methods. They frequently define and serve new market segments that established companies have failed to recognize.

There are two final external variables to consider in the evaluation of national competitive advantage: chance and government.

Other Forces Acting on the Diamond

Two additional elements of Porter's model to consider in the evaluation of national competitive advantage are chance and government. In addition, there are nonmarket forces that are part of the environment and that should be considered as an expansion of or supplement to government and chance.

CHANCE Chance events play a role in shaping the competitive environment. Chance events are occurrences that are beyond the control of firms, industries, and usually governments. Included in this category are such things as wars and their aftermath, major technological breakthroughs, sudden dramatic shifts in factor or input cost (e.g., the oil crisis), dramatic swings in exchange rates, and so on.

Chance events are important because they create major discontinuities in technologies that allow nations and firms that were not competitive to leapfrog over old competitors and become competitive—even leaders—in the changed industry. For example, the development of microelectronics allowed many Japanese firms to overtake American and German firms in industries that had been based on electromechanical technologies.

From a systemic perspective, the role of chance events lies in the fact that they alter conditions in the diamond shown in Figure 9-4. The nation with the most favorable diamond, however, will be the one most likely to take advantage of these events and convert them into competitive advantage. For example, Canadian researchers were the first to isolate insulin, but they could not convert this breakthrough into an internationally competitive product. Firms in the United States and Denmark were able to do that because of their respective national diamonds.

GOVERNMENT Although it is often argued that government is a major determinant of national competitive advantage, the fact is that government is not a determinant but rather an influence on determinants. Government influences determinants by virtue of its role as a buyer of products and services and by its role as a maker of policies on labor, education, capital formation, natural resources, and product standards. It also influences determinants by its role as a regulator of commerce (for example, by telling banks and telephone companies what they can and cannot do).

By reinforcing positive determinants of competitive advantage in an industry, government can improve the competitive position of the nation's firms. Governments devise legal systems that influence competitive advantage by means of tariff and non-tariff barriers and laws requiring local content and labor.

Other Nonmarket Factors

In addition to government and chance, there are other nonmarket forces that affect the strategy system. The nonmarket forces, in addition to government, include interest groups, activists, and the public. These nonmarket forces are part of a noneconomic strategy system that operates on the basis of social, political, and legal forces that interact in the nonmarket environment of the firm.[10] An understanding of these forces is especially complicated and critical to the success of global strategies that are implemented in many different countries and cultures. The nonmarket environment differs from the market environment in many ways. For example, the market environment is principally one involving economic exchange, whereas the nonmarket environment includes regulatory bodies, interest groups, and others whose motives are often political rather than economic. For example, in some countries, environmental groups have promoted regulations that dramatically increase capital and operating costs for businesses that operate manufacturing plants. In the pharmaceutical industry, religious groups have impeded progress in genetic research. Competing companies operating in different national or geographic markets that do not have these limitations or costs have a competitive advantage.

THE SYSTEM OF DETERMINANTS It is important to view the determinants of national competitive advantage as an interactive system in which activity in any one of the four points of the diamond impacts on all the others and vice versa. This interplay between the determinants is depicted in Figure 9-5. The interaction of all of the forces is presented in Figure 9-6.

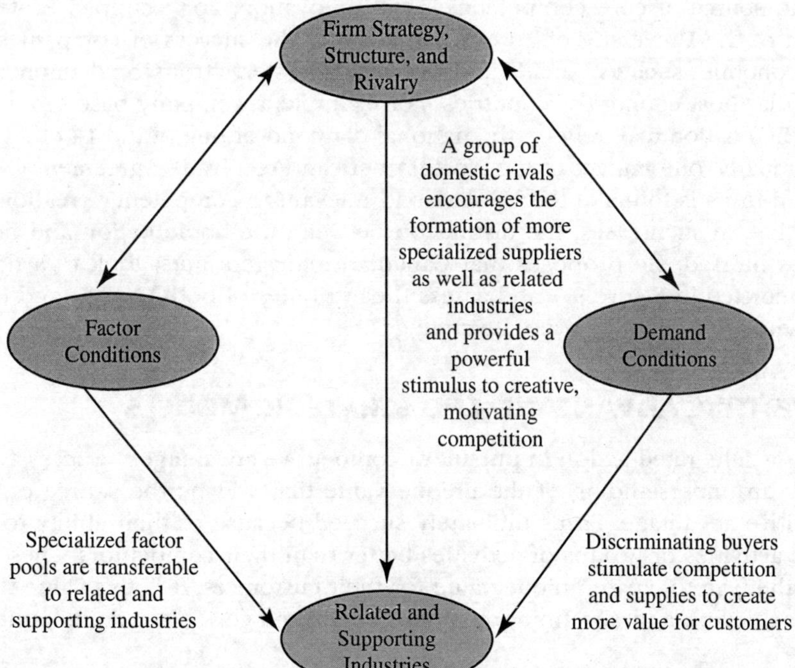

FIGURE 9-5 Influences on the Development of Related and Supporting Industries

[10] David P. Baron, "The Nonmarket Strategy System," *Sloan Management Review*, 37, no. 1 (Fall 1995): 73–85.

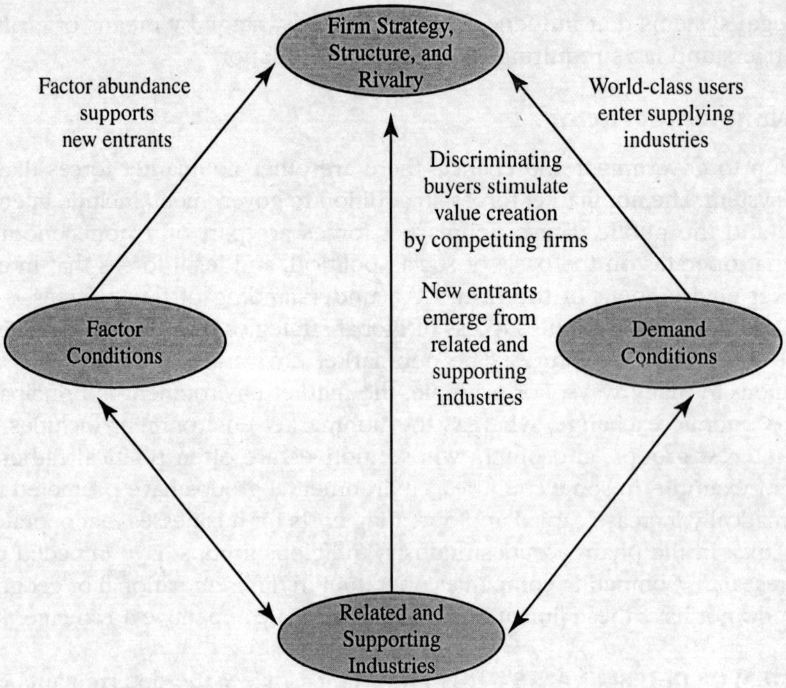

FIGURE 9-6 Influences on Domestic Rivalry

Single or Double Diamond?

Other researchers have challenged Porter's thesis that a firm's home-base country is the main source of core competencies and innovation. For example, Professor Alan Rugman of the University of Toronto argues that the success of companies based in small economies such as Canada and New Zealand stems from the diamonds found in a particular host country or countries. For example, a company based in a European Union (EU) nation may rely on the national diamond of one of the 14 other EU members. Similarly, one impact of the North American Free Trade Agreement (NAFTA) on Canadian firms is to make the US diamond relevant to competency creation. Rugman argues that, in such cases, the distinction between the home nation and host nation becomes blurred. He proposes that Canadian managers must look to a double diamond depicted in Figure 9-7 and assess the attributes of both Canada and the United States when formulating corporate strategy.[11]

COMPETITIVE ADVANTAGE AND STRATEGIC MODELS

Strategy is integrated action in pursuit of competitive advantage.[12] Successful strategy requires an understanding of the unique value that will be the source of the firm's competitive advantage. Firms ultimately succeed because of their ability to carry out specific activities or groups of activities better than their competitors. These activities enable the firm to create unique value for their customers. It is this value that is central to achieving and sustaining competitive advantage. This unique value must be

[11] See Alan M. Rugman and Alain Verbeke, "Foreign Subsidiaries and Multinational Strategic Management: An Extension and Correction of Porter's Single Diamond Framework," *Management International Review,* 33, no. 2 (Special Issue 1993): 71–84.

[12] See George Day, *Market Driven Strategy: Processes for Creating Value* (New York: Free Press, 1990).

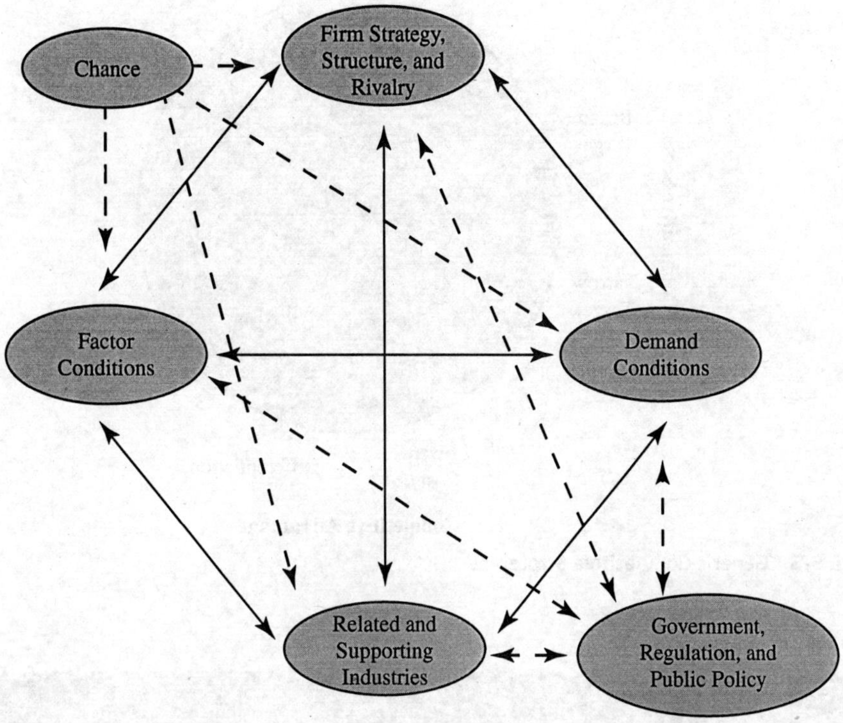

FIGURE 9-7 The Complete System

something that competitors will not be able to easily match. The uniqueness and magnitude of the customer value created by a firm's strategy are ultimately determined by customer perception. Operating results such as sales and profits are measures that depend on the level of psychological value created for customers: the greater the perceived consumer value, the stronger the competitive advantage, and the better the strategy. A firm may market a better mousetrap, but the ultimate success of the product depends on customers deciding for themselves whether to buy it. Value is like beauty—it is in the eye of the beholder. In sum, competitive advantage is achieved by creating more value than the competition, and value is defined by customer perception.

Two different models of competitive advantage have received considerable attention. The first offers generic strategies, which are four alternative positions that organizations can seek in order to offer superior value and achieve competitive advantage. According to the second model, the generic strategies alone do not explain the astonishing success of many companies in recent years. A more recent model, based on the concept of strategic intent, proposes four different sources of competitive advantage. Both models are discussed next.

Generic Strategies for Creating Competitive Advantage

In addition to the five-forces model of industry competition, Porter developed a framework of so-called generic business strategies based on two sources of competitive advantage: low cost and differentiation. Figure 9-8 shows that the combination of these two sources with the scope of the target market served (narrow or broad) or product mix width (narrow or wide) yields four generic strategies: cost leadership, product differentiation, focused differentiation, and cost focus.

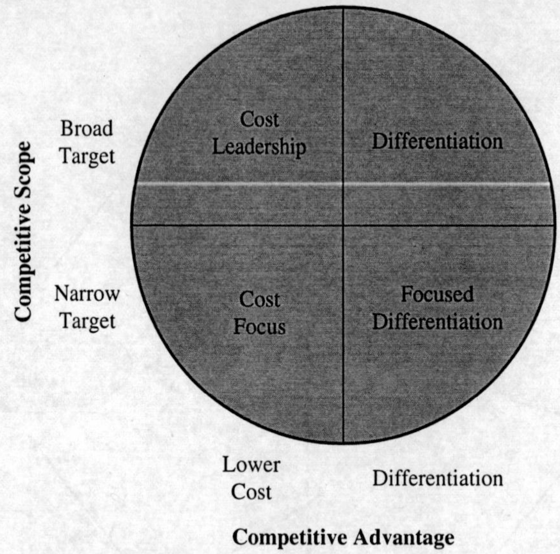

FIGURE 9-8 Generic Competitive Strategies

BOX 9-2

Side Bar: IKEA Achieving Strategic Advantage[13]

IKEA, the Swedish furniture company described in the chapter introduction, is an example of the cost-focus strategy. Notes George Bradley, president of Levitz Furniture in Boca Raton, Florida, "[IKEA] has really made a splash. They're going to capture their niche in every city they go into." Of course, such a strategy can be risky. As Bradley explains, "Their market is finite because it is so narrow. If you don't want contemporary, knockdown furniture, it's not for you. So it takes a certain customer to buy it. And remember, fashions change." The issue of sustainability is central to this strategy concept. As noted later in the chapter, cost leadership is a sustainable source of competitive advantage only if barriers exist that prevent competitors from achieving the same low costs. Sustained differentiation depends on continued perceived value and the absence of imitation by competitors. Several factors determine whether focus can be sustained as a source of competitive advantage. First, a cost focus is sustainable if a firm's competitors are defining their target markets more broadly. A cost focuser does not try to be all things to all people: competitors may diminish their advantage by trying to satisfy the needs of a broader market segment—a strategy that, by definition, means a blunter focus. Second, a firm's differentiation-focus advantage is sustainable only if competitors cannot define the segment even more narrowly. Also, focus can be sustained only if competitors cannot overcome barriers that prevent imitation of the focus strategy, and if consumers in the target segment do not migrate to other segments that the focuser does not serve.

[13] http://www.ikea.com/us/en/about_ikea/newsitem/IKEA_Group_Announces_Growth_2010_Press_Release; Tim Burt, "IKEA Chief Breaks Silence to Tell Home Truths," *The Financial Times*, August 18, 1998: 17; Tim Burt, "IKEA's Expansion Includes Move into Russia," *The Financial Times*, July 22, 1998: 16; George Nichols, "IKEA Will Never Be Listed," *The Financial Times*, March 23, 1999: 29; Loretta Roach, "IKEA: Furnishing the World," *Discount Merchandiser* (October 1994): 46, 48; "Furnishing the World," *The Economist*, November 19, 1994: 79–80; Jack Burton, "Rearranging the Furniture," *International Management* (September 1991): 58–61; Ela Schwartz, "The Swedish Invasion," *Discount Merchandiser* (July 1990): 52, 56; Lisa Marie Petersen, "The 1992 Client Media All-Stars: John Sitnik, IKEA," *Mediaweek*, December 12,1992: 25; Michael E. Porter, *The Competitive Advantage of Nations* (New York: Free Press, 1990): 158.

IKEA's approach to the furniture business has enabled it to rack up impressive growth in an industry in which overall sales have been flat. Sourcing furniture from more than 2,000 suppliers in more than 60 countries helps the company maintain its low-cost position.

IKEA's international growth has been quite successful but probably would not have been possible if the company had gone public, according to its founder, Ingvar Kamprad. He does not feel a need to show constant profits and, therefore, can take more investment risks. Since the 1990s, IKEA has opened stores in Central and Eastern Europe (Poland is one of its fastest-growing markets) and has expanded into Russia. Because many consumers in those regions have relatively low purchasing power, the stores offer a smaller selection of goods; some furniture was designed specifically for the cramped living styles typical in former Soviet bloc countries. Kamprad firmly believes in long-term investment and states, "It will take 25 years to furnish Russia." He believes that investment in Russia would not have been possible if the company had been a public company, which often suffers from a need to show short-term profits. Throughout the world, IKEA benefits from the perception that Sweden is the source of high-quality products.

Industry observers predict that North America will eventually be one of IKEA's largest markets. The company opened its first US store in Philadelphia in 1985; today, IKEA has outlets in many major metropolitan areas. Notes Jeff Young, chief operating officer of Lexington Furniture Industries, "IKEA is on the way to becoming the Wal-Mart stores of the home-furnishing industry. If you're in this business, you'd better take a look." Some American customers, however, are irked to find popular items are sometimes out of stock. Another problem is the long lines resulting from the company's no-frills approach. Complained one shopper, "Great idea, poor execution. The quality of much of what they sell is good, but the hassles make you question whether it's worth it."

Goran Carstedt, president of IKEA North America, responded to such criticism by referring to the company's mission. "If we offered more services, our prices would go up," he explains. "Our customers understand our philosophy, which calls for each of us to do a little in order to save a lot. They value our low prices. And almost all of them say they will come back again." Although it is a common industry practice to rely heavily on newspaper and radio advertising, two-thirds of IKEA's North American advertising budget is allocated for TV. John Sitnik, an executive at IKEA's US company, says, "We distanced ourselves from the other furniture stores. We decided TV is something we can own."

Generic strategies aiming at the achievement of competitive advantage demand that the firm make choices. The choices are the position it seeks to attain from which to offer unique value (based on cost or differentiation) and the market scope or product mix width within which competitive advantage will be attained.[14] The nature of the choice between positions and market scope is a gamble and involves risk. By choosing a given generic strategy, a firm always risks making the wrong choice.

Broad Market Strategies

COST-LEADERSHIP ADVANTAGE When the unique value delivered by a firm is based on its position as the industry's low-cost producer, in broadly defined markets or across a wide mix of products, a cost-leadership advantage occurs. This strategy has become increasingly popular in recent years as a result of the popularization of the experience curve concept. A firm that bases its competitive strategy on overall cost leadership must construct the most efficient facilities (in terms of scale or technology) and obtain the largest share of market so that its cost per unit is the lowest in the industry. These advantages, in turn, give the producer a substantial lead in terms of experience with building the product. Experience then leads to more refinements of the entire process of production, delivery, and service, which lead to further cost reductions.

[14] Porter, *The Competitive Advantage of Nations*, 12.

Whatever its source, cost-leadership advantage can be the basis for offering lower prices (and more value) to customers in the late, more competitive stages of the product life cycle. In Japan, companies in a range of industries—35 mm cameras, consumer electronics and entertainment equipment, motorcycles, and automobiles—have achieved cost leadership on a worldwide basis. Cost leadership, however, is a sustainable source of competitive advantage only if barriers exist that prevent competitors from achieving the same low costs. In an era of process reengineering and increasing technological improvements in manufacturing, manufacturers constantly leapfrog over one another in pursuit of lower costs. At one time, for example, IBM enjoyed the low-cost advantage in the production of computer printers. Then the Japanese took the same technology and, after reducing production costs and improving product reliability, gained the low-cost advantage. IBM fought back with a highly automated printer plant in North Carolina, where the number of component parts was slashed by more than 50 percent and robots were used to snap many components into place. Despite these changes, IBM ultimately chose to exit the business and the plant was sold.

DIFFERENTIATION When a firm's product delivers unique value because of an actual or perceived uniqueness in a broad market, it is said to have a differentiation advantage. This can be an extremely effective strategy for defending market position and obtaining above-average financial returns; unique products often command premium price. Examples of successful differentiation include Maytag in large home appliances, Nike in athletic shoes, and almost any successful branded consumer product. Among motorcycle manufacturers, Harley-Davidson stands out as the market leader in the US market but must adjust its marketing strategy in various countries depending on the local competition. Figure 9-9[15] shows Harley-Davidson's revenue by region and product line in 2011. Note that 95.7 percent of Harley's sales are in high-income countries, and the remaining 4.3 percent of its sales are to high-income customers in other countries.

Narrow Target Strategies

The preceding discussion of cost leadership and differentiation considered only the impact on broad markets. By contrast, strategies to achieve a narrow-focus advantage target a narrowly defined market or customer. This advantage is based on an ability to create more customer value for a narrowly targeted segment and results from a better

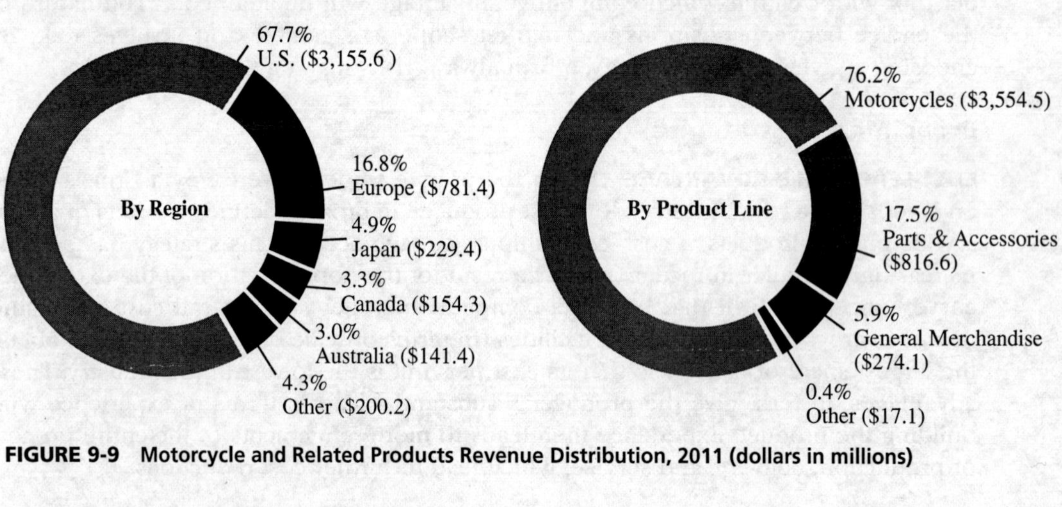

FIGURE 9-9 Motorcycle and Related Products Revenue Distribution, 2011 (dollars in millions)

15 Harley Davidson, 2011 Annual Report, 18.

understanding of customer needs and wants. A narrow-focus strategy can be combined with either cost- or differentiation-advantage strategies. In other words, whereas cost focus means offering a narrow target market low prices, a firm pursuing focused differentiation will offer a narrow target market the perception of product uniqueness at a premium price.

FOCUSED DIFFERENTIATION The German Mittelstand companies have been extremely successful pursuing focused-differentiation strategies backed by a strong export effort. The world of high-end audio equipment offers another example of focused differentiation. A few hundred companies, in the United States and elsewhere, make speakers and amplifiers and related hi-fi gear that cost thousands of dollars per component. The market for high-end audio equipment is global, and offers an opportunity for small, specialized companies to grow while retaining their narrow focus on highly differentiated products.

COST FOCUS The final strategy is cost focus, when a firm's lower-cost position enables it to offer a narrow target market lower prices than the competition. In the shipbuilding industry, for example, Polish and Chinese shipyards offer simple, standard vessel types at low prices that reflect low production costs.[16]

STRATEGIC POSITIONS

Strategic positions that provide competitive advantage are based on the activities that a firm chooses to perform and where it chooses to perform them.[17] From these positions, a firm can deliver unique value to its customers. A position is based on a set of activities that combine to create unique value for a market. Porter has identified three classifications for strategic positions.[18] A firm may choose to develop one or a combination of these positions as the basis of its competitive advantage. The three positions and the related generic strategy are shown in Table 9-1.

Variety-Based Positioning

Variety-based positioning is based on a firm's decision to carry out a limited number of activities related to delivering a limited product or service. This type of position is built by a firm, such as Southwest Airlines, that chooses to deliver value to its

TABLE 9-1 Strategic Positions

Position	Examples	Generic Strategy
1. Variety based Producing a subset of an industry's product or service	Vanguard Bic Jiffy Lube	Cost leadership
2. Customer needs based	IKEA	Differentiation
3. Customer access based Segmenting customers who are accessible in different ways	Carmike Cinemas	Segmentation

[16] Porter, *The Competitive Advantage of Nations*, 39.
[17] Not to be confused with positioning, a marketing action which focuses on efforts to position a product or company in the minds of consumers and customers.
[18] Michael Porter, "What Is Strategy," *Harvard Business Review* (November–December 1996): 65–67.

customers by limiting its product offering (point-to-point service, no baggage transfer service, no seat reservations, no meals, etc.) in order to minimize its prices and maximize its reliability and efficiency. Another example is GIVI, an Italian company that makes luggage for motorcycles. GIVI's product is unique in design, integration, and fabrication. It is premium priced, but given its unique design and quality, it is a value winner in the motorcycle luggage marketplace. The company is successfully expanding from its European variety-based position to a world variety-based position.

Needs-Based Positioning

Needs-based positioning occurs when a company attempts to deliver value to a specific customer segment by carrying out activities to satisfy a comparatively broad set of needs of those customers. This position is well developed by firms such as IKEA, which offers everything the young (or young-at-heart), budget-conscious consumer might need to furnish an apartment or home. Another example of a company with a clear positioning strategy is Purdue Pharma, a world leader in narcotic analgesics for severe pain. Purdue has focused on a need, alleviation of pain, and developed an integrated program for addressing this need. It has developed products that offer more relief with fewer side effects. In addition to focusing on the need, Purdue has created the world's best-trained field sales force to call on doctors and answer their questions on how to effectively use Purdue's products. It has also been able to get its products listed on the formulary of hospitals, managed-care organizations, and government agencies. All of these activities are driven by the company's focus on the need to alleviate pain.

Access-Based Positioning

The ability of a firm to uniquely or preferentially reach a specific market is an access-based position. For example, international management recruitment firms, such as Korn/Ferry International, establish relationships with executives and track them throughout their careers. They know where these executives are located and help their clients get to them. Access consideration can be a critical knockout factor. The first level of all international expansion is about access. Global marketing strategy must deal with barriers to access to national markets that are typically created by governmental authorities. Access to national markets is restricted by regulations, tariffs, distance, and a host of nontariff barriers, which include ways of doing business and openness to new entrants. As a prerequisite to international expansion, firms must develop the ability to carry out the activities that deal with these barriers to access. However, developing the ability to operate in many national markets does not necessarily confer global competitive advantage on a firm. This is not the same as access-based positioning, which refers to the advantage that can be gained by preferential access or control of access to customers. In order to gain competitive advantage in the target market, the entrant must establish a perceived unique value to its customers. If other competitors can gain access or are already established in the market, it is not enough to merely be present in a market.

The annals of international business failures are replete with examples of companies that did not understand this message. The companies who failed believed that all they needed to do was show up. When the market told them that they had a competitive disadvantage, they simply packed up and retreated. Renault did this in the US automobile market in the 1960s, and Federal Express did it again in the express delivery market in Europe in the 1980s. FedEx has regrouped and restrategized its European entry. Renault's setback in the United States in the 1960's sent it back to Europe, where it was a regional/international player in a globalizing industry. Today with its operations in Brazil and its control of Nissan, it is a global player in a global industry. Renault is a good example of a company that did not let an initial setback derail its globalization strategy. With the resources from its success in the European market, it has been able to establish itself as a global company.

Which Position to Take?

All real strategies are a combination of all three positions: every winning strategy is based on a combination of doing the right thing (activity based), meeting a need (needs based), and access. Nevertheless, it is valuable and useful to identify the principal thrust of a strategy: activity, need, or access. Company winners have followed the von Clausewitz maxim: "The best strategy is always to be very strong, first generally then at the decisive point."

COMPETITIVE INNOVATION AND STRATEGIC INTENT

An alternative framework for understanding competitive advantage focuses on competitiveness as a function of the pace at which a company implants new advantages deep within its organization. This framework identifies strategic intent, growing out of ambition and obsession with winning, as the means for achieving competitive advantage. Writing in the *Harvard Business Review,* Hamel and Prahalad note:

> Few competitive advantages are long lasting. Keeping score of existing advantages is not the same as building new advantages. The essence of strategy lies in creating tomorrow's competitive advantages faster than competitors mimic the ones you possess today. An organization's capacity to improve existing skills and learn new ones is the most defensible competitive advantage of all.[19]

This approach is founded on the principles of W. E. Deming, who stressed that a company must commit itself to continuing improvement in order to be a winner in a competitive struggle. For years, Deming's message fell on deaf ears in the United States, whereas the Japanese heeded his message and benefited tremendously. Japan's most prestigious business award is named after him. Finally, however, US manufacturers are starting to respond.

The significance of Hamel and Prahalad's framework becomes evident when comparing Caterpillar and Komatsu. As noted earlier in the chapter, Caterpillar is a classic example of differentiation. The company became the largest manufacturer of earth-moving equipment in the world because it was fanatic about quality and service. Caterpillar is the world's leading manufacturer of construction and mining equipment, diesel and natural gas engines, industrial gas turbines, and diesel-electric locomotives.

The differentiation advantage was achieved with product durability, global spare parts service (including guaranteed parts delivery anywhere in the world within 48 hours), a strong network of loyal dealers, and the lowest total life-cycle cost of ownership in the industry.

Caterpillar has faced a very challenging set of environmental forces. Many of Caterpillar's plants were closed by a lengthy strike in the early 1980s; a worldwide recession at the same time caused a downturn in the construction industry. This hurt companies that were Caterpillar customers. In addition, the strong dollar gave a cost advantage to foreign rivals.

---

[19] Gary Hamel and C. K. Prahalad, "Strategic Intent," *Harvard Business Review* (May–June 1989): 69. See also Gary Hamel and C. K. Prahalad, "The Core Competence of the Corporation," *Harvard Business Review* (May–June 1990): 79–91.

Compounding Caterpillar's problems was a new competitive threat from Japan. Komatsu was the world's number-two construction equipment company and had been competing with Caterpillar in the Japanese market for years. Komatsu's products were generally acknowledged to offer a lower level of quality. The rivalry took on a new dimension after Komatsu adopted the slogan *Maru-C,* meaning "encircle Caterpillar." Emphasizing quality and taking advantage of low labor costs and the strong dollar, Komatsu surpassed Caterpillar in earth-moving equipment sales in Japan and made serious inroads in the United States and other markets. Yet, the company continued to develop new sources of competitive advantage even after it achieved world-class quality. For example, new-product development cycles were shortened, and manufacturing was rationalized. Caterpillar struggled to sustain its competitive advantage because many customers found that Komatsu's combination of quality, durability, and lower price created compelling value. Yet even as recession and a strong yen put new pressure on Komatsu, the company sought new opportunities by diversifying into machine tools and robots.[20]

The Komatsu/Caterpillar saga is just one example of how global competitive battles are shaped by more than the pursuit of generic strategies. Many firms have gained competitive advantage by disadvantaging rivals through competitive innovation, defined by Hamel and Prahalad as "the art of containing competitive risks within manageable proportions." They identify four successful approaches utilized by Japanese competitors: building layers of advantage, searching for loose bricks, changing the rules of engagement, and collaborating.

Layers of Advantage

A company faces less risk in competitive encounters if it has a wide portfolio of advantages. Successful companies steadily build such portfolios by establishing layers of advantage on top of one another. Komatsu is an excellent example of this approach.

In order to build the next layer of advantage, the Japanese spent the 1970s investing heavily in marketing channels and Japanese brand names to gain recognition. This strategy added yet another layer of competitive advantage: the global brand franchise—that is, a global customer base. By the late 1970s, channels and brand awareness were established well enough to support the introduction of new products that could benefit from global marketing—videocassette recorders (VCRs) and photocopy machines, for example. Finally, many companies have invested in regional manufacturing so their products can be differentiated and better adapted to customer needs in individual markets.

The process of building layers illustrates how a company can move along the value chain to strengthen competitive advantage. The Japanese and now the Chinese began with manufacturing (an upstream value activity) and moved on to marketing (a downstream value activity) and then back upstream to basic R&D. All of these sources of competitive advantage represent mutually desirable layers that are accumulated over time.

Changing the Rules

A second approach involves changing the so-called rules of engagement and refusing to play by the rules set by industry leaders. For example, in the mobile phone market, Apple's iPhone and RIM's BlackBerry changed the rules by introducing the

---

[20] Robert L. Rose and Masayoshi Kanabayashi, "Komatsu Throttles Back on Construction Equipment," *The Wall Street Journal,* May 13, 1992: B4.

smartphone, combining the functionality of a mobile phone with Internet-based applications in the case of Apple, and office integration of e-mail, calendar, and Internet connection in the case of RIM. They took the "high ground" of the market, leaving the former leader, Nokia, with the low-price, low-margin, low-profit segment of the global market. Apple did this again when it introduced the iPad, a product that created a new market segment: smaller and lighter than a notebook, larger screen and longer battery life than a phone, available with Wi-Fi only or with cellular network capability.

Collaborating

A final source of competitive advantage is using know-how developed by other companies. Such collaboration may take the form of licensing agreements, joint ventures, or partnerships. One of the legendary licensing agreements of modern business history is Sony's licensing of transistor technology from AT&T's Western Electric subsidiary in the 1950s for $25,000. This agreement gave Sony access to the transistor and allowed the company to become a world leader. Building on its initial successes in the manufacturing and marketing of portable radios, Sony has grown into a superb global marketer whose name is synonymous with a wide assortment of high-quality consumer electronics products.

Today, China leads the world in successful collaboration. In every industry and category, the Chinese are taking advantage of collaboration to increase their competitive advantage. One path of collaboration is the purchase of an entire business: Lenovo's purchase of the IBM ThinkPad business is an example of how one Chinese company acquired an entire business. In 2005, IBM announced the agreement:

> We announced an agreement with Lenovo that creates a powerful new leader in the PC industry. Lenovo will acquire IBM's Personal Computing Division and create a new company that will bring the strengths of IBM's legendary PC business together with those of Lenovo, that will employ 19,000 people and provide the widest range of PC products and technologies to businesses, worldwide. The agreement includes a broad-based, strategic marketing alliance under which Lenovo will receive sales and marketing support from IBM, and Lenovo's products will be integrated into IBM Global Services offerings. Important for all customers of IBM to know: IBM will provide warranty service and support and financing and leasing options for PC products from the new Lenovo. IBM will take an ownership stake of 18.9 percent in Lenovo, and it will purchase PCs for its own employees from Lenovo as well. With this agreement, Lenovo becomes the world's third-largest PC company and a key, strategic IBM business partner. Lenovo will have all of the strengths of IBM's existing PC division, including research, development, design, and manufacturing capabilities.[21]

Hamel and Prahalad continued to refine and develop the concept of strategic intent since it was introduced in their groundbreaking 1989 article. Recently, the authors outlined broad categories of resource leverage that managers can use to achieve their aspirations: concentrating resources on strategic goals via convergence and

[21] See, http://www-03.ibm.com/press/us/en/pressrelease/7450.wss. For 2011 update, see, ww.lenovo.com/ww/lenovo/pdf/report/E_099220120531d.pdf.

focus; accumulating resources more efficiently via extracting and borrowing; complementing one resource with another by blending and balancing; and conserving resources by recycling, co-opting, and shielding.[22]

Hypercompetition?

In his book, Professor Richard D'Aveni suggests that the Porter strategy frameworks fail to adequately address the dynamics of competition in the twenty-first century.[23] D'Aveni notes that in today's business environment, market stability is undermined by short product life cycles, short product design cycles, new technologies, and globalization. The result is an escalation and acceleration of competitive forces. In light of these changes, D'Aveni believes the goal of strategy has shifted from sustaining to disrupting advantages. The limitation of the Porter models, D'Aveni argues, is that they provide a snapshot of competition at a given point in time. In other words, they are static models.

Acknowledging that Hamel and Prahalad broke new ground in recognizing that few advantages are sustainable, D'Aveni aims to build on their work to shape "a truly dynamic approach to the creation and destruction of traditional advantages." D'Aveni uses the term *hypercompetition* to describe a dynamic, competitive world in which no action or advantage can be sustained for long. In such a world, D'Aveni argues, everything changes because of the dynamic maneuvering and strategic interactions by hypercompetitive firms such as Microsoft and Gillette. According to D'Aveni's model, competition unfolds in a series of dynamic strategic interactions in four arenas: cost versus quality, timing and know-how, entry barriers, and deep pockets. Each of these arenas is "continuously destroyed and re-created by the dynamic maneuvering of hypercompetitive firms." According to D'Aveni, the only source of a truly sustainable competitive advantage is a company's ability to manage its dynamic strategic interactions with competitors' movements in a way that maintains a relative position of strength in each of the four arenas. The irony and paradox of this model is that, in order to achieve a sustainable advantage, companies must seek a series of unsustainable advantages! D'Aveni is in agreement with Peter Drucker, who has long counseled that the role of marketing is innovation and the creation of new markets. Innovation begins with abandonment of the old and obsolete. In Drucker's words, "Innovative organizations spend neither time nor resources on defending yesterday. Systematic abandonment of yesterday alone can transfer the resources...for work on the new."[24]

D'Aveni urges managers to reconsider and reevaluate the use of what he believes are old strategic tools and maxims. He warns of the dangers of commitment to a given strategy or course of action. The flexible, unpredictable player may have an advantage over the inflexible, committed opponent. D'Aveni notes that, in hypercompetition, pursuit of generic strategies results in short-term advantage at best. The winning companies are the ones that successfully move up the ladder of escalating competition, not the ones that lock into a fixed position. D'Aveni also is critical of the five-forces model. The best entry barrier, he argues, is maintaining the initiative, not mounting a defensive attempt to exclude new entrants.

---

[22] Gary Hamel and C. K. Prahalad, "Strategy as Stretch and Leverage," *Harvard Business Review* (March– April 1993): 75–84.
[23] Richard D'Aveni, *Hypercompetition: Managing the Dynamics of Strategic Maneuvering* (New York: Free Press, 1994).
[24] Peter Drucker, *On the Profession of Management* (Boston, MA: Harvard Business School Publishing, 1988): 12.

Summary

In this chapter, we focus on factors helping industries and countries achieve competitive advantage. According to Porter's five-forces model, industry competition is a function of the threat of new entrants, the threat of substitutes, the bargaining power of suppliers and buyers, and rivalry among existing competitors. Porter's strategic positions can be used by managers to understand how to combine activities to create unique value, the source of competitive advantage.

Hamel and Prahalad have proposed an alternative framework for pursuing competitive advantage, growing out of a firm's strategic intent and use of competitive innovation. A firm can build layers of advantage, search for loose bricks in a competitor's defensive walls, change the rules of engagement, or collaborate with competitors and utilize their technology and know-how. This framework is not necessarily inconsistent with the positions proposed by Porter. The concepts proposed by Hamel and Prahalad, as well as D'Aveni, stress the dynamic environment. Strategic positions have shorter lives than in the past and may have to be supplemented or abandoned faster than ever before.

Today, many companies are discovering that industry competition is changing from a purely domestic to a global phenomenon. Thus, competitive analysis must also be carried out on a global scale. Global marketers must also have an understanding of national sources of competitive advantage. Porter has described four determinants of national advantage. Factor conditions include human, physical, knowledge, capital, and infrastructure resources. Demand conditions include the composition, size, and growth pattern of home demand. The rate of home-market growth and the means by which a nation's products are pulled into foreign markets also affect demand conditions. The final two determinants are the presence of related and supporting industries and the nature of firm strategy, structure, and rivalry. Porter notes that chance and government also influence a nation's competitive advantage.

Discussion Questions

1. How can a company measure its competitive advantage? How does a firm know if it is gaining or losing competitive advantage?
2. Outline Porter's five-forces model of industry competition. How are the various barriers of entry relevant to global marketing?
3. What are the three strategic positions identified by Michael Porter?
4. Identify three strategic positions. Pick a successful company that you know or have read about, and identify that company's strategic position.
5. Give an example of a company that illustrates each of the four generic strategies that can lead to competitive advantage: overall cost leadership, cost focus, differentiation, and focused differentiation.
6. What is the relationship, if any, between Porter's four generic strategies and his three strategic positions?
7. Briefly describe Hamel and Prahalad's framework for competitive advantage.
8. How can a nation achieve competitive advantage?
9. Do you agree with D'Aveni that no action or strategic advantage can be sustained for long? Why? Why not?

Suggested Readings

Abegglen, James C., and George Stalk, Jr. *Kaisha: The Japanese Corporation*. New York: Basic Books, 1985.

Alexander, Marcus, and Harry Korine. "When You Shouldn't Go Global." *Harvard Business Review* (December 2008): 70–77.

Baghai, Mehrdad, Sven Smit, and Patrick Viguerie. "Is Your Growth Strategy Flying Blind?" *Harvard Business Review* (May 2009): 86–96.

Bungay, Stephen. "How to Make the Most of Your Company's Strategy." *Harvard Business Review* (January–February 2011): 132–140.

Corstjens, Marcel, and Rajiv Lal. "Retail Doesn't Cross Borders: Here's Why and What to Do About It." *Harvard Business Review* (April 2012): 104–111.

D'Aveni, Richard A. *Hypercompetition: Managing the Dynamics of Strategic Maneuvering*. New York: The Free Press, a division of Simon & Schuster, Inc., 2005.

Dyer, Jeffrey H., Prashant Kale, and Harbir Singh. "When to Ally & When to Acquire." *Harvard Business Review* (July–August 2004): 109–115.

Egelhoff, William G. "Great Strategy or Great Strategy Implementation—Two Ways of Competing in Global

Markets." *Sloan Management Review,* 34, no. 2 (Winter 1993): 37–50.

Garsombke, Diane J. "International Competitor Analysis." *Planning Review,* 17, no. 3 (May–June 1989): 42–47.

Ghemawat, Pankaj, and Thomas Hout. "Tomorrow's Global Giants? Not the Usual Suspects." *Harvard Business Review* (November 2008): 80–88.

Ghoshal, Sumantra, and D. Eleanor Westney. "Organizing Competitor Analysis Systems." *Strategic Management Journal,* 12, no. 1 (January 1991): 17–31.

Grove, Andrew S. *Only the Paranoid Survive.* New York: Doubleday, 1996.

Guillen, Mauro F., and Esteban Garcia-Canal. *Emerging Markets Rule: Growth Strategies of the New Global Giants.* New York: McGraw-Hill Books, 2013.

Guillen, Mauro F., and Esteban Garcia-Canal. "Multinationals from Emerging Markets: Making a Virtue out of Necessity." *Knowledge@Wharton*, an online business newsletter of Wharton Business School (December 17, 2012). Accessed December 25, 2012. http://knowledge.wharton.upenn.edu.

Halberstam, David. *The Reckoning.* New York: William Morrow, 1986.

Hamel, Gary, and C. K. Prahalad. "The Core Competence of the Corporation." *Harvard Business Review,* 68 (May–June 1990): 79–93.

Hamel, Gary, and C. K. Prahalad. "Strategic Intent." *Harvard Business Review,* 67 (May–June 1989): 63–76.

Hamel, Gary, and C. K. Prahalad. "Strategy as Stretch and Leverage." *Harvard Business Review,* 71, no. 2 (March–April 1993): 75–85.

Harrigan, Kathryn Rudie. "A World-Class Company Is One Whose Customers Cannot Be Won Away by Competitors: Internationalizing Strategic Management." *Journal of Business Administration,* 21, no. 1-2 (Fall 1992): 251–264.

Isenberg, Daniel J. "The Global Entrepreneur: A New Breed of Entrepreneur Is Thinking Across Borders—From Day One." *Harvard Business Review* (December 2008): 107–111.

Johnson, Bill. "The CEO of Heinz on Powering Growth in Emerging Markets." *Harvard Business Review* (October 2011): 47–50.

Kim, Chan W., and Renee Mauborgne. "How Strategy Shapes Structure: Instead of Letting the Environment Define Your Strategy, Craft a Strategy that Defines Your Environment." *Harvard Business Review* (September 2009): 73–80.

Kotter, John P. "The Big Idea: How the Most Innovative Companies Capitalize on Today's Rapid-Fire Strategic Challenges—and Still Make Their Numbers." *Harvard Business Review* (November 2012): 44–58.

Moore, Geoffrey A. *Crossing the Chasm: Marketing and Selling Technology Products to Mainstream Customers.* New York: HarperBusiness, 1991.

Moore, Geoffrey A. *Inside the Tornado: Marketing Strategies from Silicon Valley's Cutting Edge.* New York: HarperBusiness, 1995.

Moore, James F. *The Death of Competition: Leadership and Strategy in the Age of Business Ecosystems.* New York: HarperBusiness, 1996.

Ohmae, Kenichi. *Triad Power.* New York: Free Press, 1985.

Pearson, Andrall E. "Corporate Redemption and the Seven Deadly Sins." *Harvard Business Review,* 70, no. 3 (May–June 1992): 65–75.

Perkins, Anne G. "Global Competition: Confront Your Rivals on Their Home Turf." *Harvard Business Review,* 71, no. 3 (May–June 1993): 10.

Peters, Tom. "Rethinking Scale." *California Management Review,* 35, no. 1 (Fall 1992): 7–29.

Porter, Michael E. *Competition in Global Industries.* Boston: Harvard Business School Press, 1986.

Porter, Michael E. *Competitive Advantage: Creating and Sustaining Superior Performance.* New York: Free Press, 1985.

Porter, Michael E. *The Competitive Advantage of Nations.* New York: Free Press, 1990.

Porter, Michael E. *Competitive Strategy.* New York: Free Press, 1980.

Porter, Michael E. "What Is Strategy?" *Harvard Business Review* (November–December 1996): 60–78.

Rugman, Alan M., and Alain Verbeke. "Foreign Subsidiaries and Multinational Strategic Management: An Extension and Correction of Porter's Single Diamond Framework." *Management International Review,* 33, no. 2 (Special Issue 1993/2): 71–84.

Schoemaker, Paul J. H. "How to Link Strategic Vision to Core Capabilities." *Sloan Management Review,* 34, no. 1 (Fall 1992): 67–81.

Timmor, Yaron, Samuel Rabino, and Jehiel Zif. "Defending a Domestic Position Against Global Entries." *Journal of Global Marketing*, 22, no. 4 (2009): 251–265.

Von Ghyczy, Tiha, Bolko von Oetinger, and Christopher Bassford, eds. *Clausewitz On Strategy.* New York: John Wiley & Sons, Inc./A publication of the Strategy Institute of The Boston Consulting Group, 2001.

Williams, Jeffrey R. "How Sustainable Is Your Competitive Advantage?" *California Management Review,* 34, no. 3 (Spring 1992): 29–51.

Womack, James P., Daniel T. Jones, and Daniel Roos. *The Machine That Changed the World.* New York: HarperCollins, 1990.

Yip, George S. *Total Global Strategy: Managing for Worldwide Competitive Advantage.* Upper Saddle River, NJ: Prentice Hall, 1995.

Zhang, Cheng, Peijian Song, and Zhe Qu. "Competitive Action in the Diffusion of Internet Technology Products in Emerging Markets: Implications for Global Marketing Managers." *Journal of International Marketing,* 19, no. 4 (December 2011).

Zhang, Haisu, Chengli Shu, Xu Jiang, and Alan J. Malter. "Managing Knowledge for Innovation: The Role of Cooperation, Competition, and Alliance Nationality." *Journal of International Marketing,* 18, no. 4 (December 2010): 74–94.

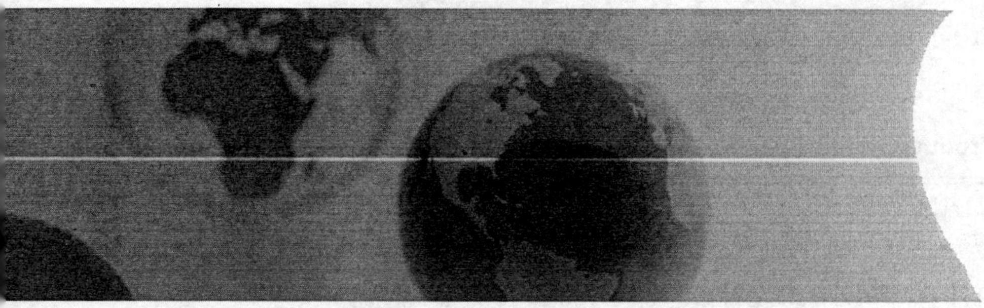

CHAPTER 10

Product Decisions

The prospects for American car manufacturers in Europe would appear to be good if they will meet the conditions and requirements of these various countries, but to attempt to do so on the lines on which business is done in America would make it a fruitless task.

—LAMES COUZENS, 1907 *Officer of the Ford Motor Company*

The fact is that all US midsize cars contain the same parts count, the same engine and transmission technology, the same safety equipment, the same ABS brakes and traction control, the same or similar seats and interiors—and many of these parts even come from the same suppliers. A Chevrolet Malibu's material cost is within a couple percent of that of a BMW 3-Series.[1]

—BOB LUTZ, 2011–*Former Executive With GM, BMW, Ford, and Chrysler*

None. It's not the consumers' job to know what they want.

—STEVE JOBS, 1955–2011, *(When asked about what market research went into the iPad.)*

Learning Objectives

1. Explain basic product concepts (299–304).
2. Discuss the general strategies for product positioning (306–307).
3. Identify the factors that influence product saturation, design, and image (308–311).
4. Describe five strategic alternatives for global product positioning (312–316).
5. Discuss the process of new product development (317–318).

[1] Mr. Lutz held senior leadership positions at GM, BMW, Ford, and Chrysler over the course of a 47-year career. From Bob Lutz, *Car Guys vs. Bean Counters: The Battle for the Soul of American Business* (Penguin Group, 2011).

BOX 10-1

Side Bar: Product Standardization at KFC

Prof Theodor Levitt, way back in 1983, advised the American companies not to be too 'local' in foreign country markets and thereby losing economics of scale through his seminal article "the globalisation of market ". When this article appeared in the Harvard Business Review, it raised a hue and cry in the international business circuit as American multinationals were prone to adaptation of business models in accordance with local taste, choice and preferences. Multinationals used to confine themselves to the respective country specific environment and miss the scale economics due to localization. According to Prof Levitt, economies of scale should have provided them the much needed cost advantages in the international business that could come from attaining bigger size, output, or standardised scale of operation resulting in decreasing the cost per unit of output as fixed costs of operation gets spread out over more units of outputs produced on a global basis. Behaving and acting as a 'local' in every country, reduced the scale of operation, hence found disadvantageous for attaining product pricing competitiveness. When Prof Levitt's sermon came during 1983, the American business of Colonel Sanders was already present across 55 different countries with 5,800 KFC outlets. Some of the important countries where KFC was present before 1983, with year of entry are as mentioned in the Table 10-1.

Even a cursory look at the table above suggests that up to 1983, KFC selected the entry in a country's market with careful consideration. It seemed the international business strategists at KFC was not in a mood to enter the countries where its business model required to be changed more than cursory level while doing business there. All the countries were dominantly non vegetarian and had strong cultural preference for Chicken based products which had been the forte of KFC. The substantial level of standardised preference of products across 55 country markets provided a wonderful opportunity for the company to enjoy the economics of scale in operation, sourcing, marketing etc. So when Prof Levitt's sermon came, the company did not feel disturbed. But things started going haywire after entering into the world's top most populous countries like China and India during the post-Levitt era. Both the countries have their strong cultural preferences compelling enough to force KFC for effecting change in its age old and successfully testing business model. After the entry in China it was a battle like situation between the existing business model of KFC and cultural preferences of Chinese customers. It soon became clear that cultural preferences were wining and the age old business model KFC was succumbing to abrupt

TABLE 10-1 KFC's International Markets Prior 1983

Continents	Countries with years of entry
Africa	South Africa (1971)
Asia	Indonesia (1979), Japan (1970), Malaysia (1973), Philippines (1967), Singapore (1977),
Caribbean and South America	Argentina (1979), Bahamas (1967),Barbados (1971), Bermuda (1975), Costa Rica (1970), Ecuador (1975), Jamaica (1964), Panama (1969), Peru (1981), Puerto Rico (1967), Trinidad and Tobago (1973), Venezuela (1977)
Europe	Germany (1963), Iceland (1980), Ireland (1971), Spain (1970), Netherland (1972), United Kingdom (1965), Czech Republic (1994)
Middle East	Bahrain (1973), Egypt (1973), Jordon (1973), Kuwait (1973), Lebanon (1973), Omman (1973), Qatar (1976), Saudi Arabia (1980), UAE (1975)
North America	Canada (1953), Mexico (1963)

Adapted from KFC India's official website, https://online.kfc.co.in/.

changes disturbing the prevailing scale economics situation of the company. KFC started offering traditional dishes like spicy chicken, rice dishes, egg tarts, fried dough sticks, soy milk drinks, fish and shrimp burgers and even extremely local dishes like Congee. Restaurants were given more floor space to allure Chinese customers for organising large gatherings in occasions. KFC went on adding local items which eventually made total products offered for Chinese customers almost double the items it offered in US. The Indian story was not much different than that of China. KFC went on altering its standard menu to accommodate localization and introduced spicier versions of products and also Chicken Curry to suit Indian preferences. Very soon it marked a huge deviation from its global nature by introducing Indianised vegetarian items like fried vegetable strips and burger patties with potato. It went to the extreme of launching a separate blue line dining which essentially was for the strict vegetarian people who do not even touch the food if those are cooked in the same kitchen space as that of non-vegetarian. As the KFC website put it "at KFC we maintain stringent standards to ensure that vegetarian and non-vegetarian offerings at our store are prepared separately. Everything from the oil, utensils, and ingredients to even the staff is segregated. We understand and respect the sentiments and beliefs of our vegetarian customers and make sure we meet their expectations".

It seems KFC strategist decided to go against Prof Levitt's sermon for successful internationalisation which he placed for American international businesses at least for these two countries. These two countries, India and China, together have 36.41% of the total world population and so it is seemingly difficult for KFC to go against cultural preferences of the population. It is quite a dilemma, as to which one will be beneficial for KFC; to go against Levitt or against cultural preferences?

INTRODUCTION

The focus of this chapter is the product, probably the most crucial element of a marketing program. To a very important degree, a company's products define its business. Every aspect of the enterprise—including pricing, communication, and distribution policies—must fit the product. A firm's customers and competitors are determined by the products it offers. Research and development (R&D) requirements will depend in part on the technologies of a company's products and in part—as is clear from the Swatch example—on the vision of its managers and executives. The challenge facing a company with global horizons is to develop product policies and strategies that are sensitive to market needs, competition, and company resources on a global scale. Product policy must strike a balance between the payoff from adapting products to local market preferences and the competitive advantages that come from concentrating company resources on a limited number of standardized products.

This chapter examines the major dimensions of global product decisions. First, basic product concepts are explored. The diversity of preferences and needs in global markets is then underlined by an examination of product saturation levels. Product design criteria are identified and attitudes toward foreign products are explored. The next section outlines strategic alternatives available to global marketers. Finally, new product issues in global marketing are discussed.

BASIC CONCEPTS

We begin our introduction to global product decisions by briefly reviewing product concepts typically covered in a basic marketing course. All basic product concepts are fully applicable to global marketing. Additional concepts that apply specifically to global marketing are also discussed in this chapter.

Products: Definition and Classification

What is a product? On the *surface*, this seems like a simple question with an obvious answer. A product can be defined in terms of its tangible, physical attributes—such things as weight, dimensions, and materials. Thus, an automobile could be defined as 3,000 pounds of metal or plastic, measuring 483 cm (190") long, 190 cm (75") wide, and 150 cm (59") high. However, any description limited to physical attributes gives an incomplete account of the benefits a product provides. At a minimum, car buyers expect an automobile to provide safe, comfortable transportation, which derive from physical features such as air bags and adjustable seats. However, marketers cannot ignore status, mystique, and other intangible product attributes that a particular model of automobile may provide. Indeed, major segments of the auto market are developed around these intangible attributes.

Similarly, Harley-Davidson riders get much more than basic transportation from their beloved "hogs." The Harley is a recreational product: even people who ride their Harleys to work are riding because it is a form of recreation. The motorcycle in low-income countries is a form of transportation. Clearly, there is a literal world of difference between the need served by a motorcycle to the recreational rider and the rider who is using the motorcycle as a form of transportation. Some companies like Harley are focused on the recreational rider whereas others, like Honda, sell to recreational riders and to the basic transportation market. Harley, however, focuses on a broad spectrum of needs: needs for status, fun, and affiliation with the Harley legend, history, and Harley riders both past and present. Harley is a luxury brand: expensive, exclusive, and special. Harley-Davidson is selling a social and personal experience. The Harley is an American bike that celebrates the romance, adventure, and camaraderie of travel. When you buy a Harley, you are eligible to become a member of the Harley Owners Group (HOG). As a HOG member, you will meet other Harley owners and share the fun and pleasure of motorcycling with others.

Honda is an example of an activity-based strategy company. If you can power it with a motor, Honda will make it, from 50 to 5000cc, from a few hundred to 75,000 dollars, from the transportation market in the developing world to the recreation market in any country.

A *product*, then, can be defined as a collection of physical, psychological, service, and symbolic attributes that collectively yield satisfaction, or benefits, to a buyer or user. It is important to note that, while most people think of a tangible object when they hear the word "product," services such as dry cleaning and financial advice or experiences such as a vacation or a concert are also included in this definition.

A number of frameworks for classifying products have been developed. A frequently used classification is based on users and distinguishes between consumer and industrial goods. Both types of goods, in turn, can be further classified on the basis of other criteria, such as how they are purchased (convenience, preference, shopping, and specialty goods) and their life span (durable, nondurable, and disposable). These and other classification frameworks developed for domestic marketing are fully applicable to global marketing. See Table 10-2 for a summary of product categorization frameworks.

Product Concept

It is useful to break a product in to different layers or components to understand it more correctly from the marketing point of view. Primarily, the marketer's wish is to believe that there are three components or layers constituting a product. They are, core component, packaging component and support service component. A number of product features, both tangible and intangible, reside in three different products

TABLE 10-2 Product Categorization Frameworks

User	Purchase Mode	Life Span	Customer Value[2]
Industrial products	Convenience products	Durable goods	Core benefit
Consumer products	Preference products	Nondurable goods	Basic product
	Shopping products	Disposable goods	Expected product
	Specialty products		Augmented product
			Potential product

components/layers. Each of these components or layers is meant to satisfy different requirements of the target customers. The features loaded in each components, tangible and intangible, are expected to provide the desired benefits to the consumers. The tangible product features can be seen as well as measured by the consumers, while the intangible ones cannot be seen or measured but can be felt only by the customers. The marketers purposefully develop both tangibles and intangibles features in each components of product so as to create customer value better than the competitors.

CORE COMPONENT It is the originating layer or building block of a product. The features, a part of this component, provide the basic benefit to the consumers. For example, in case of an automobile, the product's features that belong to the core component are product platform, design features, basic functional features etc.

PACKAGING COMPONENT The packaging component is the second layer loaded on the core layer to make the product more meaningful and relevant to the target consumers. When the second layer is loaded, the customer not only gets additional product benefits but it becomes more clearly distinguishable from the other competitive products. For example, in case of an automobile, different tangible and intangible features are loaded in this component to make the product unique. Product features like brand name of the automobile, trademark, tag lines, slogan, price, quality descriptions, style, etc are part of the packaging component.

SUPPORT SERVICE COMPONENT It is the third and outer most layer of the product. Through addition of this third layer, the marketer still adds more customer value to the product by distinguishing it from the other competitive product in the market. For example, in the support service component of an automobile, the marketers add features like delivery clauses, warranty period, spare parts availability status, maintenance instructions etc. and thereby, desire to distinguish the product from others.

Products: Local, National, International, and Global

Many global companies find that, as a result of expanding existing businesses or acquiring a new business, they have products in a single product category for sale in a single national market. For example, Kraft Foods at one time found itself in the chewing gum business in France, the ice cream business in Brazil, and the pasta business in Italy. Although each of these unrelated businesses was, in isolation, quite profitable, the scale of each was too small to justify heavy expenditures on R&D, let alone marketing, production, and financial management from international headquarters. An important question regarding any product is whether it has the potential for expansion into other markets. The answer will depend on the company's goals and objectives and on perceptions of both global and regional opportunities.

[2] Phllip Kotler and Kevin Lane Keller, *Marketing Management*, 12 ed. (2006): 372.

Managers run the risk of committing two types of errors regarding product decisions in global marketing. One error is to fall victim to the "not invented here" (NIH) syndrome, ignoring product decisions made by subsidiary or affiliate managers. Managers who behave in this way are essentially abandoning any effort to leverage product policy outside the home-country market. The second error has been to impose product decision policy on all affiliate companies on the assumption that what is right for customers in the home market must also be right for customers everywhere. German carmaker Volkswagen AG learned the consequences of this latter error; VW saw its position in the US import market erode from leader to also-ran between the 1960s and the 1980s. One industry observer in the 1980s summed up the company's main mistake this way: "Up to now, Volkswagen has thought that what works in Germany should work in the United States." In 1984, the company closed it's US assembly operations and focused on the rest of the world. Subsequently, Volkswagen opened a design studio in Los Angeles, hoping to become better attuned to the tastes of global (including American) car buyers. Today, Volkswagen is creating global cars for the global market on basic platforms. It continues to be a strong competitor in Germany and the EU and is now successfully positioned as a global brand.

The three product categories in the local-to-global continuum—national, international, and global—are described in the following section.

LOCAL PRODUCTS A local product is available in a portion of a national market. In the United States, the term regional product is synonymous with local product. These products may be new products that a company is introducing using a roll-out strategy or a product that is distributed exclusively in that region. Originally, Cape Cod Potato Chips was a local product in the New England market. The company was later purchased by Frito-Lay and distribution was expanded to other regions of the United States and then globally.

A national product is offered in a single national market. Sometimes national products appear when a global company caters to the needs and preferences of particular country markets. For example, Coca-Cola developed a noncarbonated, ginseng-flavored beverage for sale only in Japan and a yellow, carbonated drink called Pasturina to compete with Inca Cola, Peru's favorite soft drink. After years of failing to dislodge Inca Cola, Coke followed the old strategic maxim, "if you can't beat them, buy them," and acquired Inca Cola. KFC sells noodles and rice only at its Chinese stores. Similarly, Sony and other Japanese consumer electronics companies produce a variety of products that are not sold outside of Japan. Kraft, the global foods company, sells the quintessentially Australian yeast spread Vegemite predominantly in its home country. It seems that consumers outside Australia and New Zealand have trouble adjusting to its peculiar taste.

Such examples notwithstanding, there are several reasons why national products—even those that are quite profitable—may represent a substantial opportunity cost to a company. First, the existence of a single national business does not provide an opportunity to develop and utilize global leverage from headquarters in marketing, R&D, and production. Second, the local product does not allow for the transfer and application of experience gained in one market to other markets. One of the major tools available to the multicountry marketer is comparative analysis. By definition, single-country marketers cannot avail themselves of this tool. A third shortcoming of single-country product is the lack of transferability of managerial expertise acquired in the single-product area. Managers who gain experience with a local product can utilize their product experience only in the one market in which the product is sold. Similarly, any manager coming from outside the market in which the single product is sold will lack experience in the single-product business. For these reasons, purely local products should generally be viewed as less attractive than products with international or global potential.

INTERNATIONAL PRODUCTS International products are offered in multinational, regional markets. The classic international product is the Euro product, offered throughout Europe but not in the rest of the world. The Renault was, for many years, a Euro product. When Renault entered the Brazilian market, it became a multiregional company. More recently, Renault invested in Nissan and took control of the company. The combination of Renault in Europe and Latin America, and Nissan in Asia, the Americas, Europe, the Middle East, and Africa, has catapulted Renault from a multiregional to a global company. Renault is an example of how a company that maintains a strong brand and financial position in a regional market (Europe) can move overnight, through investment and or acquisition, to a global position.

GLOBAL PRODUCTS AND GLOBAL BRANDS Global products are offered in global markets. A truly global product is offered in every world region and in countries at every stage of development. Some global products were designed to meet the needs of a global market; others were designed to meet the needs of a national market but also, happily, meet the needs of a global market.

Note that a product is not a brand. For example, laptop or tablet computers, mobile phones, and portable personal sound systems are all categories of global products; Apple, Nokia and Sony are global brands. A global brand, like a national or international brand, is a symbol about which customers have beliefs or perceptions. Many companies, including Sony, make personal sound players. Sony created the category more than 30 years ago, when it introduced the Walkman. Today, portable personal sound is a product category dominated by Apple with its iPod, iPhone, and iPad products. Sony created the category but was unable to retain its leadership postion and first-mover advantage. Creating the category does not mean you own the category. "Ownership" requires constant innovation—something Apple has shown an ability to excel at repeatedly.

Global brands are created by marketers and their globe-spanning organizations; a global brand is a promise and, if successfully managed, an umbrella for introducing new products. Although Sony is a global brand, it also markets a number of local products, unlike Apple. Apple's focus on global products has allowed it to completely leapfrog and overtake Sony in the product categories where they directly compete. Part of the reason for this is that Apple redefined or invested in many of the categories where they are head-to-head competitors and has maintained leadership through constant innovation and improvement of their category offering. The irony of this is the Japanese invented constant improvement as a competitive strategy.

Figure 10-1 identifies the qualities of a global brand. A global brand has the same name in every market. The name may be the same word, as is the case of Coke, Sony, BMW, Harley-Davidson, or Samsung, to name a few. Or it may be a name with the same meaning in different languages, as is true of Unilever's Snuggle (United States) fabric softener, which carries a cuddly teddy bear logo and the local translation of a meaning identical or similar to the meaning of "snuggle" in American English. A global brand has a similar image, similar positioning, and is guided by the same strategic principles. However, the marketing mix for a global brand may vary from country to country. That means that the product, price, promotion, and place (channels of distribution) may vary from country to country. Indeed, if one tracks the examples—Coke, Sony, Mercedes, and Avon—one will indeed find that the marketing mix for these products varies from country to country. Mercedes, which is exclusively a luxury car in the United States, is also a strong competitor in the taxi market in Europe. Avon,

- Guided by the same strategic principles
- Same name, similar image
- Similar positioning
- Marketing mix may vary
  - Product
  - Price
  - Promotion
  - Place

Examples: Apple, Google, Starbucks, Coke, Disney, BMW, Mercedes

FIGURE 10-1 Global Brand Characteristics

which is a premium-priced and packaged cosmetic line in Japan, is popularly priced in the rest of the world. In spite of these variations in marketing mix, each of these products is a world or global brand.

A global product differs from a global brand in one important respect: it does not carry the same name and image from country to country. Like the global brand, however, it is guided by the same strategic principles, is similarly positioned, and may have a marketing mix that varies from country to country. Whenever a company finds itself with global products, it faces an issue: should the global product be turned into a global brand? This requires that the name and image of the product be standardized. Faced with the global success of its noncomputer products, such as the iPod, Apple Computer Inc. dropped the "Computer" and changed its name to Apple to better reflect its transformation from computers to products and product experiences,

BOX 10-2

Side Bar: Product Advantage is a Must

Toyota's popular hybrid car, Prius, has earned it not only new customers, but also an excellent status as a maker of environmentally friendly and fuel-efficient vehicles. Given the rising importance of having a green reputation, Toyota, which as of October 2012 had sold 2.8 million Prius cars worldwide, is seeing its gas-electric hybrid deliver value that goes well beyond direct sales. What's more, the carmaker's stellar eco-image, cultivated by the popular Prius, is shifting consumers' perceptions towards all Toyota models. "Toyota's fame for hybrids allows consumers to believe every one of its vehicles is the most fuel-efficient in its category—even if it isn't," according to marketing consultant Dan Gorrell.

Such competitive edge, generated by just one product, is not lost on Toyota's competitors. "We didn't appreciate the image value of hybrids," says GM's R&D boss, Larry Burns. "We missed that." The Prius, first introduced in Japan in 1997, did not seem to pose any threat to American carmakers, who were raking in high profits at the time from the sales of oversized trucks and SUVs. But, as gas prices began to rise and "green" practices gained acceptance and approval from the public, Toyota's product was well positioned to take advantage of the new trend. Now, other automakers are racing to catch up in a product category where Toyota's vision, innovation, and timing paid off handsomely.

Sources: David Kiley, "How the Hybrid Race Went to the Swift," *BusinessWeek,* January 29, 2007: 58; Toyota Motor Corporation, Annual Report, 2012.

including portable personal sound (the iPod), smartphones (the iPhone), tablets (the iPad), and retail stores.

Dilemma for Product Standardisation vs. Adaptation

Considering the unevenness in terms of marketing environment, it is difficult to offer a single standardised product in all the countries of the world. Considering this difficulty, international marketers are resorting to adaptation for their products in different country markets to create better customer value. For example, Harry Potter book, written by legendary British author J. K. Rowling, had to resort to adaptation of the book based on the country specific requirements. For USA, the writer had to change the title of the first novel, Harry Potter and the Philosopher's Stone to Harry Potter and the Sorcerer's Stone as "Sorcerer" sounded exciting to the American children while "Philosopher" sounded boring. The book had to be translated in to more than 68 languages from original English language to clock the world-wide sales figure of 450 million copies by April 2011. The marketers behind Harry Potter books had to change the name of its central character from Harry Potter to 'Hali Bote' to suite the Mandarin language pronunciation in China. In addition, since wizardry is not legally allowed to be practiced in China so the marketer of the book had to change the original background of the books to 'magic' for the China market. Chinese adaptation of the book had changed the original books' quirky names in to more acceptable ones to make it easy to be understood by the Mandarin speaking children. Many translations were effected to carry meanings that resonate well in China's rich idiomatic language.The book of Harry Potter as a product had to, therefore, undergo several adaptations for different country market. Distribution policy of the book depended more on digital format in China to make the books quickly available for the Chinese children. The adaptations were effected in all the three components viz. core component, packaging component and support service component. The adaptation of the original wizardry back ground of Harry Potter book in to magic background was effected in the core component. The adaptation of name to Mandarin friendly one, style of presentation etc for China were effected in the packaging component. The change in distribution policy of the books to reduce the time to reach the reader was an example of adaptation in the support service component. Product adaptation provides the marketers benefits in the following three important ways.

- All the mandatory and discretionary requirements can be addressed leading to better marketability in the foreign markets.
- The product becomes local and hence no clash with culture and local norms.
- In some country markets, the product may avoid ethnocentric feelings of the consumers.

However, in contrast, the product standardisation has its own advantages as stated below:

- Cost associated with adaptation can be very high particularly when adaptation is required in the core component. Also adapting a product differently for different countries gives rise to management problems.
- Global need can be addressed very fast with standardised product. Also the company can step in for developing a global brand.
- Pricing advantage can be achieved because of standardisation. As the company covers pretty large markets with identical product so the fixed cost being the same the total cost per unit is expected to come down.
- Use of technology becomes more feasible as the company is producing for the world.

PRODUCT POSITIONING

Product positioning is a communications strategy based on the notion of mental "space." Positioning refers to the act of locating a brand in customers' minds over and against other products in terms of product attributes and benefits that the brand does and does not offer. The word, first formally used in 1969 by Ries and Trout in an article that appeared in *Industrial Marketing*, describes a strategy for "staking out turf" or "filling a slot" in the mind of target customers. Several general strategies have been suggested for positioning products: positioning by attribute or benefit, quality/price, use or application, and use/user. Two additional strategies, high-tech and high-touch, have been suggested for global products.

Attribute or Benefit

A frequently used positioning strategy exploits a particular product attribute, benefit, or feature. In global marketing, the fact that a product is imported can itself represent a benefit positioning. Economy, reliability, and durability are other frequently used attribute/benefit positions. Volvo automobiles are known for solid construction that offer safety in the event of a crash. In the ongoing credit card wars, VISA's advertising focuses on the benefit of worldwide merchant acceptance.

Quality/Price

This strategy can be thought of in terms of a continuum from high fashion/quality and high price to good value (rather than low quality) at a low price. The American Express Card, for example, has traditionally been positioned as an upscale card whose prestige and service (enhanced billing for example) justifies higher annual fees than VISA or MasterCard. The CostCo American Express Card is at the other end of the continuum: no annual fee and a cash rebate to cardholders each year.

Marketers of imported vodkas such as Absolut, Finlandia, and Stolichnaya Cristall have successfully positioned their brands as premium products at double the price of "ordinary" vodka. For example, ads for Stolichnaya Russian vodka hail it as "the most distinctive vodka in the world." Vodkas also play up their national origins, demonstrating how price/quality can also be used in conjunction with other positions such as benefit/attribute. Marketers sometimes use the phrase *transformation advertising* to describe advertising that seeks to change the experience of buying and using a product—in other words, the product benefit. Presumably, the experience of buying and consuming Stolichnaya Cristall is a higher-quality experience than that of, say, buying and consuming a bar brand such as Popov.

Use/User

Positioning can also be achieved by describing how a product is used or associating a product with a similar user or class of users in every market. For example, Benetton uses the same positioning for its clothing when it targets the global youth market. Honda used the slogan "You meet the nicest people on a Honda" to attract a new segment of first-time American motorcycle buyers in the 1960s. More recently, Harley-Davidson has successfully broadened its image to reach a new class of motorcycle enthusiast: aging baby boomer professionals who wanted to adopt an outlaw persona on weekends. An ad for the upscale Range Rover showing the sports-utility vehicle on a mountaintop has the headline, "The real reason many CEOs are unavailable for comment."

Can global positioning work for all products? One study suggests that global positioning is most effective for product categories that approach either end of a "high-touch/high-tech" continuum. Both ends of the continuum are characterized by high levels of customer involvement and by a shared language among consumers.

High-Tech Positioning

Personal computers, video, smartphones, tablets, and automobiles are product categories for which high-tech positioning has proven effective. Such products are frequently purchased on the basis of physical product features, although image may also be important. Buyers typically already possess—or wish to acquire—considerable technical information. High-tech products may be divided into three categories: technical products, special interest products, and demonstrable products.

Computers, chemicals, tires, and financial services are technical products in the sense that buyers have specialized needs. Some require a great deal of product information, and share a common language. Others require the opposite: no technical information. Marketing communications for high-tech products should be informative and emphasize features and capabilities. The amount of technical information included should be tailored to the target market segment information preference.

Special-interest products also are characterized by a shared experience and high involvement among users, although they are less technical and more leisure or recreation oriented. Again, the common language and symbols associated with such products can transcend language and cultural barriers. Fuji bicycles, Adidas and Nike sports equipment, Canon cameras, and video game players and games are examples of successful global special-interest products.

High-Touch Positioning

Marketing of high-touch products requires less emphasis on specialized information and more emphasis on image.There are three categories of high-touch products: products that solve a common problem, global-village products, and products with a universal theme.

At the other end of the price spectrum from high-tech, high-touch products that can solve a problem often provide benefits linked to "life's little moments." Ads that show friends talking over a cup of coffee in a café or quenching thirst with a soft drink during a day at the beach put the product at the center of everyday life and communicate the benefit offered in a way that is understood worldwide. Upscale fragrances and designer fashions are examples of products whose positioning is strongly cosmopolitan in nature. Fragrances and fashions have traveled as a result of growing worldwide interest in high-quality, highly visible, high-priced products that often enhance social status.

Marketing of high-touch products requires less emphasis on specialized information and more emphasis on image. Like high-tech products, however, high-touch categories are highly involving for consumers. Buyers of high-touch products also share a common language and set of symbols relating to themes of wealth, materialism, and romance.

Products may have a global appeal by virtue of their country of origin. The Americanness of Levi's and Harley-Davidson enhances their appeal to cosmopolitans around the world and offers opportunities for benefit positioning. In consumer electronics, Apple is a name synonymous with innovation and "cool"; in automobiles, Mercedes, BMW, Audi, and Volkswagens are the embodiment of legendary German engineering.

Some products can be positioned in more than one way, within either the high-tech or high-touch poles of the continuum. A sophisticated camera, for example, could simultaneously be classified as technical and special interest. Other products may also be positioned in a bipolar fashion, that is, as both high-tech and high-touch. For example, Bang & Olufsen consumer electronics products, by virtue of their design elegance, are perceived as both high-tech and high-touch.

Types of Adaptation

CONVENIENCE ADAPTATION American likes to drive a car with a coffee cup and hence it is not a bad idea to put a coffee cup holder in a car. If an automobile company manufactures automobile with built in coffee cup then it is a convenience adaptation. The conveyance adaptations are all directed towards increasing users' convenience while using the product/products. These types of adaptations are mostly discretionary in nature.

ECONOMIC ADAPTATION These types of adaptations are basically executed on the products because of economic condition prevailing in the targeted country market. In high economic growth countries the products are suitably upgraded while in poor countries they are stripped off. Suzuki motor company would make all attempts to modify the auto engines to make them fuel efficient in India. But the same is not true in case of rich countries where the adaptations are mostly to increase driving comforts in rich countries.

SOCIAL SIGNIFICANCE ADAPTATION In China, the American auto mobile majors are adapting their products as per social significance. In China, people prefer to purchase longer vehicle as it would provide them social significance. Ford Motor Company, therefore, adapted their vehicles by increasing the length of the automobiles exclusively to be marketed in China. These adaptations are also very much discretionary in nature.

AESTHETIC ADAPTATION These types of adaptations are executed on the products to increase their aesthetic appeal. Aesthetic indicates towards a sense of appreciating beauty. Japanese are supposed to have a high degree of aesthetic sense. Japanese may like to have green colour beer in the morning and champagne colour beer in the evening. A beer company to create marketing appeal may like to adapt its offering according to the prevailing aesthetic sense of the people living in the country. This adaptation is totally discretionary.

MANDATORY ADAPTATION These adaptations are driven by the prevailing legal standards. About 76 countries and territories do not allow left hand drive automobiles and hence the auto companies are legally bounded to sell modified automobiles there. European countries provide mandatory instructions related to packaging of products which are required to be followed by the marketers while marketing products.

PRODUCT SATURATION LEVELS IN GLOBAL MARKETS

Many factors determine a product's market potential. In general, product saturation levels, or the percentage of potential buyers or households who own a particular product, increase as national income per capita increases. However, for markets in which income is sufficient to enable consumers to buy a particular product, other factors must be considered. For example, the sale of air conditioners is explained by income and climate. In a low-income country, many people cannot afford an air conditioner no matter how hot it is. Affluent people in a northern climate can easily afford an air conditioner but have no need for one.

According to Datamonitor,[3] many more high-definition TV sets (HDTV) are sold in the United States compared to Europe. On first glance, this may indicate to marketers of HDTV sets that Europe presents a great untapped market for them. However, the market may not seem nearly as attractive when it is considered that, unlike the United States, where 87 percent of households are serviced by a cable operator that offers HD services, very few European cable operators offer it. In addition, because of the different TV broadcast technologies in the two markets, the improvement in the picture quality with HD programming is not nearly as noticeable in Europe as it is in the United States. Given these factors, it clear why the demand for HDTV in Europe is not that high.

The existence of wide disparities in the demand for a product from one market to the next can be a good indication of the possible potential for that product in the low-saturation-level market. However, a company that is introducing a product to a new market often has to make a decision: should it change the product to make it more appealing to that market or should it try to change the market's view of the product? The gourmet coffee company Starbucks is certainly betting on the latter strategy in China. Faced with the fact that the majority of China's population drinks tea as a taste preference and a centuries-old tradition, Starbucks' coffee products and culture are not things that Chinese flock to naturally. Therefore, the company has targeted the Chuppies—the young, brand- and status-conscious professional class open to Western culture and products—and has begun introducing them to coffee and the intricacies of coffee house culture. From stocking its stores with educational brochures to holding frequent tasting sessions and passing out free samples, Starbucks is on a mission to change Chinese tastes from tea to coffee. Nevertheless, the company has also adapted in order to gain market share. It has modified its stores to offer more food and seating and has altered its product offerings to include green tea cheesecake and Chinese moon cakes during the Mid-Autumn festival. This give-and-take approach seems to be paying off. Despite a slow start, Starbucks is continuing its expansion in China.[4]

Every company should have an active global scanning system to identify potential market opportunities based on demand disparities.

PRODUCT DESIGN CONSIDERATIONS

Product design is a key factor in determining success in global marketing. Should a company adapt product design for various national markets or offer a single design to the global market? In some instances, making a design change may increase sales. However, the benefits of such potential sales increases must be weighed against the cost of changing a product's design and testing it in the market. Global marketers need to consider four factors when making product design decisions: preferences, cost, laws and regulations, and compatibility.

Preferences

There are marked and important differences in preferences around the world for factors such as color and taste. Marketers who ignore preferences do so at their own peril. For example, the Dutch brewer Heineken knew that it had to get the taste of its new Premium Light lager just right in order to make inroads with American consumers, who prefer pale and less flavorful beer than Heineken's traditional offerings.

---

[3] http://www.accessmylibrary.com/article-1G1-149965851/datamonitor-forecasts-187m-digital.html.

[4] Janet Adamy, "Different Brew: Eyeing a Billion Tea Drinkers, Starbucks Pours It On in China," *The Wall Street Journal*, November 29, 2006: A1.

After 20 trial versions and a successful marketing campaign that highlighted the new, attractive bottle design of Heineken Premium Light, the company believed it achieved its objective. Sales of the new product are 50 percent higher than projections, and analysts expect the beverage to continue to gain market share in the United States. "We've been able to deliver a beer that plays in the light beer sandbox but is true to the Heineken brand," notes Andy Thomas, Heineken USA's chief.

Sometimes, a product design that is successful in one world region does meet with success in the rest of the world. This is especially true in the luxury products category. For example, BMW and Mercedes dominate the luxury car market in Europe and are strong competitors in the rest of the world, with exactly the same design. Luxury watches, French champagne, and top designer clothes that are available in limited quantities in trendy urban centers are, in effect, designed for the luxury purchaser worldwide.

Cost

Cost is an important factor in product design beause design and specifications influence costs. The cost of producing a product will create a long-term cost floor or minimum price that will cover the cost of manufacturing and overhead costs. This is difficult to estimate for a number of reasons, including the fact that unit costs are inversely related to production volume. Experience theory, discussed in the next chapter, is supported by empirical data that indicate that costs go down forever: for every doubling of accumulated volume of production, costs will go down by a constant percentage as a function of volume. Other design-related costs—whether incurred by the manufacturer or the end user—must also be considered. The cost of maintenance and repair services varies around the world and has an impact on product design. A product that might have an acceptable maitenance/repair cost in a low- or middle-income market might have an unacceptable cost in a high-income market.

Laws and Regulations

Compliance with laws and regulations in different countries has a direct impact on product design decisions, frequently leading to product design adaptations that increase costs. This may be seen especially clearly in Europe, where one impetus for the creation of the Single Market was to dismantle regulatory and legal barriers—particularly in the areas of technical standards and health and safety standards—that prevented pan-European sales of standardized products. In the food industry, for example, there were 200 legal and regulatory barriers to cross-border trade within the EU in 10 food categories. Among these were prohibitions or taxes on products with certain ingredients and different packaging and labeling laws. The removal of such barriers reduces the need to adapt product designs and results in the creation of standardized products that usually cost less.

Compatibility

The last product design issue that must be addressed by company managers is product compatibility with the environment in which it is used. A simple thing like failing to translate the user's manual into market languages can hurt sales. Also, electrical systems range from 50 to 230 volts and from 50 to 60 cycles. This means that the design of any product powered by electricity must be compatible with the power system in the country of use.

Manufacturers of video games find that the world is a very incompatible place for reasons besides those related to electricity. The three different video game systems that dominate the world today require different standards for the video games that can be played on their consoles—the Microsoft Xbox, Sony's Playstation, and Nintendo's Wii. In addition, the different US, European, and Japanese video signal standards also prevent a game that plays in one brand's console in the United States from playing in the same brand's video game system sold in Germany, for example. Video game companies are forced to design products that comply with every single type of technical requirement in each regional market.

Measuring systems do not demand compatibility, but the absence of compatibility in measuring systems can create product resistance. The lack of compatibility is a particular danger for the United States, which is the only nonmetric country in the world. Products calibrated in inches and pounds are at a competitive disadvantage in metric markets. US companies and industries recognize this and are going ahead with metric conversion. For example, 100 percent of US automobile manufacturing is now based on metric measurements.

ATTITUDES TOWARD COUNTRY OF ORIGIN

One of the facts of life in global marketing is the existence of stereotyped attitudes towards foreign people and products. Stereotyped attitudes may either favor or hinder the marketer's efforts. German engineering and Swiss accuracy are examples of national positive brand stereotypes. In the early stages of China's entry into global markets, goods manufactured in China were considered to be cheaper because of their lower quality. (This perception has changed, making it easier for the Chinese to and move up the price/value scale in markets.) On the positive side, as one marketing expert pointed out, "German is synonymous with quality engineering, Italian is synonymous with style, and French is synonymous with chic." No country has a monopoly on a favorable foreign reputation for its products or a universally inferior reputation. For example, Japanese electronic and automobile products' cachet as reliably high quality is no longer unique. Competitors from other countries now build world-class quality products in industries in which the Japanese once had world-quality leadership. Customers in a given country will differ in terms of both the importance they ascribe to a product's country of origin and their perceptions of different countries.

Country image can be an important part of a brand. Swiss watches, for example, have a virtual monopoly on luxury watches worldwide. German engineering is part of the brand equity of German companies in both consumer and industrial markets. Switzerland and Germany acquired their country brand image and equity the old fashioned way: they worked for it. The image is a mirror of the collective success of the companies in each country and their strength.

Country stereotyping can present a considerable disadvantage to a competitor in a given market. Because of this, global marketers should consider shifting production locations to exploit country-specific advantages, or developing an international image to avoid the country-of-origin issue altogether.

A third strategy is to deliberately work on changing a negative image into a positive, or at least neutral, image. One study[5] investigated the efforts of a country and a company from that country to transform their respective images. The authors followed Taiwan's long-running marketing campaign (1990–2004) to document the country's gradual shift in reputation from a low-cost manufacturing nation into an innovative culture and a thriving, globalized economy that is contributing to the world's economy

[5] Lyn S. Amine, Mike C.H. Chao, and Mark J. Arnold, "Executive Insights: Exploring the Practical Effects of Country of Origin, Animosity, and Price-Quality Issues: Two Case Studies of Taiwan and Acer in China." *Journal of International Marketing*, 13, no. 2 (2005): 114–150.

with original, high-quality products. Taiwan-based Acer Group, started as a behind-the-scenes original equipment manufacturer (OEM), was able to build a brand that stood for quality and become a visibly strong player in the global marketplace. However, Acer was, on its initial attempt, not able to establish itself successfully in global consumer markets. Stan Shih, Acer's founder, believed that the main reason for the company's difficulties in establishing its identity had been the negative stereotype of "Made in Taiwan."

Acer did not give up. It continued to improve its quality, designs, and marketing organization. By 2009, Acer overtook Dell in global PC marketing share and ranked second in the world after HP.

Acer's experience demonstrates the alternatives available to companies when a country's manufacturers produce quality products that are nonetheless perceived as being of low quality. One option is to attempt to hide or disguise the foreign origin of the product. Package, label, and product design can minimize evidence of foreign sourcing. A brand policy of using local names will contribute to a domestic identity. The other alternative is to continue the origin identification of the product and attempt to change consumer or customer attitudes toward it. Over time, as consumers experience higher quality, the perception will change and adjust. Perceptions of quality lag changes in actual quality. A source with rising quality will have to wait for market recognition, and one with declining quality will enjoy a lagged response to their declining quality.

In some market segments, foreign products have a substantial advantage over their domestic counterparts simply because they are foreign. In the Philippines, for example, all imported products are able to command a higher price than domestic products. Additionally, one company's products that are manufactured and imported from more industrialized countries sell at higher prices than the same company's products originating in less industrialized countries.[6] This appears to be the case with beer in the United States. In one study, subjects who were asked to indicate taste preference for beer in a blind test indicated a preference for domestic beers over imports. The same subjects were then asked to indicate preference ratings for beers in an open test with labels attached. In this test, the subjects preferred imported beer. Today, many Americans still seem to have a taste for imported beers. According to Impact, a beverage industry newsletter, imports account for 5 percent of US beer sales by volume. This is in spite of the fact that, according to brewmasters, the most important factor determining the quality of beer is freshness: the fresher, the better. Imported beers, because of their long supply chain, are not as fresh as domestic beers. The preference of foreign beers appears to be based on the foreign label and not the actual quality.

GLOBAL PRODUCT POSITIONING: STRATEGIC ALTERNATIVES

Companies can grow in three different ways. The traditional methods of market expansion—further penetration of existing markets to increase market share and extension of the product line into new product-market areas in a single national market—are both available in domestic operations. In addition, a company can expand by extending its existing operations into new countries and areas of the world. The latter method, geographic expansion, is one of the major opportunities of global marketing. To pursue geographic expansion effectively, a framework for considering alternatives is required. When a company has a product/market base, it can select from five strategic alternatives to extend this base into other geographic markets or it can create

---

[6] John Hulland, Honorio S. Todino, and Donald J. Lecraw, "Country-of-Origin Effects on Sellers' Price Premiums in Competitive Philippine Markets, " *Journal of International Marketing*, 4, no. 1 (1996): 57–79.

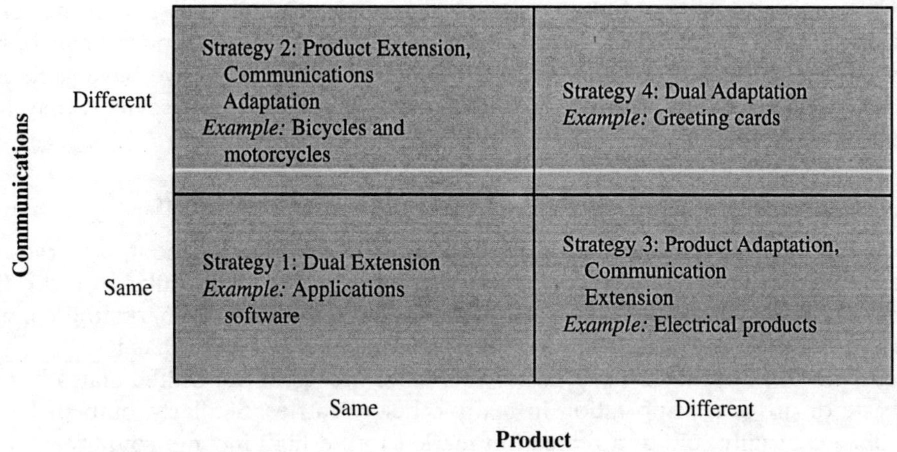

FIGURE 10-2 Global Product Planning Strategic Alternatives

a new product designed for global markets. Four of these alternatives are shown in Figure 10-2.

Strategy 1: Product/Communication Extension (Dual Extension)

Many companies employ product/communication extension as a strategy for pursuing opportunities outside the home market. Under the right conditions, this is the easiest product marketing strategy and, in many instances, the most profitable one as well. Companies pursuing this strategy sell exactly the same product, with the same advertising and promotional appeals as used in the home country, in some or all world-market countries or segments. Note that this strategy is utilized by companies in stages two, four, and five (see Chapter 8). The critical difference is one of execution and mind-set. In the stage two company, the dual extension strategy grows out of an ethnocentric orientation; the stage two company is making the assumption that all markets are alike. A company in stage four or five does not make such assumptions; the company's geocentric orientation allows it to thoroughly understand its markets and consciously take advantage of similarities in world markets.

Some marketers have learned the hard way that the dual extension approach does not work in every market. The global retailer Wal-Mart was recently forced to pull out of the German market where its standard retail model, used invariably in all new geographic markets, simply did not work. Wal-Mart's traditional practices for team building and customer service—the Wal-Mart cheer and the use of bag-packers at check out—were never fully accepted by German workers and consumers. In addition, Wal-Mart's standardized global positioning as the low-price leader did not distinguish it enough from the established German discount retailers. The ensuing price wars and damaged reputation eventually conviced the global giant to sell its remaining 85 stores to Metro AG, another global retail chain.[7]

The product/communication extension strategy has an enormous appeal to global companies because of the cost savings associated with this approach. The two most obvious sources of savings are manufacturing economies of scale and elimination of duplicate product R&D costs. Also important are the substantial economies associated with standardization of marketing communications. For a company with worldwide operations, the cost of preparing separate print and TV ads for each market

[7] Gerrit Wiesmann, "Why Wal-Mart decided to Pack Its Bags in Germany," *Financial Times,* July 29, 2006: 21.

can be enormous. Although these cost savings are important, they should not distract executives from the more important objective of maximum profit performance, which may require the use of an adaptation or invention strategy. As we have seen earlier in the chapter, product extension, in spite of its immediate cost savings, may in fact result in market failure.

Strategy 2: Product Extension/Communication Adaptation

When a product fills a different need, appeals to a different segment, or serves a different function under conditions of use that are the same or similar to those in the domestic market, the only adjustment that may be required is in marketing communications. Bicycles and motor scooters are examples of products that have been marketed with this approach. They satisfy recreation needs in the United States but serve as basic or urban transportation in many other countries. Similarly, outboard marine motors are usually sold to a recreation market in the high-income countries, whereas the same motors in most lower-income countries are mainly sold to fishing and transportation fleets. McDonald's global marketing campaigns allow for different positioning across countries. For example, in the United States, the focus is convenience; in India, "bang for the buck"; in Russia, a uniquely American experience; and in Asia, togetherness for the young and trendy.[8]

As these examples show, the product extension/communication adaptation strategy—either by design or by accident—results in product transformation. The same physical product ends up serving a different function or use than that for which it was originally designed or created.

The appeal of the product extension/communications adaptation strategy is its relatively low cost of implementation. Because the product in this strategy is unchanged, R&D, tooling, manufacturing setup, and inventory costs associated with additions to the product line are avoided. The only costs of this approach are in identifying different product functions and revising marketing communications (including advertising, sales promotion, and point-of-sale material) around the newly identified function.

Strategy 3: Product Adaptation/Communication Extension

A third approach to global product planning is to extend, without change, the basic home-market communications strategy while adapting the product to local use or preference conditions. Note that this strategy (and the one that follows) may be utilized by both stage three and stage four companies. The critical difference is, as noted above, one of execution and mind-set. In the stage three company, the product adaptation strategy grows out of a polycentric orientation; the stage three company assumes that all markets are different. By contrast, the geocentric orientation of managers and executives in a stage four global company has sensitized them to actual, rather than assumed, differences between markets.

There are many examples of products that have been adjusted to perform the same function around the globe under different environmental conditions. Soap and detergent manufacturers have adjusted their product formulations to meet local water and washing equipment conditions with no change in their basic communications approach. Household appliances have been scaled to sizes appropriate to different use environments, and clothing has been adapted to meet fashion criteria. Also, food products, by virtue of their potentially high degree of environmental sensitivity, are

[8] Michael Fielding, "Walk the Line: Global Brands Need Balance of Identity, Cultural Respect," *Marketing News*, September 1, 2006: 8–10.

often adapted. Mueslix, for example, is the name of a mushlike European health cereal that is popular in Europe. Kellogg's brought the Mueslix name and product concept to the United States but completely changed the formulation and nature of the product.

Strategy 4: Dual Adaptation

Sometimes, when comparing a new geographic market to the home market, marketers discover that environmental conditions or consumer preferences differ; the same may be true of the function a product serves or consumer receptivity to advertising appeals. In essence, this is a combination of the market conditions of strategies 2 and 3. In such a situation, a stage four/five company will utilize the strategy of product and communications adaptation. As was true about strategy 3, stage three companies will also use dual adaptation—regardless of whether the strategy is warranted by market conditions, preferences, function, or receptivity.

Gibson Guitar Corp. makes a range of guitar models that are available only in Japan—its largest international market. The Tak Matsumoto's limited edition Les Paul model, for example, is sold exclusively there and is offered in special shades such as canary yellow and suburst. The company's Japanese image conveys coolness and authenticity and inspires reverence that is not matched in its domestic market. Its fans are predominantly Japan's baby boomers. They witnessed music legends such as Jimi Hendrix play Gibson guitars in the 1970s and are now able to indulge their nostalgia by collecting this quintessentially American and quintessentially rock-'n'-roll instrument.[9]

Mobile phone giant Nokia is also using dual adaptation strategy to gain traction in India, the fastest growing market for wireless phones. The company is implementing innovations such as dust-proof keypads to make the phones usable in India's hot countryside where dusty, unpaved roads are the norm. It is also changing the way it advertises and sells its products. To avoid losing control over its marketing and advertising by distributing its phones through India's tens of thousands of small vendors, the manufacturer has hired a number of Nokia-branded vans and minivans that visit remote villages across the country on market or festival days. The Nokia representatives traveling in these vans then educate customers about the phones and sell directly to them on the spot. "You have to work with local means to reach people—even bicycles and rickshaws," says Kai Oistamo, Nokia's executive vice president and general manager for mobile phones.[10]

Strategy 5: Product Invention

Adaptation strategies are effective approaches to international (stage two) and multinational (stage three) marketing, but they may not respond to global market opportunities. They do not respond to the situation in markets where customers do not have the purchasing power to buy either the existing or adapted product. This latter situation applies to the underdeveloped markets of the world, which are home to roughly three-quarters of the world's population. When potential customers have limited purchasing power, a company may need to develop an entirely new product designed to satisfy the need or want at a price that is within the reach of the potential customer.

---

[9] Yuri Kageyama, "The Japanese Dream: Japan Market Warmly Welcomes Gibson Guitars," *Marketing News*, September 15, 2006: 48.

[10] Jack Ewing, "First Mover in Mobile: How Nokia Is Selling Cell Phones to the Developing World," *BusinessWeek*, May 4, 2007.

Invention is a demanding but potentially rewarding product strategy for reaching mass markets in poorer countries.

For example, both the microprocessor giant Intel and the nonprofit initiative One Laptop Per Child (OLPC) are developing simplified, cheap portable electronics that can be distributed in low income countires. While OLPC is focusing on developing notebooks with a unique architecture and interface that can be sold for US$100, Intel is pouring its energies into making its microchips compatible with all different types and sizes of electronic devices so that PDAs, mobile phones, and PCs will all have the same full functionality and Internet access capabilities regardless of where they are sold.[11]

The winners in global competition are the companies that can develop products offering the most benefits, which in turn create the greatest value for buyers. Value is not defined in terms of performance, but rather in terms of customer perception. The latter is as important for an expensive perfume or champagne as it is for an inexpensive soft drink. Product quality is essential, but it is also necessary to support the product quality with imaginative, value-enhancing advertising and marketing communications. Most industry experts believe that a global appeal and a global advertising campaign are more effective in creating the perception of value than a series of separate national campaigns.

Forced by competitive and financial pressures, as well as consumer trends, Ford Motor Co. worked on a global small car for its lineup for a number of years. CEO Alan Mulally has been a strong proponent of the project. He merged several far-flung development teams into a global program team tasked with developing such a product that could be sold in the European, North American, and Asian markets. Ford began selling the cars, which use a Mazda-developed platform, in the three markets.[12] While the engineering side of the project is hoping to eliminate unnecessary structural changes, reduce costs, and slim down the number of team members, a separate design team will be hard at work to develop a global design theme that will resonate with Ford customers around the world. The ultimate goal was to "be able to get off a plane anywhere in the world and say, 'Oh, yeah, there's a Ford,'" according to J Mays, Ford Motor's group vice president of design.[13]

BOX 10-3

Side Bar: Product Adaptation to Standardization: A Journey

Rice cracker is one of the various Japanese snack foods liked by the rice loving people of Japan. Traditionally, Japanese use a simple process of preparing rice cracker at home by making dough of powdered rice and then it is cooled for hardening for some time. This hardened rice cake is then cut in to pieces for necessary baking under requisite temperature to make homemade rice cracker. Senebei and OKaki varieties of rice cracker are traditionally popular amongst the Japanese as they get their favourite rice based food in a ready-made form as well. Senbei had its origin in China but there it was used to be made of flour. But Japanese love for rice made them rice based in Japan. Okaki is another variety of Japanese rice cracker made from sweet rice. Japanese make Mochi or glutinous rice sticky dough and then bake to have Okaki variety of rice cracker.

[11] David Kirkpatrick, "Intel on $100 Laptops, Smartphones, and the Net," *Fast Forward* newsletter, May 11, 2007. http://money.cnn.com/2007/05/11/technology/fastforward_inteltiny.fortune/index.htm?postversion=2007051112

[12] Amy Wilson, "Ford Will Have 1 Team for Global Small Car," *Automotive News*, March 12, 2007: 8.

[13] Amy Wilson, "Ford Brand Plans a Global Design Theme," *Automotive News*, January 22, 2007: 4.

Now a new avatar of Japanese Senebei is Dozo in the world market. One can step in any retailers in Bangkok and surely find Dozo to be there. Dozo , a crispy rice cracker, is popularly loved by the rice loving Thai population too. As advertised by the manufacturer, "Dozo, original flavour, gives you just a right full. It's delicious with genuine Japanese rice, featured with nutrition value and mixed with an authentic Japanese ingredient. Baked for long to get a good smell for the rich, well-rounded flavor. Also convenient to carry everywhere. This is the original of deliciousness".

Now the rice crackers, called Sembei in Japan, the most common snacks in the Japanese cuisine is out globally to embrace different customers of different countries. Different countries in South Asia are rice lovers so it would not take much time to capture the fancy of those people. Indian's love for rice is well known so the product has started pouring in the vast Indian market slowly but steadily.

In order to move from Japanese Rice cracker Senebei to Dozo , the product has gone through product component wise modification as stated below in the tabular form.

Product Component	Component Description	Senebei/Japan	Dozo/Global
Core component	Core component platform contains the essential technology— and all its design and functional features.	Senebei uses a kind of glutinous sticky rice which Japanese are very fond of. The product has low crispiness. It comes with several flavours, including black sesame. Small amounts of protein and low in fat makes the product healthy.	To move the product into the larger breakfast market Dozo only replaced Japanese rice by Thai rice. To make Dozo likeable by non-Japanese people, it now comes with various flavour like salted, seaweeds, etc. Functional features were made to improve by making it highly crispy to fight out competition from other snacks like biscuits. It retained low protein and low in fat nature.
Packaging component	It contains, trade mark, brand name, logo, price quality, packaging, styling	Senebei is a name of a home based product and had no brand name and professional packaging.	Dozo is a brand indicating rice cracker and comes with highly professional packaging of global standard.
Support service component	It contains delivery, warranty, support service etc.	Senebei is home based traditionally offered as home cooked product and hence devoid of information of product nutrients contents, legal certification etc.	Dozo comes with all sorts nutrients inscribed on the package. The food specific legal requirements are fulfilled and delivery through online and offline convenient stores.

HOW TO CHOOSE A STRATEGY Most companies seek a product strategy that optimizes company profits and competitive position over the long term. Which strategy for global markets best achieves this goal? There is no general answer to this question. Rather, the answer depends on the specific product–market–company mix.

Recall from Chapter 4 that, in terms of cultural sensitivity, consumer products are more sensitive than industrial products. Another rule of thumb is that food products frequently exhibit the highest degree of cultural sensitivity. What this means to managers is that some products, by their nature, are likely to demand significant adaptation, others require only partial adaptation, and still others are best left unchanged.

Companies differ in both their willingness and capability to identify and produce profitable product adaptations. In addition, there's no one unified model for global marketing strategy that can help guide them through the decision process. However,

TABLE 10-3 Major Perspectives of Global Marketing Strategy[14]

Standardization perspective	Scale economies Low-cost Simplification	Product standardization Promotion standardization Standardized channel structure Standardized price	Convergence of cultures Similarity of demand Low trade barriers Technological advances Orientation of firm	Efficiency Consistency Transfer of ideas
Configuration–coordination perspective	Comparative advantage Interdependency Specialization	Concentration of value-chain activities Coordination of value-chain activities	Low trade barriers Technological advances Orientation of firm International experience	Efficiency Synergies
Integration perspective	Cross-subsidization Competitive dislocation Rationalization	Integration of competitive moves Global market participation	Low trade barriers Orientation of firm International experience Integrated markets	Effectiveness in competition Competitive leverage

three main perspectives tend to take precedence in both the marketing literature and the business world regarding how to approach global marketing strategy. These are summarized in Table 10-3.

To sum up, the choice of product and communications strategy in international marketing is a function of three key factors: (1) the product itself, defined in terms of the function or need it serves; (2) the market, defined in terms of the conditions under which the product is used, the preferences of potential customers, and the ability to buy the products in question; and (3) the costs of adaptation and manufacture to the company considering these product/communications approaches. Only after analysis of the product/market fit and of company capabilities and costs can executives choose the most profitable international strategy.

CASE 10-1

TATA Automobile: Product Acceptance in International Market

Tata Motors or the erstwhile Tata Engineering & Locomotive Company Limited (TELCO) has been a house hold name in India and one of the best known Indian companies in terms of internationalisation. TELCO made a humble beginning during the year 1948, when the Tata's acquired an Eastern Railway Workshop to build boilers and steam locomotives for the railways. Soon it established contact with the very famous automobile company, Daimler Benz, for manufacturing support

[14] Shaoming Zou and S. Tamer Cavusgil, "The GMS: A Broad Conceptualization of Global Marketing Strategy and Its Effect on Firm Performance," *Journal of Marketing* 66, no. 4 (October 2002): 40–56.

TABLE 10-4 Automobile Production in India (Million Units)

Type of automobiles	FY 05	FY06	FY07	FY08	FY09	FY10	FY11	FY12	FY13	FY14	FY15
Passenger vehicle	1.2	1.3	1.3	1.6	1,8	2.4	3	3.1	3.2	3.1	3.2
Commercial vehicle	0.4	0.4	0.5	0.6	0.4	0.6	0.8	0.9	0.8	0.7	0.7
Three wheelers	0.4	0.4	0.6	0.5	0.5	0.6	0.8	0.9	0.8	0.8	0.9
Two wheelers	6.6	7.6	8.5	8.0	8.4	10.5	13.4	15.4	15.7	16.9	18.5

Source: SIAM website: http://www.siamindia.com/statistics.aspx?mpgid=8&pgidtrail=13, as accessed on 12 January 2017 at 12pm.

for automobiles in India. This collaboration helped TELCO to develop capability to manufacture automobile of a world-class standard. With a long outstanding business journey since independence, the company has gained a very revered place in the minds of every Indian. Tata motors became a company of consolidated revenues when it earned ₹.67,576 crores for the quarter end in March 31, 2015 which was 3.5% higher than the last year's corresponding revenue. The before tax profit of ₹.2,771 crores, the quarter end in March 31, 2015 was also indicative of the strength of the company in the automobile sector of India. In fact, this company grew with the growth of Indian automobile sector. The Indian automobile sector was very miniature at the dawn of independence. The year 1991, allowed several foreign automobile companies appearing in the Indian automobile scenario. Various Indian companies also grew up with the sector. The total production of passenger vehicles during 2004–05 was 1.2 million units which grew up to 3.2 million units during 2014–15 (refer Table 10-4). The two wheeler production grew up faster with only 6.6 million units during 2004–05 which went up to 18.5 million units during 2014–15.

AUTOMOBILE PRODUCTION IN THE WORLD

The automobile production in the world was badly hit during the 2009 recession and started recovering gradually from 2010 onwards. Respective government of the countries also came out to support the recovery phase after recession with various direct and indirect incentives. The Table 10-5 shows the production statistics of the countries of world who registered positive growth during 2014 and 2015. It primarily shows that only 30 countries of the world positively grew during the period 2014 to 2015 in terms of automobile production. France is producing the largest number of automobiles in Europe, but its growth rate during 2014 to 2015 was as low as 2.1 percent. Though Finland grew faster during the same period but the absolute volume of production was very low. Spain is the country which has respectable production volume of 2.4 million during 2014 and which grew with a pace of 13.7 percent a year later. German automobile production growth rate was a mere 2.1 percent during 2014 to 2015. In Asia there were three countries, China, India and Turkey that were managing a good show. China has been leading the pack with 23.7 million productions in 2014, which grew at the rate of 3.3 percent through 2015. India with 3.8 million productions during 2014, also manages to have a brisk growth rate of over 7 percent through 2015. Turkey also grew respectively during 2014 to 2015 at the rate of over 16 percent, but the production volume was not even clocked at 1 million. In the American continent, USA grew only at 3.8 percent during 2014 to 2015 but had a mammoth yearly production volume of 11 to 12 million per year. Mexico has a respectable production volume of over 3 million per year and had a growth pace of over 5 percent during 2014 to 2015. African nations are yet to touch the magic figure of 1 million productions.

The Table 10-6 shows the twelve countries of the world where vehicle production have gone down drastically during 2014 to 2015. Vehicle production in Brazil slowed down by 22.8 percent during 2014 to 2015. Russia, is a lso reeling under the same type of growth retardation. In Asia, Indonesia was under pressure to cut down production of automobile from 1.3 million during 2014 to 1.1 million during 2014.

TABLE 10-5 World Motor Vehicle Production by Country (2014-15) with Positive Growth

	All Countries	2014	2015	% Change
	Europe			
1	Finland	45,035	69,053	53.30%
2	Sweden (Cars Only)	1,54,174	1,88,987	22.60%
3	France—As Of 2011, Cars and LCV only	18,21,464	19,70,000	8.20%
4	Germany—As Of 2011, Cars and LCV only	59,07,548	60,33,164	2.10%
5	Italy	6,97,864	10,14,223	45.30%
6	Netherlands—As Of 2013	31,428	44,122	40.40%
7	Spain	24,02,978	27,33,201	13.70%
8	United Kingdom	15,98,879	16,82,156	5.20%
9	Czech Republic	12,51,220	13,03,603	0
10	Hungary	4,37,599	4,95,370	13.20%
11	Poland	5,93,504	6,60,603	11.30%
12	Slovakia	9,71,160	10,00,001	3.00%
13	Slovenia	1,18,591	1,33,092	12.20%
	Americas			
14	Mexico	33,68,010	35,65,469	5.90%
15	USA	1,16,60,702	1,21,00,095	3.80%
16	Colombia	71,137	78,070	9.70%
	Asia			
17	Bangladesh	536	540	0.70%
18	Azerbaidjan	247	415	68.00%
19	China	2,37,31,600	2,45,03,326	3.30%
20	India	38,44,857	41,25,744	7.30%
21	Pakistan	1,48,746	2,29,686	54.40%
22	Philippines	1,06,938	1,12,493	5.20%
23	South Korea	45,24,932	45,55,957	0.70%
24	Thailand	18,80,587	19,15,420	1.90%
25	Turkey	11,70,445	13,58,796	16.10%
26	Vietnam	48,871	50,000	2.30%
	Africa			
27	Algeria	1,244	20,000	1507.70%
28	Morocco	2,31,986	2,88,329	24.30%
29	South Africa	5,66,083	6,15,658	8.80%
30	Tunisia	540	540	0.00%

Adapted from OICA website: http://www.oica.net/category/production-statistics/, as accessed on 5 February at 3.30pm.

TABLE 10-6 World Motor Vehicle Production by Country with Negative Growth >15%

Sl No.	All Vehicles	2014	2015	% Change
1	Austria	1,52,000	1,25,500	–17.4%
2	Belgium	5,16,831	4,09,340	–20.8%
3	Serbia	1,03,150	83,630	–18.9%
4	Russia	18,87,193	13,84,399	–26.6%
5	Belarus	22,990	15,033	–34.6%
6	Kazakhstan	40,162	14,477	–64.0%
7	Ukraine	28,751	8,244	–71.3%
8	Uzbekistan	2,45,660	1,85,400	–24.5%
9	Brazil	31,46,386	24,29,463	–22.8%
10	Ecuador	5,986	4,800	–19.8%
11	Indonesia	12,98,523	10,98,780	–15.4%
12	Egypt	42,515	36,000	–15.3%

Adapted from OICA website: http://www.oica.net/category/production-statistics/, as accessed on 12 January 2017 at 12.15pm.

INDIAN MARKET AND AUTOMOBILE PLAYERS

Tata motors remained the market leader in many segments of automobile manufacturing and marketing in India. The following Table 10-7 shows that, Tata has been the market leader in MCV (Medium commercial vehicles) & HCV (heavy commercial vehicle) as well LCV (light commercial vehicle) segments in the India market. In the passenger vehicle segment, Suzuki is the market leader. In the LCV segment, the main competitor of Tata has been another Indian company, Mahindra and Mahindra (M&M). In all the segment of its presence, excepting passenger vehicle, Tata is well ahead of its competitors like M&M, Ashoke Leyland, Force, Piaggio, etc.

TABLE 10-7 Leading Auto Manufacturers in India and Market Share for the FY 14

	Tata	Hundai	M&M	Suzuki	Ashoke Leyland	Force	Piaggio	Bajaj	Hero	Honda	TVS
Passenger vehicles	8	15	10	42							
MCVs & HCVs	54.9		2.6		25.8						
LCVs	53.7		31.8			5.5	4.6				
Three wheelers			13.1				32.5	39			
Motor cycles								16.6	41.4	25.6	12.9
Scooters				6.5					16.9	54.8	15.1

Courtesy: India Brand Equity Foundation (IBEF), January 16, page 21 available at http://www.india-opportunities.es/archivos/publicaciones/Automobile-January-2016.pdf, as accessed on 12 January 2017 at 3pm.

Note: Data is for FY14 except

*Motorcycle: Data is for FY15

TABLE 10-8 Position of Tata Automobile in India Market During 2015–16

Category	Industry Sales			Company Sales			Market Share	
	Fiscal 2016	Fiscal 2015	Growth	Fiscal 2016	Fiscal 2015	Growth	Fiscal 2016	Fiscal 2015
	Units		%	Units		%	%	%
M&HCV	302,532	232,113	30.3%	157,120	126,369	24.3%	51.9%	54.4%
LCVs*	401,908	410,528	(2.1)%	169,635	191,411	(11.4)%	42.2%	46.6%
Total	704,440	642,641	9.6%	326,755	317,780	2.8%	46.4%	49.4%

Source: Society of Indian Automobile Manufactures report and Company Analysis.
*LCVs include V2 van sales

The Table 10-8 above further shows that in the MCV, HCV and LCV segment Tata further consolidated its position in India market with 49.9 percent market share.

Tata's Internationalisation

Tata is present almost everywhere around the globe. This is the Indian automobile company **which** had shown its clamour for internationalisation from the very early years of its existence in the Indian market. The strong domestic presence has helped the company to go beyond border successfully. The following are description of its international presence so far.

Tata in South Asia

In South Asia, it has a strong presence (refer Table 10-9). Way back in 1961, Tata motors exported its first vehicle to Sri Lanka. Now it has its own manufacturing/assembly operation in Bangladesh and Myanmar. Tata Motors entered Bangladesh with commercial vehicles in 1972. Today, over two-thirds of the commercial vehicles sold in Bangladesh are produced by Tata motors. Tata Nano, Tata Indigo and Tata Sumo are very popular in Bangladesh. Tata Motors has a branch office in Dhaka. Tata Motors has been operating in the Myanmar market since 2013. It has a fully operational heavy truck assembly plant in central Myanmar which has a capacity of producing 1,000 vehicles per annum initially and has the flexibility of augmenting up to 5,000 per year. TATA is also planning to set up a vehicle manufacturing base in Sri Lanka to capture the Pakistan market by taking advantage of the free trade agreement signed between Sri Lanka and Pakistan.

Tata in South East Asia

Thonburi Automotive Assembly Plant Company of Thailand, inked a JV with Tata for assembly of Xenon pick-up van. Thonburi Automotive, which builds Mercedes-Benz vehicles in Thailand has a 30 percent stake in a joint venture producing Indian Tata Motors automobiles since 2007. Tata has an assembling plant in Indonesia for cars and trucks. Tata Daewoo Commercial Vehicle Company is a wholly owned subsidiary of Tata Motors for manufacturing of commercial vehicle and is headquartered in

TABLE 10-9 Tata in South Asia

Country		
Bangladesh	M/A*	SD
Myanmar	M/A**	SD
Sri Lanka		SD
Afganistan		SD
Nepal		SD
Bhutan		SD

Adapted from http://www.tatamotors.com/worldwide/, as accessed on 12 January 2017 at 3.20pm.
*Manufacturing/Assembly operation
** Sales and distribution

TABLE 10-10 Tata in South East Asia

Thailand	JV***	SD	
Indonesia	M/A	SD	
Malaysia		SD	
South Korea			MA****

Adapted from http://www.tatamotors.com/worldwide/, as accessed on 12 January 2017 at 3.20pm.
*** Joint venture
**** Merger and Accusation

South Korea. The Daewoo Commercial Vehicle Co. Ltd which spun off from its parent Daewoo Motor Co. Ltd was acquired by Tata Motors. Tata also has a R&D centre in South Korea (Table 10-10).

Tata in Middle East

Since 1971, Tata Motors has been present in the Middle East country market. Tata vehicles are sold through sales subsidiaries in UAE, Oman, Kuwait, Qatar, Saudi Arabia, Bahrain, and Turkey through a distributor network. More than 10,000 TATA vehicles ply on Middle East roads which consists of medium bus segment, Prima trucks, Xenon pickups and Elanza school buses (refer Table 10-11).

Tata in Africa

Tata motors presence in Africa, dates back to 1965 when a batch of 20 trucks were shipped to Egypt. Thereafter, the entire Africa provided a good opportunity to the company to market its automobile. It has penetrated 43 African country markets with manufacturing facilities in South Africa and Morocco (Table 10-12). Tata adopted a 'hub and spoke' model, in capturing African markets. Mini manufacturing hubs in strategic locations and sales and distribution centres around it, allows the company to be present throughout the continent. Kenya is the largest market for the company in Africa, followed by Tanzania and South Africa. Tata Motors has an assembly line in South Africa and assembly tie-ups in Senegal, Kenya, Nigeria, and Tunisia, for specific products. It sells mostly commercial vehicles and small pick-ups like the Xenon, while its passenger vehicle business is very negligible. Tata Motors is planning to set assembly units in Nigeria as that country has made it mandatory to have local manufacturing.

Tata in Europe, Russia and Latin America

Europe has not been a very successful market for Tata but it entered UK way back in 1971. Europe for the beginning was in the steering wheel and was the originators of many innovations in the automobiles production and marketing. So Tata felt the need of presence in Europe. It set up its design and development facilities in Turin, Italy and Technical Centre in UK. Tata Motors entered Spanish market by acquiring 21% stake of a Spanish bus and coach manufacturer. In 2006, it formed a joint venture with the Brazil–based Marcopolo, to roll out fully–built buses and coaches for India and other international markets (refer Table 10-13).

TABLE 10-11 Tata in Middle East

Abu Dhabi	SD
Dubai	SD
Bahrain	SD
Oman	SD
Kuwait	SD
Qatar	SD
Turkey	SD

Adapted from http://www.tatamotors.com/worldwide/, as accessed on 12 January 2017 at 3.20pm.

TABLE 10-12 Tata in Africa

South Africa	M/A	SD		
Kenya		SD		
Tanzania		SD		
Uganda		SD		
Mozambique		SD		
Zambia		SD		
Ghana		SD		
Nigeria		SD		
Senegal		SD		
Ethiopia		SD		
Djibouti		SD		
Morocco	M/A	SD	MA	
Seychelles		SD		
Mauritius		SD		
Rwanda				HS*****
Cote d'Ivoire				HS
Niger				HS
Mauritania				HS
Mali				HS
Sierra Leone				HS
Liberia				HS
Togo				HS
Benin				HS
Gambia				HS
Burkina Faso				HS
Gabon				HS

Adapted from http://www.tatamotors.com/worldwide/, as accessed on 12 January 2017 at 3.20pm.
*****HS: Hub and Spoke model

TABLE 10-13 Tata in Europe, Russia and Latin America

UK	M/A	SD	MA
Italy		SD	
Spain		SD	MA
Poland		SD	
Russia & CIS			
Ukraine	M/A	SD	
Russia		SD	
Latin America			
Chile		SD	

Adapted from http://www.tatamotors.com/worldwide/, as accessed on 12 January 2017 at 3.20pm.

TABLE 10-14 Tata Export from 2001–02 to 2015–16

Fiscal Year	Export in number of units	YOY growth in %
2000–01	10861	–
2001–02	7481	–45.18
2002–03	6355	–17.72
2003–04	10177	37.56
2004–05	8719	–16.72
2005–06	29624	70.57
2006–07	34940	15.21
2007–08	39447	11.43
2008–09	26417	–49.32
2009–10	27667	4.52
2010–11	49558	44.17
2011–12	53783	7.86
2014–15	49936	–7.70
2015–16	58058	13.99

Adapted from Tata Motors annual reports available at http://www.moneycontrol.com/annual-report/tatamotors/TM03/2015, as accessed on 05 February 2017 at 9.30pm.

Export trend of the company

The Company's top five (quantity terms) export destinations for vehicles manufactured in India are Bangladesh, Sri Lanka, Nepal, South Africa and Indonesia which accounted for approximately 79% of the exports of commercial vehicles and passenger vehicles. The Table 10-14 above shows the trend of export automobiles from the stable of TATA.

Case Questions

1. Describe the product internationalization efforts of TATA motors.
2. Assess the product standardization/adaptation efforts of the company while internationalization and prescribe a right product strategy for more intense internationalization.

Summary

The product is a key element of a marketing program. Global marketers face the challenge of formulating a coherent global product strategy for their companies. Product strategy requires an evaluation of the basic needs and conditions of use in the company's existing and proposed markets. Marketers should be able to categorize their products according to the markets they serve (local, national, international, and global products) in order to define the opportunities for each in global markets. Whenever possible, opportunities to market global products should be given precedence over opportunities to market local or international products if the conditions for a global marketing campaign exist.

Marketers must consider many factors when designing products for global markets including preferences, costs, regulations, compatibility, and attitudes toward a product's country of origin. Five strategic positioning alternatives are open to companies pursuing global market expansion for their products: product/communications extension, product extension/communications adaptation, product adaptation/communications extension, dual adaptation, and product invention. Choosing a strategy for global market expansion should be based on analysis of the factors that would make the product most profitable in each market. Understanding that an established product in one culture may be considered an innovative product in another is critical in planning and developing products for foreign and global use. Global competition has created pressure on companies to excel at product development and innovation. Companies today must often make difficult decisions on where to locate their new product development operations in order to leverage the opportunities present in each region of the world.

Discussion Questions

1. What is the difference between a product and a brand?
2. What are the differences among a local, an international, and a global product or brand? Cite examples.
3. What criteria should global marketers consider when making product design decisions?
4. How can buyer attitudes about a product's country of origin affect marketing strategy?
5. Identify several global brands. What are some of the reasons for the success of the brands you chose?
6. Briefly describe various combinations of product/communication strategies available to global marketers. When is it appropriate to use each?

Application Exercises

Listen to the NPR story "Video Game Pioneer Kutaragi Leaves Sony" about Sony's Playstation 3 and its struggles against rivals such as Microsoft's Xbox 360 and Nintendo's Wii (http://www.npr.org/templates/story/story.php?storyId=9884088).

1. Based on the comments of the young gamers, what, besides the high price, were Sony's biggest misses in launching this product?
2. Do you believe that Sony can recover after its initial stumble in the US market? If so, what steps do you recommend that it takes?

Experiential Exercises

Select a product from your daily life that is very useful, but costs over US$100. Recommend design, production, and functionality changes that would not reduce its usefulness but would make it more affordable and practical in poorer countries. Develop a marketing strategy for this product in an underdeveloped country target market of your choice.

Suggested Readings

Anderson, Chris. *Makers: The New Industrial Revolution.* New York: Crown Publishing Group, a division of Random House Inc., 2012, and edited version of author interview, "Makers: Chris Anderson on DIY Manufacturing." *Knowledge@Wharton*, an online publication of Wharton Business School (December 17, 2012). http://knowledge.wharton.upenn.edu.

Balabanis, George and Adamantios Diamantopoulos. "Gains and Losses from the Misperception of Brand Origin: The Role of Brand Strength and Country-of-Origin Image." *Journal of International Marketing*, 19, no. 2 (June 2011): 95–116.

Barwise, Patrick, and Sean Meehan. "The One Thing You Must Get Right When Building a Brand." *Harvard Business Review* (December 2010): 80–84.

Bryce, David J., Jeffrey H. Dyer, and Nile W. Hatch. "Competing Against Free." *Harvard Business Review* (June 2011): 104–111.

Cayla, Julien, and Eric J. Amould. "A Cultural Approach to Branding in the Global Marketplace." *Journal of International Marketing*, 16, no. 4 (December 2008): 86–112.

Chen, Xiaoyun, Long W. Lam, and Huan Zou. "Antecedents and Performance Consequences of Integrated Brand Management in China: An Exploratory Study." *Journal of Global Marketing*, 24, no. 2 (2011): 167–180.

Dimofte, Claudiu V., Johny K. Johansson, and Richard P. Bagozzi. "Global Brands in the United States: How Consumer Ethnicity Mediates the Global Brand

Effect." *Journal of International Marketing*, 18, no. 3 (September 2010): 81–106.

Dinnie, Keith. *Nation Branding: Concepts, Issues, Practice.* Burlington, MA: Butterworth-Heinemann/Elsevier Ltd., 2008.

Du Preez, Johann P., Adamantios Diamantopoulos, and Bodo B. Schlegelmilch. "Product Standardization and Attribute Saliency: A Three-Product Empirical Comparison." *Journal of International Marketing,* 2, no. 1 (1994): 7–28.

Dwyer, Sean, Hani Mesak, and Maxwell Hsu. "An Exploratory Examination of the Influence of National Culture on Cross-National Product Diffusion." *Journal of International Marketing*, 13, no. 2 (June 2005): 1–27.

Elliott, Gregory R., and Ross C. Cameron. "Consumer Perception of Product Quality and the Country-of-Origin Effect." *Journal of International Marketing,* 2, no. 2 (1994): 49–62.

Eyring, Matthew, Mark W. Johnson, and Hari Nair. "New Business Models in Emerging Markets." *Harvard Business Review* (January–February 2011): 89–95.

Faulds, David J., Orlen Grunewald, and Denise Johnson. "A Cross-National Investigation of the Relationship between the Price and Quality of Consumer Products: 1970–1990." *Journal of Global Marketing,* 8, no. 1 (1994): 7–26.

Gerzema, John, and Ed Lebar. "The Trouble With Brands." *Stategy+Business* (Autumn 2009): 102–111.

Guzman, Francisco, and Audhesh K. Paswan. "Cultural Brands from Emerging Markets: Brand Image Across Host and Home Countries." *Journal of International Marketing,* 17, no. 3 (September 2009): 71–86.

Hamilton, Carl. *Absolut: Biography of a Bottle.* New York: Texere, 2000.

Johansson, Johny K., and Hans B. Thorelli. "International Product Positioning." *Journal of International Business Studies,* 16, no. 3 (Fall 1985): 57–76.

Keegan, Warren J., Sandra Moriarty, and Tom Duncan. *Marketing.* 2nd ed. Upper Saddle River, NJ: Prentice Hall, 1995.

Lee, Ruby P., Qimei Chen, Daekwan Kim, and Jean L. Johnson. "Knowledge Transfer between Multinational Corporations' Headquarters and Their Subsidiaries: Influences on and Implications for New Product Outcomes." *Journal of International Marketing*, 16, no. 2 (June 2008): 1–31.

Moskowitz, Howard R., and Samuel Rabino. "Sensory Segmentation: An Organizing Principle for International Product Concept Generation." *Journal of Global Marketing,* 8, no. 1 (1994): 73–94.

Ofek, Elie, and Luc Wathieu. "Are You Ignoring Trends That Could Shake Up Your Business?" *Harvard Business Review* (July–August 2010): 124.

Ozsomer, Aysegul, and Selin Altaras. "Global Brand Purchase Likelihood: A Critical Synthesis and an Integrated Conceptual Framework." *Journal of International Marketing* 16, no. 4 (December 2008): 1–28.

Parker, Stephen R., Diana L. Haytko, and Charles M. Hermans. "Ethnocentrism and Its Effect on the Chinese Consumer: A Threat to Foreign Goods?" *Journal of Global Marketing*, 24, no. 1 (2011): 4–17.

Powers, Thomas L., and Jeffrey J. Loyka. "Adaptation of Marketing Mix Elements in International Markets." *Journal of Global Marketing*, 23, no. 1 (2010): 65–79.

Ritson, Mark. "Should You Launch a Fighter Brand?" *Harvard Business Review* (October 2009): 87–94.

Robinson, William T., and Claes Fornell. "Sources of Market Pioneer Advantages in Consumer Goods Industries." *Journal of Marketing Research* (August 1985): 305–317.

Roll, Martin. *Asian Brand Strategy: How Asia Builds Strong Brands.* New York: Palgrave Macmillan, 2006.

Rosenbloom, Alfred, and James E. Haefner. "Country-of-Origin Effects and Global Brand Trust: A First Look." *Journal of Global Marketing*, 22, no. 4 (2009): 267–278.

Samiee, Saeed. "Customer Evaluation of Products in a Global Market." *Journal of International Business Studies,* 25, no. 3 (Third Quarter 1994): 579–604.

Schneider, Joan, and Julie Hall. "Why Most Product Launches Fail." *Harvard Business Review* (April 2011): 20–23.

Schulling, Isabelle, and Jean-Noel Kapferer. "Real Differences between Local and International Brands: Strategic Implications for International Marketers." *Journal of International Marketing*, 12, no. 4 (December 2004): 97–112.

Shankar, Venkatesh, Leonard L. Berry, and Thomas Dotzel. "A Practical Guide to Combining Products and Services." *Harvard Business Review* (November 2009): 95–99.

Smith, Alan D. "Competitive Approaches to New Product Development: A Comparison of Successful Organizations in an Unstable Economic Environment." *Team Performance Management*, 17, no. 3/4 (2011): 124–145.

Svendsen, Mons Freng, Sven A. Haugland, Kjell Gronhaug, and Trond Hammenvoll. "Marketing Strategy and Customer Involvement in Product Development." *European Journal of Marketing*, 45, no. 4 (2011): 513–530.

Unruh, Gregory, and Richard Ettenson. "Growing Green: Three Smart Paths to Developing Sustainable Products." *Harvard Business Review* (June 2010): 94–100.

Wakayama, Toshiro, Junjiro Shintaku, and Tomofumi Amano. "What Panasonic Learned in China." *Harvard Business Review* (December 2012): 109–113.

White, Katherine, Rhiannon Macdonnell, and John H. Ellard. "Belief in a Just World: Consumer Intentions and Behaviors toward Ethical Products." *Journal of Marketing*, 76, no. 1 (January 2012).

CHAPTER 11

Pricing Decisions

The real price of everything is the toil and trouble of acquiring it.

—Adam Smith, Wealth of Nations (1776)

Price is what you pay. Value is what you get.

—Warren Buffet

Pricing is a subject which has baffled the student and teacher alike.

—Alfred Oxenfeldt[1]

Learning Objectives

1. Discuss basic pricing concepts (329–334).
2. Identify the environmental factors that influence pricing decisions (335–339).
3. Compare and contrast the objectives and methods of global pricing strategies (340–341).
4. Discuss the issues associated with gray marketing (343–344).
5. Explain the causes and effects of dumping (344–345).
6. Discuss transfer pricing issues and alternatives (347–349).
7. Distinguish between three global pricing policies (350–351).

[1] Former Professor Emeritus of Marketing, Columbia Business School, New York, NY

INTRODUCTION

Price is the only area of the global marketing mix where policy can be changed without direct cost implications. It does not cost anything to raise or lower prices: at least not immediately. If the price is too high or too low, the consequences of the error in pricing may not be evident. If the price is too high, total profits and competitive position are less than they could be if the price were "right." If it is too low, the same thing is true: profits are reduced and competitive position is weakened. This, plus the fact that most consumers are sensitive to price, underlines the importance of pricing decisions, which should be made carefully and never as a quick fix. The goal of pricing policy and strategy should be to set the right price, and the right price is the price that creates the greatest value for customers and the strongest competitive position for the company.

Pricing for global markets is a challenge. The global pricing policy and strategy of a company must address the challenge of setting the right price in each country. Rarely, if ever, is the right price for each country the home-country price or the same price in a single currency translated into the currency of target markets. In each country costs, competition, and the value of a company's product or service is different.

The global manager must develop pricing systems and pricing policies that address price floors, price ceilings, and optimum prices in each of the national markets in which her company operates.

BASIC PRICING CONCEPTS

In any country, three basic factors determine the boundaries within which market prices should be set: cost, competition, and demand. The first is product cost, which establishes a long-run price floor, or minimum price. The second is competition, which of course is defined by customers: your competitors are those companies whose products compete with your products from the consumer's point of view. The third consideration is demand and value: price is a cue for value and, in the case of luxury products, is part of value. A cheap luxury watch is an oxymoron: there is no luxury without a luxury price.

BOX 11-1

Side Bar: Apple Pricing in India and World

Do you remember when the first iPhone had come out, making its first appearance to the world? Company chairman Steve Jobs spoke during the Apple's annual Macworld expo in San Francisco, USA, and let the world know about a mobile phone known as an iPhone, which could not only play music but allowed the user to surf the Web during January 2007. When it actually came out during June 2007 for sale, the retail price of this gadget was fixed between $499 and $599 depending on the features. Initially, on its appearance, the iPhone was sold through company owned Apple stores. The first off-line apple store was opened in USA in 2001 which used to sell Macintosh personal computers, software, iPod, iPad etc. Apple also had its online apple store from November, 1997. Apple by now has 486 retail stores in 19 countries and an online store available in 39 countries for marketing its product around the world. The pricing of the products varied across different countries due to various factors such as distribution channel used, marketing reasons like discount offered, logistics cost differentials etc. The following table captures the ultimate price of iPhone 5S price in USD including taxes etc which prevailed during 2012 for 40 countries of the world (Indrayan, 2013). A simple analysis of the price of iphone during 2012 shows that iphone price in Brazil was 36.57 percent high than it's median price.

continued

Country/Region	iPhone 5S price in USD (including taxes)	Above and below median price in USD	Above and below median price in percentage	GDP per capita (PPP) in USD*	iPhone 5S price as % of GDP per capita (PPP)
Brazil	1200	321.325	36.57	44,598	2.69%
Turkey	1054	175.325	19.95	44,208	2.38%
Hungary	1007	128.325	14.60	39,788	2.53%
Italy	1002	123.325	14.04	11,909	8.41%
Denmark	995	116.325	13.24	42,533	2.34%
France	975	96.325	10.96	9,233	10.56%
Poland	970	91.325	10.39	26,590	3.65%
Austria	961	82.325	9.37	42,086	2.28%
Finland	961	82.325	9.37	38,655	2.49%
Germany	961	82.325	9.37	36,104	2.66%
Ireland	961	82.325	9.37	40,901	2.35%
Netherlands	961	82.325	9.37	51,946	1.85%
Portugal	961	82.325	9.37	22,119	4.34%
Spain	961	82.325	9.37	3,876	24.79%
Belgium	959	80.325	9.14	4,956	19.35%
Sweden	957	78.325	8.91	43,592	2.20%
Norway	936	57.325	6.52	33,111	2.83%
Luxembourg	913	34.325	3.91	35,178	2.60%
Russia	912	33.325	3.79	91,388	1.00%
United Kingdom	895	16.325	1.86	17,143	5.22%
Switzerland	876	−2.675	−0.30	16,731	5.24%
China	871	−7.675	−0.87	43,198	2.02%
Czech Republic	869	−9.675	−1.10	32,219	2.70%
New Zealand	866	−12.675	−1.44	65,640	1.32%
India	860	−18.675	−2.13	4,410	19.50%
South Korea	836	−42.675	−4.86	22,162	3.77%
Mexico	822	−56.675	−6.45	25,411	3.23%
Singapore	787	−91.675	−10.43	23,501	3.35%
Phillipines	779	−99.675	−11.34	61,803	1.26%
Australia	777	−101.675	−11.57	30,801	2.52%
Canada	767	−111.675	−12.71	32,682	2.35%
Taiwan	760	−118.675	−13.51	43,180	1.76%
Thailand	745	−133.675	−15.21	53,367	1.40%
Malaysia	742	−136.675	−15.55	38,357	1.93%
Vietnam	742	−136.675	−15.55	9,820	7.56%
Hong Kong	721	−157.675	−17.94	18,348	3.93%
Indonesia	719	−159.675	−18.17	42,080	1.71%
United Arab Emirates	708	−170.675	−19.42	36,901	1.92%
United States	702	−176.675	−20.11	49,965	1.40%
Japan	696	−182.675	−20.79	3,635	19.15%
	35147			878.675	

Source: Gunjan Indrayan. (2013, December 15). Re: A comparison of iPhone 5S pricing across the globe [Web log comment]. Retrieved from https://wirelesstelecom.wordpress.com/2013/12/15/a-comparison-of-iphone-5s-pricing-across-the-globe-2/
Range calculations are from authors to provide understanding about price fluctuations.
**Source:* World Bank 2012 data.

Japan was the country which had the lowest price of iphone 5S and which was about 20.79 percent lower that its median price. United States as the originator country also enjoyed lower price which was 20.11 percent less that the median price. Indian price of iphone 5S was about 2.13 percent lower than the median price. In a way, it can be said that the iphone 5S price varied between 36.57 percent and 20.79 percent lower than the median price across 40 countries of the world.

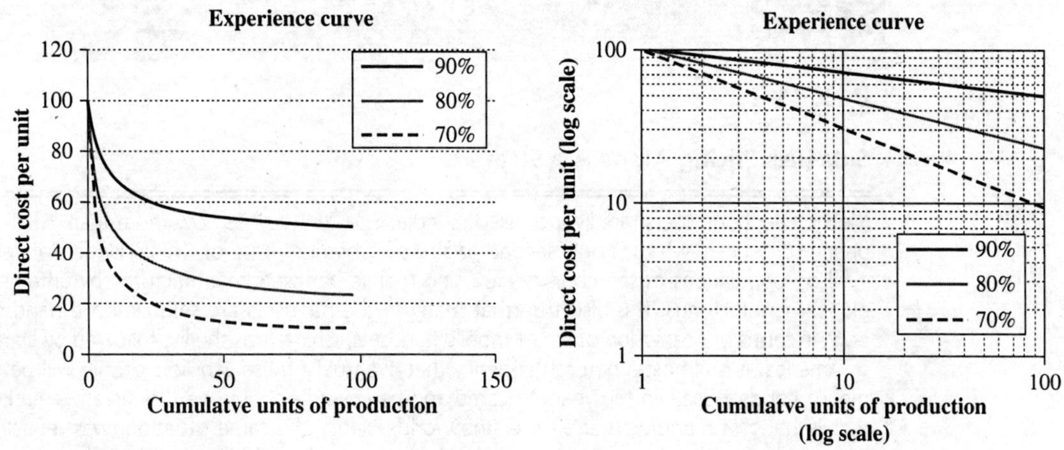

FIGURE 11-1 Experience Curve

Cost

Although it is certainly possible to price a product below the cost boundary, few firms can afford to do this for extended periods of time. Pricing below cost can be part of a strategy to achieve a leading market position which will be profitable in the long term. Amazon priced e-books below its cost in order to capture market share of the e-book market for books and readers. In the case of manufactured products, pricing below cost, or "target" pricing, can be justified by experience theory which is, simply put, an empirical finding that as the total volume of production (for all manufacturers) of a product rises, when measured by accumulated volume (that is total production volume of all manufacturers), costs go down as a constant percentage. In other words, costs go down forever. When Bruce Henderson, founder of the Boston Consulting Group, learned about the experience effect, he was one of the early advocates of experience theory pricing and pointed out that if costs go down forever, there are clear implications for management: pricing should be based not on historical or even current costs, but rather on costs that are incurred at the time of production. Especially for new products, accumulated production volume is small, meaning that continued production will double at a rapid rate in the early stages of the product's life cycle.

Every time total production volume is doubled, prices decline on a curve that can be used to forecast future costs.

The Experience Curve

The experience curve effect is broader in scope than the learning curve effect, encompassing far more than just labor time. It states that the more often a task is performed, the lower will be the cost of doing it. The task can be the production of any good or service. Each time cumulative volume doubles, value-added costs (including administration, marketing, distribution, and manufacturing) fall by a constant and predictable percentage.

Competition

Second, competitive prices for comparable products create a price ceiling, or upper boundary. International competition always puts pressure on the prices of domestic companies. A widespread effect of international trade is to lower prices. Indeed, one of the major benefits to a country of international business is the favorable impact of international competition on national price levels and, in turn, on a country's rate of inflation and standard of living. Between the lower and upper boundaries for every

BOX 11-2

Side Bar: Pricing Alone is a Strategy!

Mobile telephone users rapidly increased in India. The country has now more than 1 billion mobile phone subscribers which is only second to size of subscriber base of China. Understandably, these 1 billion populations of the country are using mobile handsets manufactured by different local or global manufacturers. It is also true that many of the handsets are smart mobile handsets. As of now, in terms of possession of smart mobile handsets, China tops the list followed by United States of America. It is almost a natural tendency that eventually these 1 billion people will be the smart mobile handset users in the years to come and hence India should be the lucrative market for the mobile handset manufacturer all over the world. Exactly the same situation, was reflecting in the smart mobile market where the competition is getting red hot. With the introduction of smart phone in India, a different type of competition was noticed amongst the handset manufacturers which was based on different features incorporated in the smart phones. Smart handsets competed on the basis of features like RAM, ROM, pixel size of camera, single sim or duel sim, different android versions used by mobile sets etc. Local manufacturing companies like Micromax used pricing and feature combination strategy and used low pricing with comparatively high features to woo the Indian consumers. The company was fairly successful in the Indian market by efficient use of this duel strategy. However, it seems that such strategy can't continue to do marketing miracle as other manufacturing companies will be ready for offering smart phones with more or less similar features. So the smart mobile handsets manufactures will be heavily dependent on innovative pricing strategy.

The Table 11-1 indicates that in the recent years China has been able to penetrate Indian mobile handset market. During 2011, China exported 62.71 percent of the total Indian import. During 2015 about 86.67 percent of total Indian import was met by the Chinese manufacturers based in China. If Hong Kong, Chinese Taipei and China together are considered, then 91.36% of the total import requirement of India came from them only.

TABLE 11-1 Top 10 Exporting Countries of Mobile Telephones for Cellular Networks to India (Values are in US Dollar Thousand and for HS Code 85171290)

	Exporting countries	Imported value in 2011	Imported value in 2012	Imported value in 2013	Imported value in 2014	Imported value in 2015	Importing country by share 2015	Importing country by share 2011
	World	5783598	4591359	5934103	7433805	6949614		
1	China	3627110	3181553	4528044	6229414	6023304	86.67%	62.71%
2	Viet Nam	348521	376150	922548	654544	455211	6.55%	6.03%
3	Hong Kong	171234	87316	134766	156776	255775	3.68%	2.96%
4	Singapore	55676	58823	6515	2242	76757	1.10%	0.96%
5	Taipei,	150045	134147	154384	205170	70378	1.01%	2.59%
6	S.Korea,	448561	131060	98093	98812	49805	0.72%	7.76%
7	Mexico	88512	78317	26353	25172	4187	0.06%	1.53%
8	Malaysia	57059	38875	4320	3740	2944	0.04%	0.99%
9	USA	150915	104917	1815	3459	1787	0.03%	2.61%
10	Sweden	10297	6708	39770	31037	1722	0.02%	0.18%
							99.89%	88.32%

Source: Trade data base and author's calculation

continued

Chinese brands like Vivo, Oppo, Huawei, Xiaomi and Lenovo are there to stay and play in the Indian market successfully because of their competitive pricing strategy alone. Example set by China's "Apple" Xiaomi by selling record 1 million smart phones in India only in a span of 18 days during pre Diwali period, 2016. The Indian and South Korean manufacturers have to learn this strategy very quickly. Though South Korean suppliers increased its share of Indian import of mobile handsets from 0.72% during 2011to 7.76% during 2015 but it looks dwarfed by the Chinese quantum of marketing success.

product there is an optimum price, which is a function of the demand for the product as determined by the willingness and ability of customers to buy. As the gray marketing example illustrates, however, sometimes the optimum price can be affected by arbitrageurs who exploit price differences in different countries.

Demand

The third consideration in pricing decisions is demand and value. The price of any product or service can never be higher than the demand for the product or service, and demand is a function of perceived product value. Demand will depend upon the competition and the perceived relative value of a company's product or service. Perceived value will depend upon the product itself, the channels of distribution, integrated marketing communications, and the price of the product: in other words, on the Four Ps of the marketing mix.

The task of determining prices in global marketing is complicated by fluctuating exchange rates, which may bear only limited relationship to underlying costs. According to the concept of purchasing power parity, in the long run, changes in domestic prices will be reflected in the exchange rate of the country's currency. Thus, in theory, fluctuating exchange rates should not present serious problems for the global marketer because a rise or decline in domestic price levels should be offset by an opposite rise or decline in the value of the home-country currency and vice versa. In the real world, however, exchange rates do not move in lockstep fashion with inflation. This means that global marketers are faced with difficult decisions about how to deal with windfalls resulting from favorable exchange rates, as well as losses due to unfavorable exchange rates.

A firm's pricing system and policies must also be consistent with other uniquely global constraints on demand. Pricing decisions must take into account international transportation costs, middlemen in elongated international channels of distribution, and the demands of global accounts for equal price treatment regardless of location. In addition to the diversity of national markets in all three basic dimensions—cost, competition, and demand—the international executive is also confronted by conflicting governmental tax policies and claims as well as various types of price controls. These include dumping legislation, resale price maintenance legislation, price ceilings, and general reviews of price levels. For example, Procter & Gamble (P&G) encountered strict price controls in Venezuela. Despite increases in the cost of raw materials, P&G was granted only about 50 percent of the price increases it requested; even then, months passed before permission to raise prices was forthcoming. As a result, detergent prices in Venezuela were less than what they were in the United States.

The approach outlined earlier is used in part or in whole by most experienced global firms, but it must be noted that the inexperienced or part-time exporter does not usually go to all this effort to determine the best price for a product in international markets. Such a company will frequently use a much simpler approach to pricing, such as the cost-plus method explained later in this chapter. As managers gain experience and become more sophisticated in their approach, however, they realize that the factors identified previously should be considered when making pricing decisions.

There are other important internal organizational considerations besides cost. Within the typical corporation, there are many interest groups and, frequently, conflicting price objectives. Divisional vice presidents, regional executives, and country managers are each concerned about profitability at their respective organizational levels. Similarly, the director of international marketing seeks competitive prices in world markets. The controller and financial vice president are also concerned about profits. The manufacturing vice president seeks long runs for maximum manufacturing efficiency. The tax manager is concerned about compliance with government transfer pricing legislation, and company counsel is concerned about the antitrust implications of international pricing practices.

Compounding the problem is the rapidly changing global marketplace and the inaccurate and incomplete nature of much of the available information regarding demand. In many parts of the world, external market information is distorted and inaccurate. It is often not possible to obtain the definitive and precise information that would be the basis of an optimal price. The same may be true about internal information. In addition to a lack of complete information, there are other problems. When attempting to estimate demand, for example, it is important to consider product appeal relative to competitive products. Although it is possible to arrive at such estimates after conducting market research, the effort can be costly and time consuming. Company managers and executives have to rely on intuition and experience. One way of improving the estimates of potential demand is to use analogy. As described in Chapter 6, this approach basically means extrapolating potential demand for target markets from actual sales in markets judged to be similar.

COST BASED PRICING METHOD

Full Cost Pricing Method

This is rather an easy method of pricing. Under this method cost of the production is taken as the datum. From the cost of production one can arrive at the cost of sales by adding promotion and distribution cost to the cost of production cost value. Then in order to find the price of a product one need to know mark-up profit and add it up to the cost of sales. Usually, there is an industry standard in terms of mark-up profit and this process of calculating the price of a product is not difficult but very straightforward. However one cannot rule out the possibility of not correctly estimating all cash and non-cash costs and arrive at the actual product cost subtotal.

Cost based pricing = cost of production + promotion and distribution cost + mark-up profit as per industry standard.

Marginal Cost Pricing Method

The is also a cost based pricing method but under this method costs associated with production are segregated in to variable cost and fixed cost and there after uses variable cost as pivot for pricing. Fixed costs are those costs which are fixed in nature at least to certain level of production. It consists of costs like factory rental, capital equipment loan repayment costs and salaries for staffs of permanent nature etc which are going to remain of same volume in the short or medium term irrespective the volume of production, remain unchanged regardless of the level of output achieved. The variable costs unlike fixed costs would directly vary with the volume of production. This costs consists of raw material costs, wages, electricity costs etc. When a company earns a volume revenue equals to cover both fixed and variable costs, then the company is in the zone of no profit and no loss. Technically, this point is known as breakeven point. At this point, total revenue is equal to total costs. When production volume reaches above breakeven, then post break even volume requires to cover the variable cost only. So a company can fix price of products, after breakeven by considering only the variable cost associated with production.

ENVIRONMENTAL INFLUENCES ON PRICING DECISIONS

Global marketers must deal with a number of environmental considerations when making pricing decisions. Among these are currency fluctuations, inflation, government controls and subsidies, competitive behavior, and market demand. Some of these factors work in conjunction with others; for example, inflation may be accompanied by government controls. Each consideration is discussed in detail next.

Currency Fluctuations

Fluctuating currency values are a fact of life in international business. The marketer must decide what to do about this fact. Are price adjustments appropriate when currencies strengthen or weaken? There are two extreme positions; one is to fix the price of products in country target markets. If this is done, any appreciation or depreciation of the value of the currency in the country of production will lead to revenue gains or losses for the seller. The other extreme position is to fix the price of products in home-country currency. If this is done, any appreciation or depreciation of the home-country currency will result in price increases or decreases for customers, with consequences for the seller. Assuming that the price before the currency fluctuation was correct, the consequences could be negative.

In practice, companies rarely assume either of these extreme positions. Pricing decisions should be consistent with the company's overall business and marketing strategy. If the strategy is long term, then it makes no sense to give up market share in order to maintain export margins. When currency fluctuations result in appreciation in the value of the currency of a country that is an exporter, wise companies do two things: they accept that currency fluctuations may unfavorably impact operating margins and they double their efforts to reduce costs. In the short run, lower margins enable them to hold prices in target markets, and in the longer run, driving down costs enables them to improve operating margins.

For companies that are in a strong, competitive market position, price increases can be passed on to customers without significant decreases in sales volume. In more competitive market situations, companies in a strong-currency country will often absorb any price increase by maintaining international market prices at pre-revaluation levels. In practice, a manufacturer and its channels of distribution may work together to maintain market share in international markets. Either party, or both, may choose to take a lower profit percentage. The channels may also choose to purchase more product to achieve volume discounts; another alternative is to maintain leaner inventories if the manufacturer can provide just-in-time delivery. By using these approaches, it is possible to remain price competitive in markets in which currency devaluation in the importing country is a price consideration.

The crisis that occurred with the Russian ruble is another good example of how currency fluctuations can affect marketing. Prior to the devaluation of the ruble, the market share for Russian shampoos, face care products, hair coloring, toothpaste, deodorants, and soaps in Russia was only 27 percent. When the price of imported products rose dramatically, many Russian women switched to local products. The market share of local products rose to 44 percent and forced some foreign producers out of the market.

TABLE 11-2 Global Pricing Strategies[2]

When Domestic Currency Is Weak	When Domestic Currency Is Strong
1. Stress price benefits.	1. Engage in nonprice competition by improving quality, delivery, and after-sale service.
2. Expand product line and add more costly features.	2. Improve productivity and engage in cost reduction.
3. Shift sourcing to domestic market.	3. Shift sourcing outside home country.
4. Exploit market opportunities in all markets.	4. Give priority to exports to countries with stronger currencies.
5. Use full-costing approach but employ marginal-cost pricing to penetrate new or competitive markets.	5. Trim profit margins and use marginal-cost pricing.
6. Speed repatriation of foreign-earned income and collections.	6. Keep the foreign-earned income in host country; slow down collections.
7. Minimize expenditures in local or host-country currency.	7. Maximize expenditures in local or host-country currency.
8. Buy advertising, insurance, transportation, and other services in domestic market.	8. Buy needed services abroad and pay for them in local currencies.
9. Bill foreign customers in their own currency.	9. Bill foreign customers in the domestic currency.

Table 11-2 provides a synopsis of pricing strategies to use when domestic currency is weak and when it is strong.

Exchange-Rate Clauses

Many sales are contracts to supply goods or services over time. When these contracts are between parties in two countries, the problem of exchange-rate fluctuations and exchange risk must be addressed.

An exchange-rate clause allows the buyer and seller to agree to supply and purchase at fixed prices in each company's national currency. If the exchange rate fluctuates within a specified range, say plus or minus 5 percent, the fluctuations do not affect the pricing agreement that is spelled out in the exchange-rate clause. Small fluctuations in exchange rates are not a problem for most buyers and sellers. Exchange-rate clauses are designed to protect both the buyer and the seller from unforeseen large swings in currencies. An example of actual clauses used by one company is shown in Table 11-3.

TABLE 11-3 Exchange-Rate Clauses

- Purpose: To protect parties from unforeseen large swings in currencies.
- Exchange rate review is made quarterly to determine possible adjustments for the next period.
- Comparison basis is the three-month daily average and the initial average.

[2] S. Tamer Cavusgil, "Pricing for Global Markets," *Columbia Journal of World Business*, 31, no. 4 (Winter 1996): 69. Reprinted with permission.

The basic design of an exchange-rate clause is straightforward: review exchange rates periodically (this is determined by the parties; any interval is possible, but most clauses specify a monthly or quarterly review), and compare the daily average during the review period and the initial base average. If the comparison produces exchange-rate fluctuations that are outside the agreed range of fluctuation, an adjustment is made to align prices with the new exchange rate. If the fluctuation is greater than a limit, say 5 to 10 percent, the parties agree to discuss and negotiate new prices. In other words, the clause accepts the foreign exchange market's effect on currency value, but only if it is within the range of 5 to 10 percent. Anything less than 5 percent does not affect pricing, and anything more than 10 percent opens up a renegotiation of prices.

Pricing in an Inflationary Environment

Inflation, or a persistent upward change in price levels, is a worldwide phenomenon. Inflation requires periodic price adjustments. These adjustments are necessitated by rising costs that must be covered by increased selling prices. An essential requirement when pricing in an inflationary environment is the maintenance of operating profit margins. Regardless of cost accounting practices, if a company maintains its margins, it has effectively protected itself from the effects of inflation.

Within the scope of this chapter, it is possible only to touch on the major accounting issues and conventions relating to price adjustments in international markets. In particular, it is worth noting that the traditional FIFO (first-in, first-out) costing method is hardly appropriate for an inflationary situation. A more appropriate accounting practice under conditions of rising prices is the LIFO (last-in, first-out) method, which takes the most recent raw material acquisition price and uses it as the basis for costing the product sold. In highly inflationary environments, historical approaches are less appropriate costing methods than replacement cost. The latter amounts to a next-in, first-out approach. Although this method does not conform to generally accepted accounting principles (GAAP), it is used to estimate future prices that will be paid for raw and component materials. These replacement costs can then be used to set prices. This approach is useful in managerial decision making, but it cannot be used in financial statements. Regardless of the accounting methods used, an essential requirement under inflationary conditions of any costing system is that it maintain gross and operating profit margins. Managerial actions can maintain these margins subject to the following constraints.

Government Controls and Subsidies

If government action limits the freedom of management to adjust prices, the maintenance of margins is definitely compromised. Under certain conditions, government action is a real threat to the profitability of a subsidiary operation. In a country that is undergoing severe financial difficulties and is in the midst of a financial crisis (e.g., a foreign exchange shortage caused in part by runaway inflation), government officials are under pressure to take some type of action. In some cases, governments will take expedient steps rather than getting at the underlying causes of inflation and foreign exchange shortages. Such steps might include the use of broad or selective price controls. When selective controls are imposed, foreign companies are more vulnerable to control than local businesses, particularly if the outsiders lack the political influence over government decision making possessed by local managers.

Government control can also take the form of prior cash deposit requirements imposed on importers. This is a requirement that a company has to tie up funds in the form of a noninterest-bearing deposit for a specified period of time if it wishes to import products. Such requirements clearly create an incentive for a company to minimize the price of the imported product; lower prices mean smaller deposits. Other government requirements that affect the pricing decision are profit transfer rules that restrict the conditions under which profits can be transferred out of a country. Under such rules, a high transfer price paid for imported goods by an affiliated company can be interpreted as a device for transferring profits out of a country.

Government subsidies can also force a company to make strategic use of sourcing to be price competitive. In Europe, government subsidies to the agricultural sector make it difficult for foreign marketers of processed food to compete on price when exporting to the European Union. In the United States, some, but not all, agricultural sectors are subsidized. In Japan, rice growers are protected.

BOX 11-3

Side Bar: Price is Elastic in Nature

The Indian Prime Minister, Narendra Modi, in January 2015, described the LED bulb as "Prakash Path"—"way to light". A simple act of changing of the one light bulb to LED at South Block, Prime Minister's office, heralded a movement in the entire country for considering the same change. The initiative is part of the Government of India's efforts to spread the message of energy efficiency in the country. UJALA scheme aims to promote efficient use of energy at the residential level; enhance the awareness of consumers about the efficacy of using energy efficient appliances and aggregating demand to reduce the high initial costs thus facilitating higher

TABLE 11-4 List of Top Ten Supplying Markets for a Product Imported by India

Product: 9405 Lamps and lighting fittings, incl. searchlights and spotlights, and parts thereof, n.e.s; illuminated ...
Unit: US Dollar thousand

Exporters	Imported value in 2011	Imported value in 2012	Imported value in 2013	Imported value in 2014	Imported value in 2015	Share of import 2015	YOY Growth of import in % (2014 to 2015)
World	235808	266858	302801	359543	576114		
China	144698	173359	210822	278280	487789	85%	75%
Korea, Republic of	2834	3162	16584	15088	19419	3%	29%
Germany	16176	19101	16774	13548	13597	2%	0%
Italy	11137	10015	11447	9522	10605	2%	11%
Hong Kong, China	3910	5012	4570	7574	7338	1%	−3%
United States of America	8610	9171	9715	5769	5855	1%	1%
Czech Republic	567	2359	1362	1000	3339	1%	234%
Spain	3939	3865	4859	3790	3102	1%	−18%
United Kingdom	6204	4262	3294	4416	2812	0%	−36%

Source: Trade data base and author's calculations

continued

uptake of LED lights by residential users. It may be noted that the scheme was initially labelled DELP (Domestic Efficient Lighting Program) and was re-launched as UJALA. Every domestic household having a metered connection from their respective Electricity Distribution Company is eligible to get the LED bulbs under the UJALA Scheme. The consumer can purchase the LED on EMI payment (monthly/bi-monthly instalments in electricity bill) or on upfront payment by paying the full amount.

The UJALA scheme of replacing all inefficient bulbs with these energy-efficient lamps has changed the market of LED bulbs. "With India selling 770 million LED bulbs every day, the country will soon become the LED capital of the world. Prices of LED bulbs have come down to 55 pence (Rs 52) from over 3.5 pounds (Rs 332) two years ago," quipped the Indian Power Minister, Piyush Goyal, in the backdrop of a conference in London. Under this scheme, more that 9.7 crore LED bulbs have been distributed so far. UJALA, has brought down the price of an LED bulb to Rs 85 for a 9-watt on an average. Some states have received even lower prices during bidding. "UJALA is providing technically the best lamps of nine watt capacity. Let's say you can get an LED bulb for an average $1.25 in India against $3.5-4 two years back," Industry expert quipped referring to Goyal's pound-denominated pricing for his London audience.

The sudden rise of LED bulb is met by import which has opened India as a lucrative market in terms of China. The above Table 11-4 indicates that during 2015 almost 85 percent of Indian imports of LED bulb are exported by China. Also year on year growth of Chinese export imports during 2014 and 2015 has gone up to 75 percent. The Republic of Korea, stood second in terms of its share of Indian import market but with only 3%. But sudden demand in Indian market has also allowed them to have export growth of 29 percent during 2014 and 2015. Interestingly, the huge importation rush affected the price stability of the product in Indian market and the high supply lowered the market price.

Source: http://timesofindia.indiatimes.com/business/india-business/India-headed-for-top-slot-in-global-LED-bulb-market/articleshow/51918389.cms

Competitive Behavior

As noted at the beginning of this chapter, pricing decisions are bounded not only by cost and the nature of demand but also by competitive action. If competitors do not adjust their prices in response to rising costs, management—even if acutely aware of the effect of rising costs on operating margins—will be severely constrained in its ability to adjust prices accordingly. Conversely, if competitors are manufacturing or sourcing in a lower-cost country, it may be necessary to cut prices to stay competitive.

Price and Quality Relationships

Is there a relationship between price and quality? Do you, in fact, get what you pay for? During the past several decades, studies conducted in the United States have indicated that the overall relationship between price and quality as measured by consumer testing organizations is quite weak. A recent four-country international study found a high degree of similarity with the results from the US studies. The authors conclude that the lack of a strong price–quality relationship appears to be an international phenomenon.[3] This is not surprising when one recognizes that consumers make purchase decisions with limited information and rely more on product appearance and style and less on technical quality as measured by objective criteria.

[3] David J. Faulds, Orlen Grunewals, and Denise Johnson, "A Cross-National Investigation of the Relationship between the Price and Quality of Consumer Products, 1970–1990," *Journal of Global Marketing*, vol. 8, no. 1 (1994): 7–25.

BOX 11-4

Side Bar: Pricing can Make as well as Break!

People don't value things that don't have value. In India there is a common saying tuned with this line, "even if gold is offered for free people will not value it". While pricing a product this universal wisdom needs to be taken care of. A product launched in the category of luxury product can not even think of reducing the price as it would have adverse impact on marketing. Can you imagine Apple iphone 7 getting launched in India at ₹5000-10000 per handset? It would be suicidal for the American company as it would be treated below par and hence there will be difficulty in selling the product. Mr Shiva Khera, the great motivational speaker priced his three days training programme on leadership at Rs, 40,000/- per participant. This programme has takers who pay the fees and participate. Of course some relaxation in pricing is provided but in disguise so that it does not make the prospective buyers believe that "it does not have value". Usual terms to lower price in disguise are 20% discount on fee for institutions sponsoring more than 5 participants or 15% discount for non-sponsored individual participant, 50 percent discount for those who have shown exceptional leadership in working situation etc. These allow people to feel great as well enjoy the low price. Just think of a possible marketing campaign during the launch of the greatly hyped Tata group's small car Nano, "discount available for those who have genuine concern for environment". Nano, the moment it publicised the car as the cheapest car in the world from then onwards the prospective customers started feeling the brunt of being labelled as 'poor person' in the society. This extraordinarily high class designed car failed to get market even amongst the rural segment for whom the manufacturers tried its level best to produce the car at the cheapest possible. It was a real marketing agony as huge possibilities wasted simply because of a pricing mistake. Ratan Tata, the legendary entrepreneur of India, quipped rightly, "Maybe it (Nano) gets launched in another country like Indonesia, where it doesn't have the stigma and the new image comes back to India. Or maybe as a changed product that gets marketed in Europe. There's a lot of interest in Nano outside India". Alas! Whatever you, as a marketer, do now to re launch the product Nano, it would be difficult to come out of the image as "cheapest car of the world".

GLOBAL PRICING OBJECTIVES AND STRATEGIES

A number of different pricing strategies are available to global marketers. An overall goal must be to contribute to company sales and profit objectives worldwide. Customer-oriented strategies such as market skimming, penetration, and market holding can be used when consumer perceptions, as determined by the value equation, are used as a guide. Global pricing can also be based on other external criteria such as the escalation in costs when goods are shipped long distances across national boundaries. The issue of global pricing can also be fully integrated in the product design process, an approach widely used by Japanese companies. Prices in global markets are not carved in stone; they must be evaluated at regular intervals and adjusted if necessary. Similarly, pricing objectives may vary, depending on a product's life-cycle stage and the country-specific competitive situation.

MARKET BASED PRICING METHODS

Cost based pricing methods have often been criticised for its simplicity and inward looking nature i.e. production orientation. Thinkers in this important subject have often advised to be market oriented in terms of fixing price as price affects the consumer behaviour and the product life in the market place. Under market based pricing method the price of a product is fixed based on the desired consumer behaviour. Four prominent methods of market based pricing are discussed below.

PENETRATION PRICING METHOD Under this method price of a product is fixed based on the understanding that comparatively low price would allow the product to rapidly reach a large number of consumers of the market and resultant word of mouth publicity allow sufficiency market penetration while launching a product in a new market. Later, after persisting with low price for some time, strategically switch over to normal range of price or more to recover the loss, if incurred, because of low pricing strategy adopted. Now the change in price would not encourage customers to switch over to other brands because of product quality by now has made the existing users loyal.

SKIMMING PRICING METHOD This method is just reverse of penetration pricing method. Under this method relatively higher price is fixed for a product or service while launching in a market to skim off the profit during the initial period and then lowers the price over time. It is a method of pricing when a company expecting imminent fierce competition and hence temporal version of price discrimination was required to generate profit at a brisk speed.

PRESTIGE PRICING METHOD Prestige pricing plays on the psychology of the prospective consumers. Under this method artificially the price of a product is hiked to the likings of the expectations of a niche class of customers who psychologically associate higher prices with superior quality. These customers then think that possession of the product would bring them higher prestige or status in the society.

FACTORS EFFECTING PRICE IN INTERNATIONAL MARKETS

There are various factors which the international marketers need to consider before fixing the price of a product in the international markets. Some important factors are as stated low.

Prejudice Against Products Manufactured in Developing Countries

Country of manufacturing (COM) is an important indicator for a product placed in international markets and assessed by prospective consumers regarding its worth. For example, if the COM is Germany or Japan it immediately attracts respect from the prospective consumers around the world and hence they ready to pay higher price to own it. Reversely, if COM is a least developing country then prospective consumers of developing or developed country would automatically be skeptical about the product quality and hence not willing to purchase the product with even normal price.

Product Differentiation

How many variety of products are being offered for a country market? An automobile, say sports utility vehicle (SUV) may be offered for Australian market under several varieties, from strip off version to luxury all frill version, and thereby allowing the prospective customers to have options for choice. This enable the automobile marketers to have a range of price for a product. Reversely, some target country may not provide enough marketing opportunity to place a whole range of product differentiated on different counts. Hence pricing felicity would automatically will be low in such situation.

Brand Image

Country of brand (COB) is an important indicator of quality in the international market. COB provides an image which allow the international marketers to charge higher price for a product. For example, Toyota has huge COB image in the international markets which M&M of India will not have and hence pricing flexibility of M&M would be much less in a distant market.

Order Size

The size of the market contemplated to be targeted also influence the pricing of a product. A large country market allow a company to set its expected sales target at a higher level than a small country where possible market size is inherently small. A larger expected sales provides flexibility in terms of fixing price of a product.

Presumed Relationship between Quality & Price

Culturally in some countries the consumers feel that higher the price more would be the quality. Quality comes at a cost and hence low price cannot bring good quality. In these countries consumers are likely to reject a quality product if price is not elevated to a higher level.

After Sales and Before Sales Services

Since international marketer markets its products in different countries it would be difficult for them to position similar after sales and before sales services in all the countries it markets its products. Tata Motors may not able to provide equally efficient after sales and before sales services in all the 117 country markets of its presence. A country where after sales and before sales services is less efficient the company may not be able to charge higher price.

Consistency/Continuity of Supplies

It is difficult for the international marketers to maintain consistency and continuity of supplies in all the distant country markets with equal efficiency. Several logistics and distribution related problems are often found to responsible for supply break down. Countries where consistency and continuity of supplies could be maintained provide opportunities to retain pricing flexibility.

PARALLEL IMPORTS INFLUENCING PRICE

Parallel importing also known as grey marketing may affect fixing of price in international markets. In parallel importing branded or trademarked goods of one country enter in another country illegally and without authorisation of the brand or trade mark owner. These illegal entry allow them to enjoy low price in the country market and thereby distorting the competitive pricing structure of the market place. So, under parallel importing, the consumers are exposed to same products being offered at different prices; one lowly priced but not sold through legally authorised shops and two, higher priced products available in the legal or authorised shops. If parallel importing is prevalently present in a country then it would force international marketers to react to the situation and lower price of its own product to combat the situation.

GRAY MARKET GOODS[4]

Gray market goods are trademarked products that are exported from one country to another, where they are sold by unauthorized persons or organizations. Sometimes, gray marketers bring a product produced in one country—French champagne, for example—into a second-country market in competition with authorized importers. The gray marketers sell at prices that undercut those set by the legitimate importers. This practice, known as *parallel importing,* may flourish when a product is in short supply or when producers attempt to set high resale prices. This has happened with French champagne sold in the United States; it is also true in the market for pharmaceuticals, where prices vary widely from country to country. In some countries, parallel imports account for more than 10 percent of the sales of some pharmaceutical brands.

In another type of gray marketing, a company manufactures a product in the home-country market as well as in foreign markets. In this case, products manufactured abroad by the company's foreign affiliate for sales abroad are sometimes sold by a foreign distributor to gray marketers. The latter then bring the products into the producing company's home-country market, where they compete with domestically produced goods. For example, Caterpillar's US dealers found themselves competing with gray market construction equipment manufactured in Europe. A strong dollar provided gray marketers with an opportunity to bring Caterpillar equipment into the United States at lower prices than domestically produced equipment. Even though the gray market goods carry the same trademarks as the domestically produced ones, they may differ in quality, ingredients, or some other way. Manufacturers may not honor warranties on some types of gray market imports such as cameras and consumer electronics equipments.[5]

As these examples show, the marketing opportunity that presents itself requires gray market goods to be priced lower than goods sold by authorized distributors or domestically produced goods. Clearly, buyers gain from lower prices and increased choice. In the United Kingdom alone, for example, total annual retail sales of gray market goods are estimated to be as high as $1.6 billion. A case in Europe resulted in a ruling that strengthened the rights of brand owners. Silhouette, an Austrian manufacturer of upscale sunglasses, sued the Hartlauer discount chain after the latter obtained thousands of pairs of sunglasses that Silhouette intended for sale in Eastern Europe. The European Court of Justice found in favor of Silhouette. In clarifying a directive, the court ruled that stores cannot import branded goods from outside the EU and then sell them at discounted prices without permission of the brand owner. The *Financial Times* denounced the ruling as "bad for consumers, bad for competition, and bad for European economies."[6]

In the United States, gray market goods are subject to a 80-year-old law, the Tariff Act of 1930. Section 526 of the act expressly forbids importation of goods of foreign manufacture without the permission of the trademark owner. There are, however, several exceptions spelled out in the act; the US Customs Service, which implements the regulation, and the court system have considerable leeway in decisions regarding gray

---

[4] Per-Henrik Mansson, "Supreme Court Upholds Gray Market Champagne," *Wine Spectator,* July 15, 1988: 5; James E. Inman, "Gray Marketing of Imported Trademarked Goods: Tariffs and Trademark Issues," *American Business Law Journal* (May 1993): 59–116; Paul Lansing and Joseph Gabriella, "Clarifying Gray Market Gray Areas," *American Business Law Journal* (September 1993): 313–337.

[5] James E. Inman, "Gray Marketing of Imported Trademarked Goods: Tariffs and Trademark Issues," *American Business Law Journal* (May 1993): 59–116; Paul Lansing and Joseph Gabriella, "Clarifying Gray Market Gray Areas," *American Business Law Journal* (September 1993): 313–337.

[6] Peggy Hollinger and Neil Buckley, "Grey Market Ruling Delights Brand Owners," *Financial Times,* July 17, 1998: 8.

market goods. For example, in 1988 the US Supreme Court ruled that trademarked goods of foreign manufacture such as champagne could legally be imported and sold by gray marketers. In many instances, however, the court's interpretation of the law differs from that of the Customs Service.

DUMPING

Dumping in international trade is predatory pricing. It occurs when manufacturers export a product at a price that is lower than that charged in its home market. Many countries have national policies and procedures for protecting national companies from dumping. The US Antidumping Act of 1921, which is enforced by the US Treasury, did not define dumping specifically but instead referred to unfair competition. However, Congress has defined dumping as an unfair trade practice that results in "injury, destruction, or prevention of the establishment of American industry." Under this definition, dumping occurs when imports sold in the US market are priced either at levels that represent less than the cost of production plus an 8 percent profit margin or at levels below those prevailing in the producing country.

Dumping was a major issue in the Uruguay Round of GATT negotiations. Many countries disapproved of the US system of antidumping laws, in part because the Commerce Department historically almost always ruled in favor of a US company filing a complaint. Another issue was the fact that US exporters were often targeted in antidumping investigations in countries with few formal rules for due process. The US negotiators hoped to improve the ability of US companies to defend their interests and understand the bases for rulings.

The result of the GATT negotiations was an Agreement on Interpretation of Article VI. From the US point of view, one of the most significant changes between the agreement and the 1979 code is the addition of a standard of review that makes it harder to dispute US antidumping determinations. There were also a number of procedural and methodological changes. In some instances, these have the effect of bringing regulations more in line with US law. For example, in calculating fair price for a given product, any sales of the product at below-cost prices in the exporting country are not included in the calculations; inclusion of such sales would have the effect of exerting downward pressure on the fair price. The agreement also brought GATT standards into line with US standards by prohibiting governments from penalizing differences between home-market and export-market prices of less than 2 percent.

As the nature of these issues and regulations suggests, in some cases dumping legislation is used as a tool to protect local enterprise from predatory pricing practices by foreign companies. In other cases, it is used as tool for limiting foreign competition in a market. The public policy rationale for legitimate dumping legislation is that dumping is harmful to the orderly development of enterprise within an economy. Few economists would object to long-run or continuous dumping. If this were done, it would be an opportunity for a country to take advantage of a low-cost source of a particular good and to specialize in other areas. However, continuous dumping rarely occurs; the sale of agricultural products at international prices, with farmers receiving subsidized higher prices, is an example of continuous dumping. The type of dumping practiced by most companies is sporadic and unpredictable and does not provide a reliable basis for national economic planning. Instead, it may hurt domestic enterprise.

There has been a shift in the countries bringing charges of dumping. In 1998, the United States, EU, Australia, and Canada brought approximately one-third or 225 of the cases opened. This is down significantly from the late 1980s when these same countries accounted for four-fifths of all cases.[7] The leading countries bringing suit were South Africa, the United States, India, the European Union, and Brazil. Nearly 20 percent of the cases were brought against the EU or member countries, followed by China and Korea.

INCO TERMS AND PRICING IMPLICATIONS

The International Commercial Terms or INCO terms are widely used in international commercial transactions. These terms were first published in 1936 by the International Chamber of Commerce (ICC) and subsequently revised several times to reflect the need of the time. The recent revision by ICC, effective from January 1, 2011. INCO terms are used to indicate and communicate clearly the tasks, costs and risks associated with the transportation and delivery of goods, the pricing decisions are also affected by the specific terms used.

The INCOTERMS 2010 are as follows:

1. EXW—EX WORKS (... named place of delivery) Description: The seller's only responsibility is to make the goods available at the seller's premises. The buyer bears full costs and risks of moving the goods from there to the destination.
2. FCA—FREE CARRIER (... named place of delivery) Description: The seller delivers the goods cleared for export, to the carrier selected by the buyer. The seller loads the goods if the carrier pickup is at the seller's premises. From that point, the buyer bears the costs and risks associated with moving the goods to destination.
3. CPT—CARRIAGE PAID TO (... named place of destination) Description: The seller pays for moving the goods to destination. From the time the goods are transferred to the first carrier, the buyer bears the risks of loss or damage.
4. CIP—CARRIAGE AND INSURANCE PAID TO (... named place of destination) Description: The seller pays for moving the goods to destination. From the time the goods are transferred to the first carrier, the buyer bears the risks of loss or damage. The seller, however, purchases the cargo insurance.
5. DAT—DELIVERED AT TERMINAL (... named terminal at port or place of destination) Description: The seller delivers when the goods, once unloaded from the arriving means of transport, are placed at the buyer's disposal at a named terminal at the named port or place of destination. "Terminal" includes any place, whether covered or not, such as a quay, warehouse, container yard or road, rail or air cargo terminal. The seller bears all risks involved in bringing the goods to and unloading them at the terminal at the named port or place of destination.
6. DAP—DELIVERED AT PLACE (... named place of destination) Description: The seller delivers when the goods are placed at the buyer's disposal on the arriving means of transport ready for unloading at the named place of destination. The seller bears all risks involved in bringing the goods to the named place.
7. DDP—DELIVERED DUTY PAID (... named place) Description: The seller delivers the goods—cleared for import—to the buyer at destination. The seller bears all costs and risks of moving the goods, including the payment of customs duties and taxes.
8. FAS—FREE ALONGSIDE SHIP (... named port of shipment) Description: The seller delivers the goods to the origin port. From that point, the buyer bears all costs and risks of loss or damage.

[7] Guy de Jonquieres, "Poor Nations Starting More Dumping Cases," *Financial Times,* May 6, 1999: 5.

9. FOB—FREE ON BOARD (... named port of shipment) Description: The seller delivers the goods on board the ship and clears the goods for export. From that point, the buyer bears all costs and risks of loss or damage.
10. CFR—COST AND FREIGHT (... named port of destination) Description: The seller clears the goods for export and pays the costs of moving the goods to destination. The buyer bears all risks of loss or damage.
11. CIF—COST INSURANCE AND FREIGHT (... named port of destination) Description: The seller clears the goods for export and pays the costs of moving the goods to the port of destination. The buyer bears all risks of loss or damage. The seller, however, purchases the cargo insurance.

BOX 11-5

Side Bar: Premier Pricing as a Strategy

India is a very lucrative country as far as air conditioner market is considered. The increasing levels of affluence of the Indian middle class consumers are much known to the air conditioner manufacturers of the world. Almost all the global big names like Daikin, Hitachi, Fujitsu General, Carrier Toshiba, Panasonic, Mitsubishi Electric, Mitsubishi Heavy Industries and Sharp, Carrier, Trane and Whirlpool are present in the Indian market. To make the situation competitive enough, there are Indian companies like Voltas, Blue Star, Godrej, Videocon, Fedders Lloyd and Onida who are also fighting for their share of the market. As usual Chinese players like Carrier Midea and Haier are also present to fight out competition with pricing advantage. The Korean conglomerate, LG and Samsung, have already proved to be strong players in the Indian market.

Air-conditioning market in India has been predicted to be one of the top three in the world by 2012. About 3.8 million units were sold by these companies during 2013 which jumped to about 4 million in 2014. Highest sold, was high wall splits AC (24, 45,000) followed by Window ACs. Inverter AC just started but had good acceptance as evident by 6 percent market during 2014 (refer Table 11-5).

The powerful player, Japanese conglomerate Hitachi Ltd, further developed strength through joining the partnership with the American industrial major, Johnson Controls, for its air conditioning business. The American Japanese JV, is all set to conquer the Indian market in the coming summer of 2017 and increase its present market share from about 11 percent in the home air conditioning segment to about 30 percent. The company has readied its product line with inclusions of premium energy-efficient ACs. Indians, according to the company, prefer to

TABLE 11-5 Indian Market Size for ACs

Type of AC	Units sold 2014	% Share
VRV/VRF	25,000	1%
high wall splits	24,45,000	71%
Ductables and packaged units	90,000	3%
floor mounted	15,000	0%
cassettes	80,000	2%
inverter ACs	2,00,000	6%
Window ACs	6,05,000	17%

continued

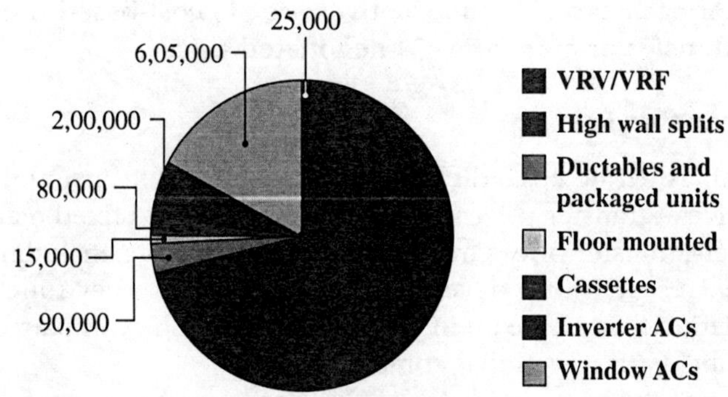

purchase energy efficient ACs only. The company manufactures, compressors for the products within India, which surely would be helpful in achieving the target. However, the company pricing strategy as usual will be premier pricing. In this strategy, the products would be offered in a higher price bracket to indicate that the products are "exclusive". The company expects that this would gel well with the Indian middle class consumer psychologically as well. The positioning would be - energy efficient, high and latest technology, higher price, global image–which will not allow Indian middle class consumers to escape.

For a positive proof of dumping to occur in the United States, both price discrimination and injury must be demonstrated. The existence of either one without the other is an insufficient condition to constitute dumping. Companies concerned with running afoul of antidumping legislation have developed a number of approaches for avoiding the dumping laws. One approach is to differentiate the product sold from that sold in the home market. An example of this is an auto accessory that one company packaged with a wrench and an instruction book, thereby changing the accessory to a tool. The tariff rate in the export market happened to be lower on tools, and the company also acquired immunity from antidumping laws because the package was not comparable to competing goods in the target market. Another approach is to make non-price-competitive adjustments in arrangements with affiliates and distributors. For example, credit can be extended and essentially have the same effect as a price reduction.

TRANSFER PRICING

Transfer pricing refers to the pricing of goods and services bought and sold by operating units or divisions of a single company. In other words, transfer pricing concerns intracorporate exchanges—transactions between buyers and sellers that have the same corporate parent. For example, Toyota subsidiaries sell to, and buy from, each other. The same is true of other companies operating globally. As companies expand and create decentralized operations, profit centers become an increasingly important component in the overall corporate financial picture. Appropriate intracorporate transfer pricing systems and policies are required to ensure profitability at each level. When a company extends its operations across national boundaries, transfer pricing takes on new dimensions and complications. In determining transfer prices to subsidiaries, global companies must address a number of issues, including taxes, duties and tariffs, country profit transfer rules, conflicting objectives of joint venture partners, and government regulations.

There are three major alternative approaches to transfer pricing. The approach used will vary with the nature of the firm, products, markets, and the historical circumstances of each case. The alternatives are (1) cost-based transfer pricing, (2) market-based transfer pricing, and (3) negotiated prices.

Cost-Based Transfer Pricing

Because companies define costs differently, some companies using the cost-based approach may arrive at transfer prices that reflect variable and fixed manufacturing costs only. Alternatively, transfer prices may be based on full costs, including overhead costs from marketing, research and development (R&D), and other functional areas. The way costs are defined may have an impact on tariffs and may impact duties on sales to affiliates and subsidiaries by global companies.

Cost-plus pricing is a variation of the cost-based approach. Companies that follow the cost-plus pricing method are taking the position that profit must be shown for any product or service at every stage of movement through the corporate system. In such an instance, transfer prices may be set at a certain percentage of fixed costs, such as "110 percent of cost." While cost-plus pricing may result in a price that is completely unrelated to competitive or demand conditions in international markets, many exporters use this approach successfully.

Market-Based Transfer Price

A market-based transfer price is derived from the price required to be competitive in the international market. The constraint on this price is cost. However, as noted previously in the chapter, there is a considerable degree of variation in how costs are defined. Because costs generally decline with volume, a decision must be made regarding whether to price on the basis of current or planned volume levels. To use market-based transfer prices to enter a new market that is too small to support local manufacturing, third-country sourcing may be required. This enables a company to establish its name or franchise in the market without committing to a major capital investment.

Negotiated Transfer Prices

A third alternative is to allow the organization's affiliates to negotiate transfer prices among themselves. In some instances, the final transfer price may reflect costs and market prices, but this is not a requirement.[8] The gold standard of negotiated transfer prices is known as an arm's-length price: the price that two independent, unrelated entities would negotiate.

Tax Regulations and Transfer Prices

Because the global corporation conducts business in a world with different corporate tax rates, there is an incentive to maximize system income in countries with the lowest tax rates and to minimize income in high-tax countries. Governments, naturally, are well aware of this situation. In recent years, many governments have tried to maximize national tax revenues by examining company returns and mandating reallocation of income and expenses.

Although a full treatment of tax issues is beyond the scope of this book, students should understand that a basic pricing question facing global marketers is, "What can a company do in the international pricing area in the light of current tax laws?" It is important to note that US Treasury regulations do not have the weight of law

---

[8] Charles T. Horngren and George Foster, *Cost Accounting: A Managerial Approach* (Upper Saddle River, NJ: Prentice Hall, 1991): 856.

TABLE 11-6 Transfer Pricing Methods for Selected Countries[9]

Methods	United States	Canada	Japan	United Kingdom
1. Cost based	46%	33%	41%	38%
2. Market price based	35%	37%	37%	31%
3. Negotiated	14%	26%	22%	20%
4. Other	5%	4%	0%	11%
	100%	100%	100%	100%

until they are upheld by the courts. Global marketers must examine the regulations carefully, not only because they are the tax laws but because they guide the Internal Revenue Service (IRS) when it reviews transactions between related business organizations. In the United States, Section 482 of the tax code and the accompanying regulations are devoted to transfer pricing. The complete text of Section 482 appears in Appendix 1 at the end of this chapter.

SALES OF TANGIBLE AND INTANGIBLE PROPERTY Section 482 of the US Treasury regulations deals with controlled intracompany transfers of raw materials and finished and intermediate goods, as well as intangibles such as charges for the use of manufacturing technology. The general rule that applies to sales of tangible property is known as the arm's-length formula, defined as the prices that would have been charged in independent transactions between unrelated parties under similar circumstances. Three methods—listed next in order of priority—are spelled out in the regulations for establishing an arm's-length price. The regulations require that a company disprove the applicability of one method before utilizing a lower-priority one.

According to the comparable uncontrolled price method, uncontrolled sales (between unrelated seller and buyer) are considered comparable to controlled sales (sales between related parties) if the property and circumstances involved are identical or nearly identical to those in controlled sales. Frequently, no comparable uncontrolled sale is available to use as a reference. In such instances, it may be necessary to determine an applicable resale price, that is, the price at which property purchased in a controlled sale is resold by the buyer in an uncontrolled sale. Using this approach, which is sometimes referred to as retail price minus, an arm's-length price can be established by reducing the applicable resale price by an amount that reflects an appropriate markup. This is the resale price method of determining transfer prices. The third and lowest priority method is the cost-plus method. When the quest for an arm's-length price brings a global company to cost-plus pricing, it has come full circle to the basic transfer pricing methods described earlier in the chapter.

Table 11-6 summarizes the results of recent studies comparing transfer pricing methods by country. As shown in the table, nearly half of US-based companies doing business internationally use some form of cost-based transfer pricing.

COMPETITIVE PRICING Because Section 482 places so much emphasis on arm's-length price, a manager at an American company who examines the regulations might wonder whether the spirit of these regulations permits pricing decisions to be made with regard to market and competitive factors. Clearly, if only the arm's-length

[9] Adapted from Charles T. Horngren and George Foster, *Cost Accounting: A Managerial Approach* (Upper Saddle River, NJ: Prentice Hall, 1991): 866.

standard is applied, a company may not be able to respond to competitive factors existing in every market, domestic and global. Fortunately, the regulations provide an opening for the company that seeks to be price competitive or to aggressively price US-sourced products in its international operations. Many interpret the regulations to mean that it is proper for a company to reduce prices and increase marketing expenditures through a controlled affiliate to gain market share even when it would not do so in an arm's-length transaction with an independent distributor. This is because market position represents, in effect, an investment and an asset. A company would invest in such an asset only if it controlled the reseller—that is, if the reseller is a subsidiary. The regulations may also be interpreted as permitting a company to lower its transfer price for the purpose of entering a new market or meeting competition in an existing market either by instituting price reductions or by increased marketing efforts in the target markets. Companies must have and use this latitude in making price decisions if they are to achieve significant success in international markets with US-sourced goods.

IMPORTANCE OF SECTION 482 REGULATIONS Whatever the pricing rationale, it is important that executives and managers involved in international pricing policy decisions familiarize themselves with the Section 482 regulations. The pricing rationale must conform with the intention of these regulations. In an effort to develop more workable transfer pricing rules, the US Internal Revenue Service (IRS) issued regulations calling for contemporaneous documentation that supports transfer price decisions. Such documentation will require participation of management and marketing personnel in transfer pricing decisions, as opposed to the tax department. Companies should be prepared to demonstrate that their pricing methods are the result of informed choice, not oversight.

It is true that US Treasury regulations and IRS enforcement policy often seem perplexingly inscrutable. However, there is ample evidence that the government simply seeks to prevent tax avoidance and to ensure fair distribution of income from the operations of companies doing business internationally. Still, the government does not always succeed in its efforts to enforce Section 482 by reallocating income. In one recent court decision, Merck & Co. sued the US government on the grounds that the IRS's allocation of 7 percent of the income from a wholly owned subsidiary to the parent company was "arbitrary, capricious, and unreasonable." The IRS had argued that Merck artificially shifted income to the subsidiary by sharing costs associated with research and development, marketing facilities, and management personnel. The court agreed with Merck and ordered the IRS to issue a tax refund.

As the Merck case demonstrates, even companies that make a conscientious effort to comply with the regulations and that document this effort may find themselves in tax court. Should a tax auditor raise questions, executives should be able to make a strong case for their decisions. Fortunately, consulting services are available to help managers deal with the arcane world of transfer pricing.

Transfer pricing to minimize tax liabilities can lead to unexpected and undesired distortions. A classic example is a major US company with a decentralized, profit-centered organization that promoted and gave frequent and substantial salary increases to its divisional manager in Switzerland. The reason for the manager's rapid rise was his outstanding profit record. His stellar numbers were picked up by the company's performance appraisal control system, which in turn triggered the salary and promotion actions. The problem in this company was that the financial control system had not been adjusted to recognize that a Swiss tax haven profit center had been created. The manager's sky-high profits were simply the result of artificially low transfer pricing into the tax haven operations and artificially high transfer pricing out of the Swiss tax haven to operating subsidiaries. It took a team of outside consultants to discover the situation. In this case, the company's profit and loss records were a gross distortion of true operating results. The company had to adjust its control system and use different criteria to evaluate managerial performance in tax havens.

Duty and Tariff Constraints

Corporate costs and profits are also affected by import duties. The higher the duty rate, the more desirable a low transfer price. The high duty creates an incentive to reduce transfer prices to minimize the customs duty. Many companies tend to downplay the influence of taxes when developing pricing policies. There are a number of reasons for this. First, some companies consider tax savings to be trivial in comparison with the earnings that can be obtained by concentrating on effective systems of motivation and corporate resource allocation. Second, management may consider any effort at systematic tax minimization to be unethical. Another argument is that a simple, consistent, and straightforward pricing policy minimizes the tax investigation problems that can develop if sharper pricing policies are pursued. According to this argument, the savings in executive time and the costs of outside counsel offset any additional taxes that might be paid using such an approach. Finally, after analyzing the worldwide trend toward harmonization of tax rates, many chief financial officers (CFOs) have concluded that any set of policies appropriate to a world characterized by wide differentials in tax rates will soon become obsolete. They have, therefore, concentrated on developing pricing policies that are appropriate for a world that is very rapidly evolving toward relatively similar tax rates.

Joint Ventures

Joint ventures present an incentive to set transfer prices at higher levels than would be used in sales to wholly owned affiliates because a company's share of the joint venture earnings is less than 100 percent. Any profits that occur in the joint venture must be shared. The increasing frequency of tax authority audits is an important reason for working out an agreement that will also be acceptable to the tax authorities. The tax authorities' criterion of arm's-length prices is probably most appropriate for the majority of joint ventures.

To avoid potential conflict, companies with joint ventures should work out pricing agreements in advance that are acceptable to both sides. The following are several considerations for joint venture transfer pricing:[10]

1. The way in which transfer prices will be adjusted in response to exchange-rate changes.
2. Expected reductions in manufacturing costs arising from learning curve improvements and the way these will be reflected in transfer prices.
3. Shifts in the sourcing of products or components from parents to alternative sources.
4. The effects of competition on volume and overall margins.

[10] Timothy M. Collins and Thomas L. Doorley, *Teaming Up for the 90s: A Guide to International Joint Ventures and Strategic Alliances* (Homewood, IL: Business One Irwin, 1991): 212–213.

BOX 11-6

Side Bar: Prestige pricing in India[11]

When Reebok, the world's number two athletic shoe company, decided to enter India in 1995, it faced several basic marketing challenges. For one thing, Reebok was creating a market from scratch. Upscale sports shoes were virtually unknown, and the most expensive sneakers available at the time cost 1,000 rupees (about $23). Reebok officials also had to select a market entry mode. The decision was made to subcontract with four local suppliers, one of which became a joint venture partner. Only a limited number of distribution options were available. Bata, a Canadian company with global operations, was the sole shoe retailer with national coverage. American-style sports stores were unknown in India. To reinforce Reebok's high-tech brand image, company officials decided to establish their own retail infrastructure. There were two other crucial pieces of the puzzle: product and price. Should Reebok create a line of mass-market shoes specifically for India and priced at Rs 1,000? The alternative was to offer the same designs sold in other parts of the world and price them at Rs 2,500 ($58), a figure that represented the equivalent of a month's salary for a junior civil servant.

In the end, Reebok decided to offer Indian consumers about 60 models chosen from the company's global offerings. The decision was based in part on a desire to sustain Reebok's brand image of high quality. Management realized that the decision would limit the size of the market. Despite estimates that India's "middle class" was comprised of 300 million people, the number who could afford premium-priced products was estimated to be about 30 million. Reebok's expensive shoes were priced at about Rs 2,000 per pair. Nevertheless, customer response was very favorable, especially among middle-class youths. As Muktesh Pant, Reebok's regional manager, noted, "For Rs 2,000 to Rs 3,000, people feel they can really make a statement. It's cheaper than buying a new watch, for instance, if you want to make a splash at a party.

Reebok was also pleased to discover that demand was strong outside of key metropolitan markets such as Delhi, Mumbai, and Chennai. The cost of living is lower in small towns, so consumers have more disposable income to spend. In addition, inhabitants of rural areas have had less opportunity to travel abroad and therefore have not had the opportunity to shop for trendy brands elsewhere. Reebok now has about 100 branded franchise stores that sell about 300,000 pairs of athletic shoes in India each year. The company exports twice that number of Indian-made shoes to Europe and the United States. As Pant observed, "At first, we were embarrassed about our pricing. But it has ended up serving us well."

CASE 11-1

Go to the Basics and Apply the Methods of Pricing

Indian Sports Utility Vehicle (SUV) Scorpio, has been the flagship product of the Indian multinational Mahindra and Mahindra Limited (M&M). After fighting out Indian competition in the home turf, this SUV was in preparation to take on its competitors in the sports utility vehicle segment in United States of America. The vehicle proved its credibility in Indian market by occupying more than fifty percent market share. The market of the vehicle was also successfully extended to Europe, South America, Australia, Africa and Asian countries. Now, the company decided to launch the vehicle in the Mecca of vehicle i.e. the US

[11] Mark Nicholson, "Where a Pair of Trainers Costs as Much as a Cow," *Financial Times,* August 18, 1998: 10.

TABLE 11-7 Pricing for Scorpio in India and US

Scorpio & Indian competitors	Pricing in Indian market in USD	Scorpio & US competitors	Pricing in US market in USD	Willingness to pay (from survey)
Scorpio	19603	Scorpio	?	$15.000 (40 % says)
Tata Safari Dicor	16684	Ford Explorer	$28,190	$20,000 (33 % says)
Ford Endeavor	34732	Jeep Grand Cherokee	$19,370–$23,385	$25,000 (10 % says)
Honda CRV	42190	Toyata 4Runner	$27,500	Wouldn't buy one at any price (14 percent says)
Mitshubishi Outlander	43255	Kia Sorento	$19,995–$28,895	
Suzuki Grand Vitara	30044	Nissan Rogue	$20,148–$22,905	

market. Though there was a strong skepticism regarding the selection of recession time of 2009 as the timing of hitting the ever competitive US market but the company successfully defended by saying that the best time to hit enemy is when it is weak. During the recession it was a turbulent time in the US automobile sector when a number of global car manufactures had slowed down introduction of new models fearing the consumers' mood against spending big amount for acquiring a new vehicle. At the same time, M&M was targeting to register a global sale of around 20 per cent of total business by 2012 against barely 5 per cent of 2007-08 and 7 percent of 2008-09.

At this juncture the company was deciding on the pricing of the SUV in the US market at launch. M&M was fully aware of the challenge of fixing the price as it could make or break the future of the SUV in the US market. The international marketing team at M&M, loaded with the task of fixing the price for the product, first reviewed the pricing of different competitors of Scorpio in the US market as well as Indian market (refer Table 11-7). This exercise revealed that when it competed in India, 'Scorpio ', was not the least cost vehicle in the market. However, there were many other SUVs from global players like Mitsubishi or Ford Motor Company whose price were much above the price of 'Scorpio ' in the Indian market.

Therefore, from the Indian pricing strategy viewpoint which was suggested was that regarding the pricing for Scorpio in the India market the company played somewhat a safe strategy and did avoid direct pricing war with its competitors. Should the company then price its Scorpio much less than the competitors or keep the Indian Price intact for the foreign market? At this stage the international marketing team was thinking about, 'how international pricing can be determined for a product and on what factors it depends'. The team found that there are several 'internal factors' as well as 'external factors' that were required to be considered as they had a significant effect on pricing (refer Table 11-8).

After understanding the internal and external factors related to international pricing, the team worked out different pricing scenario using different methods of pricing usually recommended by the text book of international pricing in the following way.

(a) Full Cost Pricing

It ensures full recovery of the cost of sales

Selling price = Cost of landing + distribution cost + promotion cost + standard mark up profit

= 21000$ + 2000$ + 1000$ + 15% of cost of sales

= 21000$+ 2000$ + 1000$ + 3600$ = 27600$

Implication: As per pre launch opinion survey there are no buyers at this price.

(b) Marginal cost pricing

Variable cost per car (VC) 90 % of cost of production i.e. 20000$ = 90% of 20000$ = 18000$

The sales price per car (SP) in home country = 19603$

Contribution margin per car= SP- VC= 1603$

Fixed expenses per year = $ 64 million

Breakeven volume = Fixed expenses for a year/ Contribution margin per car

= 64 million$/ 2603$ per unit= 30.73

= 39925 units

Scorpio sales in India were about 50000 units per year in India. So, the US bound cars already were covered of the fixed cost. Hence, it provided the flexibility of 2000$ while pricing.

TABLE 11-8 Internal and External Factors for International Pricing

Different Factor Influencing International Price	Significance
External Factors	
What is the level of price competition in the target market?	In price war like situation, pricing alone can be greater importance than marketing.
What is the level of promotional competition?	High order of promotional campaign by the competitors may force a new entrant to be subdued.
Is there a global aspiration for the firm?	In case of a global aspiration, the new entrant may not like to be involved in price war but rather follow a 'standard pricing for all the market' strategy.
Is there a demand variability?	In case of a demand certainty the pricing could be uppish.
Are they enforcing regulations?	Regulation put a tight jacket around pricing flexibility.
Is there a country of origin effect (COE) on the competitors	For technical product COE effect could be pronounced and hence force to settle for a lower price.
Consumer willingness to pay	Important to understand through market survey while deciding the price
Internal	
Is there an emphasis to maximize on short run profit	If yes, the skimming pricing would be favoured.
What is the landed cost and distribution cost of the product in the foreign market?	It will help to decide the threshold price below which there could be loss.
How many promotional effects are positioned I	High degree of promotion may provide a cover in case of pricing is comparatively higher than the competitors.
What sell off is expected by the company in the first year?	If the off take of the product is considerably higher than the profit percentage per product could be sacrificed for a limited time.
Local positioning strategy	If local positioning is based on extraordinary quality of a product then initially pricing may be kept low to get a foot hold in the market.
Sales internationally for off load short term overcapacity in home country.	It may help to resort to marginal cost pricing even.

So, selling price for USA = 27600\$ - 2000\$
= 25600\$

Implication: As per pre launch opinion survey, there is about 10 percent buyers at this price and company can still make profit.

(c) Skimming pricing

It refers to launching of product at an artificially hiked price and skims the market within one year or so. Skimming pricing cannot be used for USA bound Scorpio as the company already decided not to launch any aggressive advertisement for US market.

(d) Penetration Pricing

It refers to penetrate the market at a low cost but superior quality product. The condition of recovering the lost money after one year or so may not be easy as the competitors were all offering excellent quality product in the market.

(e) Loss Leader Pricing

It refers to loss made on one product recovered from the profit of others. However, M&M was not launching different version of the SUV initially. So this method of pricing cannot be used.

At the end of the exercise, the marketing team was somewhat delighted as they could understand the possible pricing scenario in details and implications thereof. The team then suggested sticking to marginal cost pricing while launching the SUV for US market. This pricing would allow the company not to comprise with the profit margin as well as initially there could be about 10 percent of willing customers in the US market to buy the SUV.

Case Questions

1. What pricing objective the company should have for the US market?
2. If you were the marketing manager of the company then at what price you would have launched the SUV in the US market? Justify your answer.

Summary

Pricing decisions are a critical element of the marketing mix that must reflect costs and competitive factors. There is no absolute maximum price, but for any customer, price must correspond to the customer's perceived value of the product. The aim of most marketing strategies is to set a price that corresponds to customers' perceptions of value in the product and at the same time does not "leave money on the table" (i.e., set a price that is lower than consumers are willing to pay for a product or service). Generally, a company must charge what a product is worth to the customer, cover all costs, and provide a margin for profit in the process. Pricing strategies include market skimming, market penetration, and market holding. Pricing decisions must also take into account the price escalation that occurs when products are shipped from one country to another.

International pricing is complicated by the fact that businesses must conform to different laws and different competitive situations in each country. Each company must examine the market, the competition, its own costs and objectives, and local and regional regulations and laws when setting prices that are consistent with the overall marketing strategy. Dumping—selling products in international markets at prices below those in the home country or below the cost of production—and parallel importing are two particularly contentious pricing issues. Company managers must also set transfer prices that are appropriate to company profitability objectives and that also conform to tax regulations in individual country markets.

Discussion Questions

1. What are the three basic factors affecting price in any market? What considerations enter into the pricing decision?
2. Identify some of the environmental constraints on global pricing decisions.
3. What is dumping? Is it an important trade issue? Is dumping an attractive competitive price strategy for a company?
4. What is a transfer price? What is the difference, if any, between a transfer price and a regular price? What are three methods for determining transfer prices?
5. What are the three alternative approaches to global pricing? Which one would you recommend to a company that has global market aspirations?
6. If you were responsible for marketing computed axial tomography (CAT) scanners worldwide and your sourcing country (location of manufacture) was experiencing a strong and appreciating currency against almost all other world currencies, what options are available for adjusting prices to take into account the strong currency situation?

Suggested Readings

Anderson, Chris. *Free: The Future of a Radical Price.* New York: Hyperion Books/HarperCollins, 2009.

Bryce, David J., Jeffrey H. Dyer, and Nile W. Hatch. "Competing Against Free." *Harvard Business Review* (June 2011): 104–111.

Cannon, Hugh M., and Fred W. Morgan. "A Strategic Pricing Framework." *Journal of Business and Industrial Marketing,* 6, no. 3,4 (Summer–Fall 1991): 59–70.

Cavusgil, S. Tamer. "Pricing for Global Markets." *Columbia Journal of World Business,* 31, no. 4 (1996).

Eccles, Robert G. *The Transfer Pricing Problem: A Theory for Practice.* Lexington, MA: Lexington Books, 1985.

Johnson, Mark W., and Hari Nair. "New Business Models in Emerging Markets." *Harvard Business Review* (January–February 2011): 89–95.

Samiee, Saeed, and Patrik Anckar. "Currency Choice in Industrial Pricing: A Cross-National Evaluation." *Journal of Marketing,* 62, no. 3 (1998): 112–127.

Samli, A. Coskun, and Laurence Jacobs. "Pricing Practices of American Multinational Firms: Standardization vs. Localization Dichotomy." *Journal of Global Marketing,* 8, no. 2 (1994): 51–74.

Simon, Hermann. "Pricing Opportunities—and How to Exploit Them." *Sloan Management Review,* 33, no. 2 (Winter 1992): 55–65.

Tan, Qun, and Carlos M. P. Sousa. "Research on Export Pricing: Still Moving Toward Maturity." *Journal of International Marketing,* 19, no. 3 (September 2011): 1–35.

Wessel, Maxwell, and Clayton M. Christensen. "Surviving Disruption." *Harvard Business Review* (December 2012): 56–64.

APPENDIX[12]

Trade Documentation and Getting Paid

While marketers need to understand the unique character of each international market and develop effective marketing plans to sell and serve that market, they also need to ensure that their terms of sale are competitive and that payment is received. The importance of getting paid for one's product or service should be obvious, but many managers new to international trade consider this only as an afterthought. One should never minimize the impact of not receiving timely payment on a significant sale on one's company, its employees, banking relationships, and stakeholders. The consequences can be dire and put the viability of the company (and the marketer's career) at risk. Experienced international managers consider the financial and shipping terms of a transaction as a normal part of negotiation with clients. When launching into international business, managers should already have an understanding of the specialized vocabulary and instruments of trade finance and documentation. This knowledge will be important to the manager's credibility and ability to work globally.

For instructional purposes, we will use the example of an imaginary export of, say, modern milking equipment from an American exporter to a farmers cooperative in rural Turkey.

Compared to domestic transactions, international trade carries more complexity and risk. The importer and exporter (buyer and seller) often have little knowledge of each other, or ability to judge each other's credit risk. They often lack even a basic understanding of one another's legal and political environment. Therefore, concerns naturally arise. What if one company sends payment and the other fails to ship the product? Similarly, what if one company goes to the time and expense of producing and shipping the product, but the importer does not or cannot pay? Understandably, both importer and exporter are reluctant to put their companies at risk.

Trade can be entered into with different levels of risk—from the exporter accepting full or no transaction risk to the importer absorbing full or no transaction risk (*exposure*). If there is an established relationship between the two companies, the exporter may agree to operate on an "**Open Account**" basis. In this case, the Turkish importer orders a product; the American exporter produces and ships it and then invoices the customer for the sale. Upon the product's arrival, our Turkish importer simply wire-transfers payment to the American exporter. In this scenario, the exporter takes on the full risk of nonpayment by the customer. Open Account is commonly used domestically, but is rarely appropriate internationally—especially when the importer and exporter have little knowledge of each other. For the American exporter to have no risk, it may require prepayment—known as "**Cash in Advance**" or "**Cash with Order**." Here the American exporter receives an up-front payment and the Turkish importer bears the full financial risk should the exporter not ship as promised. If the Turkish importer has had limited dealings with the exporter, the importer is unlikely to accept such a risk. Also, like most purchasing managers in the United States, the Turkish importer is likely to seek credit terms beyond the receipt of the goods or services. As an edge over a global competitor (such as a Swedish producer of milking equipment), our American exporter may indeed need to provide extended payment terms.

In most transactions, neither party will wish to absorb the risks of nonperformance by the exporter or nonpayment by the importer. How can this be resolved so that beneficial trade can proceed? Here the commercial parties can look to the international banking system. Acting in an intermediary role, international banks can remove the transaction risk

[12] Prepared by Christopher J. Nagel, Assistant Professor of Business and Director of International Management at Concordia University, Irvine, California. His prior corporate experience includes the positions of Marketing Manager–Asia for International Paper Company and Vice President–Commercial Development for Servrite International.

from both the exporter and importer. Banks can, for a fee, provide assurance to the Turkish importer that the American exporter will perform as required and, concurrently, that the American exporter will receive payment for its products. In removing financial risk from the transaction, the banking system increases the volume and efficiency of international trade to the advantage of both the United States and Turkey.

Managing risk is a key attribute of international banks, and the "**Letter of Credit**" is a standard financial instrument used to achieve this. It is commonly referred to as an "**L/C.**" It is important to note that the banking system works with and makes payments against *documents*, not contracts or relationships between companies; thus the L/C is also known as a *documentary credit*. Here, the exporter is assured of payment so long as it meets all terms and documents listed in the L/C that was opened in its favor, and the importer is not obligated to pay until the exporter has shipped the desired products.

A word of caution: marketers have a responsibility to protect the interests of their company and should not allow themselves to be pressured away from requiring L/Cs for payment. This is good business practice and does not demonstrate a lack of trust or cultural bias against a prospective customer. Working out the terms of the L/C should be seen as a regular part of a commercial sale. Furthermore, if the local bank of the importer is reluctant to open an L/C in favor of the exporter (under the process outlined below), this may reflect either on the financial health of the importer or the soundness of the importer's bank, or even on possible constraints on that country's foreign exchange. Such reluctance by the importer's local bank should signal the exporter to be especially diligent with this transaction.

International marketers recognize that, other than in the most advanced economies, there is no effective legal recourse should a problem develop with an overseas customer. The L/C and the banking system can remove such "local" exposure. In removing the risks of nonperformance and nonpayment, the international banking system significantly promotes the expansion of global trade. In our imaginary case, both our American exporter and Turkish importer have international trade experience and understand that discussing and finalizing the terms of an L/C is actually a very useful discipline—one that will minimize future misunderstandings or conflicts.

Our imaginary exporter and importer have worked out the following commercial terms for their transaction:

- The American exporter will ship a specific set of milking equipment priced at 5 million US dollars.
- The sale will be priced CIF (cost, insurance, freight) Istanbul. This means that in addition to the price of the equipment, the American exporter (or its Freight Forwarder) will arrange for product delivery from its US factory to the port of Istanbul and has included in its price the cost of ocean freight and insurance for the shipment.
- The American exporter will send the equipment in one shipment within two months of the L/C being opened in its favor and will be paid in US dollars.
- The exporter will accept payment six months after the milking equipment ships from a US port.
- The Turkish importer agrees to arrange for an Irrevocable L/C and pay local Turkish bank fees.
- Both parties will advise each other of the banks with which each will work in this transaction.

In a standard CIF quote, the *importer,* not the exporter, is responsible for the costs of local delivery from its domestic port, including local duties and fees. In most cases, L/Cs are *Irrevocable,* meaning that the importer cannot subsequently revoke the L/C created in favor of the exporter. In reality, Revocable L/Cs are rarely used. In our transaction, the L/C document will note that it is *Irrevocable.*

The L/C will specify what is to be shipped, when and to where shipment is to be made, the associated documents required, terms of sale (Ex-Works, FOB, CIF, etc.), the currency of payment, credit terms, the form of L/C (Irrevocable, Revocable, Stand-By) and who will pay the L/C and bank fees.

Now, let's now look at how these commercial terms are converted into a documentary credit (the L/C), a process that has greatly enabled international commerce through the years. There are four general steps:

Step 1. The Turkish importer asks its local Turkish bank to "open" a US$ 5 million Irrevocable Letter of Credit "in favor" of the American exporter (known now at the L/C's "beneficiary"). The L/C is payable upon the American exporter meeting the L/C documentary requirements. If the Turkish importer has good financial standing, the Turkish bank opens the L/C.

Key point: The Turkish importer's credit has now been replaced by the credit of the Turkish bank;

the exporter relies on the bank's promise of payment, not the importer's.

To ensure the American exporter performs as agreed, the importer will stipulate that the credit only be payable upon presentation of a set of documents agreed to by both exporter and importer. Again, this is why it is called a documentary credit. A basic list of documents noted in an L/C can include:

1. Signed Commercial Invoices (reflecting the price and product)
2. Time Drafts (instructing the importer to pay an amount at a future date)
3. Full set of Ocean Bills of Lading
4. Packing List
5. Insurance Certificate
6. Certificate of Origin (provided by the Chamber of Commerce)

These documents will evidence shipment of the milking equipment from the Port of Baltimore. The L/C will also state that partial shipments are not allowed and that payment in US dollars is to be made 180 days from date of the **Bill of Lading**—commonly referred to as a "**B/L**." This is a very specialized document that can serve as a receipt for the goods, a contract to transport the goods, and actual title to the goods. A B/L is date-stamped when the common carrier accepts the export cargo for shipment. Also, like many companies, our American exporter uses the services of a specialized company known as a Freight Forwarder. Such companies arrange the logistics and insurance for shipments and help prepare the document package required under the L/C.

In our example, the American exporter can expect payment 180 days from the B/L date. The Turkish importer will not receive title (the Bills of Lading) to the shipment until either payment to the Turkish bank has been made or future payment (after 180 days from B/L date in our transaction) has been assured. Note: If immediate payment had been agreed upon, the terms in the L/C would have said payable "at sight" and "Drafts" would be listed in the document package, not "Time Drafts." When Drafts and the other documents are presented to the importer's bank, the credit in favor of the American exporter will be honored immediately—"at sight."

Step 2. The Turkish bank, known as the "Issuing bank" or "Opening bank," then advises the American exporter's bank that the above L/C has been opened in favor of the exporter. The American bank, now known as the "Advising bank," advises the American exporter that the credit is in place.

Step 3. The American exporter carefully reviews the terms in the L/C to ensure they match those previously agreed to (even misspellings are problematic). Should corrections be needed, an Amended L/C will need to be generated by the issuing bank. If the exporter believes it can meet the terms of the L/C, it will proceed to produce and ship the modern milking equipment.

Step 4. Once the milking equipment ships from the Port of Baltimore, the complete documentary package is delivered to and reviewed by the exporter's advising bank, which then sends the package on and presents it to the opening bank in Turkey. The Turkish bank checks the documents and, if all is in order, formally "accepts" the Time Drafts. The bank has thus "honored" the credit and will remit $5 million, less an "acceptance" fee, to the exporter via the exporter's bank in 180 days from the B/L date. After securing a promissory note from the importer, the Turkish bank passes the B/L (which serves as title to the milking equipment) to the importer. The importer then arranges to pick up the equipment at the Turkish port. It is important to note that if the documents do not conform exactly to the terms given in the L/C, payment will not be made unless and until the Turkish importer agrees to allow the discrepancy.

Key point: Before our exporter receives payment, documents must be presented to the importer's bank evidencing that what was agreed upon has actually been shipped. If the documents are correct, the exporter is assured of payment, independent of any action by the importer.

If an importer is concerned that an exporter may not ship what was anticipated, an independent agency may be retained to physically inspect the goods before shipment. Such an agency then issues an inspection certificate vouching that the shipment matches the packing list. Such certificates can be included as part of the documentary package named in the L/C.

The above four steps are critical to commercial success in international trade. The credit risk of the transaction has been absorbed by the banking system (whose business is managing risk). Both the exporter and importer benefit from the commerce, both are protected from their commercial partner's failure to perform, and both have protected their company's future.

One should make three additional comments:

- The credit underlying this transaction is that of the Turkish importer's bank. Should the American exporter have concern over the soundness of that credit, it can ask its bank, the American advising bank, to "confirm" the Turkish bank's L/C. If the American bank agrees to confirm the Turkish bank's L/C (naturally, for a fee), the credit and guarantee of the American bank is added to that of the Turkish bank. This provides an additional level of comfort for the exporter. The American bank then becomes known as the "confirming" bank, and the L/C is now a Confirmed Irrevocable Letter of Credit. The American bank's fee is often taken as a deduction from the ultimate payment to the exporter. A further benefit of such confirmation is that the exporter is now also protected against shortages of hard currency or the imposition of exchange controls by the foreign government after the cargo has shipped.
- Remember that our American exporter agreed to accept payment 180 days after shipping the milking equipment. Even though payment is assured, the exporter has to wait six months to receive the funds. Fortunately, when the Turkish bank "accepted" the above Time Draft, it also created what is known as a "**Bankers Acceptance**" or "**B/A**," a negotiable money market instrument. Our exporter has the option to hold the B/A for 180 days and then simply receive payment. Or, for cash flow purposes, the exporter may wish to have these funds on hand immediately and will sell this Banker's Acceptance (a receivable) at a discount in the money market. In providing extended payment terms to its Turkish customer, the exporter will likely have built the cost of this discount into its pricing.
- Finally, recall that the Turkish importer agreed to make payment in US dollars. What would happen if the importer had insisted on paying with local Turkish pounds? Under the original L/C, the *importer* accepted the risk of currency fluctuations between US dollars and pounds. If payment is to be in pounds, our American exporter will bear the currency exposure and risk. Now, if the US dollar *appreciates* against the pound in the time between when the pound-denominated L/C is opened and ultimately paid, each pound received by the US exporter would convert into less US currency. The importer still pays a set amount in terms of pounds, but our American exporter receives less than anticipated in terms of dollars—possibly even creating a loss on the sale. Fortunately, the international banking system is able to limit not only credit risk, but also this currency exposure. To protect itself against a negative currency move, the American exporter could enter into a forward currency contract with its bank. Here the bank agrees to convert the future payment in Turkish pounds into US dollars at a specific exchange rate (for a given number of pounds on a specific date). Thus the exporter can lock-in the exchange rate and be assured of its dollar receipts in 180 days. So, if required to accept payment in pounds, our capable American exporter would have worked closely with its bank and then included the cost of the forward contract or "cover" in its CIF pricing. Similarly, under our initial scenario where payment for the shipment was to be in dollars, our experienced Turkish importer could also secure a "forward cover" to protect itself. International bankers are happy to provide advice and a ready market for such contracts.

CHAPTER 12

Global Marketing Channels

Unlike US companies, which can focus on developing their products before raising capital, and on distribution problems after doing so, Indian entrepreneurs have to tackle both before they can woo skeptical investors. That makes starting up in India at least twice as hard as it is elsewhere in the world.

—SAMIR PATIL, SERIAL ENTREPRENEUR

Moral Essays to Helvia on Consolation

Learning Objectives

1. Discuss the development of global marketing channels and current distribution trends (362–364).
2. Identify the factors that affect channel strategy decisions (366–367).
3. Describe the characteristics of consumer and industrial distribution channels (368–372).
4. Describe the features of global retail channels (376–379).
5. Discuss physical distribution issues and logistics (380–382).
6. Explain the causes and effects of global channel innovations (383–386).

INTRODUCTION

Big parking lots, huge department stores, and people strolling through air-conditioned suburban shopping malls with hundreds of retail stores offering both local and global products. Such places can be found in Kansas, Dubai, Indonesia, and in New Delhi! The emergence of a large, affluent middle class in India combined with an ever-increasing exposure to outside cultures has driven a change not just in terms of what products consumers buy but also in terms of how, when, and where they buy them. These suburban retail centers mirror similar retail centers abroad, often surrounded by upscale guard-gated residential communities. A consumer driving through such a neighborhood may be forgiven if they forget whether they are in India or in Irvine, California.

The emerging retail consolidation throughout the Indian subcontinent does not mean that traditional Indian retail formats like mom-and-pop stores and street vendors are disappearing quietly. Indian street vendors have even demonstrated a willingness to resort to arms to fight for their continued relevance and to protest the arrival of Western-style, large-scale retail outlets. Moreover, many foreign retailers still face difficult legal hurdles if they want to expand into markets in India, even if Indian regulation has loosened up to some extent. One recent regulatory relaxation allows foreign-majority-owned "single-brand" stores such as Nike and Gucci to establish retail stores in India.

In 2006, the world's largest retailer Wal-Mart decided it could no longer ignore the enormous Indian retail market estimated at 400 billion dollars and set up an Indian business liaison office to study market opportunities more closely. Wal-Mart found a way around the ban on foreign company retailing of multiple brands in multiple categories. Instead of operating retail stores oriented to consumers, Wal-Mart formed a 50:50 joint venture with Indian company Bharti to run a "wholesale cash-and-carry" business supplying retailers large and sometimes very small with inventory. Bharti's job was to focus on the store-operation side of the business while Wal-Mart took responsibility for all back-end operations such as order delivery and fulfillment services. Here, Wal-Mart could leverage its world-class expertise in areas such as information systems, logistics, and supply-chain management. The stores are called "Best Price Modern Wholesale," and the first store opened up in Amritsar in 2009.

These examples serve as a few glimpses into today's challenging environment with respect to how global marketing channels and physical distribution can be effectively structured in different markets throughout the world. It used to be the case that retailing was a predominantly local and culturally idiosyncratic activity. Today, consumers with more and more exposure to and appreciation of international retailing alternatives expect to have such choices available to them in their home markets.

In this chapter, we will discuss how global marketing channels can be analyzed and understood given the complexities of the global marketplace. In doing so, we will explore how global competition is becoming more pervasive in local markets and highlight risks and challenges of going global, such as hostile reception from existing channel members, local market leaders, and even consumer disinterest.

BOX 12-1

Side Bar: Hypermarkets[1]

In the United States, retailing channels are quite diverse. In addition to long-entrenched shopping malls and discount stores, there are wholesale clubs such as Costco and Sam's Club, offering rock-bottom prices, and "category killers" with wide selections in a defined product category such as Toys "Я" Us. Undeterred by such competitors, Euromarché opened its first American hypermarket in October 1984. Bigg's, in Cincinnati, was one and a half times the size of a football field, with 75 aisles, 40 checkout lanes, and 60,000 different items available at low prices. One shopper summed up the advantage of shopping at Bigg's: "I can buy bread, lunchmeat, and electrical equipment all at the same place." In February 1988, Carrefour opened its own US hypermarket, a gigantic store in Philadelphia with 330,000 square feet of floor space. Not to be outdone, several

continued

[1] Laurie M. Grossman, "Hypermarkets: A Sure-Fire Hit Bombs," *The Wall Street Journal*, June 25, 1992: B1; Steven Greenhouse, "'Hypermarkets Come to U.S.," *The New York Times*, February 7, 1985: 29; Anthony Ramirez, "Will American Shoppers Think Bigger Is Really Better?" *The New York Times*, April 1, 1990: sec. 3, p. 11.

American retailers soon followed suit. Wal-Mart opened several Hypermart USA stores; Kmart called its version American Fare.

Before long, however, many of the big stores were floundering. The problem? Not surprisingly, many shoppers found the stores too big and too overwhelming. Moreover, the big scale changed the economics of profitable operation. For example, consultants for Kmart noted that its hypermarket near Atlanta could succeed only if it attracted four times as many shoppers as a regular discount department store and if the average transaction equaled $43—double the average for discount stores. Meanwhile, costs associated with running the huge stores translated into gross margins of around 8 percent—half the margin of the typical discount store. Last but not least, Americans just did not take to mixing food and nonfood purchases in one location. As retail consultant Kurt Barnard noted, "One-stop shopping did not take hold easily. Working parents don't have time for their kids, let alone a shopping expedition that takes hours." The lesson from hypermarkets in the United States is clear: just because a format has succeeded in one country or region does not ensure that it will be accepted globally. As always, in global marketing, everything matters.

The American Marketing Association defines *channel of distribution* as "an organized network of agencies and institutions which, in combination, perform all the activities required to link producers with users to accomplish the marketing task."[2] Distribution is the physical flow of goods through channels; as suggested by the definition, channels are comprised of coordinated groups of individuals or firms that perform functions adding utility to a product or service.

Distribution channels in markets around the world are among the most highly differentiated aspects of national marketing systems. They range from big-box stores (from 5,000 to 20,000+ sq. meters) including hypermarkets (Carrefour), which sell a broad range of food, apparel, and other items under one roof; to Wal-Mart, which offers general merchandise, groceries, and services such as pharmacies, opticians, and banks; to small stores (in Latin America called *pulperias*) or street vendors who display their goods on a cart or on the ground. The diversity of channels and the wide range of possible distribution strategies can present challenges to anyone designing a global marketing program. Channel strategy is the element of the marketing mix that many companies understand the least. To a large extent, channel selection is an aspect of the marketing program that is locally led through the discretion of the in-country marketing management group. Nevertheless, it is important for managers responsible for global marketing strategy to understand the nature of international distribution channels. Channels and physical distribution are integral parts of the total marketing program and must be appropriate to the product design, price, consumer purchase behavior, and communications aspects of that program.

DIFFERENT FORMS OF INTERMEDIARIES IN THE INTERNATIONAL MARKETS

Distribution intermediaries are important for manufacturers. An international company may like to produce products in a least cost country and market the products in distant foreign markets. For example, Indian automobile giant Mahindra & Mahindra (M&M), has its own manufacturing plant for utility vehicles in South India but required distribution intermediaries to market it's Scorpio brand, sports utility vehicles in India as well as various foreign countries of the world. Marketing and distribution intermediaries are essential to do various essential jobs like owning the

[2] Peter D. Bennett, *Dictionary of Marketing Terms* (Chicago: American Marketing Association, 1988): 29.

ownership of the product, allowing a link to be developed between consumers of one country with producer of another country, bulk breaking, and publicising about a foreign product in local as well as foreign markets. Some of the important types of intermediaries like wholesalers and retailers present in different country markets are stated below.

Intermediaries	Purpose	Remark
Merchant Wholesalers	They act as temporary owner of the products before they resale the products to the retailers. Often they cater to particular line of business.	They usually serve relatively small geographic areas.
Speciality Wholesalers	Do the same think as merchant wholesalers but they stick to a particular line of business.	Speciality allows them to cover a wide geographic area and offer more specialized service to the retailers
Discount Wholesalers	These wholesalers purchase the products at some opportune time to avail least cost and resale the product at least cost.	The retailers as well as the consumers may get service from discount wholesalers
Cash-and-carry wholesalers	These wholesalers just act as conduit to pass on products to the retailers by breaking bulk and expecting margin of profit for the services rendered to both manufacturer and retailers.	The retailers are encouraged to pay in cash so that the realisation can be transferred back to the manufacturers.
Mom and pop stores	Family owned retailer located in residential area and catering to the neighbourhood population	'Kirana' stores are very important for distribution of products in Indian market as they are huge in number all over India.
Department Store	A type of retailers where product assortment width is high but depth is low.	Product assortment means the collection of goods or services the retailers offering to the ultimate consumers.
Supermarkets	A type of retailers where product assortment width is high but depth is more than departmental stores.	Width of product assortment means that the retailer caters to a number of product lines.
Hyper market	A type of retailers where both product assortment width and depth are high.	Depth of product assortment means that retailer has a number of product varieties within each product line.

CHALLENGES OF REACHING CUSTOMERS IN THE EMERGING MARKETS

The emerging country markets are very much alluring for international marketers because of economic growth prospects. Emerging countries like India, China, Russia etc are all having fast growing cities with middleclass and high income segments. However, the emerging markets pose distribution challenge much more than the developed country markets.

1. *Over dependency on Mother and pop-types of retail outlets*: Mom and pop types of stores have the greatest reach of the consumers. In India, 'Kirana' type of stores concentrate on accounts for more than 90 percent retailing and these retailers inherently have a lot of operational informality.

2. *Highly informal and unorganised*: Mckinsey study[3], executed during 2011, shows that highest informality is present in India, followed by other emerging markets like Indonesia, Philippines, Argentina, Venezuela, Thailand, Turkey, Brazil, Russia, South Africa, Mexico and China.
3. *Entry of modern retailing is slow*: Behind the presence of traditional informal retailing, there exist, though quite a few in number, modern formal retailing outlets like super and hyper markets. The entry of modern type of retailers' to these markets is quite slow.
4. *Skewed towards informality*: The contrast between the operational styles of these two types of outlets is quite perplexing for the international marketers. Hence, it is difficult to arrive at an optimum distribution retail mix when designing a distribution channel in emerging markets.

BOX 12-2

Side Bar: The Apple Stores—Something New Under the Sun[4]

When Steve Jobs announced the first Apple Store in Tysons Corner, Virginia, many people thought he was crazy. *Bloomberg Businessweek* ran the headline, "Sorry, Steve: Here's Why Apple Stores Won't Work."[5] The reason given for why Apple would fail is that each store would have to sell $12 million per year just to pay the rent. This appeared to the critics to be an unattainable level of sales. In fact, Apple's sales far exceeded the critics' expectations.

Steve Jobs, the founder of Apple, did not invent the retail store, but he did reimagine retail and apply the strategic concept of marketing described in Chapter 1. Recall that in the strategic concept of marketing the goal is to create unique value for customers. The Apple Stores offer a unique integration of value for customers: product, place, time, form, and information, all in the Apple Store. The stores are an extension of the Apple brand and promise: "insanely" great products and "think different." Customers love them.

More people now visit Apple's 326 stores in a single quarter than the 60 million who visited Walt Disney Co.'s four biggest theme parks last year, according to data from Apple and the Themed Entertainment Association. Apple's annual retail sales per square foot have soared to $4,406—excluding online sales, according to investment bank Needham & Co. Add online sales, which include iTunes, and the number jumps to $5,914. That's far higher than the sales per square foot and online sales of jeweler Tiffany & Co. ($3,070), luxury retailer Coach Inc. ($1,776), and electronics retailer Best Buy Co. ($880), according to estimates.

With their airy interiors and attractive lighting, Apple's stores project a carefree and casual atmosphere, yet Apple keeps a tight lid on how they operate. Employees are ordered to not discuss rumors about products, technicians are forbidden from prematurely acknowledging widespread glitches, and anyone caught writing about the Cupertino, California, company on the Internet is fired, according to current and former employees. Behind Apple Stores was Ron Johnson, who left Apple to become CEO of J.C. Penney Co.

The Apple Stores are different in many aspects of customer service and store design. According to several employees and training manuals, sales associates are taught an unusual sales philosophy: not to sell, but rather to help customers solve problems. "Your job is to understand all of your customers' needs—some of which they may not even realize they have," one training manual says. To that end, employees receive no sales commissions and have no sales quotas.

continued

[3] Alejandro Diaz, Max Magni, and Felix Poh, 'From oxcart to Wal-Mart: Four Keys to reaching emerging-market consumers', http://www.mckinsey.com/industries/retail/our-insights/from-oxcart-to-wal-mart-four-keys-to-reaching-emerging-market-consumers, as accessed on 20 January 2017 at 7.00pm.

[4] "Secrets from Apple's Genius Bar: Full Loyalty No Negativity," *Wall Street Journal*, June 15, 2011, http://online.wsj.com/article/SB10001424052702304563104576364071955678908.html.

[5] Cliff Edwards, "Commentary: Sorry, Steve: Here's Why Apple Stores Won't Work," *BusinessWeek,* May 20, 2001, http://www.businessweek.com/magazine/content/01_21/b3733059.htm.

The Genius Bar is a particularly valued feature of the Apple Stores. If you have a question or a problem with an Apple product, an Apple Genius will solve it. If the problem is the Apple product under warranty, it will be replaced on the spot. "You were never trying to close a sale. It was about finding solutions for a customer and finding their pain points," said an employee who worked at an Apple Store in Arlington, Virginia.

TABLE 12-1 Apple Store Locations[6]

The first two Apple Stores opened in the United States in 2001 (see details up to 2017 in the Table 12-1 below). In 2003, Apple expanded its operations into Japan, opening the first store outside of the United States. This was followed by the opening of stores in the United Kingdom, Canada, Italy, Australia, China, Switzerland, Germany, France, and Spain. In 2010, a major effort to expand sales in China was announced along with the opening of a store in Shanghai. The first Apple Store in Hong Kong, the 100th overseas store outside the United States, opened in 2011.

Country	First openings	Open stores
United States	May 19, 2001	269
United Kingdom	November 20, 2004	39
China	July 19, 2008	40
Canada	May 21, 2005	29
Australia	June 19, 2008	22
France	November 7, 2009	21
Italy	March 31, 2007	16
Germany	December 6, 2008	14
Spain	September 4, 2010	11
Japan	November 30, 2003	8
Hong Kong	September 24, 2011	6
Switzerland	September 25, 2008	4
Netherlands	March 3, 2012	3
Sweden	September 15, 2012	3
Brazil	February 15, 2014	2
Turkey	April 5, 2014	2
United Arab Emirates	October 29, 2015	2
Belgium	September 19, 2015	1
Macau	June 26, 2016	1
Mexico	September 24, 2016	1
Singapore	2017	1 (Upcoming)
Total		494

[6] http://en.wikipedia.org/wiki/Apple_Store.

PROBLEMS OF IDENTIFICATION AND SELECTION OF INTERMEDIARIES

L'Occitane, the French cosmetic giant, wanted to enter Indian market during 2002 to market its highly celebrated skin care products. The company decided to export its products in-to Indian market. It was needed by them to design an optimum distribution channel structure so as to reach its target customers mainly located in different cities of India. In order to do that, the company's officials made several visits to India and picked up a Delhi based lifestyle chain as its importer and distributor. It did take just a year for the company to understand that the importer and distributor was not the right match for them. There were several clash of interests between the French producer and the Indian distributor. Ultimately, the company had to snap all ties with its Indian intermediary. This caused the company both image and financial losses in the highly prospective market like India.

Why the French company faltered in finding the right intermediary for a foreign market like India? The reasons were varied and a few important reasons are stated below:

LACK OF KNOWLEDGE OF FOREIGN COUNTRY DISTRIBUTION SYSTEM The distribution system of any country evolves over a period of time and nourishes from the economical, political and social system prevailing in the country. Therefore, the distribution system sufficiently varies from country to country and the variations are manifested in terms of its operational characteristics. For example, Japan has a multi tier distribution system which grew up over the years under the socio political patronage. The entrant company of another country usually finds it difficult to understand the system.

AVAILABILITY OF RIGHT TYPE OF CHANNEL Countries differ in terms of availability of different types of intermediaries. A company who always uses hypermarket to off load its products, may find that some of the African countries lack in this respect. As a result the company may try to find out some easy way out which may not be the right match for its requirements.

GEOGRAPHICAL DISTANCE The geographical distance between the place of manufacturing to the point of sale and complicacy a company foresees in terms of delivery delay, lost shipment, stock-out etc, force for a compromised solution. Hence, the selections of intermediaries are not always based on objective of attaining efficiency.

LACK OF INFORMATION SOURCE It is difficult to get detailed information about the structure of the distribution channel of a foreign country. Rather, there is no single data base available, online or off line which provides information to the entrant company to understand the foreign country's channel dynamics and its structure before entering the market.

ETHNOCENTRIC ORIENTATION Many a times, the entrant company perceives that the channel structure and intermediary behaviour in the targeted host country market would be similar to its home country. For example, the French company expected the Indian intermediary to behave and function in a French way or at least in an European way because of ethnocentrism. The ethnocentrism ultimately did not do well for the company as it had to leave the Indian market altogether. The difference of commitments due to cultural reasons may pose a serious threat to the entrant company in a new market.

BOX 12-3

Side Bar: A Case of Wine—Adding Utility Through Distribution Channels

Each year, wine and spirits worth more than US$1 billion are exported from France, Germany, Italy, and other European countries to all parts of the world. Have you ever wondered how a case of wine finds its way from, say, France, to your local liquor store? In fact, after leaving the winery, the wine may pass through the hands of brokers, freight forwarders, shipping agents, export agents, shippers, importers, wholesalers, and distributors before it finishes its journey at your local retailer.

In France, the structure of the wine industry is quite complex. An intermediary called a *négociant* plays an important role that varies according to region. *Négociants* sometimes act as brokers and have standing contracts to buy specified quantities of finished wine on behalf of various American importers. The *négociant* also functions somewhat like a banker, paying the producer as much as 25 percent in advance of delivery. *Négociants* may also buy grapes from growers to make their own wine, blending and bottling them under their own labels. Wine may be bottled and packed in cases by the producer or by the *négociant*.

Wine destined for France or other European markets travels by truck. If the wine is to be exported to the United States or Japan, a freight forwarder or shipping agent sends a truck to the winery to pick up the wine. For the largest producers, the simplest type of consolidation takes place at the winery itself; a truck carrying a 20- or 40-foot shipping container is backed up to the door of the winery and loaded there for the ocean voyage. For smaller producers, the wines are picked up and then delivered to a warehouse. There the shipping agent consolidates various deliveries to fill a container for the shipping line of the importer's choosing.

Shipping dates and rates will vary depending on the availability of containers. In general, a 20-foot container can hold 800 cases of wine; a single 40-foot container can take up to 1,300 cases. The weight of the wine is a consideration when determining how many cases to ship in a given container. Not only do wine bottles vary in size (750-ml bottles are the most common, with 12 bottles in a case), but there is likely to be a difference in weight between two cases of different types of wine. For example, heavier bottles are required for champagne and other sparkling wines since the contents are under pressure; bottles of fine Bordeaux are packaged in wooden crates that weigh more than ordinary cardboard cartons.

Shipping wine is a challenging venture because of the volatile and perishable nature of the product. Proper storage and transportation are vital; light, heat, and temperature fluctuations are wine's worst enemies. Ideally, wine should be kept at a constant temperature near 55 degrees. To prevent improper shipping from ruining a shipment, temperature-controlled containers (known as reefers) are often used, even though they add about $3 per case to the cost of the shipment. To further protect the wine, some importers avoid shipping during the hot summer months. Because ownership of the wine is transferred to the importer at the moment the wine leaves the French storage warehouse, it is important to insure the shipment. Wine shipments can even be insured against possible losses due to war and terrorism. The best importers arrange for proper warehouse storage even before taking title to the wines.

The trans-Atlantic trip for US-bound wine takes a week or more. The port of entry depends on the location of the importer or wholesaler/distributor. The Port of New York is used when wines are destined for the East Coast. Wine bound for the nation's midsection often enters through Baltimore, Maryland, or Norfolk, Virginia. Ships going to a western destination may chart a course through the Gulf of Mexico on their way to Houston, Texas; wines bound for the Port of San Francisco pass through the Panama Canal. Once the wine enters the United States, it must clear US Customs. Customs agents and the importer or wholesaler make sure the shipment meets all government regulations and that paperwork is properly prepared. The Bureau of Alcohol, Tobacco, and Firearms is the US government agency with jurisdiction over wines and spirits.

After it has cleared Customs, the wine is then shipped to the wholesaler's warehouse. Again, the importance of temperature-controlled shipping comes into play. If the wholesaler is

continued

too busy to pick the container up immediately, it may sit on the dock for a week or more in warm weather; without refrigeration, the wine—and the importer's investment—might be lost. If the distributor is located in Chicago, the wine often enters the country in Baltimore and completes the next leg of the trip via rail. Sometimes trucks will bring a shipment of wine to the Midwest from the East Coast and return full of meat in order to make the trip cost-effective. After the wine has been unloaded at the warehouse, the distributor's sales staff arranges for the cases of wine to be delivered by truck or van to individual retailers.

There is as much variety among retail channels for wine as there is among wine producers. Outlets vary from mom-and-pop grocery stores to wine sections in large supermarkets to huge wine and liquor discounters, with considerable variety in between. In some stores, wine is stored and displayed haphazardly, often in sunny windows or near heating vents. Other stores go to great lengths to make sure that the wine is not ruined after its long journey in protective containers. One large retailer, Big Y in Northampton, Massachusetts, even goes so far as to keep the entire store at 55 degrees year round.

There are still other factors that have a major influence on sales. One is the marketing and merchandising skill of the retailer. Point-of-sale recommendation from an informed retailer is important in selling fine wines. Also, the industry press can have a huge impact on sales. A good rating in publications such as *Wine Spectator* or *The Wine Advocate* can make the difference between obscurity and a sellout in a particular wine. Often, savvy wine retailers will display a press clipping with a positive rating right on the bin of a certain wine so that customers can educate themselves as they shop.

Channel strategy in a global marketing program must fit the company's competitive position and overall marketing objectives in each national market. If a company wants to enter a competitive market, it has two basic choices:

1. Direct involvement (its own sales force, retail stores, etc.)
2. Indirect involvement (independent agents, distributors, wholesalers)

The first choice requires the company to establish company-owned or franchised outlets. The second choice requires incentives to independent channel agents that will induce them to market the company's product. The process of shaping international channels to fit overall company objectives is constrained by several factors: customers, products, middlemen, and the environment. Important characteristics of each of these factors will be discussed briefly.

Customer Characteristics

The characteristics of customers are an important influence on channel design. Their number, geographic distribution, income, shopping habits, and reactions to different selling methods all vary from country to country and, therefore, require different channel approaches. Remember, channels create utility for customers.

In general, regardless of the stage of market development, the need for multiple channel intermediaries increases as the number of customers increases. The converse is also true: the need for channel intermediaries decreases as the number of customers decreases. For example, if there are only 10 customers for an industrial product in each national market, these 10 customers must be directly contacted by either the manufacturer or an agent. For mass-market products bought by millions of customers, retail distribution outlets or mail-order distribution is required. In a country with a large number of low-volume retailers, it is usually cheaper to reach them via wholesalers. Direct selling that bypasses wholesale intermediaries may be the most cost-effective means of serving large-volume retailers. These generalizations apply to all countries, regardless of stage of development; however, individual country customs will vary. For example, Toys "Я" Us faced considerable opposition from Japanese toy manufacturers that refused to sell directly to the American company after it built its first stores in Japan.

Product Characteristics

Certain product attributes such as degree of standardization, perishability, bulk, service requirements, and unit price have an important influence on channel design and strategy. Products with a high unit price, for example, are often sold through a company sales force because the selling cost of this expensive distribution method is a small part of the total sale price. Moreover, the high cost of such products is usually associated with complexity or with product features that must be explained in some detail, and this can be done most effectively by a controlled sales force. For example, mainframe computers are expensive, complicated products that require both explanation and applications analysis focused on the customer's needs. A company-trained salesperson or sales engineer is well suited to the task of creating information utility for computer buyers.

Mainframe computers, photocopiers, and other industrial products may require margins to cover the costs of expensive sales engineering. Other products require margins to provide a large monetary incentive to a direct sales force. In many parts of the world, cosmetics are sold door to door; company representatives call on potential customers. The reps must create customer awareness of the value of cosmetics and evoke a feeling of need for this value that leads to a sale. The sales activity must be paid for. Companies using direct distribution for consumer products rely on wide gross selling margins to generate the revenue necessary to compensate salespeople. Amway and Avon are two companies that have succeeded in extending their direct-sales systems globally.

Bulky products usually require channel arrangements that minimize the shipping distances and the number of times products change hands between channel intermediaries before they reach the ultimate customer. Soft drinks and beer are examples of bulky products whose widespread availability is an important aspect of an effective marketing strategy.

Middleman Characteristics

Channel strategy must recognize the characteristics of existing middlemen. Middlemen are in business to maximize their own profit and not that of the manufacturer. They are notorious for cherry picking, that is, the practice of taking orders from manufacturers whose products and brands are in demand to avoid any real selling effort for a manufacturer's products that may require push. This is a rational response by the middleman, but it can present a serious obstacle to the manufacturer attempting to break into a market with a new product. The cherry picker is not interested in building a market for a new product. This is a problem for the expanding international company. Frequently, a manufacturer with a new product or a product with a limited market share is forced to set up some arrangement for bypassing the cherry-picking segment of the channel. In some cases, manufacturers will set up an expensive direct-distribution organization to obtain a share of the market. When they finally obtain a share of the target market, they may abandon the direct-distribution system for a more cost-effective intermediary system. The move does not mean that intermediaries are better than direct-distribution. It is simply a response by a manufacturer to cost considerations and the newly acquired attractiveness of the company's product to independent distributors.

An alternative method of dealing with the cherry-picking problem does not require setting up an expensive direct sales force. Rather, a company may decide to rely on a distributor's own sales force by subsidizing the cost of the sales representatives the distributor has assigned to the company's products. This approach has the advantage of holding down costs by tying missionary and support selling in with the distributor's existing sales management team and physical distribution system. With this approach, it is possible to place managed direct-selling support and distribution support behind a product at the expense of only one salesperson per selling area. The distributor's incentive for cooperating in this kind of arrangement is that he or she obtains a free sales representative for a new product with the potential to be a profitable addition to his or her line. This cooperative arrangement is ideally suited to getting a new export-sourced product into distribution in a market.

SELECTION AND CARE OF DISTRIBUTORS AND AGENTS The selection of distributors and agents in a target market is a critically important task. A good commission agent or stocking distributor can make the difference between realizing zero performance and performance that exceeds what is expected. At any point in time it is likely that some of any company's agents and distributors will be excellent, others will be satisfactory, and still others will be unsatisfactory and in need of replacement.

To find a good distributor, a firm can begin with a list provided by the home country's Ministry of Trade or Department of Commerce or the local chamber of commerce or trade associations. Talk to end users of industrial products or the retailers of consumer products and find out which distributors they prefer and why they prefer them or get this information from someone in the country who can do the research for you. If the product is a consumer product, go to the retail outlets and find out where consumers are buying products similar to your own and why. Two or three names will keep coming up. Go to these two or three and see which of them would be available to sign. Before signing, make sure there is someone in the organization who will be the key person for your product. The key person is someone who will make it a personal objective to achieve success with your product.

This is the critical difference between the successful distributor and the worthless distributor. There must be a personal, individual commitment to the product. The second and related requirement for successful distributors or agents is that they must be successful with the product. Success means that they can sell the product and make money on it. In any case, the product must be designed and priced to be competitive in the target market. The distributor can assist in this process by providing information about customer wants and the competition and by promoting the product he or she represents. See Figure 12-1 for a list of selection criteria for selection of distributors.

Once all important criteria are identified, more specific evaluation may be necessary. Specific criteria for any product or market depend on the nature of the firm's business and its distribution objective in any given market. The criteria selected should correspond directly to the marketer's own determinants of success—all elements that are important to gaining competitive advantage. For example, a manufacturer of consumer goods may consider the distributor's marketing management expertise and financial soundness to be of utmost importance. These indicators reflect whether the distributor is profitable and is able to perform the necessary marketing functions, such as extension of credit to customers. Financial reports may not always be complete or reliable or may lend themselves to differences of interpretation. Alternatively, an industrial goods company may consider the distributor's product compatibility, technical know-how, facilities, and service support of critical importance and the distributor's infrastructure, client performance, and attitude towards its products of less importance. A high-tech consumer-goods company, on the other hand, may favor financial

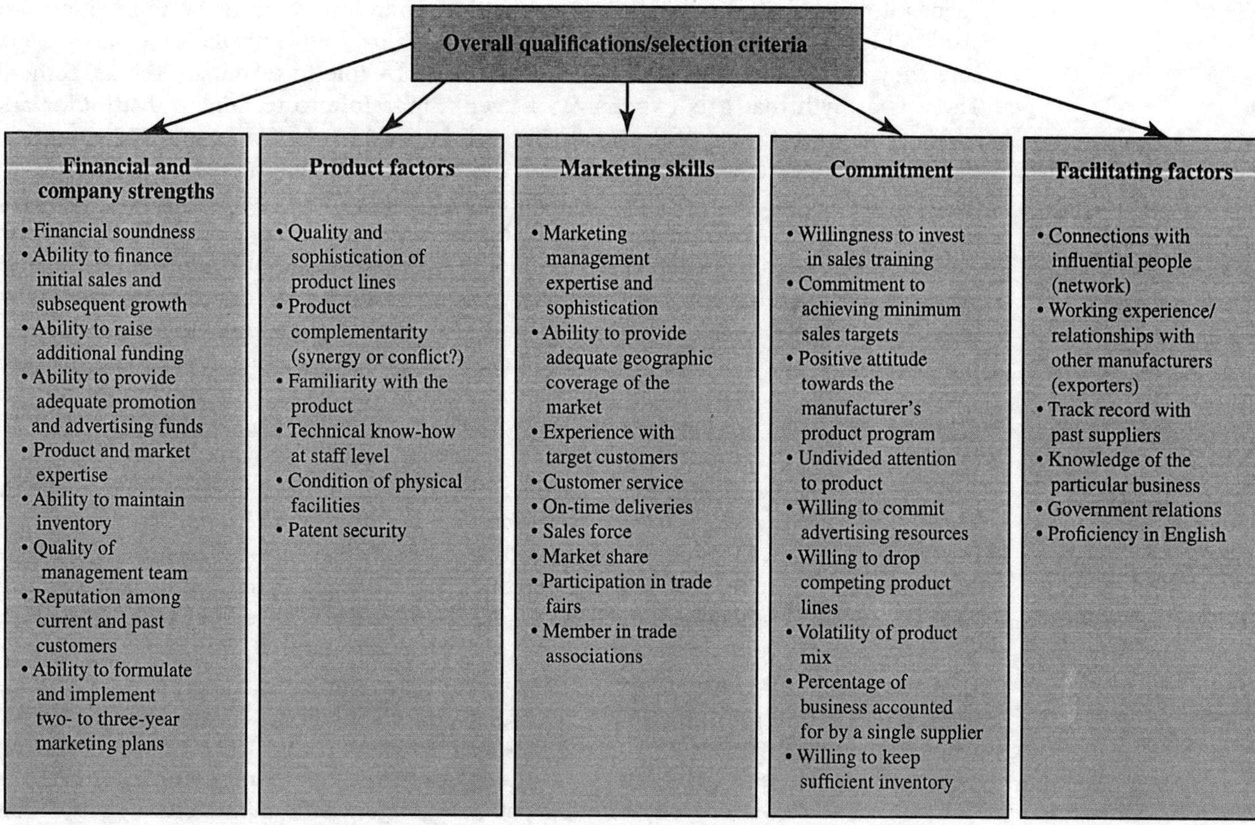

FIGURE 12-1 Criteria for Evaluating Distributors
Source: Sven Hollensen, "Global Marketing, Fifth Edition, Pearson Education Limited, 2011," Adapted from Cavusgil et al (1995).

soundness, marketing management expertise, reputation, technical know-how, facilities, service support, and government relations of special importance.

AGENT/DISTRIBUTOR PERFORMANCE Agent and distributor performance is essential if they are part of your channel strategy. A key task is to determine what you must do to motivate and support their efforts. The RF Division of Harris Corporation achieved great success in international markets with its shortwave radios. One of the reasons for its success was the quality of agents in key markets and their commitment to the Harris product. They were attracted to Harris because the company made a product that was as good as or better than any other product on the market. Also, Harris offered commissions of 33 percent on all sales—at least 15 percent higher than commissions offered by any other competitor. This was certainly one of the single most important factors in ensuring Harris's success. The generous commission motivated the agents to sell Harris products and provided the financial resources to support a strong marketing effort. There was, of course, a trade-off: Harris prices were higher, but in their target markets, this price effect was more than offset by the effectiveness of the higher margins.

TERMINATION The only way to keep a good distributor or agent is to work closely with him or her to ensure that she is making money on the product. Any distributor who does not make money on a line will drop it. It is really quite simple. In general, if a distributor is not working out, it is wise to terminate the agreement and find another one. Few companies have the capability to convert a mediocre distributor or agent into an effective business representative. Therefore, two of the most important clauses in the distributor contract are the performance and cancellation clauses. Make sure they are written in a way that will make it possible to terminate the agreement. There is a myth that it is expensive or even impossible to terminate distributor and agent agreements. Some of the most successful global marketers have terminated hundreds of agreements and know success is based on their willingness to terminate if a distributor or agent does not perform. The key factor is performance: distributors who do not perform must either shape up or be replaced.

However, termination can result in legal expenses. In some countries, companies are exposed to courts that are blatantly corrupt. In Ecuador, for example, the courts have made awards to terminated distributors of global companies that have been as high as 400 years of sales! Even if you have a termination clause, agents and distributors have rights in many jurisdictions that cannot be taken away by agreement. For example, say that your agreement gives you the right to terminate without cause with 90 days' notice. The agent, if the agreement is enforceable in New Jersey, can sue on the grounds that you have breached the good faith and fair dealing covenant of New Jersey law. This is a rule of law that holds that if a distributor is acting in good faith on the assumption that his or her appointment as a distributor is going to continue, he or she has a right to sue a manufacturer for damages if the agreement is terminated. Clearly, jurisdiction of disputes is important and any agreement should be clear on this issue. There is no substitute for the advice of qualified, local counsel when it comes to the preparation of agent/distributor agreements.

Another rule for agreements is that you should be able to read and understand the agreement. If you cannot, insist that your attorney redraft the agreement in understandable language. If you cannot understand the agreement, you may find that it will come back to haunt you. Whether you are an agent or a manufacturer, you should know what your rights and obligations are under your agreements.

Environmental Characteristics

The general characteristics of the total marketing environment are a major consideration in channel design. Because of the enormous variety of economic, social, and political environments internationally, there is a need to delegate a large degree of independence to local operating management or agents. A comparison of food distribution in countries at different stages of development illustrates how channels reflect and respond to underlying market conditions in a country. In high-income countries, several factors combine to make the supermarket or the self-service, one-stop food store the basic food retailing unit. These factors include high incomes, large-capacity refrigerator/freezer units, automobile ownership, acceptance of frozen and convenience foods, and attitudes toward food preparation. Many shoppers want to purchase a week's worth of groceries in one trip to the store. They have the money, ample storage space in the refrigerator, and the hauling capacity of the car to move this large quantity of food from the store to the home. The supermarket, because it is efficient, can fill the food shoppers' needs at lower prices than are found in butcher shops and other traditional full-service food stores. Additionally, supermarkets can offer more variety and a greater selection of merchandise than can smaller food stores, a fact that appeals to affluent consumers.

DISTRIBUTION CHANNELS: TERMINOLOGY AND STRUCTURE

Distribution channels are systems that link manufacturers to customers. Although channels for consumer products and industrial products are similar, there are also some distinct differences, as will be discussed later in the chapter. Consumer channels

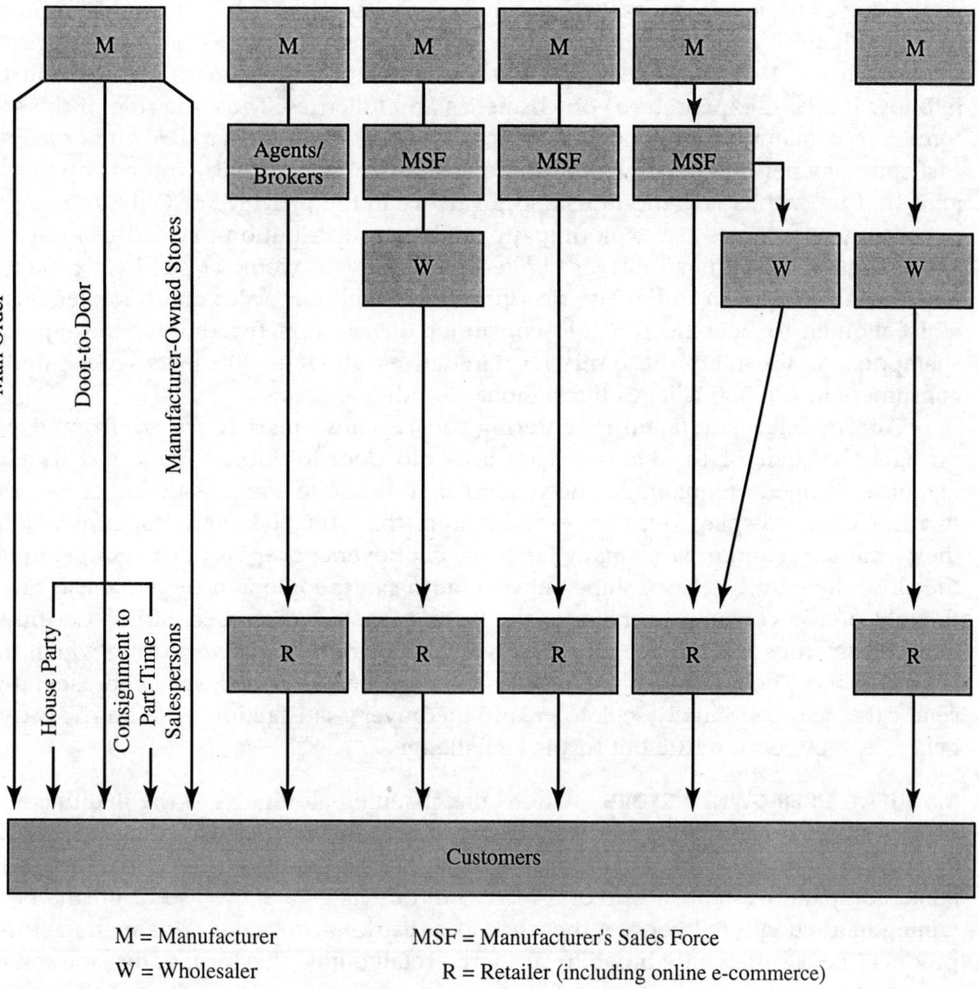

FIGURE 12-2 Marketing Channel Alternatives—Consumer Products

are designed to put products in the hands of people for their own use; industrial channels deliver products to manufacturers or organizations that use them in the production process or in day-to-day operations.

Consumer Products

Figure 12-2 summarizes channel structure alternatives for consumer products. A consumer products marketer can sell to customers directly (using a door-to-door sales force), online on the Internet, through mail-order selling (using a catalog or other printed materials), or through manufacturer-owned or independent retailers. Most companies use a combination of channels. For example, IKEA, the world's largest furniture retailer, relies primarily on its company-owned retail stores, but it also has a catalog that supports both the retail stores and online sales. IKEA annually prints 38 editions of its catalog in 17 languages.

DOOR-TO-DOOR SELLING Door-to-door selling is a relatively expensive form of distribution that, as noted earlier, requires high gross margins and can result in higher prices to the customer. In high-income countries it is a mature channel. Certain items—frozen foods, vacuum cleaners, and cosmetics—continue to be sold in this manner. Door-to-door selling, however, is growing in popularity in many countries at earlier stages of development. For example, Avon has successfully used this approach in more than 50 countries identified by company executives as having weak retail infrastructures. Also, they recognize that low levels of discretionary income translate into low levels of expenditures on cosmetics and toiletries. Thus, the role of the sales force is to communicate the benefits of cosmetics and build demand. Avon became the first company permitted to sell door-to-door in China. Since 1990, Avon has operated a joint venture with Guangzhou Cosmetics Factory in the province of Old Canton.

Many companies are exploring approaches to distribution that utilize local market strengths. Hindustan Unilever Limited partners with women's self-help groups to reach small villages in India. The firm provides training in sales and bookkeeping to assist women to become direct-to-consumer distributors for Unilever's soaps and shampoos. As a result of these very local initiatives, about 4,500 agents serve 3 million consumers in 100,000 villages throughout 15 Indian states.[7]

Automobile manufacturers entering the Japanese market are confronted with the fact that half of the nation's cars are sold door-to-door. Toyota and its eight Japanese competitors maintain showrooms that are quite small, with sometimes only two models on display, but they employ more than 100,000 car salespeople. Unlike their American counterparts, many Japanese car buyers never visit dealerships. In fact, the close, long-term relationships between auto salespeople and the Japanese can be thought of as a consumer version of the *keiretsu* system discussed earlier. Car buyers expect numerous face-to-face meetings with a sales representative, during which trust is established. The relationship continues after the deal is closed; sales representatives send cards and continually seek to ensure the buyer's satisfaction. Foreign rivals try to generate showroom traffic but this is a challenge.

MANUFACTURER-OWNED STORE A third direct-selling alternative is the manufacturer-owned store. For example, the Walt Disney Company owns stores that sell apparel, videos, toys, and other merchandise relating to the company's trademarked characters. Some companies establish one or a few retail outlets as a showcase or means of obtaining marketing intelligence rather than as a distribution strategy. If a manufacturer's product line is sufficiently broad to support a retail outlet, this form of distribution can be very attractive. The shoe store, for example, is a viable retail unit, and shoe manufacturers typically have established their own direct outlets as a major element in their distribution strategy, both at home and in important world markets. Over 30 percent of Apple Stores are outside the United States. In fact, Apple's fastest growth is occurring outside the United States, where it realized 44 percent of 2010 revenues.[8]

FRANCHISE OPERATIONS Franchise operations are a contractual agreement between a franchisor and a franchisee whereby the franchisor grants the right to sell goods and/or services to a franchisee. The franchisee agrees to operate the business according to a plan defined by the franchisor and under a trade name owned by the franchisor and, in some cases, using supplies that are provided by the franchisor. There are many reasons for a franchise company to expand internationally. The first step in becoming a global franchisor is to have a well-established and successful operation in a home market. The home-country operation must be able to support the investment required to establish a global expansion. Franchise companies must develop a capacity to support and manage their global business operations. It may make financial sense to establish regional offices. For example, there is a 13-hour difference between the United States and Asia. This means that something as simple as making a telephone call between the offices can be

---

[7] "Winning in Two Worlds: Supply Chain Flexibility," Knowledge@Wharton online newsletter (January 26, 2011), accessed February 4, 2011, http:knowledge.wharton.upenn.edu.

[8] Apple Inc., Form 10-K 2010, pg 12.

TABLE 12-2 Top 10 Global Franchises—Rankings (2016)

Rank	Franchise Name	Country	Industry
1	McDonald's	United States of America	Fast Food Franchises
2	SUBWAY®	United States of America	Sandwich & Bagel Franchises
3	KFC	United States of America	Chicken Franchises
4	Burger King	United States of America	Fast Food Franchises
5	Pizza Hut	United States of America	Pizza Franchises
6	7 Eleven	United States of America	Convenience Store Franchises
7	Wyndham Hotels and Resorts	United States of America	Hotel Franchises
8	Inter Continental Hotels and Resorts	United Kingdom	Hotel Franchises
9	Hilton Hotels & Resorts	United States of America	Hotel Franchises
10	Marriott International	United States of America	Hotel Franchises

difficult. Also, language differences require translation and adaptation of manuals, advertising, websites and training materials to ensure successful entry and expansion.

The world's best-known franchises are fast-food chains (Table 12-2). For example, McDonald's restaurants are in over 120 countries. Almost half of McDonald's volume is derived from sales outside of the United States. Over 50 percent of revenue from KFC (formerly known as Kentucky Fried Chicken), Shakey's Pizza Parlor, East Side Mario's, and I Can't Believe It's Yogurt is from sales outside of the United States.

McDonald's has both benefited and suffered from its identification as an American company. On balance, this association has supported McDonald's world growth, but there are instances when it has been, at least for a period of time, a net liability. For example, during the bombing of Serbia by NATO forces that included the United States, the McDonald's in Belgrade, Serbia, took steps to let customers know that it was Serbian owned and managed.

The strong tradition of franchising in the United States had led to the domination of global franchising by US based companies.

BOX 12-4

Side Bar: Franchising Operation in India

KFC used franchising mode for entering in to different countries of world. As of 2014, there were 18,875 KFC outlets in 118 countries and territories located across the world. KFC first wanted to get in to the nitty-gritty franchise operation in domestic market USA during 1952. This understanding allowed them to open second franchisee outlet in the neighbouring country, Canada, the following year. Thereafter, there was no looking back. KFC went on to expand its franchisee outlets across different countries of the world. KFC crossed the Atlantic Ocean to set up an overseas franchise business in the United Kingdom, during 1964. Franchisee business allowed KFC the required speed of expansion. The different franchisees of different countries invested on their own to use the big brand image of KFC and enthusiastically spend the operative expenses connected to day to day running of KFC outlets. KFC was not required to offer, directly or indirectly, the franchisees' initial investment for opening of KFC businesses in their respective countries. Rather, the franchisees

continued

of different countries are also required to pay the franchisor an initial franchisee fee, called 'royalty fees' at the rate 5% of gross revenues or a minimum of $825, whichever is greater per month, and the renewal fees and share of advertisement cost as per agreement to mark the beginning of using the KFC brand in their countries. Indian entrepreneurs are increasingly being involved in franchising businesses in different sectors like food, lifestyle, retail, business services, healthcare, communication, education, entertainment and travel. The big brands of the world are also getting interested to enter India through signing of franchising agreement with the Indian franchisors and allowing them to carefully nurture the brand image. Eventually, the sheer size of Indian market lured the big brand holders to an extent that the country is now recognised as one of the largest in the world, in terms of franchisee business. However, the big brand foreign owners are eagerly waiting for legislation in India specifically relating to franchising. This legislation would provide a clear code of franchisee conduct and hence be helpful in conducting franchise businesses with full understanding of each other's expectations and more importantly, legal connotations behind the franchising agreements. Such legal frameworks are prevalent in developed countries and have boosted franchisee businesses to flourish in an unambiguous environment.

COMBINATION STRUCTURES The other channel structure alternatives for consumer products are various combinations of a manufacturer's sales force and wholesalers calling on retail outlets, which in turn sell to customers. In a given country, at a particular point in time, various product classes will have characteristic distribution patterns associated with them. In Japan, for example, several layers of small wholesalers play an important role in the distribution of food. Attempts to bypass these apparently unnecessary units in the channel have failed because the cost to a manufacturer of providing their service (frequent, small deliveries to small grocery outlets) is greater than the margin they require. Channel patterns that appear to be inefficient may reflect rational adjustment to costs and preferences in a market, or they may present an opportunity to the innovative global marketer to obtain competitive advantage by introducing more effective channel arrangements.

Industrial Products

Figure 12-3 summarizes marketing channel alternatives for the industrial product company. Three basic elements are involved: the manufacturer's sales force, distributors or agents, and wholesalers. A manufacturer can reach customers with its own sales force, or a sales force that calls on wholesalers who sell to customers, or a combination of these two arrangements. A manufacturer can sell directly to wholesalers without using a sales force, and wholesalers, in turn, can supply customers. Finally, a distributor or agent can call on wholesalers or customers for a manufacturer. B2B sales via the Internet are a rapidly growing option.

Distribution patterns vary from country to country. Before deciding which pattern to use and which wholesalers and agents to select, managers must study each country individually. In general, the larger the market, the more feasible it is for a manufacturer to use its own sales force. Kyocera Corporation of Kyoto, Japan, successfully used its own sales force at home and in the United States to achieve leadership in the $1.2 billion global market for ceramic microchip covers. Company founder Kazuo Inamori went to great lengths to make sure the spiritual drive of Kyocera's unique corporate culture extended to all parts of the company, including the sales force.

Global Retailing

Global retailing is any retailing activity that crosses national boundaries. Today, there is a growing interest among successful retailers to expand globally, but this is not a new phenomenon. For centuries, venturesome merchants have gone abroad both to

FIGURE 12-3 Marketing Channel Alternatives—Industrial Products

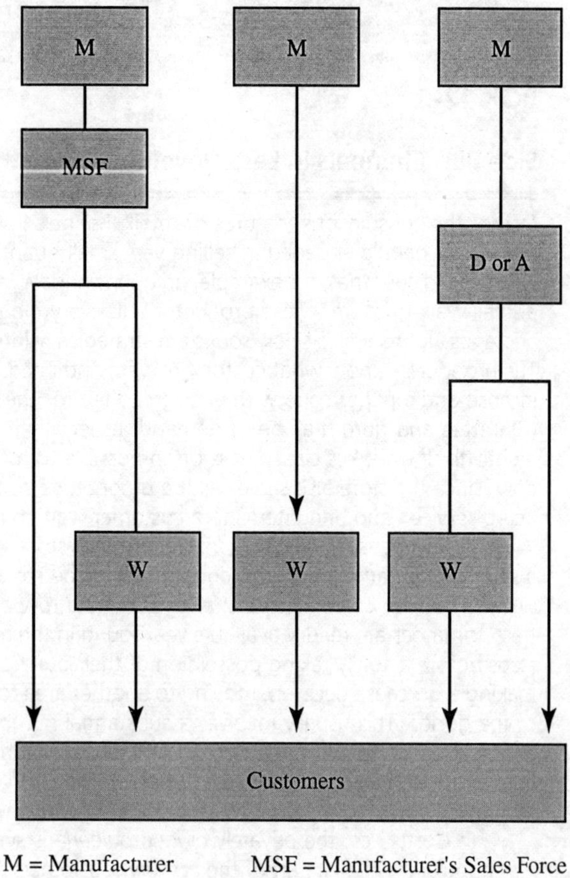

obtain merchandise and ideas and to operate retail establishments. The development of trading company operations in Africa and Asia by British, French, Dutch, Belgian, and German retailing organizations progressed extensively during the nineteenth and early twentieth centuries. International trading and retail store operation were two of the economic pillars of the colonial system of that era. Global retailing today involves the creation of global retailing organizations operating in every world region and in all of the fast-growing emerging-market countries.

Retail stores can be divided into categories according to the amount of square meters of floor space, the level of service offered, and width and depth of product offerings. In practice, stores have many different names in different countries, and definitions based on selling area also vary. A variety of terms is used to refer to large stores, including *supermarkets, discounters, superstores, big-box stores, hypermarkets, mass merchandisers, and membership stores*.

In general, countries in which the number of stores in a category is low relative to their share of turnover are those that joined the supermarket revolution many years after it began. France, Belgium, Spain, Brazil, and Colombia are some of the countries in which supermarket retailing sprang up as large, modern, highly efficient units were built. In Italy, where worker-protective legislation limiting the opening of large supermarkets is a factor, large surface stores grew in popularity more gradually. They have more than half of the grocery market share today, up from only 25 percent two decades ago. In other countries, supermarkets have existed for more than five decades. Some of the smaller units have been closed down, and new, very large stores have appeared in their place.

BOX 12-5

Side Bar: Channels in Less Developed Countries[9]

One of the conspicuous features of retail channels in less developed countries is the remarkable number of people engaged in selling very small quantities of merchandise. In Ethiopia and other East African countries, for example, an open window in the side of a building is likely to be a *souk*, a small walk-up store whose proprietor sells everything from toilet paper and playing cards to rice and eggs. To maximize sales, *souks* are strategically interspersed throughout neighborhood areas. The proprietors know what customers want and need. For example, early in the day they may sell incense and a paper cone with enough coffee for the morning coffee ceremony. In the evening, cigarettes and gum may be in demand, especially if the *souk* is located near a neighborhood nightclub. If a *souk* is closed, it is often possible to rouse the proprietor by knocking on the window, since the store also serves as the proprietor's domicile. Some *souk* owners will even provide "curb service" and bring items to a customer waiting in a car.

By comparison, government department stores in East Africa are less likely to display such a service orientation. Government stores may be stocked with mass quantities of items that are slow to sell. For example, the shelves may hold row after row of tinned tomatoes, even though fresh tomatoes are readily available year round in the market. Customers must go through several steps before actually taking possession of their purchases: determining what goods are available, making a purchase decision, moving to another area to pay, and finally, actually taking possession of the goods. This usually involves a substantial number of papers, seals, and stamps, as well as interaction with two or three clerks. Clerk jobs are highly prized in countries where jobs are scarce; compared to the *souk* proprietor, who is willing to work from dawn to dusk, the government employee works from 9:00 a.m. to 5:00 p.m., with two hours off for lunch.

In Costa Rica, the privately owned *pulperia* is similar to the Western-style general store that was popular in the first part of the century. Customers enter the store, tell clerks what items are desired, and the clerks fetch the items—which may range from chicken feed to thumb tacks. A typical *pulperia* stocks staples such as sugar and flour in 50-kilo bags, which the proprietor resells in smaller portions. Most *pulperias* have a refrigeration unit so they can sell ice cream novelties; in areas where there is no electricity, the *pulperia* owner will use a generator to provide power for the refrigerator. *Pulperias* are serviced by a fleet of private wholesalers; on any given day, the soft-drink truck, the candy truck, or the staples truck may make deliveries. The *pulperia* serves as a central gathering place for the neighborhood and generally has a public telephone from which patrons can make calls for a fee. This attracts many people to the store in communities where there are few, if any, telephones.

Both the *souk* and the *pulperia* typically offer an informal system of credit. People who patronize these shops usually live in the neighborhood and are known to the proprietor. Often, the proprietor will extend credit if he or she knows that a customer has suffered a setback such as loss of a job or a death in the family. Informally, the proprietors of private retail shops fulfill the role of a lender, especially for people who do not have access to credit through regular financial institutions.

The large number of unsuccessful international retailing ventures suggests that anyone contemplating a move into international retailing should do so with a great deal of caution. The critical question for the would-be international retailer is, "What advantages do we have relative to local competition?" The answer may be "nothing" when local laws governing retailing practice are taken into account. In such cases, there is no reason to expect highly profitable operations to develop from a venture into international retailing.

---

[9] Private communication from Brian Larson of CARE Niger.

On the other hand, the answer may indicate that potential advantages do exist. Basically, a retailer has two things to offer consumers. One is the selection of goods at a price, and the second is the overall manner in which the goods are offered in the store setting. This includes such things as the store site, parking facilities, in-store setting, and customer service. J.C. Penney is expanding retailing operations internationally for both reasons. After touring several countries, J.C. Penney executives realized that retailers in many countries lack marketing sophistication in terms of displaying products, locating aisles to optimize customer traffic, and grouping products. For example, in Istanbul, Turkey, a visiting team noted that one store featured lingerie next to plumbing equipment. Penney's advantage in such instances is its ability to develop an environment that invites the customer to shop.

GLOBAL CHANNEL INNOVATION

As noted at the beginning of this chapter, distribution channels around the world are highly differentiated. On the surface, it appears this differentiation can be explained only in terms of culture and the income level that exists in the market. However, the incidence and rate of innovation in retail channels can be explained in terms of the following four observations:

1. Innovation takes place only in the most highly developed systems. In general, channel agents in less developed systems will adapt developments already tried and tested in more highly developed systems.
2. The ability of a system to successfully adapt innovations is directly related to its level of economic development. Threshold levels of economic development are necessary to support anything beyond the most simple retailing methods.
3. When the economic environment is favorable to change, the process of adaptation may be either hindered or helped by local demographic/geographic factors, social mores, government action, competitive pressures, and infrastructure.
4. The process of adaptation can be greatly accelerated by the actions of innovative individual firms.

Self-service—the provision for customers to handle and select merchandise themselves in a store with minimal assistance from sales personnel—is a major twentieth-century channel innovation. It provides an excellent illustration of the postulates just outlined. Self-service was first introduced in the United States. The spread of self-service to other countries supports the hypothesis that the ability of a system to accept innovations is directly related to the level of economic development in the system. Self-service was first introduced globally to high-income countries. It has spread to emerging markets in every world region.

If a marketing system has reached a stage of development that will support channel innovation, it is clear that the action of well-managed firms can contribute considerably to the diffusion of the channel innovation. The rapid growth of McDonald's is a testament to the skill and competence of these firms as well as to the appeal of their products. In some instances, channel innovations are improved, refined, and expanded outside the home country. 7-Eleven stores in Japan, for example, are half the size of US stores and carry one-third the inventory, yet they ring up twice as much in sales. (Note: 7-Eleven, the parent company, is Japanese-owned.) Conversely, in China, KFC (Kentucky Fried Chicken) outlets are twice the size of those in the United States due to the greater emphasis of eating in a restaurant rather than taking food out.

PHYSICAL DISTRIBUTION AND LOGISTICS

Physical distribution and logistics are the means by which products are made available to customers when and where they want them. Distribution issues include order processing, warehousing, inventory management, and transportation. A firm's global strategy for logistics management depends in great part on the infrastructure and logistics services available in each country market. For global firms, *logistical integration* refers to the coordination of production and distribution across markets. Moving away from the more traditional country-based siloed structures for production, sales, warehousing, distribution, and logistical integration allows for more efficient and cost-effective supply-chain operations.

The Internet has shifted the balance of power between and among consumers, retailers, distributors, manufacturers, and service providers. Consumers can now easily search for price offers, the physical distribution industry is expanding its capacity to deliver goods at lower costs in less time in high-income countries, the cost of internet access continues to decline, and the access speeds continue to rise. These changes have led to enhanced consumer online shopping and delivery experience. Brick and mortar retailers are facing increasing competitive pressure from e-commerce channels. As an example of what can happen to market channel share, in one of the strongest categories of e-commerce in the United States, e-books accounted for 22 percent of all book spending in 2012, up from 14 percent in 2011. Amazon.com, the largest e-book seller, had a 27 percent share of the e-book market.[10]

This process of *disintermediation* is one which will continue into the future, perhaps increasing as manufacturers compete with their resellers and create *channel conflict* to reach the ultimate end users most efficiently and on their terms. Failure to move to new means of information dissemination, including mobile telephony, tablets, direct-to-consumer products, service order capabilities, and digital distribution networks, where applicable, certainly means decreased profitability and relevancy for companies staying with declining distribution methods.

Order Processing

Activities relating to order processing provide information inputs that are critical in fulfilling a customer's order. Order processing includes order entry, in which the order is actually entered into a company's information system; order handling, which involves locating, assembling, and moving products into distribution; and order delivery, the process by which products are made available to the customer.

Warehousing and Inventory Management

Traditionally, logistics strategy involved anticipating demand based on forecasting tools as well as using often proprietary software to manage inventory. Proper inventory management ensures that a company neither runs out of manufacturing components or finished goods nor incurs the expense and risk of carrying excessive stocks of these items. With the now ubiquitous use of information technology, EDI or electronic data interchange, as well as intermodal transportation, just-in-time (JIT) delivery is now more prevalent than ever. Where warehousing continues to be needed, it is used to store goods until they are sold; another type of facility, the distribution center, is designed to efficiently receive goods from suppliers and then fill orders for individual stores. A company may have its own warehouses and distribution centers or pay a specialist to provide these facilities.

---

[10] http://www.publishersweekly.com/pw/by-topic/digital/retailing/article/54609-e-books-market-share-at-22-amazon-has-27.html, accessed January 27, 2013.

Transportation

Finally, transportation decisions concern which of five methods a company should use to move its products: rail, truck, air, water, or pipeline. When contemplating market expansion outside the home country, management's inclination may be to configure these aspects of the value chain exactly as they are at home. However, this may not be the most effective solution because the organization may lack the necessary skill and experience to conduct all value-chain activities in target markets. A company with home-market competitive advantages in both upstream activities and downstream activities—manufacturing and distribution, for example—may be forced to reconfigure distribution activities to successfully enter new global markets.

Among American companies, 3M does an excellent job managing the physical distribution aspects of the value chain to support global market exports. Outbound logistics, for example, represent just one aspect of the company's overall global strategic plan to support burgeoning exports to Europe. In St. Paul, 3M's international distribution center receives more than 5,000 orders per week. In 1985, export orders took 11 days to get through the center. By 1990, only 5.5 days were required, and shipping mistakes were cut 71 percent, despite the fact that volume was up 89 percent. In Europe, meanwhile, 3M set up a distribution center in Breda, the Netherlands, to receive containers from Norfolk, Virginia, and other ports. Logistics managers convinced 3M to spend as much as $1 million per year for additional trucks to provide daily delivery service to each of 3M's 19 European subsidiaries. The outlay was approved after the managers demonstrated that savings could be achieved—due to lower inventories and faster deliveries—even if trucks were not filled to capacity.[11]

Laura Ashley, the global retailer of traditional English-style household linen and clothing for women, recently reconfigured its supply chain. The company has more than 300 company-owned retail stores around the world, supplying them with goods manufactured in 15 different countries. In the past, Laura Ashley's suppliers all sent goods to the company's distribution center in Wales. This meant that blouses manufactured in Hong Kong were first sent to Wales; blouses bound for the company's Tokyo store then had to be sent back to the Far East. Not surprisingly, this was not an effective arrangement; Laura Ashley stores were typically sold out of 20 percent of goods even though the company's warehouses were full. To cut costs and improve its inventory management, Laura Ashley subcontracted physical distribution to FedEx's Business Logistics Service. FedEx's information system is tied in with the retail stores; when a Laura Ashley buyer orders blouses from Hong Kong, FedEx arranges shipment from the manufacturer directly to the stores.[12]

Global firms exist in a "two-speed world." One has a lower rate of growth and high per capita income (for example, developed regions such as Europe and North America); the other has much higher growth and low per capita income (for example, emerging economies such as China, India, and Indonesia). These divergent growth patterns have significant implications for a global firm's supply and channel management processes and operations. The challenge of this "two-speed world" is in the need for both flexibility and adaptability in supply-chain creation and management. In high-growth emerging markets, this means managing channels of distribution capable of delivering high volumes of low-cost and oftentimes low-margin products

[11] Robert L. Rose, "Success Abroad: 3M, by Tiptoeing into Foreign Markets, Became a Big Exporter," *The Wall Street Journal,* March 29, 1991: A10.

[12] Stephanie Strom, "Logistics Steps onto Retail Battlefield," *The New York Times,* November 3, 1993: D1, D2.

profitably even where there is little infrastructure to support it. In low-growth, mature economies, including Western Europe, North America, and Japan, it means developing innovative and cost-competitive logistics in order to surpass competitors and defend or steal market share without sacrificing profit margins. While mature markets support innovation with up-to-the-minute, aggregated sales metrics created by computerized, integrated supply-chain management systems, in the fast-growing markets of the developing countries, less reliable data make distribution and channel management even more challenging.

In light of these challenges, companies are rethinking their sourcing and distribution facilities and partnerships, often looking to "near-shore" production for the added value of providing better service and more innovative products that will allow the firm to charge premium prices. To do this, companies are learning that they need to move quickly without the burden of distance, work with the most efficient and highly trained suppliers, develop the right products for a target audience, and get them to market faster than competitors. Coordination with partners is critical. For example, Procter & Gamble has a number of employees working near Wal-Mart's Bentonville, Arkansas, headquarters to facilitate and collaborate with Wal-Mart on planning and promotion. This enables P&G to more quickly respond to increasing or decreasing supply of specified product on an as-needed basis.[13]

BOX 12-6

Side Bar: India's Retailing Sector is Changing!

Retail stores are important because ultimately all the manufactured products would ultimately reach the consumers through them. There are various retail formats who actively support this process of product transfer. Traditionally in India, kirana stores or mom and pop stores played a very important role in transferring the manufactured products to consumers. These retail formats are small, individually run outlets but with penetration across length and breadth of the country. According to an estimate of Boston Consulting Group, the concentration of Kirana stores has been 10 stores per 1,000 Indians. Neighbourhood convenient stores like 7-11 of Japan or Thailand would be an upcoming dark horse in Indian urban situation simply because the convenience and ease they can provide for the busy Indian consumers living in urban areas. The department stores has played its important role in Indian market but right now seems to be in the decline stage. Different shopping malls are very active in the Indian market and provide a vast array of shopping experience to the modern Indians. Global hypermarket chains were set to rush to India once the country's policy on multi-brand retail regarding tough sourcing norms were relaxed. E-retailing is really making the Indians enthused and increasingly the manufacturing are using this channel to send products to the consumers particularly in product categories like food & beverage, beauty products for both male and female, and infant care. All these led to a "retail boom" in the Indian market. The 2016 Global Retail Development Index (GRD Index), published by A.T. Kearney, is also indicative of the fact that the whole world now recognises the retail potential of the country. The Table 12-3 captures the countries who made it to the top ten ranked countries in terms of their retail strength. The index ranks of emerging countries based on more than 25 macroeconomic and retail-specific variables. The variables included in the calculation of the GRD index are economic and political risk, retail market attractiveness, retail saturation levels, and modern retailing sales area and sales growth of the countries.

continued

[13] See, for example, "Winning in Two Worlds: Supply Chain Flexibility," Knowledge@Wharton online newsletter (January 26, 2011), accessed February 4, 2011, http:knowledge.wharton.upenn.edu.

TABLE 12-3 Global Retail Development Index

Rank 1995	GRDI 1995	Rank 2006	GRDI 2006	Rank 2011	GRDI 2011	Rank 2015	GRDI 2015	Rank 2016	GRDI 2016
1	South Korea	1	India	1	Brazil	1	China	1	China (1)
2	Poland	2	Russia	2	Uruguay	2	Uruguay	2	India (15)
3	Brazil	3	Vietnam	3	Chile	3	chile	3	Malaysia (9)
4	Chile	4	Ukraine	4	India	4	Qatar	4	Kazakhstan (13)
5	Taiwan	5	China	5	Kuwait	5	Mangolia	5	Indonesia (12)
6	Indonesia	6	Chile	6	China	6	Georgia	6	Turkey (11)
7	Malaysia	7	Latvia	7	Saudi Arabia	7	UAE	7	UAE (7)
8	Argentina	8	Slovenia	8	Peru	8	Brasil	8	Saudi Arabia (17)
9	Thailand	9	Croatia	9	U.A.E.	9	Malaysia	9	Peru (16)
10	Czech Republic	10	Turkey	10	Turkey	10	Armenia	10	Azerbiajan (22)

Source: A.T. Kearney GRD index
Note: figures in the bracket shows the rank of the countries during 2015.

During 1995, India was nowhere in the list of top ten countries as per the GRDI score. However, strong economic growth allowed the country to be number two in the world during 2004. Thereafter, by 2011 India slipped to the 4th rank. During 2015 India again disappeared from the top ten list of GRD index and placed it as 15th country out of 30 emerging countries ranked by A.T. Kearney. But the current 2016 GRDI index by A.T. Kearney just ranked the country second only after China. India's economy was backed by strong GDP growth and openness shown by the policymakers regarding FDI regulations. GRDI's strong ranking of India actually shows the increased optimism in retail market which India is witnessing.

DISTRIBUTION CHANNEL STRUCTURE IN DIFFERENCE IN COUNTRIES

The Table 12-4 shows the basic structural difference between four countries like India, Japan, South Korea and United states. The Indian wholesalers, retailers are independent and not controlled by manufactures as well as by the government of the country unless otherwise legal issues are involved. Though the modern type of retailers like super market, hyper markets are speedily coming in the retailing landscape but overall there exists a huge concentration of Mom and Pop stores where lots of operational informality could be noticed. Both margin and relationship drives the channel members like mom and pop stores, convenience stores, wholesalers etc present in the Indian market. Japanese channel members like wholesalers and retailers show absolute allegiance to the manufacturers following "keiretsu" system of networking originated by big manufacturers. Keiretsu in Japanese means a conglomeration of businesses bonded by cross-shareholdings leading to the development of a robust corporate structure. There is dominance of small retailers in Japan and hence retail stores per thousand populations are highest in Japan. The "keiretsu" system is very strong and completely manufactures' driven system. Interpersonal relationship amongst the keiretsu members do not rely on individual decision making but keep faith on collective wisdom. Multiple wholesalers and

TABLE 12-4 Characteristics of Distribution System in Four Countries

Characteristics	Indian	Japanese	Korean	US
Openness	Wholesalers, retailers are independent and not controlled by manufactures	Wholesalers, retailers are controlled by manufactures	Korean distribution system is characterized as Chaebol driven	Wholesalers, retailers are independent and not controlled by manufactures
Retailers' concentration	large number of small-scale "mom-and-pop" retail stores	Dominated by small retail stores	Large number of small-scale "mom-and-pop" retail stores	Balanced representation of small, medium and big retailers
Motivational force	Both margin and relationship driven	Relationship driven, "keiretsu" network	Relationship driven	Totally margin-driven
Cultural dominance	No significant effect of culture	Highly soaked in culture	Highly soaked in culture	Came out of cultural impact

retailers take part in a chain down to consumers making the distribution chain inefficient and eventual rise of ultimate product price. Korean distribution system is dominated by small-scale "mom-and-pop" retail stores. Unlike Japan, the industry-specific and manufacture driven retail chains are relatively shorter but like Japan they are controlled by "Chaebol" which means a business in which family controls the distribution chain. In contrast, in USA the wholesalers, retailers participating in a distribution chain are completely independent and hence take their own distribution related decisions. Also the representation of small, medium and big retailers is quite balanced.

DISTRIBUTION CHANNEL IN CHINA

China's retailing landscape is comprised of different types of retailing formats, different sizes ranging from very small to medium sized retailers, different ownership status like Chinese-owned to joint venture with foreign chain or exclusively foreign enterprises. Though there are many single units small retailers spread across different parts of the country but simultaneously various chain retail stores have been growing ever since Chinese government liberalised the sector. These chain stores operate under direct and unified management from the headquarters. Up to 1986, Chinese distribution system, comprised of wholesalers and retailers, was controlled by various state owned marketing channels. The state owned national or regional distribution agencies not only regulated but also distributed products and commodities across the country through second level wholesalers in the provincial level. During 1994, these wholesalers came out of the government control. A number of collectively owned as well privately owned wholesale enterprises filled up the space. Simultaneously, there were reforms in the retail sector. Different types of retail formats came up under different ownership structures like private, co- operative basis, joint venture between foreign and Chinese owners. Wholesale businesses were involved in bulk breaking and acting as conduit through which products and commodities were transferred to the retailers and then to the consumers for daily use. The wholesaler might have ownership of the commodities for wholesale and trade in the name of the company. The wholesaler also acted as a commission agent or commodity broker without the ownership

TABLE 12-5 Status of Chinese Retail Chian Store (2009–2014)

Different Chain Retail Store	No of stores (units) 2009	No of stores (units) 2014	Growth in number (2009–14)	Total sales of commodities in 100 million Yuan 2009	Total sales of commodities in 100 million Yuan 2014	Growth in sales (2009–14)
Convenient stores	15779	16832	6%	269.8	346	28%
Discount stores	859	377	−128%	37.2	29.5	−21%
Supermarket	33224	33202	0%	2569.5	2981.8	16%
Hyper Market	2493	9481	74%	2443.5	4647.2	90%
Ware house club	179	108	−66%	142.5	240.9	69%
Departmental stores	5304	4689	−13%	2498.3	3806.1	52%
Speciality stores	82704	108809	24%	13373.9	23345.8	75%
Gas stations	29345	34985	16%	8996.2	16786.3	87%
Franchised stores	24075	22854	−5%	697.3	1400.3	101%
Building material store	102	69	−48%	63.3	50.9	−20%
Factory outlet	410	309	−33%	1.5	16.4	993%
Other stores	10548	9685	−9%	143	475.7	233%
Total	2,05,022	241400	15%	31236	54126.9	73%

Adapted from http://www.stats.gov.cn/tjsj/ndsj/2010/indexeh.htm, as accessed on 20 January 2017 at 7.02pm.

of commodities, as the case may be. The Table 12-5 above depicts the status of retail chain store formats in China which throws light on the performance of different retail formats in China during a period from 2009 to 2014.

It can be seen from the above table that different types of retail formats ranging from convenience stores to hyper market grew up over the years to take the advantage of the economic prosperity of the country. During the period 2009-2014, convenient stores grew at the rate of 6 percent in numbers with sales growth of 28 percent during the same period. Discount stores, like in any part of the world were dying, as also in China as a retail form. Not surprising that in an affluent country like China both super market and hyper market flourished. The sales revenue of hyper market grew by 90 percent during the period 2009-14 indicating consumers' preference for this particular retail format. Discount stores were declining in numbers possibly because of onslaught of off line retailers. Franchised stores revenue also grew up very fast during the period 2009-14 indicting rush of foreign retailers to enter the country by taking franchise route.

EFFECT OF CULTURE ON DISTRIBUTION CHANNEL RELATIONSHIP

There is a great deal of understanding required between a manufacturer of one country and its distributors located in other countries in order for marketing to happen harmoniously. Who else better than Reinold Geiger, the 69 years old CEO of French cosmetics major L'Occitane, could understand that! The Austrian born and a French passport holder CEO kept on guessing what actually went wrong between the French company and its Indian importer distributor Ravissant. "Our first seven years in India was really like not being here. The company that represented us were nice gentlemen (Ravissant). I even met them in Paris twice. But they did not understand the skincare business." Reinold Geiger with all his understanding deeply rooted in French culture was referring to the great business loss that the company had to face in Indian market but used peculiar 'French way' of describing serious things with satire. The professional relationship between L'Occitane and its distributors Ravissant came to an all time low and the French company decided to walk out of Indian market. This was a great loss for the company as the growing affluence of Indian middle class population wanted upscale French cosmetics products. But alas! the French company and its Indian channel member were not only geographically distanced but culturally as well and failed to understand each other's voice. As per Hofstede, cultural understanding of India and France are distanced on two counts: individualism and uncertainty avoidance. With the high individualism score of 71 in France, Reinold Geiger would have preferred to have clarity in conversations and communication from Ravissant which were denied by Indian CEO of Ravissant having individualism score of only 48. Similarly with uncertainty avoidance score of 71 for France, Reinold Geiger made him almost roasted in absence of clear communication from Indian CEO of Ravissant about its plan of action related to marketing L'Occitane products in Indian market. However, Ravissant was completely unaware of the anxiety level of its French counterpart and maintained the famous 'jo hoga dekha jayega' attitude leaving L'Occitane with little to fall back upon. Misunderstanding between the French producers and Indian distributors reached to its maximum point as none of the involved party were prepared to handle cross country misunderstanding.

CASE EXAMPLE: JAPAN

Over the years, Japan has presented an especially difficult distribution challenge to foreign companies. Japanese distribution is a highly developed system that has evolved to satisfy the needs of the Japanese consumer. The total number of retail outlets in Japan—1.14 million stores—is down from a high of 2.15 million in 1985. Approximately 90 percent of the stores were small and medium-scale operations (with less than 10 persons) with just over 50 percent being individual proprietorships. This compares to 1.12 million retail outlets for the same time period in the United States which has twice as large a population. On a per capita basis, in the mid-1990s, Japan had twice the number of wholesalers and twice the number of retailers of the United States.[14] A correspondingly high number of intermediaries, including more than 400,000 wholesalers, is needed in Japan to service this fragmented system of outlets.[15] There are changes in distribution strategies in Japan. For example, Japanese women are marrying later and living longer. To meet the needs of women, theme shopping facilities are being developed. In Tokyo, VenusFort, a huge shopping center, attracts 120,000 visitors a day, most of whom are women. It is decorated with southern European ambiance and even has a "fake sky in which the sun rises and sets every hour."[16]

The categories of wholesalers and retailers in Japan are very finely divided. For example, meat stores in Japan do about 80 percent of their business in meat items. Similar focus exists in other specialty stores as well. This kind of concentration is also true at the wholesale level. This very high degree of specialization in Japan is made possible by the clustering of various types of stores at major street intersections or stops along commuter rail lines.

---

[14] http://en.wikipedia.org/wiki/Trade_and_services_in_Japan, accessed January 7, 2012; see also Lohtia Ritu, and Ramesh Subramaniam, "Structural Transformation of the Japanese Retail Distribution System," *Journal of Business & Industrial Marketing*, 15, No. 5 (2000): 323–339.

[15] Jack G. Kaikati, "Don't Crack the Japanese Distribution System—Just Circumvent It," *Columbia Journal of World Business* (Spring 1993): 38–41.

[16] "A Land Fit for Consumers," *The Economist*, November 27, 1999: 16.

There are, of course, many instances in which overseas firms have entered the Japanese market and have been able to overcome difficulties presented by the distribution system. Unfortunately, problems in coping with and adapting to Japanese distribution have also prevented a number of firms from achieving the success they might have had. Historically, foreign marketers in Japan make two basic mistakes. The first is their assumption that distribution problems can be solved the same way they would be in the West, that is, by going as directly as possible to the customer and, thus, cutting out the middleman. In Japan, because of the very fragmented nature of retailing, it is simply not cost-effective to go direct.

The second mistake often made is in treating the Japanese market at arm's length by selling to a trading company. The trading company may sell in low volumes to a very limited segment of the market, such as the luxury segment, with the result that there is usually limited interest on the part of the trading company. The experience is likely to be disappointing to all parties involved.

Successful distribution in Japan (or any other market) requires adaptation to the realities of the marketplace. In Japan, this means, first and foremost, adaptation to the reality of fragmented distribution. Second, it requires research into the market itself, including customer needs and competitive products. Then a company must develop an overall marketing strategy that (1) positions the product vis-à-vis market segment identified according to need, price, and other issues; (2) positions the product against competitors; and (3) lays out a marketing plan—including a distribution plan—for achieving volume and share-of-market objectives.

Devising a Japanese Distribution Strategy

Shimaguchi and Rosenberg identified several considerations for any company formulating and implementing a Japanese distribution strategy. The first called for finding a Japanese partner, such as an import agent, to help navigate the unfamiliar waters. Import agents range in size from small local distributors to the giant *sogo-sosha* (general trading companies). The authors also advised companies to pursue a strategy of offering better quality, lower price, or a distinctive positioning as a foreign product. Foreigners are advised to prepare for a long-term effort and modest returns; nothing happens quickly in Japanese distribution, and patience is required. Finally, cultivate personal relationships in distribution. Loyalty and trust are important.

These considerations are still relevant today; however, some recent studies have described ways to bypass the Japanese distribution quagmire by pursuing alternative distribution channels. For example, foreign companies may wish to follow the example of Toys "Я" Us and establish their own retail stores in Japan. Toys "Я" Us attempted to circumvent the multilayered wholesale system by buying directly from manufacturers. A second approach is to use direct-marketing techniques. Although telemarketing is relatively new and has proven more successful with business-to-business rather than consumer marketing, mail order in Japan has been experiencing 17 percent annual growth. L.L. Bean, with the help of the Internet, sells a substantial amount of merchandise in Japan, despite the fact that it has never published a Japanese catalog. Door-to-door selling is a third alternative channel strategy in Japan that has been successfully pursued by Amway. Amway has established its own system of over one million independent distributors; most of the 190-plus products sold are imported from the United States. Finally, a company may wish to explore creative ways of piggybacking with other successful companies. For example, Shop America successfully launched a specialty catalog business by piggybacking with Japan's 7-Eleven convenience stores.

Summary

Channel decisions are difficult to manage globally because of the variation in channel structures from country to country. Nevertheless, certain patterns of change associated with market development offer the astute global marketer the opportunity to create channel innovations and gain competitive advantage. The characteristics of customers, products, middlemen, and environment all impact channel design and strategy. Consumer channels may be direct, via mail, door-to-door, the Internet, or direct factory/manufacturer outlets; or they may involve one or more levels of resellers. A combination of the manufacturer's sales force, agents/brokers, and wholesalers may also be used. Channels for industrial products are less varied, with the manufacturer's sales force, wholesalers, and dealers or agents being utilized.

In developed countries, retail channels are characterized by the substitution of capital for labor. This is evident in self-service stores, which offer a wide range of items at relatively low gross margins. The opposite is true in less developed countries with abundant labor. Such countries disguise their unemployment in inefficient retail and wholesale channels suited to the needs of consumers; such channels may have gross margins that are 50 percent lower than those in self-service stores in developed countries. A global marketer must either tailor the marketing program to these different types of channels or introduce new retail concepts.

Transportation and physical distribution issues are critically important in global marketing because of the geographical distances involved in sourcing products and serving customers in different parts of the world. Today, many companies are reconfiguring their supply chains to cut costs and improve efficiency.

Discussion Questions

1. In what ways can channel intermediaries create utility for buyers?
2. What factors influence the channel structures and strategies available to global marketers?
3. What is cherry-picking? What approaches can be used to deal with this problem?
4. Compare and contrast the typical channel structures for consumer products and industrial products.
5. Briefly discuss the global issues associated with physical distribution and transportation logistics. Cite one example of a company that is making efficiency improvements in its physical distribution.
6. What special distribution challenges exist in Japan? What is the best way for a non-Japanese company to deal with these challenges?

Suggested Readings

Carr, Mark, Arlene Hostrop, and Daniel O'Connor. "The New Era of Global Retailing." *Journal of Business Strategy,* 19, 3 (1998): 11–15.

Cavusgil, S. Tamer. "The Importance of Distributor Training at Caterpillar." *Industrial Marketing Management,* 19, no. 1 (February 1990): 1–9.

Coughlan, Anne T., Erin Anderson, Stern, Louis W., and Adel L. El-Ansary. *Marketing Channels,* 7th ed. Upper Saddle River, NJ: Prentice Hall, 2001.

Daugherty, Patricia J. "Review of Logistics and Supply Chain Relationship Literature and Suggested Research Agenda." *International Journal of Physical Distribution & Logistics Management,* 41, no. 1 (2011): 16–31.

Fields, George. *From Bonsai to Levi's: An Insider's Surprising Account of How the Japanese Live.* New York: Macmillan, 1983.

Gao, Tao (Tony), and Linda Hui Shi. "How Do Multinational Suppliers Formulate Mechanisms of Global Account Coordination? An Integrative Framework and Empirical Study." *Journal of International Marketing,* 19, no. 4 (December 2011).

Lee, Hau L. "Don't Tweak Your Supply Chain—Rethink It End to End." *Harvard Business Review* (October 2010): 62–69.

Mehta, Rajiv, Rolph E. Anderson, Alan J. Dubinsky, Jolanta Mazur, and Pia Polsa. "Managing Channel Partner Relationships: A Cross-Cultural Study." *Journal of Global Marketing,* 24, no. 2 (2011): 105–124.

Mollenkopf, Diane A., Hannah Stolze, Wendy L. Tate, and Monique Ueltschy. "Green, Lean, and Global Supply Chains." *International Journal of Physical Distribution & Logistics Management,* 40, no. 1–2 (2010): 14–21.

Murray, Janet Y., Masaaki Katobe, and Stanford A. Westjohn. "Global Sourcing Strategy and Performance of Knowledge-Intensive Business Services: A Two-Stage Strategic Fit Model." *Journal of International Marketing*, 17, no. 4 (December 2009): 106–109.

New, Steve. "The Transparent Supply Chain." *Harvard Business Review* (October 2010): 76–82.

Prokesch, Steven. "The Sustainable Supply Chain." Interview with Peter Senge, *Harvard Business Review* (October 2010): 70–72.

Rangan, V. Kasturi, with Marie Bell. "The Promise of Channel Stewardship." *HBS Working Knowledge*, an online newsletter of Harvard Business School (June 12, 2006). Accessed August 18, 2011. http://hbswk.edu/cgi-bin/print/5375.html.

Wang, Michael Chih-Hung, Shadab Khalil, Charles Blankson, and Julian Ming-Sung Cheng. "The Influence of the Provision of Online Channel Functions on Exporting Channel Performance: The Moderating Effect of International Experience." *Journal of Global Marketing*, 24, no. 2 (2011): 125–135.

CHAPTER 13

Global Integrated Marketing Communications

Eighteen-year-olds in Paris have more in common with eighteen-year-olds in New York than with their own parents. They buy the same products, go to the same movies, listen to the same music, sip the same colas. Global advertising merely works on that premise.

—William Roedy *Director, MTV Europe*

Learning Objectives

1. What is global integrated marketing communications? How does it differ from global advertising? (390–393).
2. Explain the advantages and disadvantages of advertising standardization and localization (396–397).
3. Discuss the global marketing methods and tools for encouraging customer engagement (402–404).
4. Identify factors to consider when choosing an advertising agency for a global marketing campaign (412–414).
5. Discuss the significance of art, copy, and culture to global advertisers (414–415).

INTRODUCTION

Marketing Communication

It is important to place products or services strategically in a target market which can provide marketing advantage over the competitors' offerings. Marketing communication, which is one of the important Ps in 4P, that helps to achieve success in this direction. Marketing communication conveys the product or service features to the targeted consumers and establishes a channel of communication between the producer and consumers. The producer acts as information source and develops message containing information about the product which is required to be communicated to the target of prospective consumers for attracting them to the products or services. The producers use the best suitable media to transmit the message effectively and efficiently to the consumers. The success of the whole process depends on how accurately the message was transmitted and understood by the targeted prospective consumers. The producer understands the success of communication when feedback is received from the consumers.

DIFFERENCE BETWEEN DOMESTIC AND INTERNATIONAL MARKETING COMMUNICATION In international marketing, the producer of a country is required to communicate to the prospective consumers of another country. In various ways the communication efficiency could be low when the producers and the consumers are geographically distanced and separated by international border. The message transmitted to the targeted consumers of other countries may not be perceived in the desired way, resulting in reduced acceptance of the product. A producer therefore, may be forced to alter the message content from country to country. This would lead to adaptation of communication as per country specific requirements. The producers in the international marketing situation would be compelled to sacrifice the benefits associated with economy of scale if several countries are candidates for communication adaptation. Therefore, in the international marketing communication, standardisation versus adaptation is a strategic decision making area. Since, a total homogeneous marketing environment is difficult to get, even in the present globalised world, so decision making revolves around the degree of adaptation affected in a marketing communication which would result in a trade off between economy of scale parameters and adaptation requirements. For example, Lux, the global brand of Unilever since 1925, maintained standardised theme of female celebrity endorsements all along in advertisements for different countries of the world but picked up country specific celebrity. During 1960, the leading Bengali Actress, Supriya Choudhury, featured as model in Lux advertisement in India whereas Janet Leigh, the American actress and author, featured in US advertisement. United Colour of Benetton attempted universal standardised advertisement when it used controversial social issues like AIDS, Gulf War casualties and so on concerning individuals living in different countries. McDonald makes cursory adaptation in different countries to suit the local requirements. For example, local cartoon characters Asterix and Obelisk were introduced in its advertisements in France.

BARRIERS OF INTERNATIONAL MARKETING COMMUNICATION While dealing with marketing communication the basic objective of any company is to reduce the distortion effect. Distortion happens in communication when the message purposefully developed to communicate the unique features of a product, either partly or fully fails to reach the target consumers, and hence marketing objective of the company suffers. The prospective consumers could not decode the underlying meaning of the message. Suzuki India's message hidden in 'Kitna deti hai' campaign, underlining its claim to make India's most fuel efficient car, was providing a solution narrative (i.e. buy the car and get rid of problems of fuel inefficiency) may not be understood by the prospective consumers of Qatar where fuel efficiency was not at all a problem. Mostly in a rich country like Qatar one can expect enhancement narrative (buy the car to make your life much more better) in an advertising message. Now, consider a situation where Suzuki India's message soaked in a solution narrative is getting exposed to the prospective consumers of Qatar. In that case, the Qatar audience would not be able to really understand the hidden code in the advertisement leading to distortion in communication. The advertising company would be unable to reap marketing benefits out of their marketing campaign. In International marketing communication, this distortion may happen for several reasons. Some of them are listed below:

Language Differences Languages, both verbal and non-verbal, are different in different countries. International marketers might even be required to advertise in as many as 389 languages in order to cover 94 percent of the population if it desires to be local everywhere. This is because though there about 6909 spoken languages in the world, but many (94%) of these languages are spoken by few only. However, 389 languages are no less in number and creating marketing communication message in 389 languages almost seems to be impossible. Marketing communication using English language may not convey the right underneath meaning of the message to the Russian speaking people even if the message has been translated to their native language. For example, American global corporation, Xerox translated its slogan, "We taught the world to copy", in Russian language for Russian population. But the target population could not relish the underneath meaning of the message and was found to be distorted when literally translated.

Government Control and Regulations Royal Stag, a semi-premium blended whisky, has been very popular in the Indian market. The French liquor company, Pernod Ricard, for marketing the products in India, released one of its advertisement featuring popular cricketer, Harbhajan Singh during 2011. In the advertisement it was shown that Harbhajan Singh, in his dream, is enjoying his cricketing gear under the brand name Royal Stag. It was a surrogated advertisement which did not mention Royal Stag as a liquor brand. It also carried a tag line "cricket gear available in select retail outlet'. However, the advertising regulator did not like the marketing communication as it was not indicative enough of the fact that Royal Stag actually was a liquor brand. They result was the discontinuation of the advertisement as it violated Indian standard. TVS Motor's, television commercial highlighting the 'body balance' advantage also violated the advertising standard of India. The company's scooter, 'Scooty Wego', was seen in the commercial as being utilised by two women doing daring stunts in regular traffic road situation. TVS Motor actually wanted to convey in the commercial that it was all about the manoeuvre technique of the particular scooter. However, the prevailing Indian advertising standard pulled the advertisement on the ground by accusing the company of instigating the teenagers to do daring stunts by risking their life.

Media Availability Media availability is not same in all the countries of the world. Presence of media like TV, radio, newspapers, magazines and internet are essential for reaching to the mass public. Internet penetration (% of population had access to internet) in China was about 52.3 % during 2015 which was 91% in Japan. The internet penetration was as low as 28.7 % in Africa. Naturally a company like Unilever, when released its internet based Dove Campaign for Real Beauty worldwide in order to bolster its marketing around the world could not make much success in Africa. Then again, Television advertisement are not equally possible in all the countries due to differential user base and government restrictions. During 2012, Chinese government clamped a ban on advertisements in the middle of television programmes lasting for 45 minutes. Media limitations may ruin an advertising campaign in one country when the same did well in others where media availability is high.

Local Norms and Sentiments Sumo wrestling is one of the oldest and most respected sports in Japan. The people in general will like it when the Sumo wrestler is portrayed in a commercial advertisement. Saffron is scared colour in India as it is associated with Hindu religion. The Indian people may not like the colour to be associated in an advertisement of non-vegetarian foods. Chinese dragon is very sacred to Chinese society and hence the advertisement released by Toyota Motor Corporation for marketing its "Prado" sports utility came under fire when the company miss understood the Chinese sentiments.

Economic Differences Burundi is one of the poorest countries in the world with an average income per capita (current prices) of US $352, whereas Luxembourg in Europe is one of the richest countries with GDP (per capita) of US$101,926.4. The way Burundian people perceive the advertising message would be substantially different than people of Luxembourg. Coco Cola came up with a campaign to create a safe haven for polar bears in the high Arctic region that would simply not create much of marketing impact in Burundi. The underneath meaning of the campaign would be highly distorted because of presence of huge economic difference in these two countries.

Concept of Communication Mix

International marketers use a number of communicating tools to reach to the targeted consumers in different countries. Advertising, both online and offline, is a very effective tool to reach a larger number of consumers in different geographies. Through personal selling, the marketers try to use their sales force to promote and motivate people to buy a particular product. Sales promotion brings the potential customer close to the physical products so that the latent needs are converted to real sales. Public relations techniques are being used by many companies to bring an all-round understanding about the company and its products. Direct marketing through mail order or telephone allows a company to reach the target consumers directly with via the channel partners. Stealth marketing allows a company to use undercover to publicise about the products though indirectly but effectively influence people to use a particular brand. All the above mentioned communication tools and techniques are like the different weapons in the hands of international marketers to adequately publicize features of products amongst target groups. However, a right mix, referred as communication mix, of these tools and techniques are required to maximise the publicising benefits in a target country market. The right communication mix may be different from different country market because the differential marketing environment prevailing the countries.

Integrated marketing communications or IMC, refers to all forms of communication used by organizations to inform, remind, explain, persuade, and influence the attitudes and buying behavior of customers and other persons. The primary purpose of marketing communications is to inform consumers and customers about the benefits and values that a product or service offers. The elements of the promotion mix are advertising, public relations, personal selling, sales promotion, and direct marketing. The media for these different forms of promotion include print, broadcast, cable, outdoor (billboards and signage, skywriting, and balloons), and online, digital communications including social networks, e-mail, display, search, and online video.

The global communications environment has changed profoundly over the last half century. The Internet and IT have been major new drivers of globalization for the past two decades. Costs have come down and service has improved steadily and dramatically. A web presence is instantly global. The global reach of credit card issuers, package delivery services, and e-business tools of broadcast video, telephony, and the ever-expanding web has created a whole new level of possibilities for global consumer and business-to-business marketing by even the smallest firms. For example, it has been traditional marketing thinking that larger brands have the scale to overwhelm smaller players for "share of voice" in the marketplace. However, with user-driven traffic across platforms and performance-driven paid advertising, smaller brands and companies can engage customers and gain a positive return on their social marketing dollars since social traffic is driven by Twitter followers, Facebook fans, or a viral YouTube video—all of which must be earned and cannot be purchased or scheduled. It may no longer be a sustainable strategy to just outspend competitors with advertising dollars; competitive advantage now comes from the ability to optimize social media, not only scale of advertising spend.[1] The web is now a critical component of IMC.

This growth is reflected in the annual advertising expenditures. In 2009, world advertising expenditures exceeded $365 billion. This amount is expected to approach $550 billion by 2016. Internet advertising will account for $71 billion in global advertising during 2011 and is projected to reach $117 billion by 2016, rising from 17 percent of the global total to 21 percent.[2] During this time, it is forecasted that the largest advertising markets will remain the same with United States, Japan, Germany, the UK, and China dominating. However, China's growth will propel it to account for 9 percent of the world's online advertising by 2016, up from 5 percent in 2011.[3] Now, Norway, Australia, Switzerland, and the United States have the greatest advertising revenue per person. In the future, India and China, now in the lowest quintile of advertising per person, will be instrumental in the future growth of global advertising.[4]

Television is a primary medium vehicle, especially for global firms and global brands competing on brand attributes. TV advertising accounts for 41 percent of global advertising dollars, with the United States, Japan, China, Italy, and Brazil being the five largest markets. TV dollars are projected to capture 44 percent of the advertising and communications market globally by 2016. The increasing availability of multichannel TV, including Pay TV delivered through cable, satellite, or other emerging means, has and will continue to cause fragmentation of national, regional, and global audiences. It is anticipated that Pay TV will rise from 26 percent to 32 percent of total TV advertising between 2011 and 2016.[5] In mature markets, including Western Europe and North America, the negative impact of the switch from live to DVR recorded video, which allows fast forward skipping of commercial advertising, even at the 50 percent penetration level, may be offset by both rising middle-class populations and consumption levels.[6] In addition, Internet-delivered television such as online video and high-speed broadband may continue to fragment the audience market. Despite varying mobile devices and capabilities defining consumer experiences throughout the world, mobile media will continue to converge with the more conventional fixed-location web. With $2.7 billion in mobile advertising spend in 2011, it is anticipated that advertising in the

---

[1] Jonathan Shapiro, "Why Social Media Lets David Kick Goliath's Ads," ClickZ online newsletter (November 18, 2010), accessed November 18, 2010, http://www.clickz.com/clickz/column/1898114/social-media-david-kick-goliaths-ads.
[2] http://www.neoadvertising.com.
[3] Ibid.
[4] Ibid.
[5] Ibid.
[6] Ibid.

mobile sphere will balloon to $6.6 billion by 2016, with an average annual growth rate of 19.4 percent over this period of time.[7] Fixed location outdoor media now includes digital billboards and a growing number of "faces" on buildings and public transit systems as innovation drives digital display to new realms. Take, for example, the use of augmented reality to reintroduce the VW Beetle to the Canadian market in the fall of 2011. The campaign consisted of several very large billboards in Toronto's Dundas Square, in addition to posters on transit shelters throughout Toronto and Vancouver. Passersby downloaded a free app which they could use to make the cars come to life—racing through a tunnel and then crashing through the shelter itself. The introduction of the Beetle "with attitude" is reflected in the advertising and messaging, with social media used to alert people to the billboards.

The environment in which marketing communications programs and strategies are implemented also varies from country to country. For example, print media, including newspapers, magazines, and digital text, will benefit from raising literacy rates in countries like India where literacy is below 65 percent but rising rapidly. Digital communication can also provide growth opportunities when more traditional publishers embrace digital distribution. Although it is projected that magazine advertising will decline in each of the world's 10 largest markets,[8] strong magazine advertising will continue in countries like Brazil and Russia, which will support product awareness-building programs during market entry or expansion in these countries. In Latin America, for example, government policies continue to favor several larger media industry players such as Televisa/Azteca in Mexico and broadband, Pay TV. Television continues as the dominant media, with newspapers and magazine advertising continuing to grow. Outdoor advertising is also constrained by regulation in this region, especially in Brazil. Compare this with Asia, where governments have shifted their sights to the domestic consumer to continue double-digit growth. Advertising across mediums in China will surpass that of Japan by 2012, as companies in these countries turn to Internet-based advertising in light of low rates of Pay TV penetration and the high use among many demographics of inexpensive consumer electronic devices to access Internet-delivered content.[9]

The challenge of effectively communicating across borders is one reason leading companies are embracing integrated marketing communications (IMC). Adherents of an IMC approach explicitly recognize that the various elements of a company's communication strategy must be carefully coordinated.[10] In this chapter, IMC will be examined from the perspective of the global marketer.

BOX 13-1

Side Bar: Avoid Communication Mishaps

Can you play with the sentiment of a vast majority of population in India? Even more so, when it is connected with patriotism. Indians don't even want to debate any more about the Kashmir's integration with India. Every Indian feels Kashmir is rightfully a part of India. Since independence

continued

[7] Ibid.

[8] Ibid.

[9] Ibid.

[10] Thomas R. Duncan and Stephen E. Everett, "Client Perception of Integrated Marketing Communications," *Journal of Advertising Research* (May–June 1993): 119–122.

and till date Indians successfully rebutted all the claim of Pakistan as their part of land. You ask every Indian in the road, and all will be equivocally saying that Kashmir is an integral part of India and everybody will fight tooth and nail with Pakistan if there were any attempts to forcefully detach Kashmir from India. This wasn't known to the British confectionery giant, Cadbury during 2002. The British company made a great mistake by comparing Kashmir with Cadbury brand of chocolate 'temptation' and describing both as "too good to share". The company wanted to use 'Kashmir' to reach millions of Indians who are emotionally corrected with Kashmir and time and again reiterate their stand to fight out any evil design of Pakistan on this issue. Cadbury's, Temptations brand's newspaper campaign used India's geographical map showing the area of Jammu and Kashmir shaded over. It also had a catch line "I'm good. I'm tempting. I'm too good to share. What am I? Cadbury's Temptations or Kashmir?".

This comparing of Kashmir with Cadbury and the question of sharing it with Pakistan, as an obvious reference irked Indians. It soon became the talk of the town and politicians jumped in to roast their bread in the fire. Political parties cutting across political line started demanding an apology from Cadbury. The company was labelled spreading anti national feelings and some parties were considering legal action against the company. There was a general sentiment across India that the company toyed with the sacrifice of so many Indian jawans(soldiers), who sacrificed their lives for the cause of Kashmir. Some Indians came up with more blatant rhetoric. "Had such a thing happened in other countries of the world, people would have rejected the product altogether and Cadbury's stock and sales would have burrowed deep in the ground". The tone of people's outburst was increasing day by day since the advertisement campaign was released. The London headquarters was watching the development cautiously and did not waste any time further. It came out with apology for the advertisement saying it was issued "entirely in good faith, with no intention whatsoever to offend the sentiments of the public", and stopped publishing the advertisement further.

Standardisation of Communication

International marketing communication standardisation is an attempt to push an universally applicable marketing communication with single content, message, theme, logo, tune, jingle, background etc. in different countries of the world using different media like Television. Radio. Print publications, internet etc. A company can achieve the following primary benefits out of standardisation of International marketing communication.

GLOBAL IMAGE A single brand can manage countries around the world. However, it requires large budgets, efficient use of new techniques such as social media, etc. to stand a common image across the countries of the world.

ECONOMY OF SCALE Since a large market is to be covered with single advertisement so the fixed cost of developing the advertisement comes down considerably leading to scale economics.

Customisation of Communication

The customisation of the international marketing communication, is an attempt to push marketing communication with partly or fully customised content, message, theme, logo, tune, jingle, background etc. in accordance with country specific requirements using different media like television, radio, print publications, internet etc. A company can achieve the following primary benefits out of customisation of international marketing communication.

REDUCE THE NOISE IN COMMUNICATION The underneath meaning of a message contained in an advertisement, requires to be fully decoded or understood by the targeted consumer segment. Several barriers like language differences, government control and regulations, media availability, local norms and sentiments, economic differences etc. act in the situation of international marketing which create 'noise' in the system of communication. The noise distorts the underneath meaning of the message which the producer of one country wanted to convey to its target consumer of another country. Customisation of international marketing communication reduces the noise in the communication system and allows the different country consumers to understand the communicated message correctly.

LOCAL EVERYWHERE Communication customisation in international marketing allows foreign country brand image to grow 'locally' in every country. Different country consumers feel closeness to the brand as if it is their own country brand. A global producer may, therefore, take advantage of this closeness and convert it towards marketing advantage.

THE EXTENSION VERSUS ADAPTATION DEBATE

Communication experts generally agree that the overall requirements of effective communication and persuasion are fixed and do not vary from country to country. The same is true of the components of the communication process: the marketer's or sender's message must be encoded, conveyed via the appropriate channel(s), and decoded by the customer or receiver. Communication takes place only when meaning is transferred. Four major difficulties can compromise an organization's attempt to communicate with customers in any location:

1. The message may not get through to the intended recipient. This problem may be the result of an advertiser's lack of knowledge about appropriate media for reaching certain types of audiences. For example, the effectiveness of television as a medium for reaching mass audiences will vary proportionately with the extent to which television viewing occurs within a country.
2. The message may reach the target audience but may not be understood or may even be misunderstood. This can be the result of an inadequate understanding of the target audience's level of sophistication or improper encoding.
3. The message may reach the target audience and may be understood but still may not induce the recipient to take the action desired by the sender. This could result from a lack of cultural knowledge about a target audience.
4. The effectiveness of the message can be impaired by noise. Noise in this case is an external influence such as competitive advertising, other sales personnel, and confusion at the receiving end, which can detract from the ultimate effectiveness of the communication.

The key question for global marketers is whether the specific advertising message and media strategy must be changed from region to region or country to country because of environmental requirements. Proponents of the "one world, one voice" approach to global advertising believe that the era of the global village is here, and that tastes and preferences are converging worldwide. According to the standardization argument, because people everywhere want the same products for the same reasons, companies can achieve great economies of scale by unifying advertising around the globe. Advertisers who follow the localized approach are skeptical of the global-village argument. Even Coca-Cola records radio spots in 40 languages with 140 different music backgrounds.[11] Coca-Cola asserts that consumers still differ from country to country and must be reached by advertising tailored to their respective countries. Proponents of localization point out that most blunders occur because advertisers have failed to understand and adapt to foreign cultures. Nick Brien, managing director of Leo Burnett, explains the situation this way:

> As the potency of traditional media declines on a daily basis, brand building locally becomes more costly and international brand building becomes more cost effective. The challenge for advertisers and agencies is finding ads which work in different countries and cultures. At the same time as this global tendency, there is a growing local tendency. It's becoming increasingly important to understand the requirements of both.[12]

During the 1950s, the widespread opinion of advertising professionals was that effective international advertising required assigning responsibility for campaign preparation to a local agency. In the early 1960s, this idea of local delegation was repeatedly challenged. For example, Eric Elinder, head of a Swedish advertising agency, wrote: "Why should three artists in three different countries sit drawing the same electric iron and three copywriters write about what after all is largely the same copy for the same iron?"[13] Elinder argued that consumer differences between countries were diminishing and that he would more effectively serve a client's interest by putting top specialists to work devising a strong international campaign. The campaign would then be presented with insignificant modifications that mainly entailed translating the copy into language well suited for a particular country.

COMMUNICATING BRAND PERSONALITIES ACROSS COUNTRIES

Brand personality is the human face of a brand. Every human because of certain traits- physical, mental and behavioural- develops a unique personality. Similarly, a brand because of its certain traits also develops a unique personality. According to renowned professor, Jennifer Aaker, the brand personality differs on account of five different brand traits like sincerity, excitement, competence, sophistication, and ruggedness and a particular personality allowed to be developed by the marketers. For example, Tata, as a brand has a trait leaning towards 'sincerity' in India as well as neighbouring countries. Tata represents 'honesty' in India. Godrej, as a brand in India is inclined towards 'competence' trait. Hence Godrej brand is perceived by Indian consumers as reliable, intelligent, and successful. The company **Godrej Consumer Products Limited** uses its product name, tag line, symbol, logo, manufacturing country image, character, packaging, slogan etc in its marketing communication to build 'Godrej' brand and nurture its 'competence' type of personality in India. When a company of one country enters to another country primarily, it seems difficult to transfer the brand personality maintained in home country to the destination country. For example, Godrej of India would be struggling to built and retain its 'competence' personality in Indonesia on entry. In initial phase of entry, the Indonesian consumers would be undergoing through 'halo effect' by dint of which they would be relying more on country of origin cues like familiarity with the country, image of producing

---

[11] The Coca-Cola Company 1999 Annual Report, p. 18.

[12] Meg Carter, "Think Globally, Act Locally," *Financial Times,* June 30, 1997: 12.

[13] Eric Elinder, "International Advertisers Must Devise Universal Ads, Dump Separate National Ones, Swedish Ad Man Avers," *Advertising Age* (November 27, 1961): 91.

country, country's expertise in production, its standard, reputation in the field etc. At this stage they would place more importance on their belief about the country of origin, and hence discard all other product information provided by the Indian company. In the next phase, the Indian brand would enter in to the 'default heuristic effect' when the consumers would not discard the marketing communications totally but additionally bring them in a back-and-forth manner without forgetting the country of origin related cues. In the next phase of "product attribute effect," it can be expected to have a level playing field when marketing communications released by the Indian company would get its legitimate space in the minds of the foreign country consumers. It is the time for brand like Godrej to overcome negative, if any, country of origin effect or strategically bring in to support its brand personality building exercise in the foreign country like Indonesia. In this stage marketing communications would be weighted by the consumers in terms of their merits but without totally forgetting the country of origin cues. So, in a sense, every brand has to cross three somewhat overlapping phases to transfer its home country grown brand personalities to the other countries of the world.

TAG LINE EFFECTIVENESS IN COUNTRIES

Tag line is a catchphrase or slogan used in advertising. Some of the successful tagline of Indian companies are: Amul: The taste of India; Tata Safari, Reclaim Your Life; Rasna: I love you Rasna; MRF: Tyres With Muscle; Fevicol: Fevicol ka mazboot jod hai Tootega nahi!; Big Bazar: Isse sasta aura cha kahin nahi, Videocon: The Indian Multinational. Now operating in different countries provokes the companies to translate its tag line in to local language. HSBC bank made a blunder when it tried to translate it tag line 'assume nothing' in to local languages when operating overseas. It simply did not do much impact in the foreign countries because it was perceived to be vague in many countries. One can imagine Tata Safari's tag line 'Reclaim Your Life' may not be correctly translated in to Chinese language as many Chinese might not understand the meaning of it. The German automaker did the right thing to retain its tag line "Das Auto" without translating it in different country markets. McDonald was strategic in terms of using its tag line in different country market. The company used a Spanish translated version in Spanish speaking countries which actually meant "I really like it" to make the slogan culturally meaningful. In countries of low context culture, people prefer to communicate in ways that are explicit and do not rely heavily on the aura built around the tag line.

BOX 13-2

Side Bar: Campaign Adaptations to Appeal Consumers

Certain consumer products lend themselves to advertising extension. If a product appeals to the same need around the world, there is a possibility of extending the appeal to that need. The list of products "going global," once confined to a score of consumer and luxury goods, is constantly growing. Global advertising is partly responsible for increased worldwide sales of disposable diapers, diamond watches, shampoos, and athletic shoes. Some longtime global advertisers are benefiting from fresh campaigns. Jeans marketer Levi Strauss & Company racked up record

continued

sales in Europe in 1991 on the strength of a campaign extended unchanged to Europeans, Latin Americans, and Australians. The basic issue is whether there is, in fact, a global market for the product. If the market is global, appeals can be standardized and extended. Soft drinks, Scotch whiskey, Swiss watches, and designer clothing are examples of product categories whose markets are truly global. For example, Seagram's recently ran a global campaign keyed to the theme, "There will always be a Chivas Regal." The campaign ran in 34 countries and was translated into 15 languages to enhance the universal appeal for Chivas. The theory: The rich all over will sip the brand, no matter where they made their fortune.

Gillette Company took a standardized "one product/one brand name/one strategy" global approach when it introduced the Sensor razor in 1990. The campaign slogan was "Gillette: The Best a Man Can Get," an appeal that was expected to cross boundaries with ease. Peter Hoffman, marketing vice president of the North Atlantic Shaving Group, noted in a press release: "We are blessed with a product category where we're able to market shaving systems across multinational boundaries as if they were one country. Gillette Sensor is the trigger for a total Gillette megabrand strategy which will revolutionize the entire shaving market." In the Japanese market, Gillette's standardized advertising campaign differs strikingly from that of archrival Schick. Prior to the Sensor launch, Gillette custom-made advertising for the Japanese market; now, except that the phrase, "The Best A Man Can Get," is translated into Japanese, the ads shown in Japan are the same as those shown in the United States and the rest of the world. Schick, meanwhile, uses Japanese actors in its ads.

As the decade of the 1980s began, Pierre Liotard-Vogt, former CEO of Nestlé, expressed similar views in an interview with *Advertising Age*.

> *Advertising Age:* Are food tastes and preferences different in each of the countries in which you do business?
>
> *Liotard-Vogt:* The two countries where we are selling perhaps the most instant coffee are England and Japan. Before the war, they didn't drink coffee in those countries, and I heard people say that it wasn't any use to try to sell instant coffee to the English because they drink only tea and still less to the Japanese because they drink green tea and they're not interested in anything else.
>
> When I was very young, I lived in England, and at that time, if you spoke to an Englishman about eating spaghetti or pizza or anything like that, he would just look at you and think that the stuff was perhaps food for Italians. Now on the corner of every road in London you find pizzerias and spaghetti houses.
>
> So I do not believe [preconceptions] about "national tastes." They are "habits," and they're not the same. If you bring the public a different food, even if it is unknown initially, when they get used to it, they will enjoy it too.
>
> To a certain extent we know that in the north they like a coffee milder and a bit acid and less roasted; in the south, they like it very dark. So I can't say that taste differences don't exist. But to believe that those tastes are set and can't be changed is a mistake.[14]

The standardized-versus-localized debate picked up tremendous momentum after the publication in 1983 of Professor Ted Levitt's *Harvard Business Review* article titled "The Globalization of Markets," noted in earlier chapters. In contrast to the view expounded by Levitt and Liotard-Vogt, some recent scholarly research suggests that the trend is toward the increased use of localized international advertising. Kanso reached that conclusion in a study surveying two different groups of advertising

[14] "A Conversation with Nestlé's Pierre Liotard-Vogt," *Advertising Age* (June 30, 1980): 31.

managers—those taking localized approaches to overseas advertising and those taking standardized approaches.[15] Another finding was that managers who are attuned to cultural issues tended to prefer the localized approach, whereas managers less sensitive to cultural issues preferred a standardized approach. Bruce Steinberg, ad sales director for MTV Europe, has discovered that the people responsible for executing global campaigns locally can exhibit strong resistance to a global campaign. Steinberg sometimes has to visit as many as 20 marketing directors from the same company to get approval for a pan-European MTV ad.[16]

As Kanso correctly notes, the controversy over advertising approaches will probably continue for years to come. Localized and standardized advertising both have their place and both will continue to be used. Kanso's conclusion: What is needed for successful international advertising is a global commitment to local vision. In the final analysis, the decision of whether to use a global or localized campaign depends on recognition by managers of the trade-offs involved. On the one hand, a global campaign will result in the substantial benefits of cost savings, increased control, and the potential creative leverage of a global appeal. On the other hand, localized campaigns have the advantage of appeals that focus on the most important attributes of a product in each nation or culture. The question of when to use each approach depends on the product involved and a company's objectives in a particular market.

BOX 13-3

Sidebar: Understand Country Specific Requirements for Effective Communication

China has always been an important market for the global automobile producers. Almost all the foreign automobile companies are rushed to China to take advantage of growing market. As per the estimates of China Association of Automobile Manufacturers, nearly 80-85 percent of the demand are being met by Foreign-origin brands. A number of foreign companies have come forward to set production facilities in China to become as close as possible to the market. The global companies were also getting its pie from China market. One estimate shows, that General Motors of USA has been the biggest beneficiary of the automobile boom in China followed by German car maker, Volkswagen. The growth story of China is continuing and by 2020 Chinese automobile growth will reach the peak. Companies seem to be readying themselves for the eminent battle for the market, however there always been a problem of marketing communication in China. The following two cases demonstrate the nature of the communication problem that exists in China.

Case 1: Toyota Advertising in China

Toyata openly says that if they have manufactured good automobiles in the world then Prado SUV is one of them. During 2003 it was banking on Chinese car market to earn good revenue from the sale of flagship car Prado. Prado was well accepted in other countries of the world for its look as well as power. But alas! One advertisement from another advertising giant, **Saatchi & Saatchi**, ruined its marketing possibilities in China. The advertisement was released in leading

continued

[15] Ali Kanso, "International Advertising Strategies: Global Commitment to Local Vision," *Journal of Advertising Research* (January–February 1992): 10–14.
[16] Wells, "Selling to the World," A1.

auto magazines in China to attract immediate attention of the SUV lovers. It was shown in the advertisement, that a Prado SUV was entering China while sacred Chinese snow lion was saluting the automobile. As a tag line it was written in Chinese whose translated meaning was "You can't help but be ruled by Prado's power," "The Prado's power will take you over," or "You have to admire and respect Prado's supreme quality." This irked the Chinese. There were huge protests across the country on the line of patriotic chord. Many blamed the Japanese company of resorting to purposeful line of offending the Chinese national pride, the snow lion. The situation went out of control when the state machinery had get involved to ensure that all the Prado SUVs are taken away from the country.

Case 2: Mercedes Benz in China

Mercedes-Benz is a respected German company in the automobile world best known for its luxury vehicles, buses, coaches, and trucks. It is an automobile brand of German company, Daimler AG. With the rising affluence level in China the company found that there exist a big opportunity to market its luxury world famous automobiles. Karl Friedrich Benz was a German automobile engineer who actually patented the name "Benz"for the motorcar during 1886 and henceforth it became the symbol of the world famous luxury car. The German company was also sure the brand name Mercedes Benz would be enough to attract Chinese potential customers because of the enduring reputation attached to the brand name. But the way the company thought, it did not happen in reality. Company found that the Chinese translation for Mercedes-Benz was Bensi in Mandarin, which actually conveys the meaning as "Rush to your death" The company's official was in a fix for the simple reason that under such a brand name which indicates "rushing to death", no automobile could be marketed. They rushed back to the company head quarters at Stuttgart, in Germany. For the first time in the history of Mercedes Benz the company agreed to rebrand its products as "Ben Chi" which translates more properly i.e. "Dashing speed".

CUSTOMER ENGAGEMENT

The future of marketing is about relevance and engagement. The bottom line here, as it has been highlighted throughout this book, is that the web, particularly the social web, is about value exchange. In conversations about brands, product categories, or services, the web makes transparent those offerings of value backed by emerging universal principles of quality, durability, and environmental sustability.[17] Traditional marketing has been very good at differentiating products and building brands. It continues to be marketing's role to identify and segment customers, differentiate and position products, and build value propositions by encouraging demand and interaction with customers. A firm's assets are not only intellectual property (IP), but also it's relationship assets (RA) including, most importantly, customers. The challenge is recognizing that relationships are assets.

Why does engagement matter? Marketing has always addressed wants and needs—as the driver of a connection between potential customers and the company's offerings. We are witnessing a second consumptive shift—from the mass consumption of Henry Ford's era to addressing the needs of the individual. Increases in standards of living around the globe, more education for more people, social stratification, and longevity all support the expression of individual self-realization. The consumption of

[17] Dave Evans, "Social Media, Business and the Exchange of Value," ClickZ online newsletter (January 19, 2011), accessed January 19, 2011, http://www.clickz.com/clickz/column/1937866/social-media-business-exchange-value. See also, John Gerzema and Michael D'Antonio, *Spend Shift How the Post-Crisis Values Revolution is Changing the Way We Buy, Sell and Live* (San Francisco, CA:Young and Rubicam Brands, Jossey-Bass, 2011) where focus on value is not the same as "low cost."

products and services is increasingly influenced and enabled by interactive technologies.[18] In the era of mass consumption, wealth creation started with the organization which focused on a common need, cost reduction, growth, and returns on investment. In the new era, wealth creation starts and ends with the individual. The task of marketing is connecting to individuals, understanding them and creating products and services that meet their needs and wants.

Today, around the world, people surfing the Internet are not anonymous.[19] While Web 2.0 was built on user-generated content creating an information-based web, Travis Katz, founder and CEO of the travel site Gogobot, predicts that in the future, "every page [of the Internet] is going to be personalized" creating a "people web"[20] or a phenomenon referred to at Facebook as "social design."[21] Social media is, in fact, a disruptive innovation "When there are low-friction ways for people to interact directly with each other based on their real identities, it is a revolution."[22]

As engagement channels proliferate, it is important to understand which channels customers choose to use and for what reasons. Understanding this creates the foundation for designing what are called engagement strategies, growing directly out of the identification of consumer needs and wants. How does the global marketer identify the most pressing needs driving engagement and what channels are selected to satisfy these needs? While we know that "digital" shifts control towards the consumer and away from the marketer, a 2011 Customer Engagement Report, created by the interactive marketing and technology firm Razorfish,[23] found that consumers are looking to satisfy needs in their online relationships with brands, companies, and product and service categories. Importantly, the study defined the term *engagement* from the perspective of the consumer—what is a positive engagement experience–instead of the marketer's perspective—usually measureable constructs such as time spent on a site, site visits, page views, or search keywords. The study found that the six most important needs consumers demonstrate in their outreach and engagement is feeling valued, trust, efficiency, consistency, relevance, and control. The top three were consistent across gender, age, or preferred channel. Threfore, the most important reason for engagement across channels and touch points is the need to feel valued by the companies people seek to do business with, followed by getting needs addressed quickly and efficiently, and feeling that the company is trustworthy. Interestingly, control came in last out of the six most important cited needs. The study also found that although social platforms such as Facebook and Twitter, and geolocation services such as Foursquare, are being adopted quickly, consumers don't view them as important vehicles for engaging with brands or product categories in themselves Accordingly, engagement is not about the selected channel—it is about the relationship with the channel being subservient to satisfying needs. In addition, channels of choice people use to meet their engagement needs varied across age groups, although there was some overlap.

---

[18] Shoshanna Zubhoff, "Creating Value in the Age of Distributed Capitalism," *McKinsey Quarterly, Online Journal of McKinsey & Company* (September 2010), accessed September 10, 2010, http://www.mckinseyquarterly.com/Creating_value_in_the_age_of_distributed_capitalism_2666.

[19] "Web 3.0: The 'Social Wave' and How it Disrupts the Internet," Knowledge@Wharton online newsletter (July 6, 2011), accessed August 24, 2011, http://knowledge.wharton.upenn.edu/article.cfm?articleid=2808.; "More than 250 million Facebook users log on each day and each of their pages looks completely different."

[20] Ibid. Quote by Ethan Beard, Facebook's director of platform partnerships.

[21] Ibid. Ethan Beard.

[22] Ibid. Quote by Mitch Kapor, entrepreneur and Lotus 1-2-3 designer.

[23] "Liminal: The 2011 Razorfish Customer Engagement Report," accessed September 13, 2011, http://liminal.razorfish.com/.

The study also found that the most important customer engagement channels are transactional e-mail, company websites, traditional word-of-mouth, and e-mail; the least important for engagement were social networking sites such as Twitter, LinkedIn, Facebook, or geolocation-based social networking sites. Accordingly, although people are increasingly using social media sites, these sites do not reflect strength in addressing the need to feel valued; instead, they score well in addressing the needs for control and relevance. Not surprisingly, face-to-face interaction excels at delivering trust and making customers feel valued, whereas company websites are strong at efficiency and consistency.[24] Again, not surprisingly, transactional e-mails deliver strong relevance and control to the consumer; postal mail, print ads, mobile applications, and real-time chat with customer service representatives perform the lowest of all channel categories.

As this study shows, the task for the global marketer is to optimize channel selection and develop an engagement strategy that speaks to the touch points that best address the company's high-value constomer needs of engagement. In additon, it is important to look at the language being used in social media platforms; credible, participatory, humble, personal, and authentic voices need to define a brand or product category's "social voice." Types of influences are also important when populating social media channels. It is important to distinguish types of influences—blogs, anonymous reviews, or off-line peers—who will impact brand or product affinity and purchase intent through the purchase decision funnel.[25]

BOX 13-4

Sidebar: Respect Country Specific Advertising Standard

Advertising Standards Council of India (ASCI) is the nongovernmental watch dog for advertisements released in India by different agencies. The main stake holders like Advertisers, advertising agencies and media came together to form this independent NGO to uphold the sanctity of the advertisement in India. ASCI follows four basic principles while scrutinising the sanctity of an advertisement released by a company in India. They are, a) honest representations b) non-Offensive to Public and c) against Harmful Products/Situations.

A good example of violation of the ASCI principle was made by Procter & Gamble (P&G) during P&G was envying the market leader Clinic Plus from the stable of Hindustan Unilever in shampoo category. In fact, Clinic Plus was the largest selling shampoo brand in India. The company's strategic decision to launch Rs. 1 shampoo sachet and its promise to remove dandruff seemed to have won the target consumers. Quickly, the Clinic Plus brand occupied 25 percent of the shampoo market in India. P&G with its Head & Shoulder brand was struggling to have a space in the market as well as in the prospective consumers' mind. P&G wanted to topple Clinic Plus desperately. It came out with a TV commercial displaying visual Head & Shoulder brand sachet and a write up in Hindi. In English it meant:"your Rs. 1 shampoo is not capable of removing dandruff even after third wash but Head & Shoulder can remove dandruff in a single wash." In the left hand side of the screen, a visual of lookalike Clinic plus shampoo sachet was shown with

continued

[24] See, for example, Lauren Price, "Is the Corporate Website a Digital Dinosaur?" ClickZ online newsletter (September 15, 2011), accessed September 15, 2011, http://www.clickz.com/clickz/column/2109229/corporate-website-digital-dinosaur.

[25] "New Razorfish Study Finds Brands Aren't Doing Enough to Engage Consumers on Social Platforms," PRWeb (July 13, 2009), accessed August 14, 2009, http://www.prweb.com/releases/2009/07/prweb2631374.htm (Accessed.

write up "Leading Rs. 1 Shampoo", ASCI found that the Head & Shoulder violated the ASCI code on the following counts.

- Head & Shoulders was impinging on the long standing goodwill and reputation of Clinic Plus shampoo as dandruff remover.
- Head & Shoulders shampoo was not designed to provide anti-dandruff benefits.
- Showing a pack similar to Clinic Plus was a deceptive practice.
- Superiority claim of Head& Shoulders over Clinic plus was not based on solid proof.
- Showing of lookalike Clinic plus sachet was also an infringement on intellectual property rights of Hindustan Unilever Ltd.

SOCIAL MEDIA CONTENT AND TARGETING

Encouraging engagement and building value for the customer puts the creation of *content* at the forefront of social media and digital marketing planning. It is one of the more important elements of customer experience. Content must be contextually relevant to the targeted audience to create value. With relevant content, the global marketer can establish "thought leadership" in a product category or can increase a brand's visiblity or buzz activity, for example. Interestingly, basic customer focused research can highlight the content which might be most useful, entertaining, or informative for a consumer segment. "By recognizing online user behaviors and how and where they are interacting with content, utilities, applications...we can create timely solutions, increasing consumer engagement and, yes, value."[26] Content done well actually begins to blur the line between creating communications messaging and developing relationships. As such, content becomes part of the media mix in social media marketing.[27] As important as content, *context,* or where and when the content is delivered, is crucial. Marketing to the targeted audience, perhaps of one, at the point of need—the right time, place, and message—is all part of the content strategy.[28] So, for example, content may be targeted to consumer research phase channels, including company websites and company-owned blogs, search engines, e-mail newsletters, industry blogs, social networks, and even competitor websites. Or, content can be targeted to the post-purchase phase channels which might include opt-in e-mail newsletters, noncompany-owned product reviews, customer service and online assistance, company-owned discussion forums, and opt-in SMS texts.

With ever-expanding convergence, integrated marketing programs and their content become all the more important. Convergence has been defined as "the flow of content across multiple media platforms, the cooperation between multiple media industries, and the migratory behavior of media audiences who will go almost anywhere in search of the kinds of entertainment experience they want."[29] The importance of convergence for the global marketer is, of course, the media audience and what makes it tick, along with understanding the best use of various media platforms. The dream of convergence was to bring together all electronic media into one device that

[26] Amy Manus, "If Content is King, Then Context is Queen," ClickZ online newsletter (April 13, 2011), accessed April 14, 2011, http://www.clickz.com/clickz/column/2042624/content-king-context-queen.

[27] Jessica Richards, "Content is a Tangible Media Strategy," ClickZ online newsletter (June 14, 2011), accessed June 14, 2011, http://www.clickz.com/clickz/column/2076924/content-tangible-media-strategy.

[28] Ibid.

[29] Quote by Henry Jenkins, author and leading thinker on the topic of convergence, in "Notes on the Convergence," Gary Stein, ClickZ online newsletter (May 14, 2010), accessed May 17, 2010, http://www.clickz.com/clickz/column/1718227/notes-convergence.

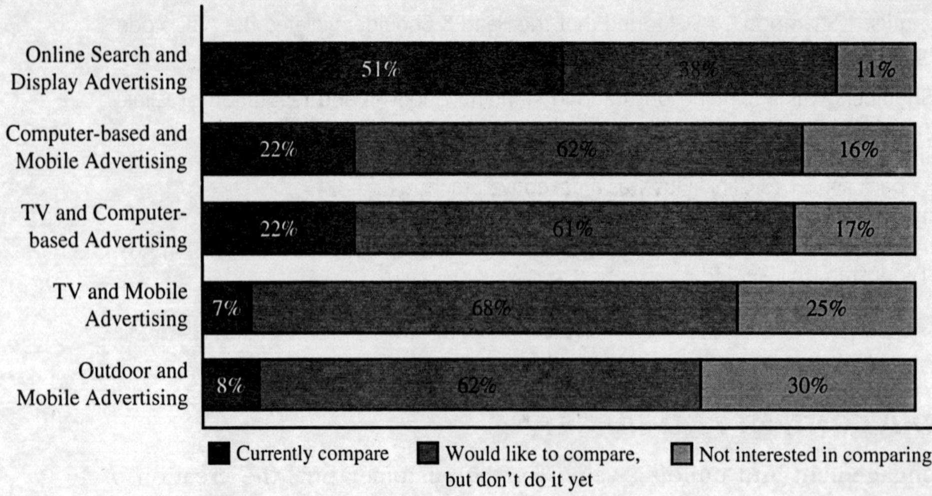

FIGURE 13-1 Cross-Channel Performance Data Comparison

provides easy access to that media.[30] The smartphone, with its ability to provide a standard platform for electronic media, its ubiquity, ease of use, always-on data collection, and, perhaps most importantly, its ability to be the intersection of the "virtual" and "real" worlds, may be that device.[31]

A recent study conducted by MediaMind, formerly Eyeblaster (a global provider of ditigital advertising solutions), and TNS (a leader in market research, global market information, and business analysis) found that more than two-thirds (67%) of global marketing executives indicated they were already running digital cross-channel ad campaigns, but only 12 percent were integrating their cross-channel performance data during their planning, execution, and measurement initiatives.[32] This finding reveals a large gap between running a campaign on multiple channels and integrating those performance data in a unified manner. Respondents cited the lack of suitable metrics to measure impact (44%), lack of case studies showing effectiveness across channels (37%), and lack of technology (34%) as barriers to data integration across channels. Interestingly, the study demonstrates not only interest in cross-channel execution but also that cross-channel integration is a high priority for marketers—both digitally and off-line. At this time, however, reporting across channels for media campaigns is more prevalent in the Asia-Pacific region, with 44 percent of firms requiring it compared with 23 percent in North America, where the market for cross-channel data may be less developed.[33]

This data suggests that firms are moving beyond digital siloed campaigns where search and display remain distinct from each other. For example, 51 percent of respondents indicated they are analyzing cross-channel data derived from search and display advertising (see Figure 13-1). The study also revealed that marketers tend to rely on more established techniques such as rich media banners, for example, in lieu of newer strategies such as mobile.

A misconception among some marketers is that brands are built and sustained off-line and that customer response is driven by online initiatives. Participants showed

---

[30] Sean Carton, "Convergence Comes in Small Packages," ClickZ online newsletter (February 29, 2011), accessed March 1, 2010, http://www.clickz.com/clickz/column/2029068/convergence-comes-packages.

[31] Ibid.

[32] "The Digital Horizon: A Chasm Between Expectation and Execution," Eyeblaster, Inc. and TNS, 2009, www.eyeblaster.com; see also, "Marketers Frustrated by Digital Cross-Channel Chasm" (June 18, 2009), accessed June 23, 2009, http://www.mediabuyerplanner.com.

[33] Ibid.

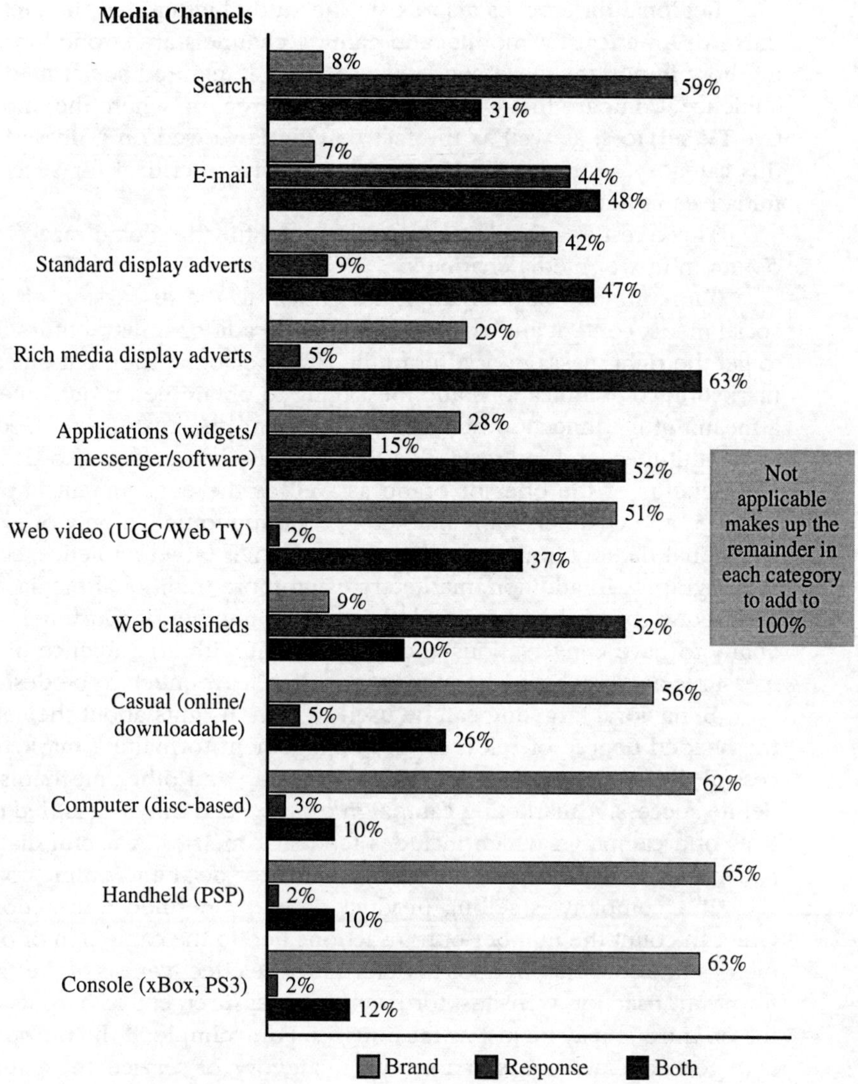

FIGURE 13-2 Percentage Influence of Media Channels on Brand and Customer Response
Source: "The Digital Horizon: A Chasm Between Expectation and Execution," Eyeblaster, Inc. and TNS, 2009, www.eyeblaster.com; see also, "Marketers Frustrated by Digital Cross-Channel Chasm" (June 18, 2009), accessed June 23, 2009, http://www.mediabuyerplanner.com.

a predispostion toward the use of web video and online gaming when the goal was to build brands and the use of search and classifieds when the objective was to drive customer response. However, results of the MediaMinds and TNS study suggest that whether online or off-line, all media channel choices support both brand building and response, although to differing degrees. For example, in the emerging computer gaming channels, many media choices build both brand growth and customer response as seen in Figure 13-2.[34]

As perceptions and expectations shift among both marketing professionals and customers, digital tools as well as off-line techniques will support both brand growth and customer response, albeit to differing degrees.

[34] Ibid.

Regional differences also exist. The study highlighted the fact that, for example, in North America, TV, mobile, and gaming channels are strong brand builders, revealing how important these channels are to an integrated social media strategy for this audience. Compare this with the Asia-Pacific region, where the importance of interactive TV services, as well as the fact that TV is viewed on a myriad of devices, makes this category a strong customer response driver—critical for successful social media initiatives in that region.

These results raise important questions for the global marketer in search of the optimum mix of media channels.

Targeting and segmentation are critical to the discussion of the effectiveness of social media content and channel selection. Traditional marketing's fundamental role is to get the right message or offer to the right person at the right time. Targeting enables marketing communications and messaging to obtain better outcomes through creating a meaningful connection between an offer and the customer's needs, purchase intentions, attitudes, and interests. The effectiveness of an offer also depends on the value and benefits of the offer or brand as well as the engagement impact of the creative message and channel. Many marketers continue to utilize only one or two of the more traditional demographic measures to reach their target audience, such as age, gender, or geography. In addition, marketers using more traditional media often rely on reach and frequency modeling to reach the greatest number of consumers. However, with the ability to have conversations and engagement with an audience of one, demographic measures and reach and frequency modeling leave much to be desired.

Behavioral targeting can be used to gain insights about the consumer and create the needed degree of relevacy and engagement to make a marketing campaign successful. Before discussing behavioral targeting and other mechanisms, one must first define success. A marketing campaign can succeed only if it is tied to goals and objectives of a campaign which includes feedback metrics. A useful distinction here is between measuring *outcomes* and *outputs* in the social and online context.[35]

If a company is selling product online, a defined transactional context exists. One can count the number of transactions tied to the campaign or one can use various metrics like conversion ratios to determine the effectiveness of the campaign. However, for nontransaction websites, for example, measurement of outputs or activities occuring on the site may be just as meaningful. For example, if the purpose of the campaign is to generate awareness of a product, category, or service, the actual number of visits to the site, number of pages viewed or downloaded, or number of contacts made via the Contact Us page or using an e-mail link, may reveal, via a web analytics system, important information for the company. Further measurement could include surveys or questions highlighting the impact of the materials on the site and whether it has changed behavior or attitudes, demonstrating to the marketer the role and influence of the site and its content. As companies move toward increasing socialization and collaboration with their digital initiatives, user engagement metrics will become imore important for marketers.

Underpinning digital campaign success is the data that has been used to create the link between the company's offer and the consumer's needs. Before addressing other forms of targeting data, there are two basic digital categories: *declared data* and *observed data*.[36] *Declared data* is information that is contributed by consumers themselves to databases such as social media profiles, answers to online surveys or

---

[35] Neil Mason, "Measuring Outcomes and Not Just Outputs," ClickZ online newsletter (February 15, 2011), accessed February 15, 2011, http://www.clickz.com/clickz/column/2025904/measuring-outcomes-outputs.

[36] Rob Graham, "Campaign Targeting Data and Target Audiences," ClickZ online newsletter (March 9, 2011), accessed March 21, 2011, http://www.clickz.com/clickz/column/2031839/campaign-targeting-target-audiences.

questionnaires, or personal information such as name and e-mail contact when visiting webpages. *Observed data* is collected from website visits where companies data mine points of contact and interactions such as dates and times of visits, topical webpages visited, keywords used to find information, time spent on selected pages, and the technology and IP address used, which may reveal the device used for access or geographical information about the location of the visitor.

Observed data can be expanded to include metrics such as *search volume* and *social intensity*[37] as key performance indicators (KPIs). With metrics such as page views, unique visitors, time-on-site, or banner ad impressions, there may be only a loose connection of these tools to ultimate sales, at best. For example, number os page views or time-on-site may not be indicative of purchase intent. Video viewing might account for longer time spent on the site or, alternatively, viewing only a short number of pages may be indicative that someone was successful in finding what they were searching for. Increases in *search volume* surrounding a Super Bowl ad are similarly not indicative of campaign success over time. For example, four days after an ad aired on "Denny's free breakfast" during Super Bowl XLIII, none of the top 100 Google searches related to the ad.[38] On the other hand, *social intensity* may be best for measuring "brand lift,"[39] as this metric reveals actions taken by targeted customers based on their knowledge of the product, brand, or message. Social activity can include actions such as blogging, recommending, sharing, and reviewing. Apple is one of the best examples of brands with strong social intensity over time.

With online channels capable of delivering massive reach, audiences are becoming more fragmented and topics are becoming more niche to address their needs and interests. As a result, the target audience continues to get increasingly smaller. Global brands often struggle with how to better define their target audience and segment and personalize messaging and communications around their offering. Knowledge of the customer provides the foundation for what has been termed *behaviorial* marketing programming. Reaching unique or overlapping markets that have different levels of product awareness, for example, or brand maturity, require programming differentiation, not standardization. Varying cultural norms and decision making around a purchase may best be addressed by offering multiple content options, allowing customers to self-select their level of interaction and, in this way, begin to behaviorally profile the target audience.[40]

Geographic location or geotargeting has become essential across many mediums, from search, site content, and social media, to mobile devices and apps, many of which are GPS driven. Raw data is tracked through not only global positioning systems, but also by cell towers or local Wi-Fi networks. New kinds of cartography are in the works, indentifying places not by land masses but by what kinds of people inhabit or spend their time in those locations. These geo-rich types of information will become a treasure trove for marketers seeking targeted audiences across social media. Current uses of

---

[37] Augustine Fou, "Social Intensity: A New Measure for Campaign Success?" ClickZ online newsletter (February 11, 2009), accessed February 12, 2009, http://www.clickz.com/clickz/column/1712215/social-intensity-a-new-measure-campaign-success.

[38] Ibid.

[39] Adrian Tompsett, "Moving Beyond the Click to Measure and Optimize Brand Lift," ClickZ online newsletter (December 22, 2010), accessed January 4, 2011, http://www.clickz.com/clickz/column/1933501/moving-click-measure-optimize-brand-lift. Quoting Dan Beltramo, CEO and cofounder of Vizu, "Brand lift metrics, or the lift in performance of the branding objectives, bring the same metrics used to measure and optimize advertising effectiveness in the off-line world to the online medium in a more robust way.... Online brand advertising optimization is the ability to tune various aspects of an online media buy to generate the greatest amount of brand lift for the given media spend."

[40] Andrea Fishman, "Using Geography and Demographics to Enhance Behavioral Targeting," Clickz online newsletter (February 24, 2010), accessed February 24, 2010, http://www.clickz.com/clickz/column/1708996/using-geography-demographics-enhance-behavioral-targeting.

geotargeting focus on a designated market area such as a metropolitan region. Custom targeting involves designating a boundary or drawing a circular radius around a selected location. Keywords can simultaneously be utilized to target the selected audience. With the exponential growth of smartphone adoption and mobile applications, "check-in" services, for example, powered by social web technology, encourage people to share what they think others would like to know about the place they are now in the context of any decision they are making or have made. Data left by prior consumers is used when someone "checks in," effectively sharing what's in the area, recommendations, and who else might be nearby. Location relevancy is driven to a whole new sphere and depth. Mobile data including location-based services, commerce, visual search, and recommendations from peers create a virtual bridge between the physical and digital worlds. And, as people overwhelmingly trust personal recommendations more than ads, already the social search category has begun to eclipse paid search advertising. It will influence future advertising across all media, especially in the consumer goods category. By understanding mobile rich media, its interactivity, and the special benefits of mobile devices, including cameras, video, speakers, and accelerometers, its use can be positioned to deliver experiential brand value. The rise of Groupon and Foursquare reflect the value and interest in local content and create the opportunity to personalize the user experience without extensive segmentation or targeting strategies.

Search marketing has grown to become the largest online advertising tool, in great part due to its ability to deliver a targeted message to a potential customer at the most opportune time—when they are actively seeking information on a company's product or service. With the rapid evolution of mobile platforms and applications, search is quickly becoming social to stay relevant with, for example, targeted ad opportunies through Facebook and links through Google to social networks and media such as Twitter and LinkedIn, Facebook, Flickr, or YouTube. Therefore, search engines which already take behaviorial data and search history into account will move toward social and networked relationships. Introducing the social context into search will make reputation management and listening on the part of any company a continuing priority as consumers publicly share their recommendations, affinities, and stories.[41]

BOX 13-5

Sidebar: Role of Culture in Communication

In high power distance countries, a majority of population having enjoyed less power in society believe that they are naturally to be ruled by the more powerful people. They also believe that these powerful people form the views in the society and others are there to follow them. According to Geert Hofstede, the famous anthropologist, the following countries are amongst the countries with high power distance countries as expressed by cultural Index score of respective countries. The more score of the index, the more will the power distance prevailing in the country.

As the Table 13-1 indicates Slovakia, China, India, Saudi Arabia, Guatemala, Philippines, Panama etc. are among the countries who have comparatively high power distance. In these above countries, the decision making process flows from top to down. The top notch people of the society would make decision about what is good or bad for the society. Interestingly, the

continued

[41] Rebecca Lieb, "What's Next in Search?" ClickZ online newsletter (June 5, 2009), accessed June 5, 2009, http://www.clickz.com/clickz/column/1691354/whats-next-search; see also, Vanessa Fox, *Marketing in the Age of Google*, Hoboken, New Jersey: John Wiley & Sons, Inc., 2010.

TABLE 13-1 High Power Distance Countries

Countries	Hofstede Cultural Index Score
India	77
China	80
Mexico	81
Venezuela	81
Surinam	85
Serbia	86
Kuwait	90
Romania	90
Arab Emirates	90
Albania	90
Russia	93
Bhutan	94
Philippines	94
Guatemala	95
Panama	95
Saudi Arabia	95
Iraq	95
Malaysia	100
Slovakia	100

Source: Hofstede cultural index website

followers are not supposed to ask questions about the rightness or wrongness of the decisions. The followers' purchase intentions are, therefore, influenced by the society leaders. The marketers, while releasing marketing communication took advantage of these leaders--followers cultural syndrome. For example, automobile companies in India, always wanted Bollywood leading actors to tell the followers why someone should by a particular automobile. From Hyundai Santro to Xcent, almost 16 years, Shah Rukh Khan actively took part in the advertisement of the Korean company to tell Indian people to buy Hyundai made automobiles. Cadillac wanted to do brisk business in China during 2015 and took cue from high power distance score of China and contracted Hollywood hero Brad Pitt to advertise the automobile in China. The result was that the company tripled its sale in China.

BOX 13-6

Sidebar: Communication in Collectivist Society

Collectivist countries are those where people try to live in groups without any conflict. The groups promise full safety to the members, hence the members do not deviate from the common view point of the group. Hofstede's individualism index, carries opposite meaning to collectivism index.

TABLE 13-2 High Collectivist Countries

Sl No.	Country	Hofstede Individualism index score
1	Guatemala	6
2	Ecuador	8
3	Panama	11
4	Venezuela	12
5	Colombia	13
6	Fiji	14
7	Indonesia	14
8	Pakistan	14
9	Trinidad	16
10	Ghana	15
11	Taiwan	17
12	South Korea	18
13	Thailand	20
14	China	20
15	India	48

Source: Hofstede cultural index website

Collectivist countries are Guatemala, Panama, Venezuela, Indonesia, Fiji, Pakistan South, Korea, Thailand, China etc. India is not as collectivist country like China (Hofstede individualism score is only 20) as evident from its Hofstede score of 48 (refer Table 13-2).

In collectivist countries the advertising message must conform to the requirement of groups like family, religious etc. For example, a bank while advertising for its credit card in South Korea, should read " We can enjoy dinner with the help credit card", to take care of its inclination. But the same company would be using its tag line as "enjoy lunch with your girlfriend while in USA", to take marketing advantage through efficient use of a country's cultural norms.

ADVERTISING STRATEGY

Advertising Appeals

Advertising must communicate appeals that are relevant and effective in the target market environment. Because products are frequently at different stages in their life cycle in various national markets, and because of the basic cultural, social, and economic differences that exist in markets, the most effective appeal for a product may vary from market to market. Yet, global marketers should attempt to identify situations in which (1) potential cost reductions exist because of the presence of economies of scale; (2) barriers to standardization such as cultural differences are not significant; and (3) products satisfy similar functional and emotional needs across different cultures.

Green, Cunningham, and Cunningham conducted a cross-cultural study to determine the extent to which consumers of different nationalities use the same criteria to evaluate two common consumer products: soft drinks and toothpaste. Their subjects were college students from the United States, France, India, and Brazil. Compared with France and India, the US sample placed more emphasis on the subjective and less on functional product attributes, and the Brazilian sample appeared even more concerned with the subjective attributes than did the US sample. The authors concluded that advertising messages should not use the same appeal for these countries if the advertiser is concerned with communicating the most important attributes of its product in each market.[42]

Effective advertising may also require developing different creative executions or presentations using a product's basic appeal or selling proposition as a point of departure. In other words, there can be differences between what one says and how one says it. If the creative execution in one key market is closely tied to a particular cultural attribute, the execution may have to be adapted to other markets. For example, the selling proposition for many products and services is fun or pleasure, and the creative presentation should show people having fun as appropriate for a country or culture. Lego Freestyle created a communications campaign in both Europe and the Far East. The Asian version "Build your child's mind," appealed to Asian parents' desire to have their children do well academically. The Asian educational system is highly competitive; a child not doing well is a reflection on the parents. Compare that with the European version: "What will your child make of it?" which stresses creativity instead of academic rigor.

According to one recent survey, experienced advertising executives indicated that strong selling propositions can be transferred more than 50 percent of the time. An example of a selling proposal that transfers well is top quality. The promise of low price or of value for money regularly surmounts national barriers. In the same survey, most executives indicated that they did not believe that creative presentations traveled well. The obstacles are cultural barriers, communications barriers, legislative problems (for example, children cannot be used in France to merchandise products), competitive positions (the advertising strategy for a leading brand or product is normally quite different from that for a minor brand), and execution problems.

Food may be the product category most likely to exhibit cultural sensitivity. Thus, marketers of food and food products must be alert to the need to localize their advertising. A good example of this is the effort by H. J. Heinz Company to develop the international market for ketchup. Heinz's strategy called for adapting both the product and advertising to target country tastes.[43] In Greece, for example, ads show ketchup pouring over pasta, eggs, and cuts of meat. In Japan, they instruct Japanese homemakers on using ketchup as an ingredient in Western-style food such as omelets, sausages, and pasta. Barry Tilley, London-based general manager of Heinz's Western Hemisphere trading division, says Heinz uses focus groups to determine what foreign consumers want in the way of taste and image. Americans like a relatively sweet ketchup, but Europeans prefer a spicier, more piquant variety. Significantly, Heinz's foreign marketing efforts are most successful when the company quickly adapts to local cultural preferences. In Sweden, the made-in-America theme is so muted in Heinz's ads that "Swedes don't realize Heinz is American. They think it is German because of the name," says Mr. Tilley. In contrast to this, American themes still work well in Germany. Kraft and Heinz are trying to outdo each other with ads featuring strong American images. In a Heinz TV commercial, American football players in a restaurant become very angry when the 12 steaks they ordered arrive without ketchup. The ad ends happily, of course, with plenty of Heinz ketchup to go around.[44]

---

[42] Robert T. Green, William H. Cunningham, and Isabella C. M. Cunningham, "The Effectiveness of Standardized Global Advertising," *Journal of Advertising* (Summer 1975): 25–30.

[43] Gary Levin, "Ads Going Global," *Advertising Age* (July 22, 1991): 4, 42.

[44] Gabriella Stern, "Heinz Aims to Export Taste for Ketchup," *The Wall Street Journal,* November 20, 1992, B1.

In general, the fewer the number of purchasers of a product, the less important advertising is as an element of the promotion mix. For example, successful marketing of expensive and technically complex industrial products generally requires a highly trained direct sales force. The more sophisticated and technically complicated an industrial product is, the more necessary this becomes. For such products, there is no point in letting national agencies duplicate each other's efforts. Advertising of industrial products—computers and telecommunications equipment, for example—does play an important role in setting the stage for the work of the sales force. A good advertising campaign can make it significantly easier for a salesperson to get in the door and, once inside, make the sale.

Art

Art direction is concerned with visual presentation—the body language of print and broadcast advertising. Some forms of visual presentation are universally understood. Revlon, for example, has used a French producer to develop television commercials in English and Spanish for use in international markets. These commercials, which are filmed in Parisian settings, communicate the universal appeals and specific advantages of Revlon products. By producing its ads in France, Revlon obtains effective television commercials at a much lower price than it would have to pay for similar-length commercials produced in the United States. PepsiCo has used four basic commercials to communicate its advertising themes. The basic setting of young people having fun at a party or on a beach has been adapted to reflect the general physical environment and racial characteristics of North America, South America, Europe, Africa, and Asia. The music in these commercials has also been adapted to suit regional tastes, ranging from rock 'n' roll in North America to bossa nova in Latin America to high life in Africa.

The international advertiser must make sure that visual executions are not inappropriately extended into markets. Benetton encountered a problem with its "United Colors of Benetton" campaign. The campaign appeared in 77 countries, primarily in print and on billboards. The art direction focused on striking, provocative interracial juxtapositions—a white hand and a black hand handcuffed together, for example. Another version of the campaign, depicting a black woman nursing a white baby, won advertising awards in France and Italy. However, because the image evoked the history of slavery in America, that particular creative execution was not used in the US market.

Copy

A global strategy of using a global appeal requires the translation of copy, the written text of an advertisement, and has been the subject of debate in advertising circles. The clearer the basic appeal, the greater is the possibility that it can be executed globally in translation. One of the advantages of a global company is the fact that successful global appeals must be clear and compelling if they are going to be subject to translation. Copy should be relatively short and avoid slang or idioms. Low literacy rates in countries seriously compromise the use of print as a communications device and require greater creativity in the use of audio-oriented media.

It is important to recognize overlap in the use of languages in many areas of the world (e.g., the EU, Latin America, and North America). Capitalizing on this, global advertisers can realize economies of scale in producing advertising copy with the same language and message for these markets. Of course, the success of this approach will depend in part on avoiding unintended ambiguity in the ad copy. On the other hand, in some situations ad copy must be translated into the local language. Advertising slogans often present the most difficult translation problems. The challenge of encoding and decoding slogans and tag lines in different national and cultural contexts can lead to hilarious errors. For example, Kentucky Fried Chicken's "Finger-lickin' good" came out in Chinese as "Eat your fingers off"; the Asian version of Pepsi's "Come Alive" copy line was rendered as a call to bring ancestors back from the grave.

Advertising executives may elect to prepare new copy for a foreign market in the language of the target country, or to translate the original copy into the target language. A third option is to leave some (or all) copy elements in the original (home-country) language. In choosing from these alternatives, the advertiser must consider whether a translated message can be received and comprehended by the intended foreign audience. Anyone with a knowledge of languages realizes that the ability to think in a language facilitates accurate communication. One must understand the connotations of words, phrases, and sentence structures, as well as their translated meaning, in order to be confident that a message will be understood correctly after it is received. The same principle applies to advertising, perhaps to an even greater degree. A copywriter who can think in the target language and understands the consumers in the target country will be able to create the most effective appeals, organize the ideas, and craft the specific language, especially if colloquialisms, idioms, and humor are involved. For example, in southern China, McDonald's is careful not to advertise prices with multiple occurrences of the number four. The reason is simple: In Cantonese, the pronunciation of the word *four* is similar to that of the word *death*.[45] In its efforts to develop a global brand image, Citicorp discovered that translations of its slogan "Citi Never Sleeps" conveyed the meaning that Citibank had a sleeping disorder such as insomnia. Company executives decided to retain the slogan but use English throughout the world.[46]

When formulating television and print advertising for use in high-income countries such as the United States, Canada, Japan, and the EU, the advertiser must recognize major style and content differences. Ads that strike viewers in some countries as irritating may not necessarily be perceived that way by viewers in other countries. American ads make frequent use of spokespersons and direct product comparisons and use logical arguments to try to appeal to the reason of audiences. Japanese advertising is more image-oriented and appeals to audience sentiment. In Japan, what is most important frequently is not what is stated explicitly but, rather, what is implied. Nike's US advertising is legendary for its irreverent, "in-your-face" style and relies heavily on celebrity sports endorsers such as Michael Jordan. In other parts of the world, where soccer is the top sport, some Nike ads are considered to be in poor taste and its pitchmen have less relevance. Nike has responded by adjusting its approach; notes Geoffrey Frost, director of global advertising, "We have to root ourselves in the passions of other countries. It's part of our growing up."[47]

---

[45] Jeanne Whalen, "McDonald's Cooks Worldwide Growth," *Advertising Age International* (July–August 1995): I4.

[46] Stephen E. Frank, "Citicorp's Big Account Is at Stake as It Seeks a Global Brand Name," *The Wall Street Journal,* January 9, 1997, B6.

[47] Roger Thurow, "Shtick Ball: In Global Drive, Nike Finds Its Brash Ways Don't Always Pay Off," *The Wall Street Journal,* May 5, 1997, A10.

Summary

Integrated marketing communications, or IMC, refers to all forms of communication used by organizations to inform, remind, explain, persuade, and influence the attitudes and buying behavior of customers and other persons. Marketing communications—the promotion P of the marketing mix—includes advertising, public relations, sales promotion, and personal selling. Although marketers may identify opportunities for global standardized advertising campaigns, local adaptation or distinct local campaigns may also be required. A powerful reason to try to create a global campaign is that the process forces a company to attempt to identify a global market for its product. In addition, the identification of global appeals and benefits forces a company to probe deeply to identify basic needs and buying motives. When creating advertising, care must be taken to ensure that the art direction and copy are appropriate for the intended audiences in target countries. Advertisers may place a single global agency in charge of worldwide advertising; it is also possible to use one or more agencies on a regional or local basis. Advertising intensity and media use varies from country to country.

We're still in the early days of the web-driven economy where consumer demand has created online blockbusters such as Facebook, Twitter, and Google with their always-on digital connectivity and personal influence. The global marketplace exhibits characteristics showing it to be far from equilibrium;[48] both newcomers–online and offline—and firms showing market staying power must strategize in light of constant change in media consumption across countries and regions as well as influences of technology on consumptive behavior. Every business will become a multichannel publisher with increasing brand and product category accountability. Service offerings will continue to grow on proprietary platforms offered via low-cost cloud computing as well as mobile devices. Communication strategies will include web-based branded content promotions and marketing campaigns and messaging that will be virally spread through socially networked friends responding to ever more targeted campaigns. Businesses with successful marketing communications strategies will be nimble and often data-driven. A business eager to take advantage of web-based communications must strategically select a business model that integrates marketing communications across both new direct marketing mediums as well as existing distribution and communication channels.

Discussion Questions

1. In what ways can global brands and global advertising campaigns benefit a company?
2. How does the standardized-versus-localized debate apply to advertising? Identify and discuss the problems with assessing advertising effectiveness in foreign markets.
3. When creating advertising for world markets, what issues must art directors and copywriters take into account?
4. How do the media options available to advertisers vary in different parts of the world? What can advertisers do to cope with media limitations or differences in media consumption in certain countries?
5. It was once said that advertising is America's greatest export. Discuss.
6. Describe the relationship between integrated marketing communications and the other elements of the marketing mix.
7. Can it be argued that social networking and social media are hybrid elements of the promotion mix because they exhibit characteristics of more traditional integrated marketing communications such as word-of-mouth? What degree of control and influence can the marketing manager have over the frequency or content of information being shared? Discuss.

[48] Jacques Bughin, "The Web's C100 Billion Surplus," McKinsey Quarterly online newsletter (January 2011), accessed January 12, 2011, http://mckinseyquarterly.com.

Suggested Readings

Becker-Olsen, Karen, Charles R. Taylor, Ronald Paul Hill, and Goksel Yalcinkaya. "A Cross-Cultural Examination of Corporate Social Responsibility Marketing Communication in Mexico and the United States: Strategies for Global Brands." *Journal of International Marketing*, 19, no. 2 (June 2011): 30–44.

Birch, Dawn, and Janelle McPhail. "Does Accent Matter in International Television Advertisements?" *International Journal of Advertising*, 18 (May 1999): 251.

Chen, Chien-Wei. "Integrated Marketing Communications and New Product Performance in International Markets." *Journal of Global Marketing*, 24, no. 5 (2011): 397–416.

Duncan, Thomas R., and Stephen E. Everett. "Client Perception of Integrated Marketing Communications." *Journal of Advertising Research* (May–June 1993): 119–122.

Evans, Philip, and Thomas S. Wurster. *Blown To Bits: How the New Economics of Information Transforms Strategy.* Boston: The Boston Consulting Group and the Harvard Business School Press, 2000.

Hanni, David A., John K. Ryans, Jr., and Ivan R. Vernon. "Coordinating International Advertising—The Goodyear Case Revisited for Latin America." *Journal of International Marketing*, 3, no. 2 (1995): 83–98.

Israel, Shel, and Robert Scoble. *Naked Conversations: How Blogs are Changing the Way Businesses Talk With Customers.* Hoboken, NJ: John Wiley & Sons, Inc., 2006.

Kalliny, Morris, and Salma Ghanem. "The Role of the Advertising Agency in the Cultural Message Content of Advertisements: A Comparison of the Middle East and the United States." *Journal of Global Marketing*, 22, no. 4 (2009): 313–328.

Kaynak, Erdener, and Lianxi Zhou. "Special Issue on Brand Equity, Branding, and Marketing Communications in Emerging Markets." *Journal of Global Marketing*, 23 (2010): 171–176.

Leong, Siew Meng, Sween Hoon Ang, and Lai Leng Tham. "Increasing Brand Name Recall in Print Advertising among Asian Consumers." *Journal of Advertising*, 25, no. 2 (1996): 65–81.

Limon, Yonca, Lynn R. Kahle, and Ulrich R. Orth. "Package Design as a Communications Vehicle in Cross-Cultural Values Shopping." *Journal of International Marketing*, 17, no. 1 (March 2009): 30–57.

Mahim, Sagar, Rishabh Khandelwal, Amit Mittal, and Deepali Singh. "Ethical Positioning Index (EPI): An Innovative Tool for Differentiated Brand Positioning." *Corporate Communications: An International Journal*, 16, no. 2 (2011): 124–138.

McCullough, W. R. "Global Advertising Which Acts Local: The IBM Subtitles Campaign." *Journal of Advertising Research*, 36, no. 3 (1996): 11–15.

Mooij, Marieke K. De. *Advertising Worldwide: Concepts, Theories and Practice of International, Multinational and Global Advertising*, 2nd ed. Upper Saddle River, NJ: Prentice Hall, 1994.

Scott, David Meerman. *The New Rules of Marketing and PR: How to Use Social Media, Online Video, Mobile Applications, Blogs, News Releases, and Viral Marketing to Reach Buyers Directly.* Hoboken, NJ: John Wiley & Sons, Inc., 2011.

Sinclair, John, and Rowan Wilken. "Strategic Regionalization in Marketing Campaigns: Beyond the Standardization/Globalization Debate." *Continuum: Journal of Media and Cultural Studies*, 23, no. 2 (April 2009): 147–157.

Spenner, Patrick. "Why You Need a New-Media 'Ringmaster.'" *Harvard Business Review* (December 2010): 78–79.

Taylor, Charles R., and Shintaro Okazaki. "Who Standardizes Advertising More Frequently and Why Do They Do So? A Comparison of U.S. and Japanese Subsidiaries' Advertising Practices in the European Union." *Journal of International Marketing*, 14, no. 1 (March 2006): 98–120.

Vollmer, Christopher. "Digital Darwinism." *Strategy + Business* (Autumn 2009): 78–89.

Wilken, Rowan, and John Sinclair. "Global Marketing Communications and Strategic Regionalism." *Globalizations*, 8, no. 1 (February 2011): 1–15.

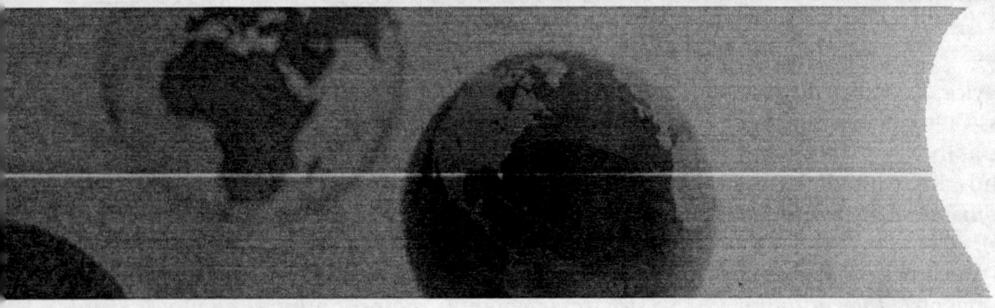

CHAPTER 14

Global Organization and Leadership: Managing the Global Marketing Effort

It seems incredible, and yet it has happened a hundred times, that troops have been divided and separated merely through a mysterious feeling of conventional manner, without any clear perception of the reason.

—Carl von Clausewitz, 1780–1831
Vom Kriege (1832–1837) *Book III, Chapter XI, "Assembly of Forces in Space"*

Learning Objectives

1. Identify the characteristics of great companies (419–420).
2. Discuss global organizational design issues (421–423).
3. Differentiate between the types of organizational structures (424–432).
4. Describe the factors that affect organizational structure (434–435).
5. Describe the stages of organizational development (434–435).
6. Discuss global marketing control practices (438).

INTRODUCTION

This chapter focuses on the integration of each element of the marketing mix into a total plan that addresses expected opportunities and threats in the global marketing environment. We begin with leadership and global vision and consider the difference between the great and ordinary companies. This is a critical distinction for any company that finds itself competing in a global industry. Only great companies become global. Ordinary local companies in globalizing industries must either change their thinking, worldview, strategy, and structure and go global or face the threat of inevitable decline and possible extinction.

The late Steve Jobs of Apple and Mark Zuckerberg of Facebook are examples of global leaders who, by their example and the success of their organizations, illustrate the critical role of leadership in a global firm. Leaders must be capable of articulating a coherent global vision and strategy that integrates local responsiveness, global efficiency, and leverage. The challenge is to direct the efforts and creativity of everyone in the company toward a global effort that best utilizes organizational resources to exploit global opportunities. Global marketing demands exceptional leadership. As we have said throughout this book, the hallmark of a global company is the capacity to formulate and implement global strategies that leverage worldwide learning, respond fully to local needs and wants, and draw on all the talent and energy of every member of the organization. This is a heroic task requiring global vision and a sensitivity to local needs. Members of each operating unit must address their immediate responsibilities and, at the same time, cooperate with functional, product, and country experts in different locations.

GREAT COMPANIES THINK DIFFERENTLY

What distinguishes the great company from the ordinary company? Perhaps the most fundamental difference is that great companies think differently. The ordinary company has a limited view of its purpose and mission: the most ordinary and lowest form of ordinary is the company that sees itself as nothing more than a money-making machine. Great companies believe that they have a much broader purpose than just making money. They see themselves as key social institutions like the family, government, religion, or not-for-profit organizations, including NGOs, operating globally. Like each of these institutions, great companies know that they create value for the world not only in the products and services they provide to their customers, but also in the contributions they make to individuals and communities all over the world through the opportunities they create for creative expression of human potential. Great companies make the world a better place and enrich the lives of their customers, communities, and society. Great global companies do this globally.[1]

The practice of using self-directed work teams to respond to competitive challenges is becoming more widespread. Reports vary as to how widely teams are being used today. One study found that 47 percent of *Fortune* 1000 companies used teams with at least some of their employees. With the increased usage of e-mail, instant messaging (IM), enhanced Voice over Internet Protocol (VoIP) and videoconferencing, team members at different locations can work together in ways that have, until the recent expansion of bandwidth and processing power, never been possible.

More and more managers agree that teams will become the primary unit of performance in high-performance organizations. The implementation of self-directed work teams is another example of the need for organizational innovation to maintain competitiveness. They represent another corporate response to the need to flatten the organization, to reduce costs and overheads, and to be more responsive. As Tom Peters put it, "You can't survive, let alone thrive, in a time-competitive world with a six- to eight-layer organization structure. The time-obsessed organization is flat—no barriers among functions, no borders with the outside."[2]

---

[1] For a discussion of the Great Company see Rosabeth Moss Kanter, "How Great Companies Think Differently," *Harvard Business Review* (November 2011): 68–78; and Anand P. Raman, "Why Don't We Try to be India's Most Respected Company?" an interview with N.R. Narayana Murthy, founder of Infosys, *Harvard Business Review* (November 2011): 80–86.

[2] Tom Peters, "Time Obsessed Competition," *Management Review* (September 1990): 18.

William J. Amelio, the CEO of Lenovo, the world's third-largest computer maker, terms his global workforce strategy "world-sourcing." Lenovo has executive offices in five cities throughout the world and organizes its workforce around hubs of expertise such as hardware designers in Japan and marketers in India. With this type of workforce structure, "you operate as if there's just one time zone...and you're always on."[3] Accordingly, managing people across borders and ensuring that visas and permits are compliant with local immigration rules has become an important task of the global firm. Reaching and maintaining global and effective scale has become critical for both productivity and efficiency.

New tools such as telepresence, which are often custom-built meeting rooms with a bank of high-definition screens and cameras, or even the presence of several mobile humanoid robots, have dramatically changed how teams interface not only across the globe but often in the same city. According to the Global Business Travel Association, the bill in 2010 for business travel was $228 billion, along with cost of thousands of gallons of jet fuel, tons of carbon dioxide poured into the environment, and missed family occasions. Trips—to make presentations, conduct site visits, meet with supply chain partners, interview employees, or attend trade shows–are based on the conviction that face-to-face contact is critical to team success. Telepresence gives participants the "sense of human presence" by "virtualiz[ing] people and resources" in real time to communicate smoothly on what may be a complex, dynamic task. Many *Fortune* 500 companies such as Bank of America, PepsiCo, Procter & Gamble, and Royal Dutch Shell have installed, often at great cost, "immersive suites" for managing meetings in real time.[4] A major role of top management is to instill important values necessary for success in a global marketplace throughout their organization. One critical value vital to an effective global organization is to have the proper mind-set for both leadership and the organization, including of course, team participants. It has been said that "global teams are like oceans: depending on how they are navigated, they can link the world together or split it apart."[5] Global teams can be assets which build on creativity and innovation by utilizing often unique skill sets, points of view, and networks of players and partners, thereby unlocking value for companies and their clients. Core company values can stress the importance of innovation, openness to new ideas and approaches, creativity, empowerment of employees and customers, and the embracement of new technologies and learning, to name a few.

Martine Haas, Professor of Management at Wharton, has studied team interaction of large organizations. Haas found that a combination of "cosmopolitans" and "locals" are key to team successes. "Locals" know a lot about the country they represent, whereas "cosmopolitans" have lived and worked in several countries or regions of the world and may speak several languages. Teams that have a representative mix of both types were found to be the most successful.[6] In addition, Haas found that several other differences drive teams apart. Along with cultural differences, barriers to communication and team building include demographic, geographic, and structural roles, that is, team member differences that arise from holding a position in the firm's hierarchy or business unit that is different than other team members and may lead to decisions to withhold knowledge or information.[7]

---

[3] Jena McGregor and Steve Hamm, "Managing the Global Workforce," *BusinessWeek*, January 28, 2008: 34.

[4] Drake Bennett, "I'll Have My Robots Talk To Your Robots," *BusinessWeek*, February 21–27, 2011: 53–61.

[5] "'Locals,' 'Cosmopolitans,' and Other Keys to Creating Successful Global Teams," *Knowledge@Wharton* enewsletter (September 2, 2009), http://knowledge.wharton.upenn.edu.

[6] Ibid.

[7] Ibid.

To achieve organization effectiveness, it is important to consider the following points:

1. Composition of the board of directors and company leadership across business units and hierarchy—mix of nationalities, international experience, language skills
2. Choice of locations for meetings
3. International experience and language skills of the chief executive, executive committee, business unit managers
4. Time spent by the CEO and key executives in world regions
5. Choice of locations for business unit headquarters
6. Proportion of middle and senior managers who are members of cross-border teams
7. Executive career ladders that reward international experience
8. Performance measurement and incentive systems that motivate managers to optimize local and global performance

ORGANIZATION

The goal in organizing for global marketing is to find a structure that enables the company to respond to relevant market environment differences while ensuring the diffusion of corporate knowledge and experience from national markets throughout the entire corporate system. The pull between the value of centralized knowledge and coordination and the need for individualized response to the local situation creates a constant tension in the global marketing organization. A key issue in global organization is how to achieve balance between autonomy and integration. Subsidiaries need autonomy in order to adapt to their local environment. However, the business as a whole needs integration to implement global strategy.[8]

When management at a domestic company decides to pursue international expansion, the issue of how to organize arises immediately. Who should be responsible for this expansion? Should product divisions operate directly or should an international division be established? Should individual country subsidiaries report directly to the company president or should a special corporate officer be appointed to take full-time responsibility for international activities? Once the first decision of how to organize initial international operations has been reached, a growing company is faced with a number of reappraisal points during the development of its international business activities. Should a company abandon its international division and, if so, what alternative structure should be adopted? Should an area or regional headquarters be formed? What should be the relationship of staff executives at corporate, regional, and subsidiary offices? Specifically, how should the marketing function be organized? To what extent should regional and corporate marketing executives become involved in subsidiary marketing management?

It is important to recognize that there is no single correct organizational structure for global marketing. Even within an industry, worldwide companies have developed very different strategic and organizational responses to changes in their environments. Still, it is possible to make some generalizations. Leading-edge global competitors share one key organizational design characteristic: their corporate structure is simple and flat, rather than tall and complex. The message is clear: the world is complicated enough; there is no need to add to the confusion with a complex internal structure. Simple structures increase the speed and clarity of communication and allow the concentration of organizational energy and valuable resources on learning, rather than

[8] George S. Yip, *Total Global Strategy* (Upper Saddle River, NJ: Prentice Hall, 1992): 179.

on controlling, monitoring, and reporting.[9] Successful global leaders seek to create an organization where people exchange ideas, processes, and systems across borders and work together to identify the best global opportunities and the biggest global problems facing the organization.

A geographically dispersed company cannot limit its knowledge to product, function, and the home territory. Company personnel must acquire knowledge of the complex set of social, political, economic, and institutional arrangements that exist within each international market. Many companies, after initial ad hoc arrangements—for example, all foreign subsidiaries reporting to a designated vice president or to the president—establish an international division to manage their geographically dispersed new business. It is clear, however, that the international division in the multi-product company is an unstable organizational arrangement. As a company grows, this initial organizational structure gives way to various alternative structures.[10]

In today's fast-changing, competitive global environment, corporations have to find new and more creative ways to organize. New forms of flexibility, efficiency, and responsiveness are required to meet the market demands. The need to be cost-effective, to be customer driven, to deliver the best quality, and to deliver that quality quickly, are some of today's market realities.

Several authors have described new organizational designs that represent responses to the competitive environment of the twenty-first century. These designs acknowledge the need to find more responsive and flexible structures, to flatten the organization, and to employ teams. There is also the recognition of the need to develop networks, to develop stronger relationships among participants, and to exploit technology. They also reflect an evolution in approaches to organizational effectiveness. At the beginning of the twentieth century, Fredrick Taylor claimed that all managers had to see the world the same way. Then came the contingency theorists who said that effective organizations design themselves to match their conditions. These two basic theories are reflected in today's popular management writings. Some theorists have focused on strategy, while others have focused on operations. Successful companies, the real global winners, have both: great strategy and great execution. Look around, and whenever you find a company that has achieved a sustainable competitive advantage and global leadership, behind that greatness is the double power of strategy and execution.

Confirming past findings, recent research has shown that twentieth-century models of organizational design, which stressed hierarchy and the importance of labor and capital inputs over intellectual pursuit and collaborative efforts, not only create undue complexity but actually work at cross-purposes to organizing talent worldwide in order to create lasting competitive advantage.[11] Gary Hamel, author of the *Future of Management*,[12] observed: "Throughout history, technological innovation has always preceded organizational and management innovation.…The old model was, 'How do you get people to serve the organization's goals?' Today we have to ask, 'How do you build organizations that merit the gifts of creativity and passion and initiative? '"[13] He goes on

---

[9] Vladimir Pucik, "Globalization and Human Resource Management," in *Globalizing Management: Creating and Leading the Competitive Organization*, V. Pucik, N. Tichy, and C. Barnett, Eds. (New York: Wiley, 1992): 70.

[10] See the classic description of this process in John M. Stopford and Louis T. Wells, *Managing the Multinational Enterprise* (New York: Basic Books, 1972).

[11] Lowell L. Bryan and Claudia I. Joyce, *Mobilizing Minds: Creating Wealth from Talent in the 21st-Century Organization* (New York: McGraw Hill, 2007).

[12] Gary Hamel. *The Future of Management* (Boston: Harvard Business School Press, 2007).

[13] Joanna Barsh, "Innovative Management: A Conversation with Gary Hamel and Lowell Bryan," *McKinsey Quarterly* online newsletter, 1 (2008), accessed March 6, 2013, https://www.mckinseyquarterly.com/Innovative_management_A_conversation_between_Gary_Hamel_and_Lowell_Bryan_2065.

to say, "In a market where talent is largely a commodity and can be bought anywhere, the secret sauce is creating an environment in which you push that frontier out, in which you can steadily raise the returns on human capital. The combination of technology and talent is a powerful catalyst for value creation."[14] Based on this assessment, Hamel states: "The outlines of the twenty-first-century management model are clear. Decision making will be more peer based; the tools of creativity will be widely distributed in organizations. Ideas will compete on an equal footing. Strategies will be built from the bottom up. Power will be a function of competence rather than of position.... You can see some of the pieces starting to come together, but we're not there yet."[15]

Organizations vary in terms of the size and potential of targeted global markets and the competence of local management in different country markets. Conflicting pressures may arise from the need for product and technical knowledge, functional expertise in marketing, finance, and operations, and area and country knowledge. Because the constellation of pressures that shape organizations is never exactly the same, no two organizations pass through organizational stages in exactly the same way, nor do they arrive at precisely the same organizational pattern. Nevertheless, some general patterns have developed.

Most companies undertake initial foreign expansion with an organization similar to that in Figures 14-1 and 14-2. When a company is organized on this basis, foreign subsidiaries report directly to the company president or other designated company officer, who then carries out his or her responsibilities without assistance from a headquarters staff group. This is a typical initial arrangement for companies getting started in international marketing operations.

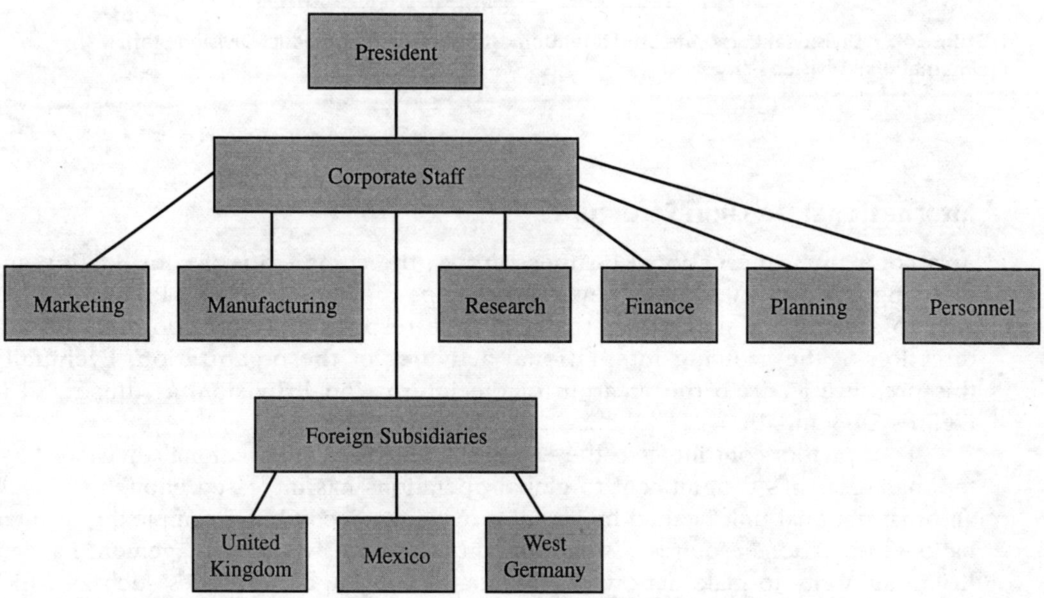

FIGURE 14-1 Functional Corporate Structure, Domestic Corporate Staff Orientation, Preinternational Division

---

[14] Ibid.

[15] Ibid.

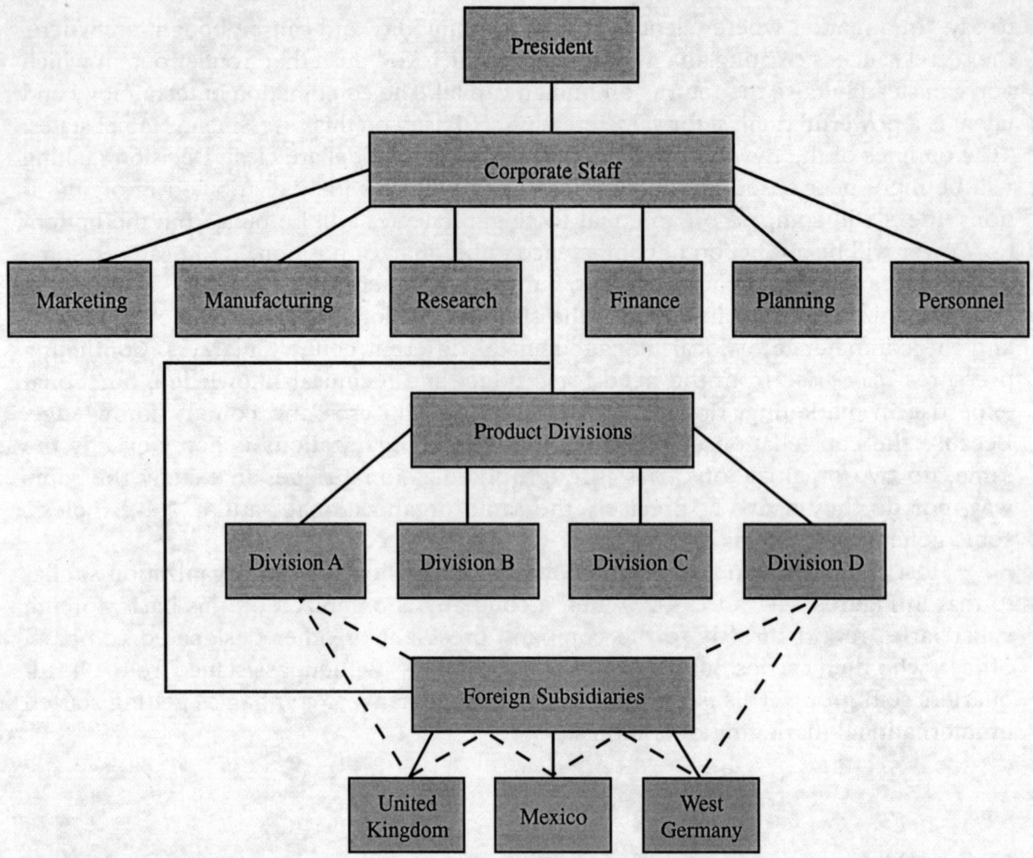

FIGURE 14-2 Divisional Corporate Structure, Domestically Oriented Product Division Staff, Preinternational Division

International Division Structure

As a company's international business grows, the complexity of coordinating and directing this activity extends beyond the scope of a single person. Pressure is created to assemble a staff group that will take responsibility for coordination and direction of the growing international activities of the organization. Eventually, this pressure leads to the creation of the international division, as illustrated in Figures 14-3 and 14-4.

Four factors contribute to the establishment of an international division. First, top management's commitment to global operations has increased enough to justify an organizational unit headed by a senior manager. Second, the complexity of international operations requires a single organization unit whose management has sufficient authority to make its own determination on important issues such as which market entry strategy to employ. Third, an international division is frequently formed when the firm has recognized the need for internal specialists to deal with the special demands of global operations. A fourth contributing factor arises when management exhibits the desire to develop the ability to scan the global horizon for opportunities and competitive threats rather than simply respond to situations that are presented to the company.

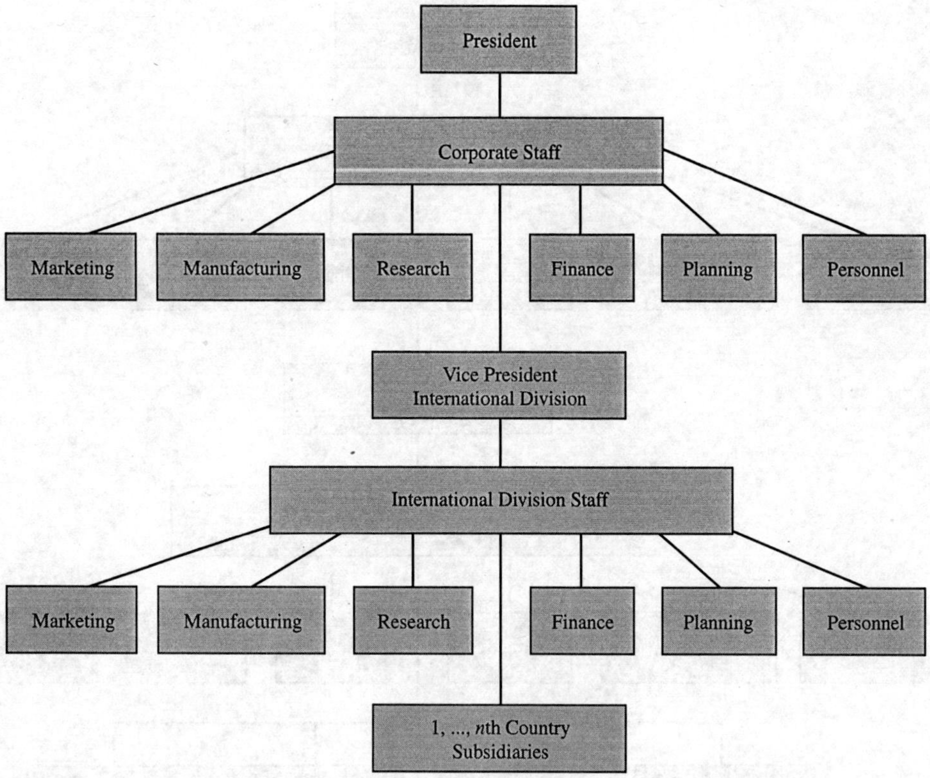

FIGURE 14-3 Functional Corporate Structure, Domestic Corporate Staff Orientation, International Division

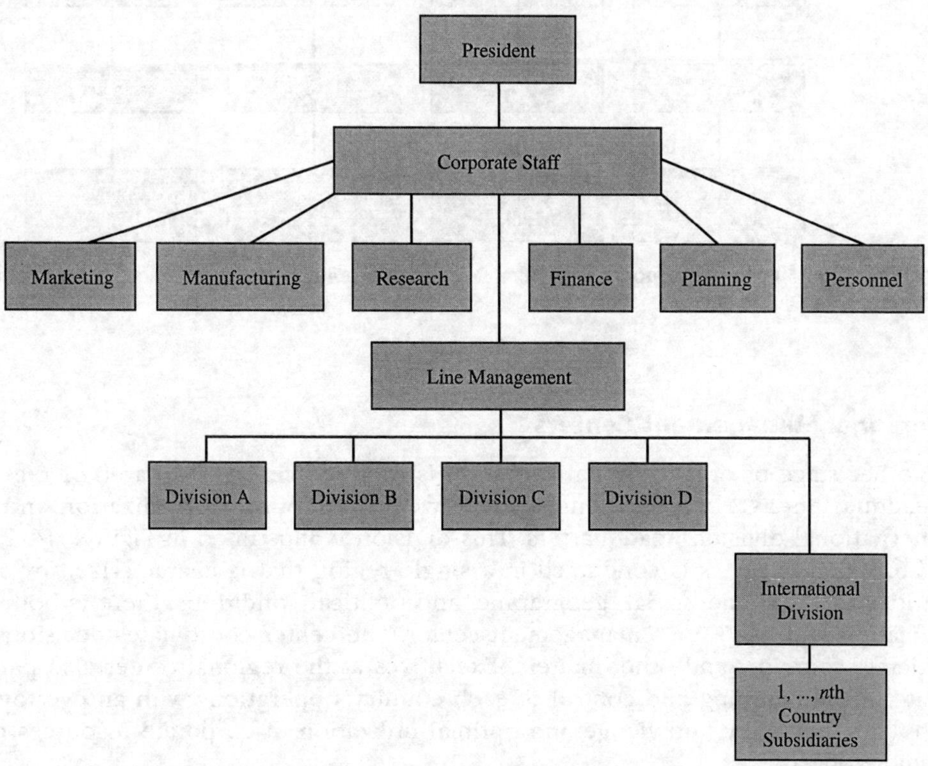

FIGURE 14-4 Divisional Corporate Structure, Domestically Orientated Corporate Staff, Domestically Oriented Product Divisions, International Division

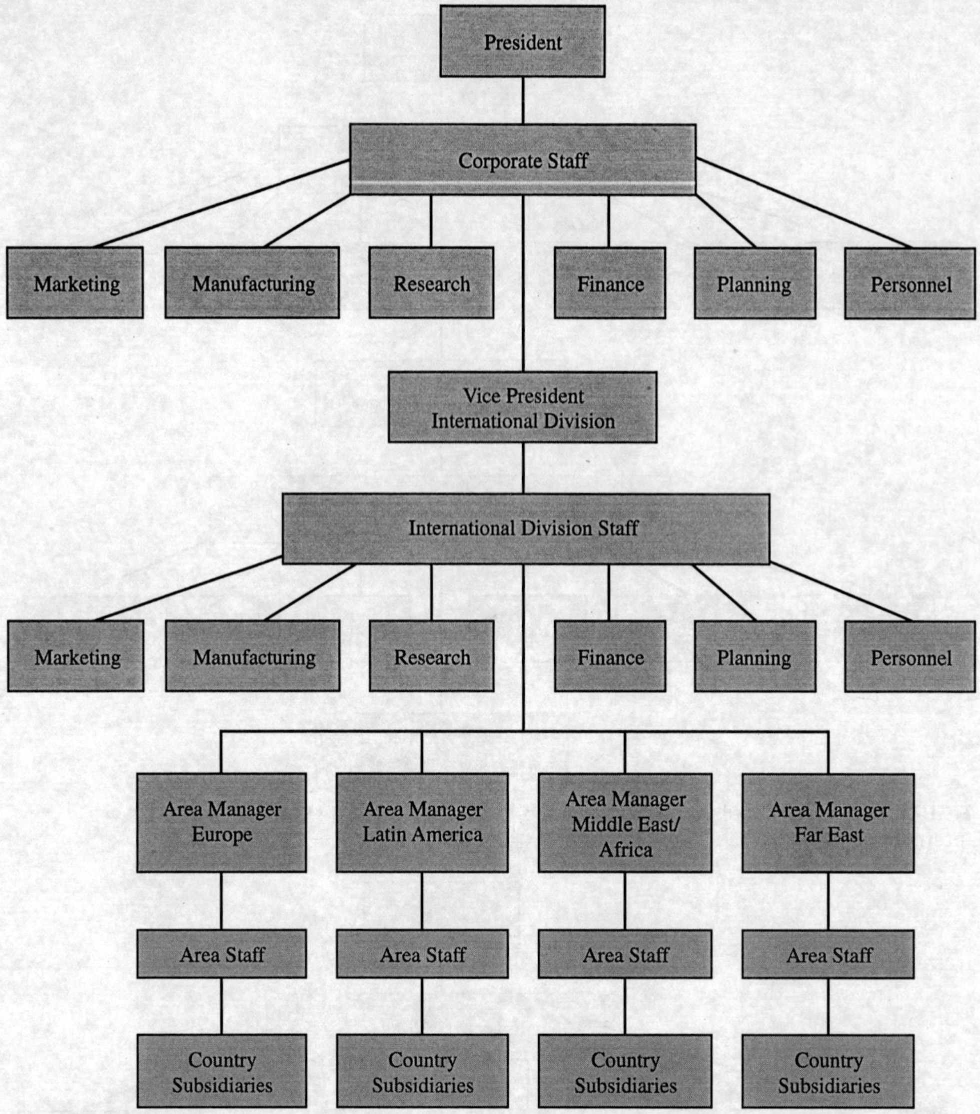

FIGURE 14-5 Functional Corporate Structure, Domestic Corporate Staff Orientation, International Division, Area Divisions

Regional Management Centers

Another stage of organizational evolution is the emergence of an area or regional headquarters as a management layer between the country organization and the international division headquarters. This division is illustrated in Figures 14-5 and 14-6. When business is conducted in a single region that is characterized by similarities in economic, social, geographic, and political conditions, there is both justification and need for a management center. The center coordinates decisions on pricing, sourcing, and other matters. Executives at the regional center also participate in the planning and control of each country's operations with an eye toward applying company knowledge and optimal utilization of corporate resources on a regional basis.

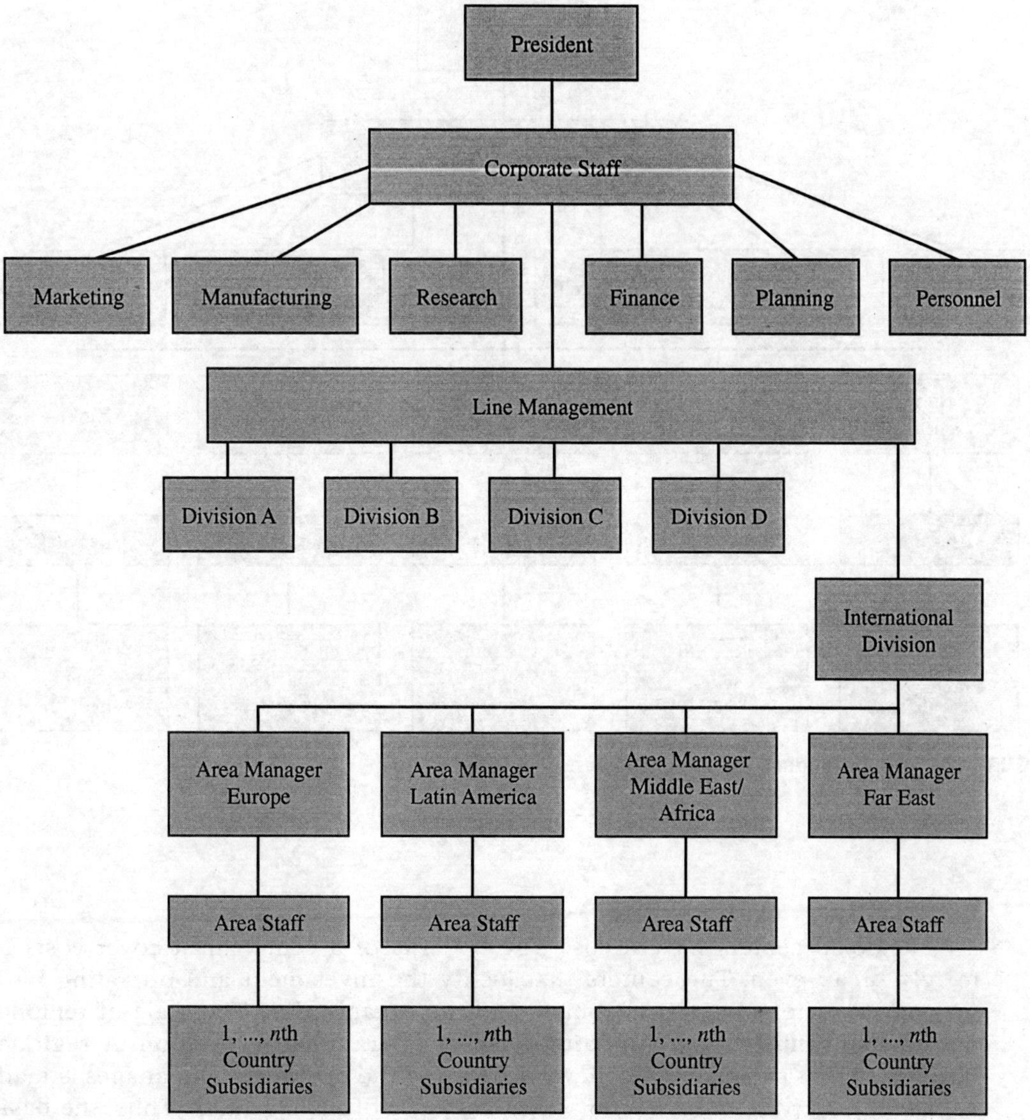

FIGURE 14-6 Divisional Corporate Structure, Domestically Oriented Corporate Staff, International Division, Area Subdivisions

Regional management can offer a company several advantages. First, many regional managers agree that an on-the-scene regional management unit makes sense when there is a real need for coordinated, pan-regional decision making. Coordinated regional planning and control is becoming necessary as the national subsidiary continues to lose its relevance as an independent operating unit. Regional management can probably achieve the best balance of geographic, product, and functional considerations required to implement corporate objectives effectively. By shifting operations and decision making to the region, the company is better able to maintain an insider advantage.

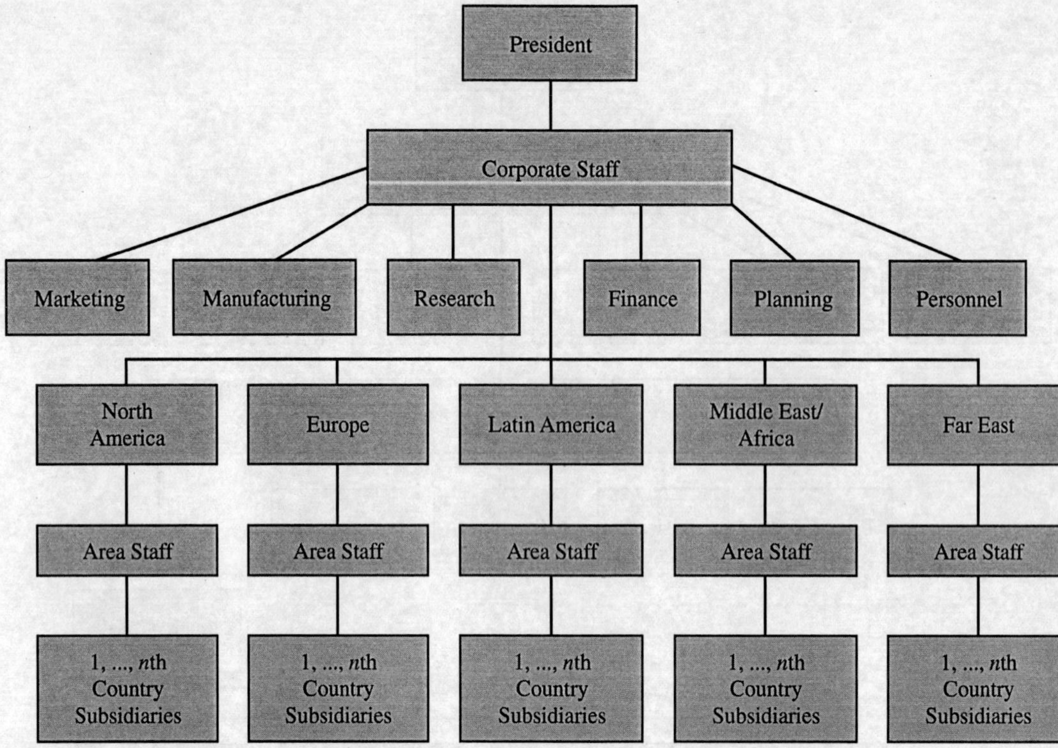

FIGURE 14-7 Single Product Division or Business Company

Regional centers have a cost. The benefits of a center must cover costs to merely break even. The centers that justify the investment and operating budgets must create value for customers and the organization. The scale of regional management must be in line with scale of operations in a region. A regional headquarters is premature whenever the size of the operations it manages is inadequate to cover the costs of the additional layer of management. Thus, the basic issue with regard to the regional headquarters is: Does it contribute enough to organizational effectiveness to justify its cost and the complexity of another layer of management?

Geographic Structure

The geographic structure involves the assignment of operational responsibility for geographic areas of the world to line managers. The corporate headquarters retains responsibility for worldwide planning and control, and each area of the world—including the "home" or base market—is organizationally equal. For the company with French origins, France is simply another geographic market under this organizational arrangement. The most common appearance of this structure is in companies with closely related product lines that are sold in similar end-use markets around the world. For example, the major international oil companies utilize the geographic structure, which is illustrated in Figure 14-7.

BOX 14-1

Side Bar: Smart Organization Structure

It was a bolt from the blue for Mr Etienne Benet, the managing director of the Swiss food giant Nestle. The information that Indian apex food regulator FSSAI, has banned Maggi on charges of containing lead and undeclared monosodium glutamate (MSG). At that time Paul Bulcke, the CEO of the company, was located in the company headquarters at Vevey, Switzerland for managing business interest across 196 countries. Nestle has 447 factories in 86 countries around the world and an employment of about 333,000 employees. To handle such a mishap in India, the organisation support was extremely necessary as well as all the wisdom of the company must come to the rescue from the mishap. The geographical expansion of activities across 196 countries increased the management complexities for the company. Different information pouring in from different countries are required to be processed at the requisite level of the company so the best decision can be taken considering suitability of the purpose. For this to happen, Nestle must have an organisation structure which is well knit for facilitating collection and accumulation of requisite information regarding different host country environment, product and functional knowledge. Also, the organisational structure must have the capacity to process them at the requisite level to take correct decisions at the correct time. For example, Nestlé's Maggi noodles mishap news immediately was processed at the right level and was sent to the CEO of the company. The CEO, Mr Paul Bulcke, communicated right away the decision to make the products off the shelf with reconfirmation of the fact that company maintained same quality standards everywhere in world where India was not an exception.

In order to take such prompt decisions for distant market like India, Nestle organisational structure adequately supported the flow of information and processing the same at the requisite hierarchical levels. As a result, correct decision came at the correct point of time which allowed the company to bring back the product Maggi in to the Indian market within a shortest possible time. A good communicable organisation structure, therefore, is an absolute necessity to help a global company in achieving its objective.

Global Product Division Structure

When an organization assigns worldwide product responsibility to its product divisions, the product divisions must decide whether to rely on an international division, thereby dividing their world into domestic and foreign, or to rely on an area structure with each region of the world organizationally treated on an equal basis. In most cases in which a divisional company shifts from a corporate international division to worldwide product divisions, there are two stages in the internationalization of the product divisions. The first stage occurs when international responsibility is shifted from a corporate international division to international departments in product divisions. The second occurs when the product divisions themselves shift international responsibility from international departments within the divisions to the total divisional organization. In effect, this shift is the utilization of a geographic structure within each product division. The worldwide product division with an international department is illustrated in Figure 14-7 as a single business or product division company, and in Figure 14-8 as a multi-business or product division company. The product structure works best when a company's product line is widely diversified, when products go into a variety of end-use markets, and when a relatively high-technological capability is required.

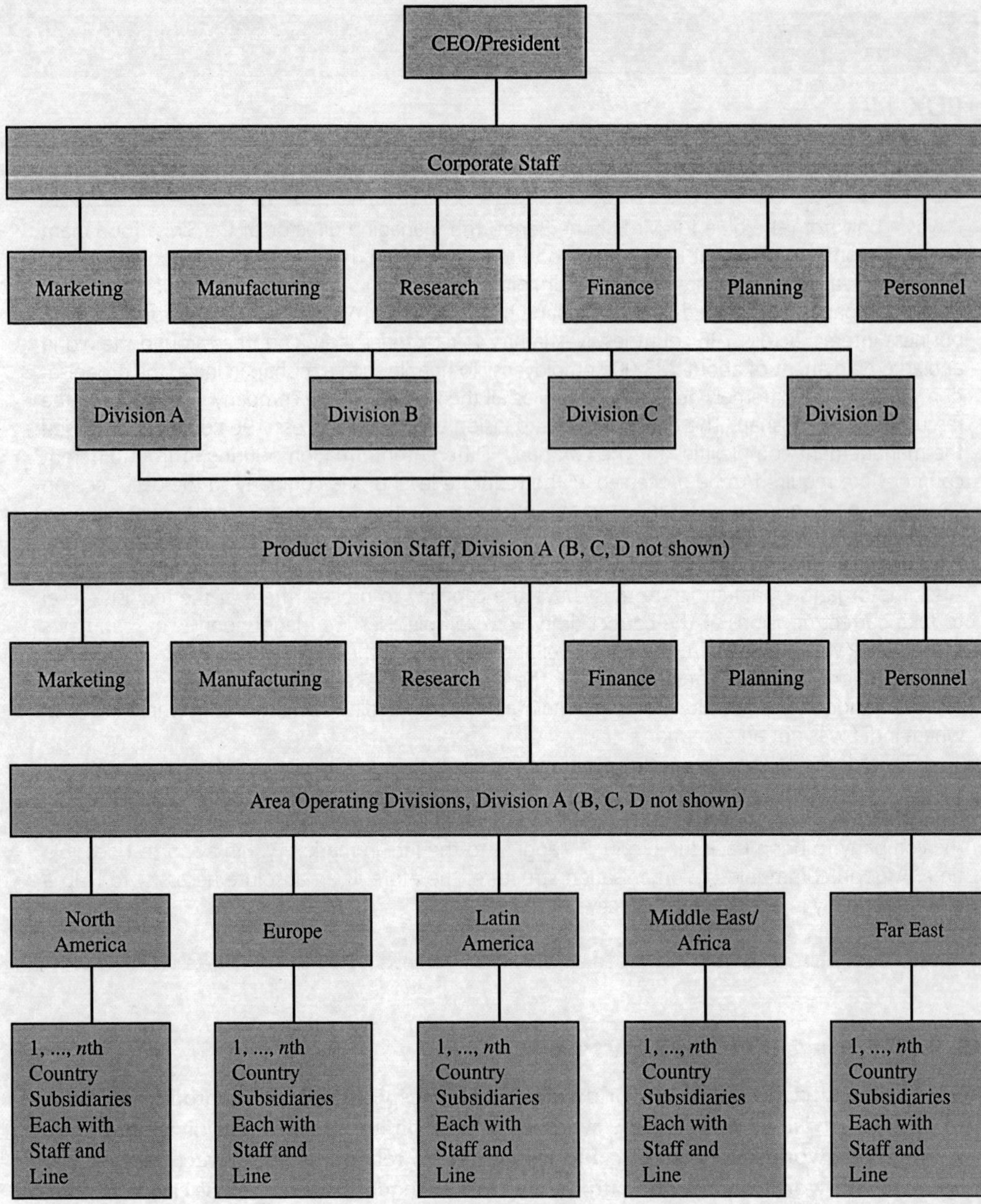

FIGURE 14-8 Multi Divisional or Multi Product Division Corporate Structure with World Corporate Staff Orientation

BOX 14-2

Side Bar: Responsive Organization Structure

"The future is ours to shape, and we need to gear up to be future-ready. The new structure could create some uncertainty, but helps in achieving its targets". Mr Guenter Butscheck, the new managing director of Tata Motors quipped in the backdrop of introducing a new organisation structure of the company. Mr Butscheck had a relook in the existing organisation structure of Tata Motor Limited (refer Figure 14-9) and opined that in order to have a turnaround in a super competitive market, it is extremely essential to have an organisation which can make faster and effective decision to reach customer segment. India's much known automobile giant was witnessing a drop in the market share of passenger vehicles nationally to an alarming 5 percent from yesteryears high of 16 percent. More stiff challenge came from commercial vehicle segment where Tata Motors always performed well but right now market share in India came down to a decades-low at 46% for the company. According to Mr Butscheck, the previous relatively tall organizational structure of the company with many levels of hierarchy and different managers with small span of control used to be slower in responding to the market needs at a fast pace. There were so much of communication exchanges within different managers, each controlling only a small group of people, that the ultimate managerial decision took the back seat. After a detailed job evaluation, it was decided that there will be only five management levels below the executive committee in the new organisational structure.

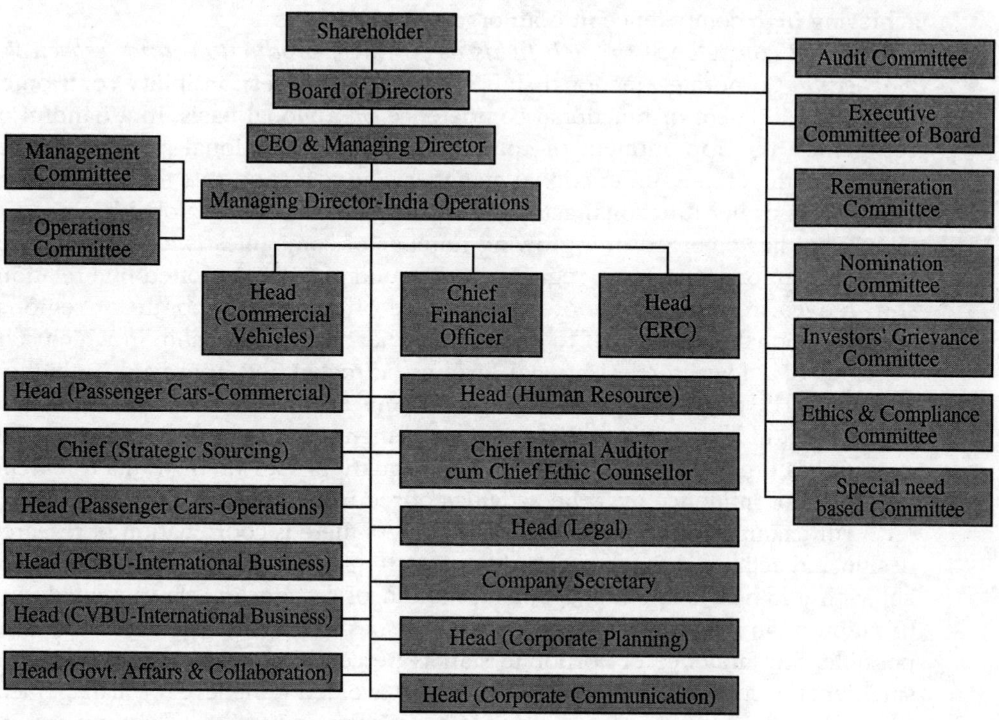

FIGURE 14-9 Tata Motors Organisation Structure Under Change

Source: http://www.tatamotors.com/investors/financials/68-ar-html/corp_gov.html, as accessed on 20 January 2017 at 2pm.

The new organisation, which was proposed to be effective from the beginning of 2017, would be much flattered with an elimination of middle management level. The span of control would now be wider. Since from top management to bottom the layers would be minimum,

continued

so decision making would be faster. Mr Butscheck was also aware of the possible ill effect of tweaking the traditional tall organisation structure of the company. "I am aware that this approach is considered disruptive and might create some uncertainty, but the right organisational formation with the best possible team is of utmost importance to achieve our game plan — in our today's competitive environment, there is no room for mediocrity and complacency," Mr Butscheck quipped.

The Integrated Structure

The most sophisticated organizational arrangement brings to bear four basic competencies on a worldwide basis. These competencies are as follows:

1. *Geographic knowledge.* An understanding of the basic economic, social, cultural, political, and governmental market and competitive dimensions of a country is essential. The country subsidiary is the major structural device employed today to enable the corporation to acquire geographic knowledge.
2. *Product and technical knowledge and know-how.* Product managers with a worldwide responsibility can achieve this level of competence on a global basis. Another way of achieving global product competence is simply to duplicate product management organizations in domestic and international divisions, achieving high competence in both organizational units.
3. *Functional competence in such fields as finance, production, and, especially, marketing.* Corporate functional staff with worldwide responsibility contributes to the development of functional competence on a global basis. In a handful of companies, the appointment of country subsidiary functional managers is reviewed by the corporate functional manager who is responsible for the development of his or her functional activity in the organization on a global basis.

   What has emerged in a growing number of companies is a dotted-line relationship among corporate, regional, and country staff. The dotted-line relationship ranges from nothing more than advice offered by corporate or regional staff to regional country staff to a much "heavier" line relationship in which staff activities of a lower organizational level are directed and approved by higher-level staff. The relationship of staff organizations can become a source of tension and conflict in an organization if top management does not create a climate that encourages organizational integration. Headquarters staff often wants to extend its control or influence over the activities of reporting staff.

   For example, in marketing research, unless there is coordination of research design and activity, the international headquarters is unable to compare one market with another. If line management, instead of recognizing the potential contribution of an integrated worldwide staff, wishes to operate as autonomously as possible, the influence of corporate staff is perceived as undesirable. In such a situation, the stronger party wins. This can be avoided if the level of management to which both line and staff report creates a climate and structure that expect and require the cooperation of line and staff and that recognize that each has responsibility for important aspects of the management of international markets.
4. *A knowledge of the customer, competition, and industry and its needs.* In sophisticated global companies, serving global customers is an integrated global effort that combines knowledge of markets and customers with the company's global knowledge and experience in order to deliver a unique value to customers in global markets.

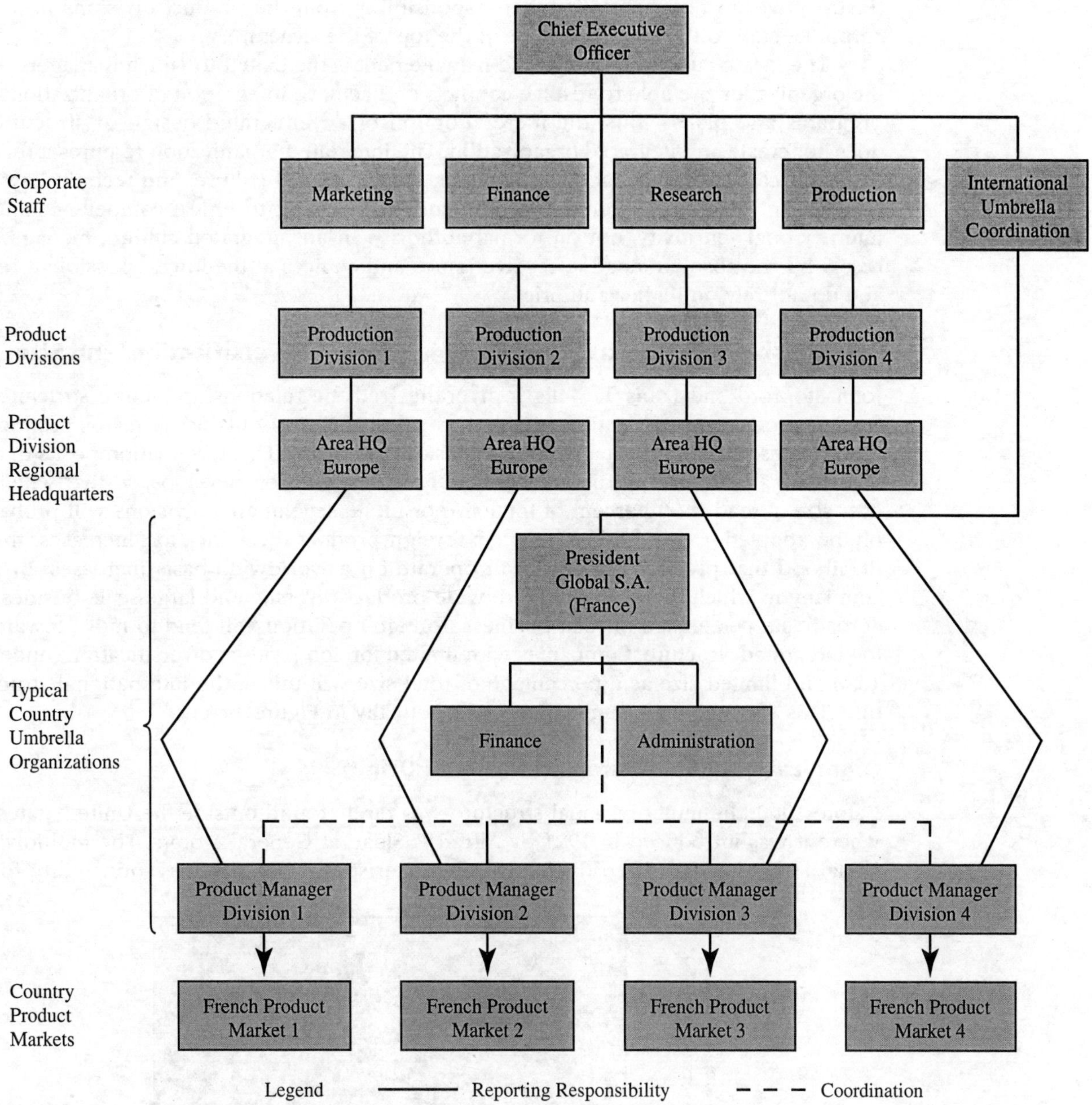

FIGURE 14-10 The Integrated Structure

In the fully developed, large-scale global company, product, function, area, and customer know-how are simultaneously focused on the organization's worldwide marketing objectives. This type of total competence is an integrated organization. In the organization, the task of management is to achieve an organizational balance that brings together different perspectives and skills to accomplish the organization's objectives. Under this arrangement, instead of designating national organizations or product divisions as profit centers, both are responsible for profitability: the national organization for country profits and the product divisions for national and worldwide product profitability. Figure 14-10 illustrates the integrated organization.

This organization chart starts with a bottom section that represents a single-country responsibility level, moves to representing the area or international level, and finally moves to representing global responsibility from the product divisions to the corporate staff to the chief executive at the top of the structure.

The key to successful integrated management is the extent to which managers in the organization are able to resolve conflicts and achieve integration of organizational programs and plans. Thus, the mere adoption of an integrated design or structure does not create an integrated organization. The integrated organization requires a fundamental change in management behavior, organizational culture, and technical systems. In an integrated organization, influence is based on technical competence and interpersonal sensitivity, not on formal authority. In an integrated culture, managers recognize the absolute need to resolve issues and choices at the lowest possible level and do not rely on higher authority.

Relationship Among Structure, Foreign Product Diversification, and Size

John Stopford and Louis T. Wells Jr. hypothesized the relationship among structure, foreign product diversification (defined as sales of a firm outside its major product line expressed as a percentage of the total sales), and size. This formulation posits that when size abroad grows, the emergence of an area division develops, so that whenever size abroad is 50 percent of total size or more, several area divisions will probably be adopted. On the other hand, as foreign product diversification increases, the likelihood that product divisions will operate on a worldwide basis increases. In a company in which there is both worldwide product diversity and large-scale business abroad as a percentage of total business, foreign operation will tend to move toward the integrated structure. Companies with limited foreign product diversification (under 10%) and limited size as a percentage of total size will utilize the international structure. This formulation is summarized schematically in Figure 14-11.[16]

Organizational Structure and National Origin

Before 1960, the multidivisional structure was rarely found outside the United States, where it was introduced in 1921 by Alfred P. Sloan at General Motors. The multidivisional structure had three distinctive characteristics. First, profit responsibility for

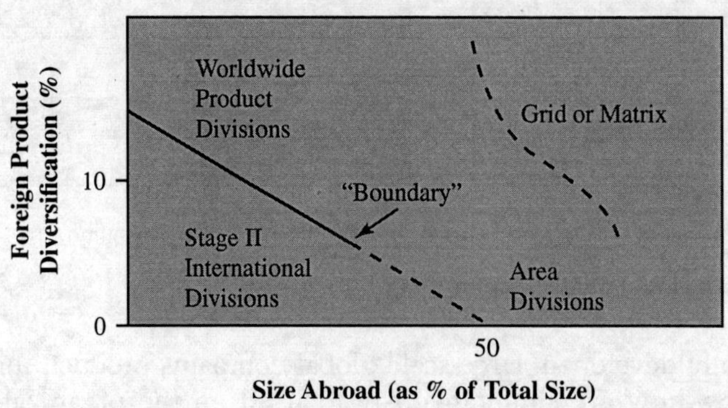

FIGURE 14-11 The Relationship Among Structure, Foreign Product Diversification, and Size Abroad (as a % of total size)

Source: Adapted from John M. Stopford and Louis T. Wells, Jr., *Managing the Multinational Enterprise* (New York: Basic Books, 1972).

[16] See also Andrew Campbell, Sven Kunisch, and Gunther Muller-Stewens, "To Centralize or Not to Centralize?" *McKinsey Quarterly* online newsletter (June 2011), accessed June 14, 2011, https://www.mckinseyquarterly.com/To_centralize_or_not_to_centralize_2815, for a discussion on whether centralization adds 10 percent to the market capitalization of profits of the group and whether it avoids risks of bureaucracy, business rigidity, reduced motivation, or distraction.

operating decisions was assigned to general managers of self-contained business units. Second, there was a corporate headquarters that was concerned with strategic planning, appraisal, and the allocation of resources among the business divisions. Third, executives at the corporate headquarters were separated from operations and were committed to the whole organization rather than the individual businesses.[17] During the 1960s, the larger European enterprises underwent a period of unprecedented reorganization and adopted the multidivisional structure.

The organizational structure of many Asian companies is quite different from the US model. Japanese organizations, for example, rely more on generalists as opposed to functional specialists, and they make greater use of project teams to design and manufacture products. They also form much closer relationships with suppliers than have American companies historically, are in a different relationship to sources of capital, and have a fundamentally different governance structure than US companies.

BOX 14-3

Side Bar: Networked Organization Structure

Changes in information and communication technologies are having significant impact on organizational change and how people work with one another, whether an enterprise is solely domestic in structure and design or spans the globe. Management today is coming to understand that collaborative Web 2.0 technologies are the basis for stronger corporate performance and productivity. A decade ago, social technologies gave rise to web-based initiatives such as YouTube and Facebook. Now, these technologies are migrating into the business enterprises with the promise of productivity gains.[18] As a recent study observes, "patterns of adoption and diffusion for the social web's enterprise applications appear to resemble those of earlier eras: a classic S curve, in which early adopters learn to use a new technology, and adoption then picks up rapidly as others begin to recognize its value."[19] Among respondents in the study, a large majority report receiving measurable business benefits from more effective marketing, including increasing customer awareness; faster access to knowledge, including experts; decreasing communication costs; and increasing satisfaction measures with suppliers and partners.

Results from the study indicate that three types of organizations realize greater levels of business benefits from their use of Web 2.0 technologies. Those termed by the study as "Internally Networked Organization" reap benefits predominantly within their own organization in employee interaction and work flows since information is shared more readily and less hierarchically and collaboration and project-based tasks are more common. "Externally Networked Organizations" gain benefits from external interactions by using Web 2.0 technologies to facilitate relationships with customers and business partners. Finally, the "Fully Networked Enterprise," only 3 percent of organizations studied, gain highest levels of business benefits from the integrated and widespread use of Web 2.0 information and communication technologies by employees, customers, and business partners. In addition, these organizations appear to have moved further along the learning curve than other enterprises by breaking down organizational barriers to information flow and use.[20]

---

[17] Lawrence G. Franko, "The Move Toward a Multidivisional Structure in European Organization," *Administrative Science Quarterly*, 19, no. 4 (December 1974): 493–506.

[18] Jacques Bughin and Michael Chui, "The Rise of the Networked Enterprise: Web 2.0 Finds Its Payday," *McKinsey Quarterly* online newsletter (December 2010), accessed December 14, 2010, http://www.mckinsey.com/insights/mgi/research/technology_and_innovation/the_rise_of_the_networked_enterprise.

[19] Ibid.

[20] Ibid.

A key question in this study involved whether these benefits translate to measurable performance improvements. Analysis of the survey results indicated market share gains were significantly correlated with the fully networked and externally networked organizations. Technology-enabled collaboration with external stakeholders enabled these organizations to gain market share from competitors as a result of closer relationships with customers, including collaboration in customer support initiatives and product development efforts.[21] Self-reported gains in operating margins correlated with the ability to make decisions lower in the decision hierarchy and the efforts of combined in-house and external stakeholder and partner teams. These suggest a more agile formal and informal organization structure where frontline staff have the ability to make decisions and firms are leveraging outside resources to raise productivity and develop more valued product and service offerings.[22] Those firms with self-reported top rankings in their industries correlated positively in the study with the Internally Networked Organizations, where Web 2.0 initiatives supported internal collaboration and therefore the greater organizational resiliency required to maintain market leadership positions.[23] Takeaways from this study include the following:

1. Integrating Web 2.0 and leading-edge information and communication technologies into employees' daily activities is a key success factor.
2. Firms should continue to drive adoption and usage both across the organization and out to external stakeholders.
3. Breaking down barriers to organizational change and collaboration is critical to market success across several important measures.

The bottom line: The social web and its use throughout the business enterprise and marketing environment is facilitating the realignment of operations and marketing in ways that tap valuable marketplace insights, synergies, and spur productivity.[24]

SME INTERNATIONALISATION

As per MSME Act 2006, the Small Medium Enterprises (SMEs) in India are defined in terms of investment in plants and machineries (refer Table 14-1). The investment limit in plant and machineries for small manufacturing enterprises is of the order of ₹25 lakhs while for service enterprises it is ₹10 lakhs. The investment limit in plant and machineries for the medium enterprises plant is ₹5 crores, while for service oriented enterprises it is ₹2 crores. The SME sectors are very important for Indian economy as over the years this sector is contributing to about 32-35 percent of the country's gross domestic product. Apart from impressive employment generating ability of this SME sector, the country also gets economic benefits of the internationalisation of SME sectors. About 34-36 percent of India's exports every year are from the SME sector only. Internationalisation per say means expansion of economic activities of a company beyond international border of its own country. This expansion could be through export, franchising, joint venture, wholly owned subsidiaries or any other means deemed fit by the company. Traditionally, the SMEs, especially small businesses, internationalise through exports only, at least in the initial stages. However, the process of internationalisation of SMEs is quite random and unpredictable. They do not follow any patterns and every small enterprise has its own way and time for internationalisation.

[21] Ibid.
[22] Ibid.
[23] Ibid.
[24] See also, Dave Evans, "Marketing and Operations Take Another Step Closer," ClickZ online newsletter (April 15, 2009), accessed April 15, 2009, http://www.clickz.com/clickz/column/1711072/marketing-operations-take-another-step-closer.

TABLE 14-1 SME Definition in India

Classification	Investment Ceiling for Plant, Machinery or Equipments — Manufacturing Enterprises	Service Enterprises
Micro	Upto ₹25 lakh ($50 thousand)	Upto ₹10 lakh ($20 thousand)
Small	Above ₹25 lakh ($50 thousand) & upto ₹5 crore ($1 million)	Above ₹10 lakh ($20 thousand) & upto ₹2 crore ($0.40 million)
Medium	Above ₹5 crore ($1 million) & upto ₹10 crore ($2 million)	Above ₹2 crore ($0.40 million) & upto ₹5 crore ($1 million)

Source: Ministry of MSME, Government of India.

SME STRUCTURE ACROSS GLOBE

In India, SMEs are classified in accordance with the quantum of monetary investment in plant and machinery. Up to 1958, India followed the two part definition for small enterprises: investment in plant and machinery as well as number of people employed in the organisation. Accordingly during 1958, the small enterprises were those with investment in plant and machinery up to ₹5 lakhs, as well as 50 workers with power or 100 worker without motive power. But as the country realised the need of more employment generation then the employment limitation criteria was removed.

Across the European Union the small enterprises are those with business turnover below or equal to 10 million Euro, employing less than 50 persons. For medium enterprises the turnover limit is extended up to 250 million Euro and employment of 250 persons. In the USA, the small enterprises are those whose annual sales are below 35.5 million USD and employed in between 10 to 499 employees. Sales turnover not exceeding RM50 million or full-time employees not exceeding 200 workers are the two conditions stipulated by Malaysia government for small enterprise category. For services and other sectors, Malaysian definition stipulates sales turnover not exceeding RM20 million or full-time employees not exceeding 75 workers as the definition of small scale service enterprises. In New Zealand, SME definition is based on employment only with 19 or fewer employees. The same is in case of Israel where a business is regarded small if it has no more than 50 employees and a medium business having between 50 to 250 workers.

EVOLUTION OF EXPORT DIVISION IN SME

Evidence across the globe suggests that SMEs' internationalisation pattern has been somewhat step by step in nature. SMEs are most likely to take export route as their first step towards internationalisation process. Once the SMEs gather sufficient experience of exporting products or services to a foreign country market then only it considers entering the country with hierarchical mode like joint venture, wholly owned subsidiary etc. This phenomena is true for the Indian SMEs as well. A large percentage of the total Indian SMEs are engaged in exporting a number of products/ services to different other countries of the world. Primarily they are involved in exporting of pearls, precious stones, metals, coins etc. electrical, electronic equipment, articles of apparel and accessories, pharmaceutical products.

There are different organisational structures for carrying out international business. For the SMEs, the initial commitment is usually for the domestic market for which suitable organisational structure exist. When the focus is somewhat shifted to the international business, the domestic manager usually takes the additional responsibility of export development. Considering the limited emphasis on export and management

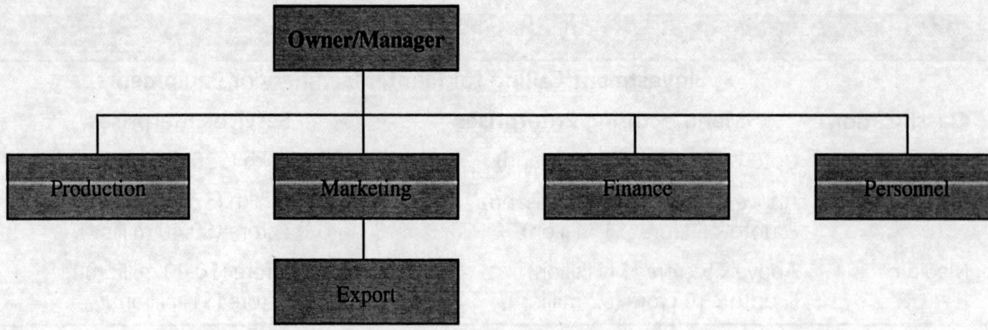

FIGURE 14-12 Export Division as a Part of the Domestic Marketing

philosophy thereof towards international marketing, a built in export department under the domestic manager comes up for the first time (refers Figure 14-12).

As the organisation gets more involved in the international business and export grows further, the built in export division cannot handle the works in totality. It requires a separate export department to handle all the activities related to export business (refer Figure 14-13). A separate export target is fixed for the export department which continues to increase with time. Eventually, it totally comes out of the control of the domestic marketing department.

MARKETING CONTROL AND SMEs

Marketing control is very vital for achieving marketing success. Any organisation plans in advance the way and process of creating customer value, for the target customers in a competitive market. Marketing control relates to the monitoring of the plan implementation and corrective action in case of any deviation from the plan. Marketing control desires to achieve the planned objectives set at the planning stage. Therefore, the degree of marketing control a company can exercise while marketing its products in a foreign country is a very important factor for ensuring business success. In this respect, different entry modes have been differentiated in terms of levels of control, it provides to the entrant company over the foreign operation. Wholly owned subsidiary, inherently provides the highest control of foreign operation, since under this entry mode the entrant company operates in the host country on its own and company management has the liberty to take marketing decisions on its own requirements. When the entry mode is under licensing arrangement, the flexibility to take marketing decisions in the host company gets curtailed as the local licensee would like to retain them fully as per licensing agreement executed. In a joint venture (JV), the marketing control gets divided between the JV partners. SMEs usually prefer to enter a foreign country through exporting as an entry mode. Inherently, the mode of entry through export provides the least marketing control to the entrant company in the host country. Therefore, SMEs, in general, have to depend on their importing partners in different countries for exercise of marketing strategy in the distant country markets.

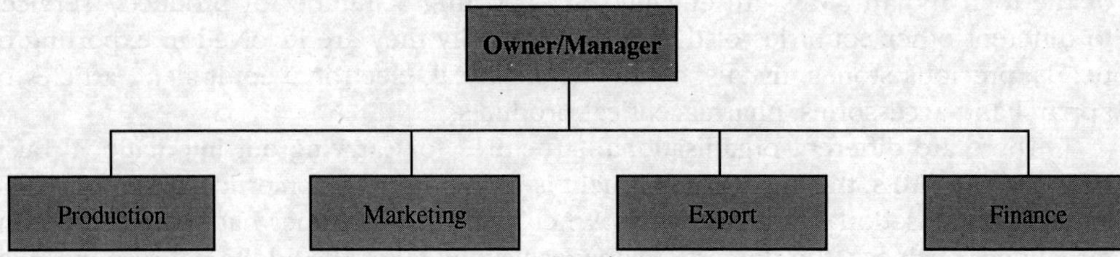

FIGURE 14-13 Independent Export Division

Summary

To respond to the opportunities and threats in the global marketing environment, a firm must have a global vision and strategy. By providing leadership, organizing a global effort, and establishing control procedures, a firm can exploit global opportunities. Leaders must have the vision, in addition to the technical resources, to build global competencies. In organizing the global marketing effort, a structure that enables the company to respond to relevant differences in international market environments and enables the company to extend valuable corporate knowledge is the goal. A balance between autonomy and integration must be established. Within this organization, firms must establish core competencies to be competitive. For global marketing control practices to be effective, differences from purely domestic control must be recognized and implemented in planning and control practices.

Discussion Questions

1. What is the difference between a great and an ordinary company?
2. Cite examples of companies that you consider to be great and ordinary companies. Explain why the companies that you selected are great or ordinary.
3. What is the major complaint of managers in subsidiary companies about the control practices of headquarters?
4. What is a global marketing audit?
5. What kind of planning problems develop in the headquarters of a global company?
6. What are the problems in planning at the country or subsidiary level in a global company?
7. How would you advise a company manufacturing a line of construction equipment to organize its business on a global scale?

Suggested Readings

Adler, Paul, Charles Heckscher, and Laurence Prusak. "Building a Collaborative Enterprise." *Harvard Business Review* (July–August 2011): 94–101.

Baetz, Mark C., and Christopher Bart. "Developing Mission Statements Which Work." *Long Range Planning,* 29, no. 4 (1996): 526–533

Bartlett, Christopher A., and Sumantra Ghoshal. *Managing Across Borders: The Transnational Solution.* Boston: Harvard Business School Press, 1989.

Becht, Bart. "Building a Company Without Borders." *Harvard Business Review* (April 2010): 103–106.

Bennis, Warren, and Patricia Ward Biederman. *Organizing Genius: The Secrets of Creative Collaboration.* Reading, MA: Addison-Wesley, 1997.

Blenko, Marcia W., Michael C. Mankins, and Paul Rogers. "The Decision-Driven Organization." *Harvard Business Review* (June 2010): 54–62.

Bodell, Lisa. *Kill the Company: End the Status Quo, Start an Innovation Revolution.* Brookline, MA: Bibliomotion Inc., 2012; and "Kill the Company: Identify Your Weaknesses Before Your Competitors Do," *Knowledge@Wharton* (December 17, 2012). Accessed December 25, 2012. http://knowledge.wharton.upenn.edu/article.cfm?articleid=3132.

Bryant, Adam. *The Corner Office: Indispensable and Unexpected Lessons From CEO's on How to Lead and Succeed.* New York: Times Books, Henry Holt and Company, LLC., 2011; and "The Corner Office: Adam Bryant on the Five Qualities of Successful Leaders," *Knowledge@Wharton*, an online business journal of Wharton Business School (December 17, 2012). Accessed December 25, 2012. http://knowledge.wharton.upenn.edu/article.cfm?articleid=3129.

Doz, Yves, Jose Santos, and Peter Williamson. *From Global to Metanational: How Companies Win in the Knowledge Economy.* Boston: Harvard Business School Press, 2001.

Dyer, Jeffrey H., Hal B. Gregersen, and Clayton M. Christensen. "The Innovator's DNA: Five Discovery Skills Separate True Innovators From the Rest of Us." *Harvard Business Review* (December 2009): 61–67.

Engelen, Andreas, and Matte Brettel. "A Cross-Cultural Perspective of Marketing Departments' Influence Tactics." *Journal of International Marketing*, 19., no. 2 (June 2011): 73–94.

Erickson, Tamara J. "Gen Y in the Workforce: How I Learned to Love Millennials (and stop worrying about what they were doing with their iPhones)." *Harvard Business Review* (February 2009): 43–49.

Erickson, Tamara J. "The Leaders We Need Now." *Harvard Business Review* (May 2010): 63–66 See also, Meister, Jeanne C., and Karie Willyerd. "Mentoring Millennials." *Harvard Business Review* (May 2010): 68–72.

Gates, Bill. *Business @ The Speed of Thought: Using a Digital Nervous System.* New York: Warner Books Inc., 1999.

Gavetti, Giovanni. "The New Psychology of Strategic Leadership." *Harvard Business Review* (July–August 2011): 118–125.

Ghoshal, Sumantra, and Christopher A. Bartlett. *The Individualized Corporation.* New York: HarperBusiness, 1997.

Hagel, John III, John Seely Brown, and Lang Davison. "Shaping Strategy in a World of Constant Disruption." *Harvard Business Review* (October 2008): 81–89.

Hammer, Michael, and James Champy. *Reengineering the Corporation.* New York: HarperCollins, 1993.

Heenan, David (2010), Bright Triumphs From Dark Hours: Turning Adversity into Success: University of Hawaii Press.

Heenan, David, and Warren Bennis. *Co-Leaders: The Power of Great Partnerships.* New York: John Wiley & Sons. 1999.

Heifetz, Ronald, Alexander Grashow, and Marty Linsky. "Leadership in a (Permanent) Crisis." *Harvard Business Review* (July–August 2009): 62–69.

Isenberg, Daniel J. "The Global Entrepreneur: A New Breed of Entrepreneur Is Thinking Across Borders—From Day One." *Harvard Business Review* (December 2008): 107–111.

Jaruzelski, Barry, John Loehr, and Richard Holman. "Why Culture Is Key." *Strategy+Business* (Winter 2011): 31–45.

Johansson, Johny K., and Ikujiro Nonaka. *Relentless: The Japanese Way of Marketing.* New York: HarperBusiness, 1997.

Kaplan, Robert S. and David P. Norton. *The Balanced Scorecard: Translating Strategy into Action.* Boston: Harvard Business School Press, 1996.

Kashani, Kamran. "Beware the Pitfalls of Global Marketing." *Harvard Business Review,* 67, no. 5 (September–October 1989): 91–98.

Katzenbach, Jon R., and Douglas K. Smith. "The Discipline of Teams." *Harvard Business Review* (March–April 1993): 111–121.

Katzenbach, Jon, and Ashley Harshak. "Stop Blaming Your Culture." *Strategy+Business,* 62 (Spring 2011): 35–43.

Katzenbach, Jon R., and Douglas K. Smith. *The Wisdom of Teams: Creating the High-Performance Organization.* Boston: Harvard Business School Press, 1993.

Kotter, John P. "The Big Idea: How the Most Innovative Companies Capitalize on Today's Rapid-Fire Strategic Challenges—and Still Make Their Numbers." *Harvard Business Review* (November 2012): 44–58.

Kumar, Nirmalya, and Phanish Puranam. "Have You Restructured for Global Success?" *Harvard Business Review* (October 2011): 123–128.

McDonald, Malcolm, and Warren J. Keegan. *Marketing Plans That Work: How to Prepare Them, How to Use Them.* Newton, MA: Butterworth Heinemann, 1997.

Meyer, Christopher, and Julia Kirby. "Leadership in the Age of Transparency." *Harvard Business Review* (April 2010): 38–46.

Mintzberg, Henry. "The Effective Organization: Forces and Forms." *Sloan Management Review* (Winter 1991).

Mintzberg, Henry. *Managing.* San Francisco: Berrett-Koehler Publishers, Inc., 2009.

Moore, James F. *The Death of Competition: Leadership and Strategy in the Age of Business Ecosystems.* New York: HarperBusiness, 1996.

Nohria, Nitin. "From Regional Star to Global Leader." *Harvard Business Review* (January 2009): 33–39.

Prahalad, C. K., and Gary Hamel. "The Core Competence of the Corporation." *Harvard Business Review,* 68 (May–June 1990): 79–93.

Prahalad, C. K., and Hrishi Bhattacharyya. "How to Be a Truly Global Company." *Strategy+Business,* 64 (Autumn 2011): 54–61.

Prokesch, Steven. "How GE Teaches Teams to Lead Change." *Harvard Business Review* (January 2009): 99–106.

Roth, Martin S., Satish Jayachandran, Mourad Dakhli, and Deborah A. Colton. "Subsidiary Use of Foreign Marketing Knowledge." *Journal of International Marketing,* 17, no. 1 (March 2009): 1–29.

Russwurm, Siegfried, Luis Hernandez, Susan Chambers, and Keumyong Chung. "Developing Your Global Know-How" (series of Interviews). *Harvard Business Review* (March 2011): 70–75.

Senge, Peter M. *The Fifth Discipline: The Art & Practice of The Learning Organization.* New York: Currency Doubleday, 1990.

Spenner, Patrick. "Why You Need a New-Media 'Ringmaster.'" *Harvard Business Review* (December 2010): 78–79.

Spreitzer, Gretchen, and Christine Porath. "Creating Sustainable Performance." *Harvard Business Review* (January–February 2012): 93–99.

Srivastava, Prashant, and Gary Frankwick. "Environment, Management Attitude, and Organizational Learning in Alliances." *Management Decision,* 49, no. 1 (2011): 156–166.

Stevenson, Howard H., and Jeffrey L. Cruikshank. *Do Lunch or Be Lunch: The Power of Predictability in Creating Your Future.* Boston: Harvard Business School Press, 1997.

Useem, Michael. "Four Lessons in Adaptive Leadership." *Harvard Business Review* (November 2010): 87–90.

Womack, James P., and Daniel T. Jones. *Lean Thinking: Banish Waste and Create Wealth in Your Corporation.* New York: Simon & Schuster, 1996.

Xu, Shichun, S. Tamer Cavusgil, and J. Chris White. "The Impact of Strategic Fit Among Strategy, Structure, and Processes on Multinational Corporate Performance: A Multimethod Assessment." *Journal of International Marketing,* 14, no. 2 (2006).

Zenoff, David B. *The Soul of the Organization: How to Ignite Employee Engagement and Productivity at Every Level.* Apress, 2013.

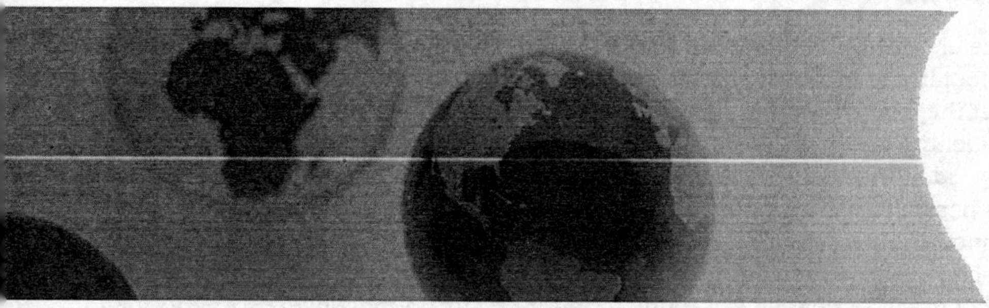

CHAPTER 15

The Future of Global Marketing

I never think of the future; it comes soon enough.

—ALBERT EINSTEIN

You must be the change you wish to see in the world.

—MAHATMA GANDHI

People want to be part of a global conversation.

—ERIC SCHMIDT, *CEO and Co-Chairman, Google*

You cannot lead unless you are future-oriented.

—C. K. PRAHALAD

Learning Objectives

1. What are the major trends shaping the future of global marketing? (443–444).
2. Explain how globalization and global marketing is influenced by the growth of information technology, technical convergence and the death of distance. (444–447).
3. How will growth of the global income and population will influence global marketing strategy. (447–451).
4. What is the trade cycle and how is it impacted by technology and factor costs? (451–452).
5. What is shared value? How does it differ from simply creating value? (453).
6. Explain the significance of sustainability and shared value to global marketing. (453).
7. Explain the relevance of an expanded set of 'C's to the global marketing effort. (Appendix) (457–461).

INTRODUCTION

Global marketers need to think about the future precisely because it will indeed happen soon enough; the global marketer needs to be prepared to seize the opportunities and meet the challenges that the future will bring. No one can predict the future, but we can identify and track major trends. Their underlying driving and restraining forces can be identified and understood. Because these trends are established and known, it is possible to anticipate, with some degree of confidence, what the world and the competitive marketplace are likely to look like in the future. Some trends are well established while others are new emerging forces. Identifying and understanding the driving forces of change is a foundation for creating a most-likely scenario for the future and a strategic marketing and business plan.

The concluding first decade of the twenty-first century saw the continued rise of the "rest of the world (ROW)," led at this stage of global development by Brazil, Russia, India, China, Indonesia, and Turkey (BRIC-IT). The high-income countries dealt with the impact of two asset bubbles, the dot-com bubble of March 2000 and the real estate bubble and great recession starting in 2008 which resulted in unemployment rates not seen since the 1930s in Europe and the Americas and that continue to depress growth as of the publication of this edition. Meanwhile, the BRIC-IT countries focused on economic growth and development to achieve their objectives of sustained high growth and GDP per capita income that is equal to or higher than the levels in existing high-income countries. At this point, the future prospects of the "rest" appear to be bright indeed. But, of course, current growth rates for these countries will not continue forever.

Japan is an example of a country that had bright prospects which have dimmed somewhat during the past two decades. Japan is the first country outside of Europe and the New World countries settled by European immigrants to demonstrate that it does not have to be European to become wealthy. By the 1980s, after Japan's spectacular post–World War II recovery, many believed that Japan was going to overtake the United States in GDP per capita. Japan's growth appeared to be unstoppable; however, the Japanese real estate and equity bubble of 1986–1991 and the country's inability to recognize and write off the bubble value collapse led to two lost decades of growth. Today, Japan's GDP per capita is less that 75 percent of that of the United States, with prime real estate in Tokyo selling at 1 percent of the bubble's peak value. Make no mistake, Japan is a large, high-income country that even today ranks third in the world in GDP after the United States and China.

But, when everyone thought that Japan was going to overtake the United States in GNP, or at the least in GDP per capita, no one imagined that Japan would be overtaken by China. There is a lesson here: trends do provide a vision of the future, until they end. Japan's rapid growth from 1955 to 1975, and its steady growth from 1975 to 1991, ended with the collapse of an asset (equity and real estate) bubble: Japan is now a case example of how a successful high-income country can manage what was long thought to be impossible: to transition from steady real economic growth to virtual economic stagnation. From 1991 to the present, Japan has struggled with slow growth.

Of course, future scenarios are only as good as our understanding of the foundation forces that are creating them. In this chapter, we will identify eight major trends: some have been established for more than a half century, and others are new ideas and changes which will shape the future of global marketing and the marketing enterprise. Implications for marketing in the world of the web, mobile telephony, entertainment and information, digitization across media and platforms, and the growing role of consumers not just as purchasers of services and products but as cocreators in product development, comarketers, and value creators, are important topics to understand in allocating future marketing dollars, planning and implementing marketing strategy, and programming. We will also suggest how to jump-start a career in global marketing.

EIGHT MAJOR TRENDS

1. **Globalization and Information Technology.** The single most important driver of globalization is information technology, which includes computers and computing; the Internet; cloud computing; wireless connectivity; social networks enabled by Facebook, LinkedIn, and Twitter; cellular phones; tablets; cheaper and cheaper connectivity; wider and wider bandwidth; and deeper and deeper penetration of world markets by information technology.
2. **The End of Distance.** Distance has been a profoundly important variable in marketing from the beginning. Over the past 10,000 years there have been many technological advances that have shrunk the world: the horse, the wheel, sail, steam, rail, roads, wagons, cars, trucks, ships, container ships, airplanes, the telegraph, telephone, radio, and most recently the Internet. The emergence of the World Wide Web has, arguably, shrunken the world more in a shorter period of time than any previous technological advance. It has eliminated distance as a barrier to communications and connection via data and voice.
3. **Technical Convergence and Connecting to the Customer.** The customer no longer separates marketing from the product or service—it is the product or experience. Although digital has been used to describe various online technologies or used interchangeably with the word online, a broader definition of digital which addresses customer experience needs to redirect marketing professionals' focus away from technology or specific devices and toward what is important to the customer, namely, addressing his or her expectations, desires, and needs.
4. **World Economic Growth and the Rise of the Rest.** The world economy has undergone revolutionary changes during the past 60 years. Perhaps the most profound change is the great rebalancing of the global economy. The extraordinary rise of Europe and the European settlements in the Americas and Asia for the past 400 years is now being met by the rise of the rest.
5. **Population Changes.** To put matters in perspective, 12,000 years ago, before the invention of agriculture, there were perhaps 1 million people in the world. It took 8,000 years to grow from 3 million to 226 million by the year 1 AD. It took 1,800 years to grow to 1 billion. The increase in population was forecast by Malthus over two centuries ago. The seventh billion was reached in 2011.
6. **The Trade Cycle Clarified.** The trade-cycle model describes the behavior of several generations of managers in some high-income countries including, most notably, the United States, who concluded that as a product matures, the location of production must shift to low-wage countries. This was never a viable strategy for sustainable competitive advantage. It provides a short-term, one–time advantage for companies who have to maintain cost competitiveness, but avoids the need to innovate to remain competitive. The result has been very costly for high-income countries in terms of labor growth and competitiveness; with trade-cycle model practices, short-term interests of companies and their home countries have diverged, leading to a general erosion of economic indicators across more mature markets.
7. **The New Paradigm: Shared Value.** Marketing is the task of creating value, and value is the relationship between customer benefits and price. We express this as V = B/P, where B = Benefits and P = Price. The equation is simple, but too many companies take a very narrow short-term view and have failed to realize that they cannot ignore the well-being of their customers over the longer term.

8. **Sustainability.** One definition of sustainability is that of the Brundtland Commission of the United Nations: "Sustainable development is development that meets the needs of the present without compromising the ability of future generations to meet their own needs."[1] The importance of sustainability is growing as the world's population and income continue to grow. Marketing should be at the vanguard of guiding companies and consumers toward more sustainable practices, products, and services.

Globalization and Information Technology

"The new electronic interdependence re-creates the world in the image of a global village." This observation, from the quotation at the beginning of this chapter, describes today's hyperconnected world. The quotation is from Marshall McLuhan's great prophetic vision published in 1967. The most important change today in marketing is the interaction of globalization and information technology. This IT driven globalization is itself driving constant productivity gains where employers everywhere are increasing their competitiveness by replacing labor with computers, machines, and robots. Workers and companies everywhere must constantly improve their productivity and performance because today, as never before in human history, all markets are exposed to global competition.

For marketers, this explosion of connectivity presents unprecedented opportunities to identify customer needs and wants and to communicate and connect with customers. Marketing is the art and science of creating value: information is the key to the task of creating value. Information is the raw material that enables marketers to identify customer needs and wants, create products that will meet these needs and wants, and communicate value propositions with existing and potential customers.

Marketing and the Web: The End of Distance

Distance has been a variable of the greatest marketing significance. As the real estate maxim has it, the three rules of property valuation are location, location, location. In global marketing, strategies and practice reflected the importance of distance. The primary trading partners of every country have been proximate neighbors: for the United States they are Canada and Mexico, for Canada and Mexico it is the United States. For France it is Germany, and for Germany it is France, and so on around the world. There has always been a positive correlation between trade and proximity. However, the Internet is totally independent of distance. Electrons traveling at the speed of light get to anywhere in the world in the same time and at the same cost. If I send an e-mail, it does not make a difference in time or cost whether the mail is addressed to my wife in the next room of our house or to someone halfway around the world. The same thing is true of a website: the location of the site does not affect the cost or speed of access. For the first time in history, the world has become a level playing field. Anyone, anywhere in the world can communicate with anyone else in the world in real time with no premium charged for distance.

These long-standing historical patterns of trade are a reflection of the importance of physical distance in global marketing. The improvement of transportation and communications technologies has been a major driver pushing the world toward greater globalization. Costs have come down and service has improved steadily and dramatically since the end of World War II. The Internet and IT have been major new drivers of globalization since the beginning of the 1990s. A web presence is instantly global. The global reach of credit card issuers, package delivery services, and e-business tools

[1] United Nations General Assembly, "Our Common Future, Chapter 2: Towards Sustainable Development," transmitted to the General Assembly as an annex to document A/42/427, "Our Common Future:Report of the World Commission on Environment and Development," United Nations General Assembly, http://www.un-documents.net/ocf-02.htm, March 20, 1987.

of broadcast video, telephony, and the ever-expanding web has created a whole new level of possibilities for global retail and business-to-business marketing by even the smallest firms. For example, in pre-web marketing, larger brands had the scale to overwhelm smaller players for "share of voice" in the marketplace. However, with user-driven traffic across web platforms and performance-driven paid advertising, smaller brands and companies can engage customers and gain a positive return on their social marketing dollars since social traffic is driven by Twitter followers, Facebook fans, or a viral YouTube video—all of which must be earned as opposed to being purchased or scheduled. It may no longer be a sustainable strategy to just outspend competitors with advertising dollars.

Technological Convergence and Connecting to the Customer

The second Generation of Internet (Web 2.0) social media companies—Facebook, Twitter, Linked/In, SalesForce—have taken users by storm and are powerful platforms for just about everything a marketer touches, including product design, feedback and dialogue, segmenting and targeting audiences, building customer loyalty and relationship, and marketing program analytics. The analogy of "Marketing's Meeting of the Waters" is a good one.[2] Just as the natural phenomenon in South America, the junction of the Amazon River and its Rio Negro tributary, do not merge at their head but coexist for several miles before combing their flows, so too traditional media and newer digital marketing platforms and tools, including mobile, currently exist side by side along with their more traditional counterparts. Differences abound from both a marketer's perspective as well as the target user's experience.[3]

For example, consumers and marketers expect "immediacy, contextual and interactive relevance, and interactive engagement" in their use of digital media as opposed to traditional platforms.[4] In addition, engagement time frames differ between the old and new, as do analytics and metrics tools.[5] In light of the expectation for deep, personalized, and immediate customer engagement, marketing organizations have created new functions and processes to integrate marketing efforts across media, from online initiatives including social networks,[6] e-mail, display, search, and online video to television, print, and the mobile experience.

No longer is it necessary to just imagine understanding the consumer across media channels; predictive modeling exists which correlates customer attributes and interests into actionable insights. With these insights and new data management systems, multichannel marketing campaigns have the capacity to deliver the most effective message to the targeted audience down to an individual at the right time and through the most effective channel, all in real time.

To truly engage customers in a fast-paced marketplace where push advertising has long lost its luster, companies must move outside of their more comfortable, traditional marketing strategy and programming. The starting point requires an organization-wide change in focus—toward customer interaction touch points and away from

---

[2] Michael Becker, "Marketing's Meeting of the Waters." ClickZ newsletter, January 31, 2011, accessed February 1, 2011, http://www.clickz.com/clickz/column/1941484/marketings-meeting-waters.

[3] Ibid.

[4] Ibid.

[5] Ibid.

[6] "Social media are the blogs, wikis, forums, public networking sites, microblogging (Twitter) audio or video sharing sites where a community model is in play and user-generated content and connections are the primary currency." "Social media marketing is the business use of social media for engaging customers, building thought leadership, creating leads, and/or driving product innovation." Allen Bonde, SearchCRM.com, accessed December 1, 2009, http://searchcrm.techtarget.com/news/2240015659/Social-media-and-CRM-The-marketing-perspective.

thinking about the customer as being "owned" by a given operational function[7]: customer relationships may not be best optimized solely by the sales department; brands may not be best managed by the marketing department without strong ties to public relations, retail operations, or media planning; the merchandising experience across multimedia may not be best suited for retailing operations.

Marketing expertise in the off-line world of TV, radio, and print, where a controlled message is carefully crafted and pushed to paid media targeting specific demographics, may not be most applicable to online initiatives, where creating value is the basis for dialogue and relationship. Public relations specialists are experts at gaining media attention, quotes from authorities in the field, and creating media bites all to push news and information. Again, creating value and relevance must be integral to online initiatives targeting social media communities. Handling positive engagement and relationship building is the expertise of the customer service department. In addition, IT efforts are critical where website and viral effort applications must function smoothly.[8] To create a cross-functional team, Philips Consumer Electronics in the Netherlands includes sales, product design, HR, and customer care joining together to create an exceptional customer experience.[9]

Understanding how people interact with all touch points with the company is imperative to designing and implementing a customer-engagement strategy. Critical to this endeavor is the fact that importance is placed on customer knowledge through systematic data-gathering and analysis. Is the marketing department the most optimal choice to assume these responsibilities? Who should they report to? Perhaps marketing should report to the head of business strategy, who will use the information to make targeting, sales, communications, pricing, and production decisions—core business choices for going to market. These and other questions raise issues of organizational design and communication and information sharing, among others, across what are often siloed functions and independent centers of decision making.

One fact is certain: the web has put the customer in charge as never before. Until the web, buyers faced obstacles in obtaining the best pricing, service, and product benefits. Producers and retailers alike guarded information. In fact, the lack of an educated consumer was a profit center for many businesses with fixed pricing as the norm. Pricing on the web permits many dynamic pricing models—from auction sites to buyer cooperatives and barter relationships—and with the advent of bots or automated shopping agents, automatic purchasing gives consumers a pricing advantage. Spurring instantaneous connection, suppliers are connected to purchasers through middlemen or infomediaries, vertical portals, or e-markets.

When a purchaser's buying preferences are identified at a specific location, dynamic pricing models, for example, may increase the opportunity for a sale. So too with the overall customer experience. Many companies are experimenting with ways to offer a better customer experience using social tools not only at point of purchase, but throughout the purchase decision process. These may take the form of Facebook fan pages, mobile apps, customer live Q&A on products and product categories, and customer service accounts on Twitter. In fact, it has been postulated that customer experience may be the most important optimization in the arsenal of marketing and business objectives.[10]

---

[7] Tom French, Laura LaBerge, and Paul Magill, "We're All Marketers Now," *The McKinsey Quarterly*, (July 2011), accessed August 24, 2011, https://www.mckinseyquarterly.com/Were_all_marketers_now_2834.

[8] Liana Evans, "Who Owns Your Company's Social Media Strategy?," ClickZ online newsletter, December 22, 2010, accessed December 22, 2010, http://www.clickz.com.

[9] Robin Neifield, "Customer Experience—Your Most Important Optimization," ClickZ online newsletter, March 9, 2011, accessed March 21, 2011, http://www.clickz.com/clickz/column/2031848/customer-experience-optimization.

[10] Ibid.

In truth, the customer no longer separates marketing from the product or service—it is the product or experience. A new definition of digital is crucial to supporting marketing's efforts to address the user's experience.[11] Although digital has been used to describe various online technologies or used interchangeably with the word online, a broader definition of digital as encompassing "the collection of habits and expectations of modern users" moves marketing professionals away from a focus on technology or specific devices and toward what is important to the customer, namely, addressing online expectations and improving the customer experience.[12] By understanding and focusing on consumer expections as they merge with off-line behavior, global marketers will strategize toward initiatives that foster dialogue and relationship building to spur loyalty and community.

World Economic Growth and the Rise of the Rest

The world economy has undergone revolutionary changes during the past 60 years. Perhaps the most profound change is the great rebalancing of the global economy. The extraordinary rise of Europe and the European settlements in the Americas and Asia for the past 400 years is now being met by the rise of the rest.

Until the great recession of 2008, the entire world was experiencing sustained economic growth. This is especially true in Asia. In 1750, Asia had more than half the world's population and economic output. By 1900, Asia's share shrank to one-fifth of the global economic output. By 2040, it is likely that Asia will return to its historical, pre-Industrial Revolution share. The exception to this global trend has been Africa south of the Sahara (excluding South Africa) where many countries have been stagnant or in economic decline. The second exception are the high-income countries that have ignored the impact of the financial collapse on consumer demand and investment and adopted austerity policies that have reduced government spending and contributed to the collapse in aggregate demand. These countries, which include Great Britain, have experienced a decline in income since the collapse.

Another important trend is world peace. Steven Pinker, Professor of Psychology at Harvard University, makes the case that there has been a decline of violence in the world.[13] Professor Pinker points out that tribal warfare was nine times as deadly as war and genocide in the twentieth century, the murder rate in medieval Europe was more than 30 times what it is today, slavery and sadistic punishments were unexceptional features of life for millennia, and were then targeted for abolition. Wars between developed countries have ended, and even in the developing world, wars kill a small fraction of the numbers they did a few decades ago. Rape, hate crimes, child abuse, deadly riots, and cruelty to animals are all substantially down.

How could this have happened? Pinker provides support for his conclusions. He argues that the inner demons that incline us to violence and the better angels that steer us away from violence have found a new balance. For example, Germany, led by a madman, was bent on world conquest only 80 years ago. A defeated Germany, rising from the ashes of total war in 1945, is today the most successful country in the EU and the undisputed

---

[11] Augustine Fou, "A New Definition of Digital," ClickZ online newsletter, September 24, 2009, accessed September 29, 2009, http://www.clickz.com.

[12] Ibid. See also Augustine Fou, "Digital Is A Philosophy," ClickZ online newsletter, March 31, 2011, accessed March 31, 2011, http://www.clickz.com/clickz/column/2037953/digital-philosophy ".... where digital becomes a 'philosophy' and its principles and insights should weave through all advertising to the point that there is no longer a distinction between traditional and digital - it is all advertising, infused and informed with digital insights, rooted in and extracted from the actions of your target consumers."; and "Digital is the DNA of All Advertising," ClickZ online newsletter, April 29, 2010, accessed April 29, 2010, http://www.clickz.com/clickz/column/1717919/digital-dna-all-advertising.

[13] Steven Pinker, *The Better Angels of Our Nature: Why Violence Has Declined* (New York: Viking, The Penguin Group, 2011).

leader of Europe. What Germany failed to achieve by arms and conquest, it has gained by focusing on markets, local and global, and creating value. So, there is of course the possibility of violence, but so far, we are living in the most peaceable era in our species' existence, and part of the reason for this happy development is global marketing!

The world economy is the dominant economic unit. The macroeconomics of the nation-state no longer control economic outcomes in countries, and even the large superpower countries such as the United States can no longer dictate to poorer countries how they should behave on the global stage. The cost of resources is determined in the global market: prices are determined by global supply and demand. With the rise of the rest, competition for resources is global and markets are global. Competition in markets is global as is competition for talent.

Today, more than ever before, there are global segment opportunities. In category after category, global efforts succeed. For example, the soft-drink industry was one of the first to successfully reach a global cola market segment and has now moved to address the fast-growing fruit-and-flavor segment. There are global segments for luxury cars, wine and spirits, every type of medical and industrial product, teenagers, senior citizens, and enthusiasts of every stripe and type, from scuba divers to snowboarders.

Global markets will grow at rates that were once thought impossible. The engine behind this accelerating growth is the high rate of growth in the emerging markets and the continued growth in high-income countries. Low- and lower-middle-income country growth leadership has been concentrated in Southeast Asia and southern Asia with China, India, and most recently Indonesia as high-growth, large countries, and Singapore, Taiwan, and South Korea at the vanguard of the smaller population high-income countries in the region. There is impressive growth in Latin America, Africa, and the Middle East. The driving forces of this growth are technology and technology transfer, education, investment, deregulation, global integration, and the triumph of marketing.

Most of the world's poor countries are getting richer. In the coming decade, the emerging countries of the world will contribute more to world growth than the developed countries. The emergence of the newly rich countries from among the ranks of the formerly less developed group breaks the long monopoly of Western Europe, North America, Australia, New Zealand, and Japan on the rich-nation status. These countries are proving that it is not necessary to be European, North American (north of the Rio Grande), or Japanese to be rich. Countries such as Singapore and Hong Kong are already high-income countries; eastern Asia in particular is home to many countries that have been growing at annual rates of 7 percent or higher. A 7 percent real growth rate will double real income in a decade. The emerging rich countries include smaller countries such as South Korea as well as the largest countries in the world, China and India, which have growing middle classes which demand goods and services from global companies. Global leaders in marketing strategy and tactics have manufacturing, product design, and marketing programming in place to meet these growing consumer segments. In fact, many of these new middle-class consumers are part of the new global customer. They have begun to look demographically more like each other across countries and regions than their own culturally unique counterparts.

It has become fashionable to compare the power of the United States to that of Britain a century ago and to predict a similar hegemonic decline. This analogy is quite misleading. It is true that Britain had global naval supremacy prior to World War I, but by World War II the country ranked fourth in its share of great power military personnel, fourth in GDP, and third in military spending as it faced rising neighbors Germany and Russia. The United States ranks first in all categories of military power, first in GDP, and it issues the world's reserve currency which allows it to borrow on exceptionally favorable terms. When you take into account immigration, higher education, the entrepreneurial culture, the many growth sectors where the United States leads, investment in R&D, the civil culture which ranks above the 90th percentile in the control of corruption, in the opinion of a leading power theorist, "the United States is not in absolute decline, and in relative terms, there is a reasonable probability that it will remain more powerful than any other state in the coming decades."[14]

The growth in the emerging markets includes Africa, where growth is especially strong in North Africa and South Africa. In Africa south of the Sahara, excluding South Africa, economic progress has been held back by corrupt, incompetent leadership and widespread ignorance, poverty, and disease. Nevertheless, for the first time in the history of the world, there is the very real likelihood of a much broader global prosperity in this region of the world in the first half of this century.

Population Changes

Twelve thousand years ago, before the invention of agriculture, there were perhaps 1 million people in the world. It took 8,000 years to grow from 3 million to 226 million by the year 1 AD. It took 1,800 years to grow to 1 billion. This increase in population was forecast by Malthus over two centuries ago. The seventh billion was reached in 2011.

We are now adding 1 billion people every 12 years and are on track to reach between 7.5 and 10.5 billion by 2050. In the preindustrial era, famine, wars, poverty, and the absence of all of the benefits of modern medicine kept death rates high, largely offsetting high birthrates. The death rate fell as governments improved sanitation and water supplies, disease control and medical science discovered vaccines that protected populations from infectious diseases, and medicines and procedures effectively treated disease and illness. Mechanized agriculture vastly expanded food production.

World population has experienced continuous growth since the end of the Bubonic Plague around the years 1348–1350. The highest rates of growth—increases above 1.8 percent per year—were seen briefly during the 1950s and for a longer period during the 1960s and 1970s; the growth rate peaked at 2.2 percent in 1963, and declined to 1.1 percent by 2009. Annual births have reduced to 140 million since their peak at 173 million in the late 1990s, and are expected to remain constant, while deaths number 57 million per year and are expected to increase to 80 million per year by 2040. Current projections show a continued increase of population (but a steady decline in the population growth rate) with the population expected to reach between 7.5 and 10.5 billion in the year 2050.[15]

The population within the developed economies of the world is continuing to gray (see Figure 15-1). The change from 1995 to the year 2050 will be quite dramatic. In 1995, nine countries had between 14 and 17.5 percent of their populations over the age of 65. In 2050, in six countries (Spain, Hong Kong, Italy, Greece, Japan, and Germany), 30 percent or more of their populations will be over the age of 65.

What impact will this graying shift have on marketing? Certainly, it will impact medical markets, but not all opportunities will be in medicines and adult diapers. Older populations are living more active, healthier lives and will be a major market for goods and services across a broad spectrum of consumer products.

Hand in hand with aging populations, the birthrate in the high-income countries is collapsing. In Japan and many European countries, the number of births has dropped to below population equilibrium level. The combination of low birthrates and wealth will drive a continuation of the global economic migration of people from poor, undeveloped countries to the rich, developed countries.

---

[14] J. S. Nye, "The Future of American Power," *Foreign Affairs,* 89, no. 6 (2010).

[15] http://en.wikipedia.org/wiki/World_population

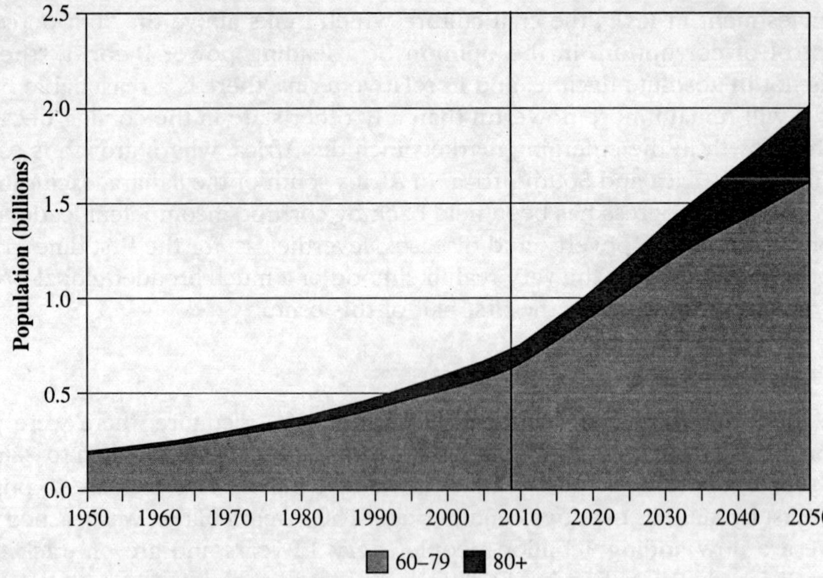

FIGURE 15-1 Projected Acceleration of World Population Aging to 2050
Source: United Nations 2009 World Population Ageing, http://www.un.org/esa/population/publications/WPA2009/WPA2009_WorkingPaper.pdf

In the industrial world, college education and increased women in the workplace have reduced birthrates to the point where population is steady or declining. The exception is the United States, which continues to have a large immigrant population. The demographic transition in the Western world to a declining population occurred between 1750 and 1950. But in the developing world, this demographic transition did not begin until the early 1900s with the introduction of modern medicines. Fertility rates have not dropped as quickly as they did in the Western world. Because these populations are so large, the world census will continue to expand until equilibrium is reached.

What this means is that there will be a dramatic change in the ranking of countries by population. The largest countries are India and China, with India growing faster. India will have over 1.6 billion people by 2050. The United States will still be the third largest country with higher birthrate immigration than the other high-income countries. The breakdown of population by area in 2050 is projected to be: Asia – 59%, Africa – 20%, South America – 9%, Europe – 7%, America – 4%.

Africa has by far the highest annualized growth. The United States is also growing quickly. But China, because of its one-child policy, has very slow growth. Europe and Japan have declining populations.

In 2008, the number of people living in urban areas surpassed those in rural areas. City dwellers are projected to double by 2050, from 3.3 billion in 2007 to 6.4 billion. Cities in the developing world are growing by about 3 million per week. Asia is only 40 percent urban today. By 2050, it will be 70 percent urban. About 38 percent of Africans live in cities today. By 2050, more than half will.

What kind of cities will they be? Good leadership can produce metropolitan areas like Singapore, whose growth and success has been phenomenal. The population of Singapore today is 5 million people. It is a thriving location for services, technology, and finances. It has no oil, yet it has become a major oil refining and distribution center. It is a global supplier of electrical components and sectors such as pharmaceuticals, medicine, and biotechnology are growing. Its 2008 GDP of $192 billion is larger than that of the Philippines, Pakistan, or Egypt.

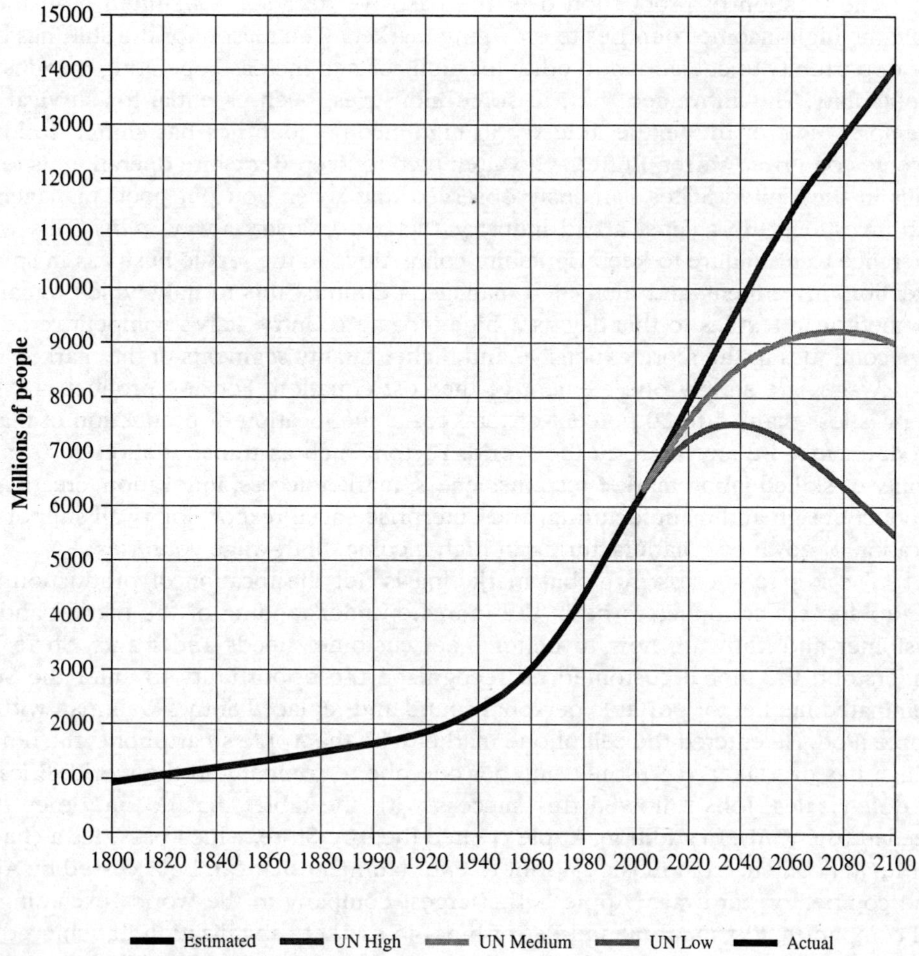

FIGURE 15-2 World Population 1800 to 2100

Contrast this with Lagos, Nigeria. Its population grew 50 percent from 2000 to 2010—from 7.2 million to 10.6 million. Unlike Singapore, Lagos is overcrowded with traffic jams, squalor, corruption, murder, and disease its hallmarks. Over the past 20 years, the city has lost much of its street lighting. There is no regular refuse collection and the road system is extremely congested. The city's sewer system is virtually nonexistent; there is inadequate safe drinking water, and half the city's dwellings suffer from routine flooding. Much of the rest of sub-Saharan Africa (excluding South Africa) is similarly run down. Unless new leadership emerges, much of this region will continue to be dilapidated, crowded, and dangerous.

Trade-Cycle Model Clarified

The trade-cycle model describes the behavior of several generations of managers in some high-income countries, including most notably the United States, who concluded that as a product matures, the location of production must shift to low-wage countries. This was never a viable strategy for sustainable competitive advantage. It provides a short-term, one-time advantage for companies who avoid the need to innovate to remain competitive. It has been a very costly practice for high-income countries; when firms across industries started shifting production, the results were a general erosion of the economy. At that time, the short-term interests of companies and the country diverged.

The location of production over the past five decades has shifted dramatically from the high-income countries to emerging markets. The reason for the shift has been the opportunity to cut labor and other location costs to increase operating margins and profitability. This movement has, in some industries, been essential for survival. For example, most of the textile industry in high-income countries has shifted to lower-income countries. Warren Buffet, who attempted to keep Berkshire operating its textile mills in the United States, famously observed that when you put good management and investment up against a bad industry, the bad industry always wins. This was a reference to his failure to keep Berkshire competitive in the textile business in spite of attention, investment, and motivated managers. Contrast this to Italy which remains a competitor in textiles to this day as a high-income country. Italy's competitive advantage continues in the more expensive and higher quality segments of the market.

Wages are simply one element of the cost equation. For any product in which labor is less than 15 to 20 percent of total costs, the location of production of mature products may be anywhere in the world. Factors such as transportation costs, availability of skilled labor, market responsiveness, market access, innovation, creativity in product design and manufacturing, and enterprise social responsibility all support the location of advanced manufacturing in high-income, high-wage countries.

The key to success in global marketing is not the location of production. The key to success continues to be in the intimate understanding of the market and the customer and knowing how to better meet customer needs and wants. Steve Jobs understood the global customer: he recognized the opportunity to enter the Sony-dominated market for portable personal sound and replaced Sony's Walkman with the Apple iPod. He entered the cell phone market with the Apple smartphone, the iPhone, which has overtaken the former number one phone company in the world, Ericsson, in dollar sales. Jobs followed this success with the tablet that no one knew they needed (the iPad). In addition, Apple created the App Store, which provides a channel for digital content from music to print to entertainment that can be accessed by Apple and competitor hardware. Apple is the largest company in the world (excluding the oil companies, Exxon Mobil and PetroChina) in market capitalization. It achieved this extraordinary position by combining insight into markets with the ability to innovate in the design and manufacture of great products to meet growing market needs.

Product maturity is a stage of the product life cycle that must be understood in a dynamic world. Automobiles today continue to be designed, manufactured, and assembled in high-income countries (Japan, Germany, France, and the United States, for example) by companies that hold and maintain strong competitive positions in global markets. The automobile is a mature product in the sense that growth has leveled in all of the high-income countries of the world. Does this mean that it is standardized? Far from it, the automobile is a highly differentiated, incredibly complicated, increasingly sophisticated, high-value product, and the way cars are designed and manufactured has been revolutionized. The result is that automobiles continue to be designed, manufactured, and assembled in high-income countries. The reason is simple: Labor is a factor in the production cost of an automobile, but as a percentage of total cost, it is not high enough to determine the location of all automobile production. In the 1980s, Swiss banks concluded that Switzerland was finished in the low end of the watch business. One man, Nicolas Hayek, disagreed. He formed the company Swatch and demonstrated that in spite of the high-wage costs in Switzerland, the country could compete in world watch markets not only in the luxury watch segment but also in the low-priced segment of fashion accessory watches. The Swiss understand the watch business, and they have been creative innovators in the design, manufacturing, and marketing of watches. All luxury watches, which account for a small percentage of volume in units but more than half of the value of world watch production, are made in Europe, and over 95 percent of European luxury watch production is in Switzerland.

In the meantime, there are mature products that have become relatively standardized in their manufacture and continue to require a relatively high percentage cost of labor to produce. These products today are made almost exclusively in lower-income countries. A good example of a product in this mature category is athletic footwear. The entire industry has shifted its production to low-income countries, and no company has been able to reverse this trend.

Shared Value: The Big New Idea in Marketing

Shared value is a big new idea for many global marketers, and a very old and accepted idea for others. The capitalist system in many countries is failing to meet the needs of society. In other countries, it is alive and well. This is good news: the companies and countries that understand and practice the application of this concept have proven that it works in today's global economy.

Companies that are not committed to shared value are trapped in an outdated and obsolete approach to value creation. These companies view value creation as something that happens in a bubble that includes only top management and shareholders. In this view, whatever is good for the bottom line is good for society. This view is justification for overlooking the well-being of employees, customers, and suppliers and the economic collapse of entire communities. It is this view that leads companies to the myopic conclusion that shifting activities to locations with lower wages is a sustainable solution to competitive challenges when it is, in reality, a short-term move that does nothing to create sustainable competitive advantage. Ignoring the concept of shared value enriches management and shareholders at the expense of society. Chapter 15 on corporate social responsibility and environmental responsibility explores this concept further.

THE Cs OF MARKETING: THREE TIMES FOUR = TWELVE

Marketers have long relied upon the three Cs as mnemonic for remembering that marketing is about Customers, Competitors, and Company. Without customers there is no market. Reaching a market successfully requires that the company develops a sustainable competitive advantage if it wishes to survive, let alone succeed and prosper. Hermawan Kartajaya, the former President of the World Marketing Federation and brilliant Indonesian marketing guru, offered his 18 guiding principles of marketing in the appendix to Chapter 1. Mr. Kartajaya shares his twelve Cs with readers of this edition, which you will find in the appendix, "The Twelve Cs of New Wave Marketing" which you will find in the appendix at the end of this chapter, "The Twelve C's of New Wave Marketing."

Sustainability

We are living in a new era. From dams impounding sediment by the gigaton, atmospheric emissions by the billions of tons, melting glaciers, rising temperatures and sea levels, stripping forests and other native habitats, increasing carbon emissions, humans are bringing about planetary change and destruction. Many scientists have concluded that we are no longer living in the Holocene but some other age, one shaped primarily by people. In 2000, Paul Crutzen, a distinguished atmospheric chemist, with colleague Eugene Stoermer suggested that this age be called the Anthropocene, "the recent age of man." The vast majority of ecosystems on the planet today reflect the presence of people. There are, for example, more trees on farms than in natural forests, and wild fish from the ocean, lakes, and streams are being replaced with farm-raised fish.

Sustainability is a response to the new Anthropocene era of man and is closely linked to shared value, the value equation, and the strategic concept of marketing. The Brundtland Commission definition "sustainable development is development that meets the needs of the present without compromising the ability of future generations to meet their own needs"[16] addresses the impact of production, consumption, and disposal/by-products on future generations. Consumption of products that are manufactured with renewable, safely recyclable resources that do not impact the earth's environment is sustainable because the resources consumed by production and consumption are replaced in a virtuous sustainable production/consumption/zero-impact cycle.

Paul Gilding, former director of Greenpeace International and now on the faculty at Cambridge University's Program for Sustainable Leadership, proposes that global warming is just one piece of an impending planetary collapse caused by our overuse of resources. According to the Global Footprint Network, we surpassed Earth's capacity in 1988, and by 2009, we needed the resources of 1.4 planets to sustain our economy; any increases in efficiencies that some claim will solve the problem are likely only to encourage humans to use more. Gilding argues that, like addicts who need to hit bottom, we, as energy users, will deny our problem until we "face head-on the risk of collapse." Gilding's confidence in our ability to transform disaster into a "happiness economy" may astonish many, but his proposal provides a refreshing, provocative alternative to the recent spate of gloom-and-doom climate-change studies.[17]

Gilding maintains that the real solution is changing world economies from spiraling growth to a steady state. The goal is to upgrade goods and services to meet needs, not to pump up a gross national product that takes no account of quality of life. He joins similar views in books such as Thomas L. Friedman's *Hot, Flat, and Crowded.*[18]

The concept of sustainability also applies to individual consumption. For example, consumption of food is a benefit up to a point, and can be harmful when it is excessive. Overeating leads to obesity which is a major health problem and cost to both the individual and society. As the AMA marketing code of ethics specifies, marketing conduct should "do no harm." Like unsustainable eating, unsustainable consumer spending will harm the health and standard of living of consumers across the globe. Marketers who are encouraging consumers to eat too much are practicing unsustainable marketing; if they are encouraging consumers to borrow too much, this is unsustainable lending.

The recent and ongoing housing bubble in many high-income countries was a joint marketing effort enabled by captive governments[19] who deregulated the financial industry. This industry proceeded to market unsustainable loans to borrowers which were securitized and sold to institutional buyers who had no idea of what they were buying.[20] Although the banks made enormous profits on the loans and the securitized loan products, because they were unsustainable, they brought grief to borrowers who lost their homes, to taxpayers who footed the bill for a bailout of the financial industry, and to citizens who lost their jobs as a result of the bubble-induced economic collapse. The only winner was the financial industry itself who was deemed "too big to fail." The industry not only survived the economic crisis which they created, it has ended up more concentrated and powerful than it was before the crisis. The securitized loans did not create shared value; in fact, they created phantom value and phantom gains *financed by US taxpayers*.

---

[16] United Nations General Assembly (March 20, 1987).

[17] Paul Gilding, *The Great Disruption: Why the Climate Crisis Will Bring On the End of Shopping and the Birth of a New World* (Bloomsbury Press, 2011).

[18] Thomas L. Friedman, *Hot, Flat, and Crowded: Why We Need a Green Revolution—and How It Can Renew America* (New York: Picador/Farrar, Straus and Giroux, 2009).

[19] A captive government is one which has been taken over by the interests and companies which governments should oversee and regulate in the public interest.

[20] Securitization is the financial practice of pooling various types of contractual debt such as residential mortgages, commercial mortgages, auto loans, or credit card debt obligations and selling said debt as bonds, pass-through securities such as collateralized mortgage obligations (CMOs), to various investors.

CAREERS IN GLOBAL MARKETING

There has never been a better time to prepare for a career in global marketing. Now that you have completed this book, the author would like to offer a few suggestions on how to jump-start your global marketing career.

First, remember, times have changed. Until very recently, one sure way to put your career at risk in many companies (especially US companies) was to go overseas. There was nothing wrong with being overseas per se, but the problem for careers was that ethnocentric management did not recognize the value of global experience and turned to executives who were close at hand when making promotions. "Out of sight, out of mind" seemed to be the operative phrase.

Today, this has changed dramatically. Global experience counts. Only the truly clueless do not recognize that we are in a global market with global competition; those with global experience have a definite advantage. Ray Viault is a good example of how to jump-start your career. Viault was a vice president of General Foods in charge of the Maxwell House coffee division. When Philip Morris acquired General Foods, it kept Viault on as president of the Maxwell House division. Later, when Philip Morris acquired Jacob Suchard, the Zurich-based chocolate and coffee company, it chose Viault as the new CEO of the acquired company. Viault was able to take his grounding (no pun intended) in the US coffee market to the European and global chocolate market and did an outstanding job of leading the global marketing effort of Jacob Suchard. Following this assignment, Viault returned to the United States to become a vice chairman of General Mills.

How do you establish a career in global marketing? There is one path with three branches:

1. Get experience with a company in an industry that prepares you for promotion to a job assignment outside your home country. In your ROW assignment, you will continue to learn more about your company and its industry, and you will gain experience in global managing and marketing. There is no substitute for solid experience in a company in an industry. Your best opportunity to get solid experience may be in your home country. You speak the language, understand the culture, and are trained in business and marketing. You are ready to learn.
2. Get a job with a company located outside of your home country. If you complete your studies in your home country, you can look for a job abroad. This will present you with a double challenge: you have no company or industry experience, and you have no experience in managing and marketing in the foreign country.
3. If you are an international student, you may choose to work in the country where you completed your studies. Your first job will give you an opportunity to learn about a company and an industry, and will also expose you to business practice in the country where you studied. Your educational experience has included exposure to the language and culture of the country where you studied, giving you valuable social and cultural experience that will enable you to be effective in a job assignment.

For many, the first choice is better than the second. For international students, the second alternative may be the best choice.

Summary

The future of global marketing will reflect seven major changes that will shape and create new directions, opportunities, and threats. All world regions will continue to grow, and world wealth will become more evenly distributed. Marketing is at the threshold of a new and exciting era: e-business, e-commerce, and e-marketing. For the first time in history, marketers have the tools to address the needs of the individual customer.

The trade cycle has not eliminated manufacturing as a source of employment and income in the high-income countries. By investing in capital equipment and by designing products for manufacturability, rich countries have proven that they can continue to successfully compete as manufacturing locations.

Global markets will continue to grow in importance as global marketers continue their quest to identify and serve global segments. This growth will enhance and expand the value of global experience for managers and executives worldwide.

There are two big new developments in marketing. The first is the concept of shared value: recognizing that companies do more than create value for customers and stockholders. Companies have stakeholders that include not only customers and stockholders and employees of the company, but also the local and global society and the environment. The concept of shared value is understood and practiced in many countries and is forgotten, unknown, or denied in others. The other big new development is sustainability: the challenge of sustainability will be a major driver of innovation and value creation and, if it is fully embraced, will ensure that future generations of consumers and marketers will enjoy fuller and richer lives.

Discussion Questions

1. Do you believe that economic democracy (free markets) will inevitably lead to political democracy? Why? Why not?
2. Why did free markets and marketing win in the competition with communism?
3. Is the trade cycle relevant to companies today? Why? Why not?
4. How have technological convergence, the Internet, and customer expectations changed the task of the global marketer? Are marketing tools and concepts discussed throughout this text relevant to the digital marketplace? If so, how? If not, why not?
5. The acceleration of population growth and aging of the world population will have an impact on marketing practices. How will these trends impact product and pricing decisions, integrated marketing communications, or other areas?
6. Are sustainability initiatives applicable to marketing? If so, how? If not, why not? What would the practice of marketing look like from a perspective where shared value is a top priority?
7. Discuss with your classroom peers where they have been residing and working. What have been their experiences with living, working, or studying in a country where they had to learn the language, the culture, and applicable industry standards? What did they find rewarding about these experiences? How have these experiences shaped their understanding of global marketing and global marketing practices?
8. Hermawan Kartajaya has outlined the Twelve Cs of New Wave Marketing in the appendix to this chapter. In your view, which are the most important Cs on his list? Why are the Cs you selected especially important?

Suggested Readings

Chouinard, Yvon, Jib Ellison, and Rick Ridgeway. "The Big Idea: The Sustainable Economy." *Harvard Business Review* (October 2011): 52–62.

Collins, James C., and Jerry I. Porras. "Building a Visionary Company." *California Management Review,* 37, no. 2 (Winter 1995): 80–100.

Comstock, Beth, Ranjay Gulati, and Stephen Liguori. "Unleashing the Power of Marketing." *Harvard Business Review* (October 2010): 90–98.

Doyle, Peter. "Marketing in the New Millennium." *European Journal of Marketing,* 29, no. 13 (1995): 23–41.

Drucker, Peter. *Management Challenges for the 21st Century.* New York: HarperBusiness, 1999.

Eyring, Matthew J., Mark W. Johnson, and Hari Nair. "New Business Models in Emerging Markets." *Harvard Business Review* (January–February 2011): 88–95.

Evans, Philip, and Thomas S. Wurster. *Blown To Bits: How the New Economics of Information Transforms Strategy.* Boston: The Boston Consulting Group and the Harvard Business School Press, 2000.

Ferguson, Niall. *Civilization: The West and the Rest.* New York: The Penguin Press, 2011.

Friedman, George, The Next Decade: Where We Have Been… And Where We Are Going. New York: Doubleday, 2011.

Israel, Shel. *Twitterville: How Businesses Can Thrive in the New Global Neighborhoods.* New York: Penguin Group, Inc., 2009.

Israel, Shel, and Robert Scoble. *Naked Conversations: How Blogs are Changing the Way Businesses Talk With Customers.* Hoboken, NJ: John Wiley & Sons, Inc. 2006.

Johnson, Simon, and James Kwak. *13 Bankers: The Wall Street Takeover and the Next Financial Meltdown.* New York: Pantheon Books, 2010.

Kanter, Rosabeth Moss. *Evolve!: Succeeding in the Digital Culture of Tomorrow.* Boston: Harvard Business School Press, 2001.

Kanter, Rosabeth Moss. "How Great Companies Think Differently." *Harvard Business Review* (November 2011): 66–78.

Kelly, Kevin. *What Technology Wants.* New York: Viking, Published by the Penguin Group, 2010.

Kotler, Philip, Hermawan Kartajaya, and Iwan Setiawan. *Marketing 3.0: From Products to Customers to the Human Spirit.* Hoboken, NJ: John Wiley & Sons, 2010.

Krugman, Paul. "Competitiveness: A Dangerous Obsession." *Foreign Affairs,* 73, no. 2 (March/April 1994).

Lewis, Michael. *Boomerang: Travels in the New Third World.* New York: W.W. Norton & Company, 2011.

McRae, Hamish. *The World in 2020: Power, Culture, and Prosperity.* Boston: Harvard Business School Press, 1994.

Meyer, Christopher, and Julia Kirby. "Run Away Capitalism." *Harvard Business Review* (January–February 2012): 66–75.

Morris, Ian. *Why the West Rules—For Now: The Patterns of History and What They Reveal About the Future.* New York: Farrar, Straus and Giroux, 2010.

Nye, Joseph S. "The Future of American Power." *Foreign Affairs,* 89, no. 6 (2010).

Pinker, Steven. *The Better Angels of Our Nature: Why Violence Has Declined.* New York: Viking: The Penguin Group, 2011.

Porter, Michael E., and Mark R. Kramer. "Creating Shared Value." *Harvard Business Review* (January–February 2011): 62–77.

Salzman, Marian, and Ira Matathia. *Next Now: Trends for the Future.* New York: Palgrave Macmillan, 2006.

Stevenson, H. H., and J. L. Cruikshank. *Do Lunch or Be Lunch: The Power of Predictability in Creating Your Future.* Boston: Harvard Business School Press, 1997.

Stiglitz, Joseph E. *Freefall: America, Free Markets, and the Sinking of the World Economy.* New York: W.W. Norton & Co., 2010.

Werbach, Kevin, and Dan Hunter. *How Game Thinking Can Revolutionize Your Business.* Philadephia, PA: Wharton Digital Press, 2012; and "'For the Win': How Gamification Can Transform Your Business." *Knowledge@Wharton*, an online business journal of Wharton Business School (December 6, 2012). Accessed December 11, 2012. http://knowledge.wharton.upenn.edu/article.cfm?articleid=3119.

Yergin, Daniel, and Thane Gustafson. *Russia 2010 and What It Means for the World.* New York: Vintage Books, 1995.

APPENDIX

The Twelve Cs of New Wave Marketing

HERMAWAN KARTAJAYA[21]

INTRODUCTION

Kenichi Ohmae, in *The Mind of the Strategist,* introduced three Cs essential in formulating strategy:[22] *Customer, Competitor,* and *Company.* Phillip Kotler and John A. Caslione, in their book *Chaotics,* build on Ohmae's original construct to include a fourth C—that of the *Change Agent.* They highlight that as information becomes more accessible and often free and markets more open, changes in the competitive marketplace become harder to predict and the roles and interplay between and among the four Cs become increasingly unclear.[23] As a result of rapid marketplace change, it is imperative for companies to be in sync with each important C. We've introduced a fifth C, *Connectors,* into the strategic equation in Chapter 16. Connections or Connectors, as we term the fifth C, enable a company to be socially connected to this rapidly changing marketplace. To highlight the importance of connections, Johan Bergendahl, the CMO of Ericsson, has said, "Without connectivity, societies stop working. Without connectivity, companies cannot do business. Without connectivity, people cannot communicate. So, without connectivity, the world

[21] Hermawan Kartajaya is founder and Chief Service Officer of MarkPlus, a leading Southeast Asia marketing and strategy consulting firm, and former president of World Marketing Association. In 2003, he was named by the United Kingdom Chartered Institute of Marketing as one of the "50 Gurus Who Have Shaped the Future of Marketing."

[22] Kenichi Ohmae, *The Mind of the Strategist: The Art of Japanese Business* (New York: McGraw-Hill, 1991).

[23] Philip Kotler and John A. Caslione, *Chaotics: The Business of Managing and Marketing in the Age of Turbulence* (New York: AMACOM, 2009).

stops."[24] Figure 15A-1 shows the traditional four "C's" and "Connector", the fifth "C"."

There are three levels of connectors: mobile connectors, experiential connectors, and social connectors. All three exist simultaneously in the off- and online world. Connectors allow global marketers to have deep connection and strong connectivity to important constituencies, including critical partners and present and future customers.

Companies should realize that online media creates excitement and informs. To deliver and build customer intimacy, relationship, and trust, a company needs to combine mobile, experiential, and social connectors. A *mobile connector* must be easy to use and accessible everywhere the customer is. US President Barack Obama used these tools effectively in his 2008 election campaign.

The second level connector is the *experiential connector,* a live experience, activity, or series of activities in multiple places and times which allow a company to connect its brand with targeted customers everywhere. Ever since the iPhone was first introduced in Macworld 2007, Apple has continued its ability to create new product launch buzz with a series of experiential connector activities, outreach, draw, and messaging to create vast word-of-mouth, curiosity, and excitement surrounding new product launches with its key spokesperson—former CEO Steve Jobs. During the launch of the new iPhone 3G and 4S, it was no surprise that buyers were—again—willing to wait for hours in front of any number of Apple Stores in order to experience and indulge in Apple's newest offering.

Social networking and social media sites provide important online support to this community of users and early purchasers/adopters. The third level connector, *social connector,* is typified by social networking sites such as Twitter and Facebook, which enjoy one-to-many social promotion from their loyal users.

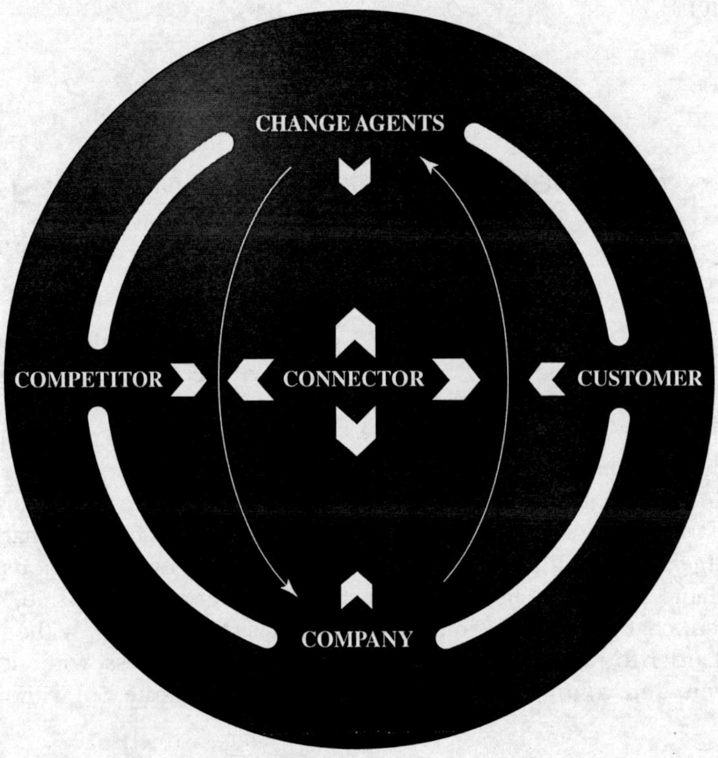

FIGURE 15A-1 The Four "C's" and "Connectors" as the Fifth "C"

[24] http://www1.ericsson.com/thinkingahead/idea/without_connectivity_societies_stop_782268019_c

With the proliferation and importance of Connectors, the fifth C, the 12 marketing practices will continue their shift from vertical and hierarchical to horizontal, flat, and integrated—all key elements of New Wave Marketing.

1. **From Segmentation to Communitization.** Traditionally, *segmentation* has been a vertical practice wholly within the realm of the company and its marketing department. Segmentation, as traditionally practiced, arises not out of relationship with customers or two-way dialogue but out of unilateral decisions based on traditional marketing research where customers are grouped according to a defined and meaningful—from the company's perspective—set of characteristics. In New Wave Marketing, companies are connected with customers and their communities. These communities are defined by the participants themselves. Communitization is the forum where meaningful and value-based relationships are built. Here, horizontal relationship and dialogue replaces more vertical or hierarchical practices where the firm dictates the 4 Ps—product, pricing, place, and promotion. Communitization fosters collaboration and insight both on the part of the company and individual consumer.
2. **From Targeting to Confirmation.** Traditional marketing practices often target customers by selecting the fastest growing and most profitable market segments. In this new connected marketspace, customers often reject being the target of unilateral marketing programming and consider the company's communication and messaging as an act of spamming and intrusion. For this reason, companies must shift to asking for a customer's permission to be a target of communications. It is the customer who decides if he or she wants to accept and Confirm the company's offer. *Confirmation* is the entry point to building relationship with the customer on the customer's terms.
3. **From Positioning to Clarification.** Since the 1980s, the concept and practice of positioning has been recognized as a battle for customer mind share. With the emergence of the New Wave landscape facilitated by new information and communication technologies, online media, mobility, digital tools, and social networking platforms, customers are able to assess and clarify the positioning promise. Companies can no longer lay unverifiable claim to their product and service positioning in marketspace. Companies can seek, through relationship and dialogue, to clarify, by consumer consensus, the positioning of the company's brand, product, or service.

   Marketing companies can position themselves as anything, but unless there is essentially a community-driven consensus, the positioning is no more than corporate, unilateral posturing. As highlighted by Larry Light, McDonald's Chief Global Marketing Officer, "Identifying one's brand position, communicating it in a repetitive manner is old-fashioned, out of date, out of touch...the end of brand positioning as we know it."
4. **From Differentiation to Codification.** Product or brand differentiation is created, defined, and shaped by companies; many customers resist the designated differentiation of an offering because they know it is not original. Therefore, differentiation must be authentic. Through the process of *codifying*—the end result of being in relationship and dialogue with customers and their communities—companies discover an authentic or original differentiation defined in the social sphere.
5. **From Product to Co-Creation.** Traditionally, companies control all product decisions from conception through design and production. Although customers may anticipate the introduction of a new product or an extension of an existing product, they are passive recipients of a finished product. There are many examples of failed products that have not met consumers' needs or wants. In light of these failures, *co-creation* can be highly beneficial for companies. Through a process of co-creation, companies are able to obtain maximum value in product conception and design by involving customers in co-creating the product platform the customers want. Afterward, companies participate with customers in their selection of how to customize the product platform, creating additional value from R&D, product extensions, or adaptations.

   "The value co-creation process involves the supplier creating superior value propositions, with customers determining value when a good or service is consumed. Superior value propositions, that are relevant to the supplier's target customers, should result in greater opportunities for co-creation and result in benefits (or 'value') being received by the supplier by way of revenues, profits, referrals, etc."[25]

6. **From Price to Currency.** *Price* is traditionally vertically set by the company; whereas in New Wave Marketing, *currency exchange* depends on value. Through consumption, customers and companies meet and define the range of the true market value of the product.

   With the proliferation of Connectors, the fifth C, the dynamics of price and cost are transparent; consumers are privy to pricing across markets and purchase venues whether on or off-line.

7. **From Place to Communal Activation.** In traditional marketing, companies develop channels and initiate flow of product, messaging, and information to customers. Through *communal activation,* community members seek access to and help to define the relevance of the product offering and contribute to its messaging, building shared experience. "Communal activation is the process whereby environmental or interpersonal circumstances activate communal thoughts or motives."[26] It is through dialogue and shared experience that social currency around the offering is built.

8. **From Promotion to Conversation.** With traditional *promotion* tactics, companies send one-way messages to present and future customers as their target audience. The result is a vertical one-to-many approach to marketing with companies broadcasting their message to the masses. In New Wave Marketing, companies develop *permission-based* marketing before effecting messaging to their audience. Seeking and receiving permission creates the context for company and customer interaction from which relationship can be developed through multi-way communication.

   This two-way *conversation* creates new opportunities for organizations to understand consumers and connect with them in a way never before possible for relatively low cost per interaction. It also allows customers to be direct influencers of consumptive choices.

9. **From Selling to Commercialization.** With *selling,* customers are objects, passive recipients of the selling proposition and persuasive tactics. In *commercialization,* the idea is to have both sides seek and obtain commercial or personal value. The objective is that companies engage with current and prospective customers as active participants in a transparent transaction of equivalent value.

10. **From Brand to Character.** Companies must realize that a brand is more than a name. A brand has a brand identity promoted through its positioning in the marketspace. This positioning is a promise (*the brand promise*) meant to create a certain perception in the customer's mind. In order for a company to exhibit true *brand integrity,* it must support this brand promise with a solid and concrete product differentiation through its marketing mix elements.

    In New Wave Marketing, branding goes beyond unilateral positioning to include the social branding of the offering or its publicly derived and supported *brand character.*

11. **From Service to Care.** In traditional service, often the measure of a company's success is through repeat visitation on the company's terms. Shifting to the *Care* approach, companies view customers as equals; instead of serving customers, a company demonstrates its genuine concern for and of the customer by listening, responding, and consistent follow-through, on terms often dictated by the customer. Care implies an ability to walk in someone else's shoes; as with individuals, "companies prosper when they tap into a power that every one of us already has—the ability to reach outside of ourselves and connect with other people."[27]

12. **From Process to Collaboration.** Process is usually developed and monitored internally by companies, which is in stark contrast to *Collaboration.* Collaboration exists when companies invite customers to take a role in the determination of process, whether it relates to channel and distribution selection, messaging

[25] Adrian F. Payne et al., "Managing the Co-Creation of Value," *Journal of the Academy of Marketing Science* 36 (2008): 83–96.

[26] Eli J. Finkel et al., "The Metamorphosis of Narcissus: Communal Activation Promotes Relationship Commitment Among Narcissists, *Personality and Social Psychology Bulletin* 35, 1271, originally published online July 21, 2009.

[27] Dev Patnaik and Peter Mortensen, *Wired to Care: How Companies Prosper When They Create Widespread Empathy* (Upper Saddle River, NJ: FT Press, 2009).

and communication vehicles and timing, or how certain expressed needs could be best met in the marketplace.

A well-known example is FedEx's Internet tracking system which involves customers in the delivery monitoring process. Another less well-known example is Uber, a recent newcomer to the US marketplace for private transportation. Uber is a start-up company based in San Francisco. They offer a cell phone application that is aimed at making a personal car service quick and responsive. When an Uber client needs a ride, the dispatch service notifies the closest car and the system informs the client of the estimated pick-up time. While waiting, the client can monitor the car's location on their phone.[28]

[28] Jenna Wortham, "With a Start-Up Company, A Ride Is Just A Tap Of An App Away," *The New York Times,* May 4, 2011, B6.

NAME INDEX

D

E

F

G

H

SUBJECT INDEX